PUSH YOUR CREATIVITY

REIMAGINING **FAIRY TALES** THROUGH ILLUSTRATION

3dtotal Publishing

3dtotal Publishing

Correspondence: publishing@3dtotal.com
Website: www.3dtotal.com

First published in the United Kingdom, 2023, by 3dtotal Publishing.

Address: 3dtotal.com Ltd,
29 Foregate Street, Worcester
WR1 1DS, United Kingdom.

Soft cover ISBN:
978-1-912843-61-9

Printing and binding:
Cambrian Printers
sales@cambrian-printers.co.uk

Visit www.3dtotalpublishing.com for a complete list of available book titles.

Managing Director: Tom Greenway
Studio Manager: Simon Morse
Lead Editor: Samantha Rigby
Lead Designer: Joseph Cartwright
Designer: Fiona Tarbet
Editor: Marisa Lewis
Cover artwork: Fatemeh "Blue Birdy" Haghnejad (front), Joshua Carson (back)

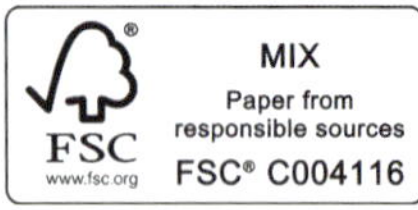

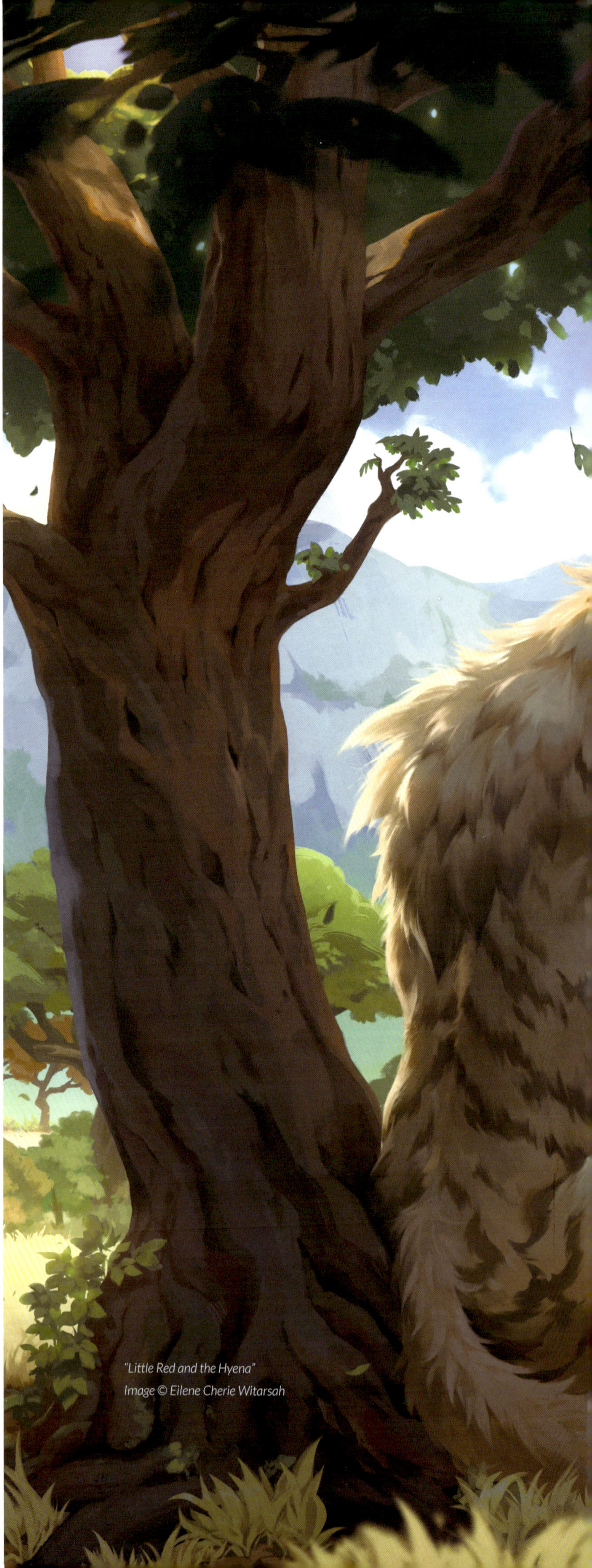

"Little Red and the Hyena"
Image © Eilene Cherie Witarsah

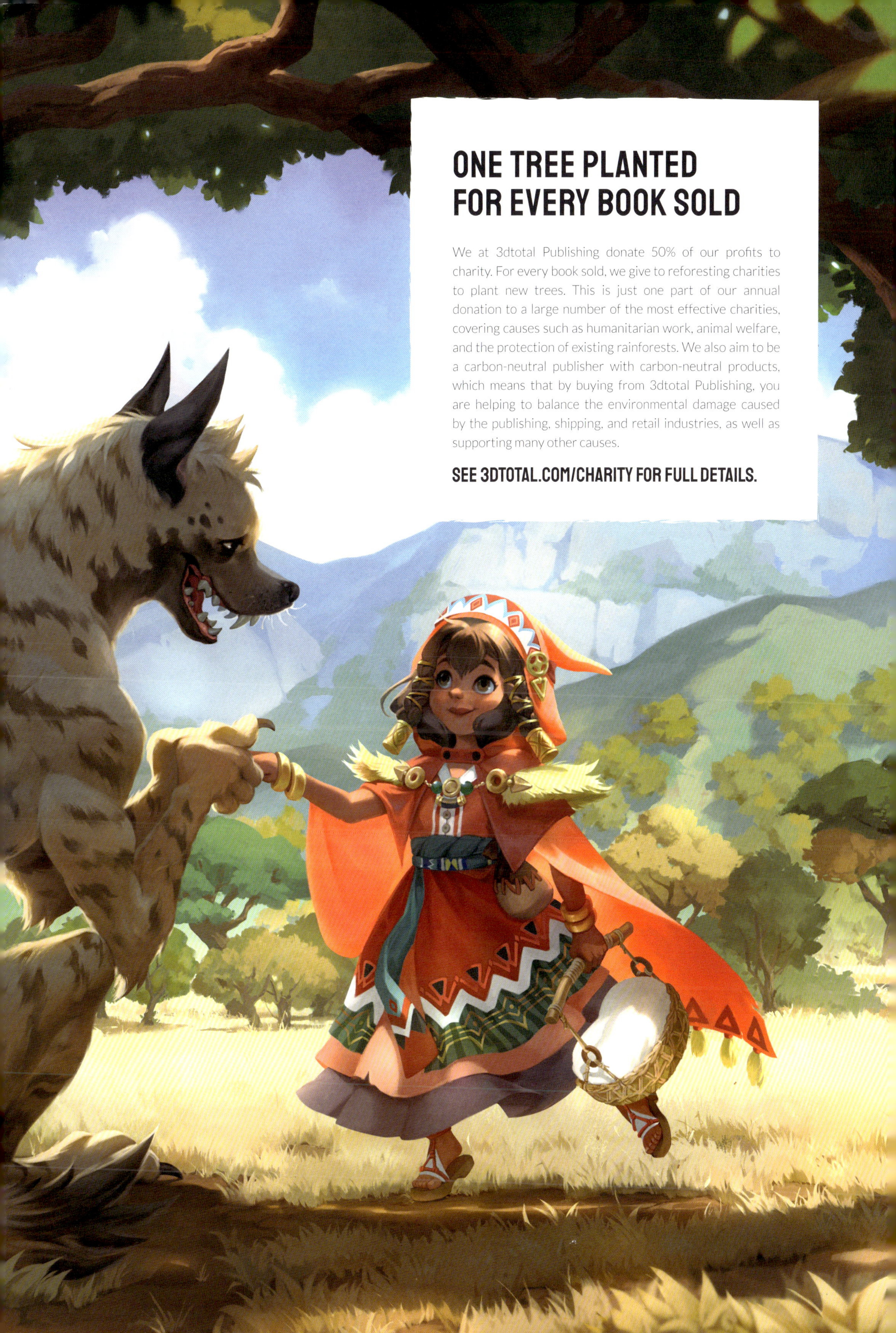

ONE TREE PLANTED
FOR EVERY BOOK SOLD
We at 3dtotal Publishing donate 50% of our profits to charity. For every book sold, we give to reforesting charities to plant new trees. This is just one part of our annual donation to a large number of the most effective charities, covering causes such as humanitarian work, animal welfare, and the protection of existing rainforests. We also aim to be a carbon-neutral publisher with carbon-neutral products, which means that by buying from 3dtotal Publishing, you are helping to balance the environmental damage caused by the publishing, shipping, and retail industries, as well as supporting many other causes.
SEE 3DTOTAL.COM/CHARITY FOR FULL DETAILS.

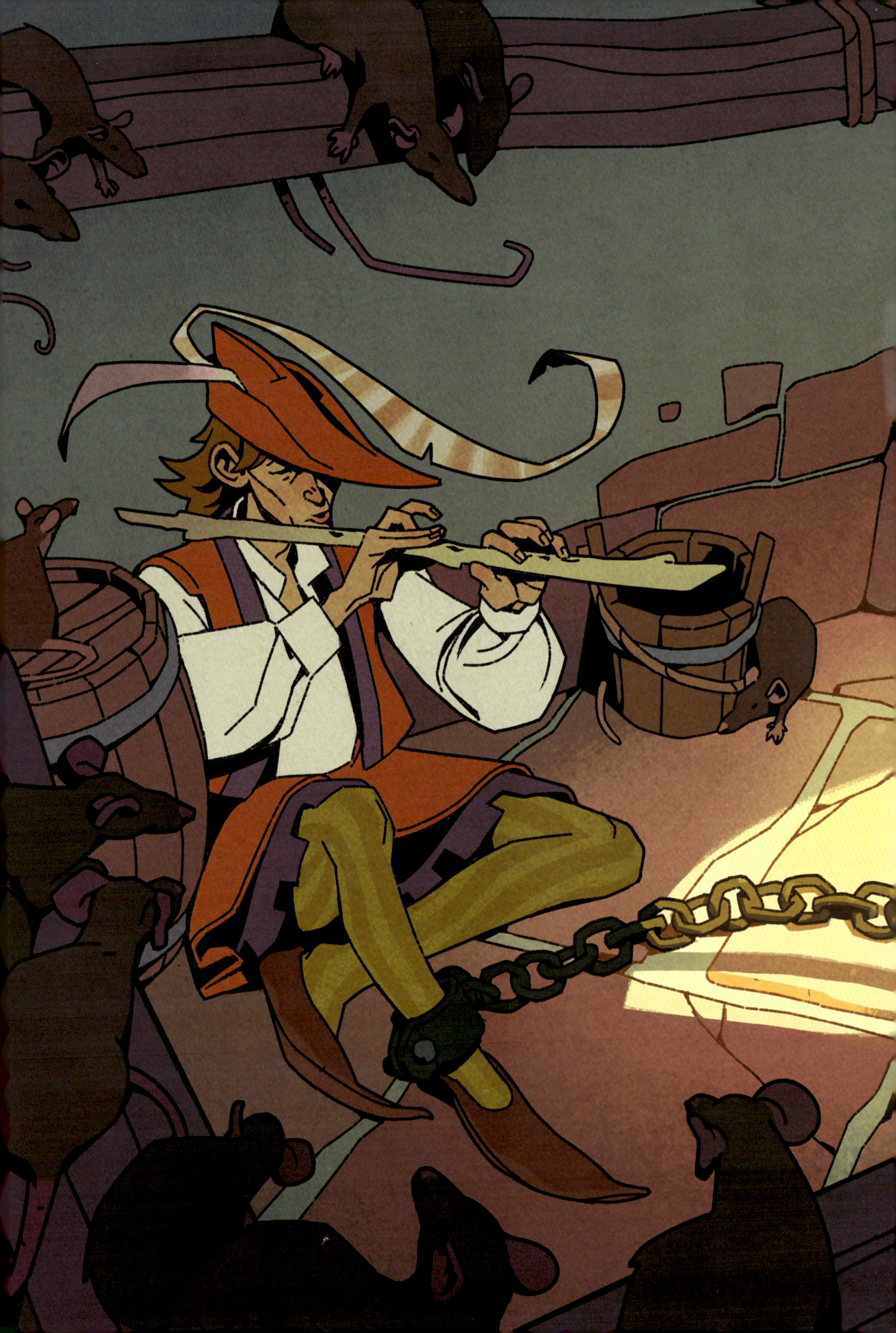

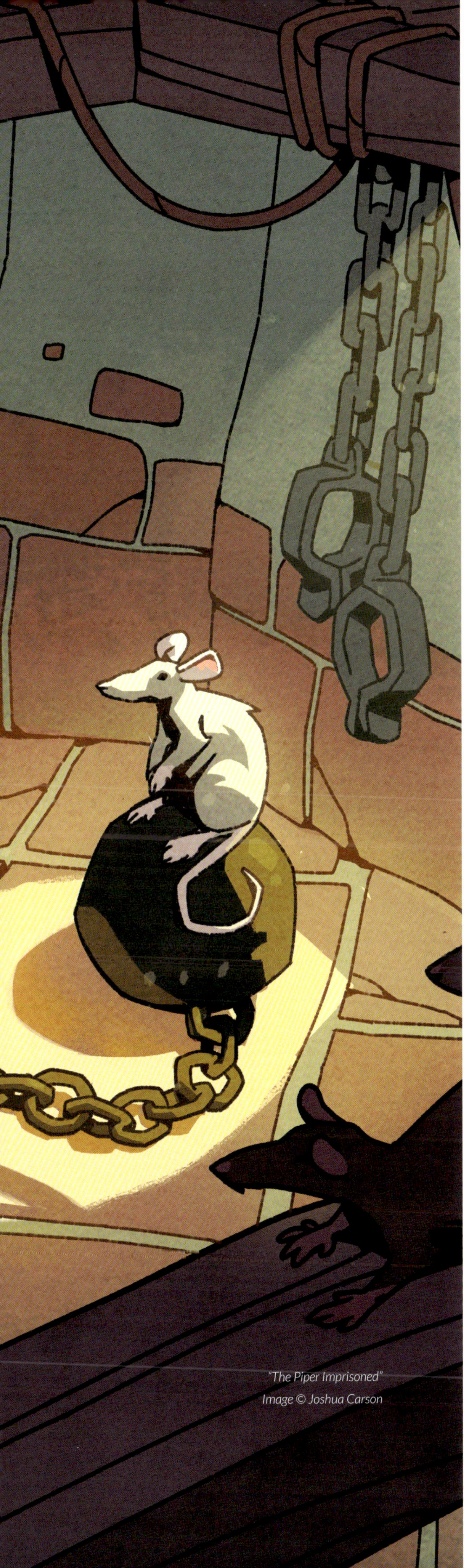

"The Piper Imprisoned"
Image © Joshua Carson

CONTENTS

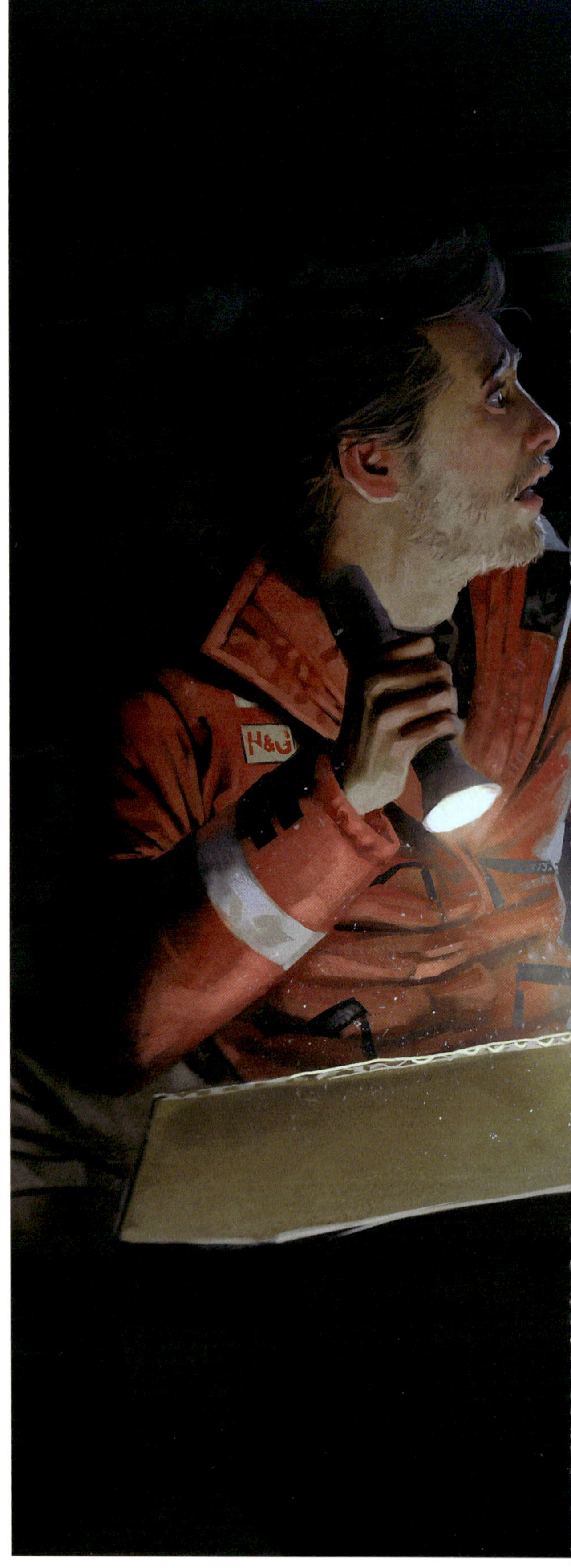

WELCOME

Fairy tales are some of the most instantly recognizable stories that we know. For many artists, books of these traditional tales are their first childhood encounter with fantasy, magic, and the imaginative power of illustration. From nursery to adulthood, we see these stories adapted, reinvented, retold, and parodied countless times – our cultural interest in them never really goes away. You may even have already tried to make your own versions of your favorite tales!

But how do creators find ways to bring something new to such old stories? If you love a story but feel like it's been well trodden by hundreds of artists before you, how can you begin to make it your own? When an idea is already so familiar and well loved, how can you make your mark on it and offer the audience something exciting, memorable, and surprising? In this book, we will discover how professional artists achieve just that. Thinking outside the box; looking at stories, situations, and designs in new ways; finding opportunities to add unique details and nuances – these are skills that all working artists need in their arsenal. Mastering them will help you elevate the humblest idea and push a merely good piece to a great one, whatever the subject matter, medium, or project.

Join our talented contributing artists as they explore five classic fairy tales: unpicking them, shaking them up, and wandering off the beaten track to find new ideas that put creative twists on familiar narratives. With the insights, methods, and tips these artists offer, you'll be able to push yourself a step further and create illustrations, concepts, and characters that thoroughly engage and intrigue your audience.

MARISA LEWIS, EDITOR
3DTOTAL PUBLISHING

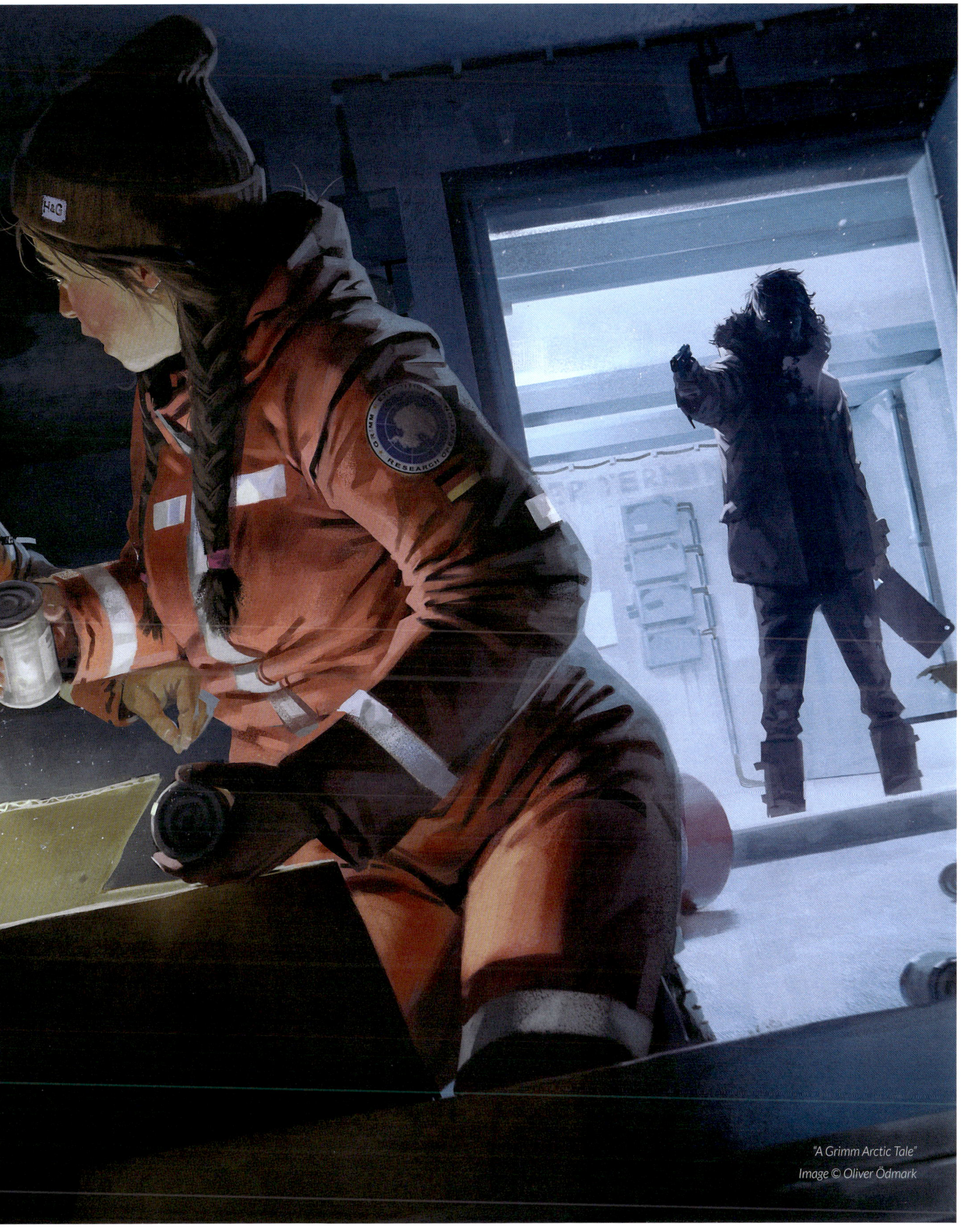

"A Grimm Arctic Tale"
Image © Oliver Ödmark

HOW TO USE THIS BOOK

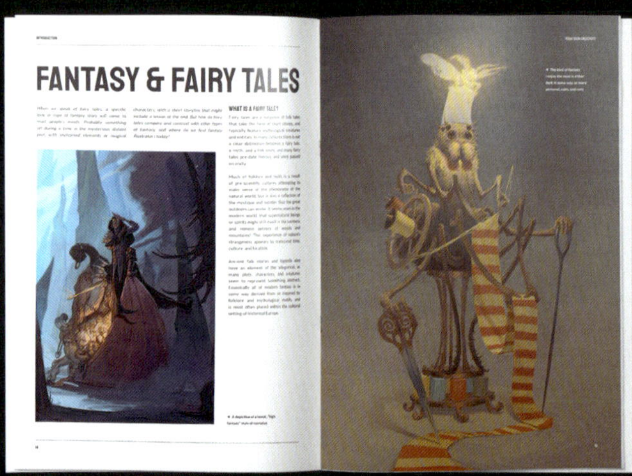
FANTASY & FAIRY TALES

◄ This book is divided into three main sections. Start with the Introduction (page 10), where illustrator Ognjen Sporin breaks down what makes a fairy tale or fantasy story, how to create stronger fantasy concepts, and some of the technical ingredients that make a successful illustration. It will whet your appetite for the tutorials and get you thinking about the types of narrative you gravitate toward.

► The tutorial chapters (starting on page 36) explore five separate classic tales. Each tale is interpreted by three different artists, each explaining their process for developing their own personal take on the story. Every artist's approach is different and shows the breadth of styles, workflows, opinions, and readings that different creators can apply to the same source material. The resulting three illustrations are shown at the end of each tale's chapter, so you can view the artists' solutions side by side and compare and contrast what they did differently or similarly.

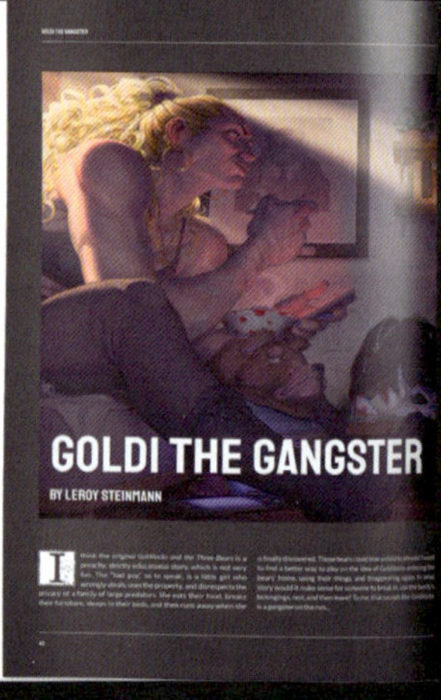
GOLDI THE GANGSTER

BY LEROY STEINMANN

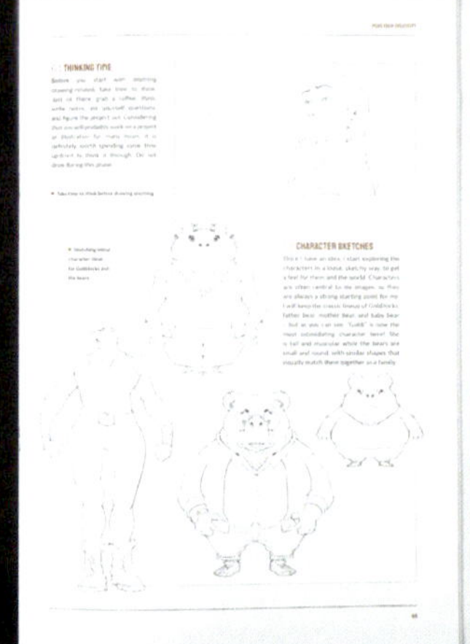

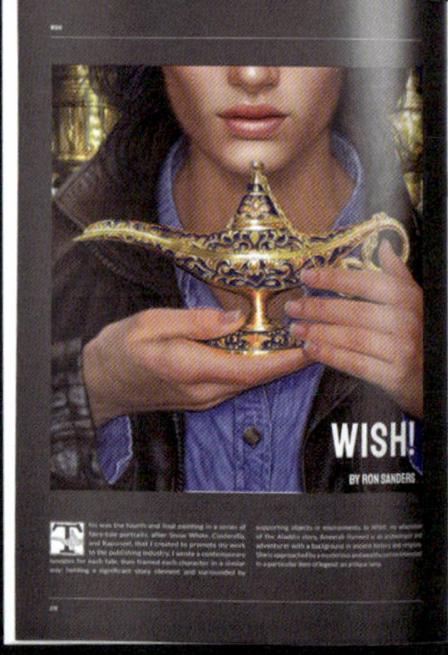
WISH!

BY RON SANDERS

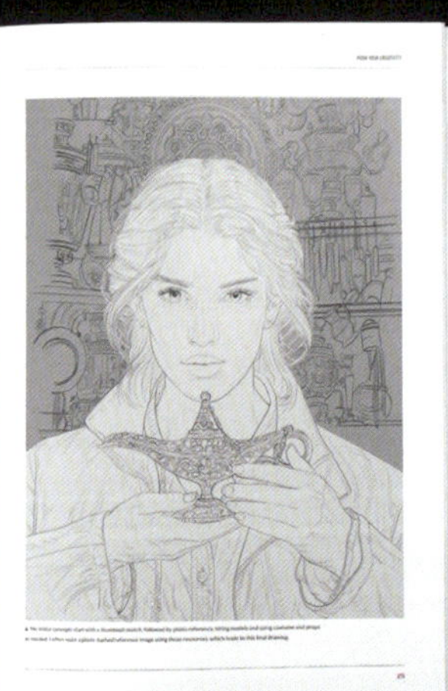

◄ The Gallery section (page 266) shows bite-sized breakdowns of fairy-tale illustrations by additional guests, looking at the ideas and works-in-progress behind their excellent portfolio pieces. Finally, the Glossary (page 286) provides quick reference for some recurring technical terms found in this book.

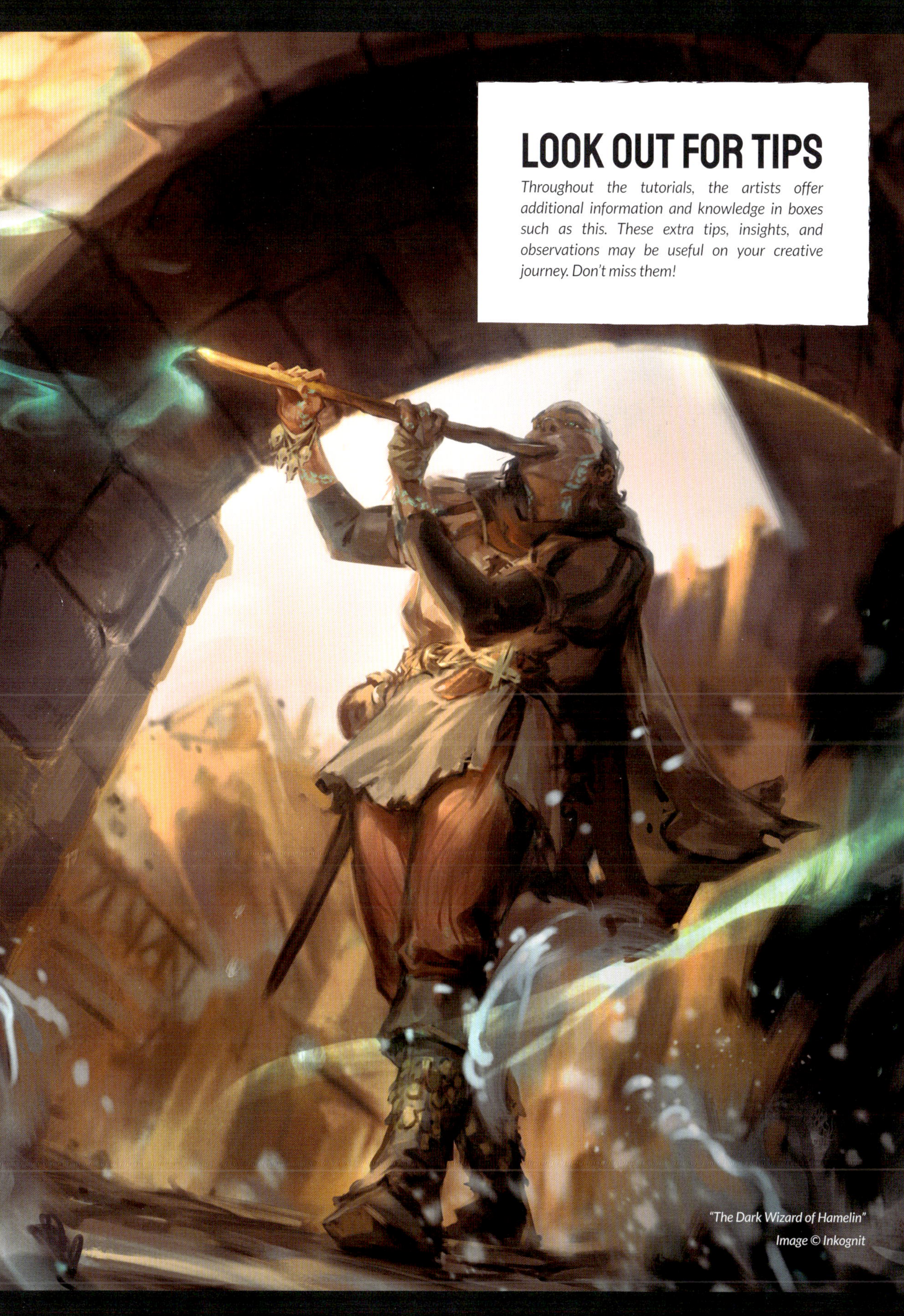

LOOK OUT FOR TIPS

Throughout the tutorials, the artists offer additional information and knowledge in boxes such as this. These extra tips, insights, and observations may be useful on your creative journey. Don't miss them!

"The Dark Wizard of Hamelin"

Image © Inkognit

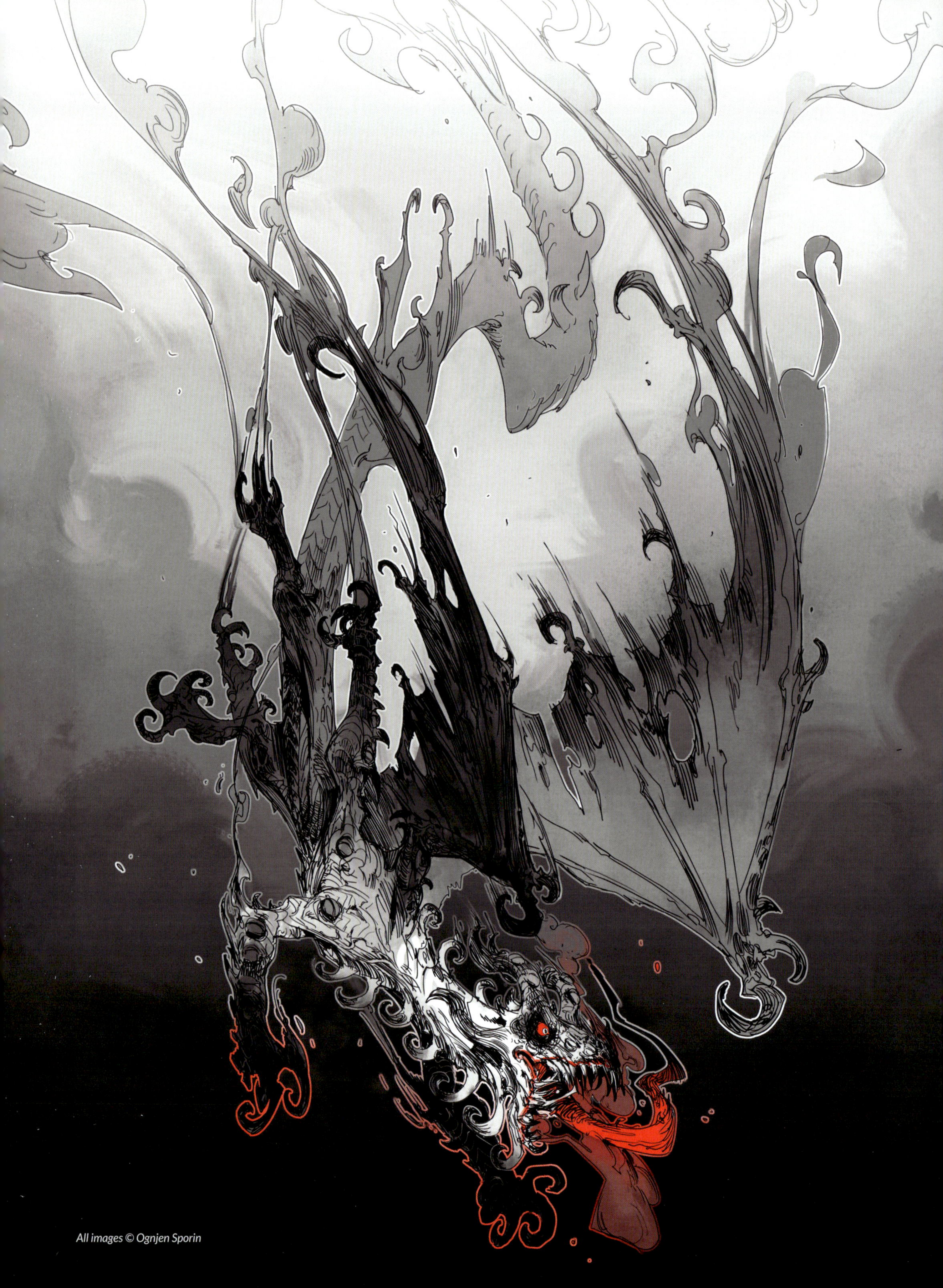

INTRODUCTION

BY OGNJEN SPORIN

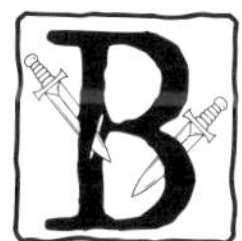efore we leap into illustrating some fairy tales, we should learn about some of the important parameters inside which this book operates. For example, what is a fairy tale? What type of story, atmosphere, or characters comes to mind when we think of fairy tales, and how can we use that knowledge to try something new and surprise the viewer? What visual ingredients work together to form an illustration, and how can you use that art-theory knowledge to make your illustrations better, more eye-catching, and more original? And finally, how can you stay motivated, creative, and inspired when the learning process gets tough? The worlds of fairy tales may be whimsical, outlandish ones where problems can be solved with luck and magic, but for fantasy artists in the real world, practice, study, and forming good habits are the keys to overcoming a challenge. Let's begin by exploring those themes and questions in this chapter.

FANTASY & FAIRY TALES

When we speak of fairy tales, a specific tone or type of fantasy story will come to most people's minds. Probably something set during a time in the mysterious distant past, with enchanted elements or magical characters, with a short storyline that might include a lesson at the end. But how do fairy tales compare and contrast with other types of fantasy, and where do we find fantasy illustrators today?

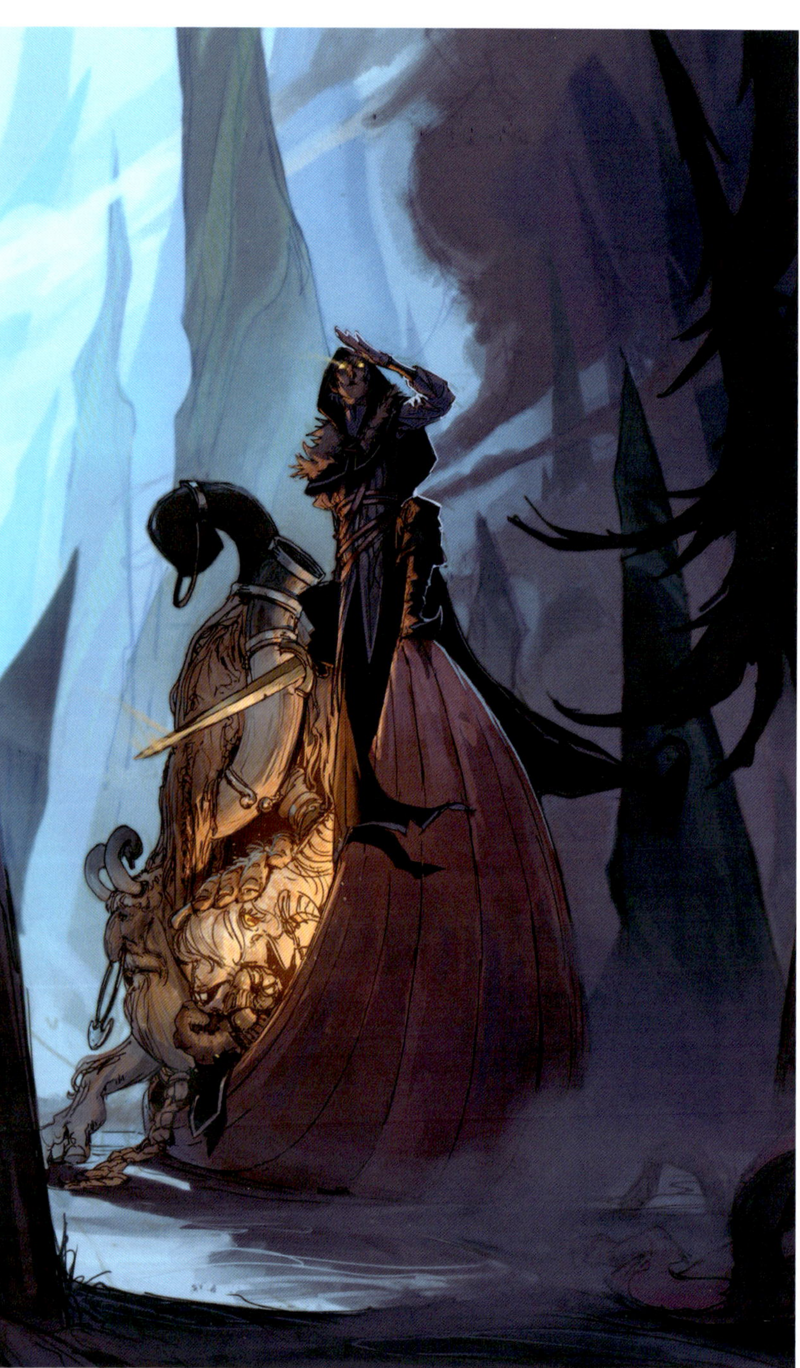

◀ A depiction of a heroic, "high fantasy" (see page 14) style of narrative

WHAT IS A FAIRY TALE?

Fairy tales are a subgenre of folk tales that take the form of short stories and typically feature mythological creatures and entities. In many cultures there is not a clear distinction between a fairy tale, a myth, and a folk story, and many fairy tales pre-date literacy and were passed on orally.

Much of folklore and myth is a result of pre-scientific cultures attempting to make sense of the phenomena of the natural world, but it is also a reflection of the mystique and wonder that the great outdoors can evoke. It seems, even in the modern world, that supernatural beings or spirits might still dwell in the vastness and remote secrecy of woods and mountains! This experience of nature's strangeness appears to transcend time, culture, and location.

Ancient folk stories and legends also have an element of the allegorical, as many plots, characters, and creatures seem to represent something abstract. Essentially all of modern fantasy is in some way derived from or inspired by folklore and mythological motifs, and is most often placed within the cultural setting of historical Europe.

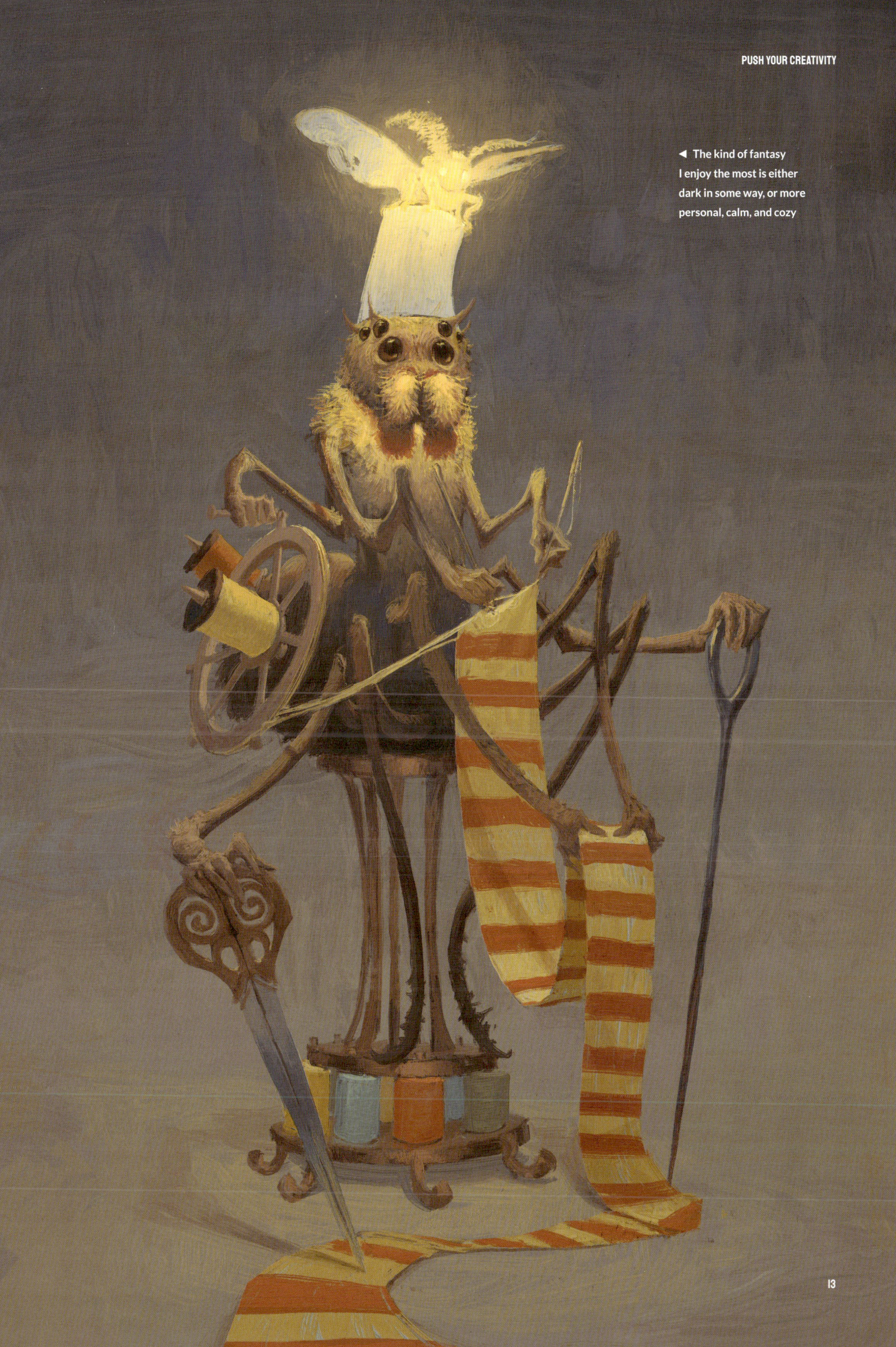

◀ The kind of fantasy I enjoy the most is either dark in some way, or more personal, calm, and cozy

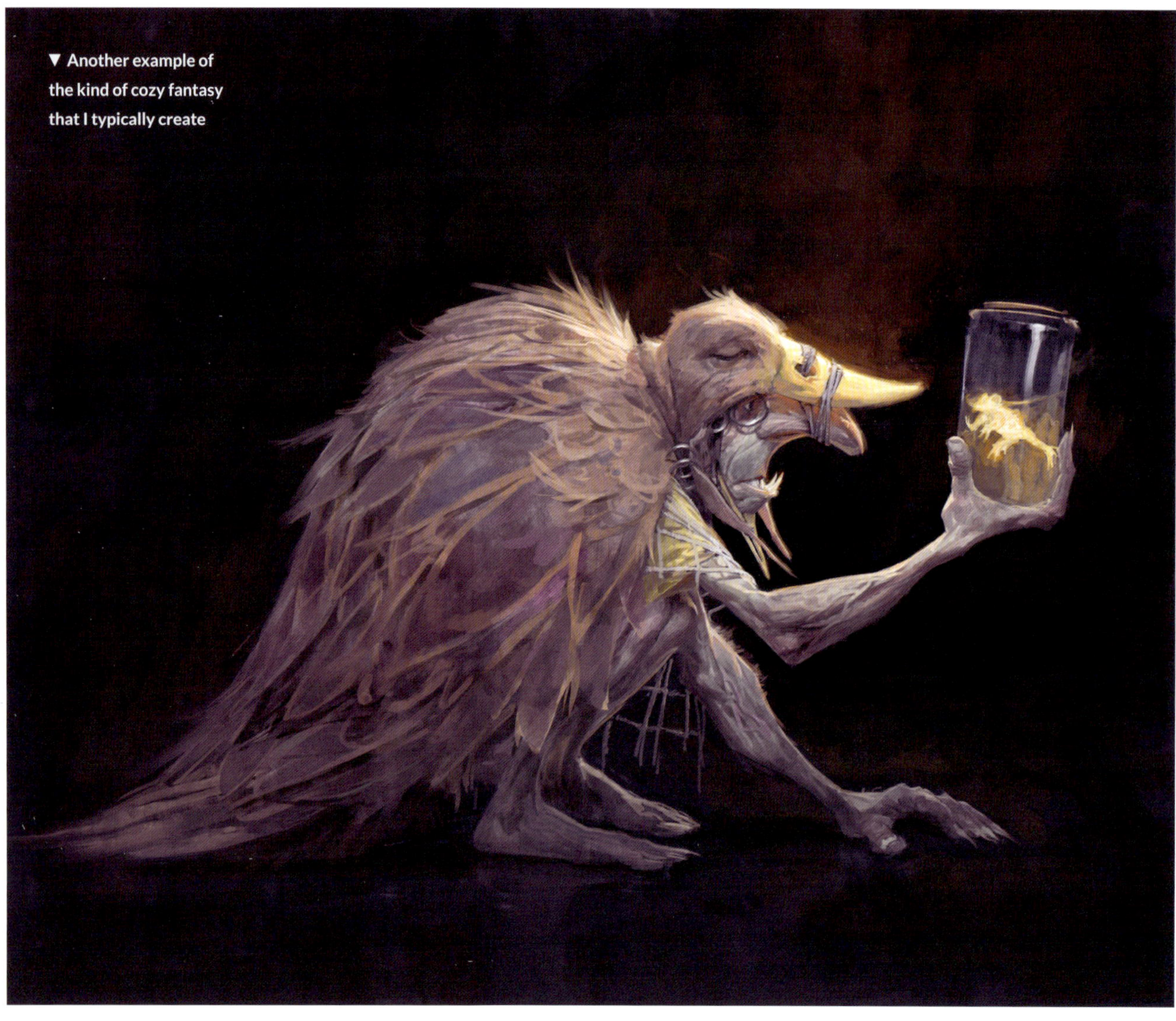

▼ **Another example of the kind of cozy fantasy that I typically create**

HIGH AND LOW FANTASY

The fantasy genre, as we think of it today, can broadly be classified into two groups: high fantasy and low fantasy. High fantasy is set within completely fantastical, epic, and expansive universes, and often deals with heroic narratives in a way that is analogous to the ancient legends of real-world cultures. Great and classic examples of this kind of fantasy are *The Lord of the Rings*, *Game of Thrones*, *The Witcher*, and *World of Warcraft*.

Low fantasy, on the other hand, is either set in the real world, or has some connection to it (such as the characters being from our own world and entering an alternate one through a gateway of some kind). Because of this relatability, the low fantasy subgenre can feel more akin to fairy tales. Examples of low fantasy settings would be *The Chronicles of Narnia*, *Harry Potter*, *Pan's Labyrinth*, and *The Spiderwick Chronicles*. Stories that are set in a wholly separate but less magical and more mundane world could also be considered low fantasy.

I personally find the more personal, mysterious and arcane atmosphere of fairy tales much more fascinating than the glamorous, epic scale of legends, and I think that shows quite clearly in my paintings, as you can see throughout this chapter. My favorite fantasy artists include Paul Bonner, Brian Froud, Jean-Baptiste Monge, Jesper Ejsing, and Petar Meseldžija.

However, we should keep in mind that there is a whole spectrum between high and low, rather than a clear division or sharp cutoff. Consider what kind of fantasy appeals to you, and where your art (or the art that you aspire to make), fits on this spectrum. This will help orient you when looking for new creative directions and avenues to explore.

FANTASY ART TODAY

There are many contexts in which we can find artists illustrating fantasy art today. Within the art industry, many fantasy projects are in the form of board games (creating card art, concept art, map art, and miniatures), card games (such as *Magic: The Gathering*), *Dungeons & Dragons* related projects, and fantasy book covers. Applying for these kinds of jobs is fairly easy – you can research suitable publishers, find the email address for applications, and just send in your art! If you think your work is at a high enough level and don't have clients, don't hesitate to find as many of these as you possibly can, and politely reach out to them with your portfolio.

▼ An easy way of creating variety and finding new ideas is to stray from the medieval European setting of fantasy and fairy tales, and exploring wider inspirations, like this swamp-dwelling Japanese yōkai

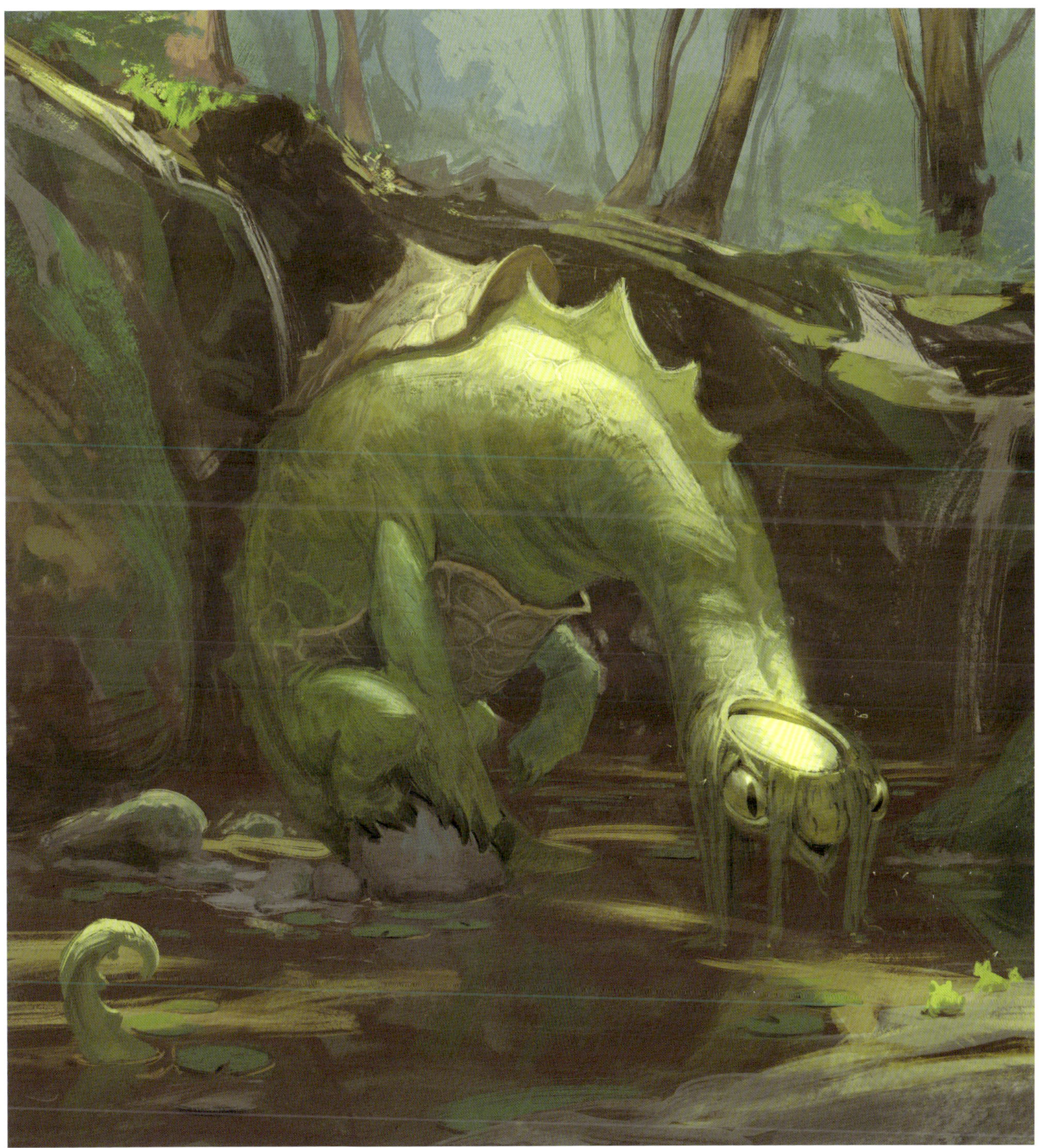

COMPOSITION

Now that we have a little more context for our fairy-tale or fantasy art, let's look at the parts that actually form an image – it is important to know these elements if you want to start bending the rules. Let's start with the foundation of composition, which is, at its simplest, the arrangement of shapes in the image to achieve an intended result. When talking about illustration, your intended aim is generally going to be to convey some kind of narrative. Within any narrative, there are elements that are more and less important; layers that ought to be seen right away and layers that are subtler and seen only upon a longer inspection. The most important elements in the image are known as its focal points.

FOCAL POINTS

When planning out an image, the most crucial question at the very beginning is always, "What is the image about? What is the image's primary focal point?" An illustration without a clear focal point will fail to engage the viewer or tell the story you are trying to convey. When you clearly determine what the image is about, you can arrange the composition accordingly. The main tool by which you create focal points is contrast: the viewer will always look at the points of highest contrast first.

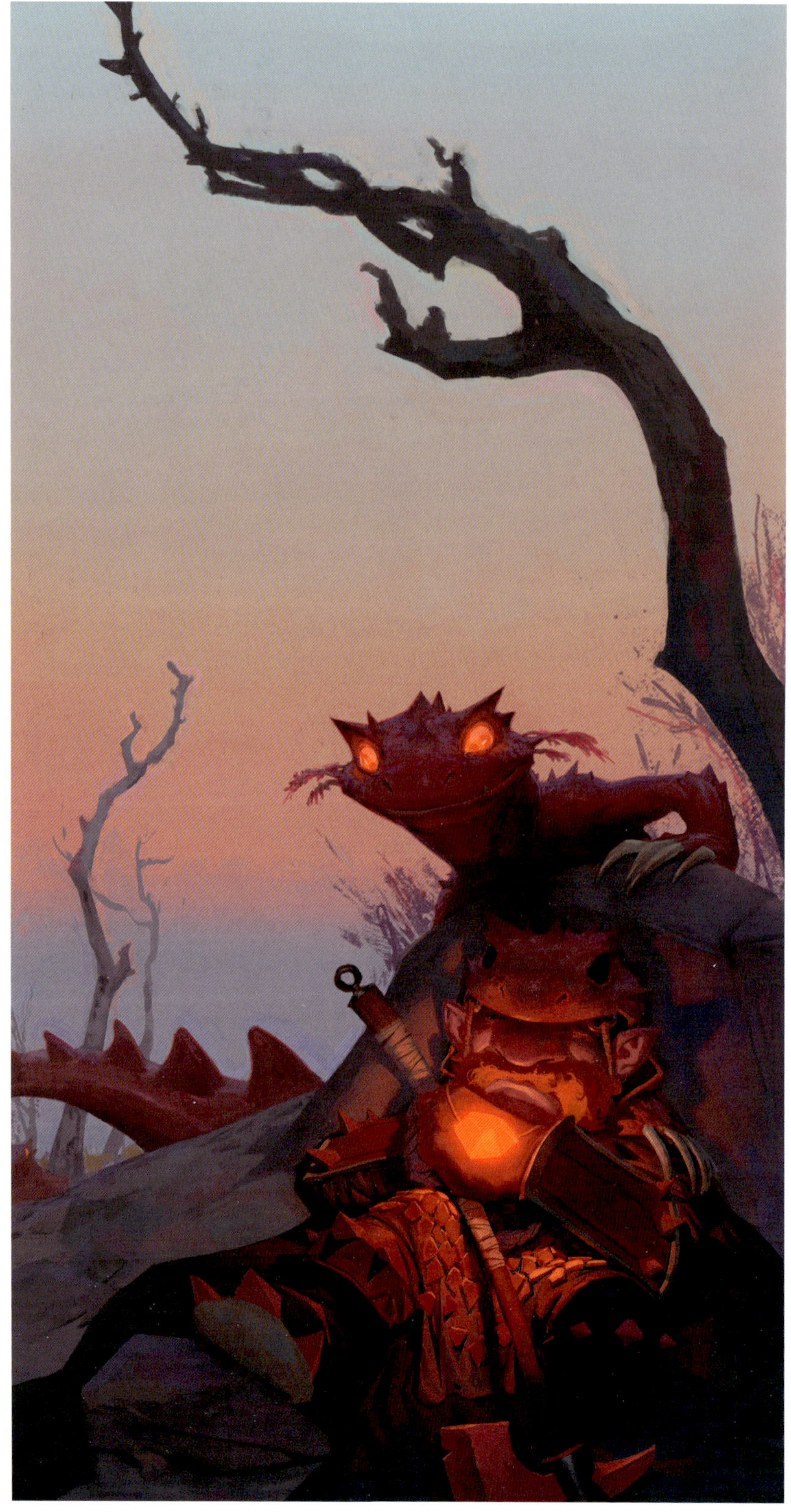

► In this image, the clear points of highest contrast are the glowing gem and the eyes, and so they are inevitably where the viewer will look first

CONTRAST

Contrast is essentially a clear difference between two or more things. In an image-making context, contrast can be achieved with any visual elements, such as value, color, saturation, texture, shape, or detail. If you put a bright value next to a dark one, a strong color next to a weak one, or a round shape next to a sharp one, you create contrast. It's also important to note that focal points are contextual and should be understood within the range of contrast of each image. For example, even if the contrast is very low throughout the entire painting, there will still be a point where the contrast is highest. That point will serve its compositional purpose as a focal point in relation to the rest of the image. When you are equipped with an awareness of the different ways you can create contrast, more creative and interesting solutions will open up to you.

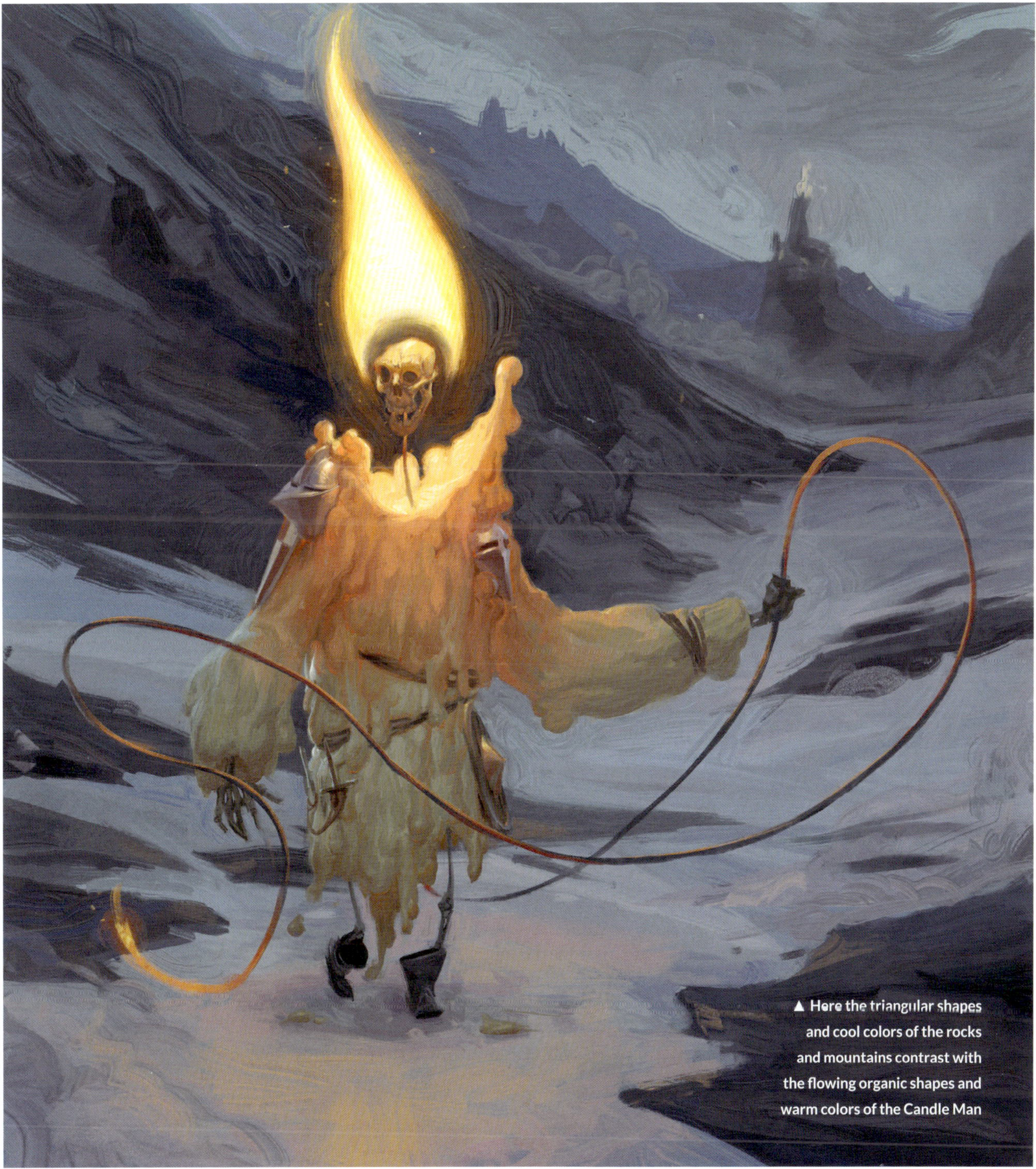

▲ Here the triangular shapes and cool colors of the rocks and mountains contrast with the flowing organic shapes and warm colors of the Candle Man

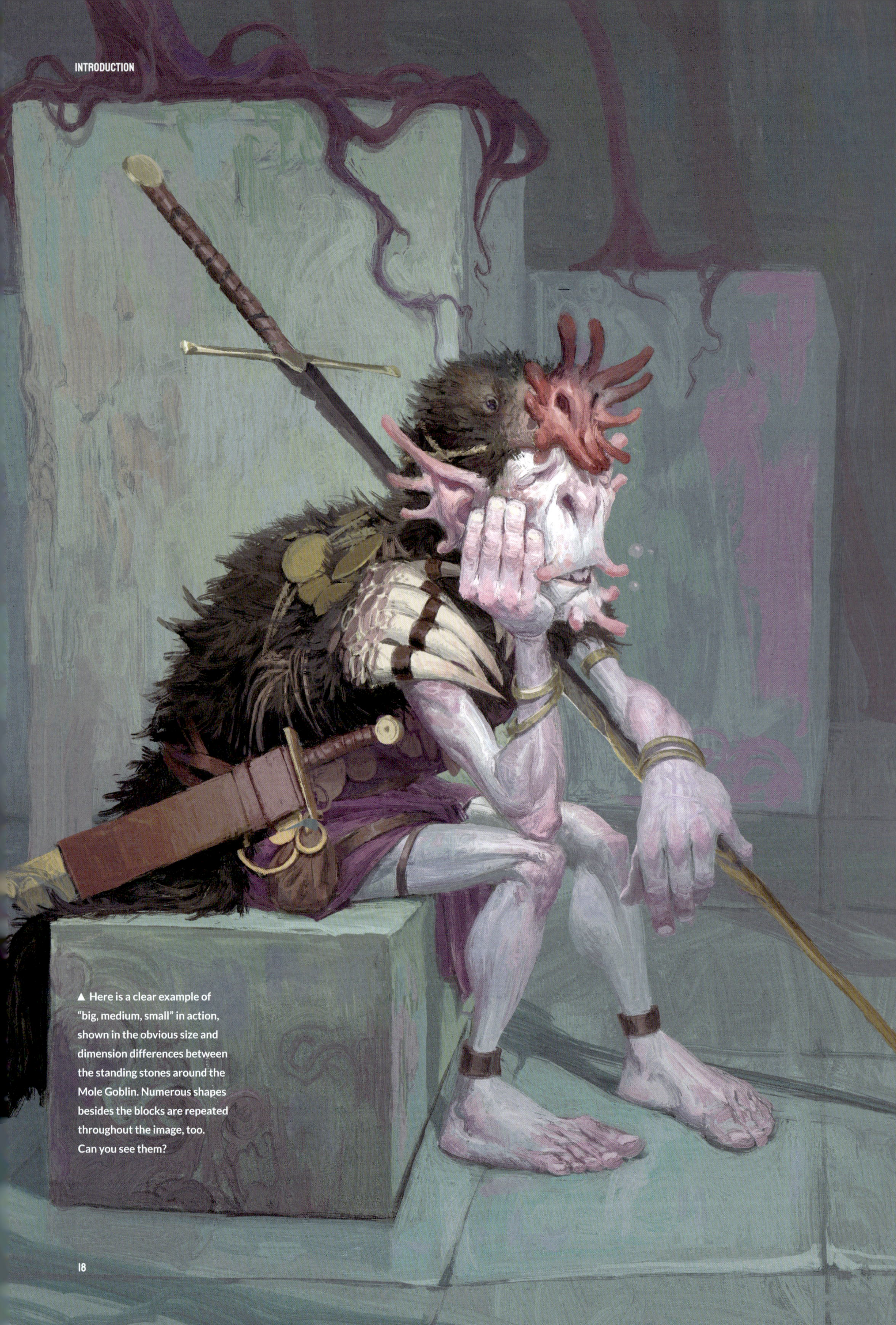

▲ Here is a clear example of "big, medium, small" in action, shown in the obvious size and dimension differences between the standing stones around the Mole Goblin. Numerous shapes besides the blocks are repeated throughout the image, too. Can you see them?

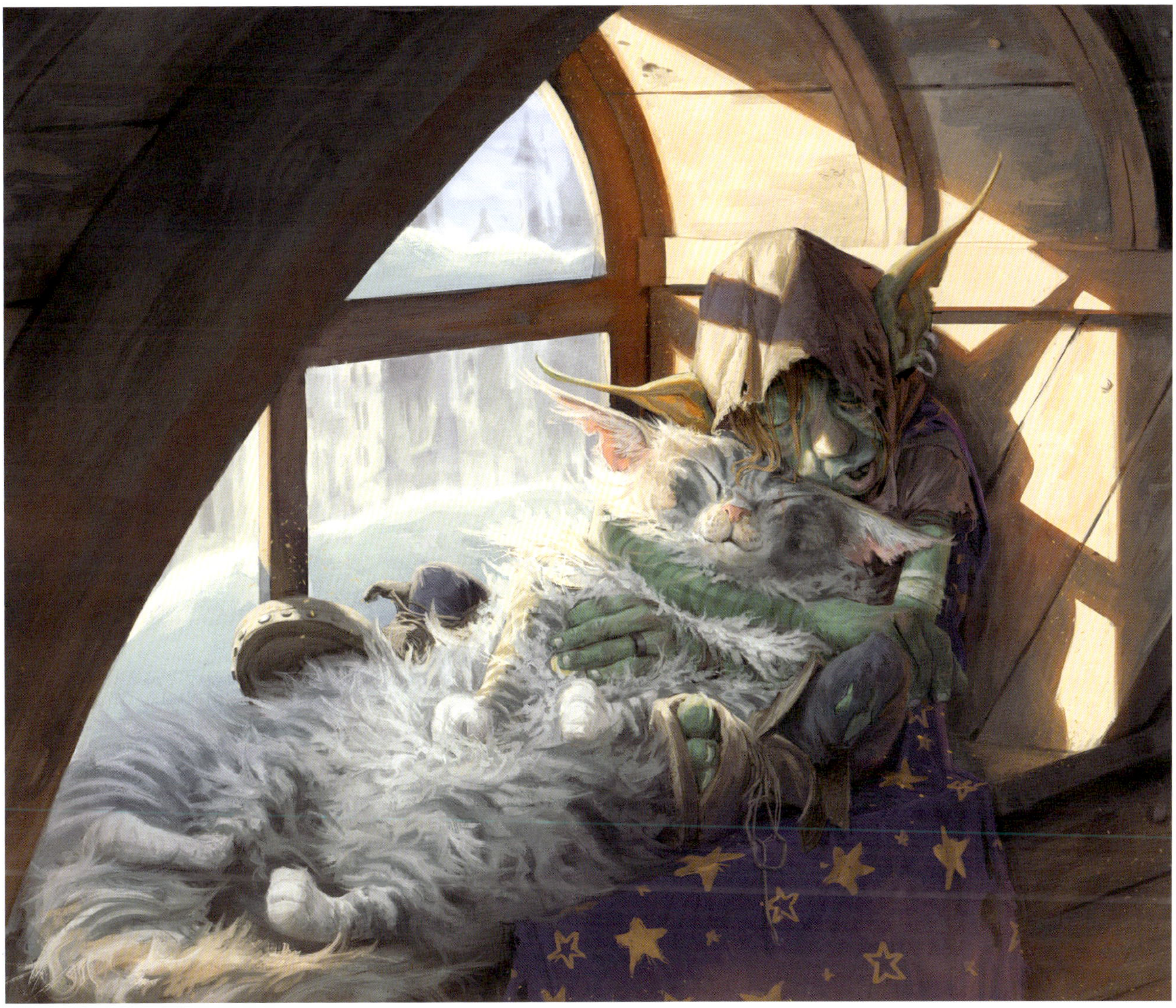

SHAPE DESIGN

As mentioned previously, a composition is simply an arrangment of shapes. The question that arises then is, "How does one create appealing shapes?"

- The first important principle of shape design is size variety. Think "big, medium, small." For shapes to be interesting in a subject, they need to be of clearly different sizes.

- The second key element of shape design is repetition or echoing. Having a primary shape that is repeated within the image creates appeal and cohesion. There might be a secondary or accent shape that stands out from the main shape language and creates a focal point.

- The third element of shape design is gesture. Every shape produces a certain visual movement within the image, and your job as a visual storyteller is to use the shapes to move the viewer's eye in and around the image.

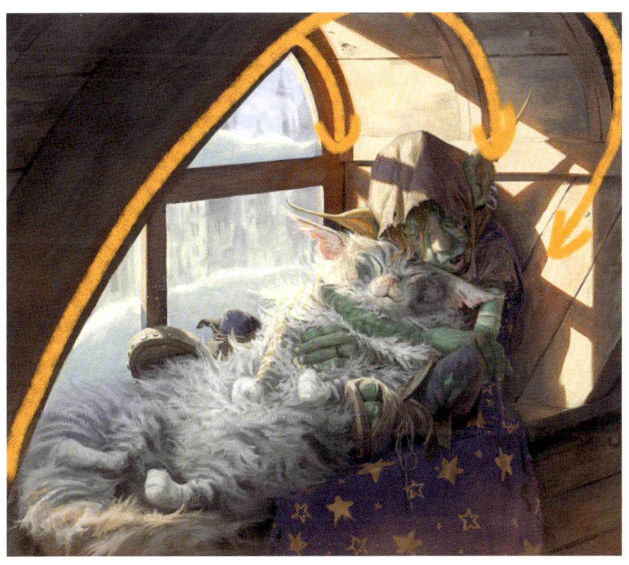

▲ In this image, the window frame is used as a compositional device to move the eye toward the characters and keep it from exiting the painting

ATMOSPHERE

When thinking about atmosphere and mood in fantasy illustration, there are really two main camps or extremes: the really epic, hero-driven, "sword and sorcery" type of fantasy, pioneered by the likes of Frank Frazetta, and the more fairy-tale-like, mysterious, and magical-feeling fantasy, such as made by John Bauer or Brian Froud. Between these extremes, there's a whole rich spectrum of different flavors of fantasy, and I think it helps to frame your images within that spectrum to more easily establish the vibe you are going for. Mood and atmosphere are somewhat abstract, but they are also tied closely to composition; because of that there are certain compositional rules of thumb that will generally help you produce a desired atmosphere within your paintings.

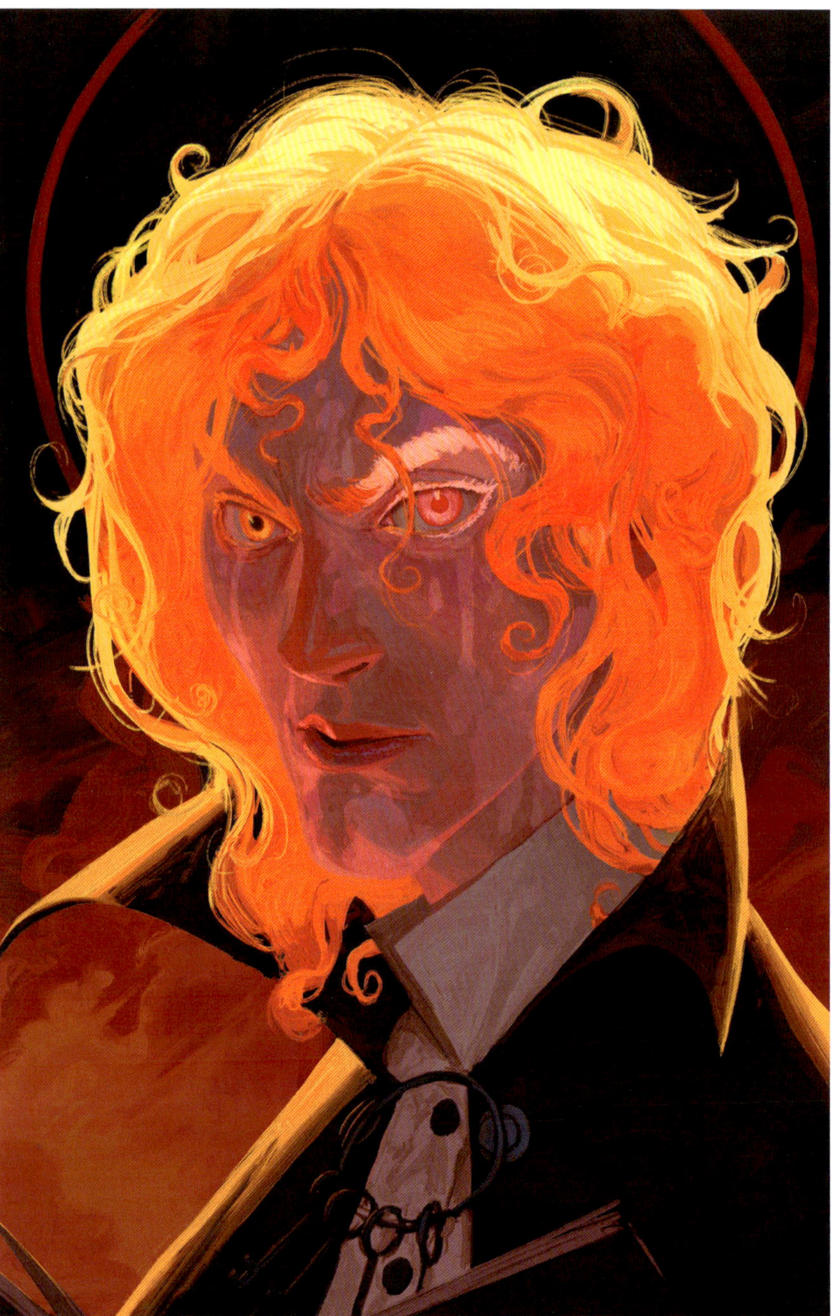

COLORS AND HUES

When using color, the most practical way to think about it is in terms of temperature. Within the context of this painting, is this a warm or a cold color? How does this temperature affect your mood? Is that mood appropriate for the character or narrative that you are trying to convey?

Each individual hue on the color wheel also has a general emotional effect that it tends to create in a viewer. Yellow and orange tend to feel very warm, cozy, and inviting; a strong red will likely evoke danger and drama; violet and turquoise might feel otherworldly or magical; and blues will obviously tend to be cold, but also calm.

As mentioned on page 17, colors are another method for creating contrast. Being conscious of your color choices and their implications is essential if you want to successfully evoke a mood or emotion in the viewer.

◀ **This painting of the angel Uriel uses dramatic lighting, warm colors, and strong contrast for a more powerful effect – apt for an angel who stands watch over the damned**

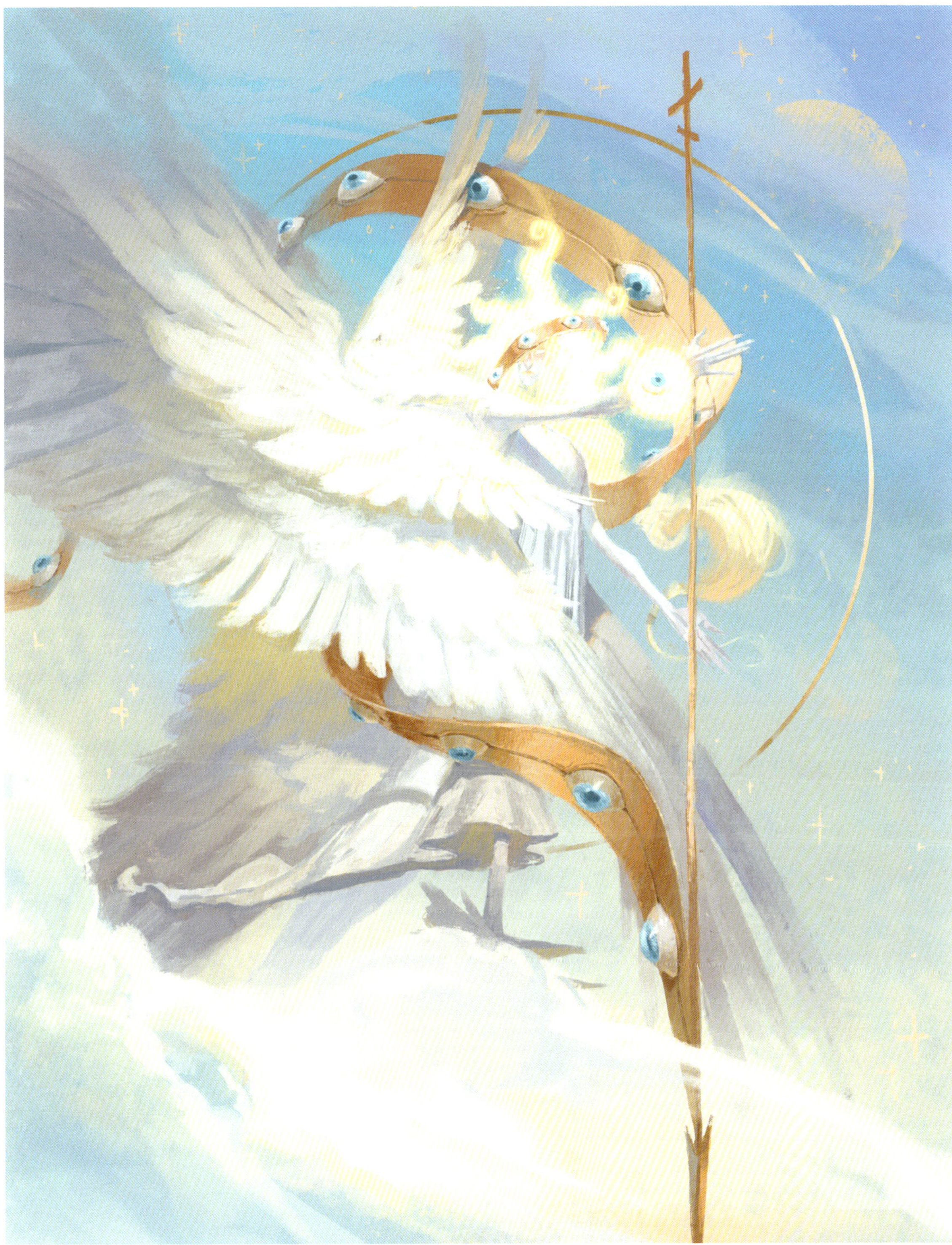

HIGH AND LOW CONTRAST

The degree of contrast is, to a large extent, what visually separates the heroic high-fantasy genre from the fairy tale. Contrast (and especially value contrast) is probably the main tool for controlling atmosphere, particularly the drama and the boldness of an image. The more drastic the range of values is in a painting, the more dramatic that painting will tend to be. The more subdued, muted, and similar the values are, the more melancholic, calm, or perhaps mysterious the mood of the image will be.

▲ Compared to the left image, the light shadows and overall low contrast in this painting create an ethereal, divine mood, fitting for a brighter depiction of an angelic being

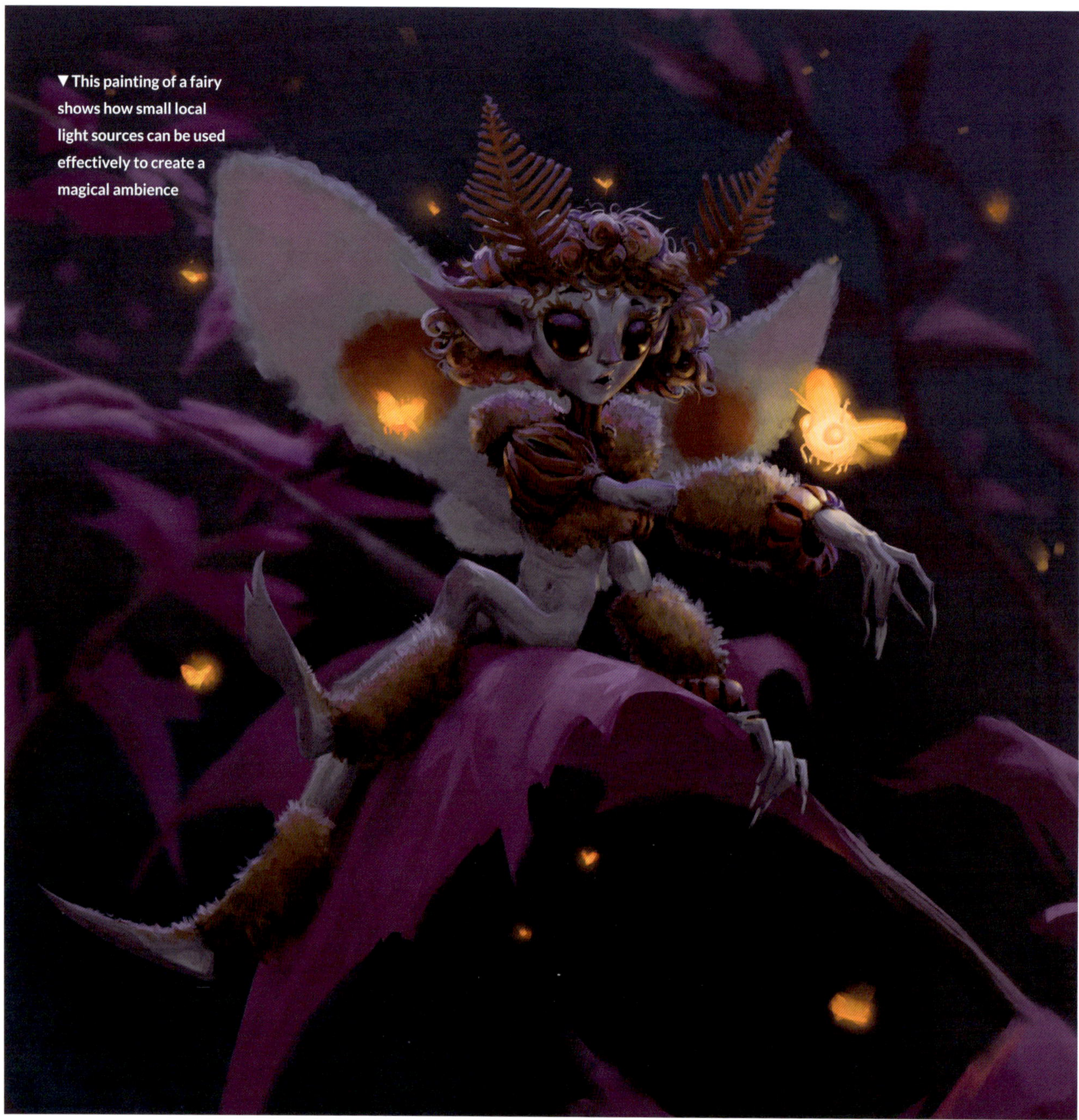

▼This painting of a fairy shows how small local light sources can be used effectively to create a magical ambience

CONTROLLING SATURATION

The stronger and more saturated the colors are in an image, the more lively and animated it will feel. However, beginner artists will often overdo the saturation throughout the entire image, leaving them with nothing to emphasize the focal points. When building up the painting, it is a good idea to start with a more toned-down palette, staying away from highly saturated colors and reserving them for the most important areas.

MOOD LIGHTING

Having "local" light sources in the image (such as lamps or candles) works incredibly well for setting a fairy-tale atmosphere. If you are creating a darker scene, try adding fireflies or lanterns! Magic effects can help create an enchanting atmosphere, too.

USING INSPIRATION

Trying to create an atmosphere that is unique and original can feel overwhelming and create a mental block for any artist. What helps with this tremendously is referencing photos, paintings, and illustrations that represent the mood you are envisioning. With a strong selection of references, you can expand or mix those inspirations to create something new.

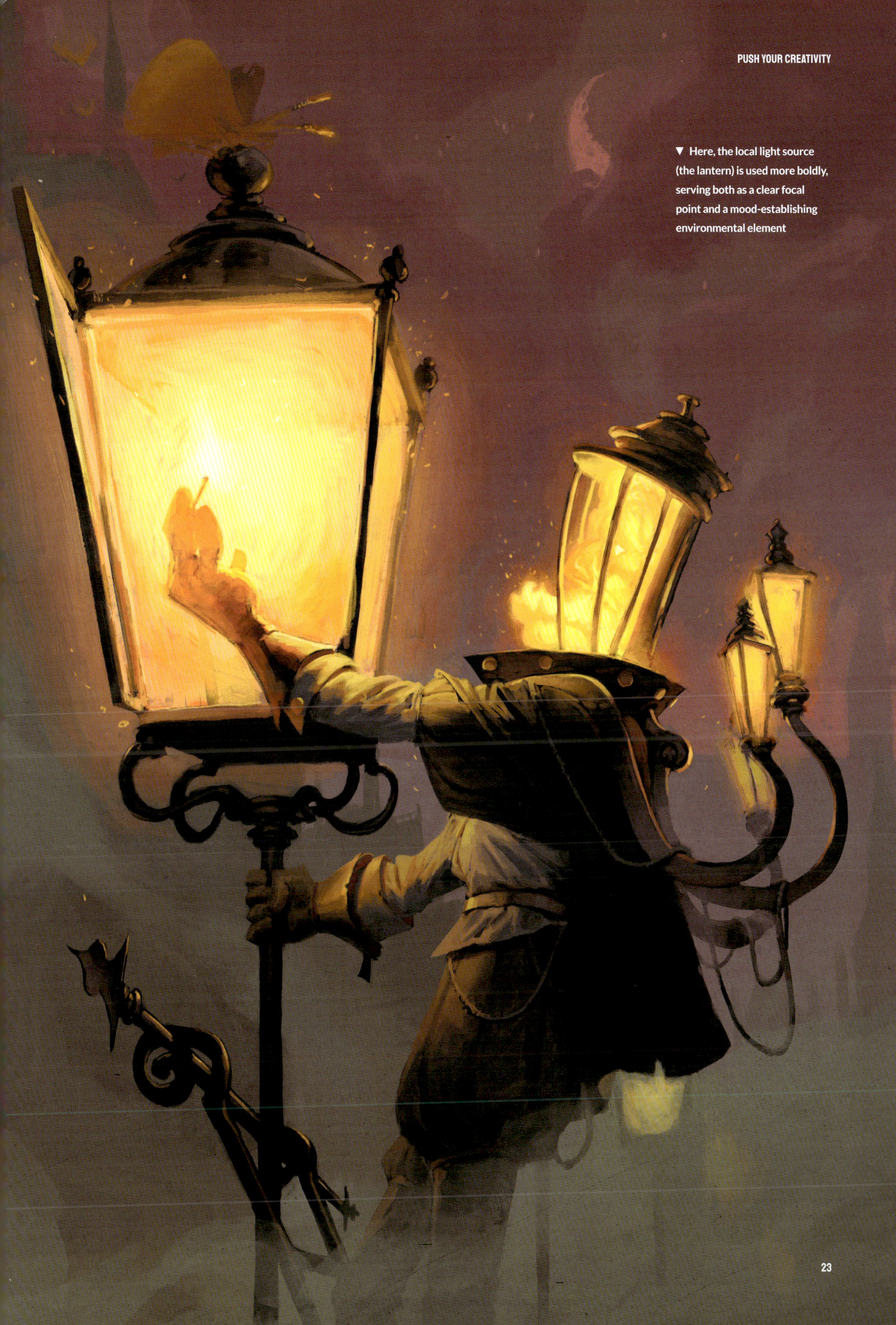

▼ Here, the local light source (the lantern) is used more boldly, serving both as a clear focal point and a mood-establishing environmental element

CHARACTER DESIGN

Character design is a very broad and somewhat intangible topic, but, as with everything, there are ways to abstract, systematize, and simplify it so that you can grasp the fundamental principles and use them reliably. When trying to break down characters, there are two main aspects to a good design: the graphic design and the narrative design. The graphic aspect is the purely visual side, concerning itself with the arrangement of shapes and colors to create a pleasing image. The narrative aspect regards the story and functionality of the design, such as the character's backstory, their place in the broader context of the world they inhabit, the practicality of their costume and tools, their traits and personality, their archetype, and other aspects that bring life and believability to the character.

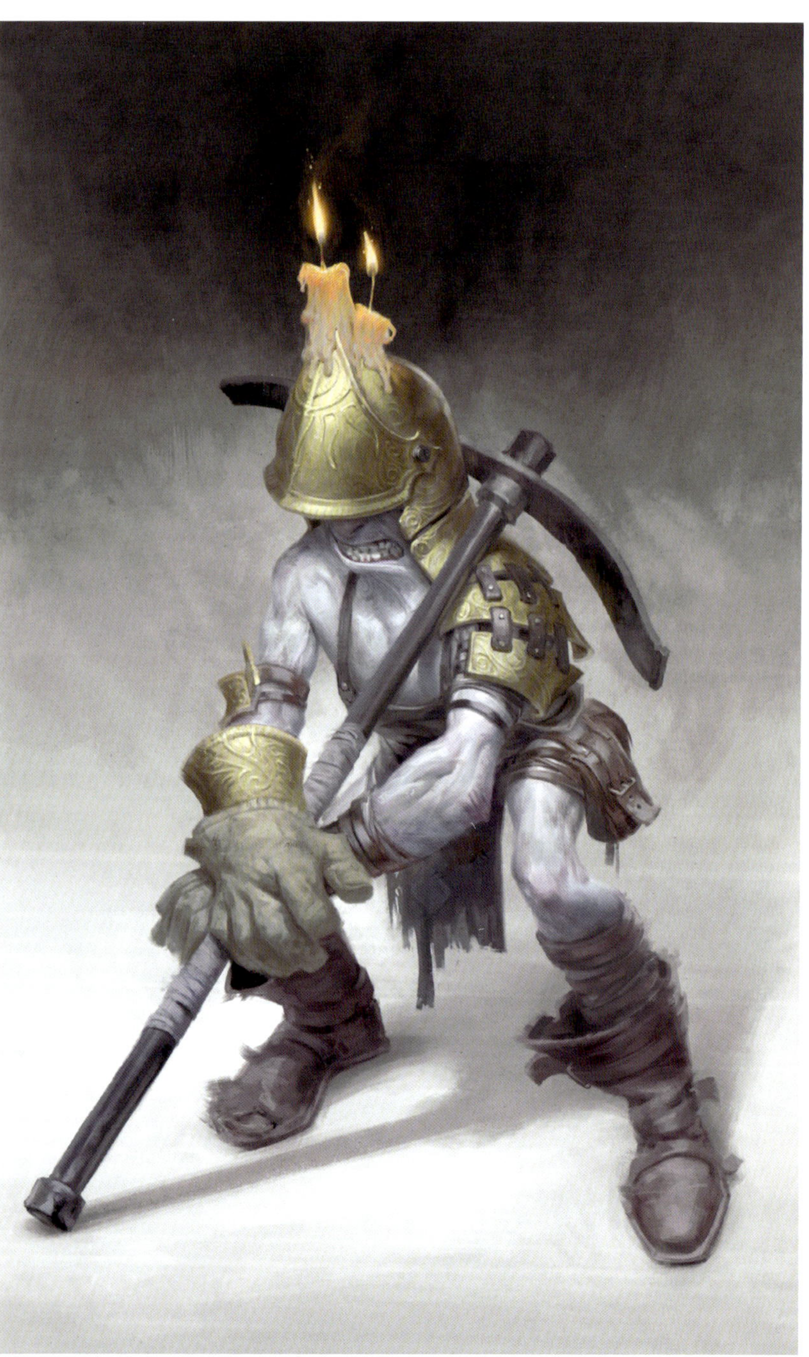

VISUAL PRINCIPLES

There are certain principles that can be used as a rule of thumb when making any sort of visual design, be that a composition for a whole illustration or a composition within a character. I have already mentioned these principles in the "Shape design" part of the Composition section (page 19), but I think they are worth reiterating in the context of designing characters:

- Use a variety of shape sizes, with a difference between big, medium, and small shapes
- Repeat a primary shape throughout the design to create cohesion and visual harmony
- Ensure your character design has clear primary and secondary points of interest – usually the head/shoulders for the former, and usually hands for the latter – and use visual contrast to emphasize those focal points.

Furthermore, all the visual elements (such as the shapes and colors) should be used to represent the character's narrative aspects in some way (such as using sharp and triangular shapes for a villain). Narrative artwork can be heavily character-driven, and the fantasy genre in particular is a playground for exciting, outlandish characters of countless types. Make sure you give your characters the attention and consideration that they need to successfully carry a story.

◀ The costumes and tools of this kobold miner clearly reflect his underground environment

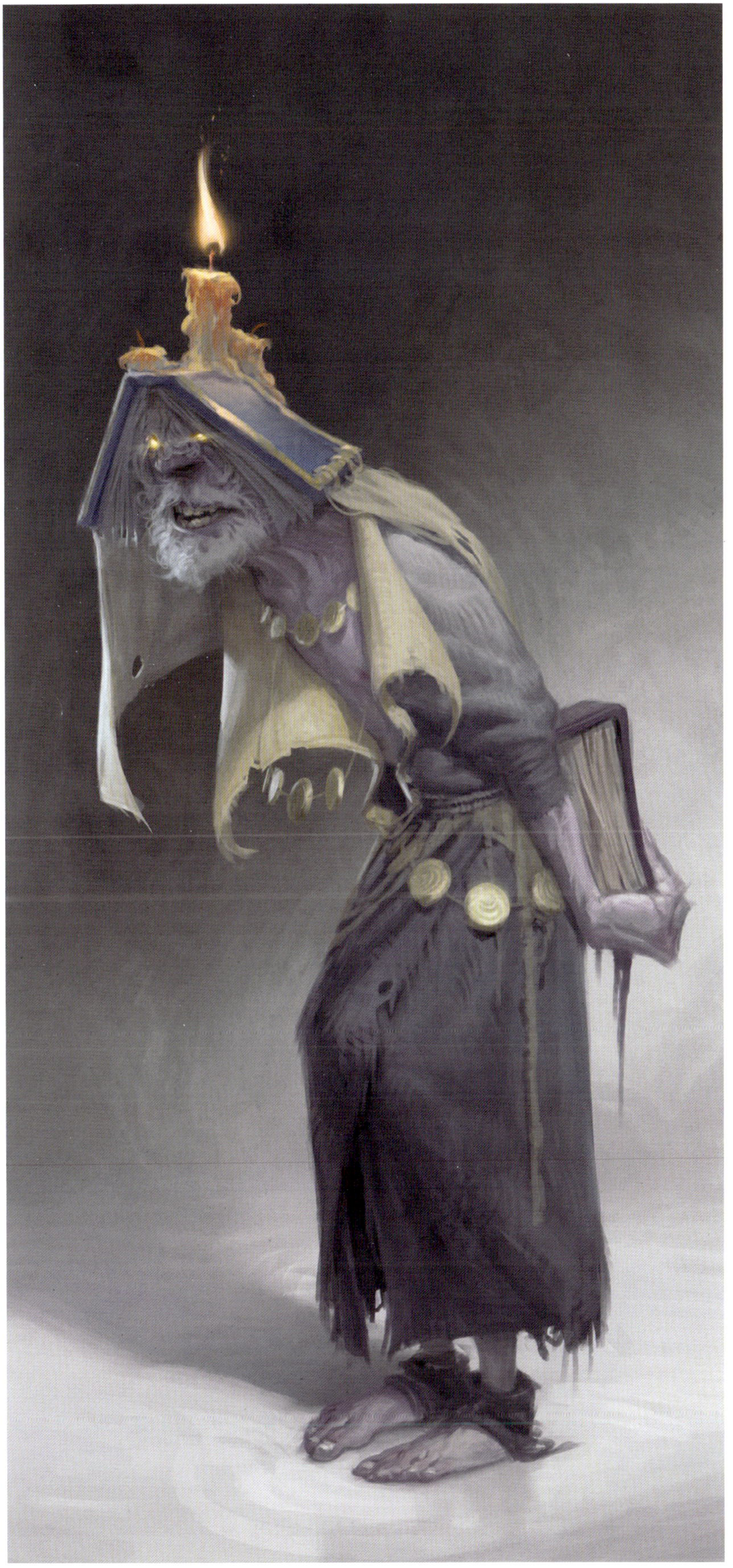

NARRATIVE PRINCIPLES

The best way to add depth, complexity, and interest to your character is to add depth and complexity to the world they inhabit and to their relationship with that world. Every character exists within and is shaped and molded by their environment to some degree, and their visual design should reflect that.

When designing a group of kobolds for a personal project (pictured left), I came up with most of their traits based around how they are affected by their environment. In my mind, they occupy a vast system of caves previously populated by a now-extinct civilization. Because they live underground with no light, their bodies are pale and milky. Their costumes are supposed to reflect the artifacts of that ancient civilization: they wear pieces of intricate golden armor that they found in the caverns, mixed with ragged, dirty clothes they have crafted themselves, reflecting a much poorer and more primitive society. I used muted, somber colors and values to make the characters mirror their environment even further.

◀ **The value contrast and saturation of this kobold priest are kept fairly low to echo the mood of the character himself**

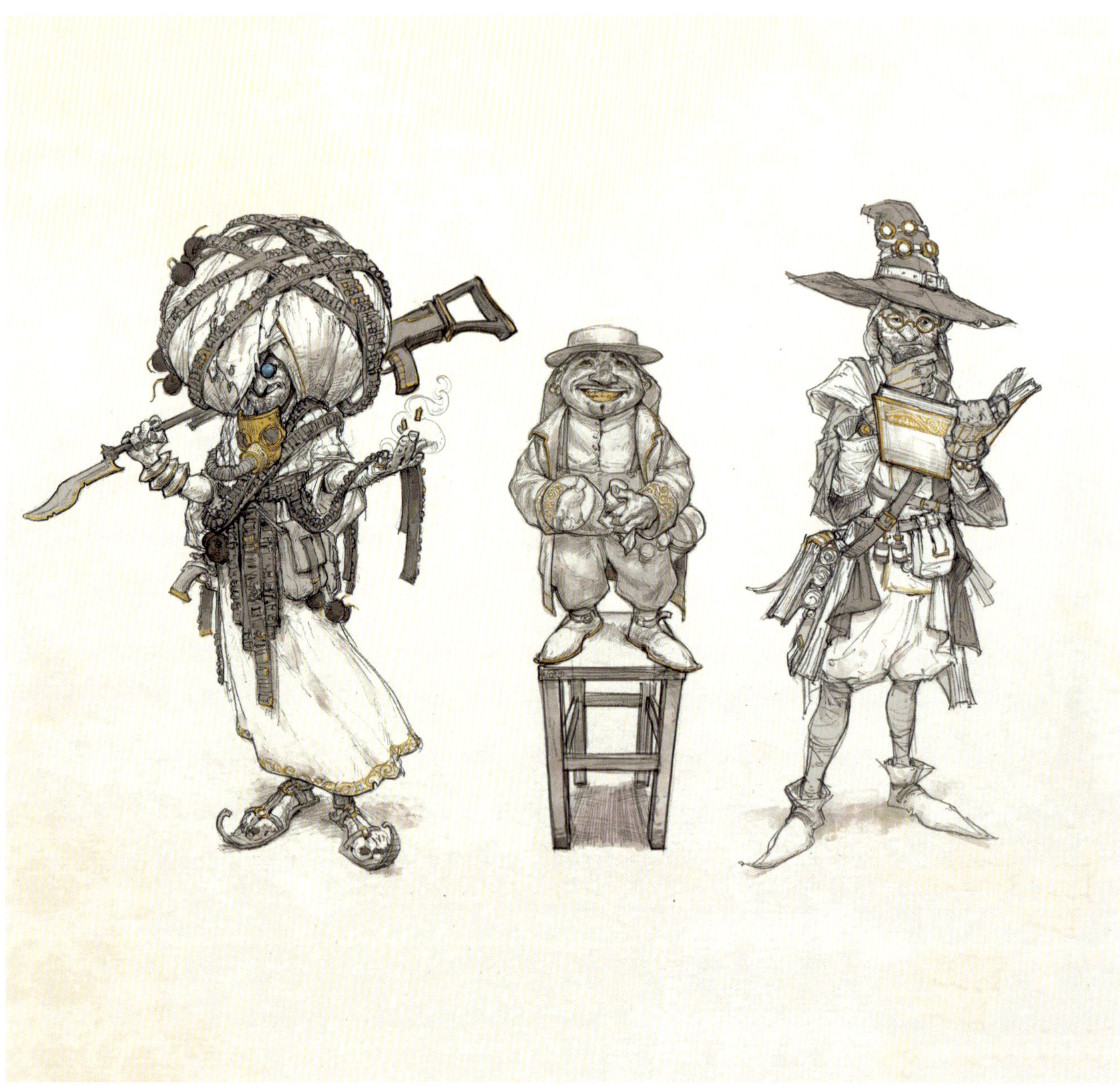

BUILDING UPON REALITY

The easiest way to come up with interesting and immersive worlds or themes for your characters is to root them in real societies and terrains. You can take a pre-existing contemporary or historical culture and use it as a base to build something more fantastical and extraordinary. Often the easiest way to do this is to combine the base culture setting with a different existing culture.

I had this exact thought process when coming up with a lineup of characters for another personal project, *Big Trouble in Hot Sands*. I mixed a Middle Eastern desert setting with a Wild West cowboy aesthetic, then took different fantasy archetypes (such as the weaponsmith, the innkeeper, and the wizard) and placed them within that world.

▲ Taking fantasy tropes or archetypes and placing them in a different setting is a great exercise, and also a great way of coming up with interesting and original designs!

► In this image, I consciously used a color palette that tries to evoke both the hot desert setting and the bloody nature of this ammo-seller character

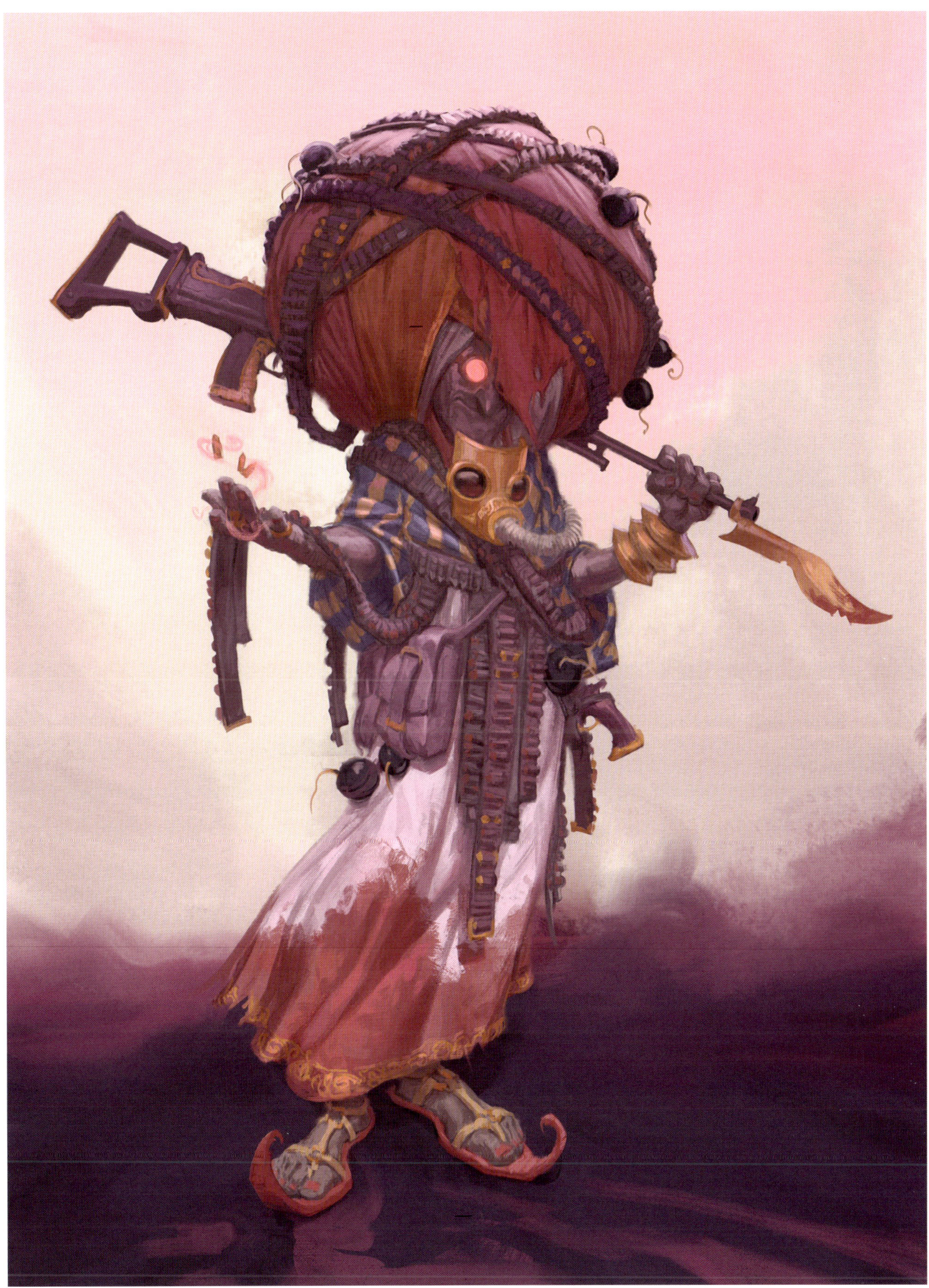

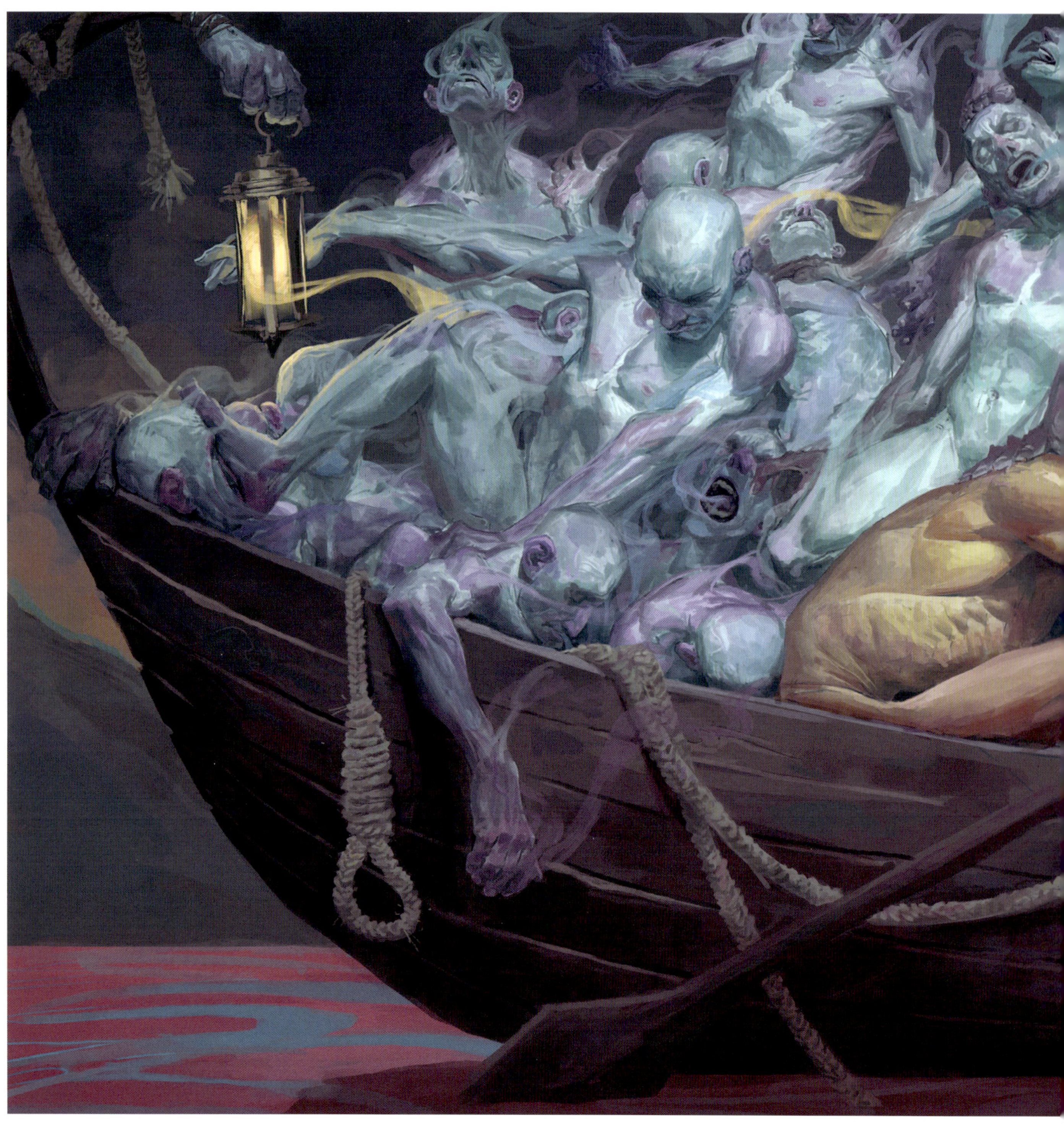

NARRATIVE

Within the context of image-making, the narrative is most often going to be a single moment, or a story beat, showing an event that takes place in a larger story. The goal of the illustrator is to showcase the broader context of the entire story within that one frame. Because of this, worldbuilding is crucial to any successful narrative. Most stories are either about a conflict or a relationship, so, when trying to come up with original narratives, a great question to ask is, "How do the characters in this story relate to each other and the world they're in?"

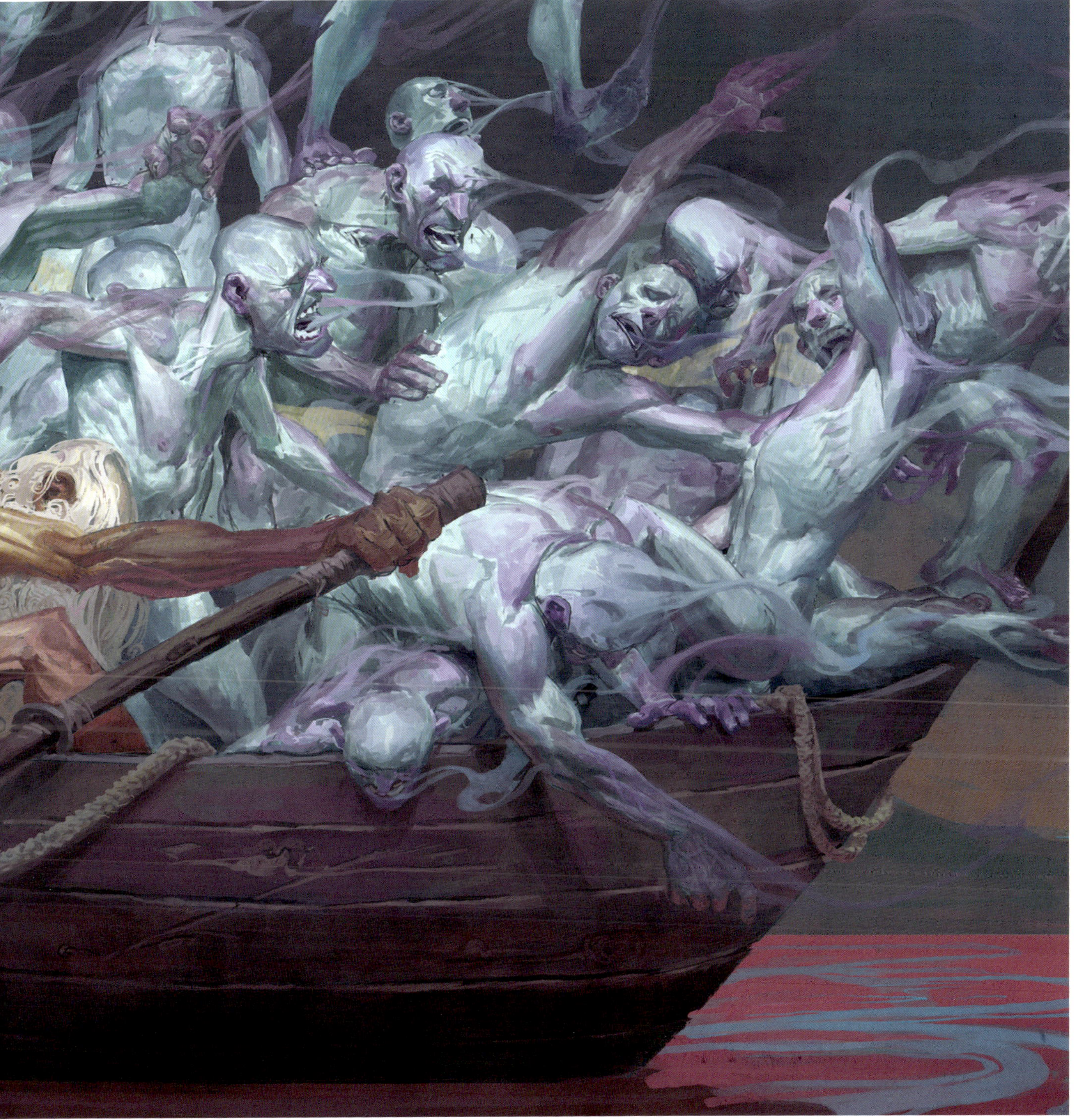

WORLDBUILDING

Worldbuilding is the process of developing an imaginary setting, usually including its geography, history, and the peoples and creatures populating it. Taking the time to think through the background of both the characters and their universe will add depth, complexity, and your own unique insight to an image. You can build from outside in, starting with the setting and placing the characters in it, or vice versa, constructing the world around a cast of characters. Even if the image is only a character design with no scenery, it's still helpful to think about the broader context and how it is shown by that character.

▲ An illustration of Charon from Dante's *Inferno* – a ferryman from Greek myth who transports the souls of the dead across the river Styx

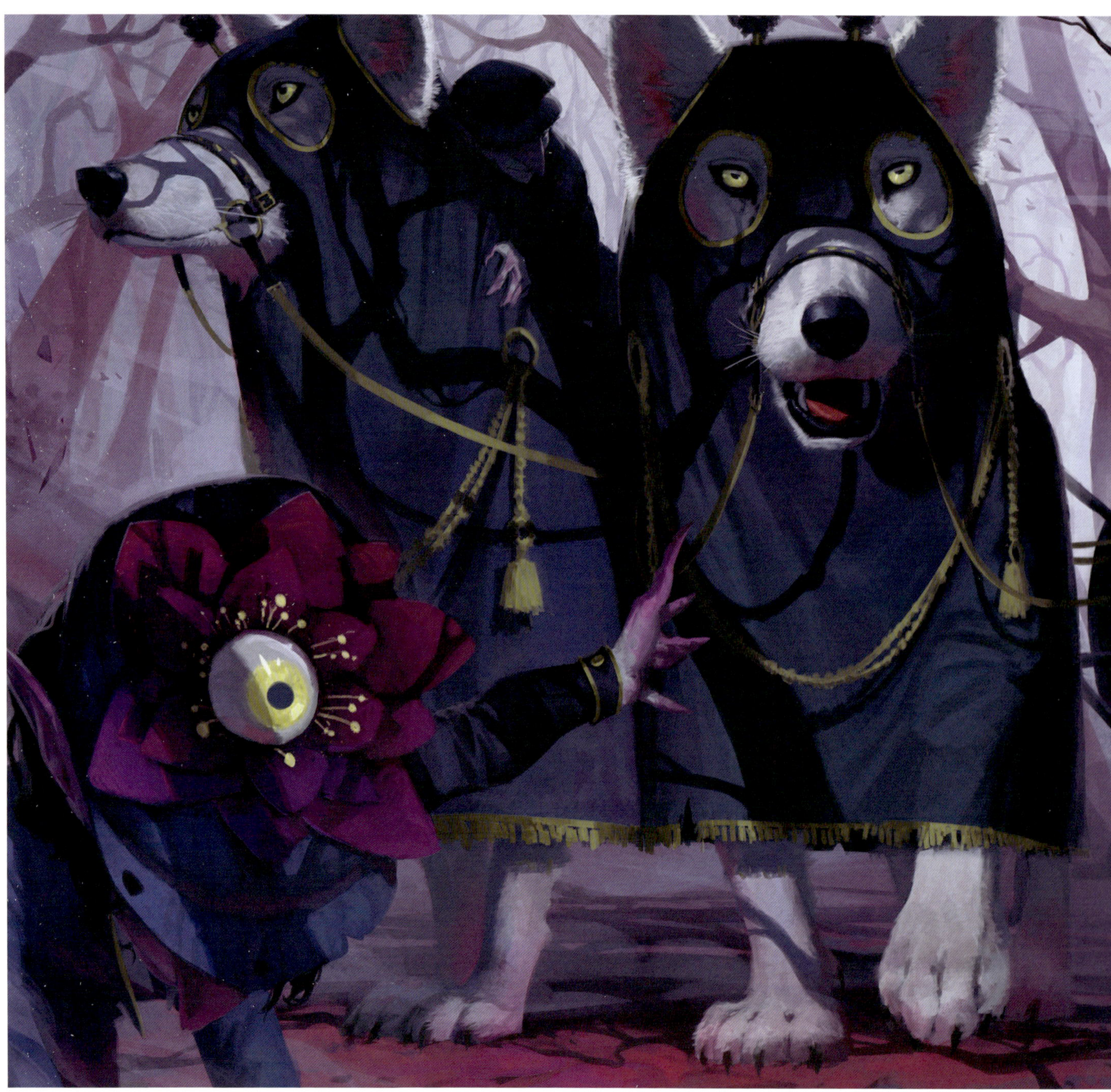

MYTHS, LEGENDS, AND ARCHETYPES

Existing fantasy works, fairy tales, myths, and legends are a rich, vast source that you can illustrate, either by depicting scenes from these tales or using them as a base to modify and build upon. Within these stories, there appear certain building blocks, or "archetypes" – a recurring symbol or motif found in a piece of art or storytelling. Fantasy stories (such as *The Lord of the Rings*) are often based upon the archetypal story structure of "the hero's journey," with commonly recurring character tropes such as the hero, the sidekick, the mentor, the villain, and the love interest. Notice here that the character's archetype is based on the narrative role they fulfill in the story. You can find interesting lists of character and story archetypes online and use those as groundwork to expand upon. Another interesting starting point for coming up with fantasy characters, and then the stories around them, is the system of character archetypes or "classes" used in roleplaying games. Generally, these roles consist of the warrior, the rogue, the ranger, the magician, and the support or healer class. More roles and sub-classes are created by mixing two or more of these, and even more variety and depth can be found by mixing narrative archetypes with roleplaying classes. For example, what would a sidekick paladin character be like?

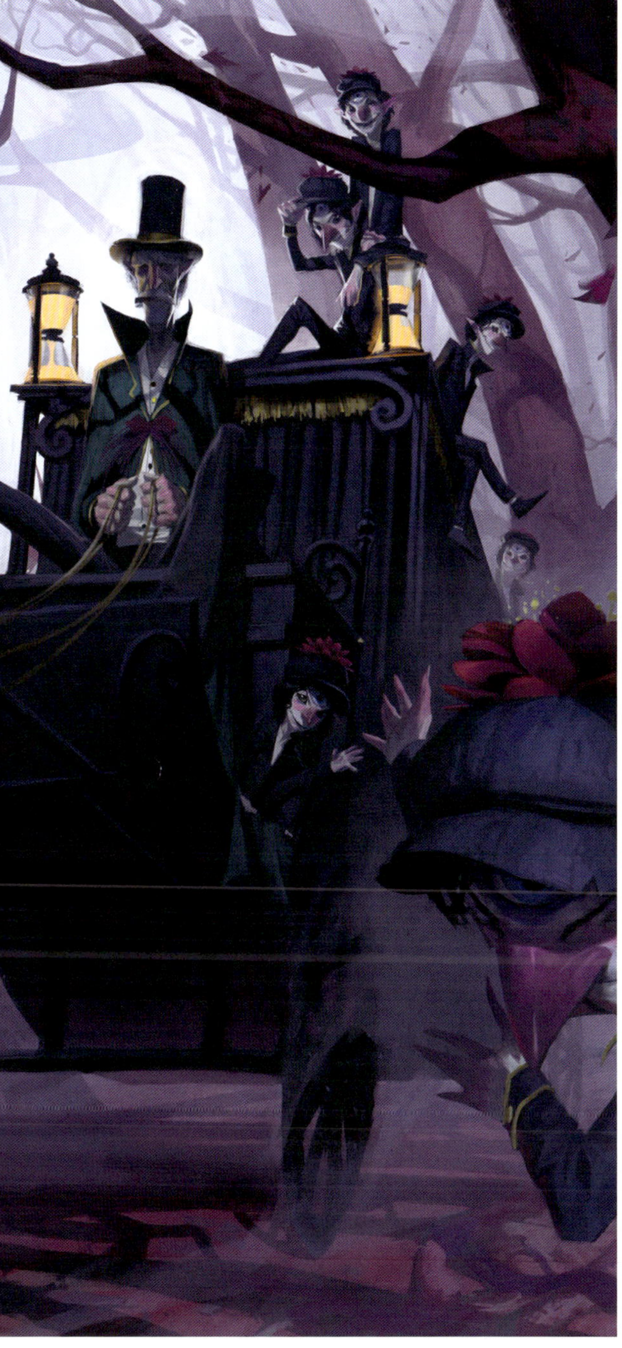

◄ This character, the Wagoner, is based on the archetype of the undertaker or Grim Reaper, similar to Charon

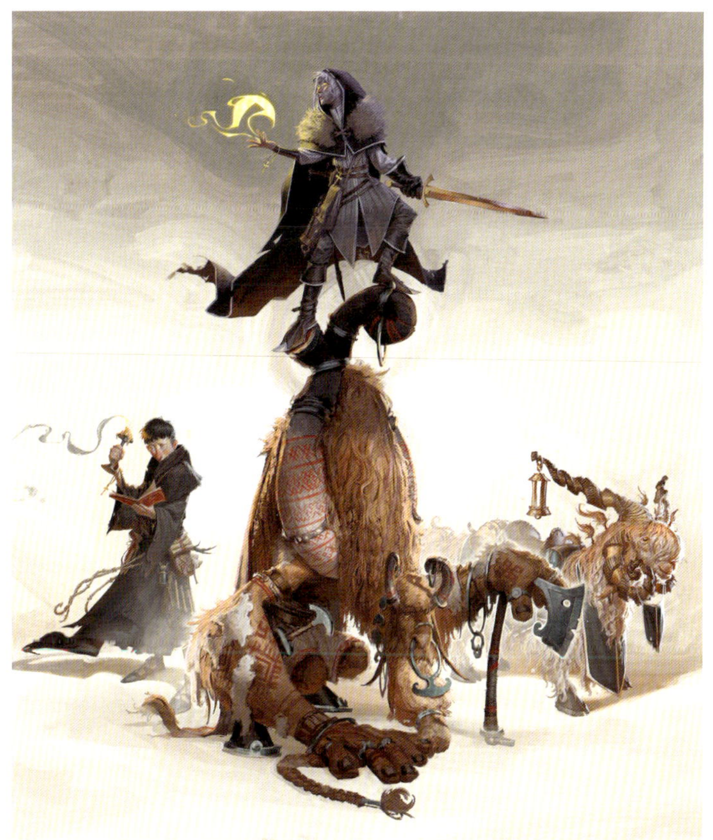

► A lineup of characters based on some archetypes of "the hero's journey": the hero before and during the journey, the companion, and the mount

ADVICE

Let's end this section with some food for thought as we prepare to enter the tutorial chapters. Improving your illustration skills, whether you are an experienced artist or a total beginner, is a never-ending process that can be non-linear, difficult, and frustrating. If you keep the following tips in mind, you will find the learning process a little easier, more manageable, and healthier to sustain.

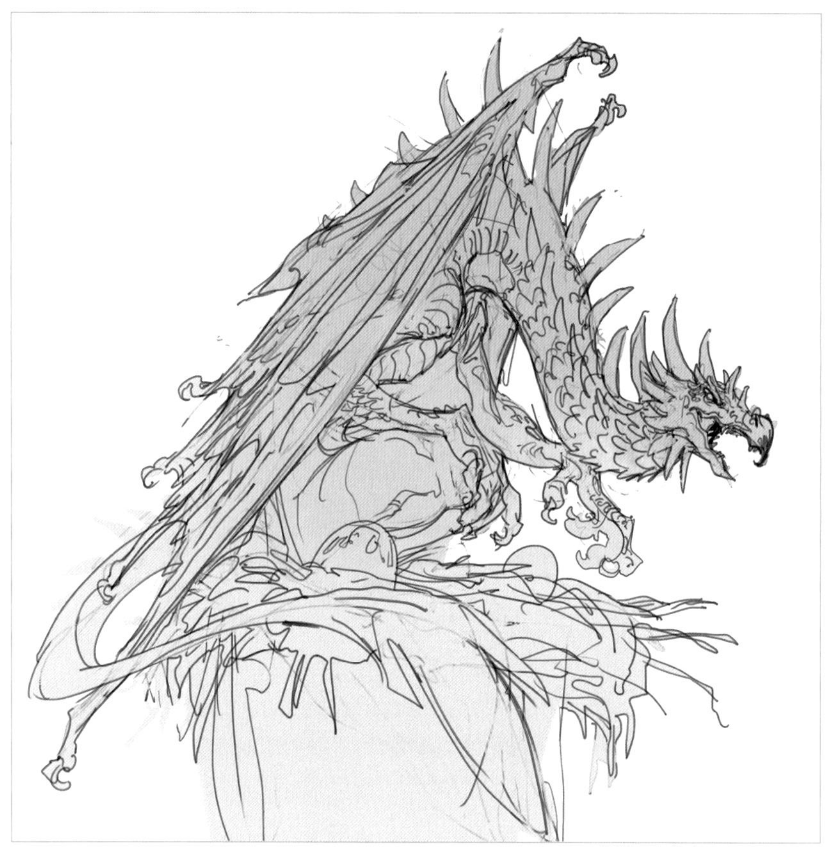

IMPROVING AT ART

First I would like to give some general advice to the aspiring fantasy illustrator about improving in art. Getting better comes from studying the fundamentals of image-making (drawing, anatomy, composition, design, light, and color), doing a lot of work (whether drawing or painting, for personal or client projects), and exploring art in different ways (such as researching art history or contemporary artists of different kinds). Improvement comes from a synthesis of these three things: study, work, and exploration. This means applying the fundamentals of art when actually producing images, while also using different eclectic influences to add depth and ingenuity to your style and narratives. It is important that your explorations and influences be broader than just the genre you inhabit.

◄ ***Explore ideas and iterations stress-free by drawing rough sketches and thumbnails***

CONSISTENCY

Consistency should always be the critical, overarching principle guiding your work, study, and exploration. Your daily aim should be to do as much art as you could if your plan was to do art every day for the rest of your life. This applies especially to studying. If you find intense study difficult or cumbersome, aim to do no more or less than you could do every day for eternity! You will slowly but steadily rack up mileage, at a consistent pace that suits you. Think of it on a large scale: even 20 minutes a day adds up to around 10 hours a month. You may even start to feel that 20 minutes is too little, and gradually become able to study more and more every day, until you find a good level to keep as a baseline.

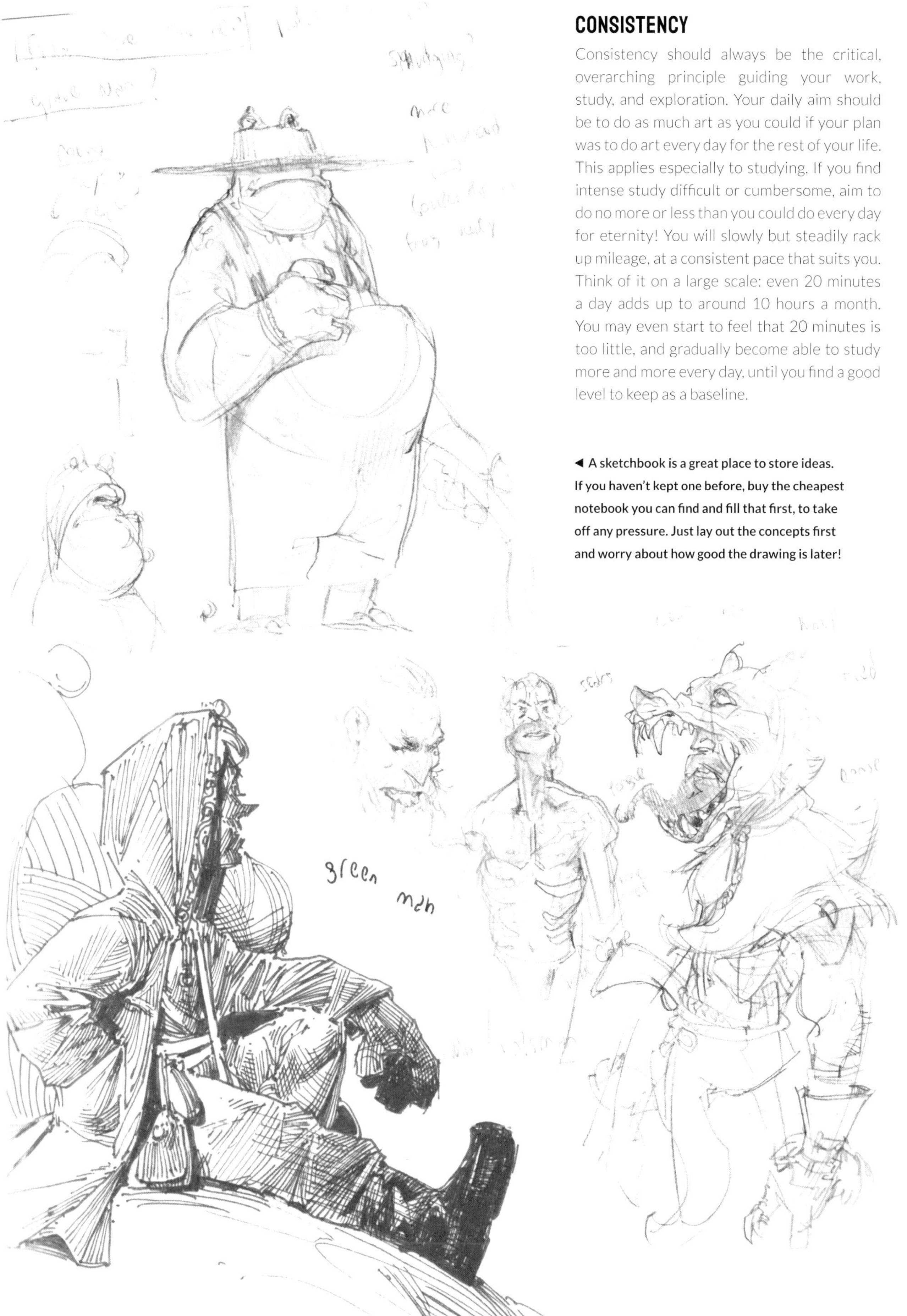

◄ A sketchbook is a great place to store ideas. If you haven't kept one before, buy the cheapest notebook you can find and fill that first, to take off any pressure. Just lay out the concepts first and worry about how good the drawing is later!

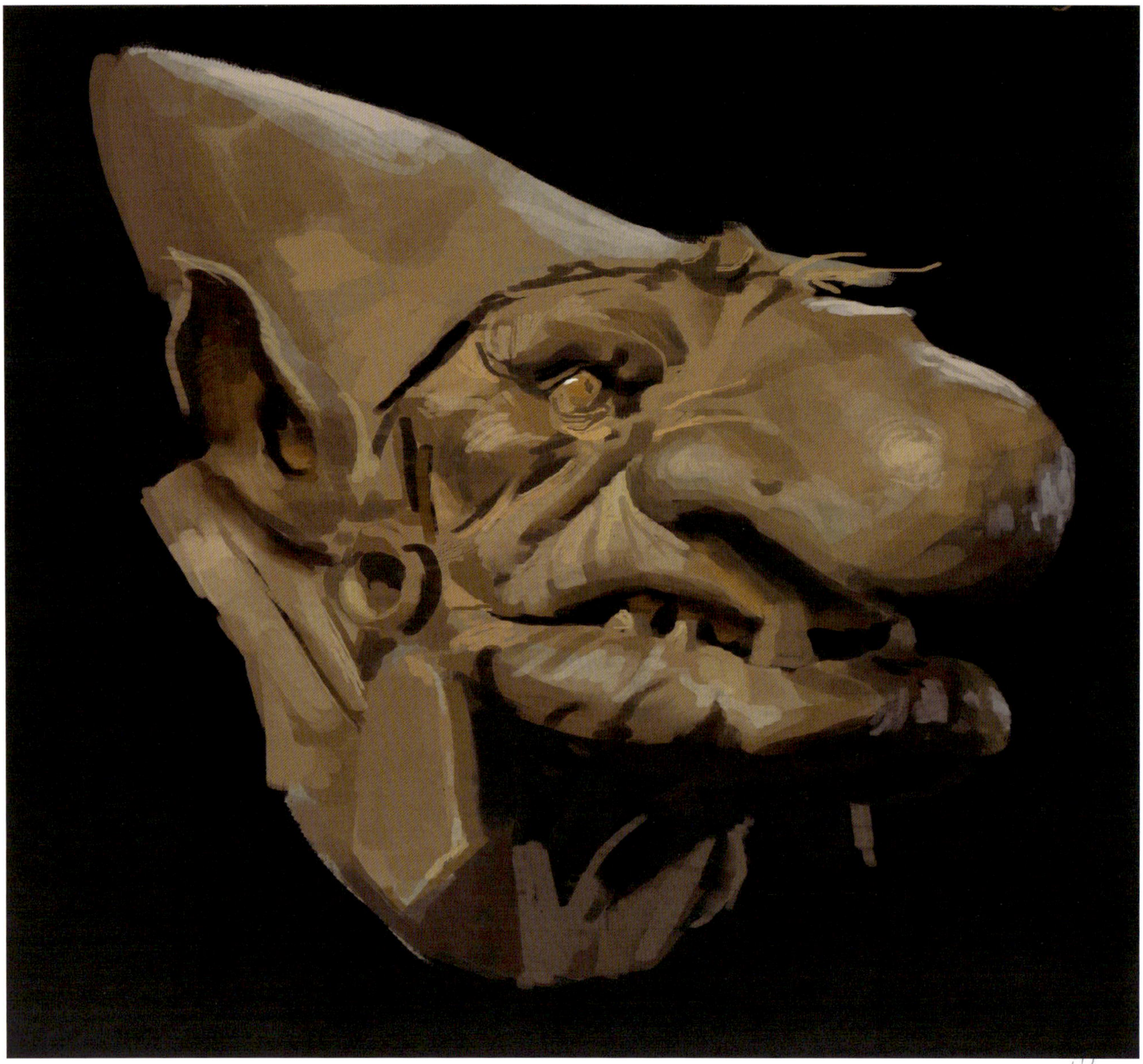

DOING WHAT YOU LOVE

If your goal is to do as much work as you can for the longest time frame possible, then it stands to reason that you would want to do the work that you find the most fulfilling and enjoyable. However, there is a certain natural fixation within artists (particularly inexperienced ones) on what they think they *should be doing*, rather than what they honestly would *like to do* the most. It is irrational and difficult to explain, but it probably has to do with comparing our own art and success to the art and outward success of others. In reality, everybody's path in art is very different. Authentic art will never stem from trying to fulfill an imagined standard, but rather from honestly and objectively looking at your own interests and passions. That authenticity and pureness in someone's art is one of the main factors that sets them apart from everyone else and creates a genuine connection with viewers.

However, you also need to extend your honesty and objectivity to your weaknesses and shortcomings. Maybe you really love horses, but you are terrible at drawing animals. This is something you need to analyze honestly and accept the reality of, and then take practical steps to improve.

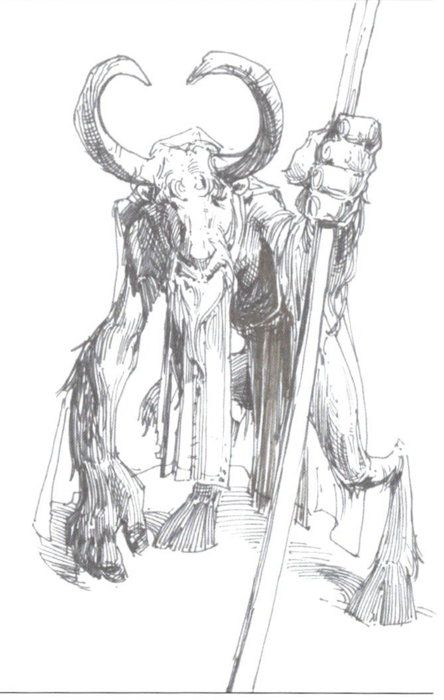

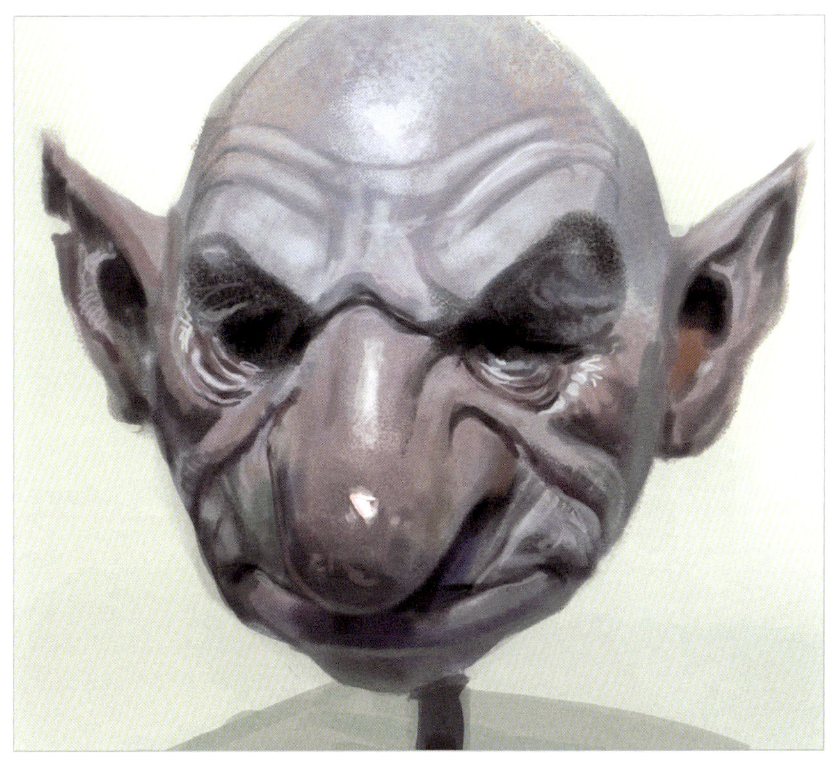

COMFORT ZONE

Your comfort zone is a limited set of fundamentals, themes, and subjects that you can reliably work within, delivering a steady level of performance, usually without a sense of risk. Goals and ambitions are, by definition, outside your comfort zone. In order to grow, you need to leave the comfort zone, but only enough to expand it – don't go so far out of your depth that you get frustrated, waste energy, and quit. Similar to consistency with working and studying, the best way to get outside your comfort zone is to consistently expand your horizons, little by little, steadily becoming more competent while avoiding burning out or beating yourself up.

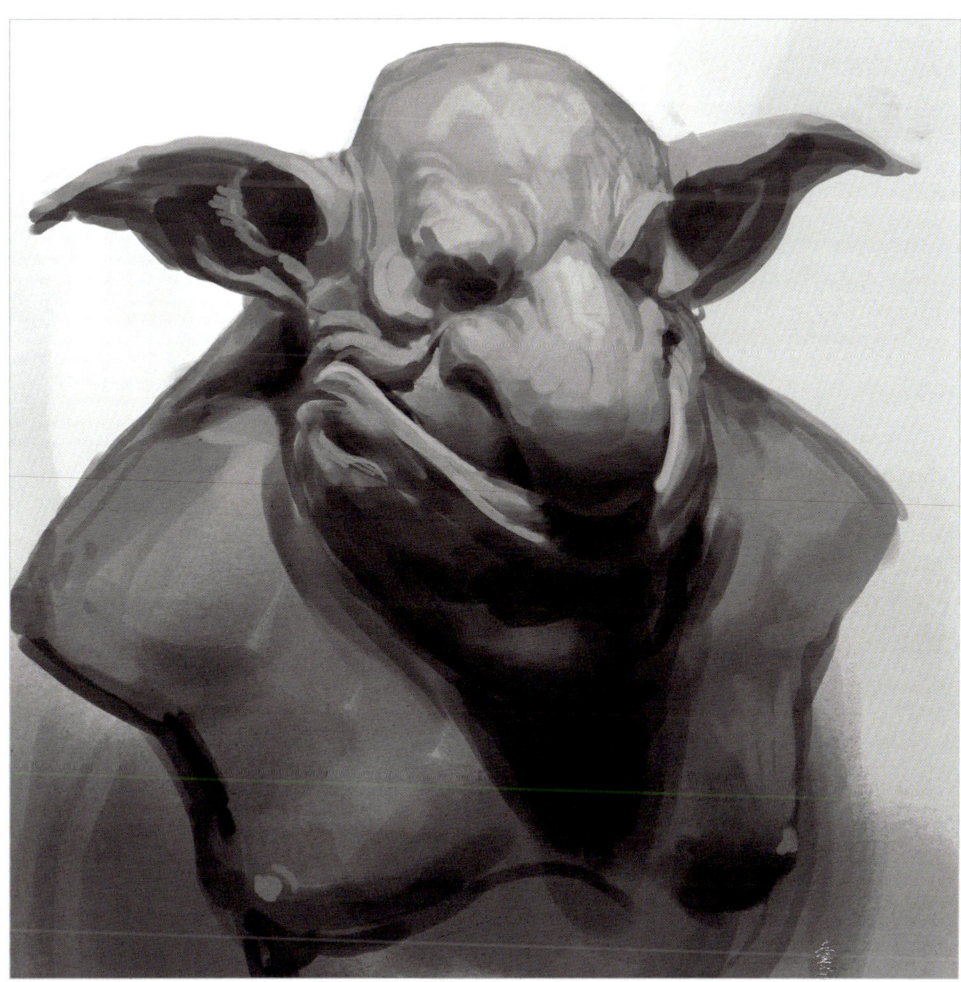

► *Study the things that you enjoy or that are practically useful for your next painting*

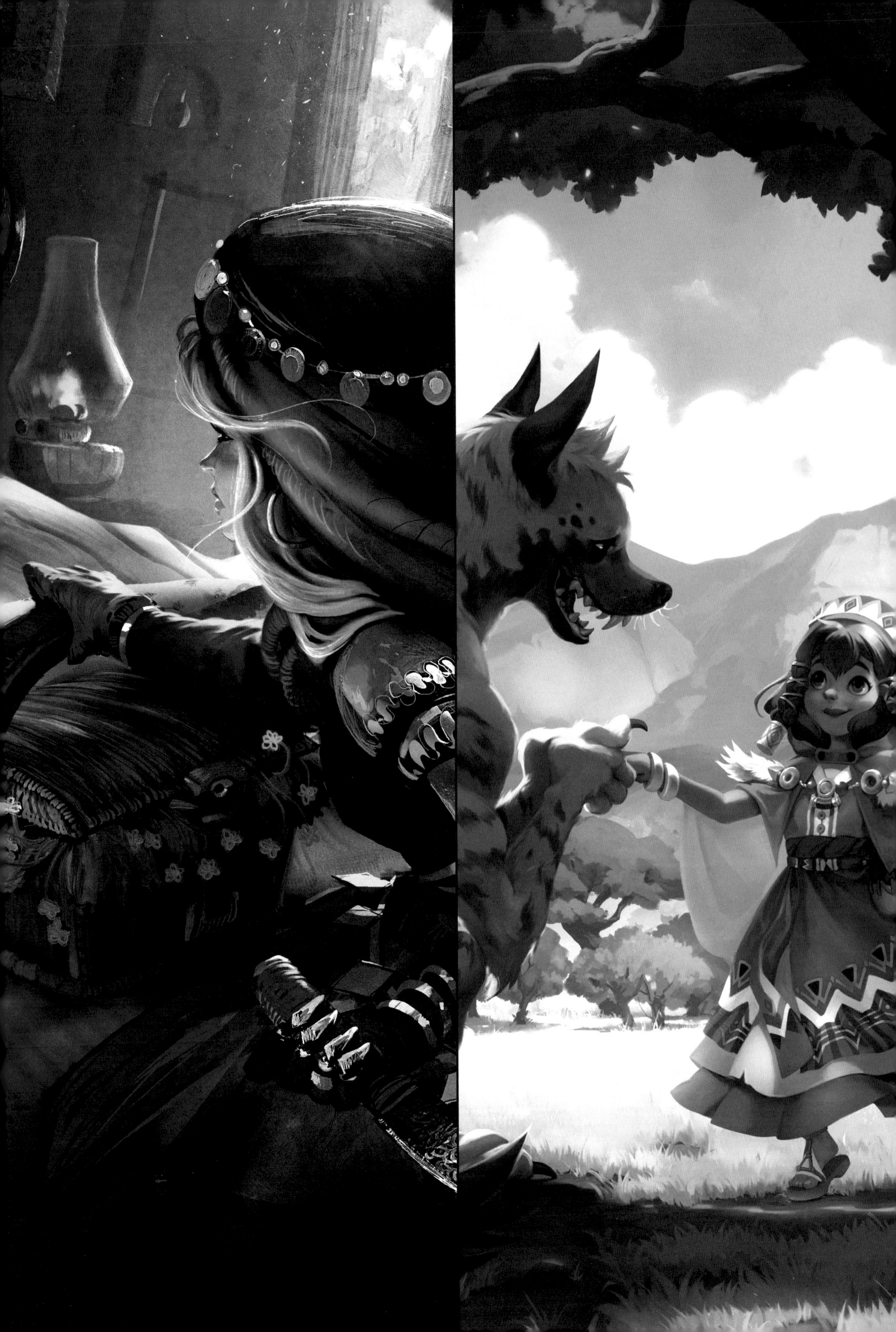

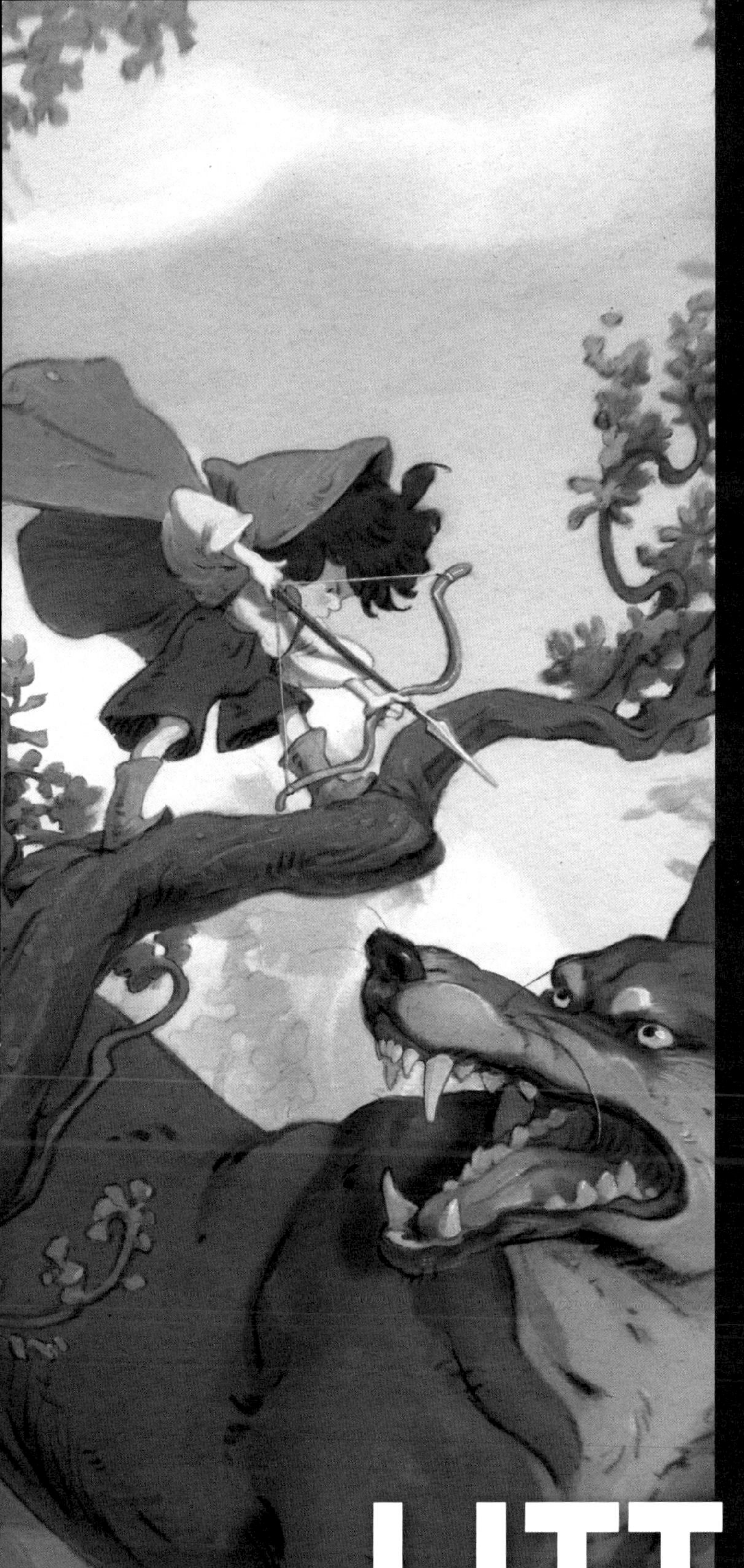

LITTLE RED RIDING HOOD

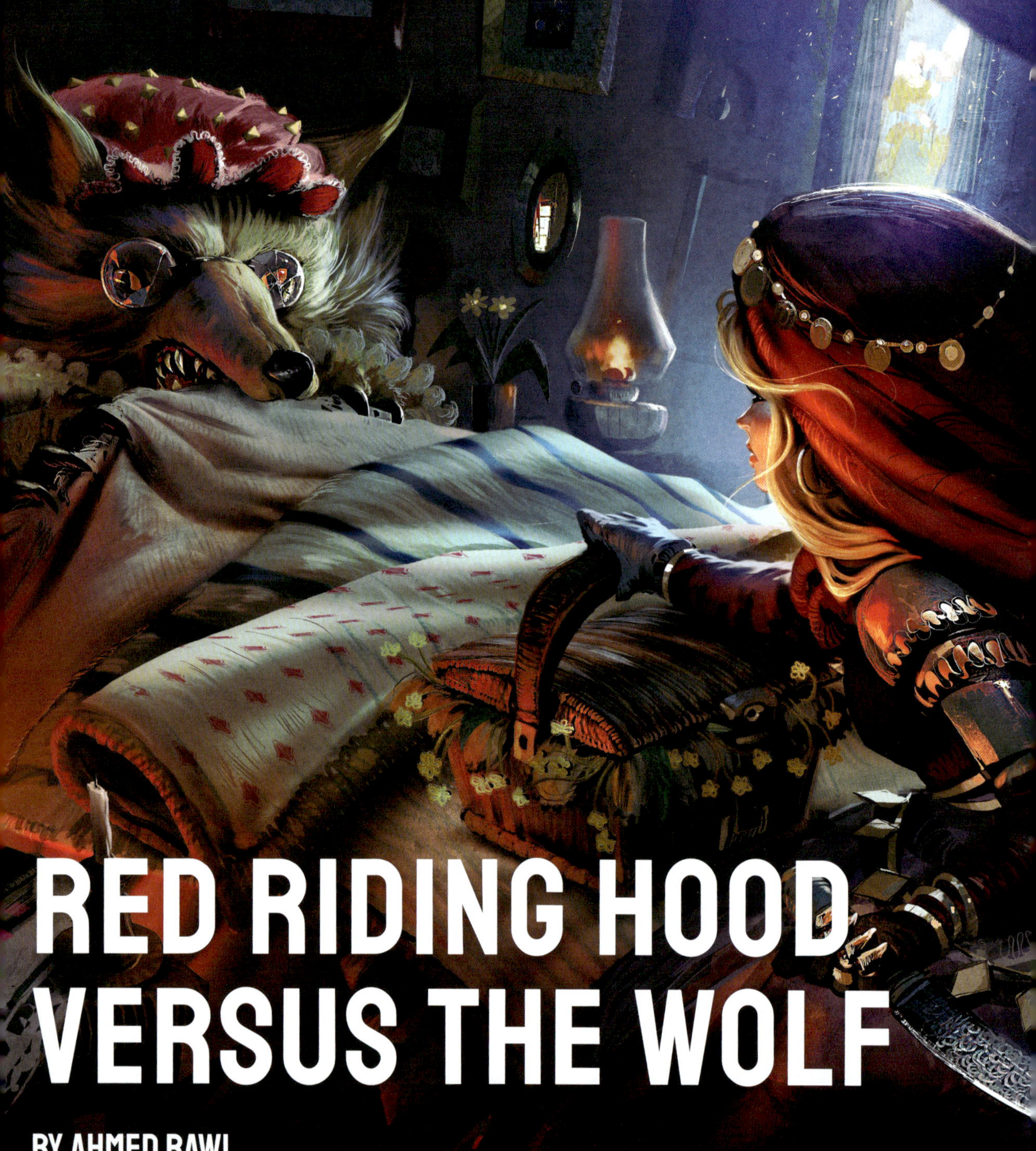

RED RIDING HOOD VERSUS THE WOLF

BY AHMED RAWI

I can't remember how old I was when I heard the original *Little Red Riding Hood*, but I think it was one of the very early stories I was told when I was little. Some of the classic illustrations I saw back then formed a good part of my artistic and emotional memory. I can't count the many versions that I have since seen of the tale, varying between serious and funny. I think the idea of finding an aggressive animal lying in bed, instead of the person you planned to visit, is quite terrifying! In my version of the story, I want to focus only on the two main characters, and put them in an interesting, suspenseful situation that puts my own twist on a key moment from the original tale.

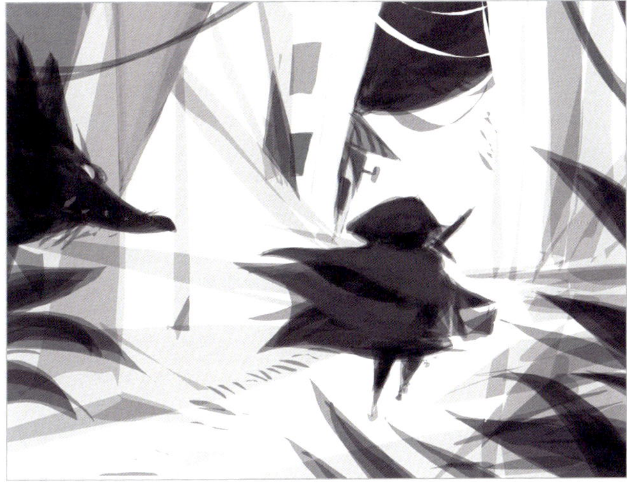

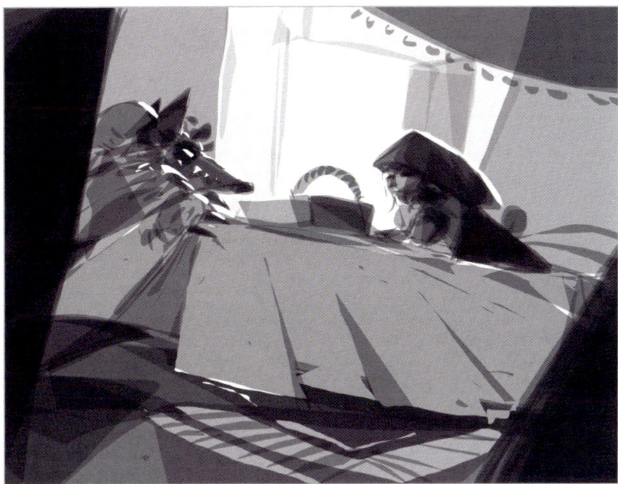

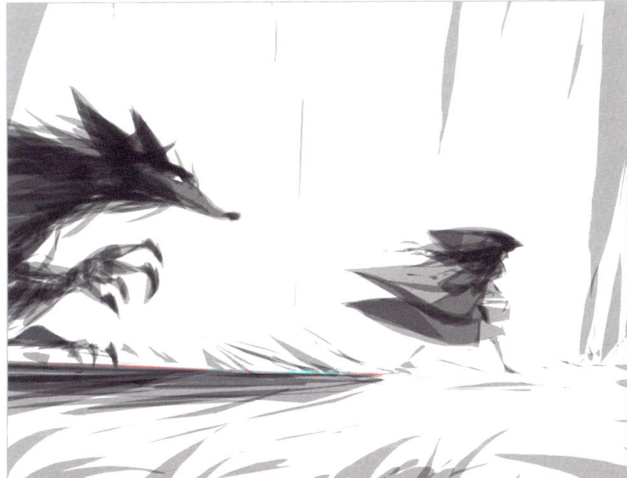

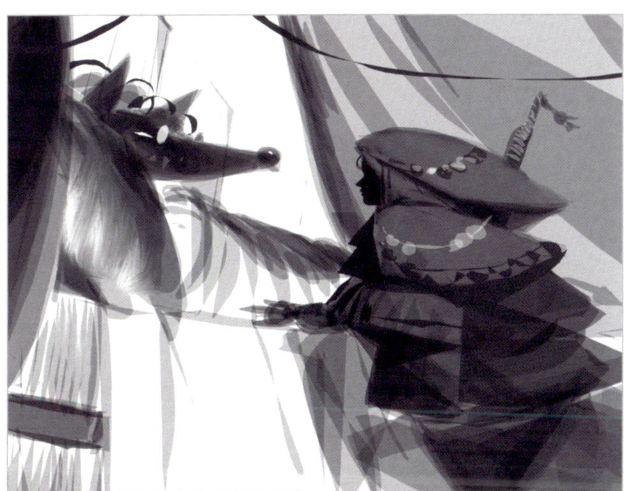

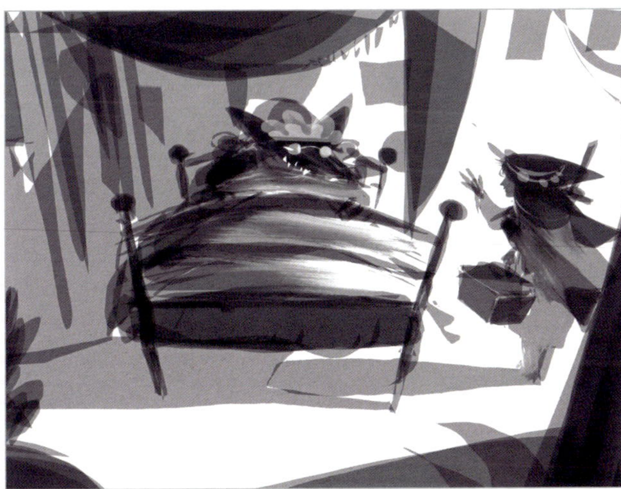

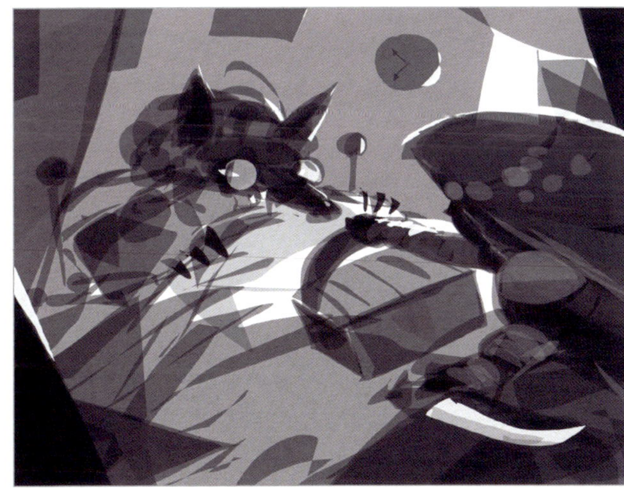

▲ Starting with thumbnailing the key events of the story

01 ONCE UPON A TIME...

First, I simply go through the classic narrative of *Little Red Riding Hood* in my mind, the way I remember it from my childhood. I allow myself to exaggerate areas of the story to give myself a clearer vision of what to change or twist. I break down the sequence as a short storyboard to pick where to focus. I start from the point where the wolf is sneakily chasing Red Riding Hood through the forest, then when the girl enters the house, and then the moment when she realizes what's going on inside. I keep my thumbnails simple, focusing only on the main action of the story. The last version is promising, placing the viewer behind Red Riding Hood.

02 QUICK THOUGHTS

This step is like a whiteboard for the illustration – just a big page of sketches and notes. Before going into any details, I have to put my thoughts and ideas roughly down, and build connections between questions, visual design options, and the twist. It's a good stage to think about the style and general theme of the characters and environment. For example, I would like to add a touch of an Arabian style to Red Riding Hood's costume and accessories, giving a slightly different look to her classic hood and cloak, which could be decorated with hanging jewelry and ornaments. I like the idea of the wolf being a clever hunter, but also a clumsy animal who is not cunning at all in covering his tracks. He might be lying in a pile of disorganized blankets, wearing the grandmother's cracked glasses that broke when he attacked her – just oblivious to the mess that might give him away! Although the grandmother will not feature in my scene, I want to show her warm personality through the setting's interior design and props.

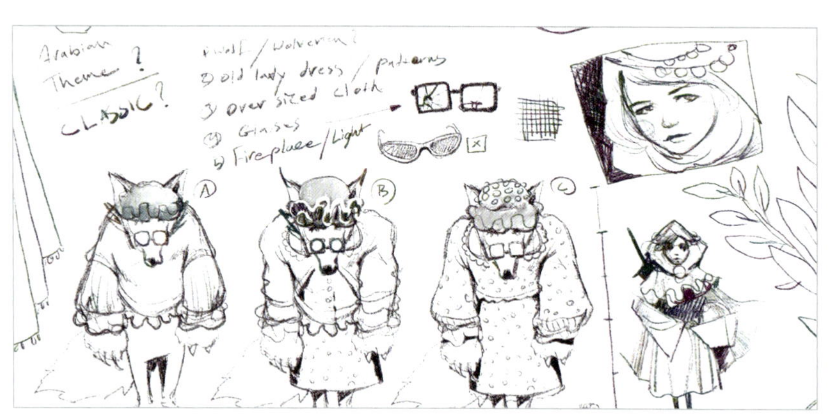

◀ Quick thoughts and preparations for the main illustration and character-design elements

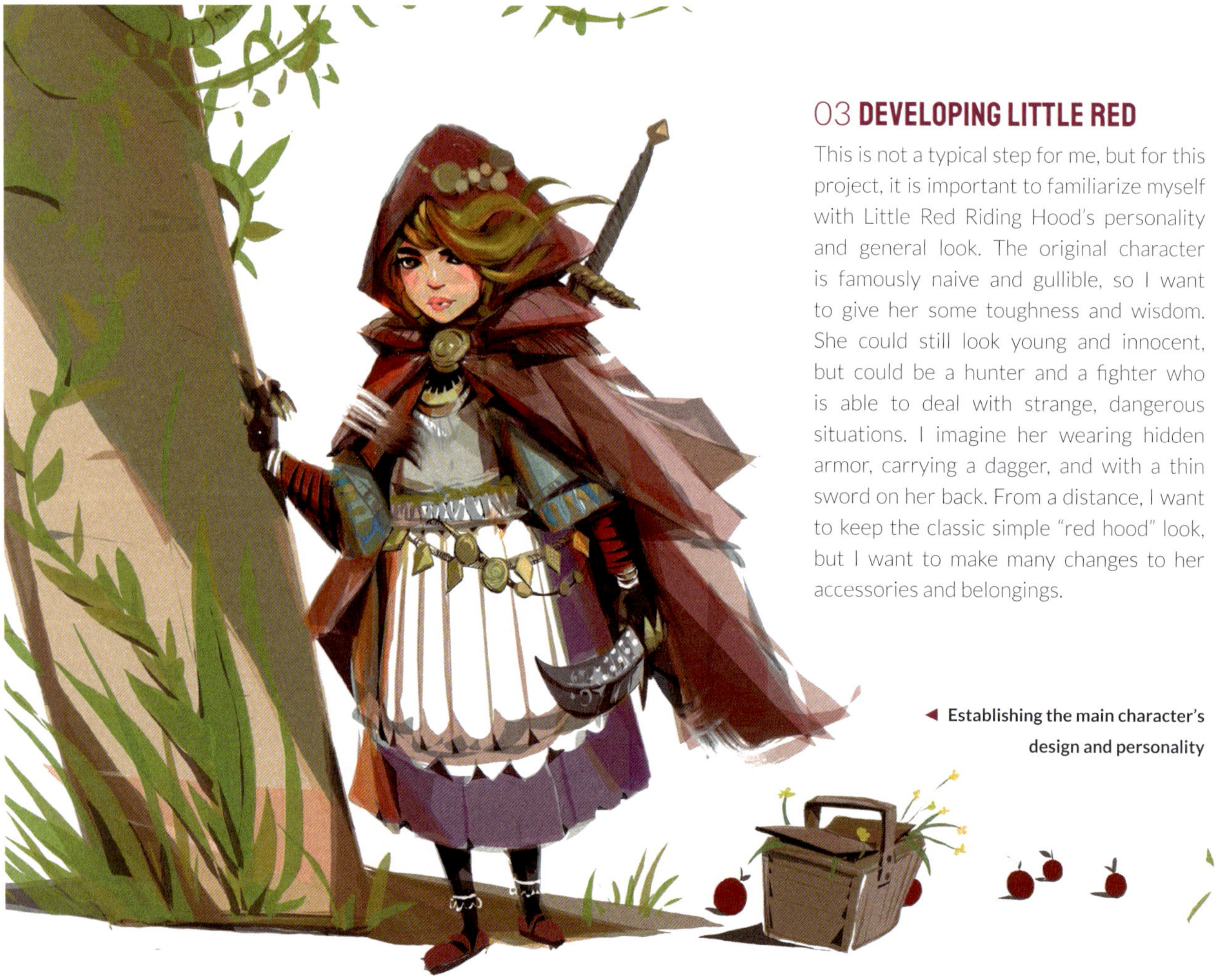

03 DEVELOPING LITTLE RED

This is not a typical step for me, but for this project, it is important to familiarize myself with Little Red Riding Hood's personality and general look. The original character is famously naive and gullible, so I want to give her some toughness and wisdom. She could still look young and innocent, but could be a hunter and a fighter who is able to deal with strange, dangerous situations. I imagine her wearing hidden armor, carrying a dagger, and with a thin sword on her back. From a distance, I want to keep the classic simple "red hood" look, but I want to make many changes to her accessories and belongings.

◀ Establishing the main character's design and personality

04 CHOOSING A KEY MOMENT

Looking at the thumbnails I made in step 01, I am very happy with them all in terms of storytelling. However, I think that only the last frame can create the story twist I am looking for. In that moment, I imagine Red Riding Hood preparing to attack the wolf with her dagger after figuring him out. She could be hiding her blade behind her food basket, just about to strike. In that same instant, the wolf is realizing with confusion that he's been discovered!

That moment of dramatic tension gives me a good idea of the character expressions, general mood, and environmental lighting I need to support the scene. I use the rule of thirds as a base for my composition, tagging the main subjects in the grid's intersections. To give Red Riding Hood the commanding role in the composition, I give her shape three times the visual weight of the wolf.

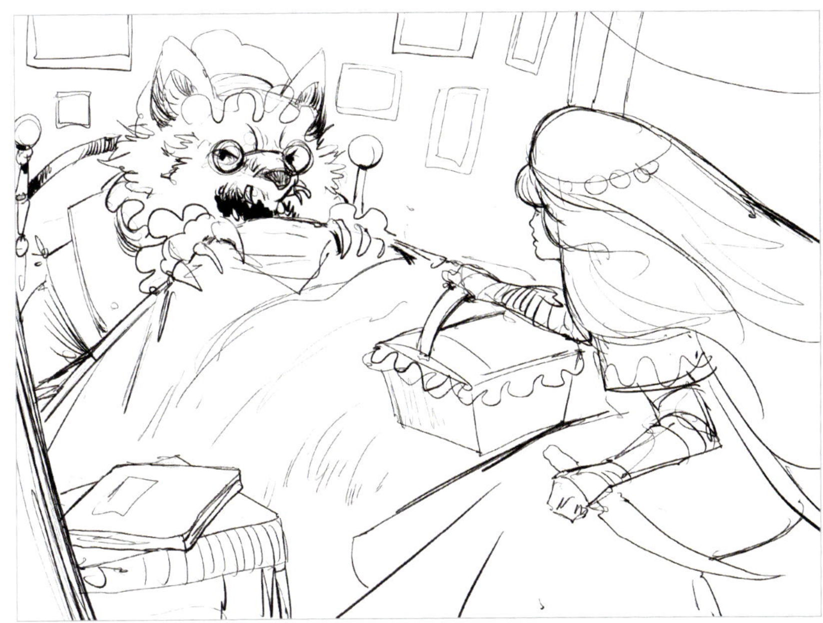

▲ Choosing a suspenseful, dramatic moment to illustrate

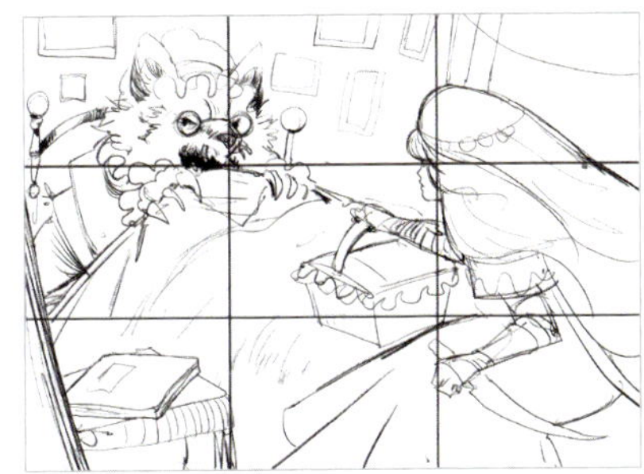

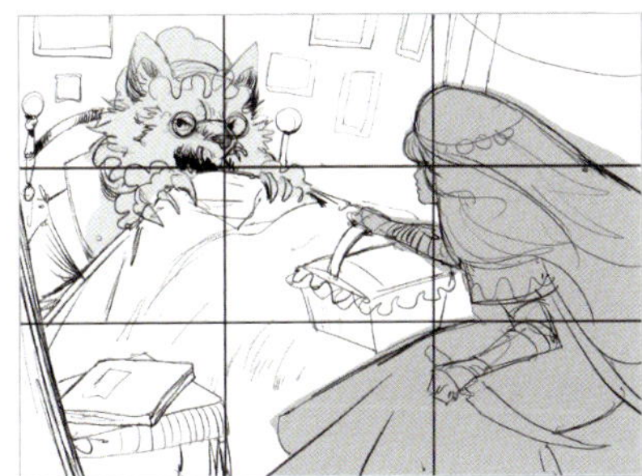

► Giving Red Riding Hood more space and visual weight in a rule-of-thirds composition

05 MAKING A BASE SKETCH

I begin making a new base sketch, starting with the awkward smile on the wolf's face, then working my way over to the broken glasses and the wall behind the bed with all the hanging frames. I try to combine the main details from the thumbnail with this new line sketch. I exaggerate the sizes of the wolf's teeth, ears, and claws for dramatic effect. When working on the wolf's facial features, I keep in mind where the key light will be coming from and where the shadows would be cast. I imagine the strongest light would be coming from the narrow opening of the door in the background.

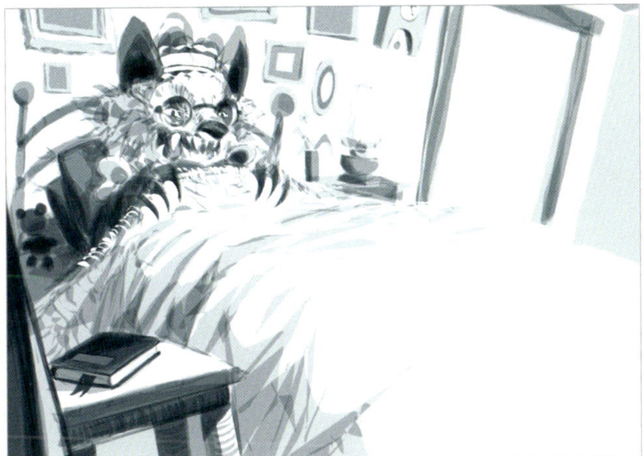

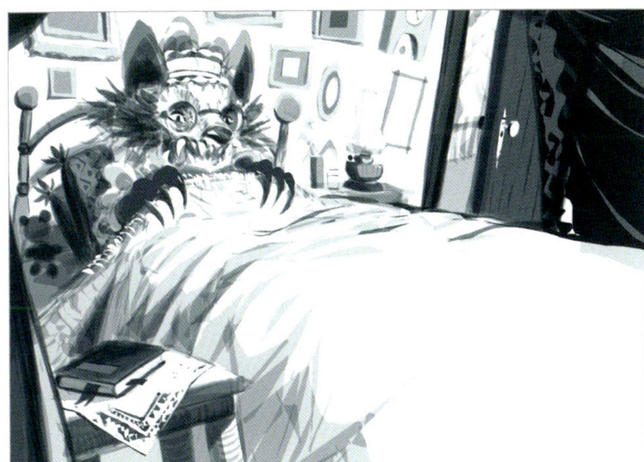

▲ Sketching out the base scene of the wolf in bed and indicating a few key shadow areas

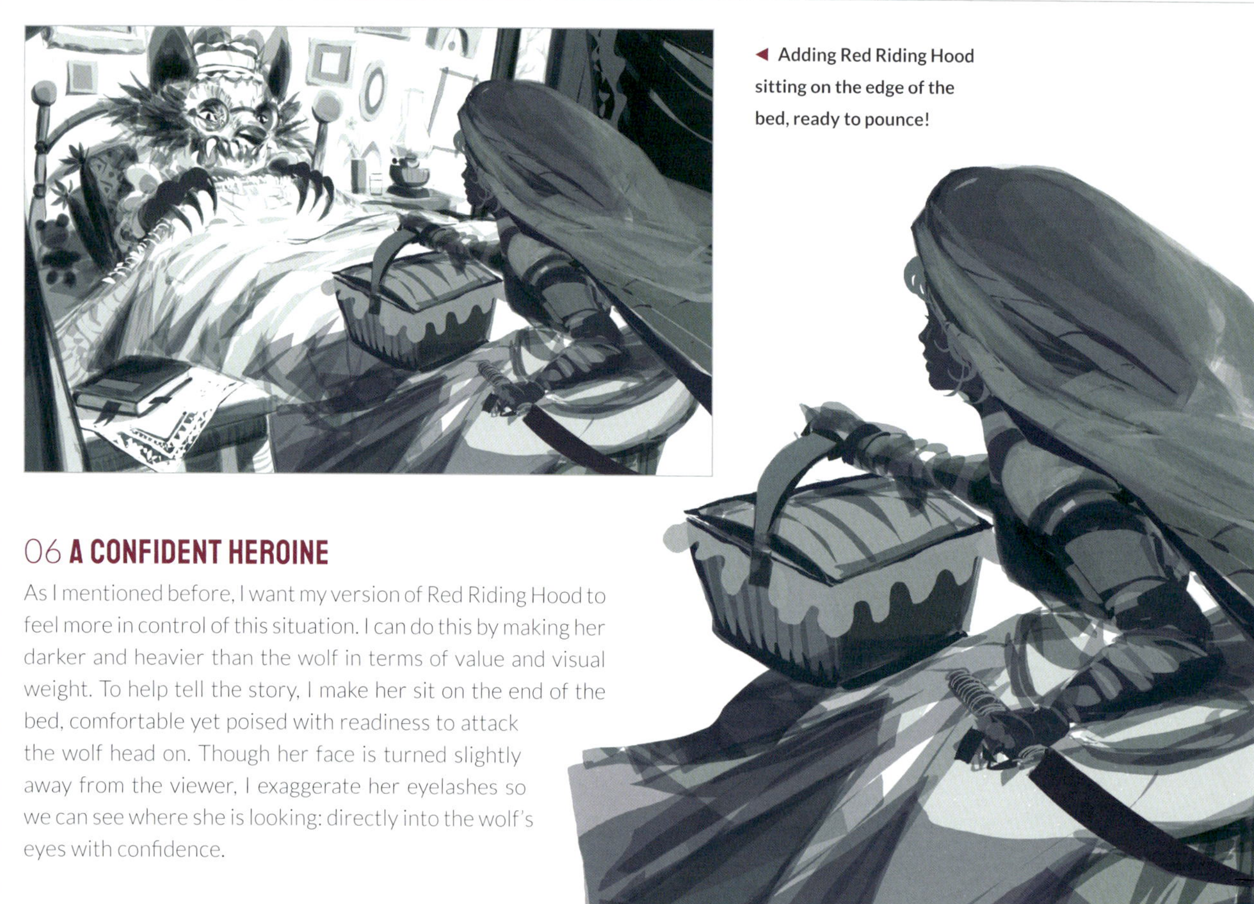

◀ Adding Red Riding Hood sitting on the edge of the bed, ready to pounce!

06 A CONFIDENT HEROINE

As I mentioned before, I want my version of Red Riding Hood to feel more in control of this situation. I can do this by making her darker and heavier than the wolf in terms of value and visual weight. To help tell the story, I make her sit on the end of the bed, comfortable yet poised with readiness to attack the wolf head on. Though her face is turned slightly away from the viewer, I exaggerate her eyelashes so we can see where she is looking: directly into the wolf's eyes with confidence.

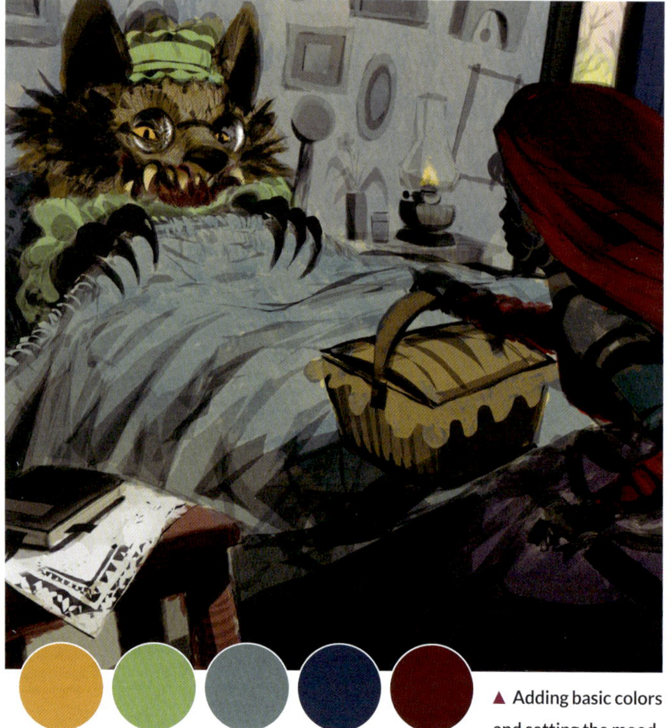

▲ Adding basic colors and setting the mood

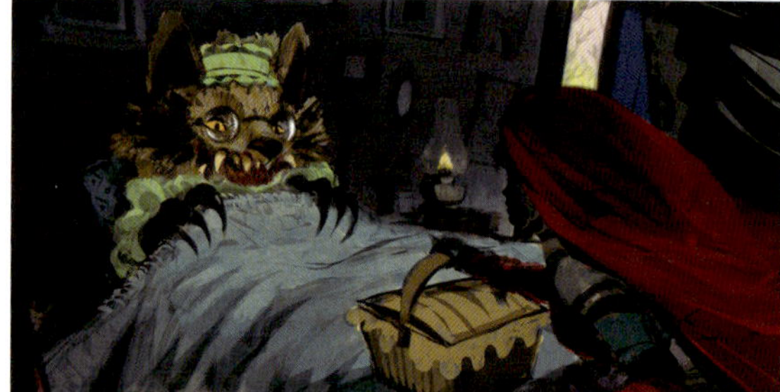

▲ Knocking back the rear wall with a temporary shadow

07 INTRODUCING COLOR

I begin lightly adding the core colors to the scene. The main character, naturally, is mostly red. The wolf will be wearing grandma's warm-looking dress and a night cap. I choose to give the wolf's fur mostly a monotone color – this gives me the scope to play further with his head shape without worrying about making the design too "busy." Although I want the back wall to be presented clearly, I do not want the decorations to become distracting, so I cover the wall with shadow for now. I will light it later with a different, subtler light source.

08 EXPLORING FACIAL FEATURES

As I continue with the first stages of coloring, two processes are taking place at once. On the one hand, I am trying to decide the best facial look for both characters – something that shows their personalities and tells the story. On the other hand, the more scientific side of my brain is calculating the lighting setup and how it will affect the volumes and visibility of the characters. For this image, I do not want to go too stylized or too realistic, but somewhere in between, especially on the wolf. For now, I only give Red Riding Hood a few quick touches of color on the face, and add a rim light from the doorway on her hood.

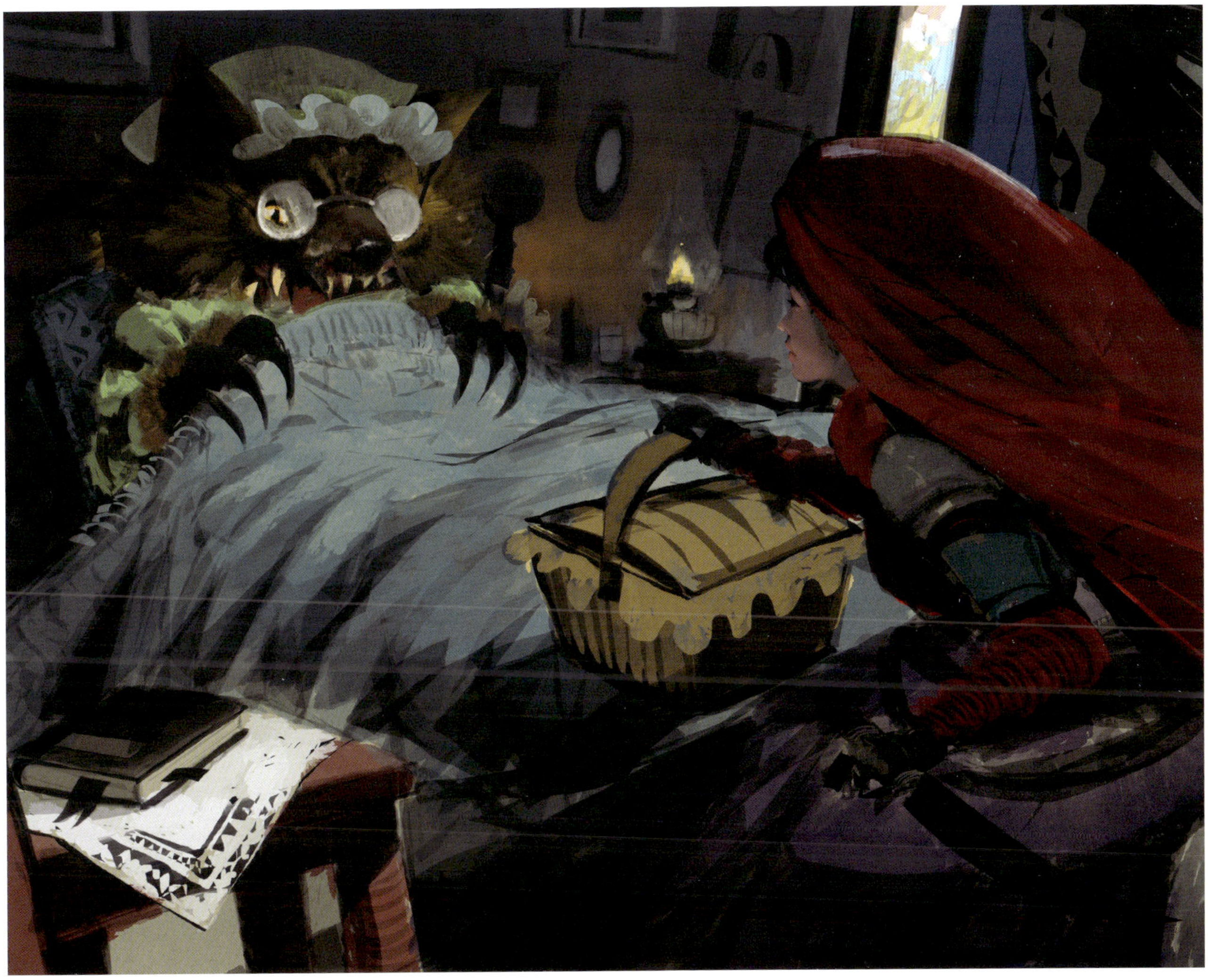

▲ Developing the characters' lighting and facial features

09 A LONGER SNOUT

During step 08, I found myself wanting something more challenging in the wolf's appearance. His face had some elements of cuteness that I wanted to take away and replace with something wicked and aggressive. I do this by adding a longer nose, wilder cheeks, and sharper teeth. I think this makes the balance fairer between the two characters, adding more tension and danger to their situation.

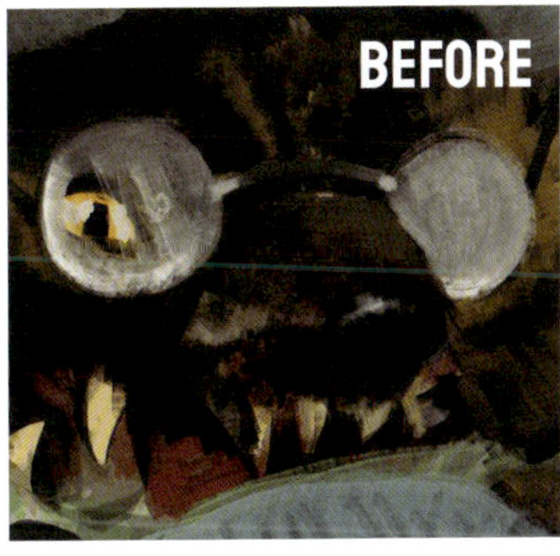

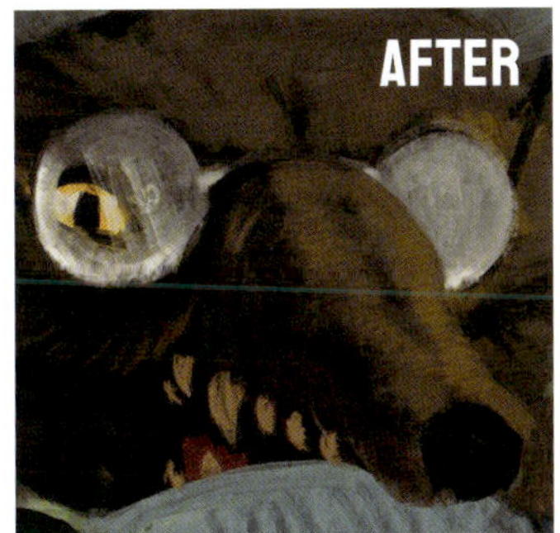

▲ Getting closer to the desired wolf face

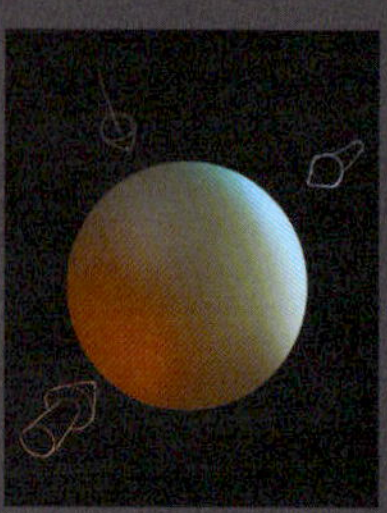
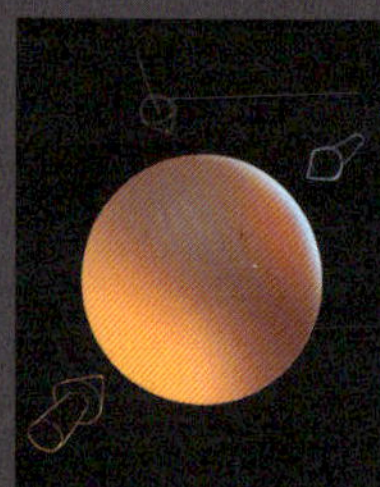

LIGHTING TEMPERATURES

Keeping the lighting consistent across a scene with different-colored light sources can be a challenge. In the example above, a cool-toned blue sphere and a warm-toned orange sphere react differently under the same lighting conditions. Inconsistent lighting can look awkward and muddy, confusing the viewer and undermining the mood of a scene. This is why it's important to place some base colors, such as in step 07, before introducing colorful atmospheric lighting – even though it can be very tempting to jump ahead!

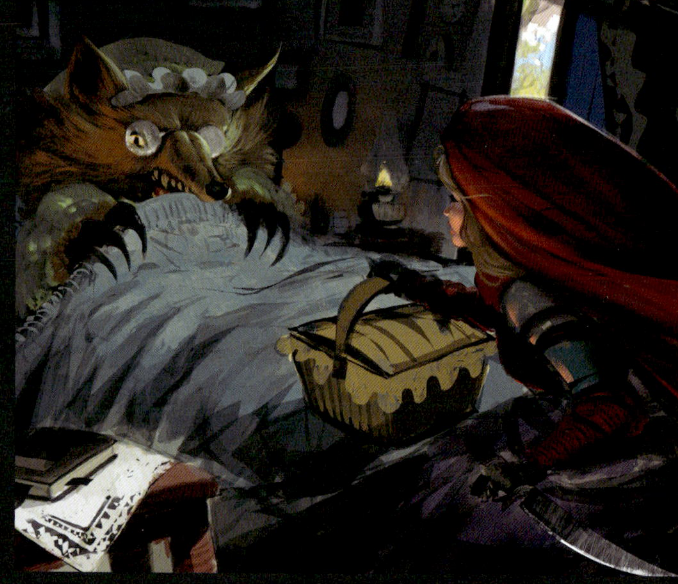

▲ Adding a warm light source for a more dramatic feel

10 WARM FIRELIGHT

I continue to develop the heroine's appearance, painting the details of her face, hair, and dagger. This scene will mainly be lit by the cool light from the doorway, but I also want to use a warm light coming from the opposite direction, as if there's a fireplace in the room. This would create a balance between cool and warm in the scene, as well as clarifying more details on this side of the characters' faces. Using an "opposite" lighting scenario like this can create a feeling of beauty and horror at the same time. That sense of drama and tension will be perfect for this story.

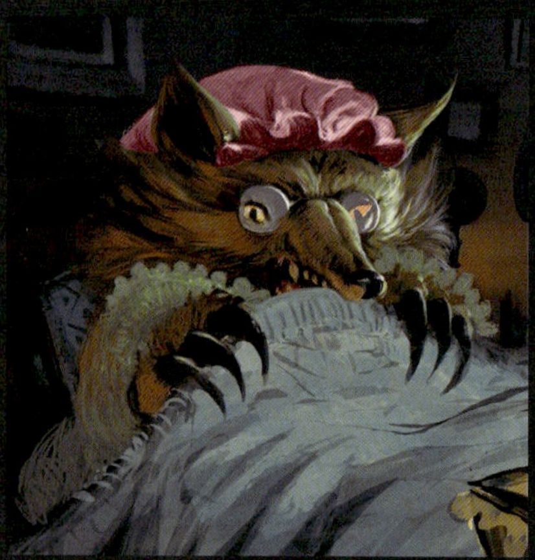
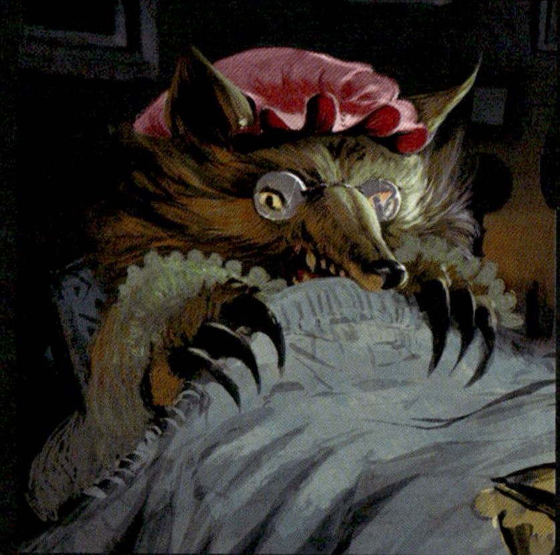
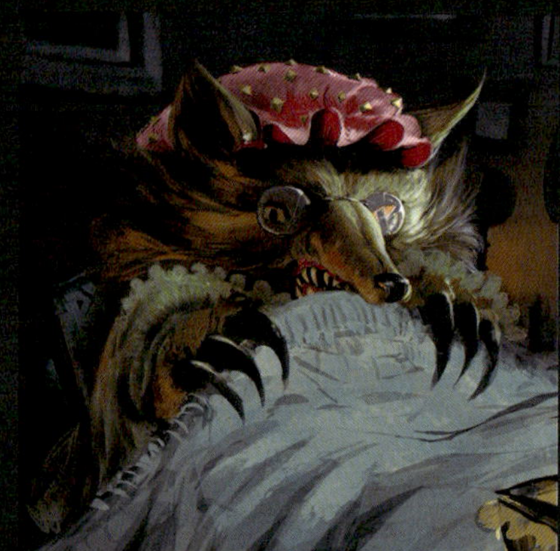

▲ Building up the details of the wolf's face and clothes

11 REFINING THE WOLF

Now that the lighting setup is clear, it becomes easier for me to add details and a new layer of polish. I change the wolf's frilly night cap to somewhat match Red Riding Hood's clothing, so that they are almost wearing the same tone (pink versus red). This balances the appearance of both characters by giving the wolf a stronger, more eye-catching costume element than in the original color sketch. Adding some cracks to the wolf's broken glasses shows the humorously clumsy side of the character, while also hinting at the grandmother's unfortunate fate. There is not a very strong, sharp light source in this scene, so I build up these details with smooth, soft shading that simulates the movement of the firelight.

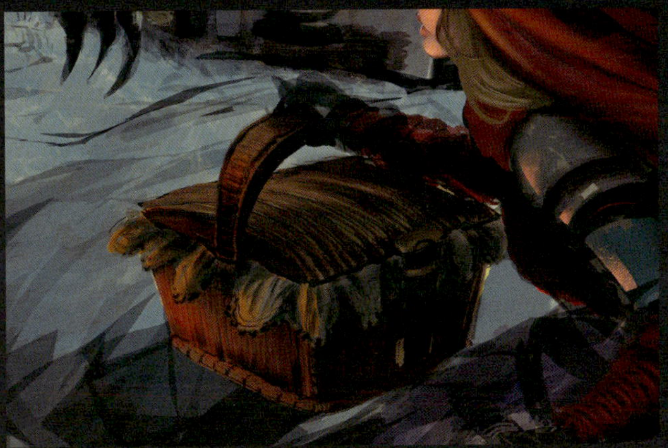

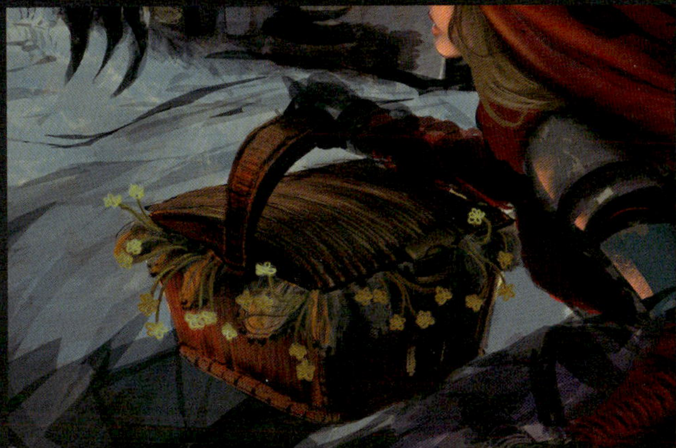

▲ Detailing Red Riding Hood's basket, one of the key objects of the tale

12 RED RIDING HOOD'S BASKET

In the original tale, the basket is one of the primary reasons for Red Riding Hood's journey: a delivery of food and drink for her ailing grandmother. In my story, it serves as a barrier to prevent the wolf from seeing our heroine's incoming attack! I give the basket an old-fashioned design with a lid for security, intriguing the viewer as to what might be inside. The frilly fabric lining the basket enhances the quaint, traditional look, echoing the grandmother's frilly clothes and creating a visual connection between those subjects. I add some chamomile flowers spilling out of the basket, as if Red Riding Hood picked them on her journey through the forest – the ideal medicinal flower for her sick grandmother to brew into a hot drink! The delicate shapes for the flowers also work well to add visual interest to the relatively empty central area of the bed. The viewer's attention is drawn to the tantalizing basket, just as the wolf's has been.

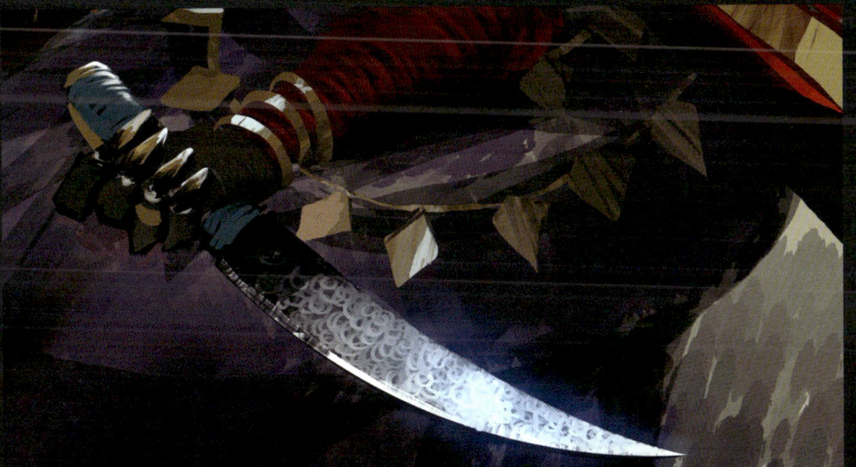

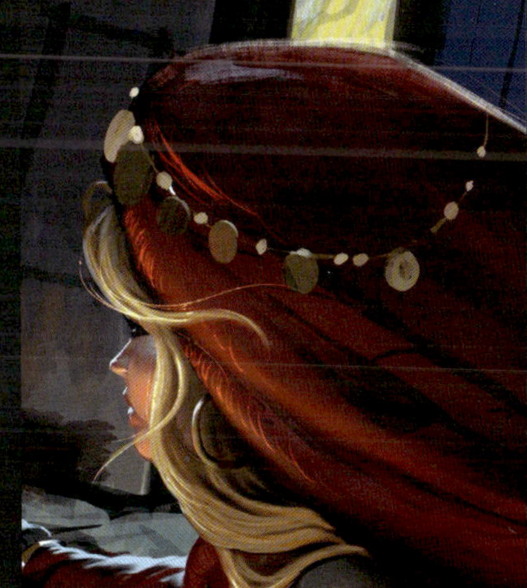

▲ Lighting and detailing the metallic elements of Red Riding Hood's costume

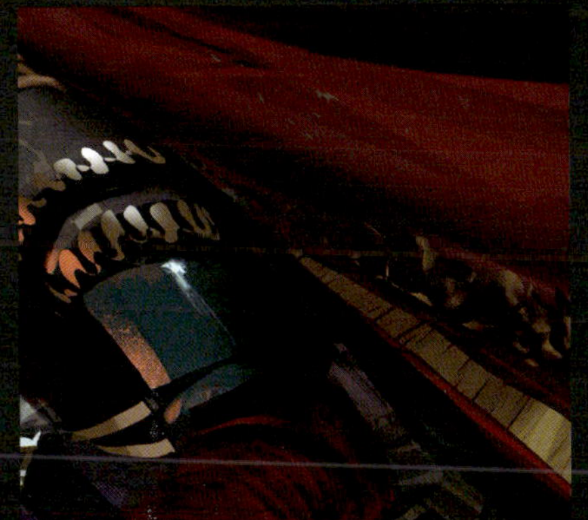

13 PUTTING THOUGHT INTO DETAILS

Now I can begin properly rendering the scene. I start with the cool light hitting Red Riding Hood's far arm and face, before moving on to the warm light, increasing the glow from the fireplace on the near side of the character. I try to capture the reflections of both these light sources on her metal accessories and armor. When detailing the dagger, I give its blade an ornate, scribbled texture, hinting that this is an unusual, specially crafted weapon that might have a bit of history to it. I always try to add extra patterns or decorative elements in a way that adds dynamism to inanimate objects, such as the direction of the golden embroidery on Red Riding Hood's scarf, or the curvature of her belts and headwear.

14 INTERIOR LIGHTING AND REFINING

Now I spread the effect of the fireplace throughout the whole room. The meeting of cool and warm light creates a feeling of beauty and drama on these two contrasting characters, but I can still heighten this sense of cold and heat. I add some fog coming through the open door and a bit of smoke coming from the fireplace. The inside of the cottage feels warm and cozy compared to the cool outdoors – the viewer can imagine how welcoming it would normally be!

Many props have now been tidied up, such as the picture frames, bed sheets, and curtain. I put a small mirror on the wall to add another dimension to the scene and give a better idea of the place's size. I find the wolf's claws are drawing a bit too much attention, so I make them smaller, and also make them pierce holes in the blanket to show the character's nervous tension.

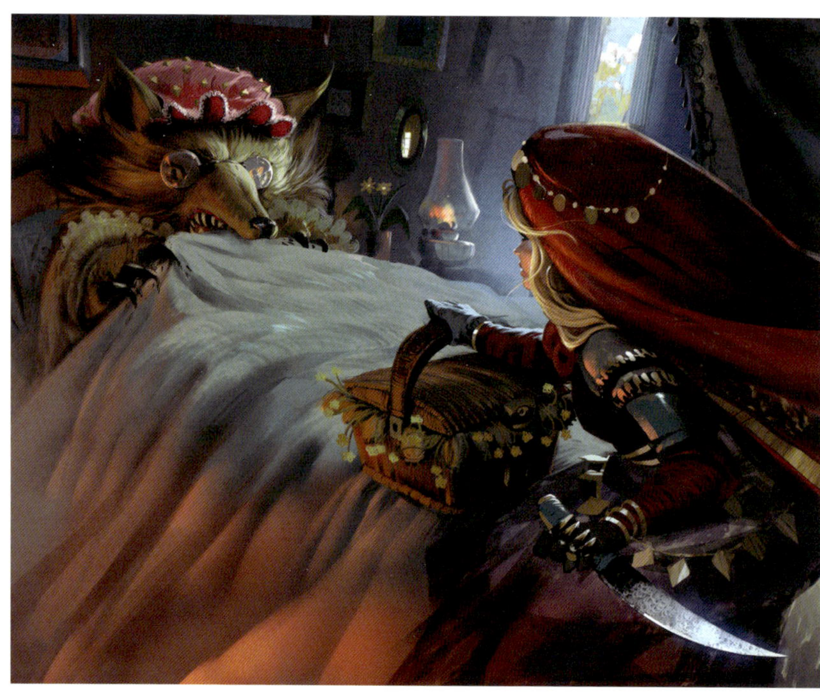

▲ Firing up the interior lighting – it makes a huge difference to the scene's atmosphere!

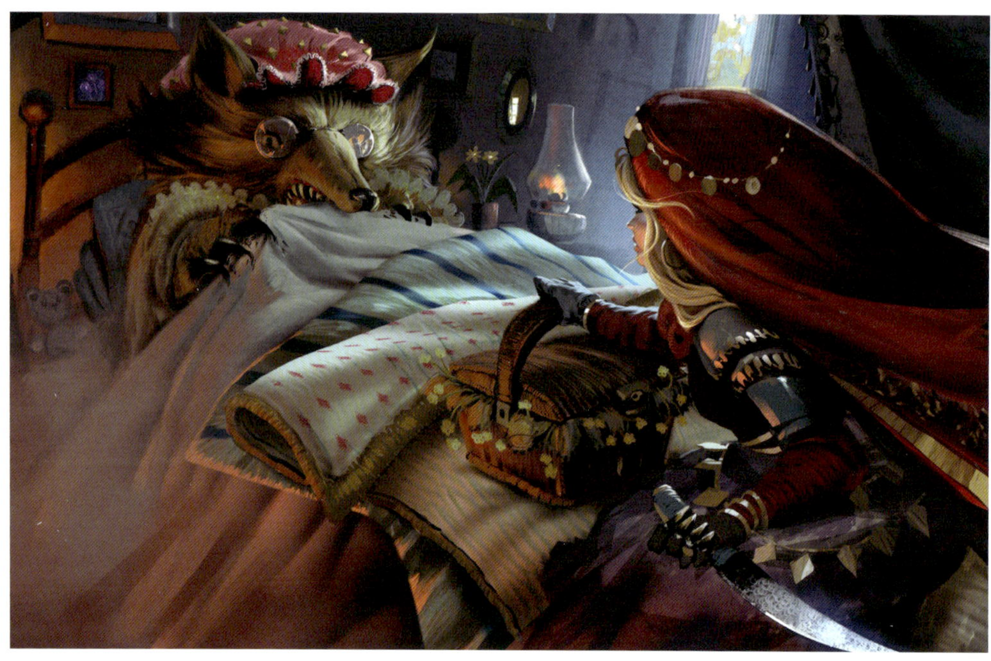

◀ Adding the crumpled blankets to increase the messiness of the scene

15 GRANDMOTHER'S BLANKETS

I imagine the wolf trying to restore the bed to normal after he attacked the grandmother, gathering random blankets and putting them messily over himself to hide his size. In his rush to hide, the blankets are still roughly folded and don't match the alignment of the bed. This is a good chance to add more variety to the scene's materials – for example, introducing some shiny satin with multiple patterns. The blankets catch the light from both sources and almost become a divider between the two opposing characters. They also tell the viewer a bit about the grandmother's character and taste. Even though she's not present in the scene, we can see her clothes, pictures, and treasured personal items, which create an affection for her, reinforcing the viewer's feeling of being on Red Riding Hood's side against this intruder.

16 STORYTELLING WITH OBJECTS

I like to present characters' stories by highlighting elements of their history or things that belong to them, even when I am not showing the characters themselves. The grandmother in this story is a strong example. Besides everything else in the room, the chair in the corner (with the book, reading glasses, and candle) tells us a lot about the grandmother's usual routine. Some bookmarks show which page she had reached, or where she had perhaps highlighted her favorite pages; we can see that she had a second pair of glasses specially for reading; we can assume that she kept a candle for emergencies if her lamp went out. From the potted plants in the scene and framed floral artwork on the wall, we can see that she loved plants and was interested in keeping them. For more lighting balance with the doorway, I add a small hint of another lamp on the left edge of the scene, which the grandmother probably used while reading in bed.

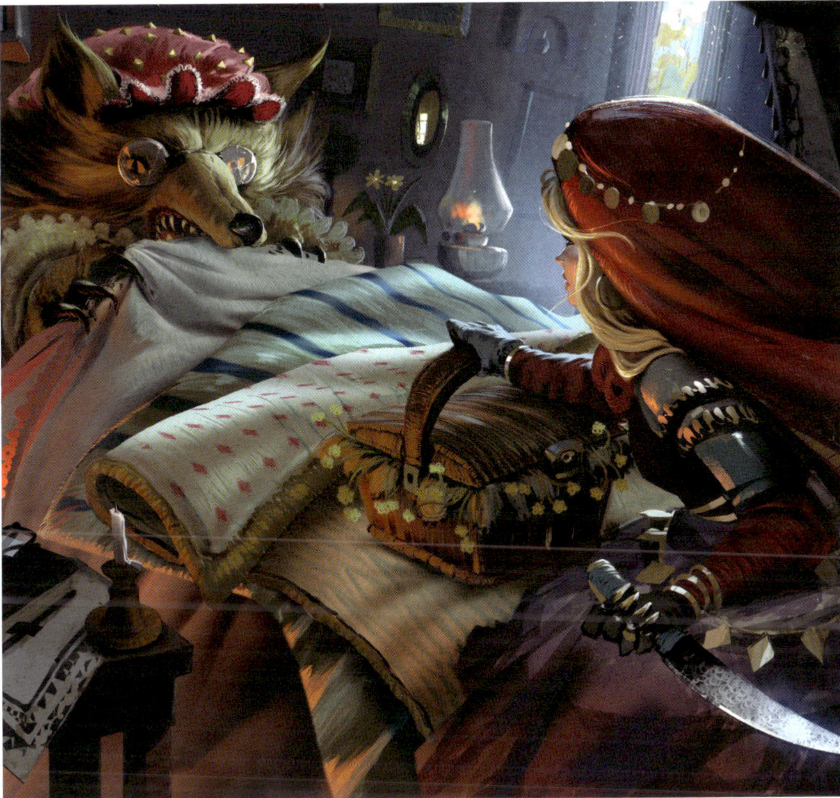

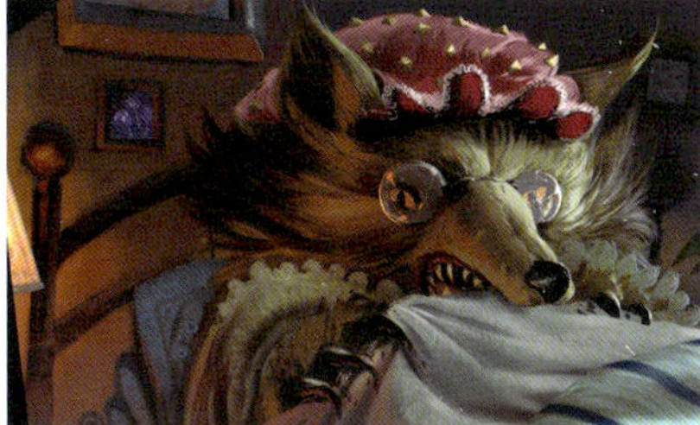

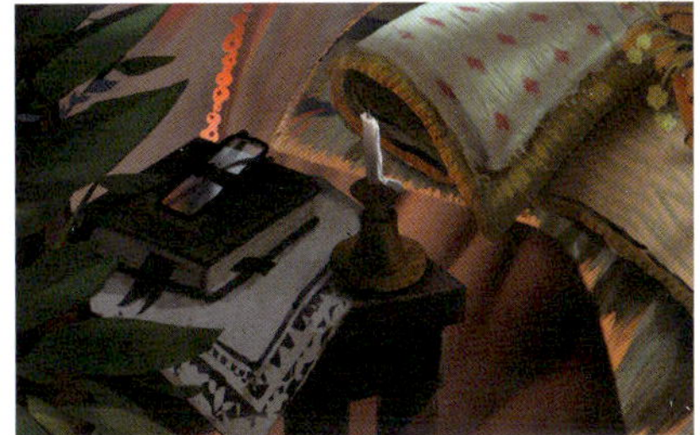

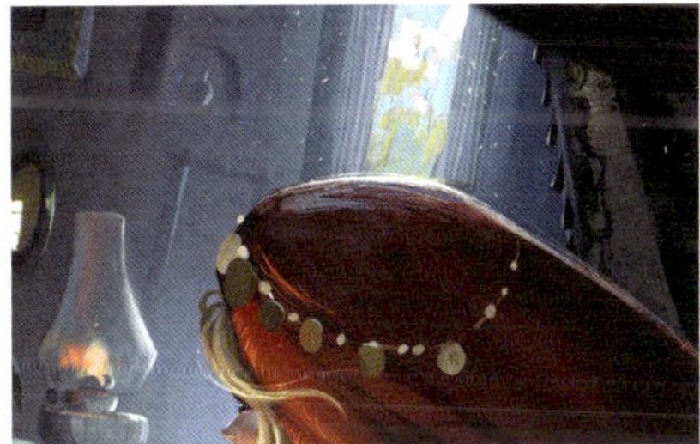

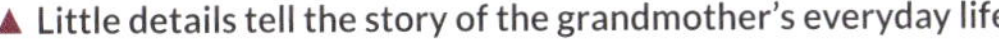

▲ Little details tell the story of the grandmother's everyday life

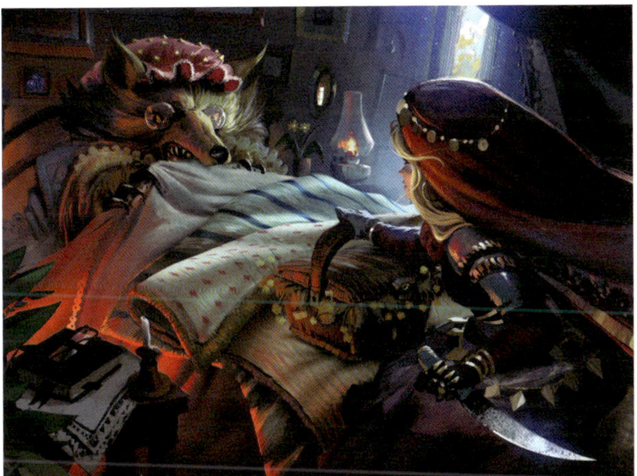

▲ Some color correction helps the scene approach a cinematic look

17 UNIFYING THE MOOD

Now it's time to properly unify the scene. I want to take the image to a cinematic level with some color corrections and lighting enhancements, with a strong central focus to give the viewer an immediate realization of what's happening at this moment of the story. After that initial recognition of the story, the viewer can then freely observe the image and arrive at a more personal analysis of it. To help achieve this focus, I slightly darken the edges of the illustration, so that the lighting and details fade away from the central focal area. I increase the saturation of the cold blue light from the door, as it's the main light source, and shift the overall shading tone to a dark navy to match it. Deeper indoors, I boost the firelight with an extra red glow, emphasizing that feeling of warmth with an undertone of danger and menace.

18 CHECKING THE VALUES

During my painting process, I always check my black-and-white values to make sure the colors, lighting, and objects are working together smoothly. It's also useful to see a non-colored version of a cinematic scene such as this one, full of tension and drama, to get a new perspective of the storytelling. For example, even without the warm/cool lighting and the heroine's iconic red hood, we can see how the characters' poses and expressions still carry the story. I also notice some areas where details could be added or refined further, such as the chair in the foreground, some extra plants, and a few areas of Red Riding Hood's hands and clothes.

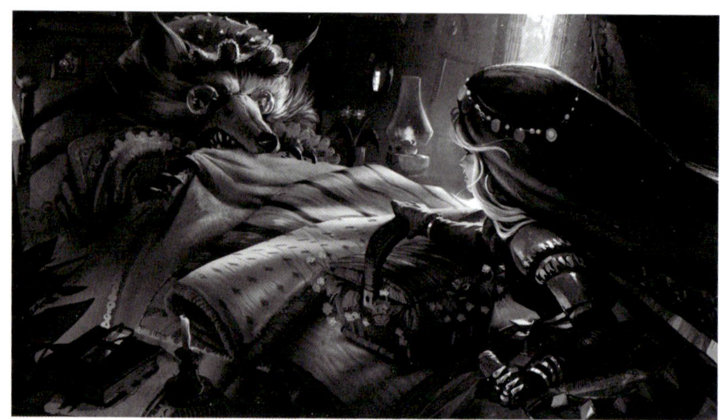

▲ A grayscale version can give you a new perspective of the scene

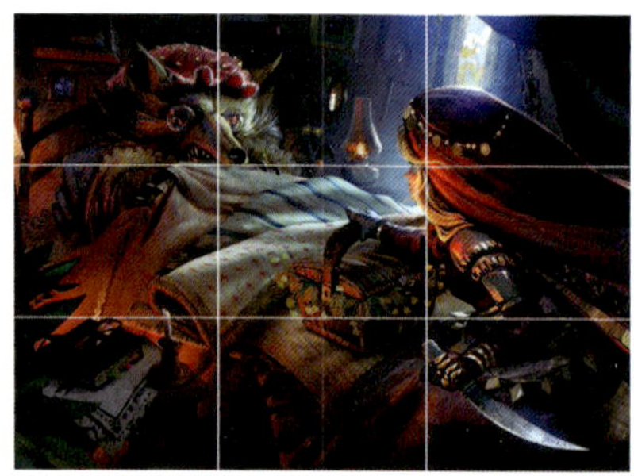

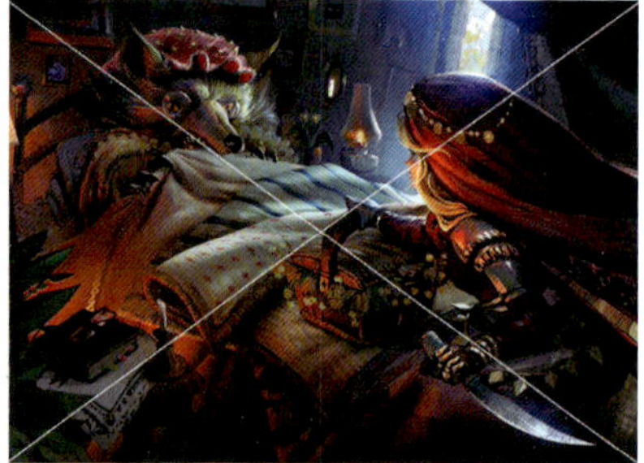

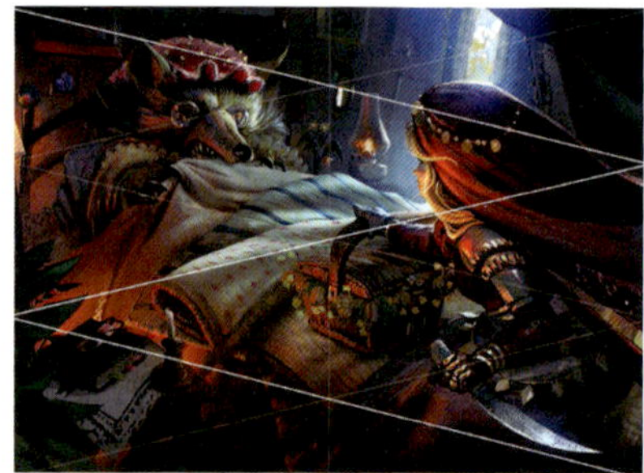

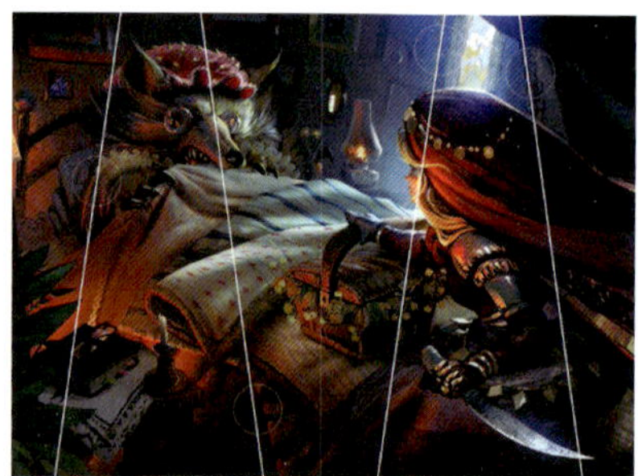

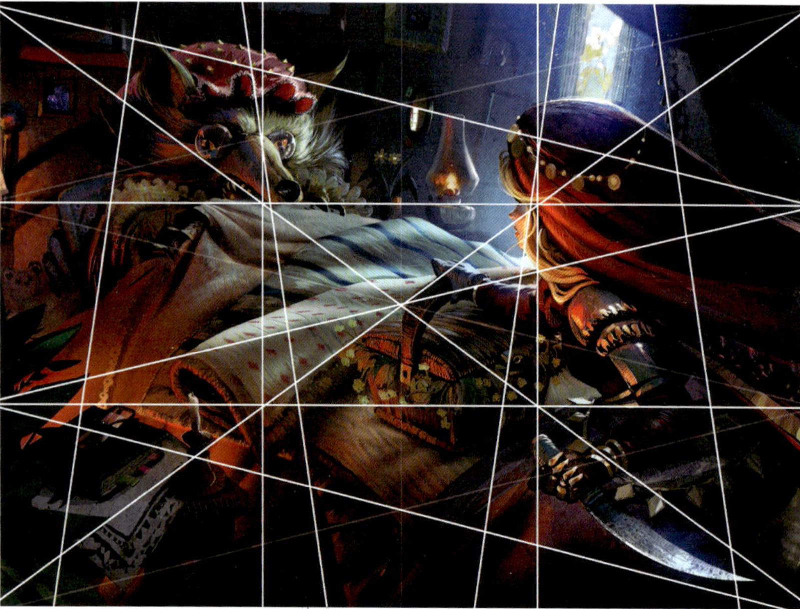

19 FINDING CONNECTIONS

Some stories don't need words to be told. Instead they need strong or soft colors, thick or thin lines, and a good variety of textures with a level of connection between them. These connections don't need to be obvious straight away – often the viewer needs to analyze or study something for a moment to discover those connections and draw their own conclusions. I already mentioned the rule of thirds in step 04, but there are other compositional devices at work here too. For example, I need some elements to work diagonally to complement or contrast with the direction of Red Riding Hood's dagger. If we look at the diagonals in the scene, we can see how the dagger leads us toward the wolf's teeth, and how the blankets align with the book on the bottom left.

We can explore more connections with a horizontal zigzag based on the rule of thirds, to find lines, patterns, and intersections that have almost the same direction and rhythm. A vertical zigzag can connect areas in the foreground, middle ground, and background. On the left you can see these guides individually and all combined. They not only help to tell a story, but to break down the scene into smaller segments that can help when cropping or reframing the image.

◀ Composition guides are not prescriptive but can be valuable for creating subtle connections in your visual storytelling

20 FINISHING TOUCHES

The image is basically complete, but I still go through some minor details to clean them up. There are always some areas that you are less focused on, so this is the time to take care of them. I ensure the lighting is consistent, make some areas sharper (such as the dagger and accessories), and make some areas smoother (such as Red Riding Hood's face and a few areas of fabric). Overall, I am happy with this level of detail, so I am careful not to over-render – I want to keep the main focus on the characters' faces, so many areas have been kept loose or even untouched since step 05, such as the piece of cloth under the book. Those details add personality to the characters and setting but can remain loosely painted so they don't distract from the story.

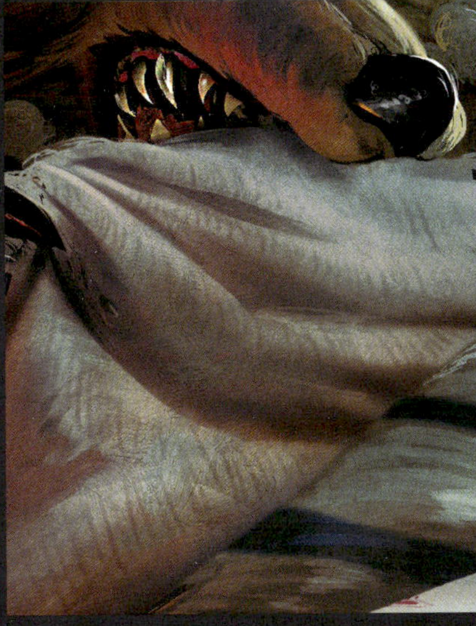

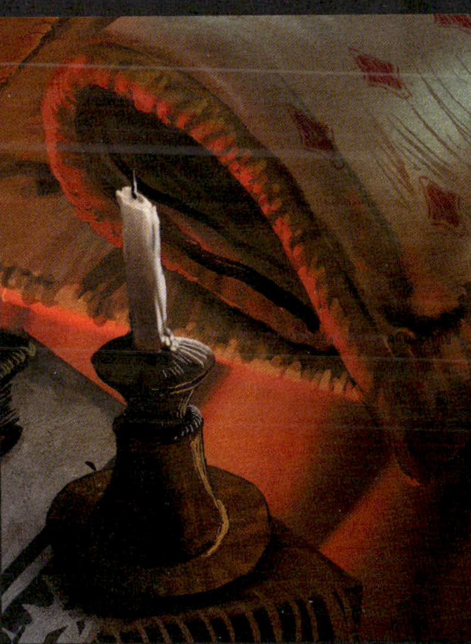

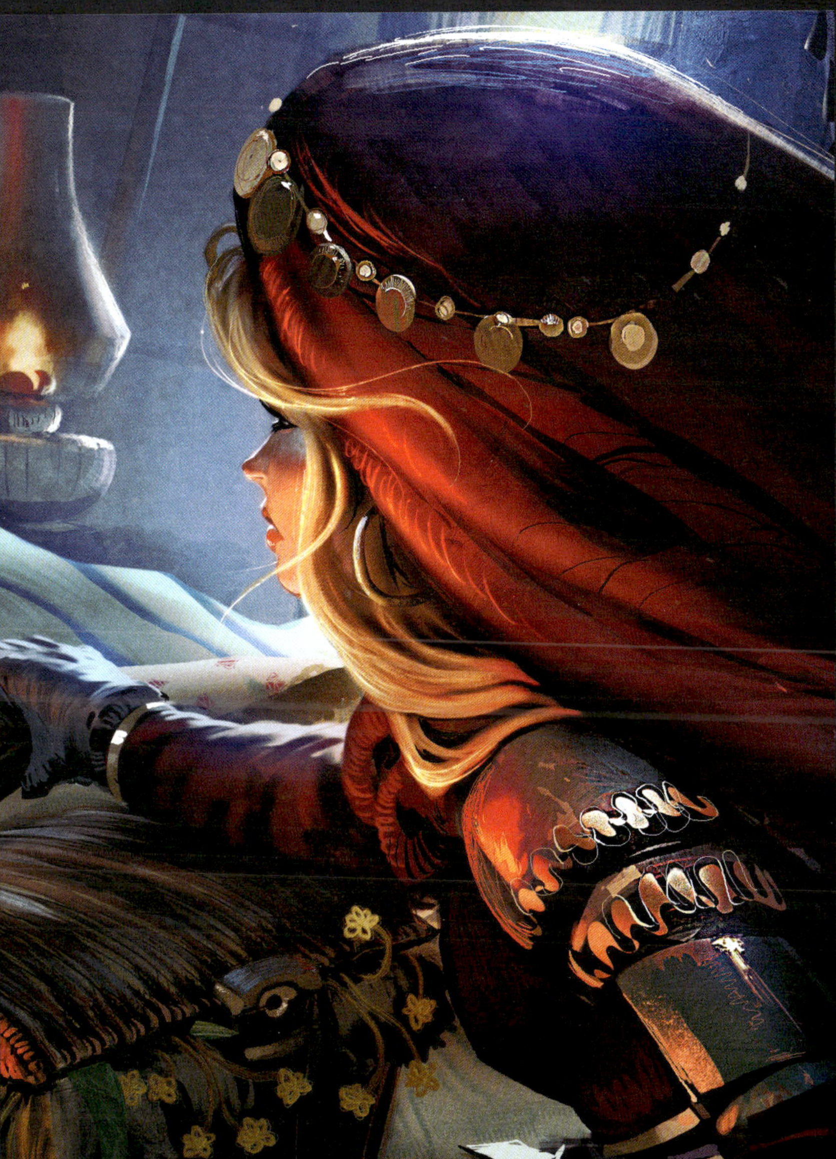

▲ Adding finishing touches to the lighting and a few rougher areas

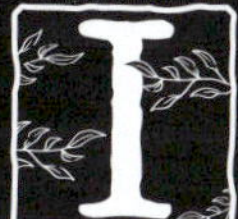

I am very glad I was able to give this story my own twist. I didn't want to change much about the classic sequence or the original visuals, as they are so iconic and effective, but I like to add my own spice to a story's recipe – keeping the same delicious flavor but adding some new ingredients. The result is a "turning of the tables" of the original story, where Red Riding Hood is a tough, well-prepared fighter with the upper hand in the confrontation, and the wolf is clumsy and caught off guard. The classic imagery of the wolf tucked up in bed with the grandmother's clothes, playing a near-fatal trick on an unsuspecting girl, now has a razor-sharp sting in its tail!

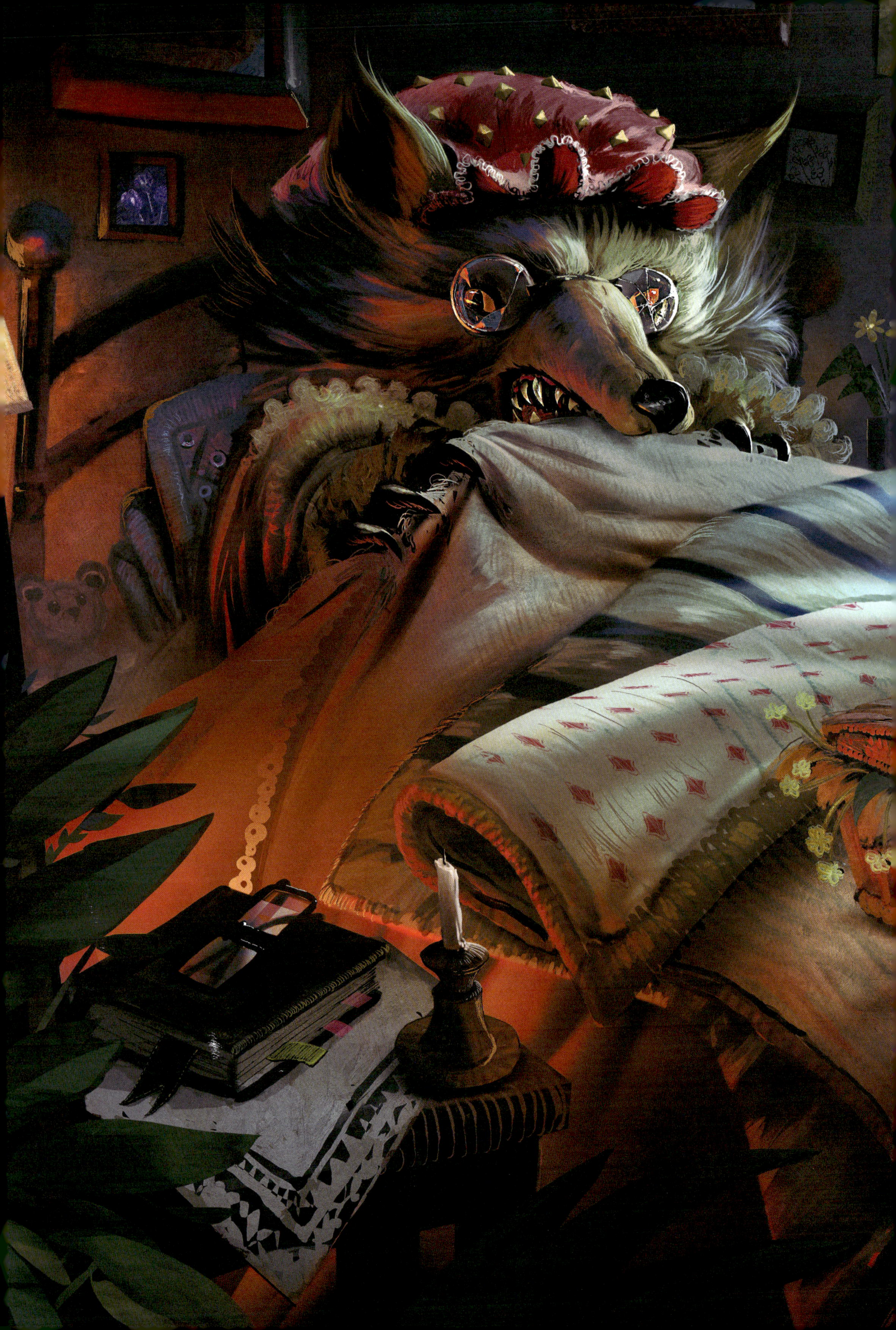

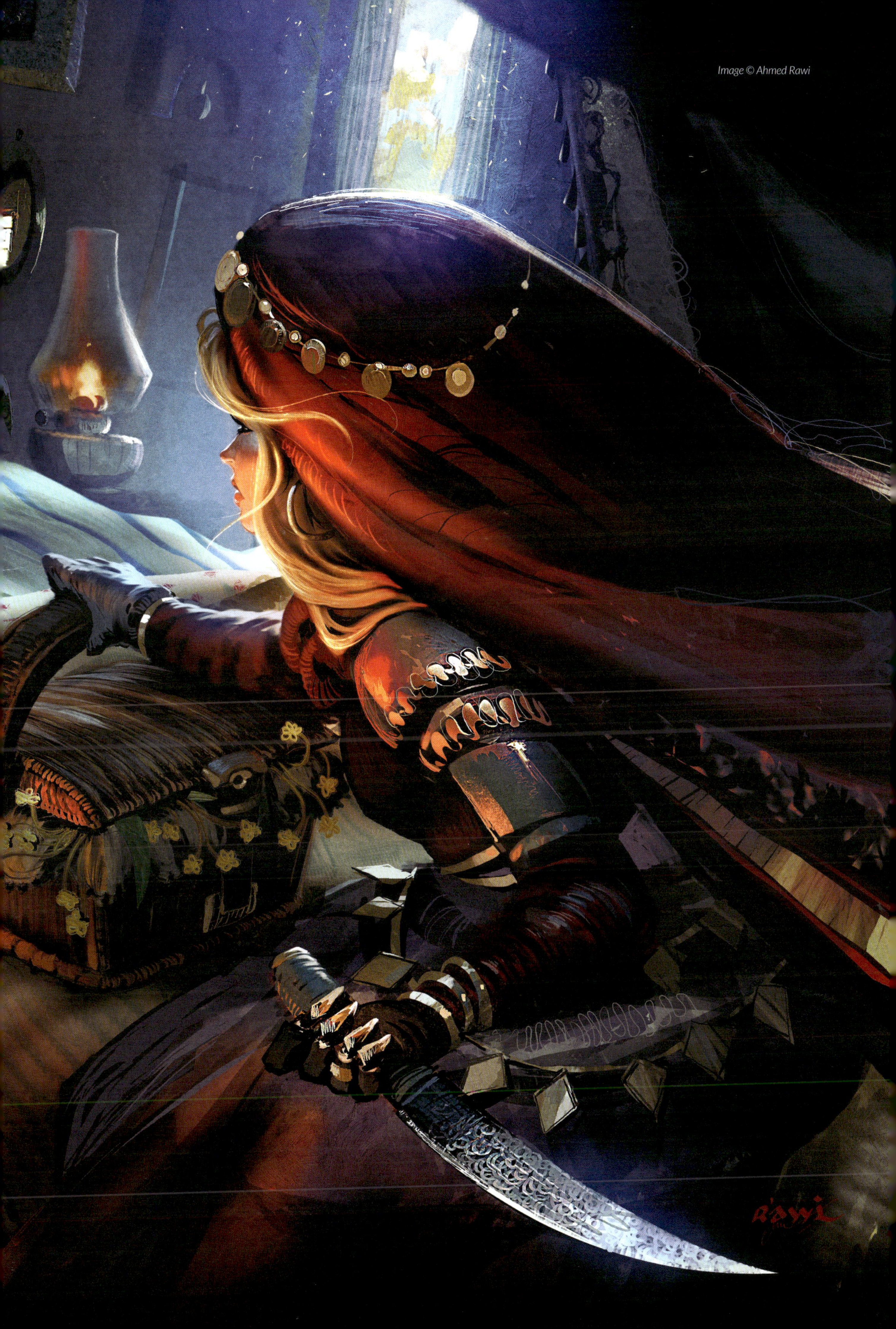

LITTLE RED AND THE HYENA

BY EILENE CHERIE WITARSAH

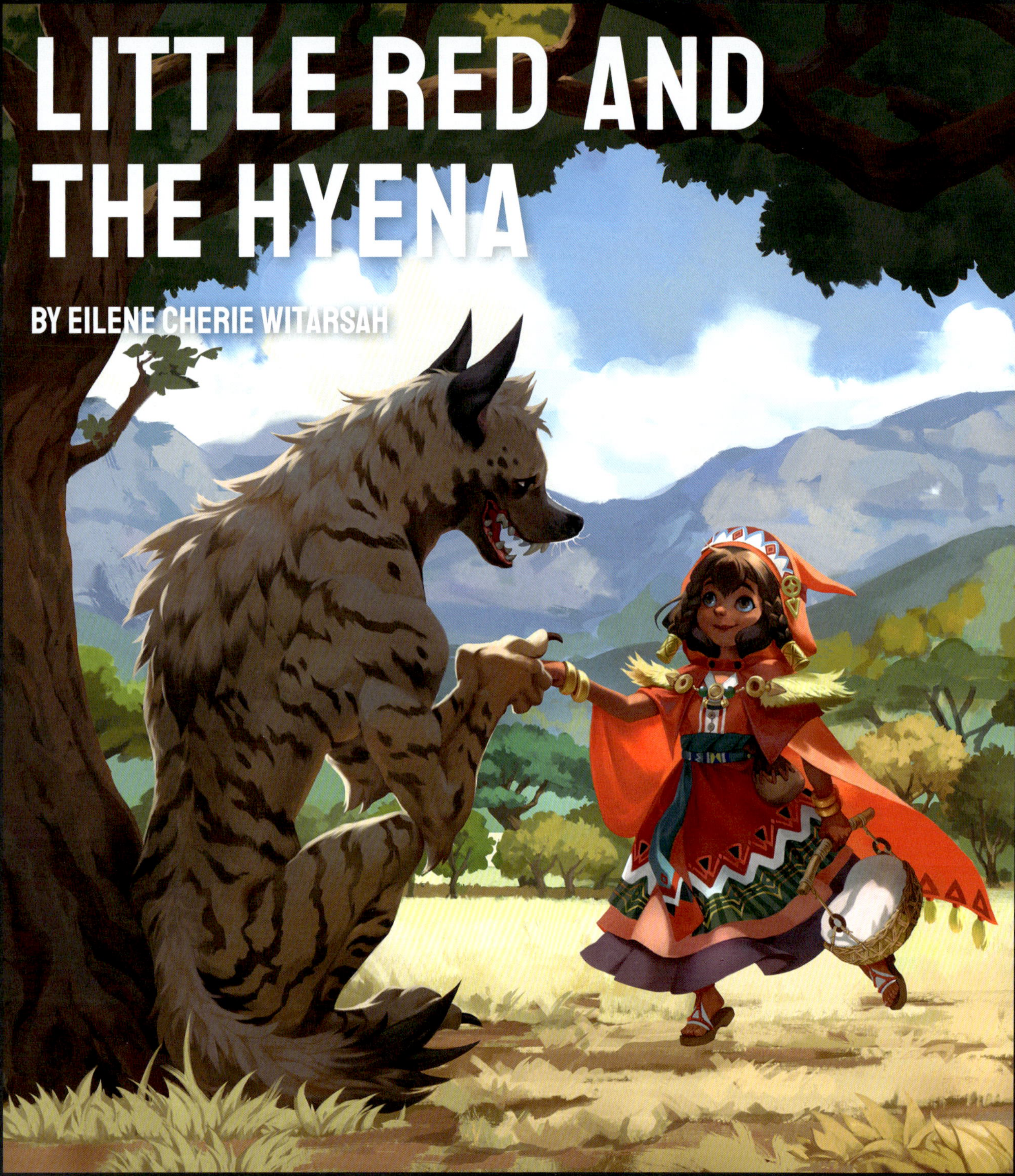

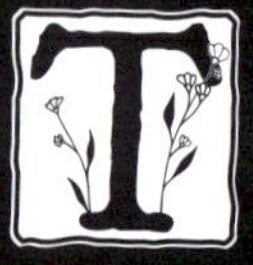

Throughout the years, the tale of Little Red Riding Hood has been retold by many authors. These versions usually share similarities in the moral of the story, which is to never trust strangers. The naive Little Red Riding Hood and the sly wolf have become iconic in the hearts of generations of readers. They are the key elements that build the entire story. Reimagining a classic tale needs to maintain the characteristics of the original story.

An original, personal work is easier in some ways, because the idea is your own and not already recognizable – but what about a classic that is already well known? When it comes to being creative, we can go wild with our ideas, but a classic story needs to be identifiable when people see our take on it. The more elements and themes we keep from the original story, the harder we have to think of alternative ways to be creative and still resonate with the audience.

01 GENERATING IDEAS

Before an art piece is created, the first thing to do is brainstorm. I usually like to come up with ideas that are fictitious, because, for me, art is a place where we can express imaginings that we cannot see in reality. If we keep thinking logically or realistically, it will limit us from finding unique ideas. Try to think of something completely contradictory, something that you think is absurd and peculiar. Don't be afraid to come up with those ideas, as everything will be figured out during the later process. Get a pen and start noting down anything that comes into mind – it can be in the form of scribbles, pictures, or words. You can keep the whole list of ideas even though some may not be suitable, since there is a possibility that those ideas can inspire you for other stuff.

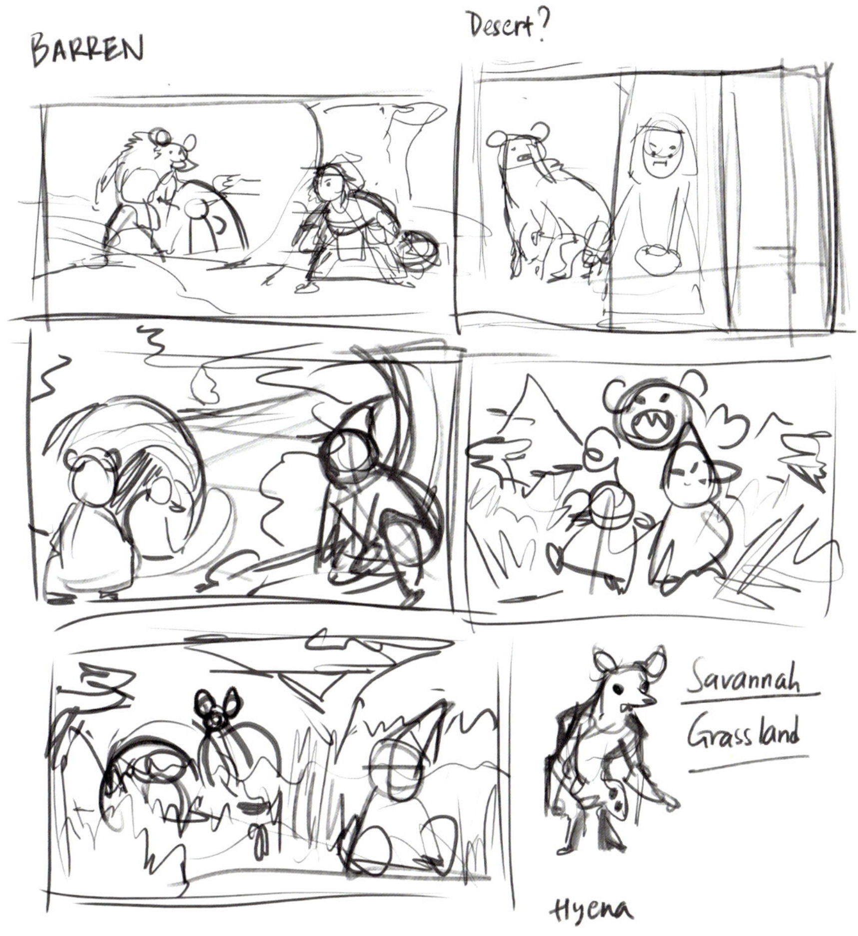

▲ Be brave and don't limit yourself when brainstorming

02 CREATIVE THINKING

If you think about the desert, your mind will automatically imagine sand stretching to the horizon. But what if, in the middle of the desert, there was a floating castle with a waterfall? That image would surely attract people's attention because it's not common – it's unexpected when you are imagining a desert landscape. The story that we always hear of Little Red Riding Hood is about her meeting the wolf in the woods, centered around a northern-European setting. What if, this time, Little Red Riding Hood's story was set in a different location? How about a place that seems contradictory to the original, like a warm savannah or barren grassland? Perhaps Little Red Riding Hood is trying to get past a hungry hyena to meet her grandmother!

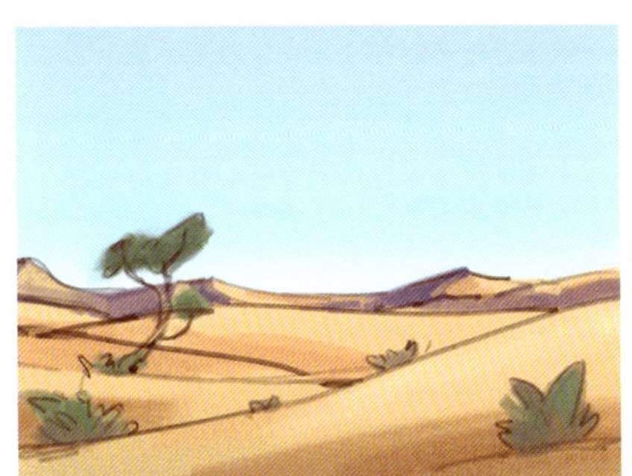

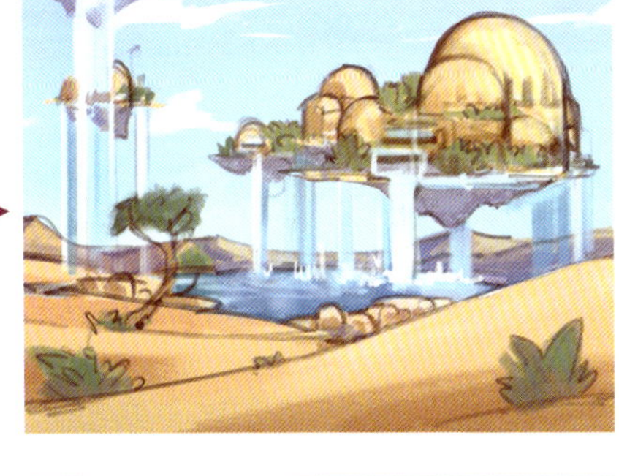

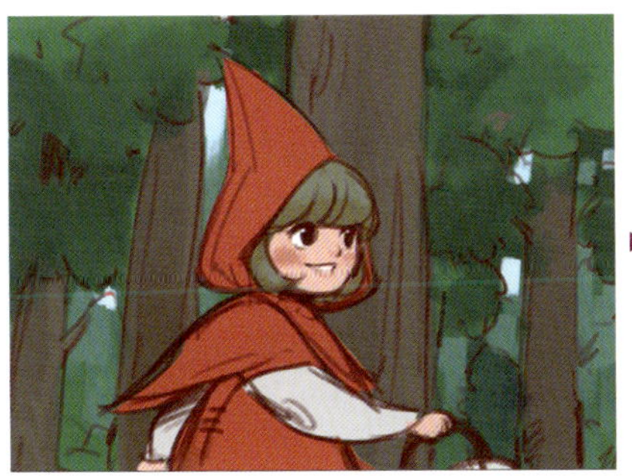

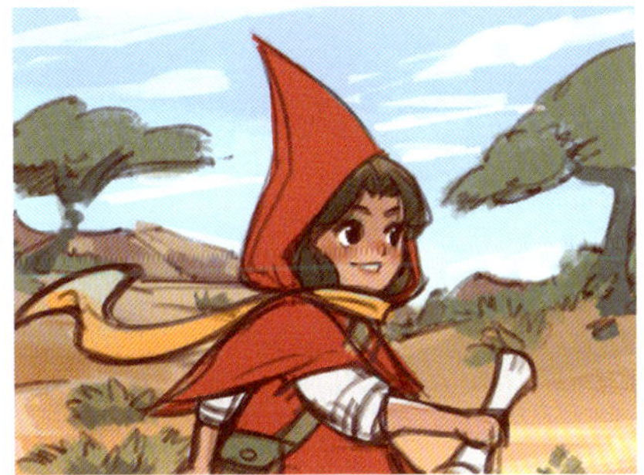

▲ Trying out fresh and different ideas is the key to creative thinking

03 FINDING REFERENCES

Researching references is essential for creating art. Whether it is photography, videos, historical paintings, or other artworks that inspire you, research helps in expanding your visual library. We cannot know or imagine things that we rarely come across in our lives – that's only natural. With references, you can reach a deeper understanding of the material you are creating and strengthen your ideas to make them more relevant. For this project, I collect references of savannah habitats, barren grasslands, deserts, hyenas, and outfits from different tribes and ethnicities that reside in grasslands around the world. By gathering all my references in one place and grouping them accordingly, I form a mini library that will assist me during the drawing process and keep me from deviating too far from my initial idea.

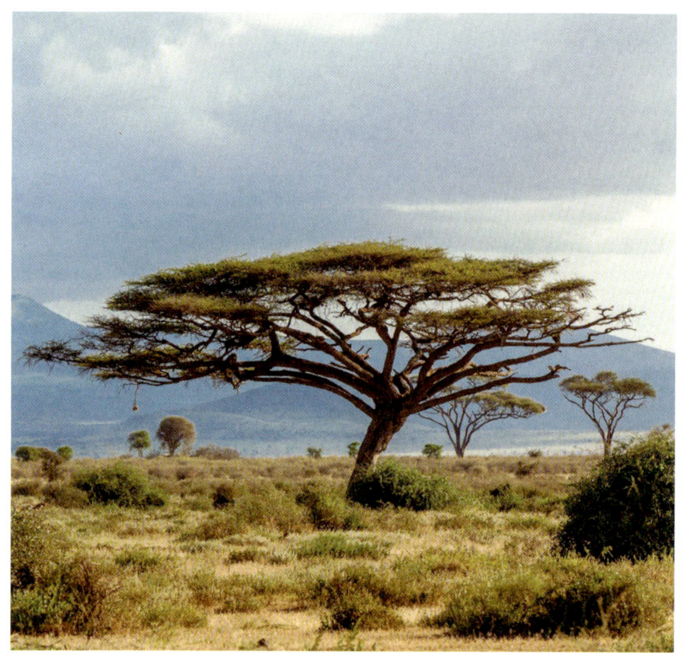

► **Always do some research before creating your art. It will definitely expand your visual library!**
Photo by Tatyana Drujinina on Abobe Stock

04 SHAPE LANGUAGE

I think Little Red Riding Hood has an iconic look, with her conical hood and red cape typically covering her whole body. I associate her design with a triangular shape. The triangle creates a look of stability because its bottom-heavy weight provides sturdiness. However, in character design, the triangle is often associated with aggressiveness due to its sharp edges, so I tone down those angular lines and give Little Red's design rounder edges to make her look friendly, young, and harmless. An inverted triangle is more suitable for the hyena. When a shape tapers down into a narrow tip, it creates a feeling of instability that is perfect for the hyena's unpredictable temperament. Adding more spiky shapes increases the design's aggressiveness, making the hyena feel more threatening. The grandmother is the most rounded character, making her feel soft, friendly, and squat.

▼ **Shape language influences the psychology of the people who see your characters**

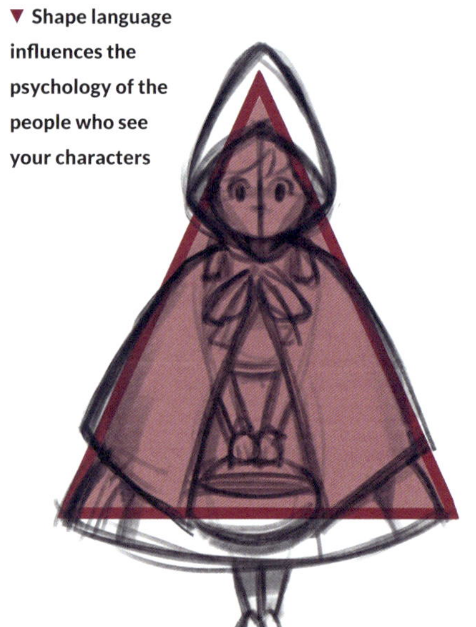

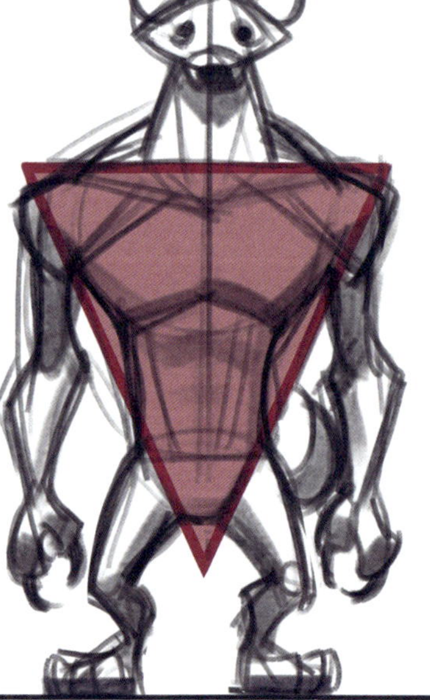

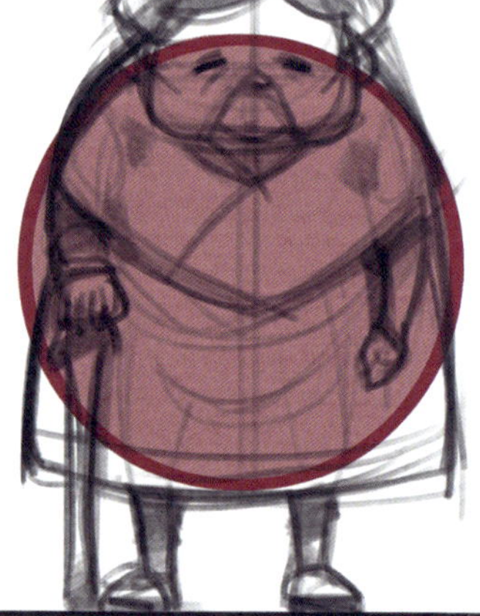

LITTLE RED RIDING HOOD
TRIANGLE

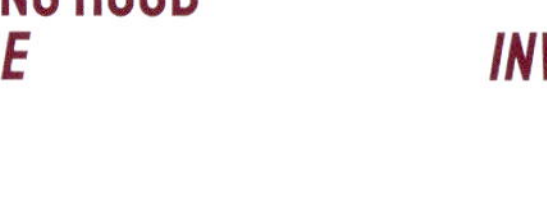

HYENA
INVERTED TRIANGLE

GRANDMOTHER
ROUND

05 FURTHER EXPLORATION

It is always fun to explore your idea by creating multiple variations of it. Every sketch you make opens a door of possibilities and different approaches for the same character. I usually start my sketches with a safer approach and then gradually develop outward from the initial idea. When I feel that I have enough ideas, I then choose the one that is the most interesting to me. Sometimes I combine the idea with different parts from other sketches to spice it up. Keep in mind that you should not forget the direction that you have settled on during the research stage.

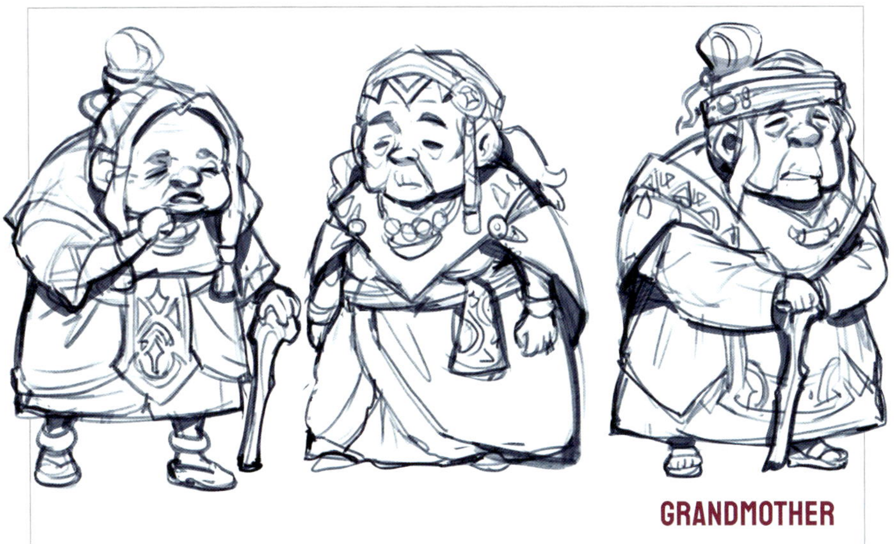

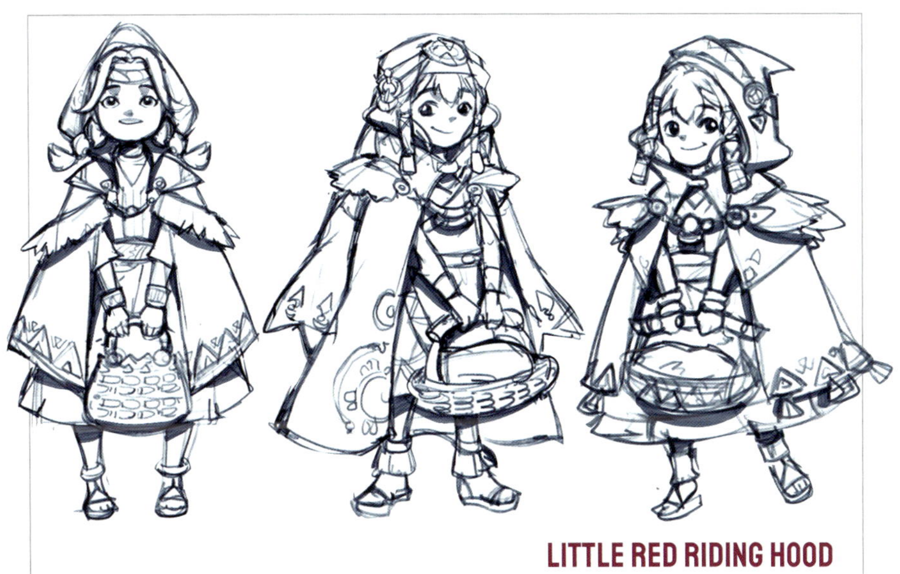

▶ The more you explore, the more possibilities you will discover

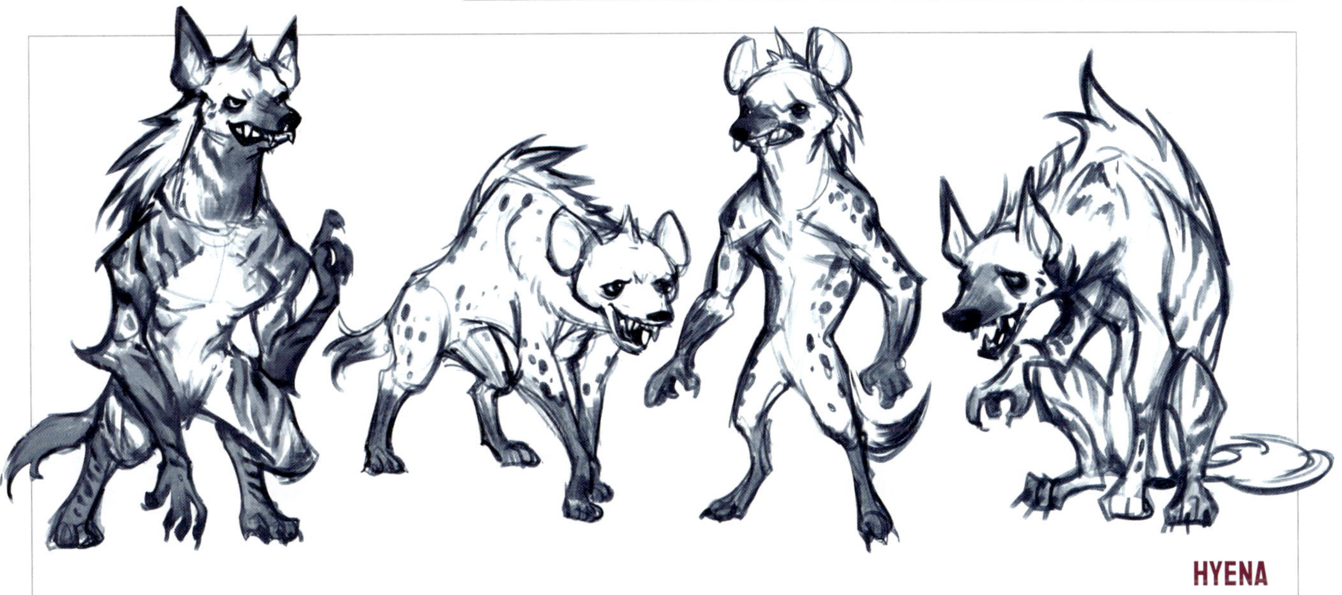

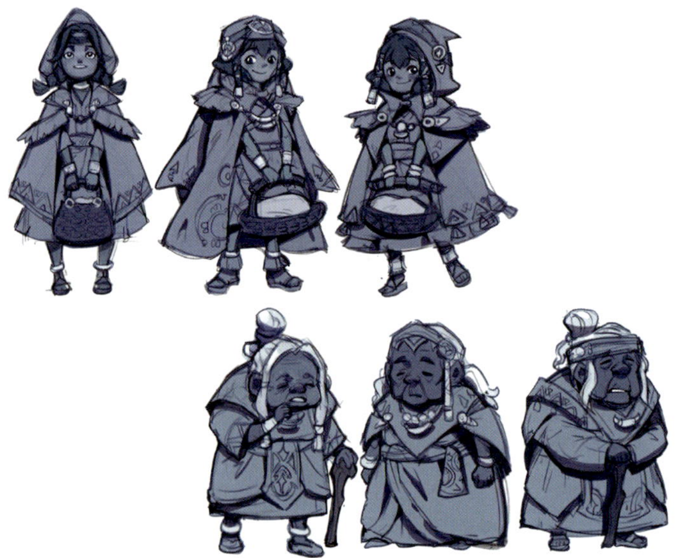

06 LITTLE RED AND HER GRANDMOTHER

As I mentioned previously, I want Little Red Riding Hood's design to maintain her iconic conical hood. When it comes to redesigning an existing character, aspects such as their likeness, behavior, attitude, shape, and silhouette are crucial. Those elements are the key to the audience recognizing the character. For me, her red hood, basket, and cheerful attitude are essential. Making her facial shape rounder emphasizes her innocence as a naive little girl. I keep a similar approach for her grandmother, giving her a round silhouette that emphasizes her kindness and softness. Their clothing and designs are inspired by several cultures that live in savannah and grassland regions throughout the world, ranging across Africa, India, the Middle East, and Central Asia.

◀ Keeping the essence of Little Red Riding Hood's classic traits and exploring possible designs for her grandmother

07 THE CUNNING HYENA

Just like the wolf, the hyena is considered an aggressive animal, making it an ideal grassland replacement for the original. Both animals are agile, cunning, and unpredictable. Giving the hyena a spiky silhouette highlights his role as an antagonist. It is a challenge to judge how far I should push the stylization of the character. Do I want the hyena to be cartoony, realistic, or monstrous-looking? I envision him being large enough to look intimidating in contrast with Little Red's small stature. I sketch different hyena types and styles, including spotted, striped, quadrupedal (more realistic), and bipedal (more humanoid).

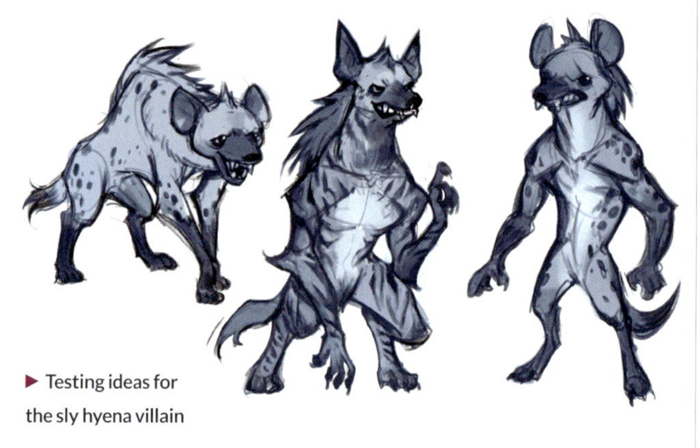

▶ Testing ideas for the sly hyena villain

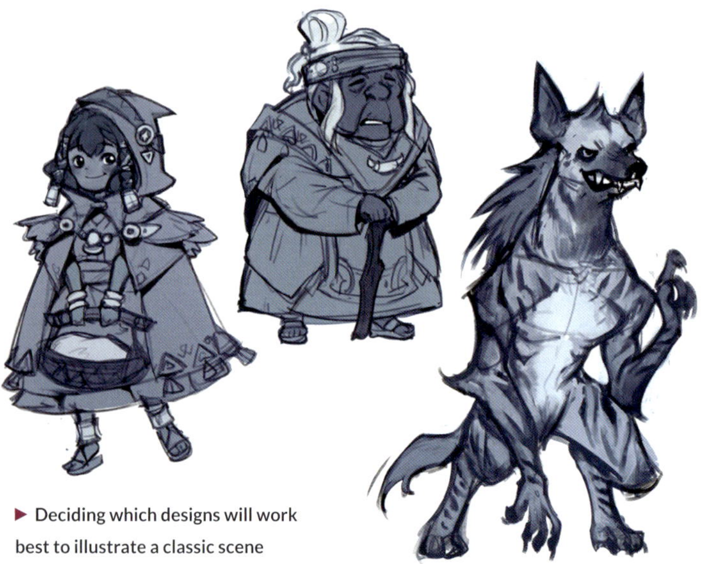

▶ Deciding which designs will work best to illustrate a classic scene

08 MAKING DECISIONS

Looking through my sketches, I begin to remove the ideas that stray too far from my initial concept, as well as ideas that may look too generic and not appeal to the audience. The designs that I choose for Little Red Riding Hood and her grandmother are the ones that I feel are the most unique while still strongly resembling the original story. They incorporate some existing cultures, mixed with fantasy elements, giving the viewer room for imagination. For the hyena, I choose a striped hyena. This species is found in Africa and throughout Asia, and has a shaggy coat and pointed ears that lend themselves well to triangular shape language. I give it a cartoonish but slightly monstrous form that is humanoid enough to communicate with the little girl, just like in the original story. This makes the character feel more lively, with many possibilities for interesting gestures that show its cunning nature.

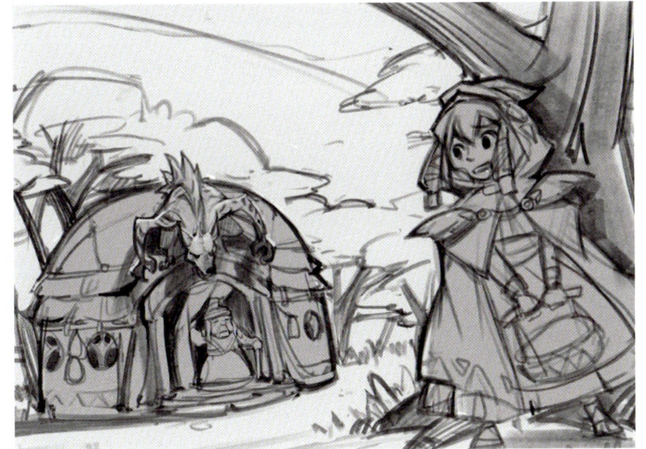

09 THUMBNAIL SKETCHES

After settling on the designs and further refining them, it's time to scribble some rough thumbnails. I always start the sketch at a small size and draw it from a distance, so that I can see the composition as a whole. I try not to focus on the cleanliness of the line art and other details first, because the main thing is to see if the scene is clear and readable from a small size. The scene must have sufficient information for the audience to understand what is happening. It is also helpful to have the light source in mind during this stage, so that you are ready for the next phase.

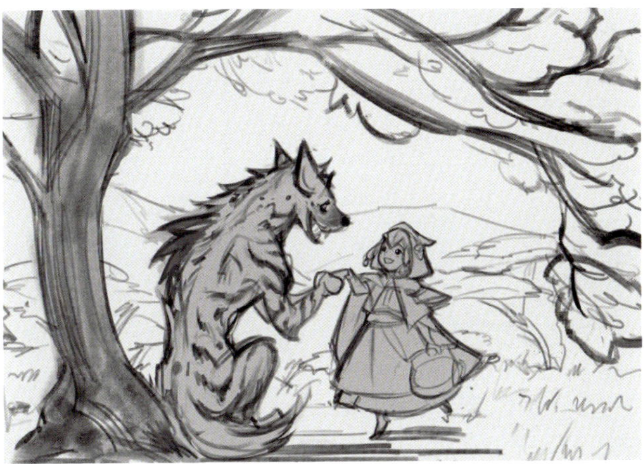

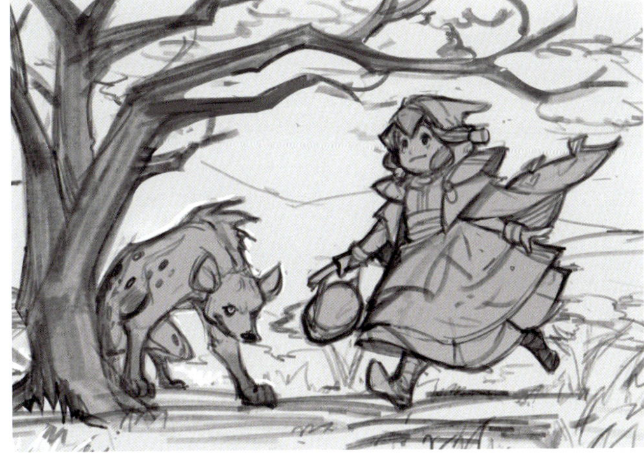

▲ Small thumbnail sketches enable me to see the illustration as a whole

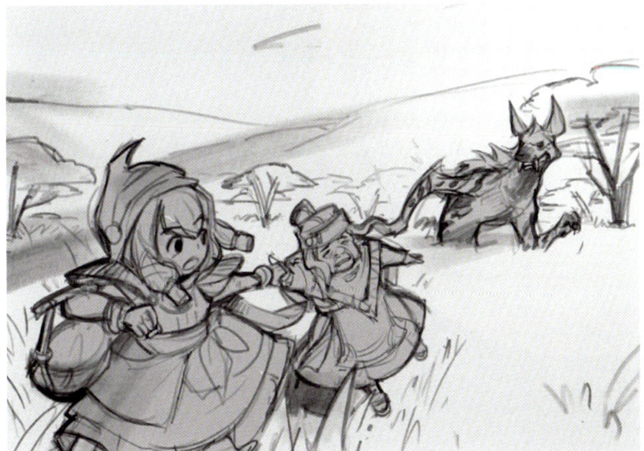

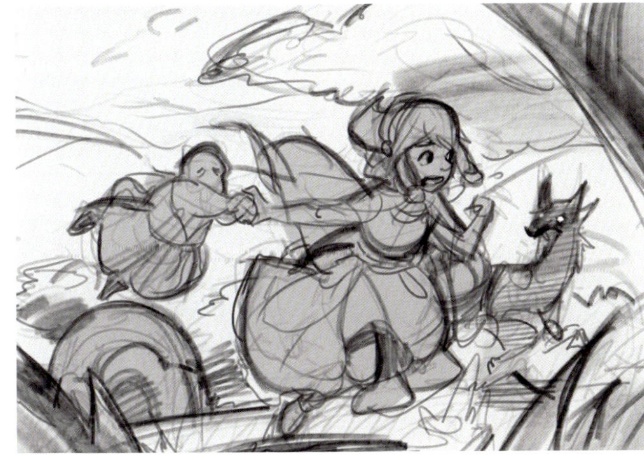

10 EXPLORING STORYTELLING

Throughout this sketching process, I am still thinking about the kind of scene that would really reflect the story of Little Red Riding Hood. The first sketch here is a plot twist exploring what would happen if the little girl arrived at the same time as the hyena. The second scene is just like the original story, where she gets acquainted with a hyena who seems very friendly. In the third scene, the hyena looms out of the darkness, ready to target the little girl for his next meal. The last scene's approach is more intense and dynamic, with Little Red helping her grandmother escape instead of waiting for someone else to save her.

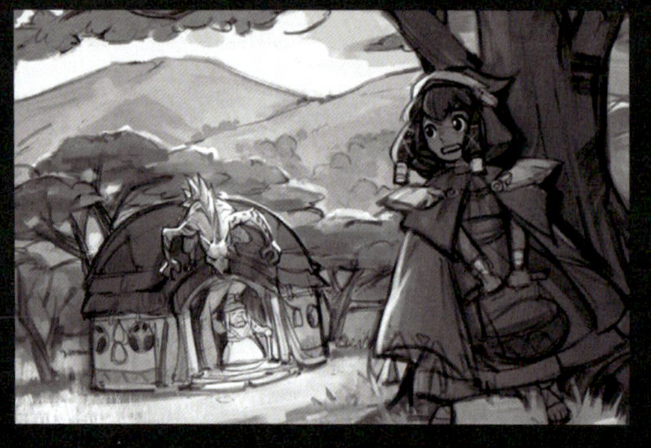
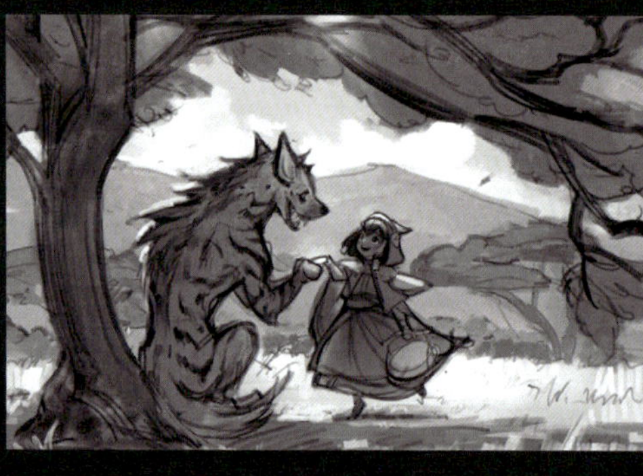
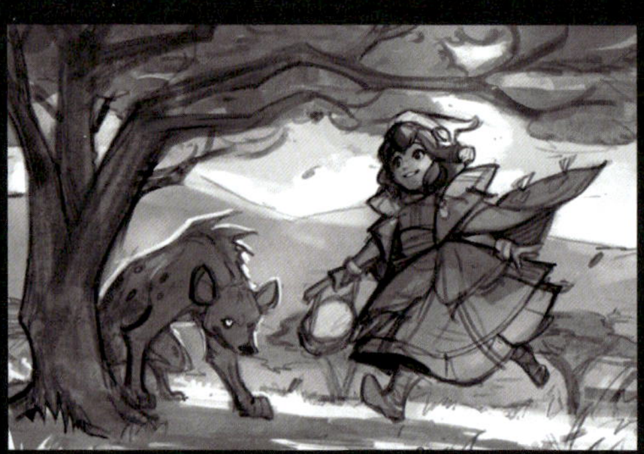
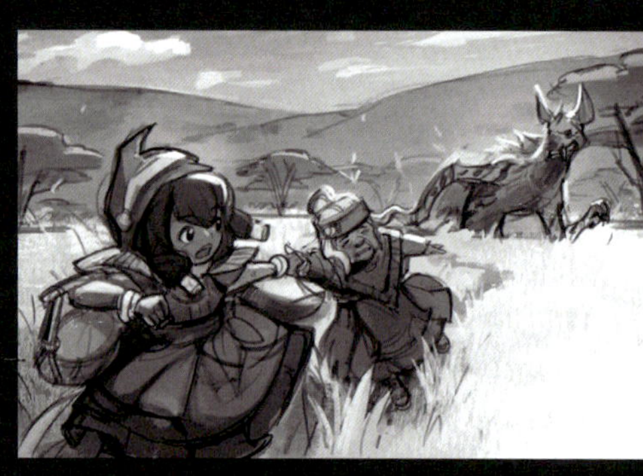

► Storytelling is always behind every illustration

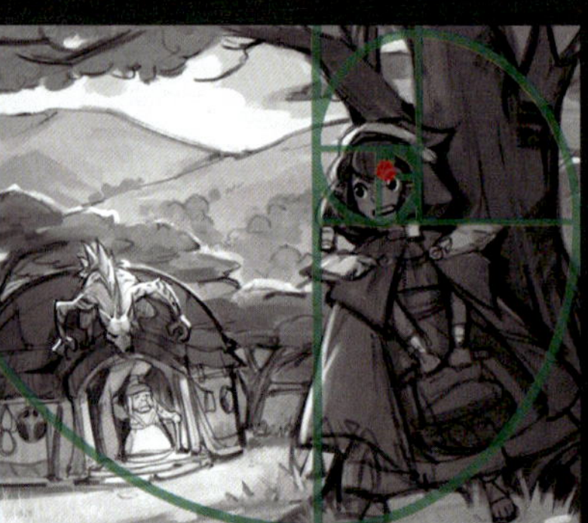
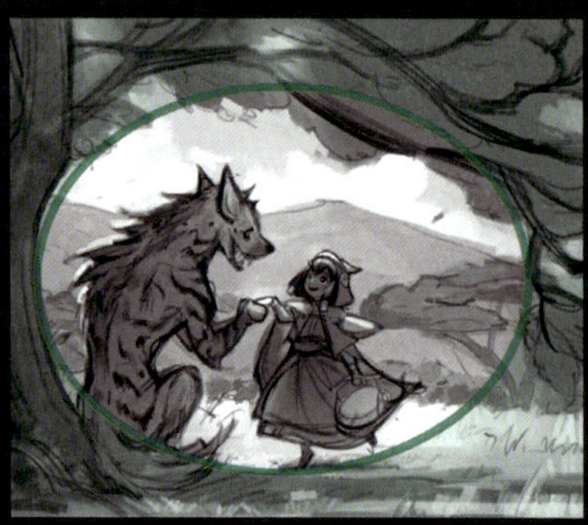
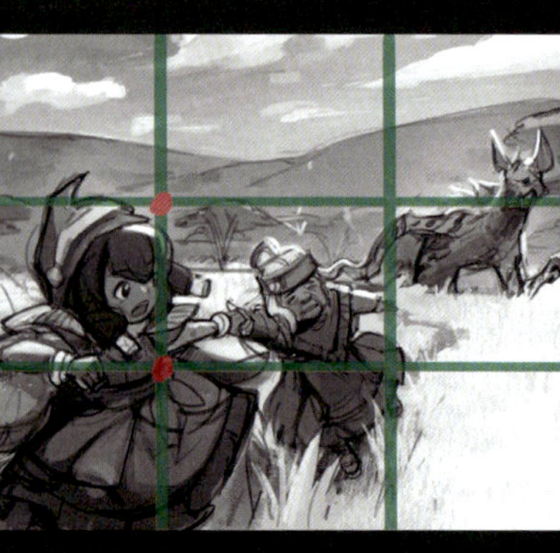
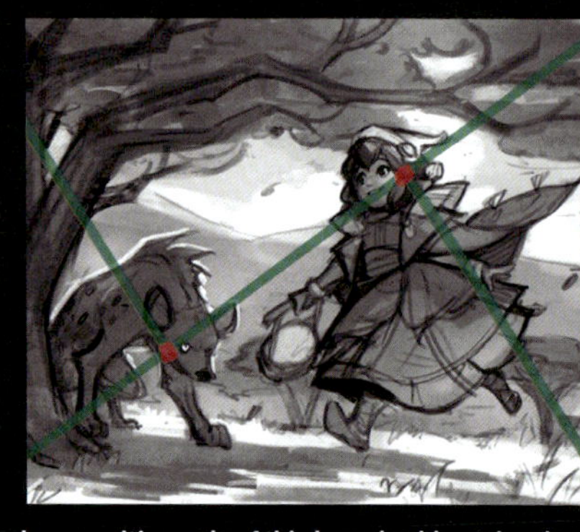

▲ From top left to bottom right: golden ratio, central composition, rule of thirds, and golden triangle

11 COMPOSITION AND FOCUS

Making an illustration is not just about ideas and painting. Composition also matters – placing the focal point of an illustration in order to attract the viewer's eye. In art theory, there are several types of guideline that are helpful for composition. You could try a central composition, the rule of thirds, the golden ratio, the golden triangle, different framings, and many more.

Personally, I often use the rule of thirds because it is well balanced. You just need to divide the canvas evenly into nine sections and place the main focus according to the guidelines. You need to take into account not only the main subject, but the negative space areas around it. Having too many objects in the background is distracting because it draws attention to unimportant details. To avoid that, you need areas of rest to give the viewer a break.

12 CHOOSING A FINAL SCENE

The narrative of *Little Red Riding Hood* centers around a particular event where a little girl meets a wolf in the woods. Therefore, I decide the second scene is the most suitable, as it's still faithful to the events of the original story. I decide against a dynamic action scene, such as the one with the grandmother, because I want to emphasize a tranquil, fairy-tale atmosphere and ensure that feeling doesn't get lost in the new setting.

This particular interaction really shows the nature of the main characters: the friendly, innocent little girl who is happy to meet the cunning hyena, not sensing any danger. I also prefer the composition of this scene, as the shapes of the tree and shadows form a frame that encircles the two characters, framing the moment in contrast against the bright background.

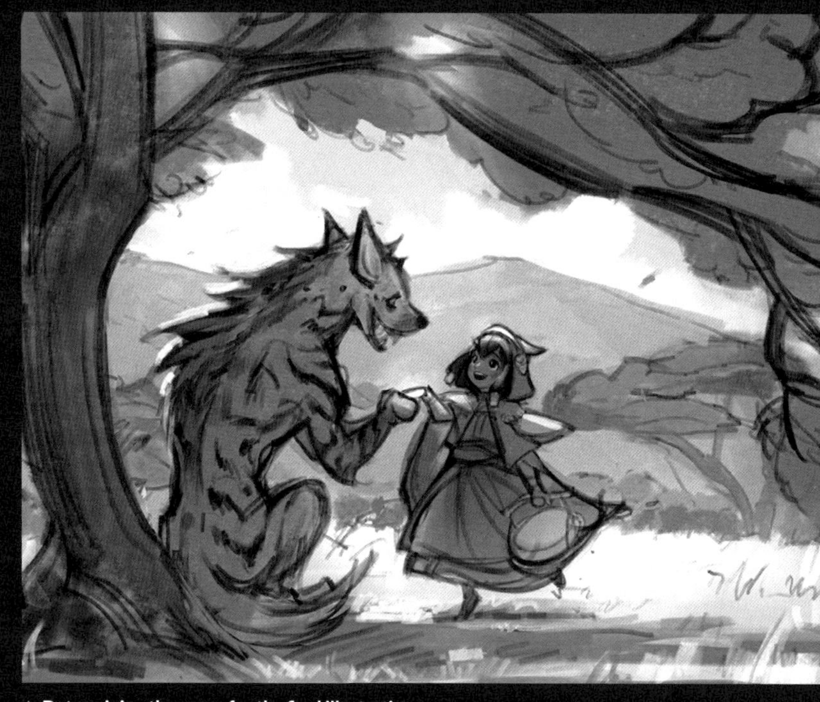

▲ Determining the scene for the final illustration

POINTS OF VIEW

Composition is influenced by perspective. Viewing the scene from a low angle, high angle, or eye level gives us different perceptions of the story. The view from a low angle may look more intense than other angles; a high angle can feel more dramatic and threatening; eye level can help the viewer feel like they are standing in the scene, with a good view of the action. Paying attention to the angles in movies or photographs can help improve your knowledge of composition.

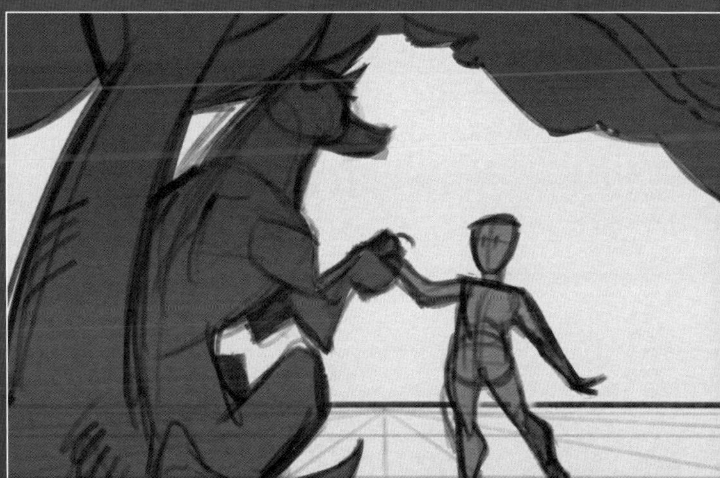

▲ The angle that you choose gives a different level of tension to the scene

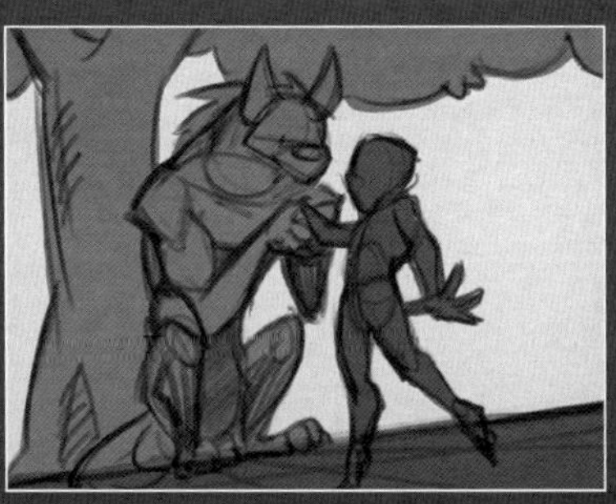

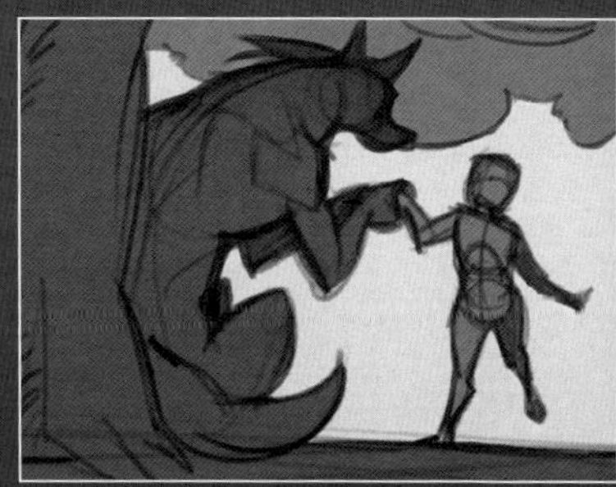

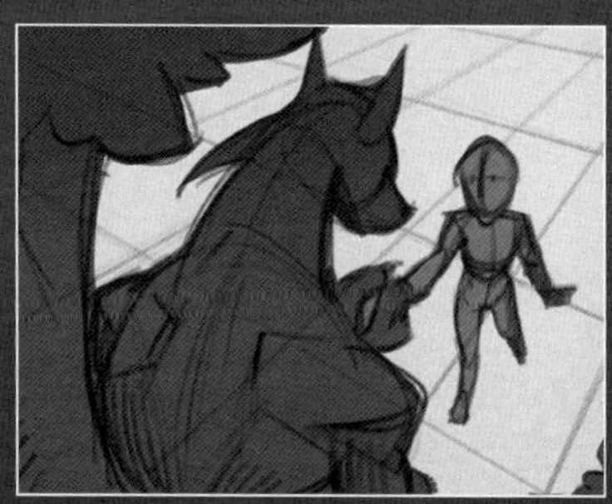

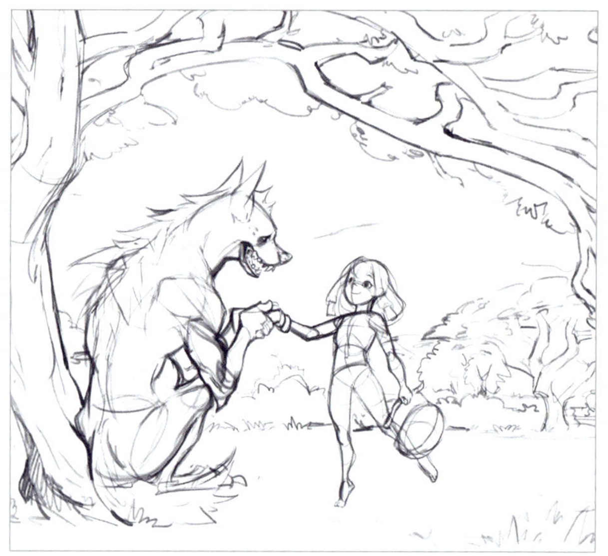

▲ Further refining the sketch will prevent you from backtracking

13 REVISING THE SKETCH

Without realizing it, the sketch that you make in a small size may be inaccurate. During the refinement process, I usually enlarge my sketch to the actual size of the final illustration and clean up the line art to make it look clearer. Planning everything properly at this stage will cut down on potential problems later. For example, drawing the full figure of a character helps to reduce uncertainty in the body proportions underneath their garments.

It's helpful to refine the sketch to around 60–70% of what you imagine for the final image, so the character designs, lighting, and composition are close to the target you have in mind. This is because if you need a major adjustment during the rendering process, you would have to backtrack. Imagine if you later realized the scenery needed changing – you would potentially have to restart almost from scratch! The bigger the change, the further back you would have to go to make the correction. You can minimize backtracking by making sure the image is well planned at this stage.

14 EXPRESSION AND GESTURE

Let's take a closer look at the expressions and gestures communicated by the characters. Little Red Riding Hood has big, sparkly eyes and her lower lip is shut tight. When a child first becomes friends with someone, they tend to be quite shy, and this expression conveys gullibility and innocence. One of her legs is slightly raised, showing her excitement as she was hopping around the grassland before meeting the hyena. In contrast, the hyena has a wicked grin and holds the girl's hand with both paws. It seems overly amused as it pulls her hand towards its chest, showing suspicious motives and the insincere body language of a flatterer.

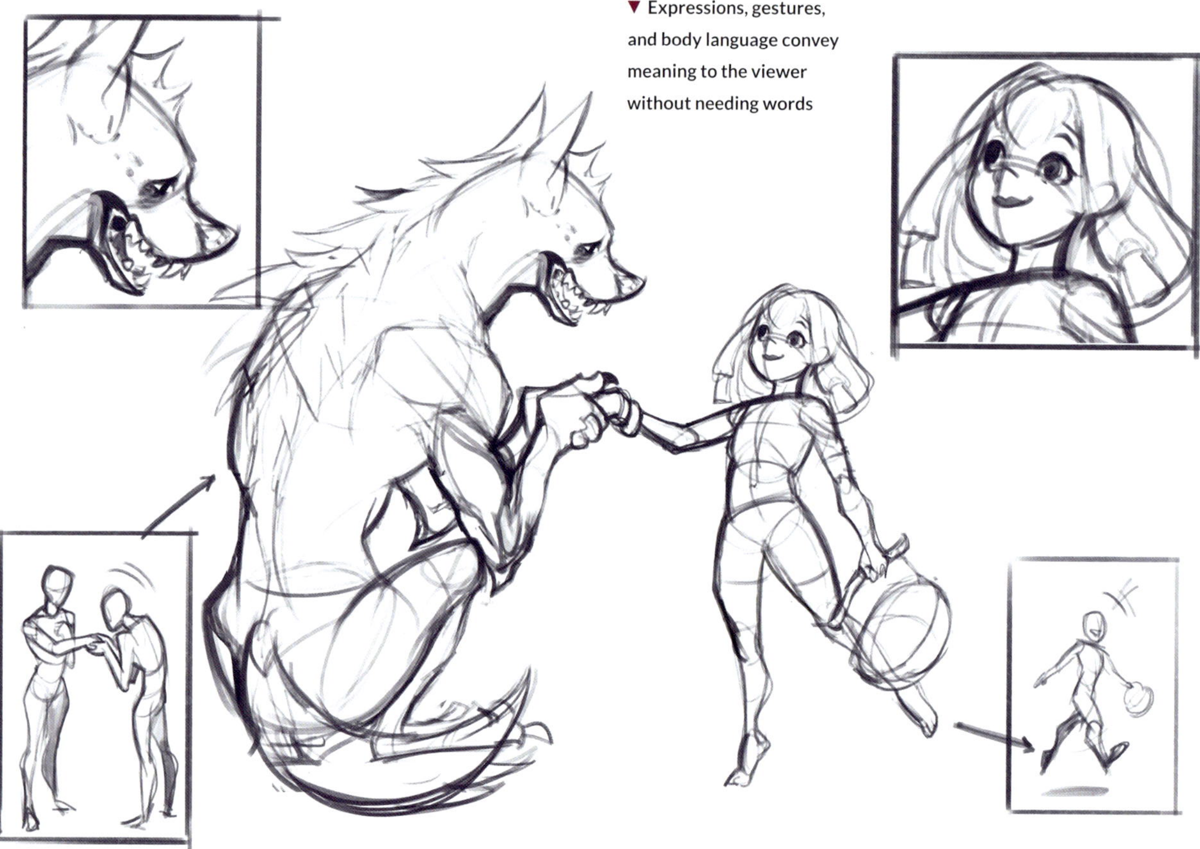

▼ Expressions, gestures, and body language convey meaning to the viewer without needing words

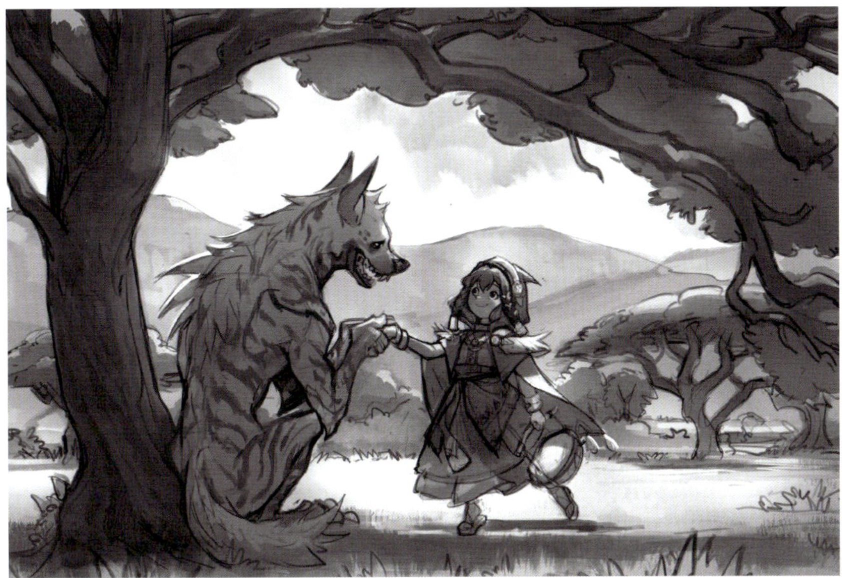

▲ Choosing the best spot for the light source to highlight the story's focal point

15 CREATING FOCUS WITH LIGHTING

The light source is something you can determine during the grayscale sketch stage. The light source is usually staged at the focal point, where you want to convey the message of the image to the viewer. Here the focus is on Little Red and the hyena, so my lighting needs to highlight the contrast between the antagonistic hyena silhouetted in the shadows and the innocent little girl standing in the light. I place the light source directly on top of Little Red, contrasting her with the hyena lurking beneath the tree. I want the viewer to think twice when they see my illustration, and wonder, "Doesn't that hyena seem suspicious?"

16 CREATING DEPTH WITH VALUES

This image's values are divided into three: the foreground, middle ground, and background values. These three layers create the effect of spatial depth, preventing the image from looking flat or two-dimensional. It also makes it easier for the viewer to distinguish the subjects you want to highlight from the background.

In this case, the foreground is the hyena and the tree; they will be the darkest, creating the highest level of contrast with the background. The middle ground is Little Red and the surrounding grassland. The mountains and other trees will stay in the background. The farther away something is, the lower the contrast, ensuring that the viewer isn't distracted by things that are less important.

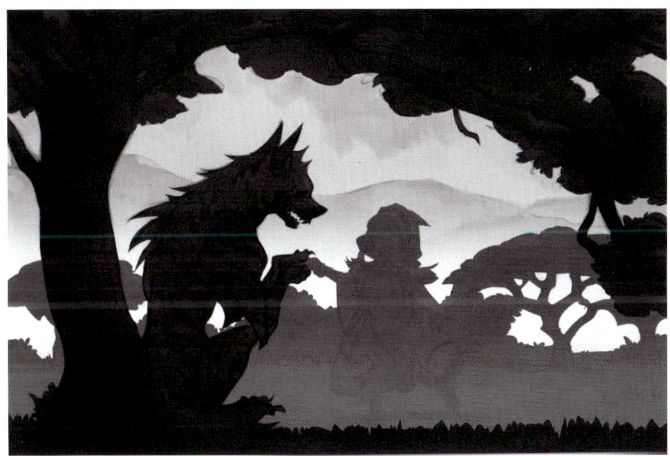

▲ Values create a sense of depth and three-dimensional space

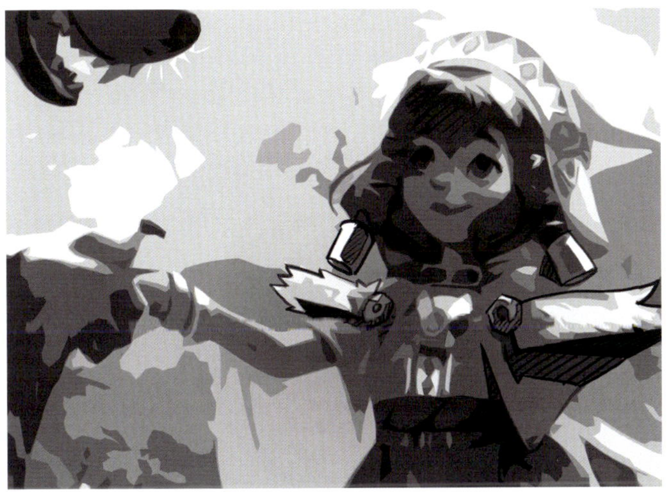

17 THREE-DIMENSIONAL FORMS

Having established all of the things mentioned previously, I proceed to the rendering stage. Taking care of the form and contour lines is often forgotten when you are concentrating on rendering an illustration. Every little thing in the image has a plane on each side, just like how we see objects in the real world. I always try to remind myself that my rendering has to look solid – this way my illustration will look more realistic instead of flat (but it depends on your own art style). Here you can see an example of how I view forms in my paintings, breaking them down into simple shapes, clarifying why it's important to have a transition of values for each subject.

◀ Creating believable forms by transitioning values from light to dark

18 FINDING THE RIGHT MOOD

Striking colors always grab the viewer's attention. Little Red Riding Hood's classic red theme is an advantage that really helps to spotlight her character. Red is an eye-catching color that complements the warm colors of the hyena and its surroundings. Hierarchically, the main subject in this story is the little girl, so everything else will be less saturated as it is less important. For the image's overall mood, a sunny day creates the perfect atmosphere – it suits the weather of a savannah or barren grassland and the cheerful, carefree character interaction taking place. It would not look right to set the scene on a gloomy day, as it could be misinterpreted as a depressing mood that isn't relevant to the story.

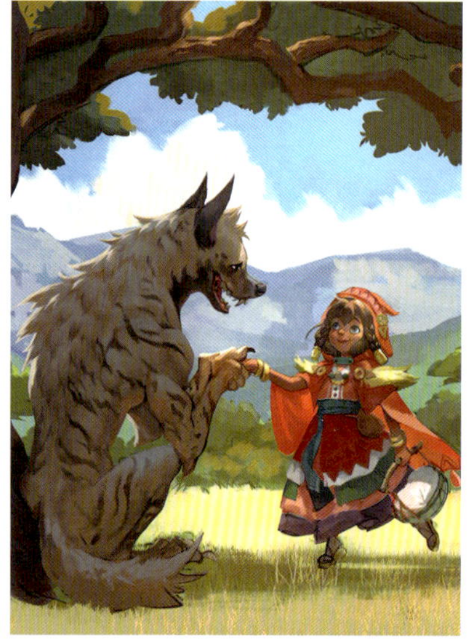

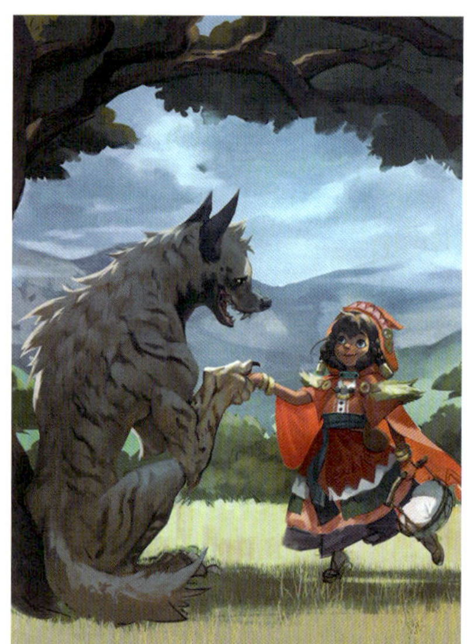

▲ Color is powerful for creating a mood that affects that viewer's feelings toward the story

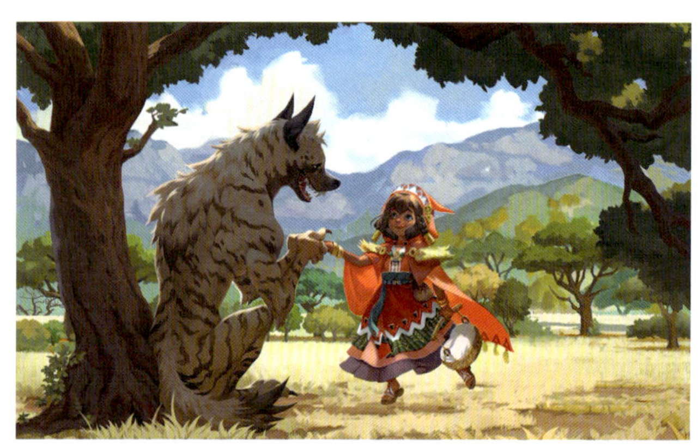

TAKING A BREAK

If you get stuck, try taking a break. Do something else to freshen up – you've been looking at your work for too long! Nothing is instant. It takes time to make progress and solving a problem cannot be forced. After sufficient rest, your eyes will be fresher than before, and you'll be able to see where things can be fixed. You can also ask people around you to give their opinions on your work. Here I am getting close to the final illustration, but I decide to take a break and think about where I could improve it.

19 MATERIALS AND TEXTURES

Illustrating a scene is challenging because many elements are combined in one space, all with different material properties. Little Red's clothes are a matte surface with low specularity, showing how the light is diffused by the soft, smooth fabric. The gold detailing is a polished, metallic surface that is flat and smooth, with high reflectivity and a strong highlight when hit by light. Leaves, fur, branches, and clouds all have different reactions to the light. Capturing these differences between surfaces – thick, thin, translucent, solid, liquid, rough, or smooth – will make your setting and characters feel immersive and believable, helping to place the viewer in the story's world.

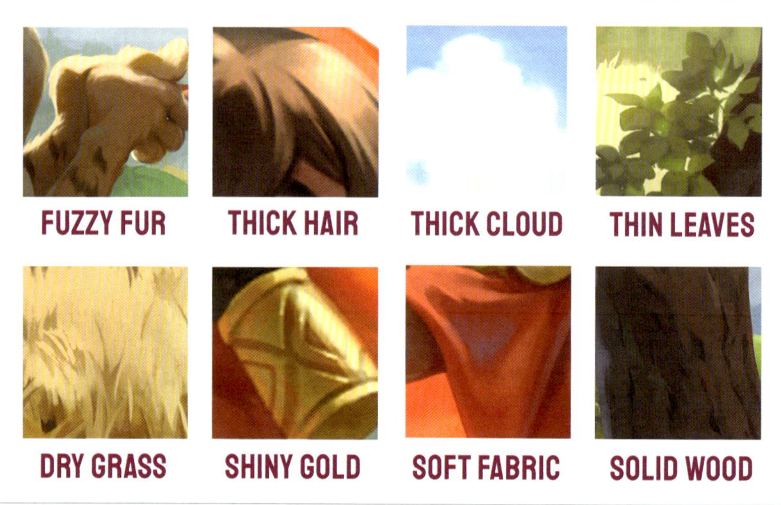

▲ Different materials and textures require different approaches to rendering

20 FINISHING TOUCHES

The final step is to examine the overall illustration and look for what can be improved. Is anything still missing? Does anything seem to be overly detailed? If there are excessive details that draw our attention away from the main event, they need to be reduced. Having everything rendered in equal detail doesn't equate to a great-looking image. When we purposefully limit the details, we can emphasize the subject we really want to highlight. For example, compare Little Red's level of detail to the mountains in the background or the out-of-focus leaves in the foreground – it is very clear where the viewer's attention should be. Conversely, if an area looks too plain, we can always add extra elements that help the illustration look more true to life. During this step, I add small details such as falling leaves, a few tears in Little Red's clothes to show her adventurous side, and some subtle scars on the hyena.

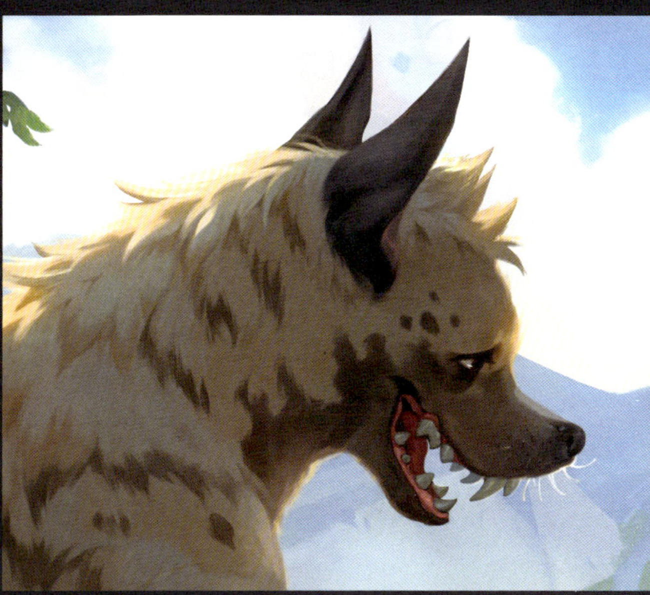

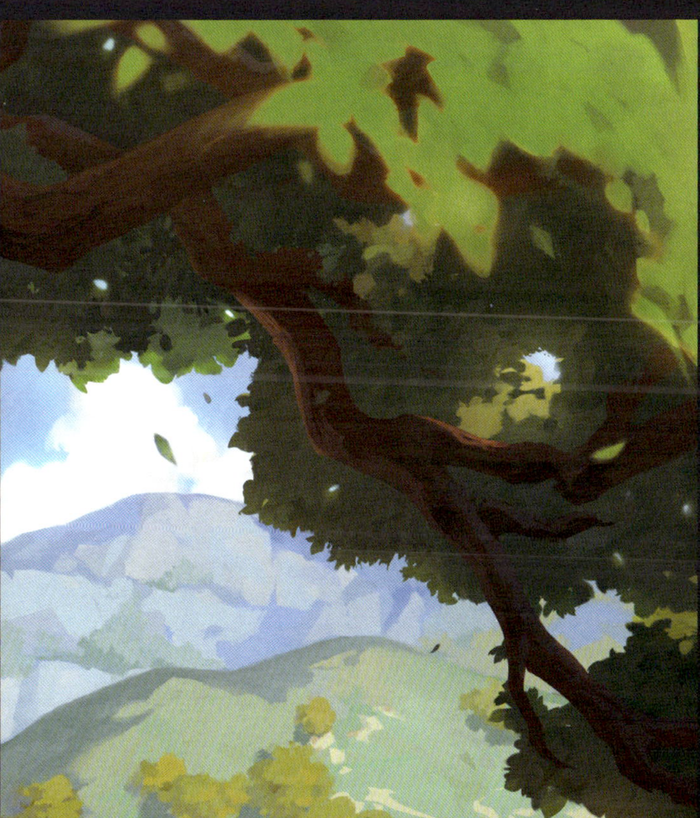

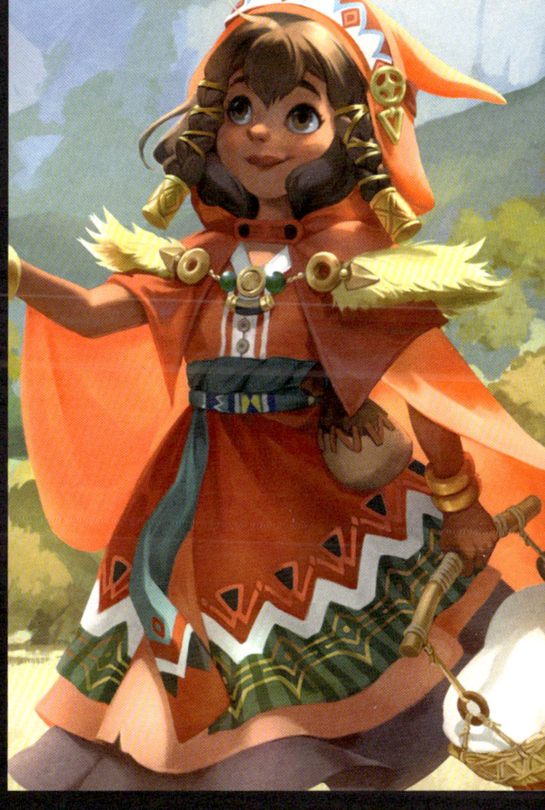

▲ Checking back over the artwork and applying finishing touches

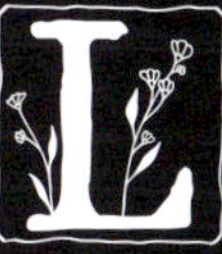

Looking back at my illustration, I am happy to have kept the event true to the original story. Even though the environment is completely different, the characters still have a resemblance to the source material, as if this fairy tale was born and grew in another part of the world. There is no wolf and no deep forest full of lurking dangers, but the characters and their roles are still instantly recognizable to anyone familiar with the original tale. I hope this tutorial has enlivened your interest in knowing more about the fundamentals of art and storytelling – I learned them through my experiences with teachers, workshops, art books, colleagues, and clients, and encourage you to pursue that knowledge too!

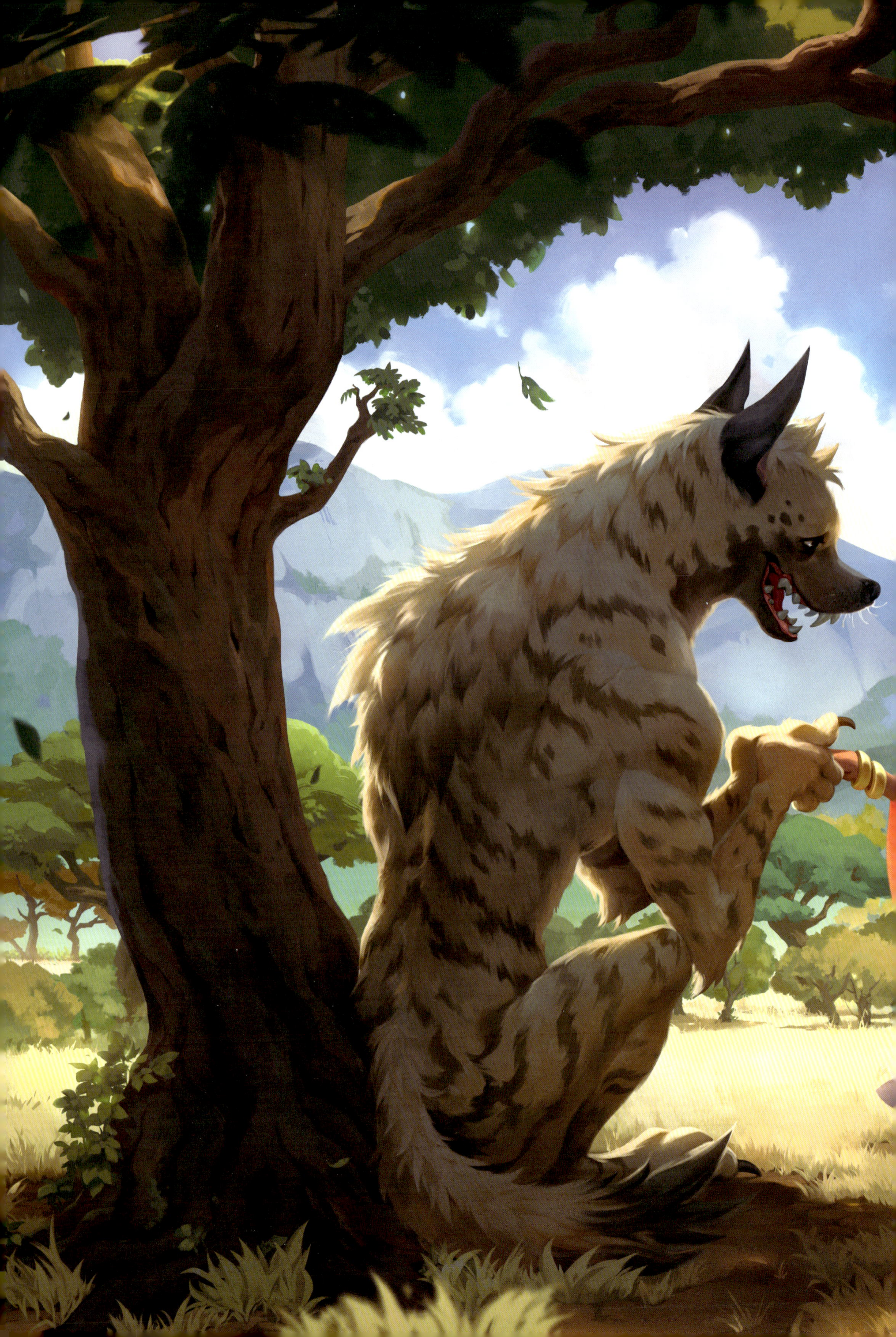

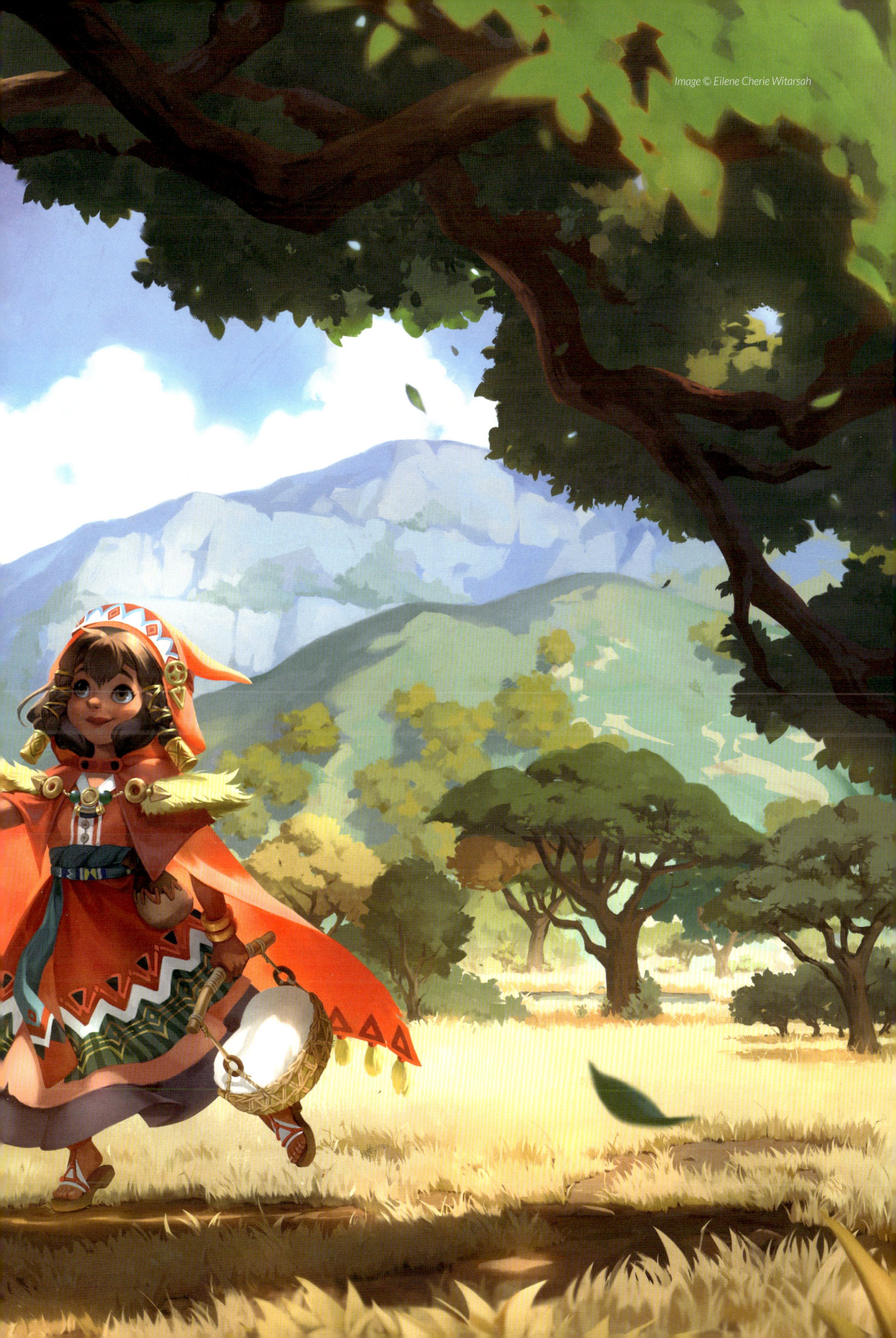

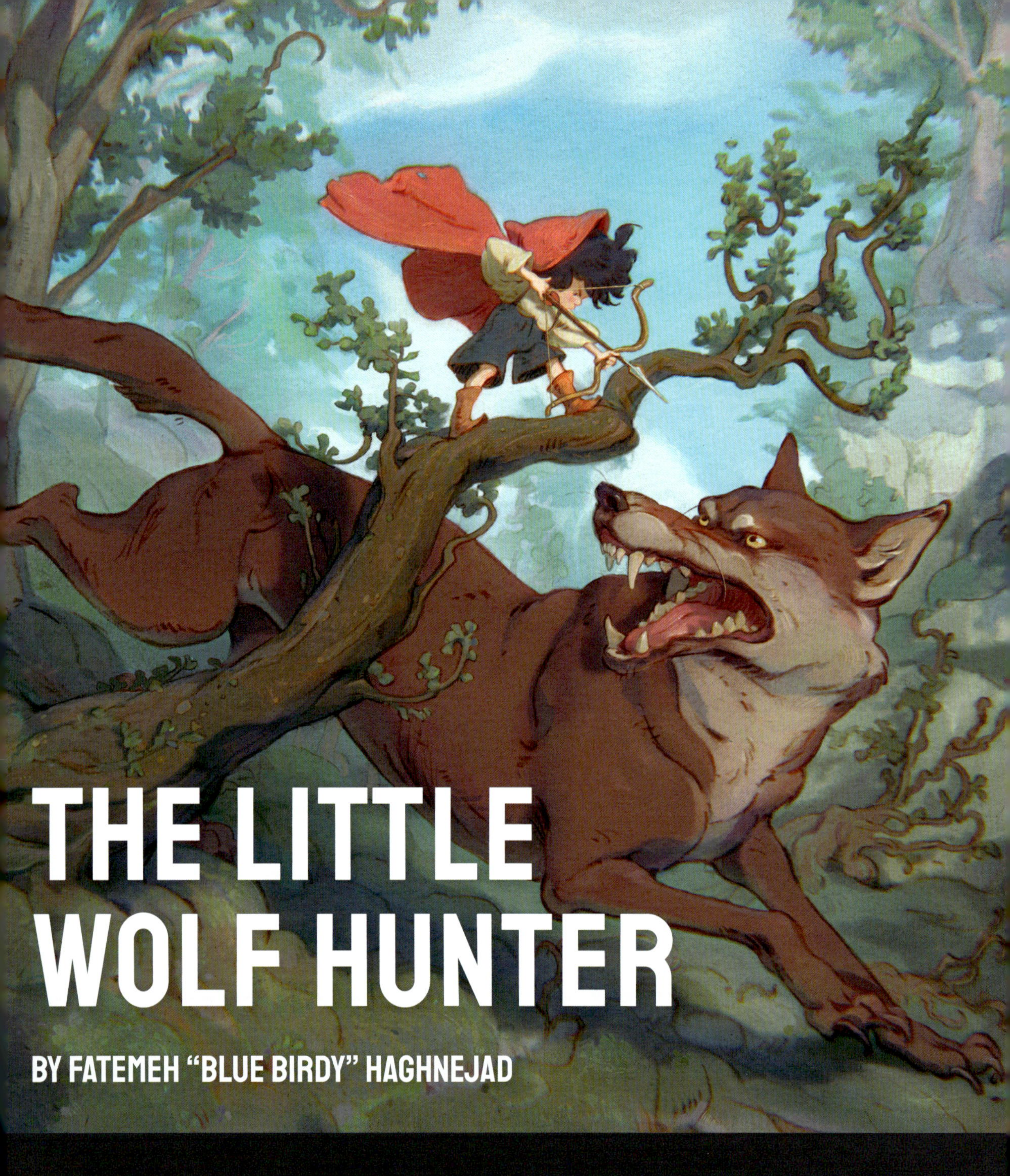

THE LITTLE WOLF HUNTER

BY FATEMEH "BLUE BIRDY" HAGHNEJAD

To start my process, I need to pick one of the many versions of the story in order to know how to subvert it. Most of us are familiar with the Brothers Grimm version of the tale, which is modified from Perrault's version, which is based on older versions in turn. I tried to find the oldest version to base my illustration on, but it was impossible, as the story originates from back before the seventeenth century! So I will base my illustration on Perrault's version, written around 1697. The key moment I would like to twist is when Little Red Riding Hood meets the wolf for the first time. I am also inspired by the amazing girls of my home country, Iran, and their strength and bravery in fighting for freedom against the darkness of our time. I want my Little Red Riding Hood to be a girl with the knowledge, tools, and bravery to stand up for herself.

01 READING THE STORY

The story of *Little Red Riding Hood* is a warning to readers about predatory strangers. Perrault concludes his fairy tale with a moral, cautioning women and young girls against the manipulation and false appearances that some men enact: "I say 'Wolf,' for all wolves are not of the same sort; there is one kind with an amenable disposition – neither noisy, nor hateful, nor angry, but tame, obliging and gentle, following the young maids in the streets, even into their homes. Alas! Who does not know that these gentle wolves are of all such creatures the most dangerous!"

If you are interested in reading different versions of the story, I recommend the poem called *The Wolf-King; or Little Red Riding Hood*, published in *Tales of Terror* around 1801. That version is close to Perrault's and is written beautifully. There is no happy ending, but I found it the most charming.

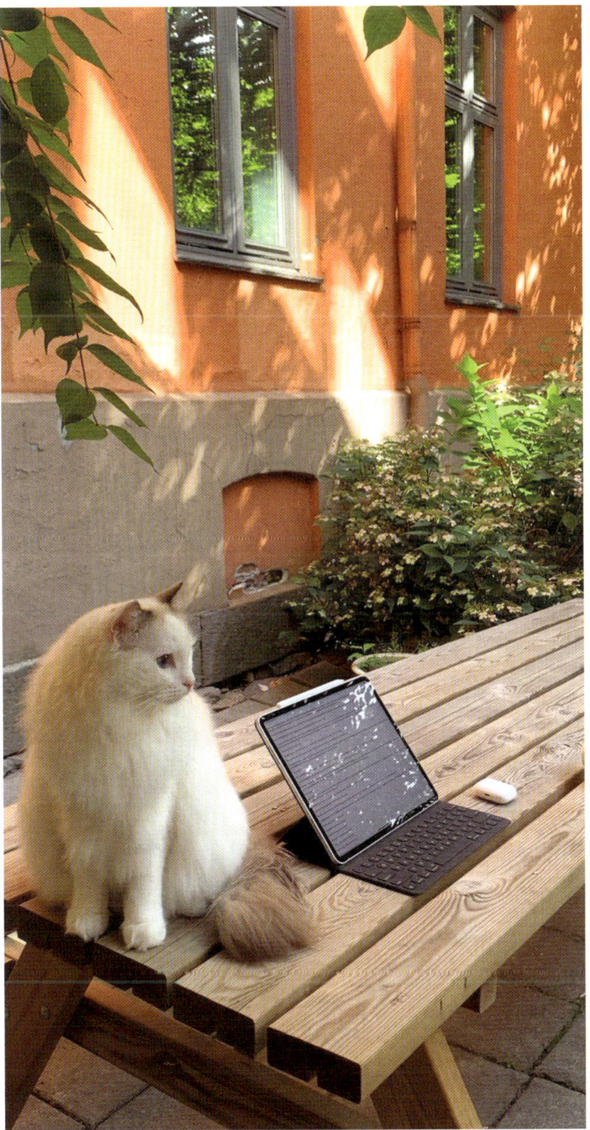

▲ Taking some time to sit and read through different versions of the story

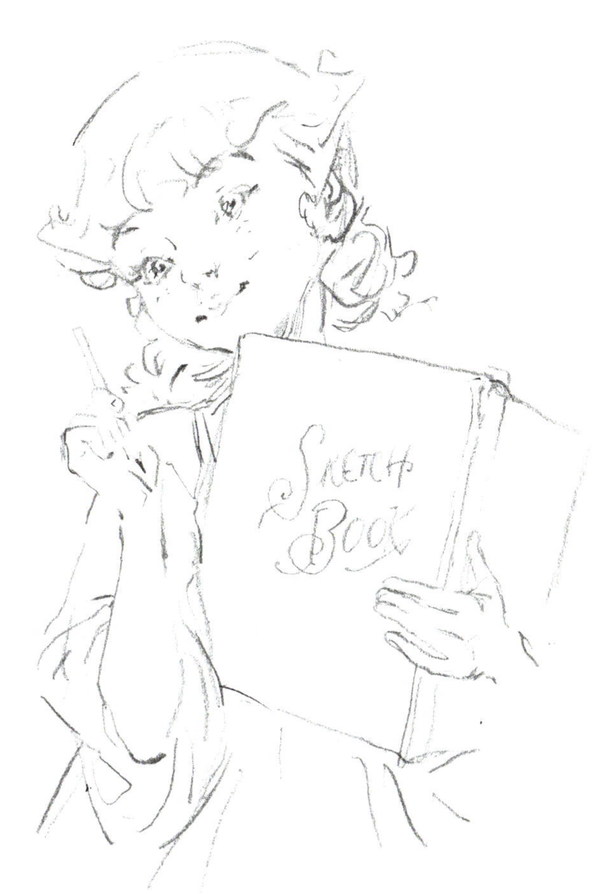

▲ Coming up with early ideas. Asking friends for inspiration helps!

02 GENERATING IDEAS

To help find an idea for the twist in the story, I share the task with my friends. Everyone comes up with an interesting twist! After giving it some thought, I decide to keep the general story but improve the main character. When Little Red Riding Hood meets the wolf in the original tale, she does not know that it is dangerous to talk to a stranger or walk into the woods unprepared. For my twist, I want her to be aware of the situation and well prepared. I have two strong ideas for this.

The first idea is locating the scene in a quiet alley, with Little Red Riding Hood wearing a red hoodie and pushing a bike with goodies for her grandma in the basket. Graffiti on the walls would capture the feeling of the woods. A man would be blocking the alley, with the neon lights in the street creating the shadow of a wolf behind him. The second idea would have a more classic fairy-tale setting, located in the woods. Little Red Riding Hood would be equipped with a bow and arrows, jumping into the trees to face the wolf.

03 TAKING NOTES

I take notes of what I want in my image and what I need to study first. This will help me tell the story in the best way I can. I write out every key detail that I can think of, as simply as possible, such as the time of day, location, mood, characters' motives, and outfits. The city scene would take place in a dark alley lit by pink neon lights and moonlight, with painted trees on the walls. Little Red Riding Hood would be wearing a red hoodie, with her grandma's goodies in the basket on her bike, confronted by a threatening man casting a wolf's shadow. The woods scene would be set at noon, viewed from above the trees, looking down at Little Red Riding Hood with the wolf running after her. She would be around ten years old, with a red cape and a bow and arrow, climbing fearlessly among the trees.

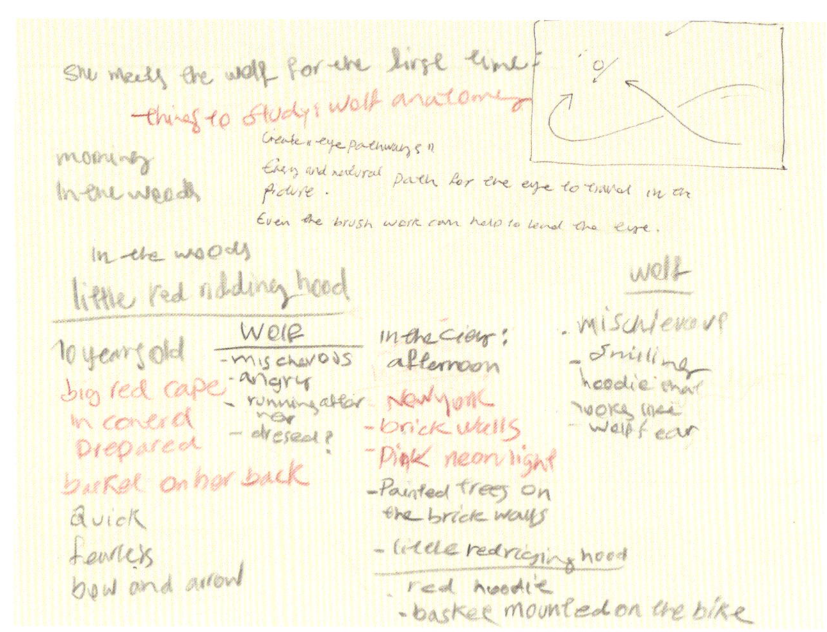

▲ Writing down all the important ideas for both scenes

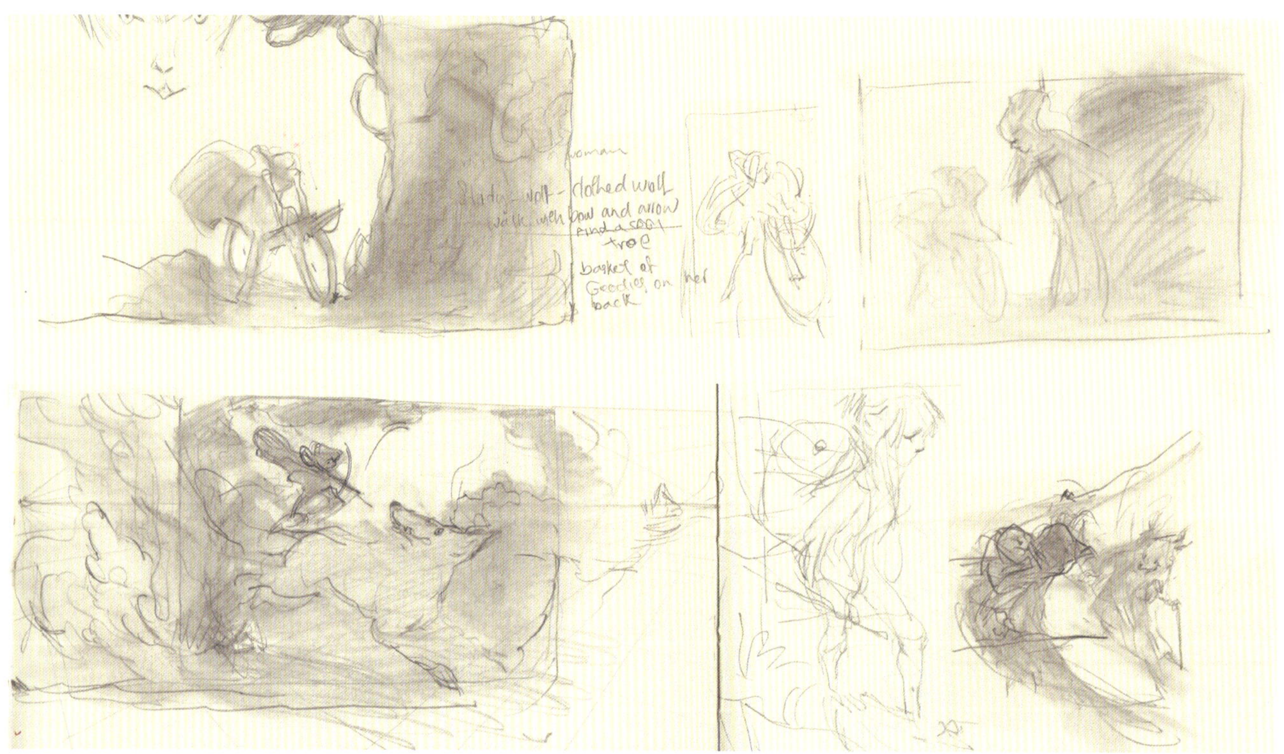

▲ Developing rough thumbnails for both scenes

04 THUMBNAIL SKETCHES

I want the viewer to recognize the story immediately, seeing the wolf and the girl in the red hood first, so I need to draw the cape and the wolf's silhouette very clearly. I make tiny sketches for both ideas, as many as I need to find the best composition. After deliberating, I decide on the second idea, set in the woods like the original – there's more freedom to create movement here. The girl jumps onto a branch, running along it with the wolf below her, looking down at him and aiming her arrow. The wolf is not clothed or anthropomorphic, but running on all fours, looking vicious and like a real predatory animal. I don't just rely on my notes, but allow the idea to develop as I sketch, trying to imagine the scene unfolding.

05 WOLF STUDIES

For this illustration I need to study wolves to understand their anatomy better – I know this will help me improve the piece. If I am familiar with wolf anatomy, it will be easier for me to draw the character as I wish. I sketch some quick studies of wolves' skeletal structure and musculature to get an idea of what's going on inside them, then find some pictures of wolves in different poses to study their overall figures. When I feel I have a better grasp of the subject, I move on to the next step.

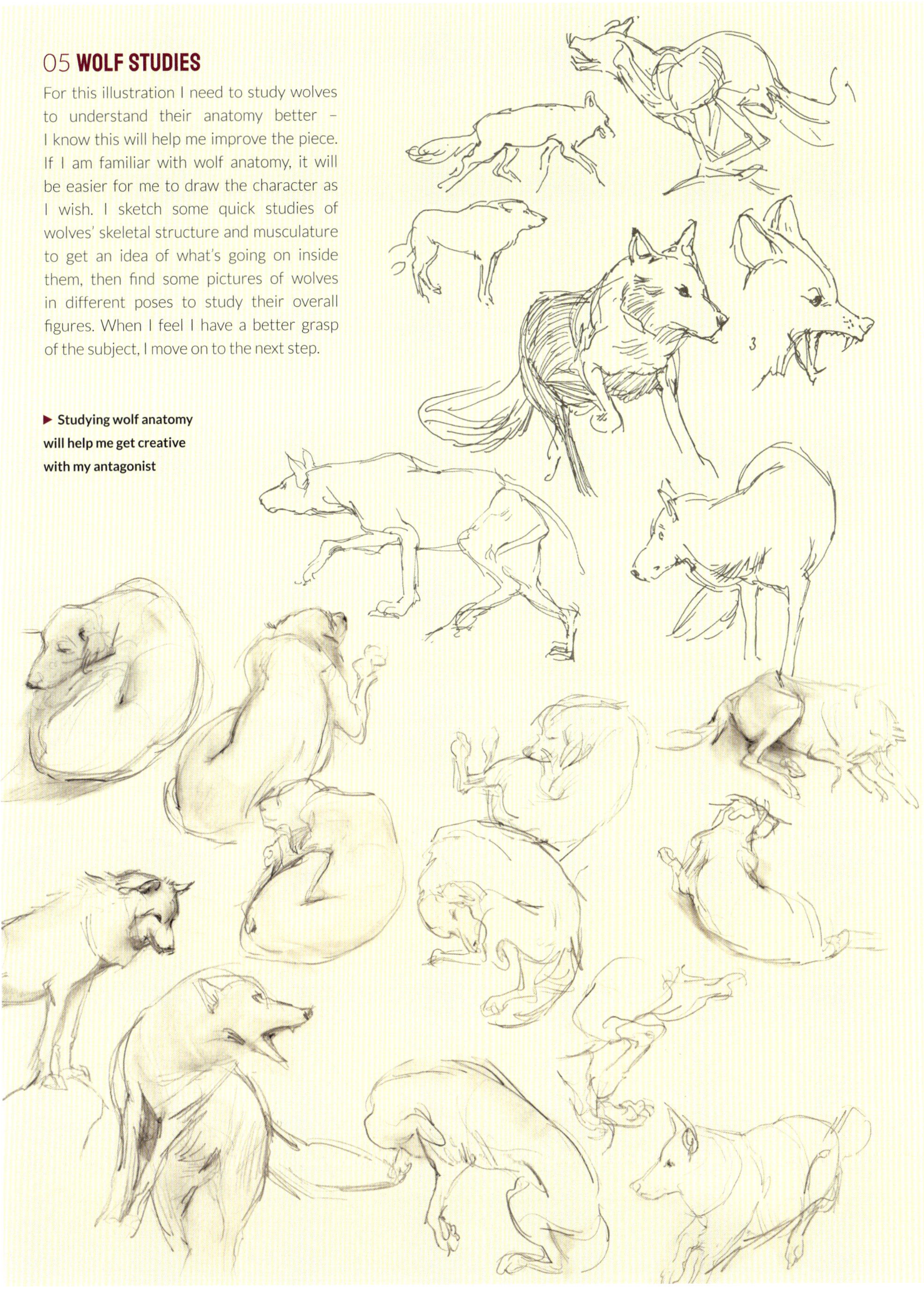

▶ **Studying wolf anatomy will help me get creative with my antagonist**

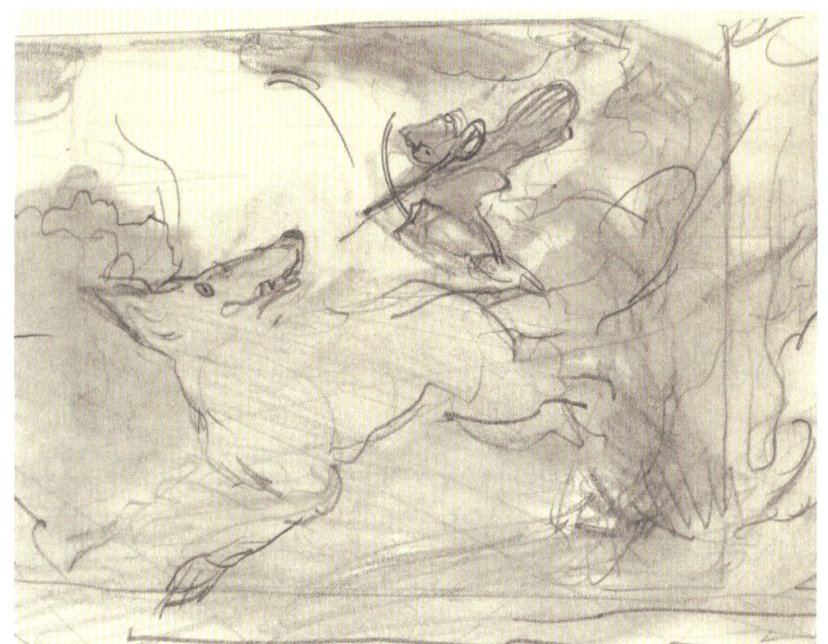

06 SKETCH DEVELOPMENT

I pick the thumbnail that I want to work with, photograph it and transfer it to Procreate, an app on the iPad. Here I can make a new layer and start to work on drawing more details into the composition. When I draw traditionally I draw the horizon line and vanishing points with a light pencil, but when I work in Procreate I can switch on its Drawing Guide function to help me adjust my perspective. Using digital media allows me to easily move things around as the composition develops. At this stage, I keep the elements as simple as possible, focusing more on creating movement and pathways for the eye.

◄ **Starting to build up a larger, cleaner sketch with better perspective**

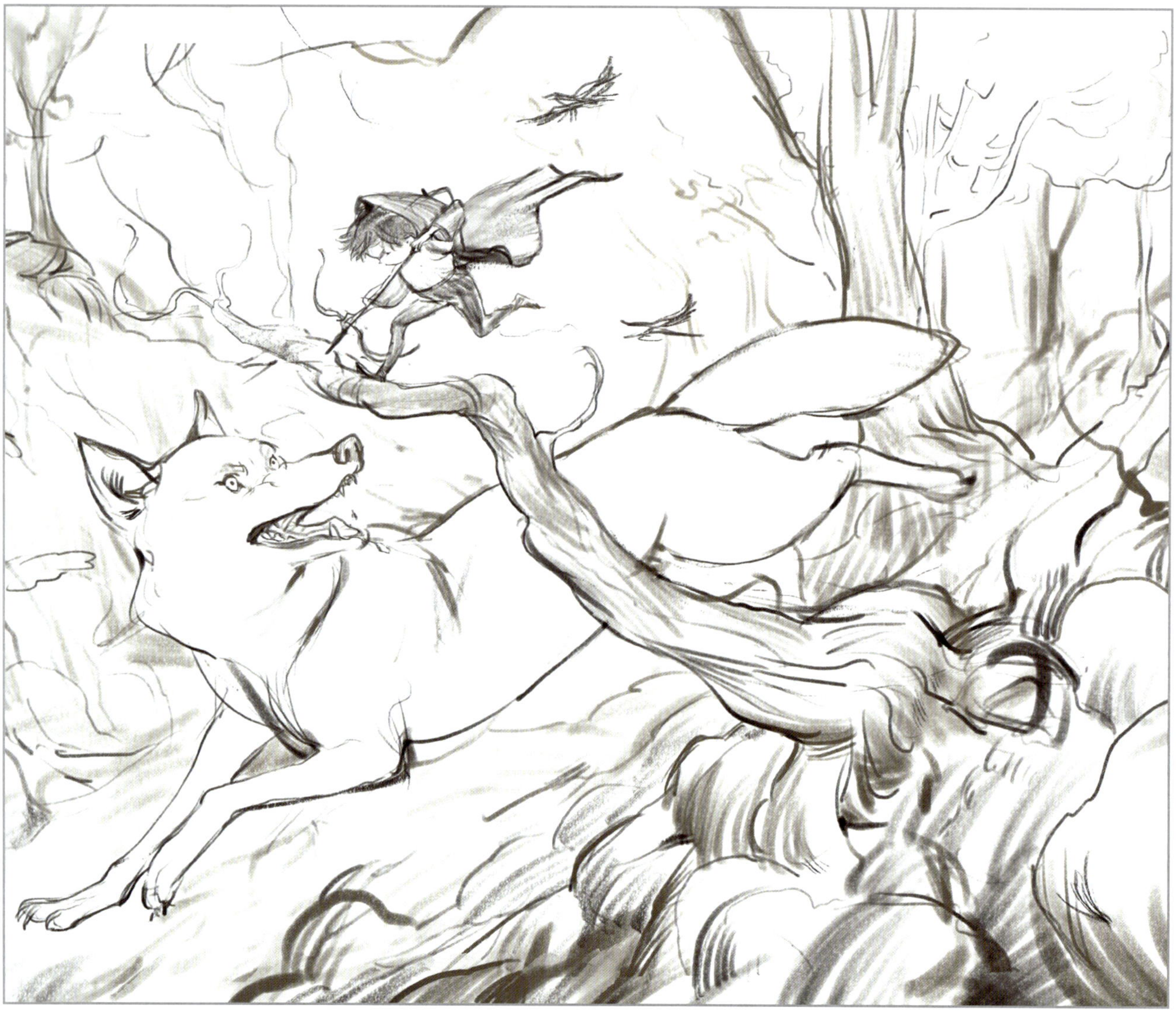

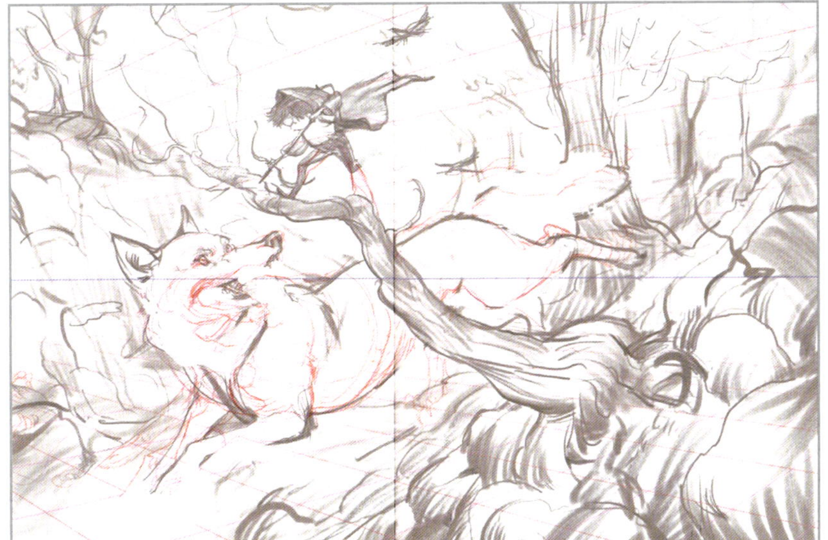

07 RETURNING TO PAPER

I want the final illustration to have a somewhat analog feel, so the process does not go fully digital yet. Instead I print out my sketch and use a light box to redraw it. I want to make the sketch as clear as possible, so that I can work on my detailed drawing with more confidence. I notice a few things that I would like to fix first, such as the wolf's mouth and Little Red Riding Hood's pose. I use white paint to remove the lines I don't need and redraw with red pencil to make the changes. I want the wolf's face to look more angry and shocked – making some quick trial sketches on a separate sheet helps me familiarize myself with the new expression before I redraw it.

▲ Using white paint and red pencil to revise the printed sketch

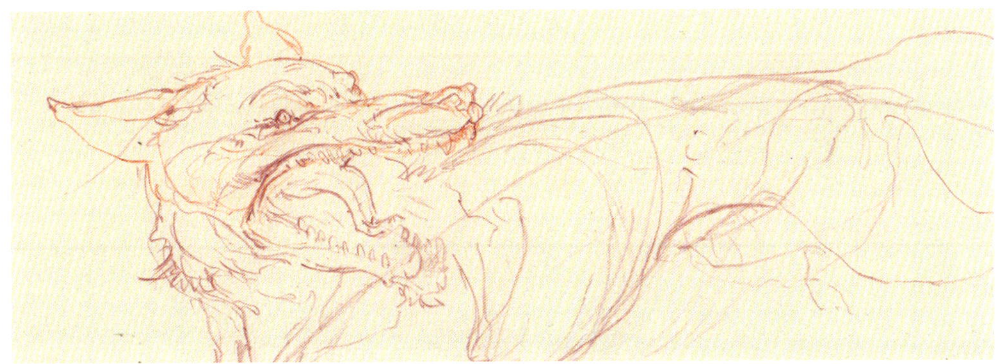

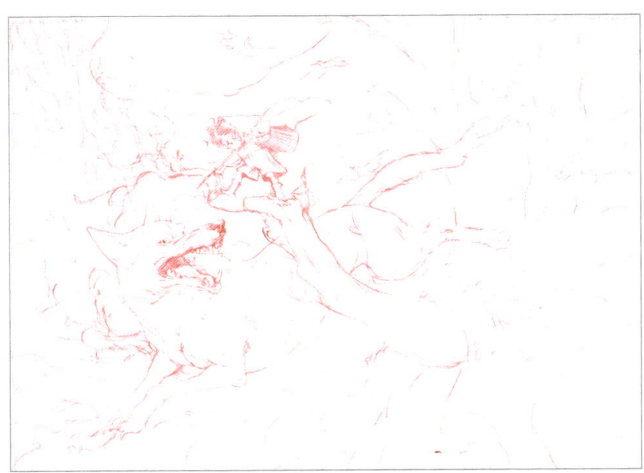

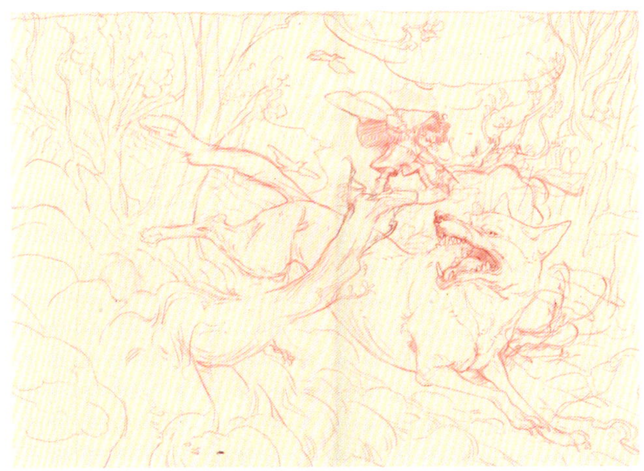

08 BUILDING UP THE SKETCH

I always find it easier to add details and immerse myself in sketching when I am working on real paper. Now that I have my foundation and elements where I like them, I can focus more on the details. I continue to use my light box to draw, still working on top of my first rough sketch, but I try not to just copy myself – I focus on improving the image as much as I can, fixing and building things as I go. I decide I want to make Little Red Riding Hood smaller to exaggerate the drama of the scene, and make my sketch even more detailed in preparation for scanning.

▲ Developing the scene until it is essentially complete

09 FINALIZING THE LINES

I scan the image again and make the character a bit smaller. She reminds me of a saying we have in Persian: "Felfel nabin che rize, beshkan bebin che tize," which means, "Don't underestimate the peppercorn for its size, try it and see how spicy it can be." Little Red Riding Hood is very small compared with the wolf, but she's very bold and strong, like a little peppercorn! I print out my drawing for the final time and use the light box to redraw it, using a dark brown pencil that will match my final color palette. I like my pencil drawings to show through in the final painting, so I want to make the lines as precise as possible.

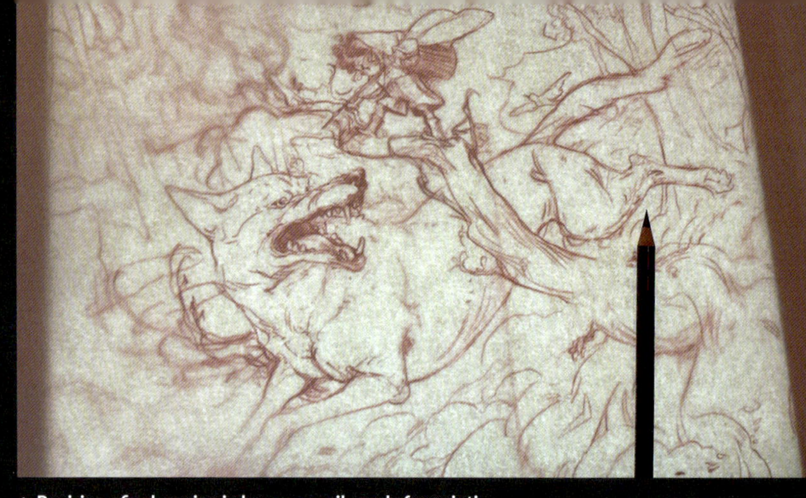

▲ Revising a final version in brown pencil, ready for painting

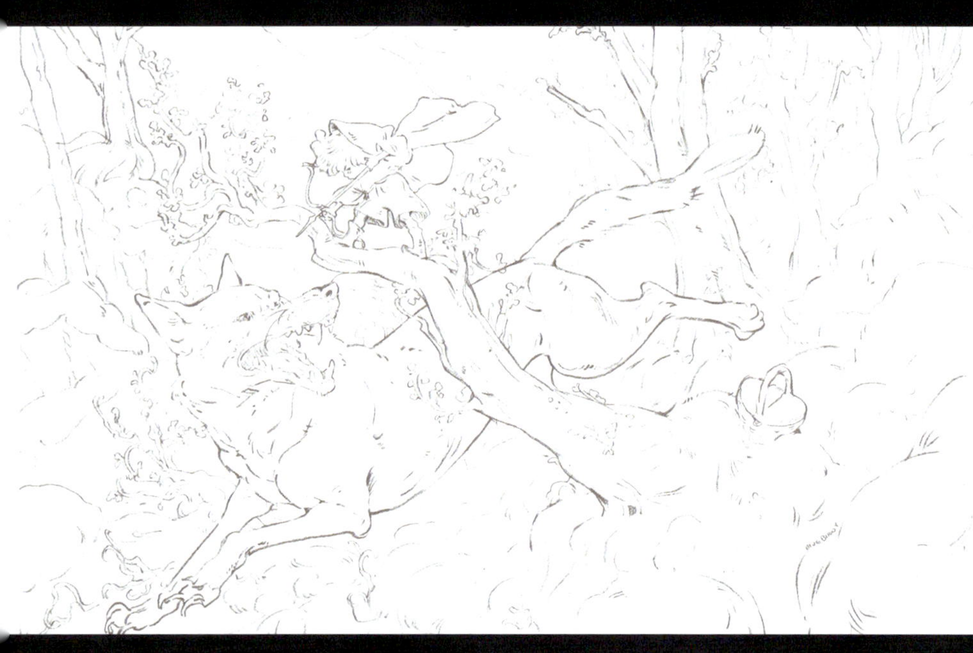

▼ Scanning the final pencil drawing and planning out value

10 VALUE TEST

I scan my finished drawing and start to work on a value test in Procreate. I start from the background trees, coloring them a light gray, and then move to the trees and stones that are one layer closer, making them a darker gray. Other than the line art, I want the wolf and arrow to have the highest contrast in the image, so I choose the darkest grays for them. These layers of value will help me keep a clear focal point and create the scene's fairy-tale atmosphere. I also start to think about where the painting's light source will be coming from, adding an arrow in the top corner as a helpful indicator.

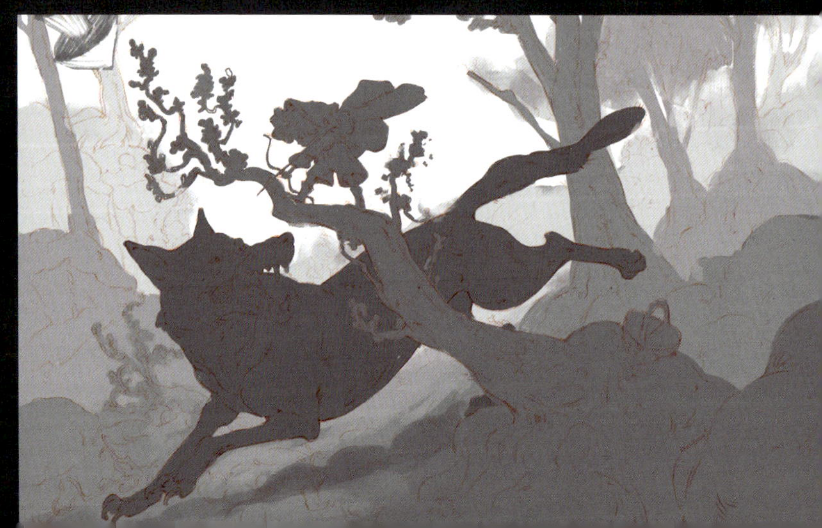

11 DEVELOPING THE VALUES

Other than the ambient light from the sky, he sun will be the image's main light source. n this value test I am free to make mistakes, so I continue to play with values and shadows o balance the image. I build up more value details, adding rough light and shadow based on my arrow guide. I keep flipping the canvas o balance the "weight" of the objects in the composition – this helps to ensure that areas of the image don't get forgotten. Now that have my value test I can use it as my value reference during my process.

► Adding more value information based on the main light source

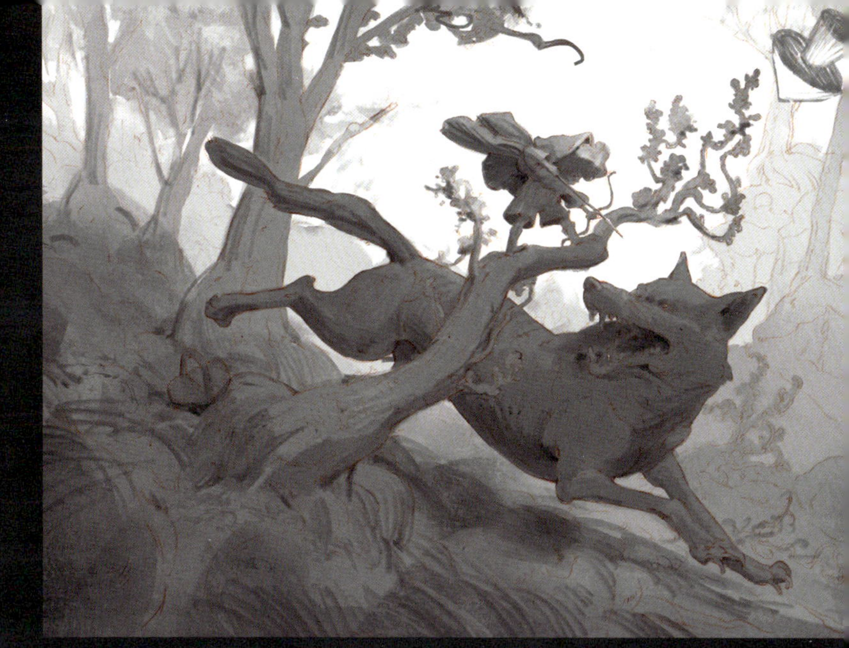

12 STARTING TO PAINT

From the beginning, I have had a clear vision of the color palette of this painting the bright blues, greens, and browns of a fairy-tale forest in the daytime. If you are less sure of your palette, it is helpful to tes a few color options and keep your chosen palette visible as reference. A single piece can sometimes span many days, while ou moods and ideas can be so changeable, so having a reference nearby will help to keep your palette clear and consistent.

I start my coloring process with the farthes thing in the background, which is the sky I try to complete as much of the sky as possible before moving to the next layer but I have the security of knowing I can still go back to that layer if I need to change anything. I paint the overall shapes and volumes of the clouds, making sure they support the composition and light direction but I may refine these later once I have placed the trees. You can see that I have flipped the painting here, which it's good to do frequently – mirroring your image can expose mistakes and imbalances that you eyes have become accustomed to seeing.

◄ Starting the painting process with the sky

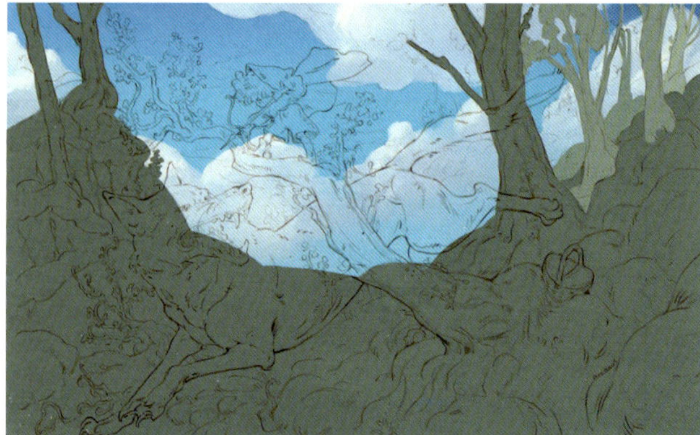

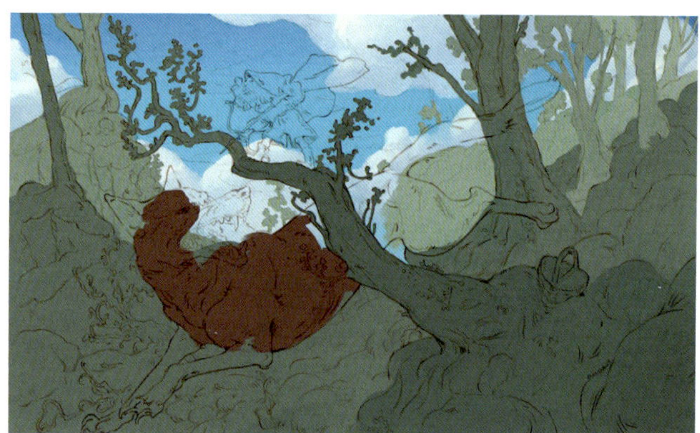

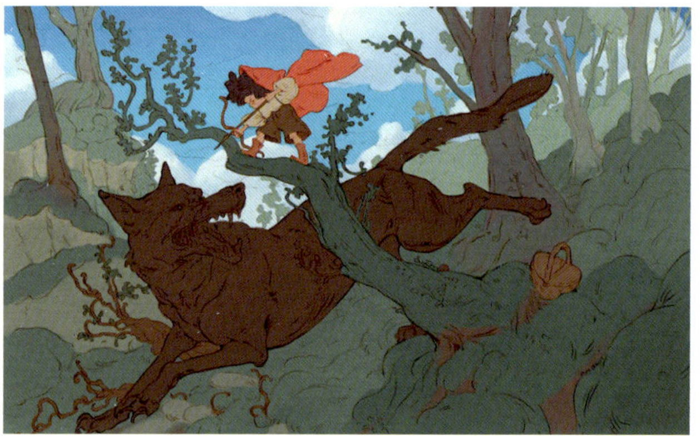

▲ Building up the colors of the environment

13 FLAT COLORS

I start painting the forest with flat colors to keep the various elements separate and clear. Using different shades of green adds variety while keeping the tones close to each other. Some sandy and brownish tones add definition to the landscape and balance the wolf's color. The most vivid color is the bright red cloak, which stands out instantly against the green forest and blue sky. The viewer's eye will naturally travel from Little Red Riding Hood's cloak, down her arrow, to the wolf's face. The rest of her clothes are more muted colors that match the earthy tones of the landscape, ensuring that the red hood is the most striking part of her outfit.

14 ADDING SHADOWS

When I have all my colors placed, I use the light source that I planned earlier as a guide for adding the cast shadows. To make this easier and clearer, I make a separate layer and change the colors of my foreground to gray, then paint my darker shadows on a layer above that, where they are easier to see. I keep the arrow for the main light source visible during this process to help me stay consistent. I add a bit of red fabric coming out of the basket, to help balance the image, but I choose a less saturated red that doesn't draw too much attention away from the red cape.

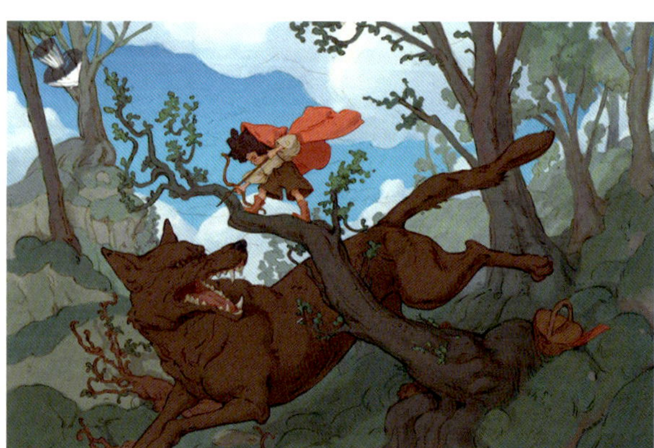

▲ Adding a smaller pop of red color for balance

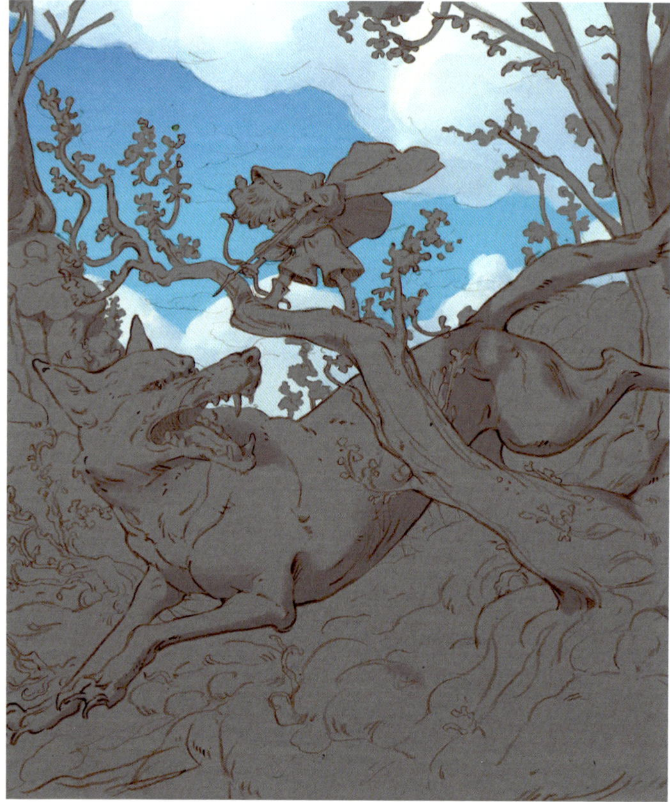

▲ Using a plain gray layer to help with visibility when painting shadows

15 BUILDING UP COLOR AND LIGHT

I feel like the palette needs to be deeper and richer, so I adjust the sky and wolf to be slightly darker. Then I continue developing the lighting and adding details to the image, such as lighter areas of the wolf's fur and more gray and green hues among the stones. To emphasize the feeling of being in a forest, I add more depth and texture to the greenery, extending some of the leafy branches and playing with different hues of green in the foliage. I notice that Little Red Riding Hood's tree is a bit too similar in color to the wolf, so I make it more of a mossy green to separate them.

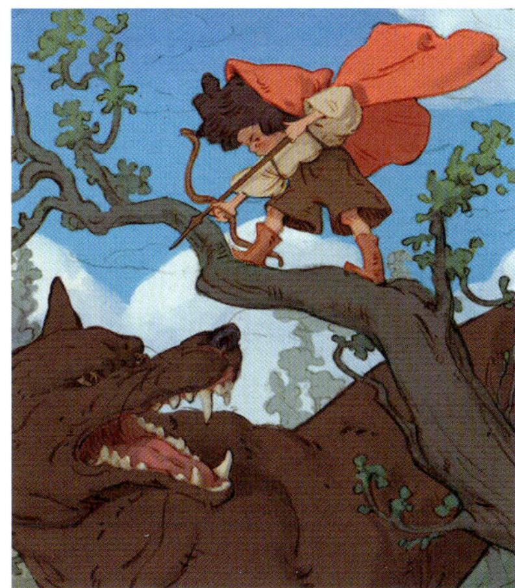

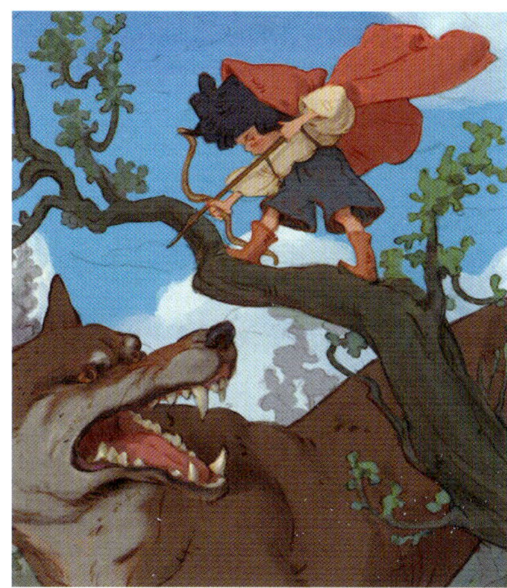

▲ Tweaking some color choices for a punchier palette, then building up form and detail

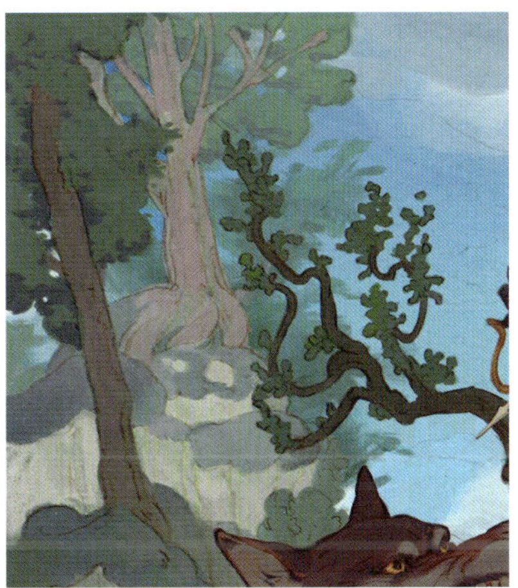

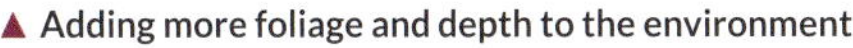

▲ Adding more foliage and depth to the environment

16 FOREST ATMOSPHERE

As I continue painting, I realize that the image isn't quite capturing the feeling of being deep in the woods. To correct this, I add another layer of background greenery and a layer of subtle gray-blue between the foreground and background. This creates an atmospheric "fog" effect, as if the forest is deeper and those distant trees are farther away. I also make the sky paler to match the palette of the forest more closely, and paint over the clouds with gray-blue, removing some of their fluffy softness and static shape. This helps add some drama and movement to the image.

17 TRADITIONAL FEEL

I want my finished illustration to have a traditional look that emphasizes its classic fairy-tale atmosphere, so I add a paper texture to my digital painting. You can do this using a blending mode such as Multiply or Linear Burn. It's always a good way to bring everything together. Painting on a single layer also helps give a more traditional look to a digital piece, so I create a merged copy of my painting and add subtle sketchy details directly onto it with a textured brush.

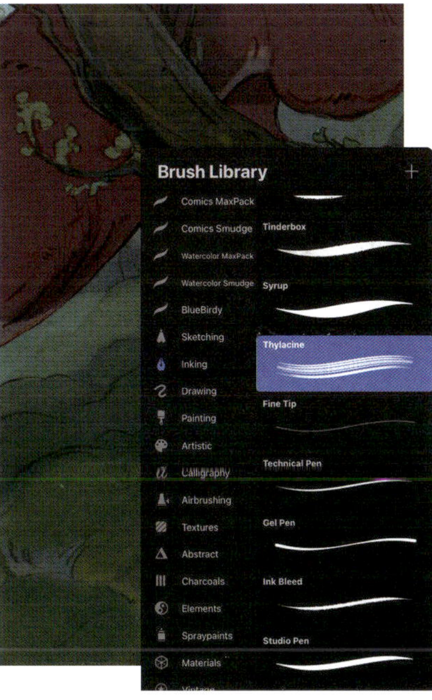

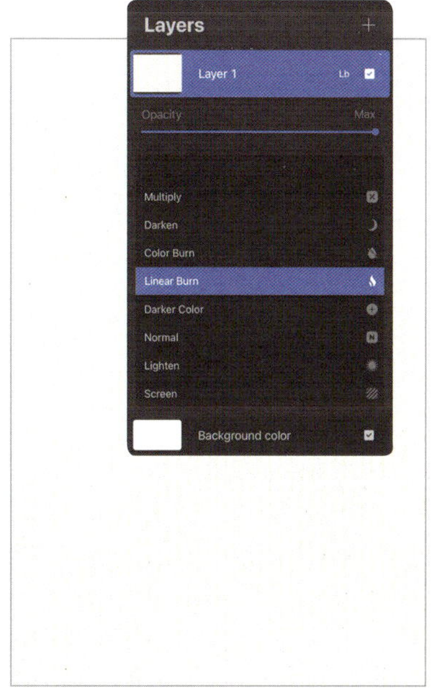

► Creating a traditional, textured feel that suits a classic fairy tale

18 TESTING LIGHT IDEAS

At this stage, I wonder whether the image needs some warm sunlight in the foreground, dropping through the trees onto the characters. As I am working digitally, I am able to make a new layer and quickly test some lighting to see what that addition might look like. If you are working on a traditional piece, you can test ideas by taking a photo of your image and editing that instead. I decide that the warm sunlight is attractive but perhaps a bit too strong; I might add some sunny warmth to the lighting in the final piece, but not in intense spotlights like this.

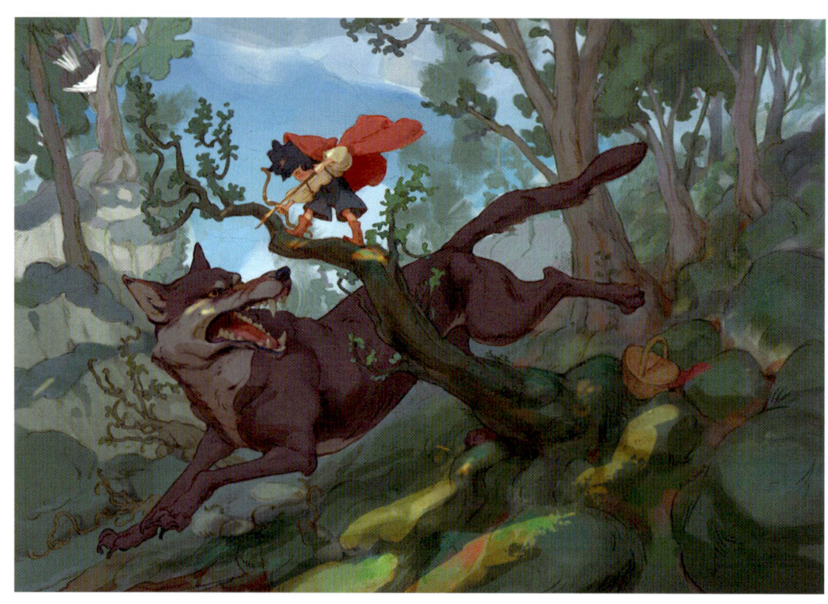

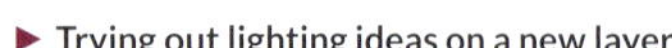

▶ Trying out lighting ideas on a new layer

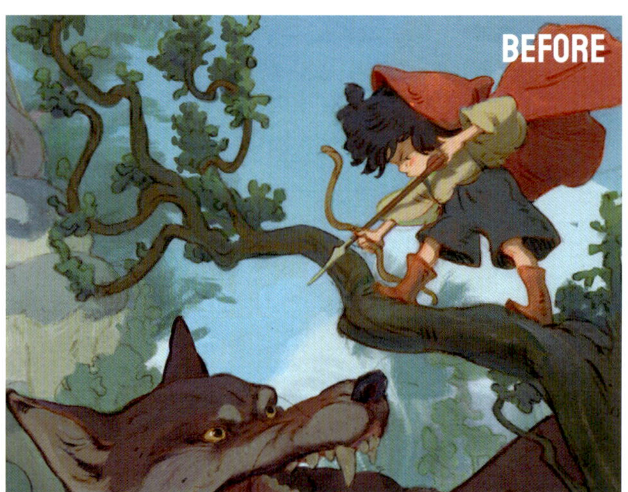

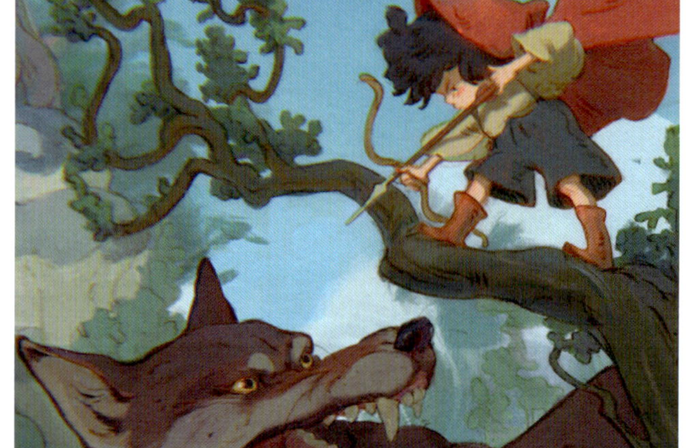

▲ Enhancing the image's texture with some chromatic aberration

19 CHROMATIC ABERRATION

I like using a "chromatic aberration" effect to give images some extra texture. Originally a glitch found in photography, this slight blurriness is often simulated by digital artists to create a cinematic texture or a dynamic, active feeling. It works well for this piece that mixes the traditional and modern in both its narrative and method. I also add a new layer, set to Color Dodge, and paint with a pale pink-orange to give some more light to the piece, particularly on Little Red Riding Hood and the wolf's face. The effect is warm and helps to emphasize the characters as the focal points, like I wanted in step 18, but is more subtle than bright light beams.

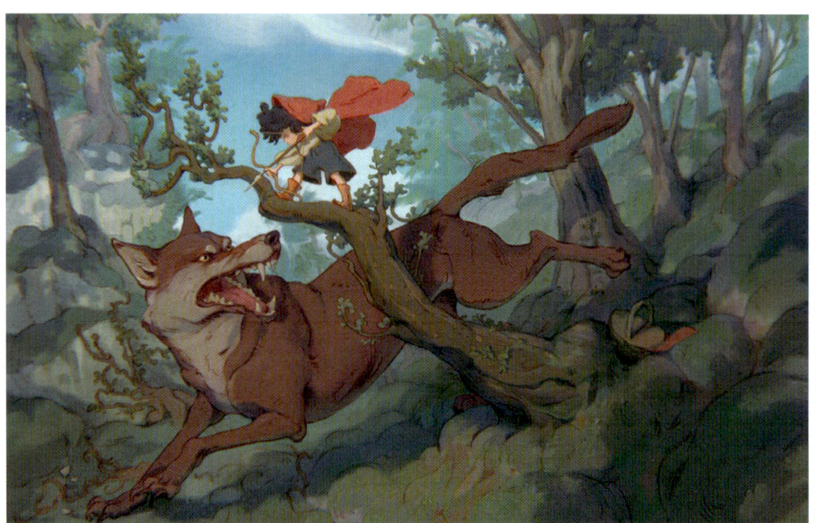

▲ Warming up the lighting as I continue to render

20 FINISHING TOUCHES

I always love the last stage of adding the final touches. This step can take me forever, so I try to set a time limit to stop myself from overworking. When comparing this version to the finished piece in my mind's eye, I decide that I only need to add some more light effects and small details, like leaves in the foreground and sharpening the wolf's eyes. I also flip the image back to the direction it faced in step 11. After finishing my details, the last thing I do is select the area around the characters and smudge it a little, just to help separate the characters from the background.

▶ **Adding final touches to the lighting and details**

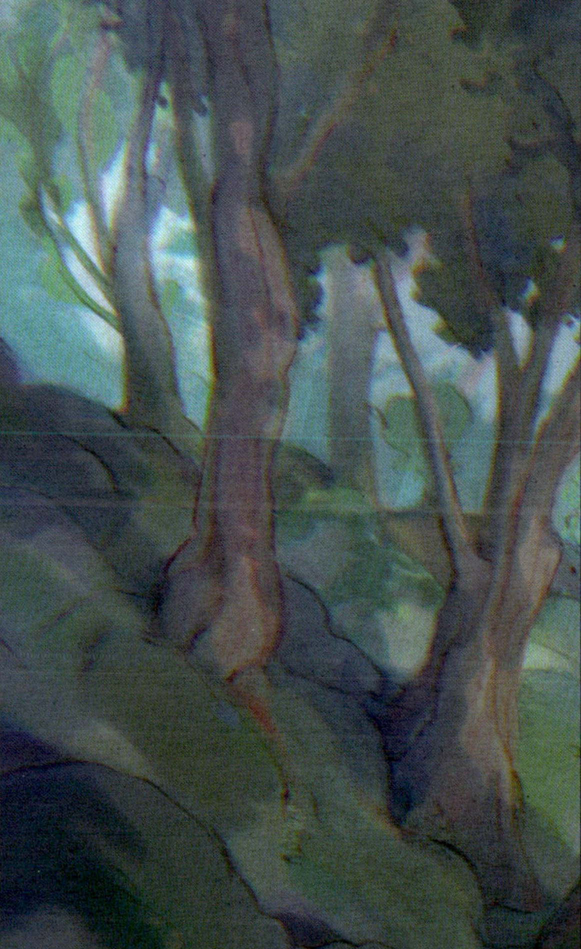

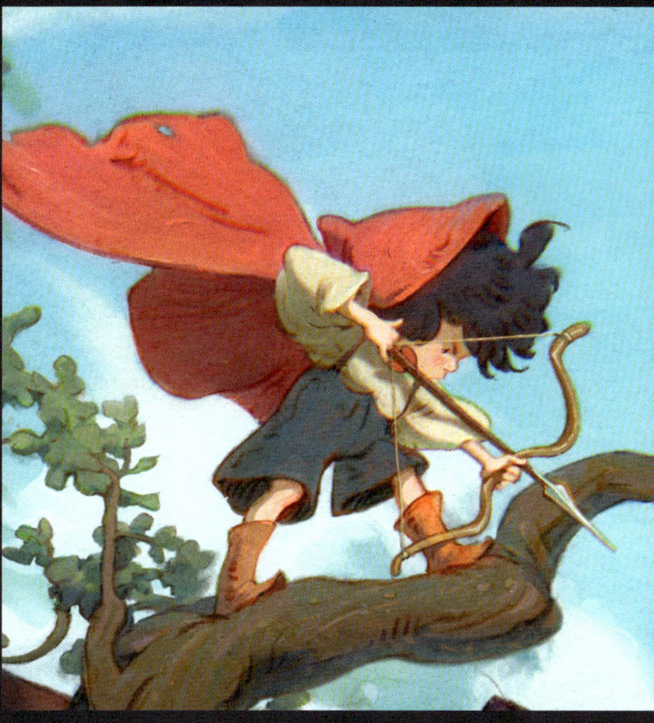

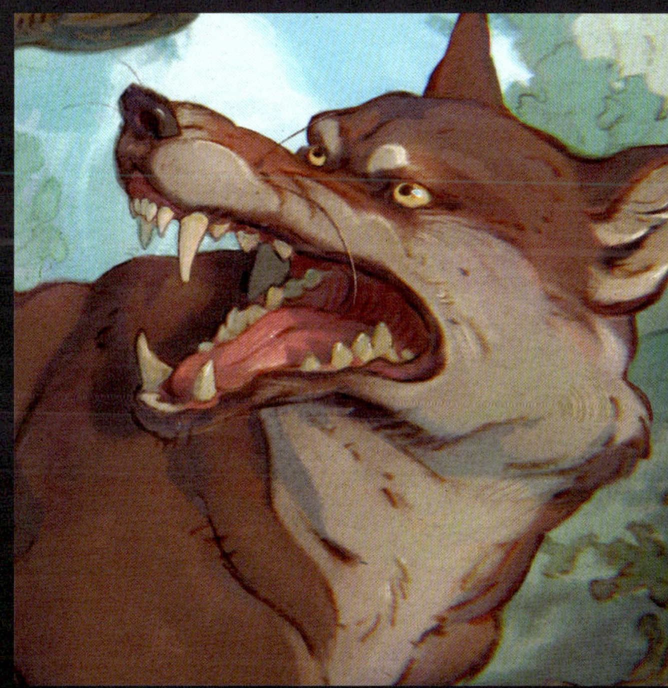

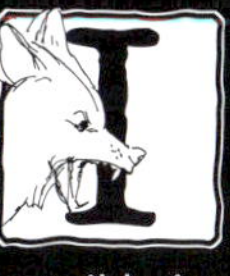

I am happy that this image went mostly as planned! Making even a single piece of art can teach you an amazing amount – any challenges or frustrations are just reminders to invest as much time as possible in studying what's needed for an image. For example, I spent time practicing wolf anatomy and am happy with the results, but in hindsight, it would have saved time to study different varieties of trees, too. In the finished image, Little Red Riding Hood is now a more satisfying character to me, with awareness and confidence that feel more modern. She can now dodge and escape from the wolf, jumping and running on tree branches as she makes for her grandmother's house. The wolf, meanwhile, looks startled to have lost the upper hand!

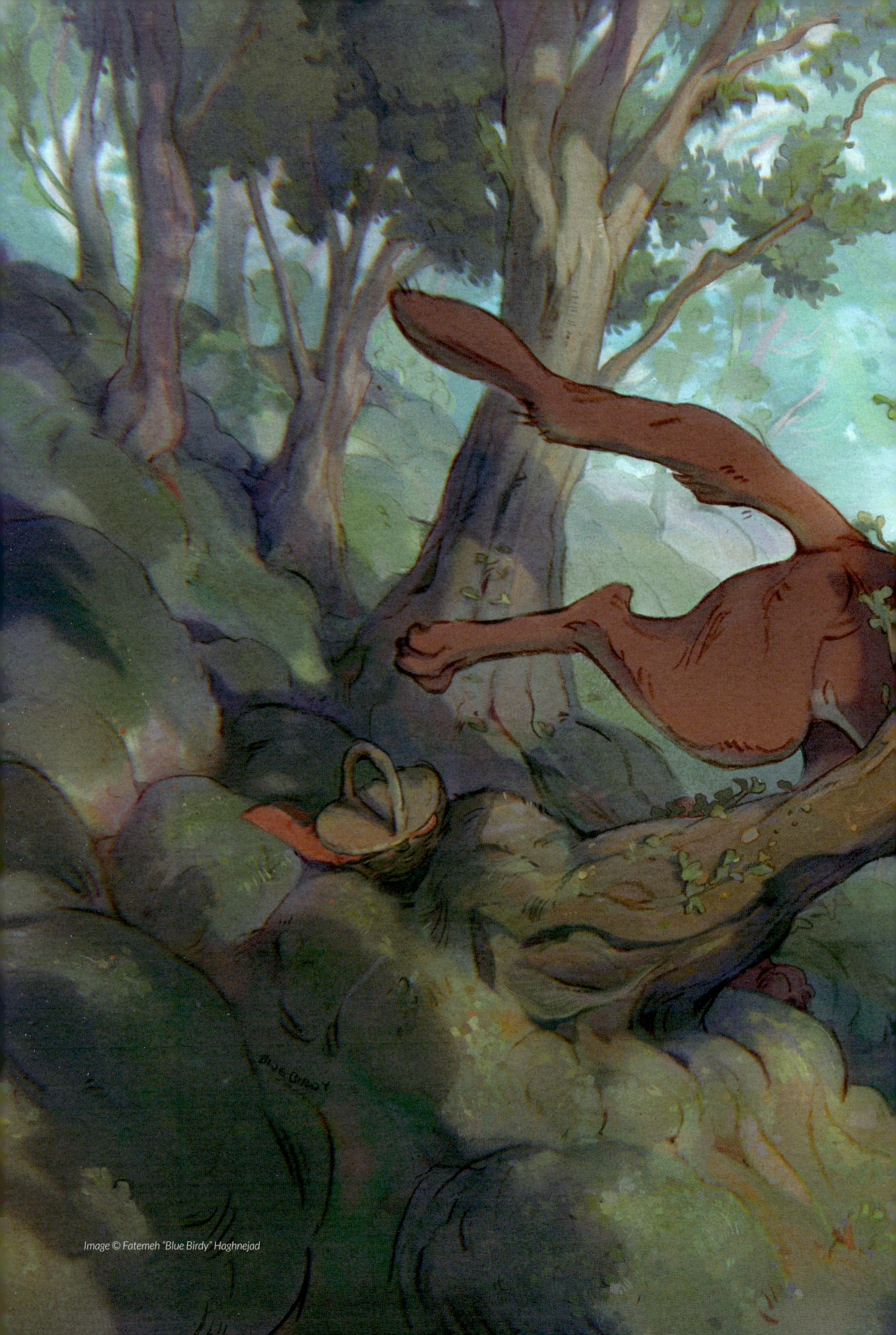
BLUE BIRDY

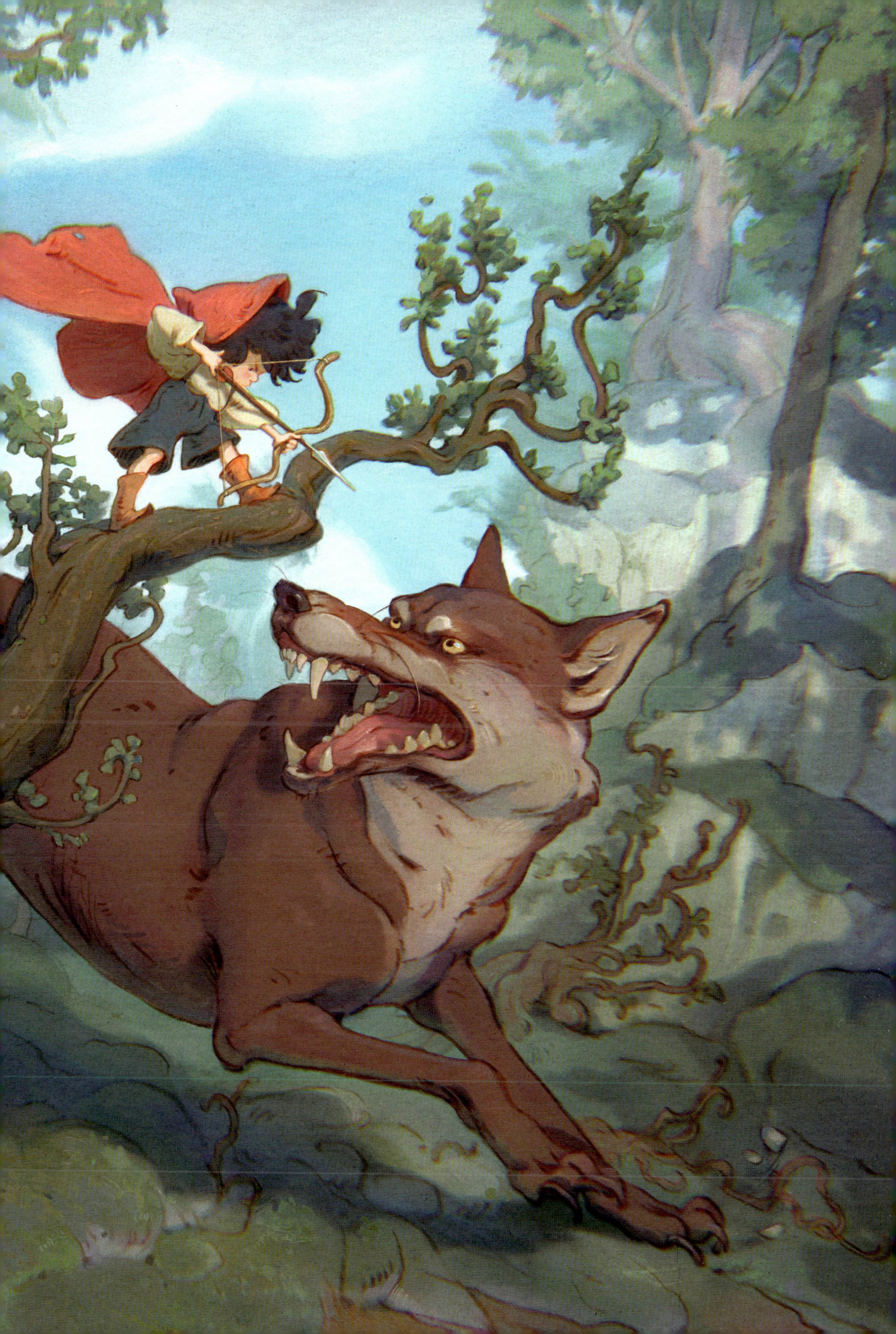

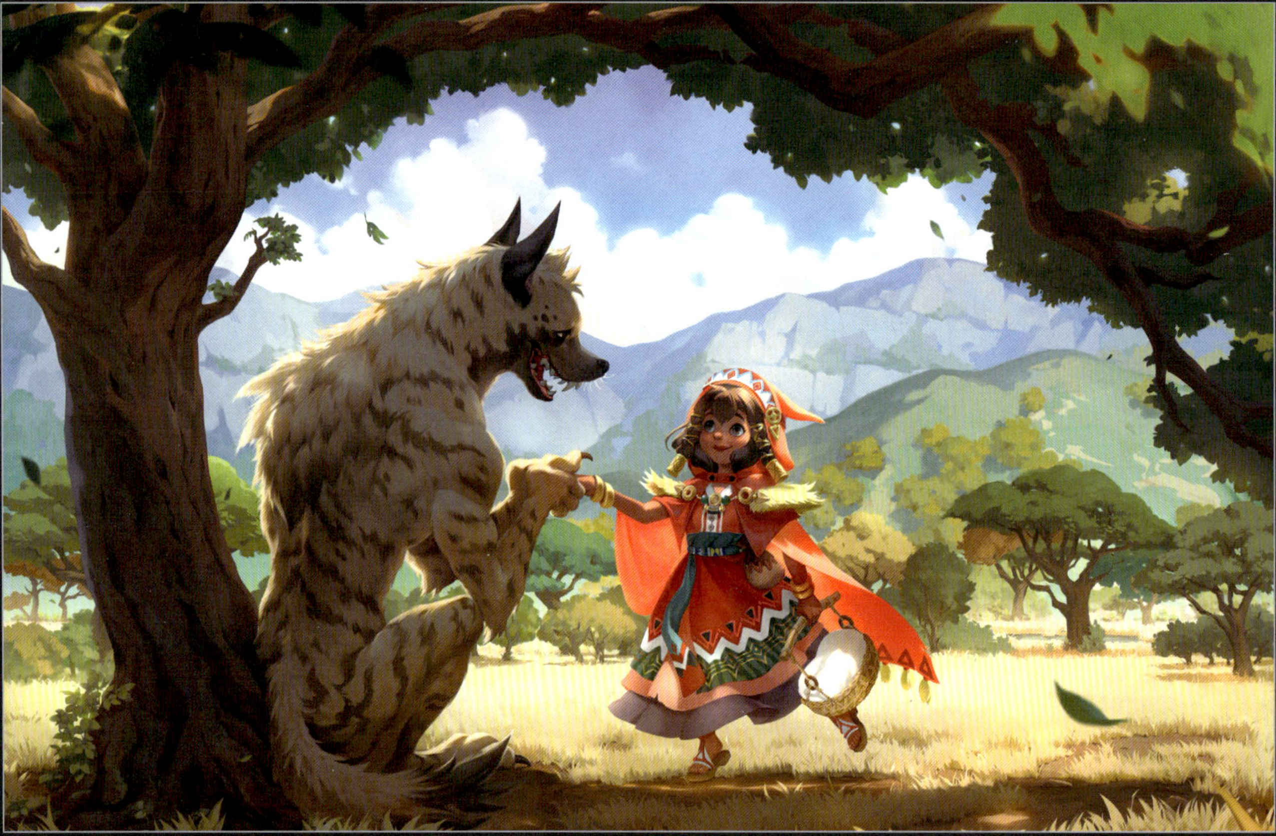

"Little Red and the Hyena." Image © Eilene Cherie Witarsah

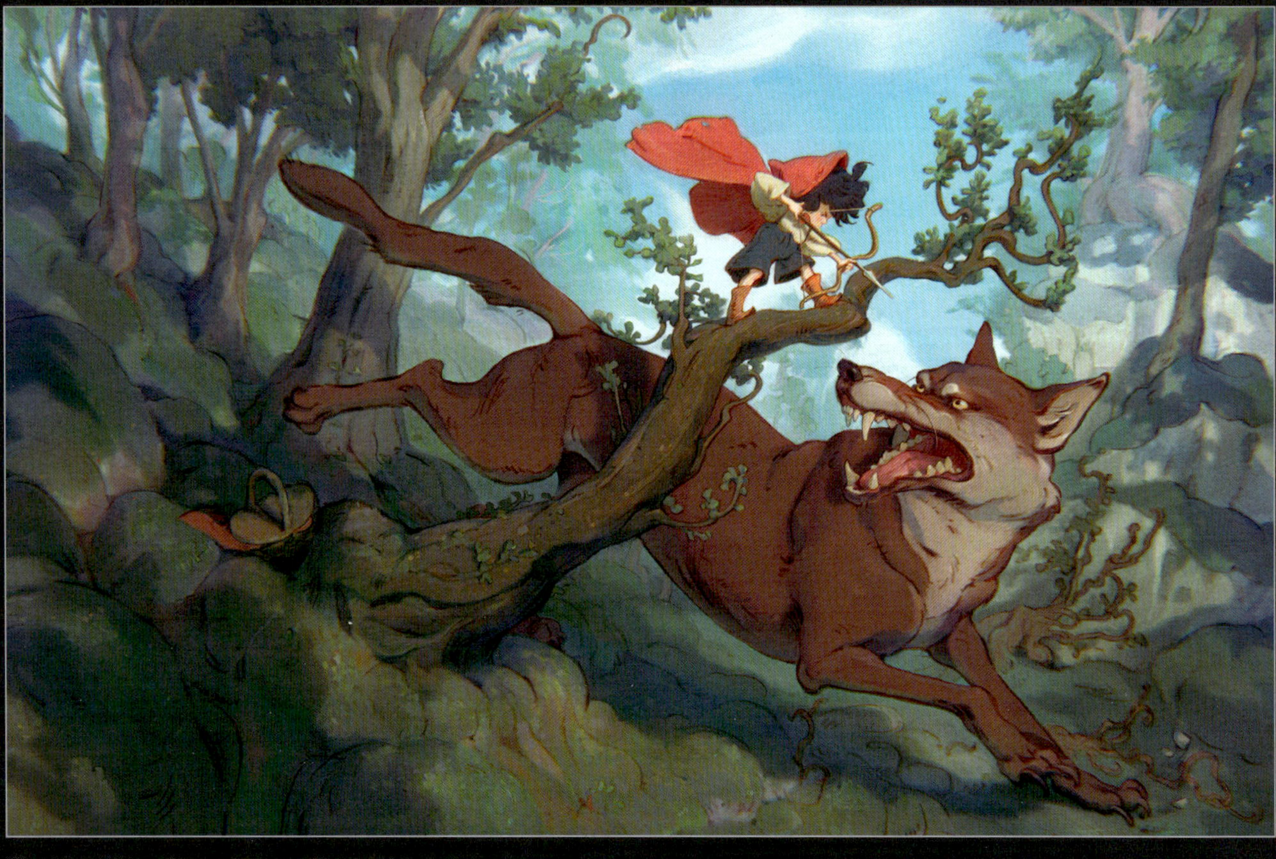

"The Little Wolf Hunter." Image © Fatemeh "Blue Birdy" Haghnejad

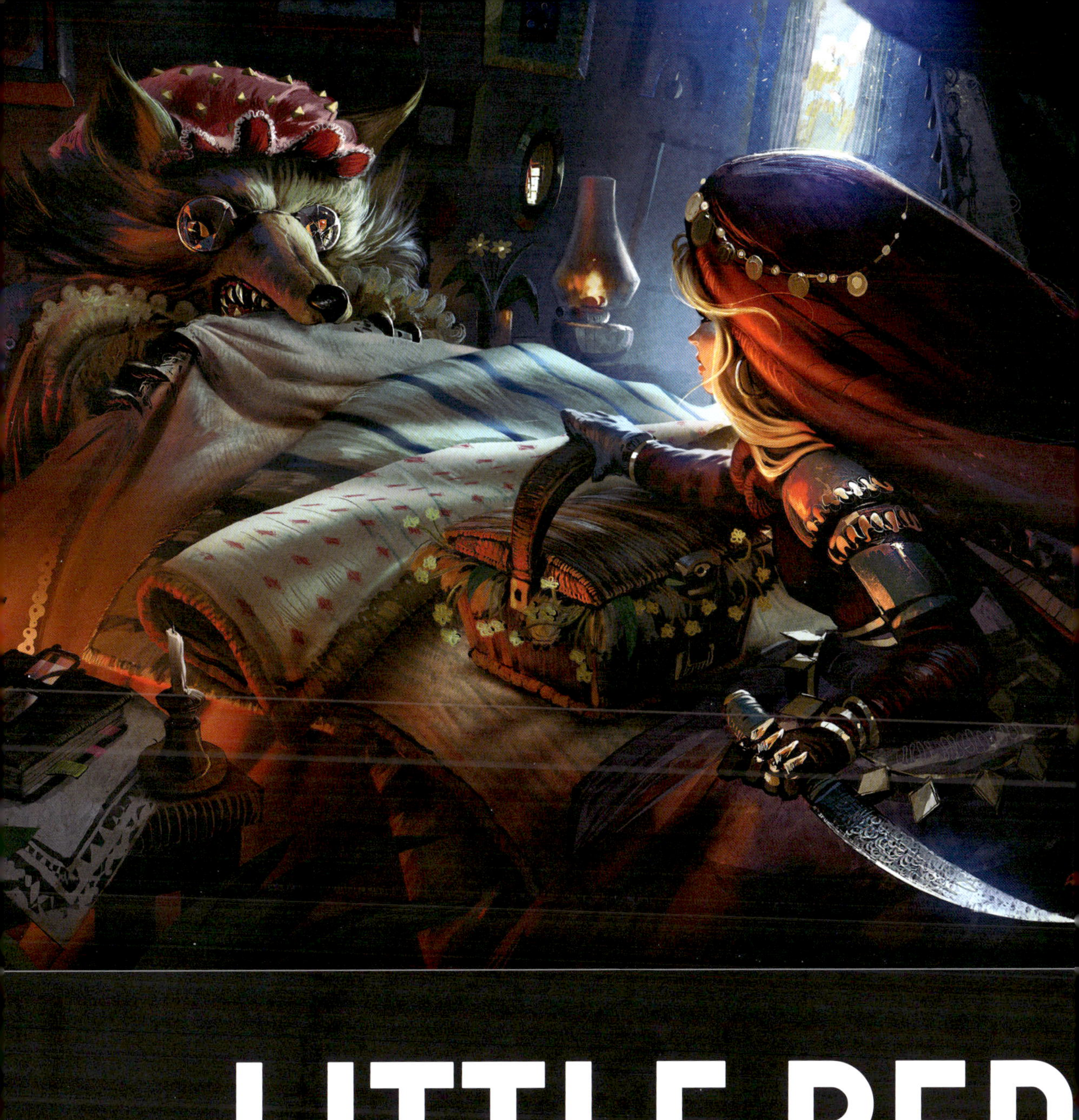

LITTLE RED RIDING HOOD

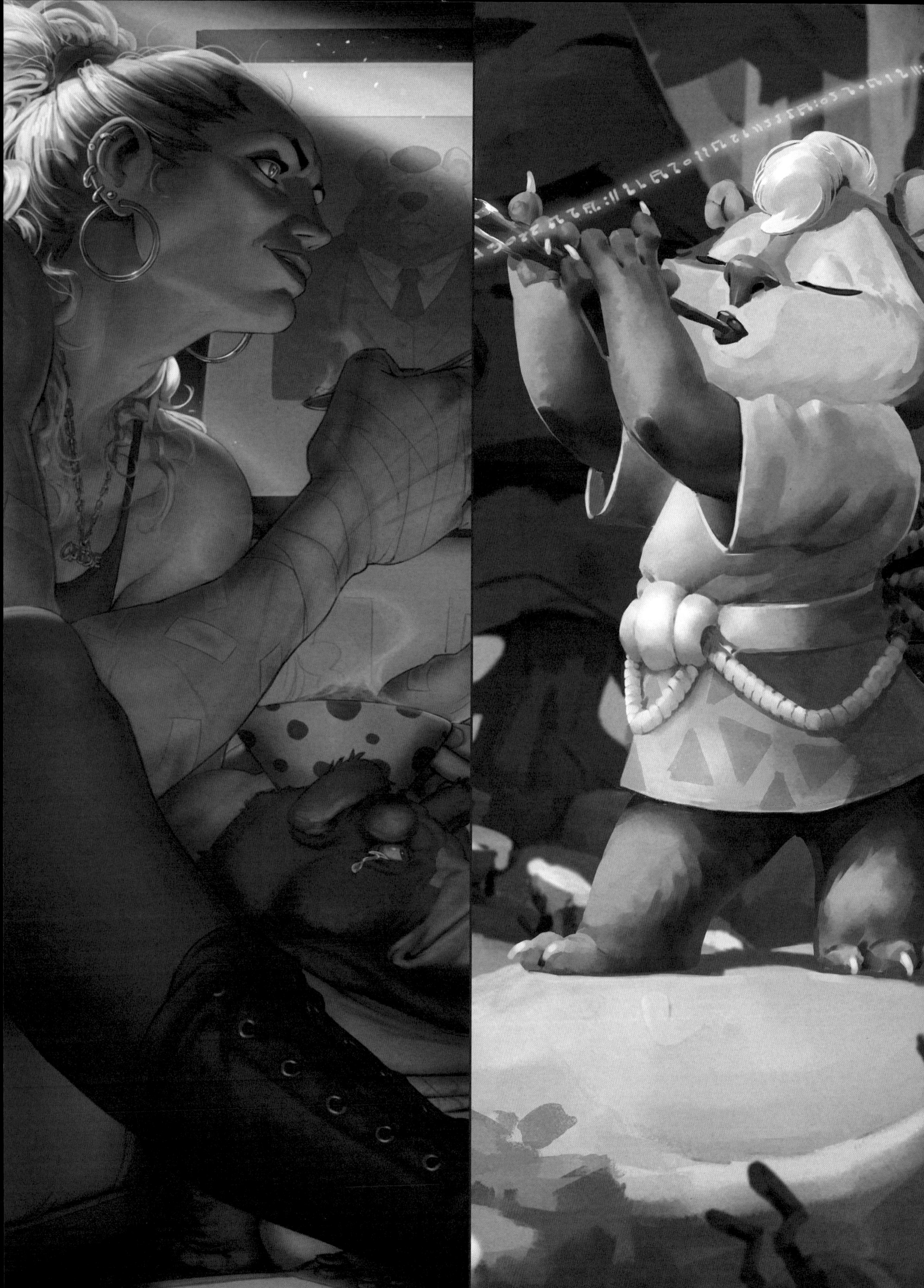

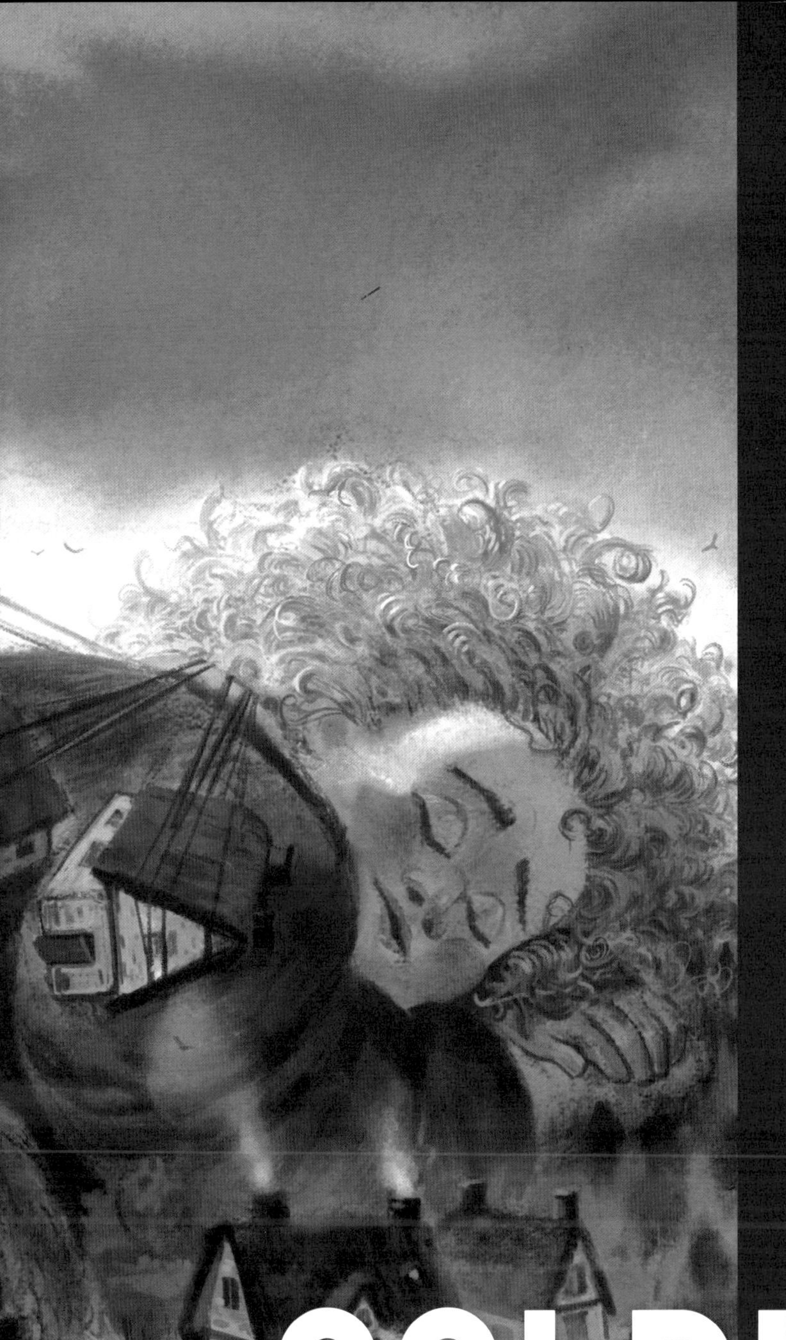

GOLDILOCKS AND THE THREE BEARS

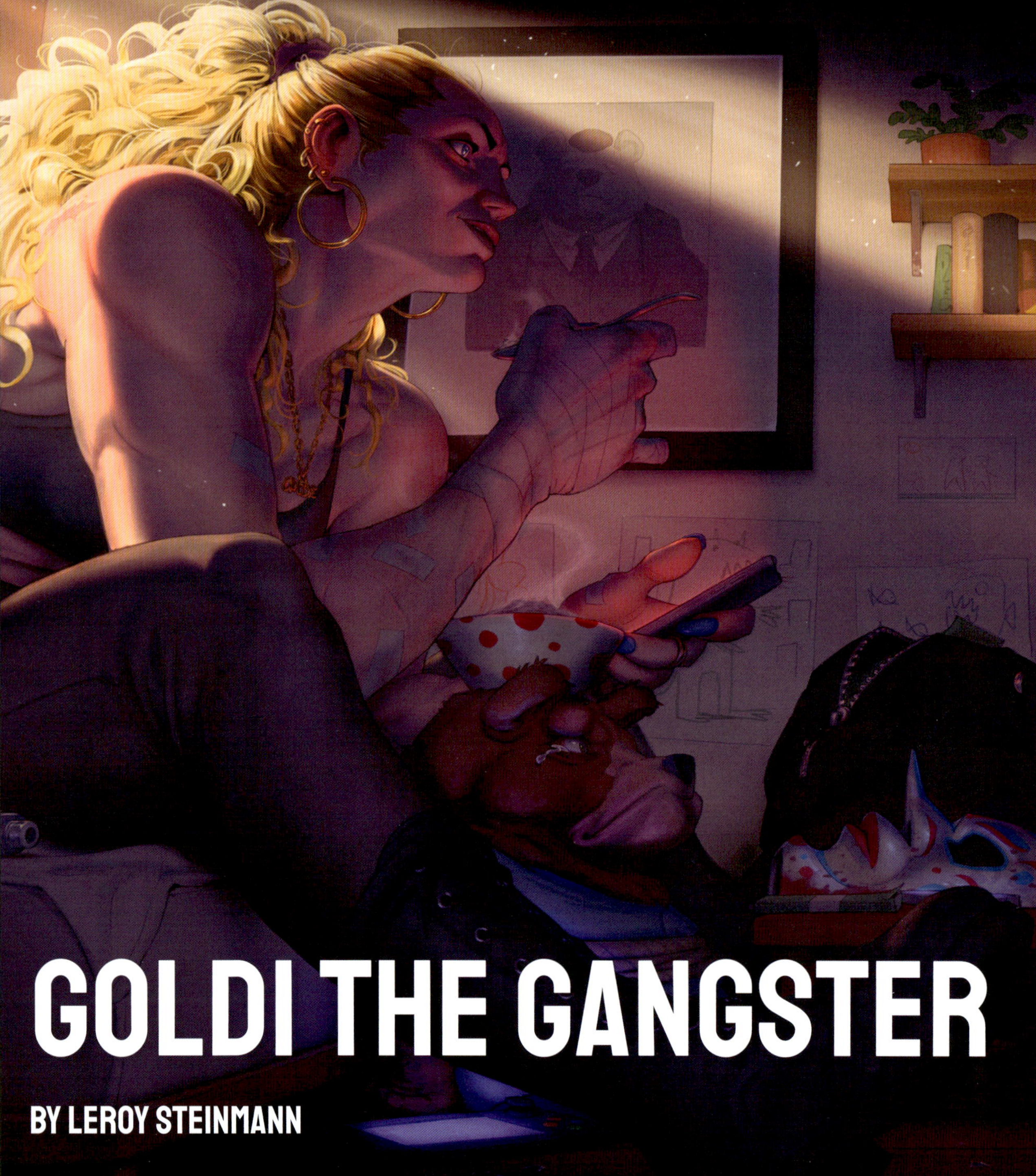

GOLDI THE GANGSTER

BY LEROY STEINMANN

I think the original *Goldilocks and the Three Bears* is a preachy, strictly educational story, which is not very fun. The "bad guy," so to speak, is a little girl who wrongly steals, uses the property, and disrespects the privacy of a family of large predators. She eats their food, breaks their furniture, sleeps in their beds, and then runs away when she is finally discovered. Those bears could tear a child to shreds! I want to find a better way to play on the idea of Goldilocks entering the bears' home, using their things, and disappearing again. In what story would it make sense for someone to break in, use the family's belongings, rest, and then leave? To me, that sounds like Goldilocks is a gangster on the run...

01 THINKING TIME

Before you start with anything drawing-related, take time to think. Just sit there, grab a coffee, think, write notes, ask yourself questions, and figure the project out. Considering that you will probably work on a project or illustration for many hours, it is definitely worth spending some time up-front to think it through. Do not draw during this phase.

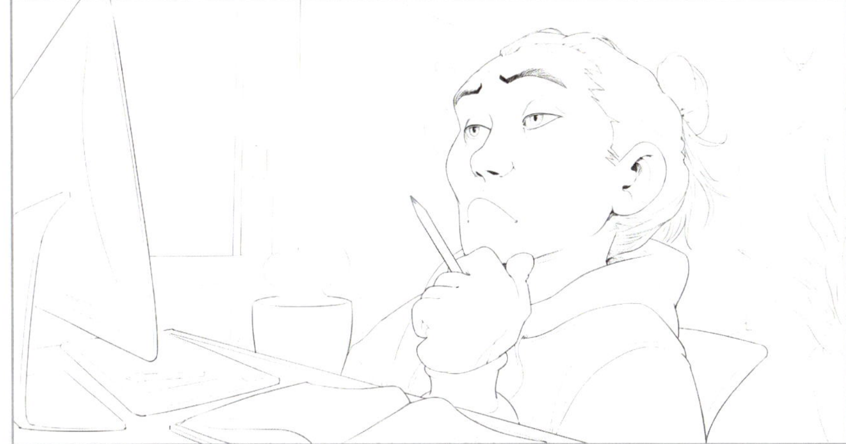

▶ Take time to think before drawing anything

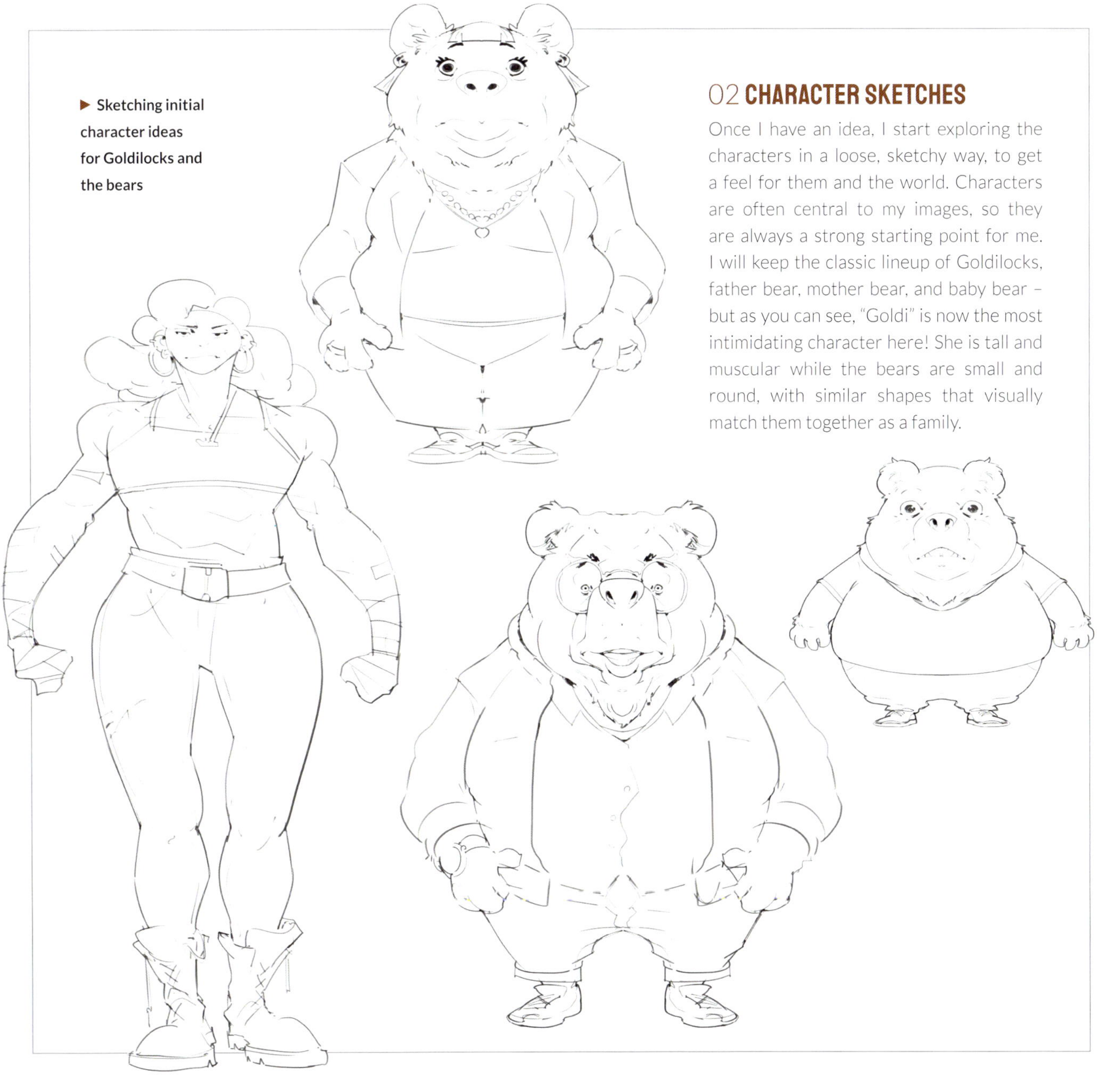

▶ Sketching initial character ideas for Goldilocks and the bears

02 CHARACTER SKETCHES

Once I have an idea, I start exploring the characters in a loose, sketchy way, to get a feel for them and the world. Characters are often central to my images, so they are always a strong starting point for me. I will keep the classic lineup of Goldilocks, father bear, mother bear, and baby bear – but as you can see, "Goldi" is now the most intimidating character here! She is tall and muscular while the bears are small and round, with similar shapes that visually match them together as a family.

03 COMPOSITIONS, ROUND ONE

With some character designs now in mind, I also start sketching composition ideas. I want to depict a scene where the bears come home and are surprised to find Goldi sitting with a bowl of porridge. I play with different angles, what those angles allow me to show, and the dynamics and moods they create. I also look at each shot in a simple, graphic way, just in terms of how much space is taken up by each volume; some scenes are dominated by Goldi, others are less so. This stage is just "visual thinking" to put my ideas on paper – I don't care about the quality of the drawings!

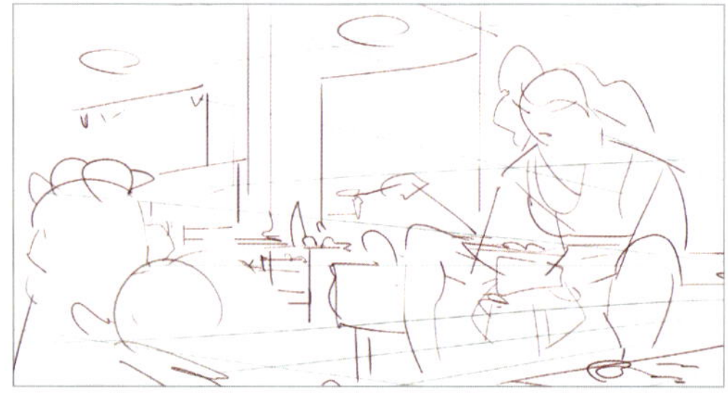

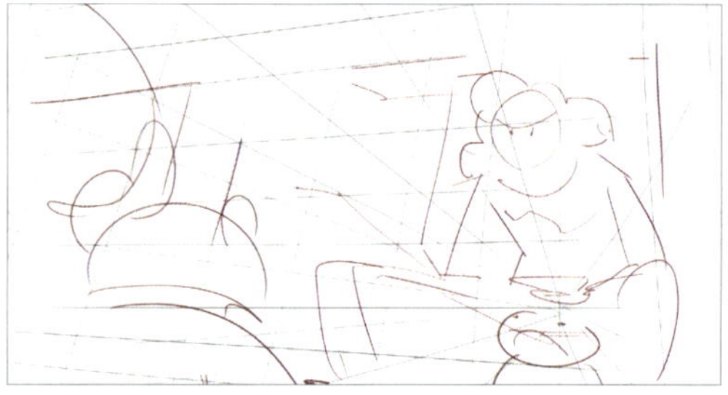

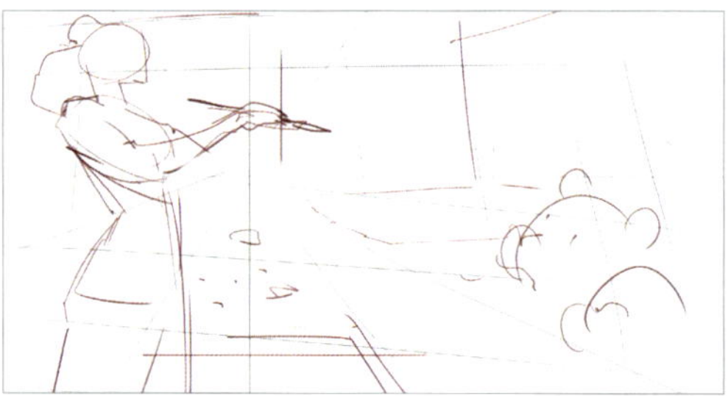

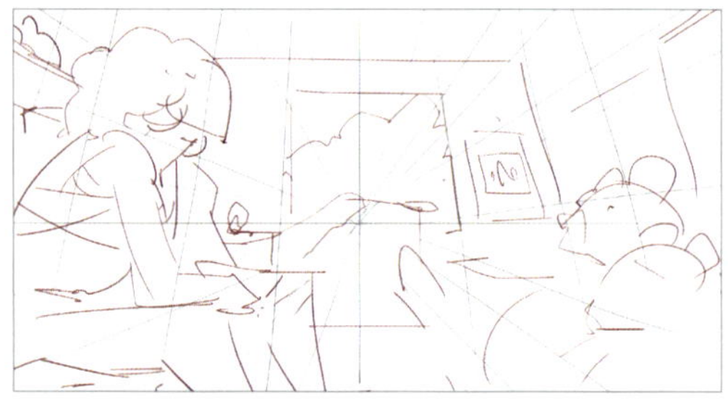

▲ Sketching some initial ideas for the composition

▼ Sketching a second round of composition ideas

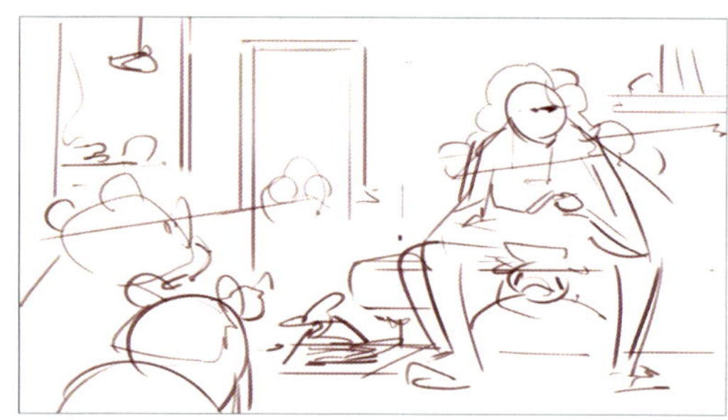

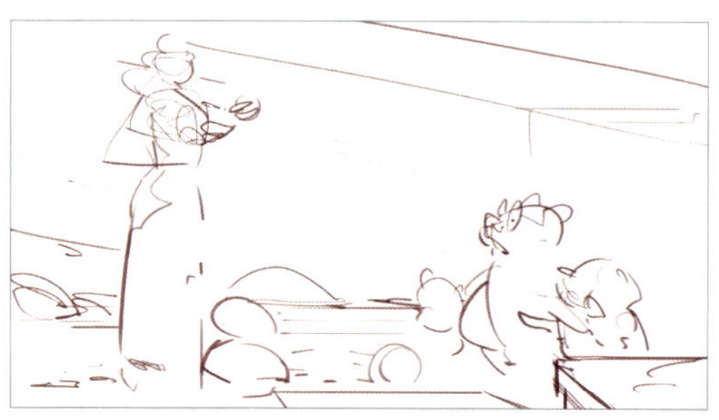

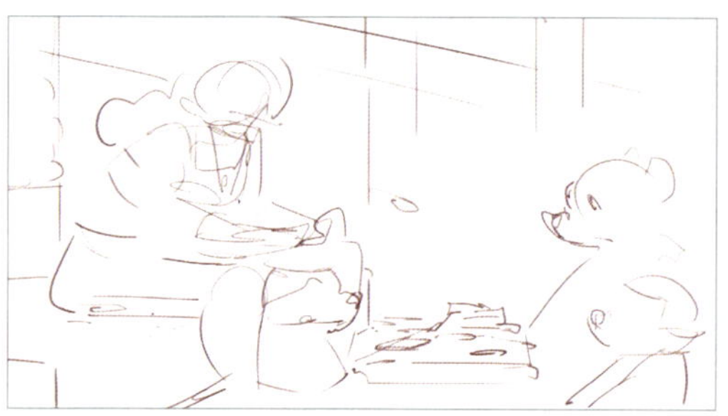

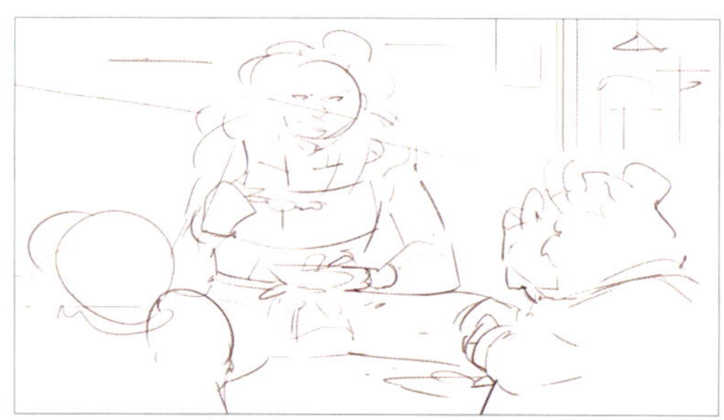

04 COMPOSITIONS, ROUND TWO

I am not happy with my first round of composition ideas, so I draw another round until I find an angle that works. The time investment per sketch is very low in this phase, so don't hesitate to make more sketches if you need to. Remember that this stage is all valuable planning and setup for later, not about making pretty pictures. I decide that a low angle helps show Goldi towering over the little bears, but I am still not sure which version to choose.

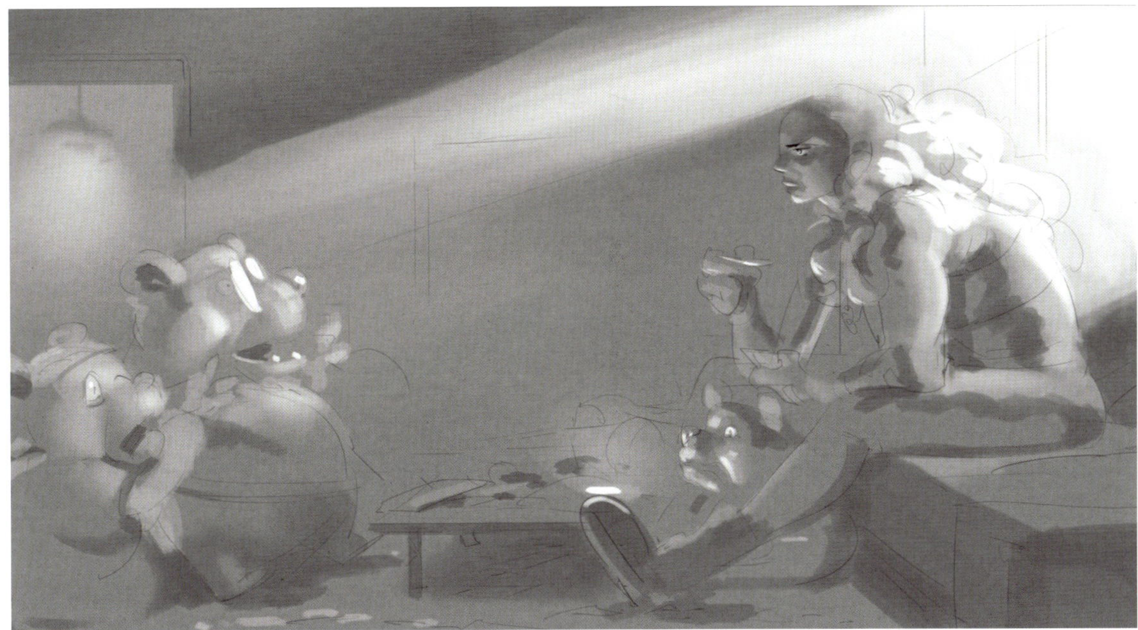

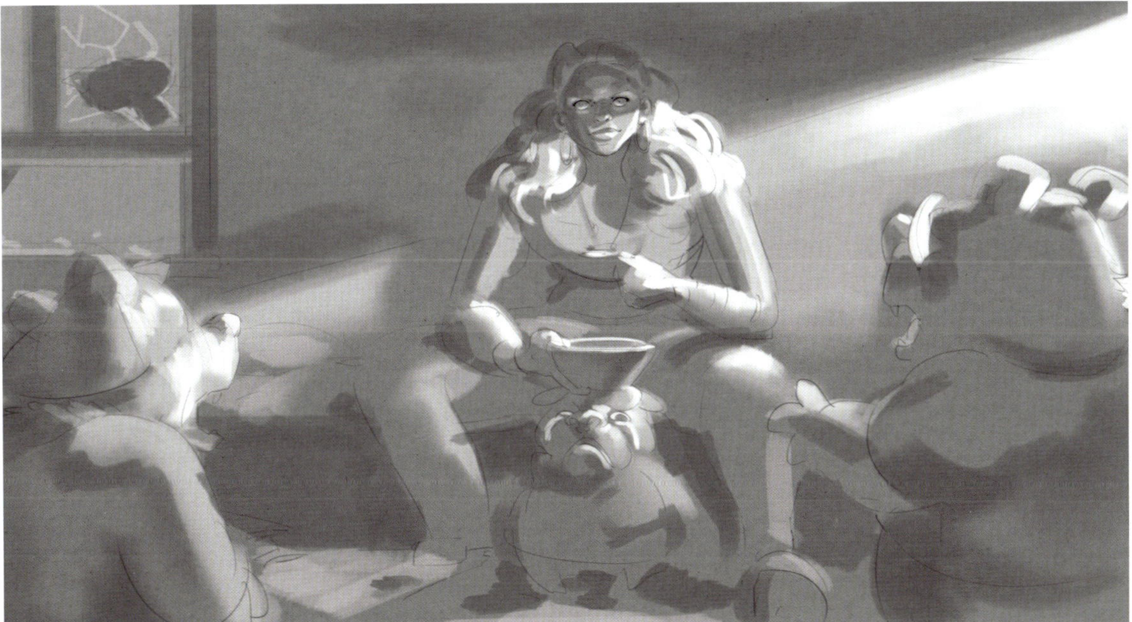

▲ Both options are strong contenders, but the side view allows for more character expression

05 CHOOSING THE BEST VIEW

I take the two thumbnails I like best a step further, to help clarify which one to pick. I also test the lighting I have in mind for both and evaluate which one I like better. The quality of the sketch is still unimportant – I am purely focused on planning and getting my ideas onto the canvas. In the first option, Goldi faces the two older bears across the room as she eats a bowl of porridge over the captive baby bear. In the second option, the older bears are in the foreground with Goldi facing the viewer. I decide that the side view is the best for storytelling, as it will clearly show the facial expressions of Goldi and all three bears.

ALWAYS PLAN AHEAD

Think and plan a lot early in the project. Answer all the questions you can ask yourself – it is time and energy that's well invested and will not be wasted. Noodling around later is much more frustrating, so stop and pause for thought and don't jump straight into drawing.

06 STOP AND STUDY

With my plan for the image basically decided, I feel good about how I am going to proceed. Now it's time for some studies. If you have anything that you feel you do not know how to draw, or that you think will be of special importance in an image, study it first. Don't just copy and don't worry about making a pretty picture. Instead, focus on learning what you need about certain aspects of your coming image. These studies are not to impress anybody, but to help you perform later. The time you put in here will absolutely be saved in the later steps, where it is easy to get lost without the knowledge you need. Studies build confidence.

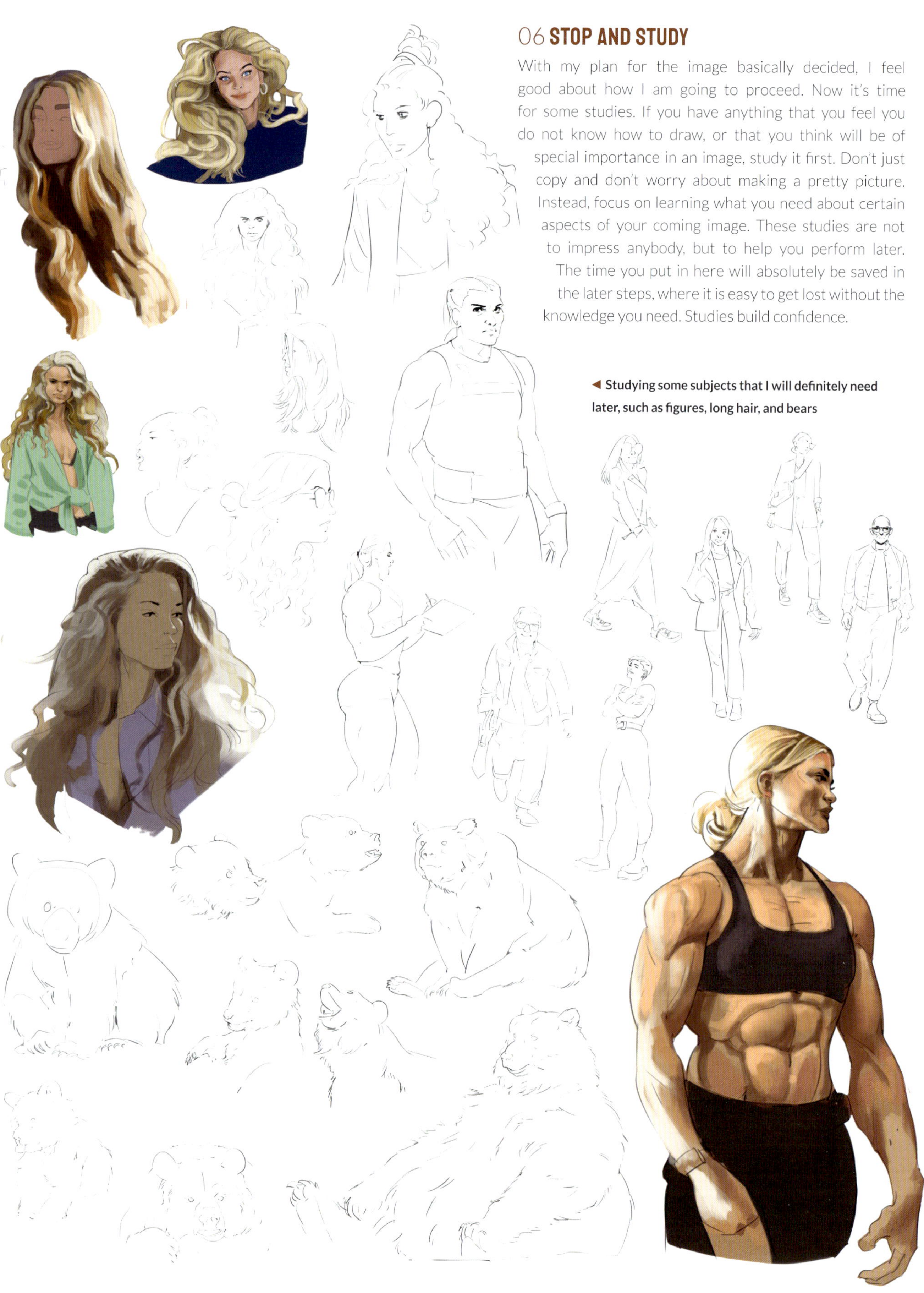

◀ **Studying some subjects that I will definitely need later, such as figures, long hair, and bears**

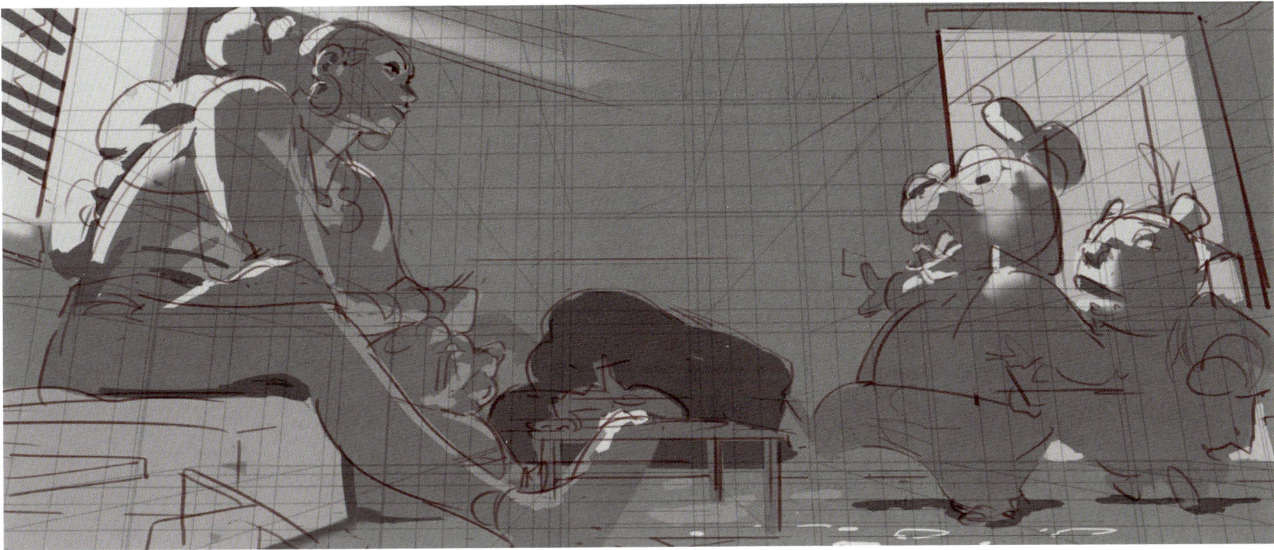

▲ Building up the rough sketch into something more workable

07 DEVELOPING THE SKETCH

Now it's time to push my composition sketch into something more legible and useful. I try to feel out the shot, what elements I can play with, and get a rough feel for the overall value setup. Where will the lights be? How do I want the shot to read? The scene will be a low shot that emphasizes Goldi's intimidating height over the bear family. The bears on the right will be framed by the light from the doorway, while Goldi will be dramatically lit by the light coming through the blinds behind her.

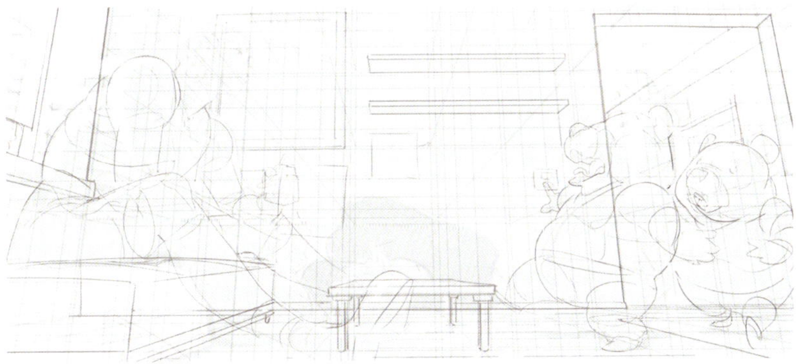

▲ Perspective guidelines help to construct a location with believable depth

08 LINE ART AND PERSPECTIVE

Now I can start building a foundation for the final line art. I use a perspective grid to draw rough volumes for everything that will be in the image: the walls, main furniture, and base forms of the characters. I introduce elements such as shelves and picture frames that will make the room – the little bear's bedroom – feel homey and lived-in. Good perspective is key for me in terms of storytelling and believability. It might seem tedious, but it pays off in terms of clarity and composition.

09 CONTINUING CONSTRUCTION

I develop the line art until everything is in perspective and I understand the volumes of the space and all the elements in it. I work from big to small, drawing the environment first; then mannequins for the characters; and then refining the faces, hands, clothing, and so on. I also lightly sketch in background details, such as books and potted plants. These little domestic touches will help heighten the feeling created by an outsider invading the bears' personal space.

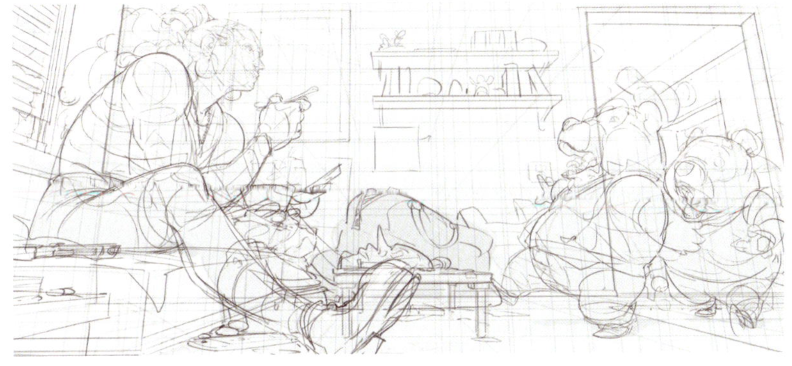

▲ Fleshing out the construction lines for the whole scene and characters

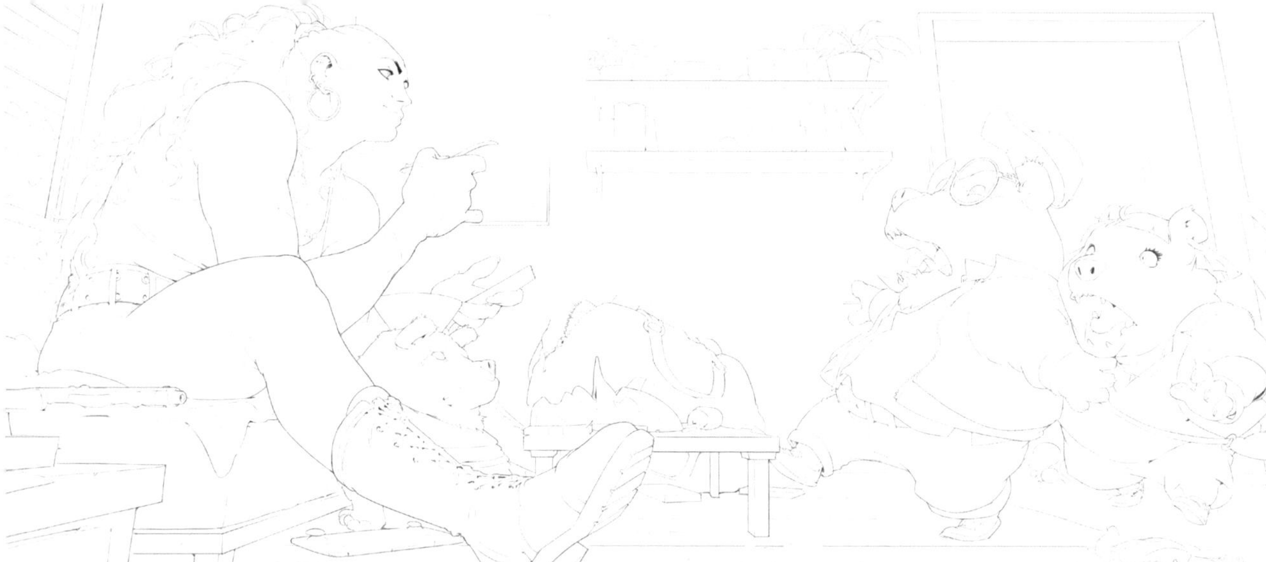

▲ The finished linework, ready for coloring and lighting

10 FINISHED LINE ART

Now it's time for the linework – an essential step for me. I am much more of a draftsman than a painter, so I rely heavily on lines and enjoy the process of drawing them. This stage gives me stability and confidence for the steps to come. I cleanly line the entire contents of the scene, including fine details and textures. The bear's room, the characters' clothes and expressions – all the objects and emotions are now fully defined. The mask and bag of cash give a strong hint as to this intruder's crime and why she's hiding out here. The hole in the window pane, bloodied knuckles and small cuts on Goldi's arm suggest how she broke in. My studies from step 06 are especially useful here, helping me tackle Goldi's long, curly hair and the bears' facial features.

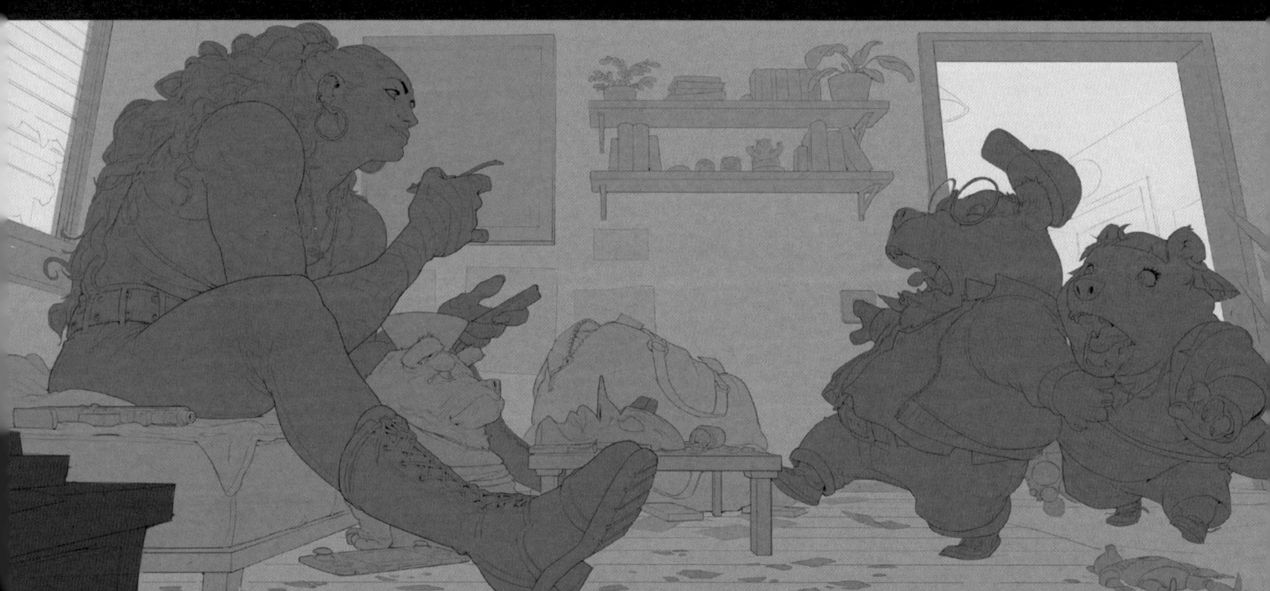

▲ Assigning a value to each subject for ease of selecting them later

11 BLOCKING OUT SUBJECTS

With the linework now fully established, I begin to block in the larger elements with simple gray values. By "larger elements," I mean I treat the objects and characters as big silhouettes – such as the two larger bears together, or all the items on the shelves together – rather than going into the fine details within those shapes. These values don't necessarily reflect the final values of the painting, but will instead be helpful for isolating and selecting subjects or areas to color later.

12 PLANNING THE COLORS

I begin to lay down the base colors of everything in the scene, unaffected by light or shadow. I keep my values on the bright or medium side, avoiding going too dark or too light, as I will need those stronger values to light the image later. This is when the characters, setting, and story start to come alive: we can see Goldi's golden hair, the bloody bandages on her knuckles, the bag of green banknotes, the colorful toys, and the patterned bowl balanced on the head of the tearful smallest bear. I also add a small chair lying in the foreground – a reference to the chair that Goldilocks breaks in the original tale, and a good way to add more disorder to the scene.

▼ Adding the base unlit colors for the whole scene

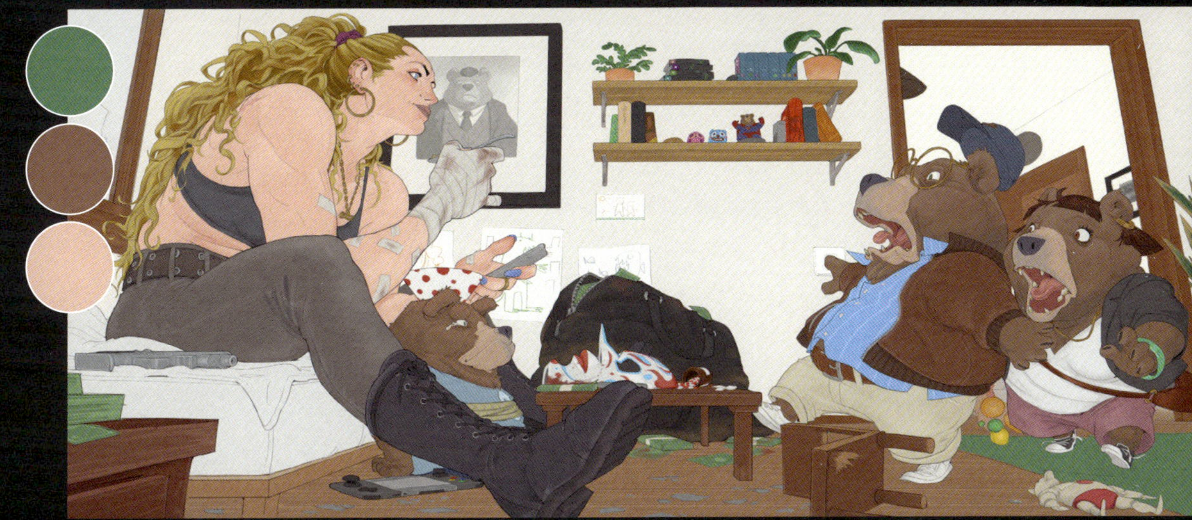

13 AMBIENT SHADOWS

I start to darken the areas of the image that would receive less light, in a fairly general ambient way, while still keeping in mind the lighting situation I planned in my sketch. For example, creases in clothing and the corners of a room will be darker in most lighting situations, as not much light can reach into them compared to a more open surface. I also darken all the surfaces slightly where the volumes turn away from the viewer, a bit like a soft light is coming from the "camera." This step adds depth and volume to the whole scene, but it isn't the "mood lighting" that will really give the image atmosphere – that will come next!

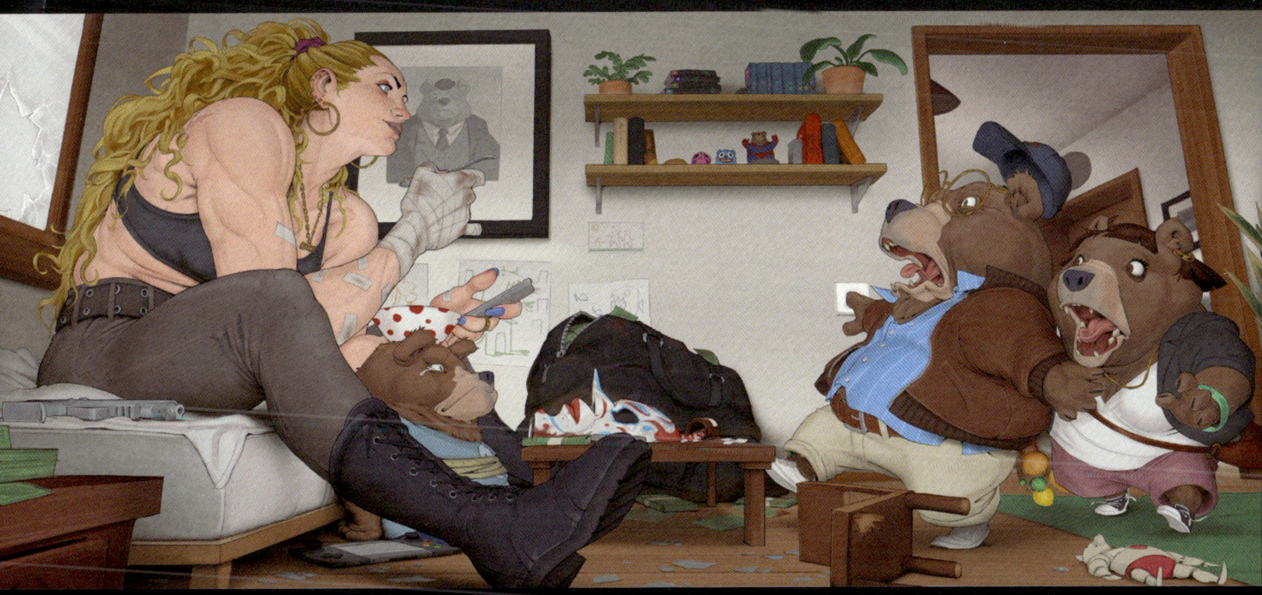

▲ Adding ambient shadows to the volumes in the scene

14 CREATING ATMOSPHERE

Now I can begin applying the main light setup, creating a darker, blue-toned duplicate of the image and erasing areas to reveal the brighter original beneath. This instantly creates a cool, mysterious, secretive atmosphere – perfectly fitting for a room with the lights switched off, dimly lit through half-closed blinds.

▼ Setting the mood by applying cool, dark shadows

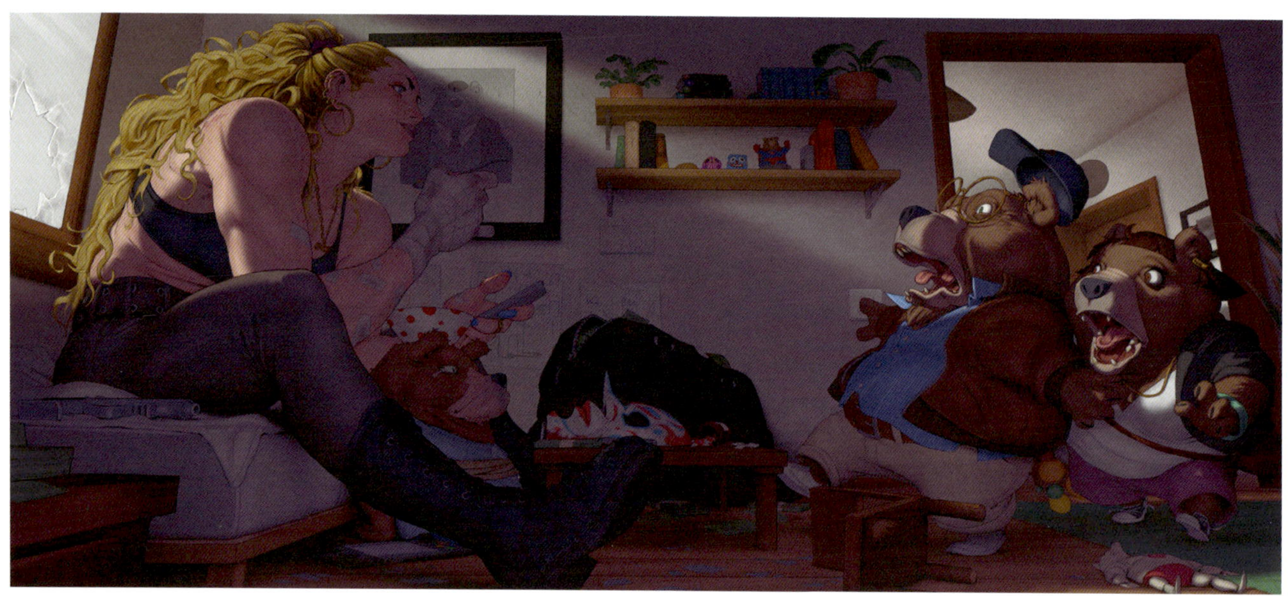

15 ENHANCING THE SHADOWS

I enhance the color and darkness of the shadows, strengthening the blue and adding a terminator shadow on the characters. This is where the shadow is strongest and most concentrated, just after the transition from main light to dark. This adds even more form and volume to the characters and objects in the scene, especially Goldi's muscled arms and the soft, rounded shapes of the bears.

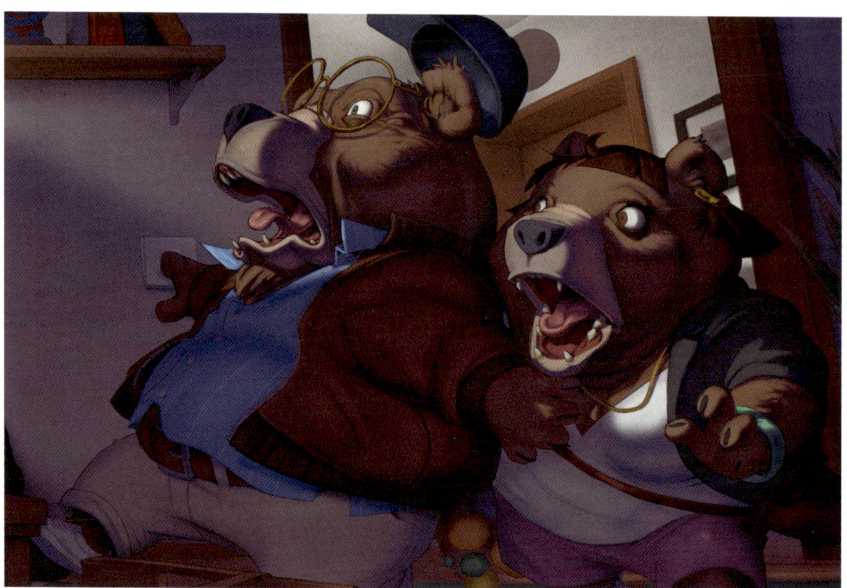

▲ Terminator shadows add another level of depth and immersion

16 TEMPERATURE CONTRASTS

I add color and brightness to the two main light sources shining from the window and back room. Their warm, welcoming hues create contrast with the cool, shadowy room where a shock awaits the returning bears. The color and intensity of the light is a major storytelling aspect of any image, creating a sense of time, place, and mood. Sometimes a slight shift toward a certain color can make all the difference, so always explore and experiment. Digital art allows us this luxury – make the most of it if you're using it!

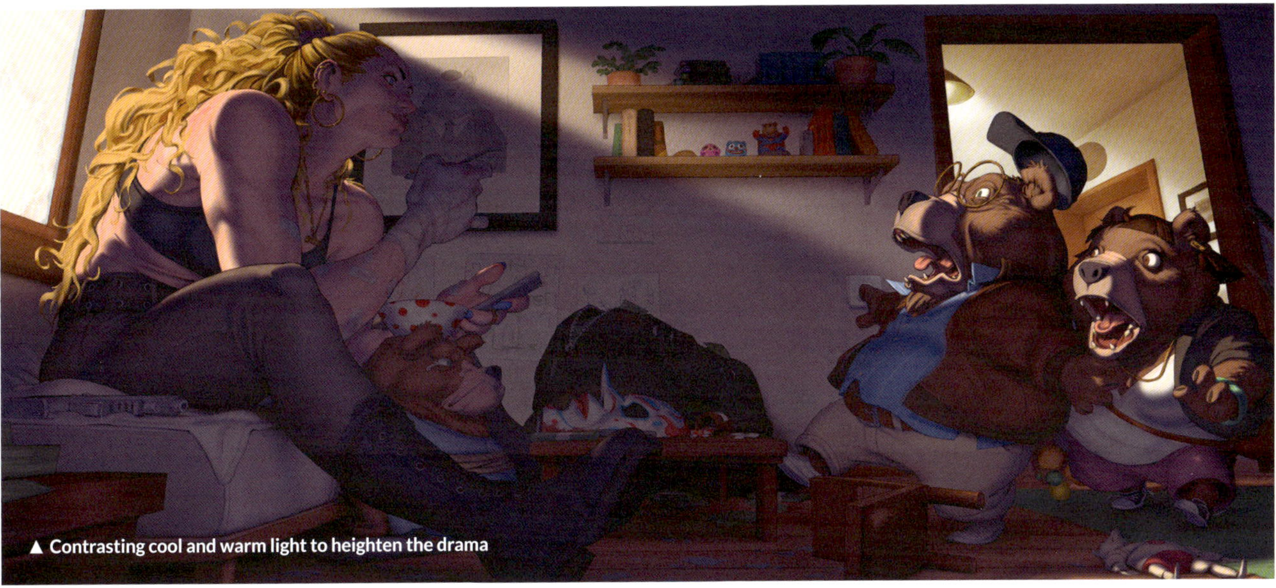

▲ Contrasting cool and warm light to heighten the drama

17 HIGHLIGHTING KEY AREAS

In the shadow areas of the image, I have certain aspects I want to "pop" for the sake of storytelling. I need to emphasize Goldi, the little bear, and the objects on the table – elements that tell us who this intruder is and what she's doing here. I do this by adding smaller light sources or enhancing existing ones, working through them one at a time: the ominous red uplighting from Goldi's phone, the little bear's games console on the floor, and the warmer lights from the window and back room.

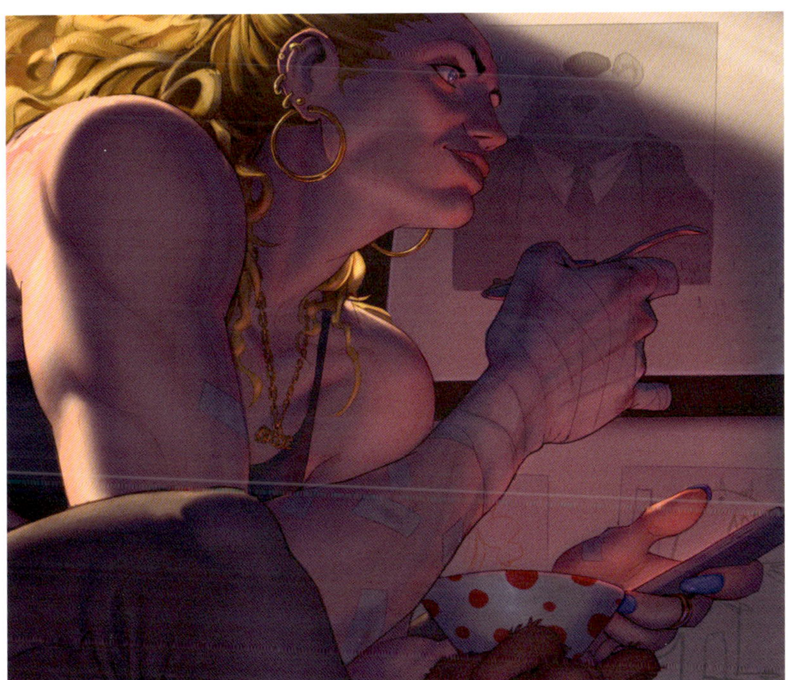

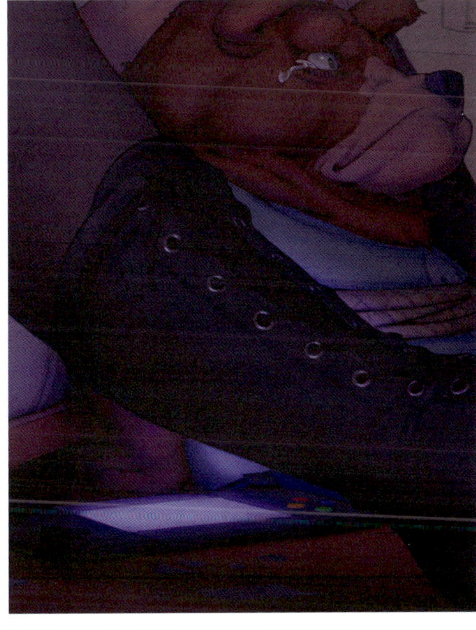

▲ Using smaller light sources and highlights to emphasize important details

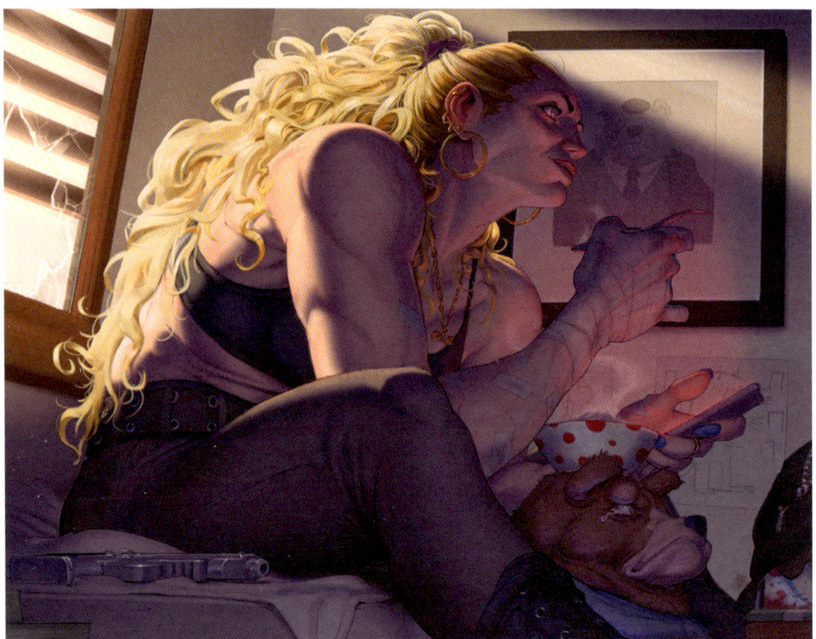

18 PAINTING FINE DETAILS

Nearing the very end of the process, I finally render some painterly elements of the image, painting over the colors and lighting I have added so far. It is not necessary to render everything in detail; I choose to work only on the areas that are important for the story, so the viewer's eye will be led there. For example, the biggest change is Goldi's curly blonde hair, glowing with light from the window, where I add wooden blinds to emphasize the closed-in feeling of the room. A wisp of steam coming from the cereal bowl gives the viewer a clue as to its hot oatmeal contents.

◀ Applying the finishing touches with a more painterly technique

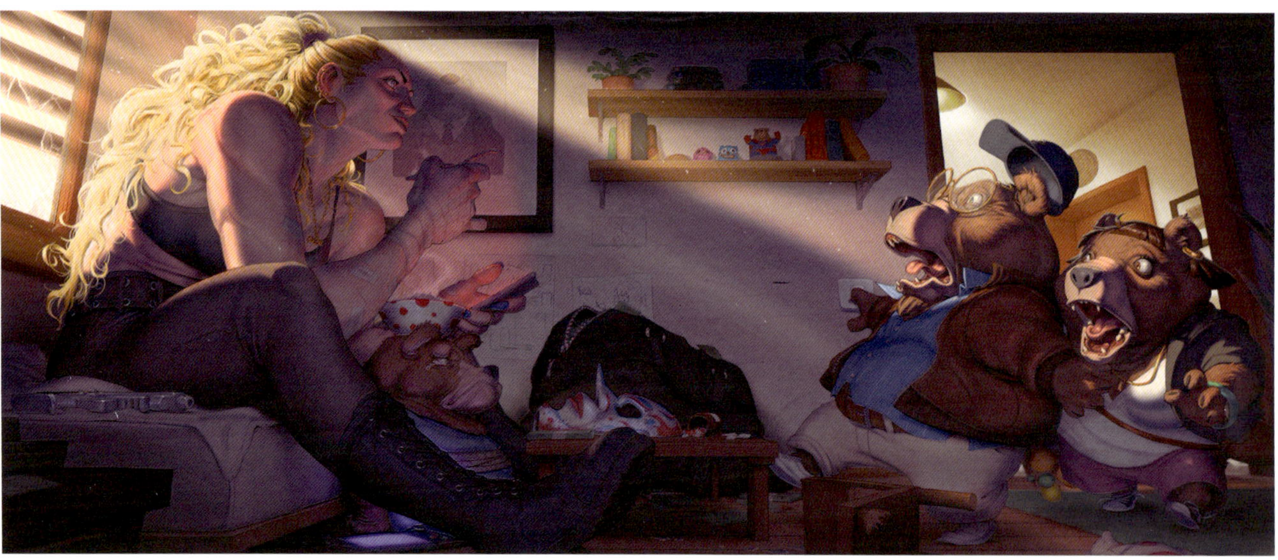

19 SPECIAL EFFECTS

I continue enhancing the light effects, adding details such as dust particles, shiny highlights, and atmospheric glows emanating from light sources. These touches seem minor but can add so much immersion for the viewer. I add a few more details to the characters, such as shiny lenses to the father bear's glasses, surprised spittle flying from his lips, and loose little strands of Goldi's hair. I save these additions until very late in the process – they often overlap many elements of the illustration, so would get in the way if I added them earlier.

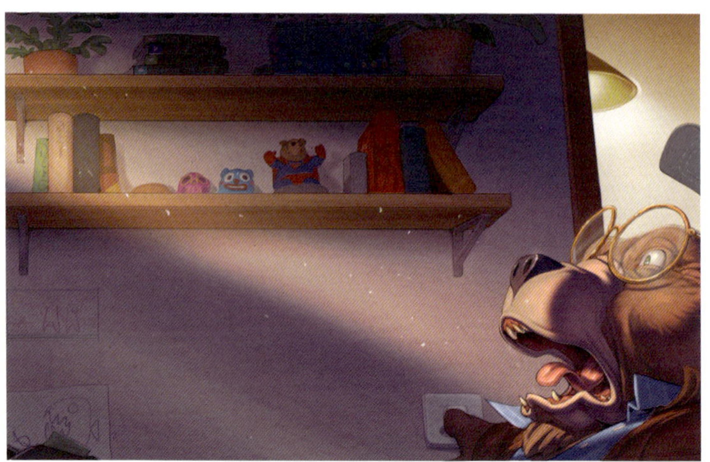

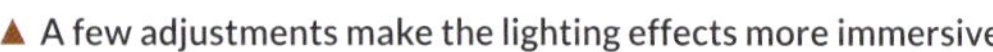

▲ A few adjustments make the lighting effects more immersive

20 THE FINAL IMAGE

I finish off the illustration by using some of Adobe Photoshop's adjustment layers, such as Curves, Hue/Saturation, and gradient maps, as if I am in a photo studio or post-production for a movie. Using these tools at a low intensity enables me to make subtle adjustments with precision. In this case, I use them to boost the overall contrast and richness of the orange and purple hues, emphasizing the scene's mood and cinematic look. The changes from the previous step are not vast, but they help to definitively wrap up the image.

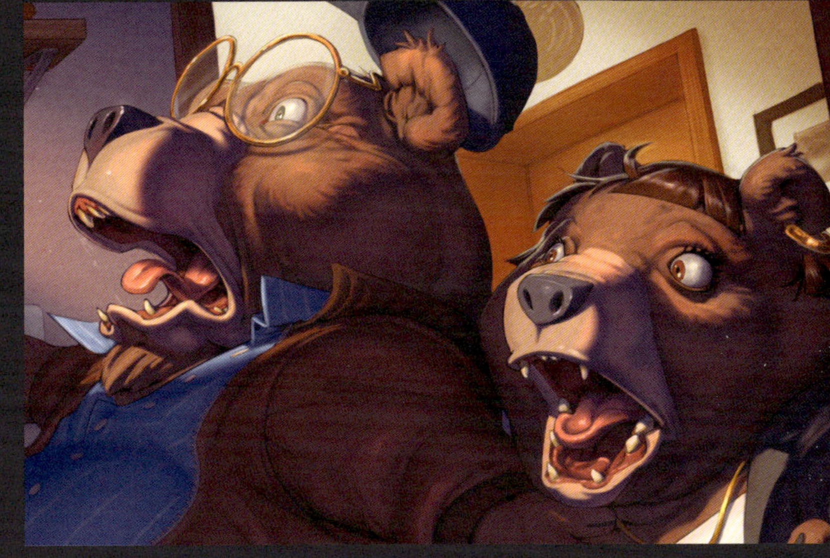

▶ Amplifying the contrast and lighting for the final version

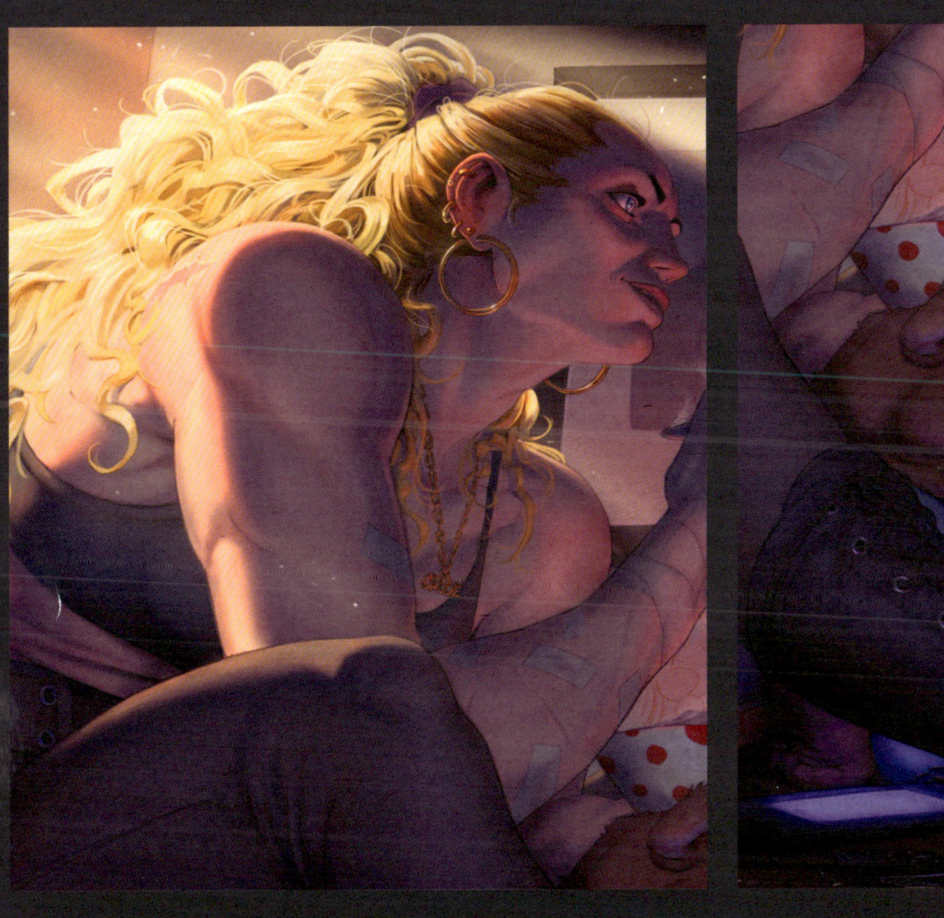

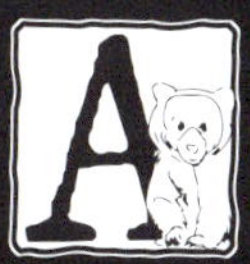

And that's a wrap! My finished illustration shows a modern take on Goldilocks – a gangster on the run, taking a quick break at a bear family's apartment. The bear parents experience quite a shock coming home to find their son held hostage. I kept the used bed, porridge, and broken chair from the original story, ensuring the tale is instantly recognizable despite the change in character dynamics. This criminal Goldi, like the original character, is still a rude intruder – but this time, she's fully aware of it and simply doesn't care! My choices of camera angle, color palette, immersive lighting, and environmental storytelling all help create the feeling of a cozy domestic setting under threat.

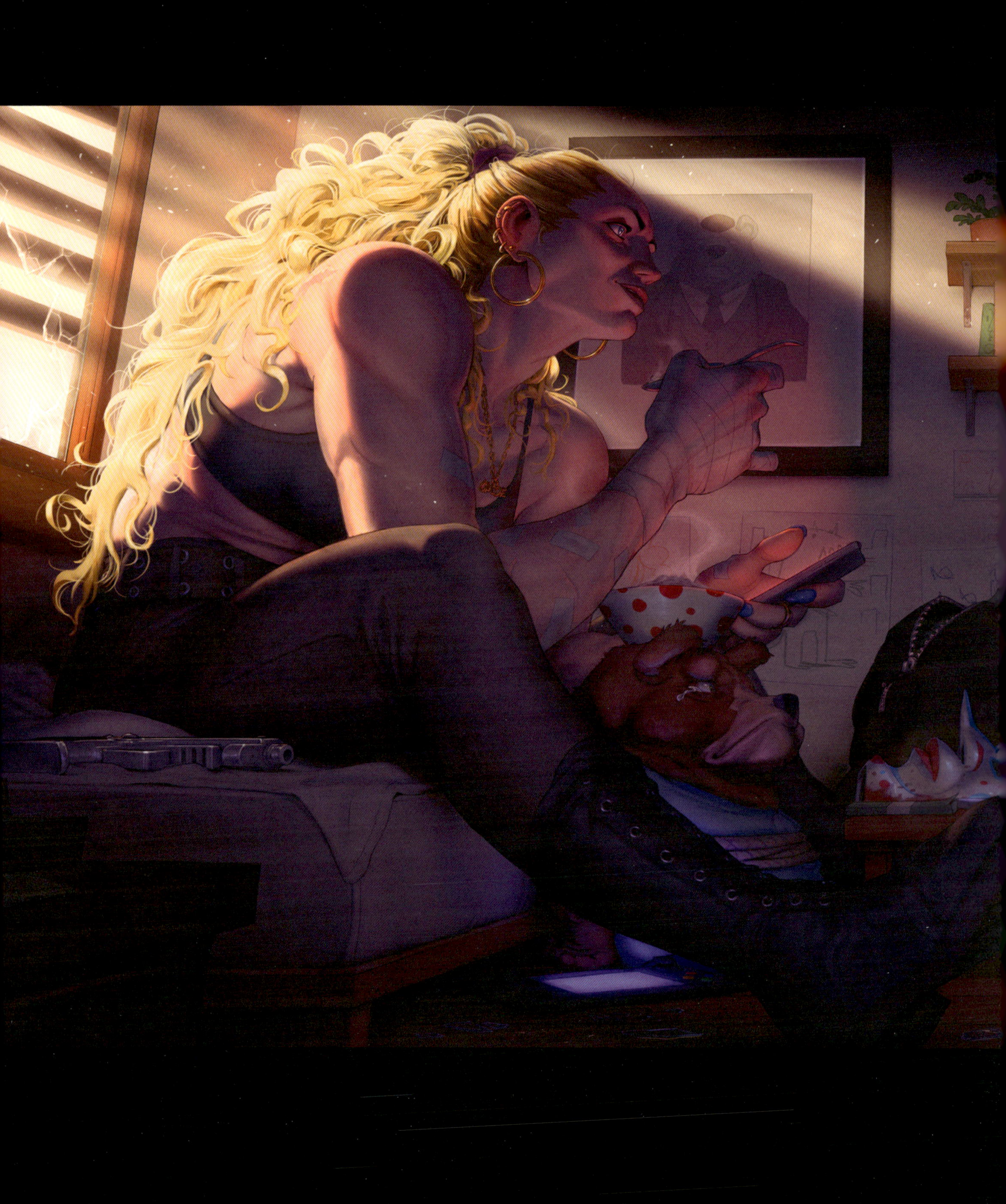

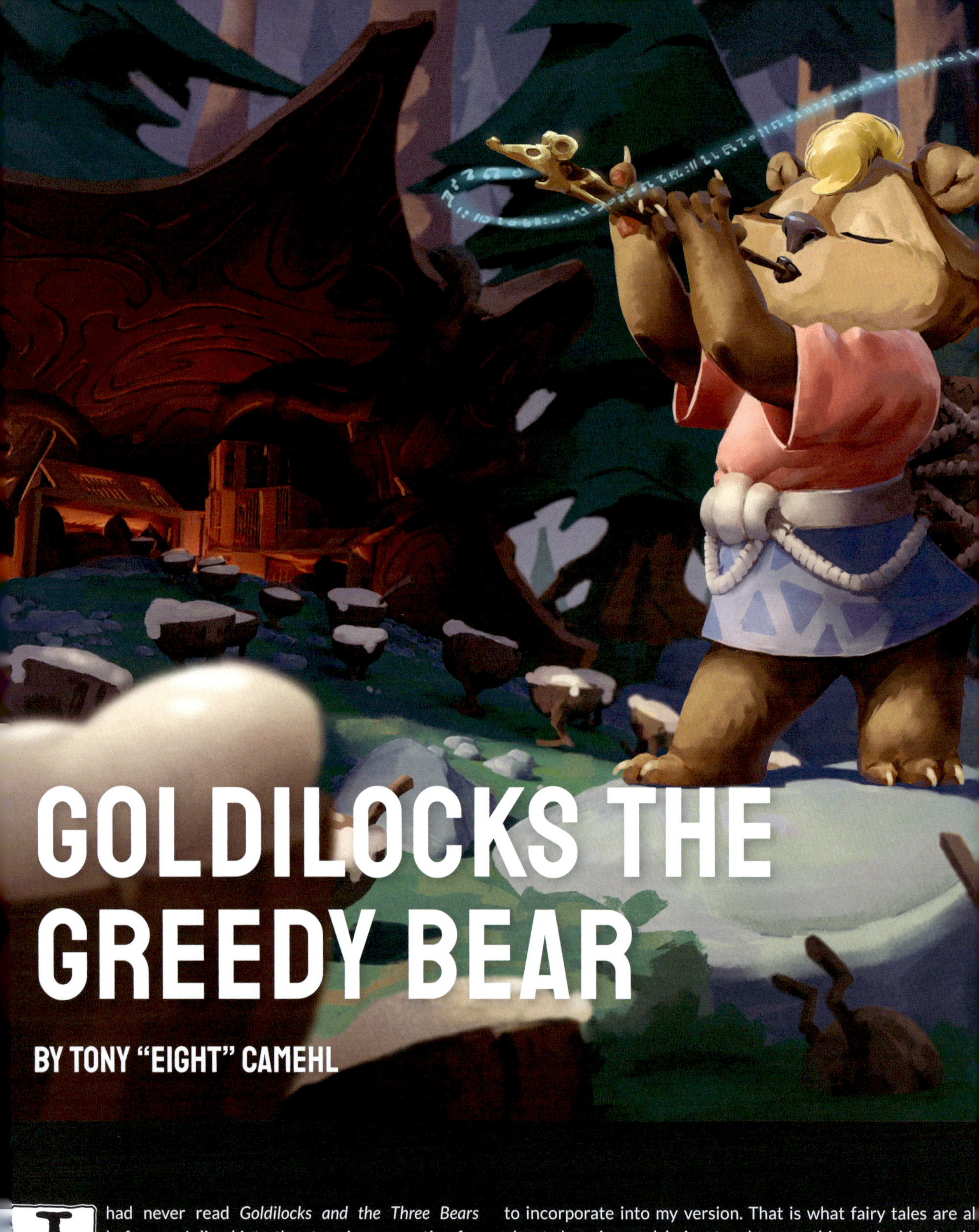

GOLDILOCKS THE GREEDY BEAR

BY TONY "EIGHT" CAMEHL

I had never read *Goldilocks and the Three Bears* before, so I dived into the story in preparation for this project. Strangely enough, I felt this particular tale felt very familiar and up-to-date with modern times. The thing I like most about fairy tales is the lessons they

to incorporate into my version. That is what fairy tales are al about: learning and being taught something valuable. In the case of this story, I feel Goldilocks' behavior was very greedy selfish, and narcissistic. These are the characteristics I want to bring into focus and illustrate in my scene, in a manner that i

GOLDILOCKS — SPOILED / SELFISH / GREEDY

▲ Starting the process by asking questions about the story

01 ASK QUESTIONS

I start by analyzing the source material – sitting down and thinking about what I have read. Before attempting to adapt a fairy tale, we first need to ask ourselves: *how* does the story make us feel? *What* is the moral of the story? And *what* are the key elements that help us connect to the story? The story makes me feel anger at Goldilocks' disrespectful behavior toward the bears. The moral of the tale is not to be greedy and selfish. The key elements would be the characters, props, and location that are familiar to us from the original. Ask as many questions as possible until you are satisfied with your understanding of the source material.

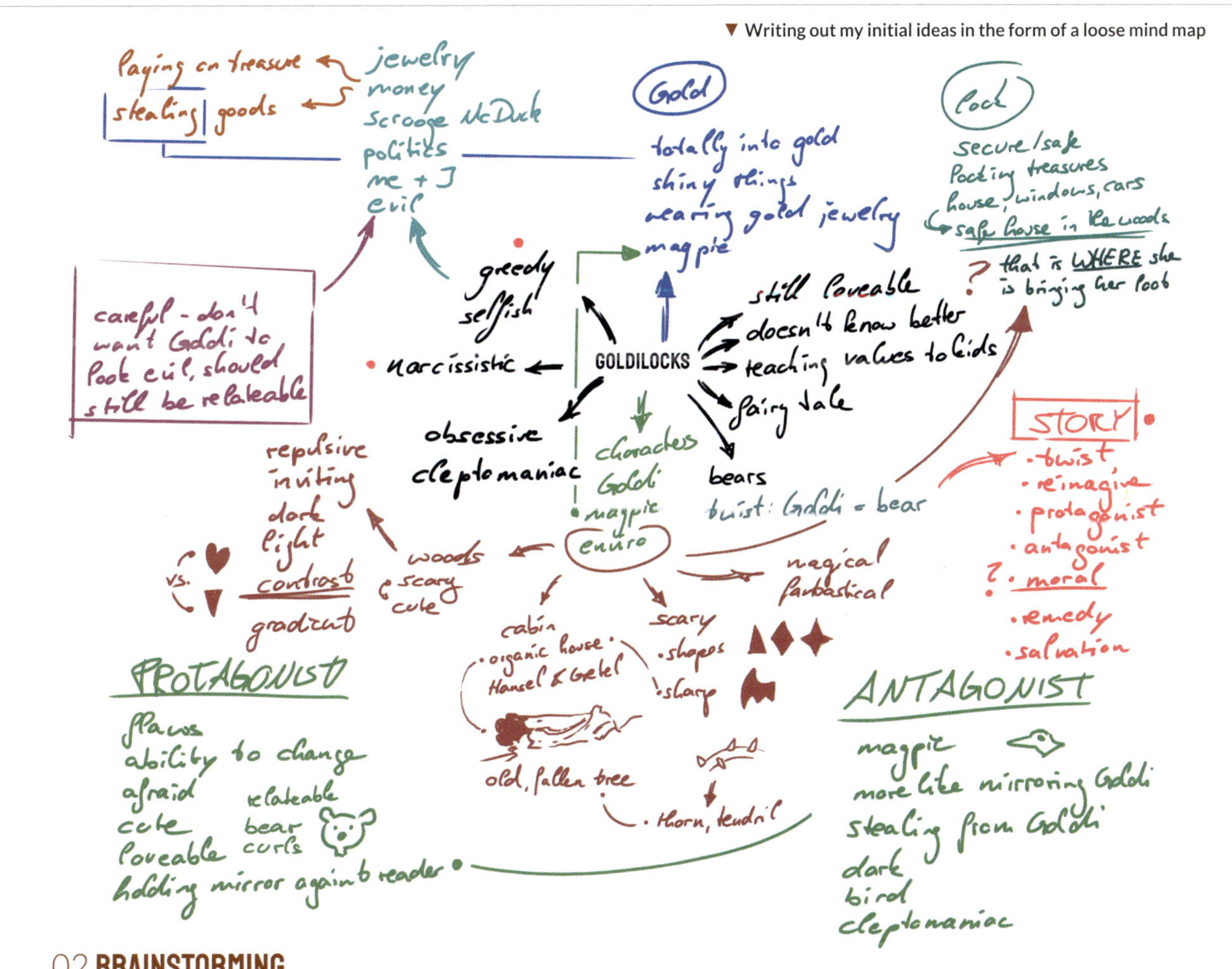

▼ Writing out my initial ideas in the form of a loose mind map

02 BRAINSTORMING

After answering my most pressing questions (you can ask more if you wish), I write down all my ideas in a brainstorming session. I let my mind wander as I scribble keywords on the page – they don't have to make sense yet. Think of this as reference-gathering, except for your narrative – gathering words that will become your road map later on.

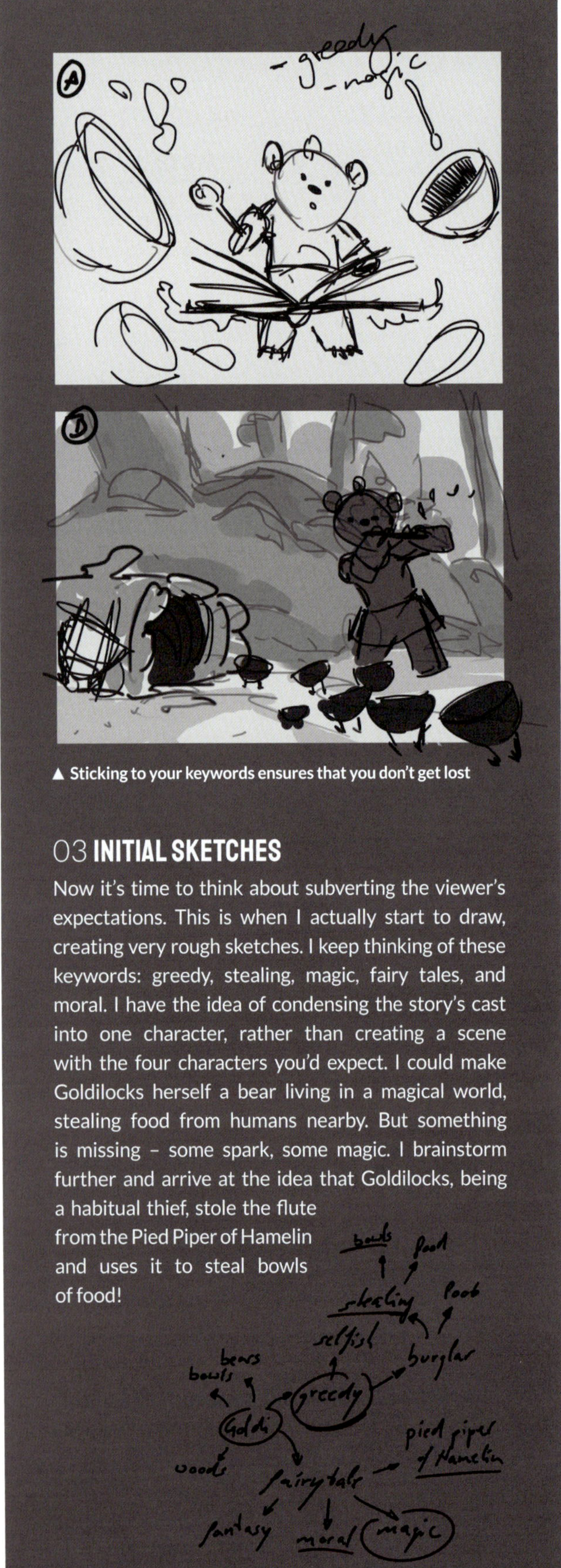

▲ Sticking to your keywords ensures that you don't get lost

03 INITIAL SKETCHES

Now it's time to think about subverting the viewer's expectations. This is when I actually start to draw, creating very rough sketches. I keep thinking of these keywords: greedy, stealing, magic, fairy tales, and moral. I have the idea of condensing the story's cast into one character, rather than creating a scene with the four characters you'd expect. I could make Goldilocks herself a bear living in a magical world, stealing food from humans nearby. But something is missing – some spark, some magic. I brainstorm further and arrive at the idea that Goldilocks, being a habitual thief, stole the flute from the Pied Piper of Hamelin and uses it to steal bowls of food!

04 THREE-POINT STORYTELLING

I want to talk about three-point storytelling, which is something I intend to build into my scene. Three-point storytelling is the idea of having three elements that interact with each other to visually tell a story. For example, in this sketch, we have Goldilocks, the Pied Piper's flute, and the bowls of porridge she is stealing. All three elements interact with each other by guiding the viewer around the drawing, creating a much more powerful way of telling the story. Whatever final composition I choose, I will keep a three-point structure in mind and use it to strengthen my illustration.

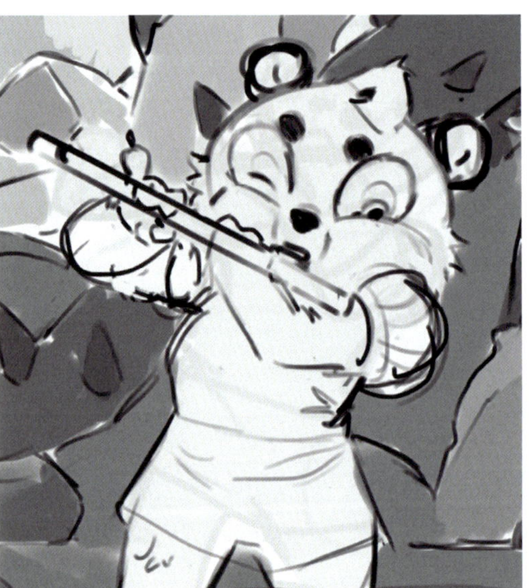

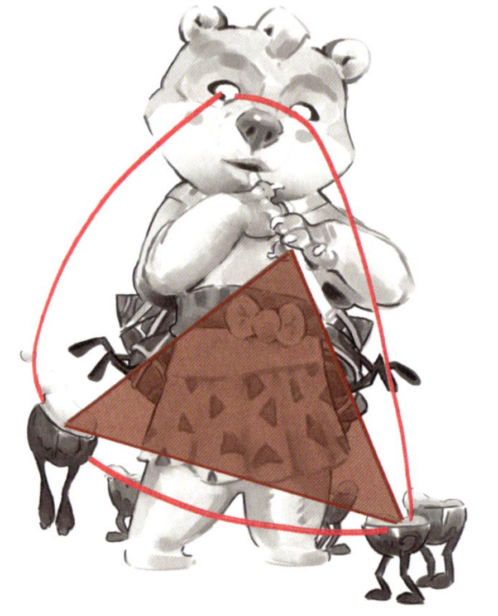

▲ Using three elements to communicate a story to the viewer

05 THE STORY'S MORAL

Illustration helps us tell a story visually, but keep in mind that the story must always come first. I keep coming back to the original tale's moral to see how my ideas are holding up. In both the original story and my version, Goldilocks is greedy and spoiled, stealing food from other people. I personally want to portray Goldilocks as a character who is only doing bad things because she does not know any better – she is selfish but not terrible, and can still change her ways. The tone and style of the illustration should be quite playful and not too dark. I will keep this in mind later on, once I start designing the character. For now, I use a mix of painting and very simple 3D to visualize my ideas of a greedy bear. This particular idea isn't working at all!

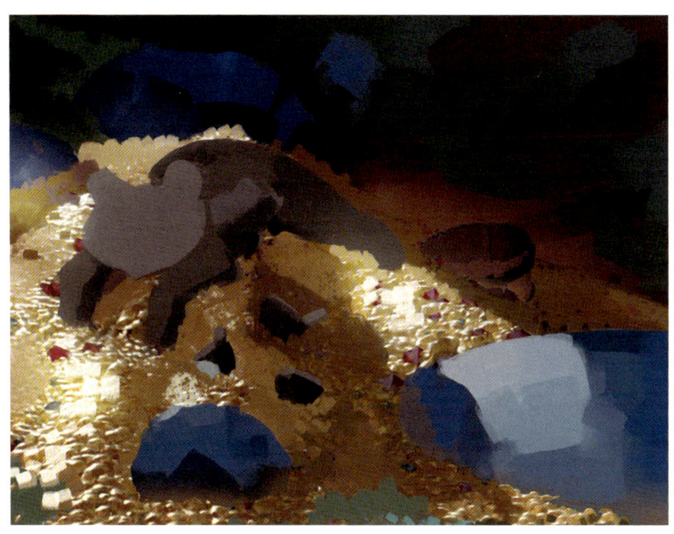

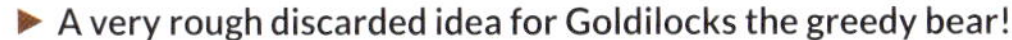

▶ A very rough discarded idea for Goldilocks the greedy bear!

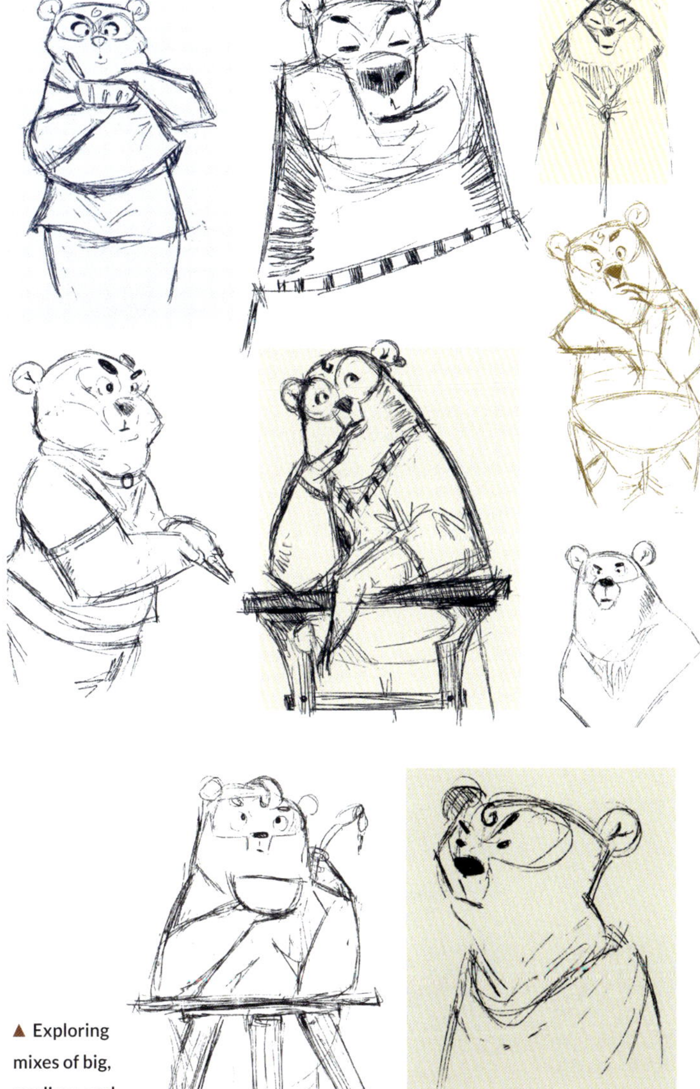

▲ Exploring mixes of big, medium, and small shapes

06 BIG, MEDIUM, SMALL

Now I can pick up my pencil and really get to work on Goldilocks' design. I always think in big, medium, and small shapes, starting from an overall silhouette and then working inward to the finer details.

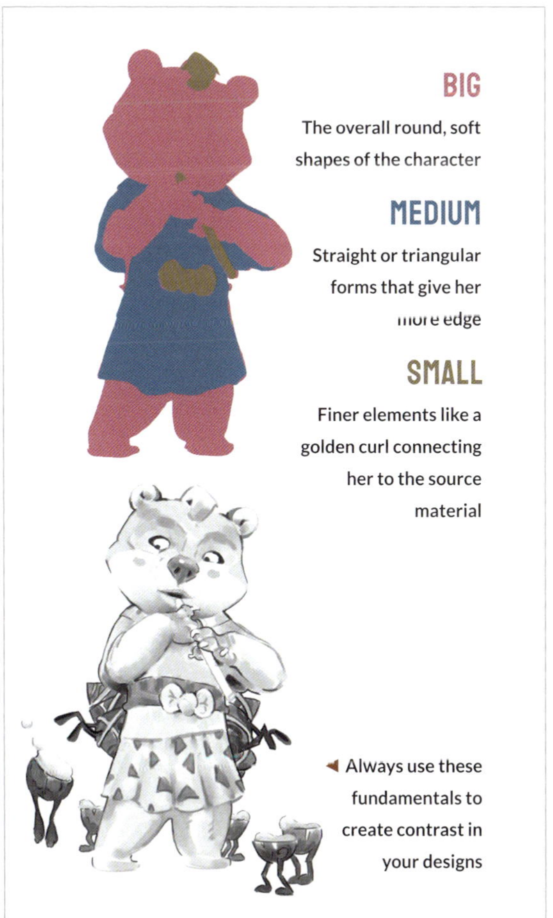

◀ Always use these fundamentals to create contrast in your designs

07 THE PORRIDGE BOWLS

Remember the three-point storytelling from step 04? Now that I have designed Goldilocks, I start thinking about the other two "characters" that will be the other elements of interest. In this case, I have identified the bowls and the Pied Piper's flute as additional characters, though they are more like special props. The porridge bowls need to feel innocent and cute, since they are playing the victim role in this fairy tale. They have round, simple shapes, and walk along on magical legs when summoned by Goldilocks' enchanted flute. There will be many bowls in the scene, so simplicity is key.

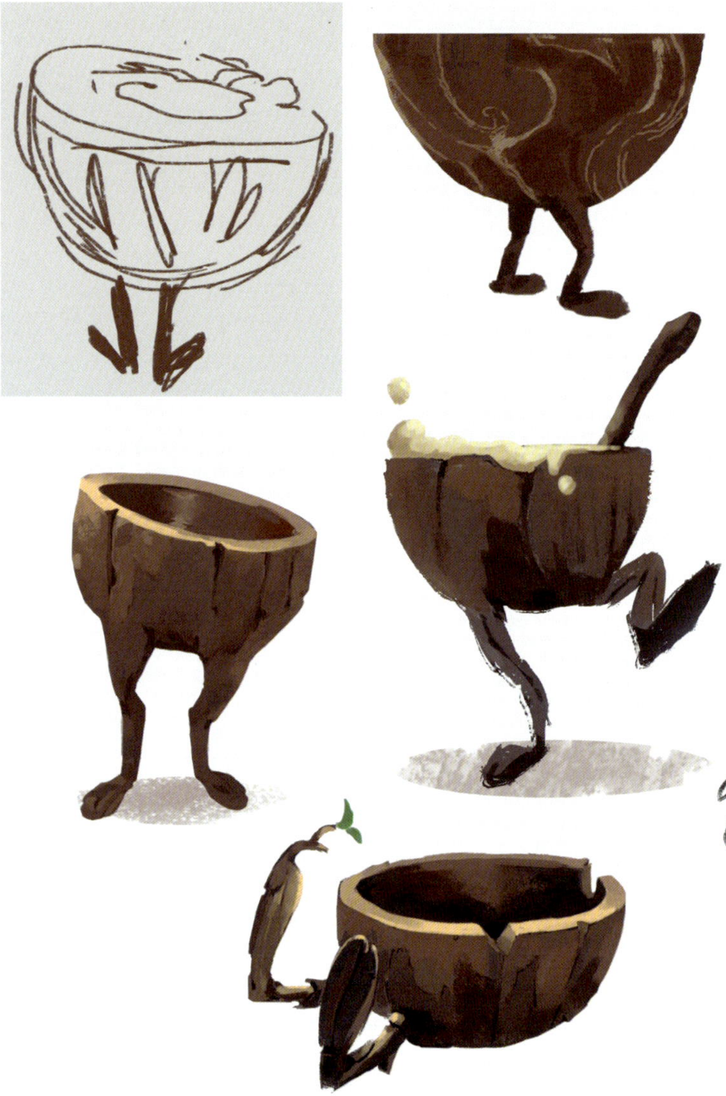

◀ Working out a design for the porridge bowls

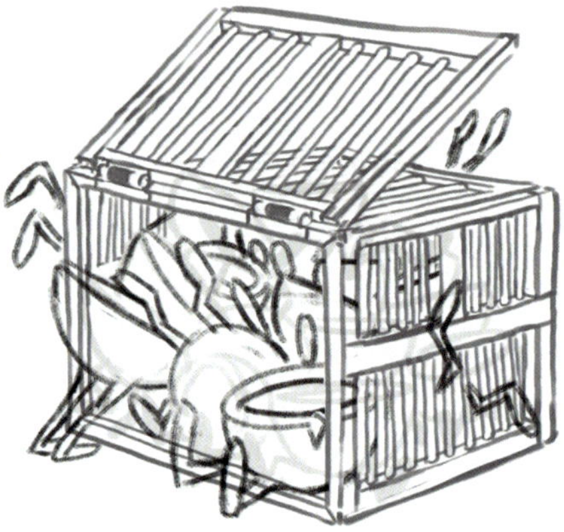

08 THE MAGIC FLUTE

Designing the Pied Piper's flute will be a little bit trickier compared to the other designs. Since I am "borrowing" the flute from another fairy tale, I want it to feel like it belongs to the world of the Pied Piper, but it also shouldn't feel out of place in Goldilocks' world. Finding an effective balance always comes down to having enough knowledge to make your decisions. In the first act of the Pied Piper's tale, he is enchanting rats to follow him out of town, so having a carved rat's head as a focal point of the flute will help make the connection between the stories. Creating "character sheets" like this is helpful for getting to know your designs – it's like a meet-and-greet event for each element!

▶ Designing the Pied Piper's flute

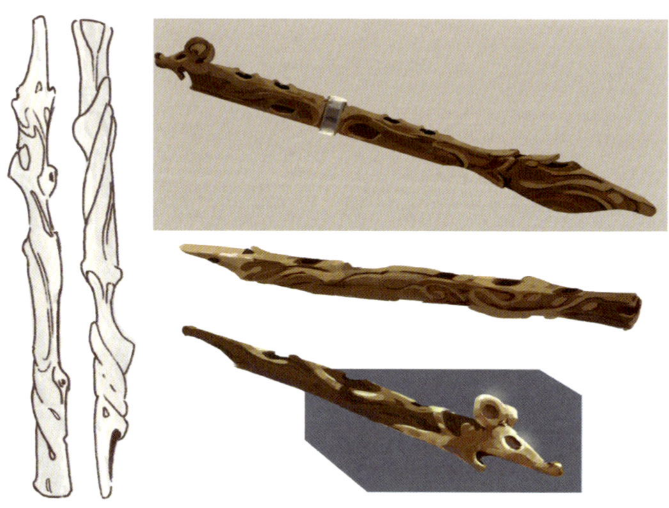

09 ENVIRONMENT DESIGN

Now that I have finished designing the characters, it is time to start designing the environment. This can be tough if you don't have much information on what it should look like or what purpose it will serve in the final illustration. However, we can assume that Goldilocks, being a bear, will live in the woods. I start with quick, exploratory thumbnails to help teleport me into Goldilocks' world. I treat this step like a visual hiking trip, making sketches and paintings while traveling an imaginary world, rather than coming up with a setting straight away. These do not have to be the final designs.

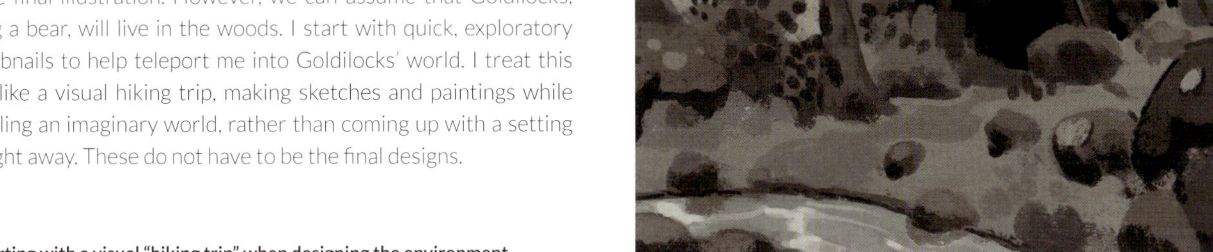

▶ **Starting with a visual "hiking trip" when designing the environment**

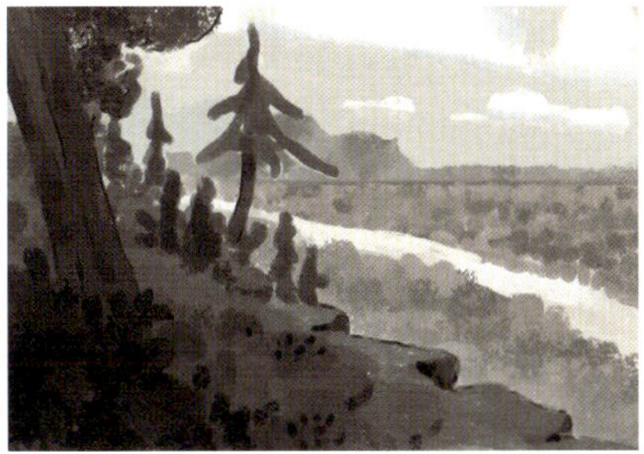

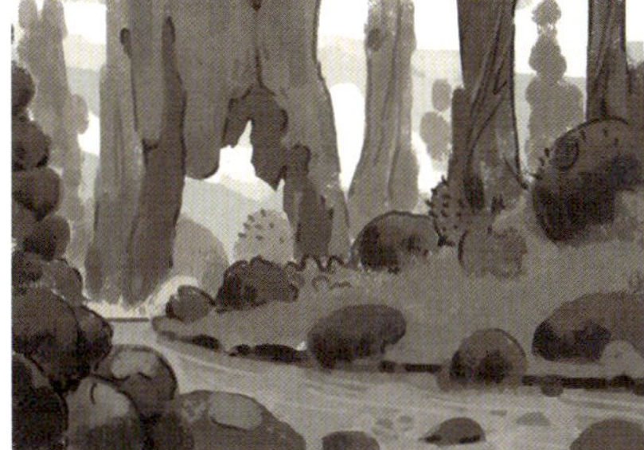

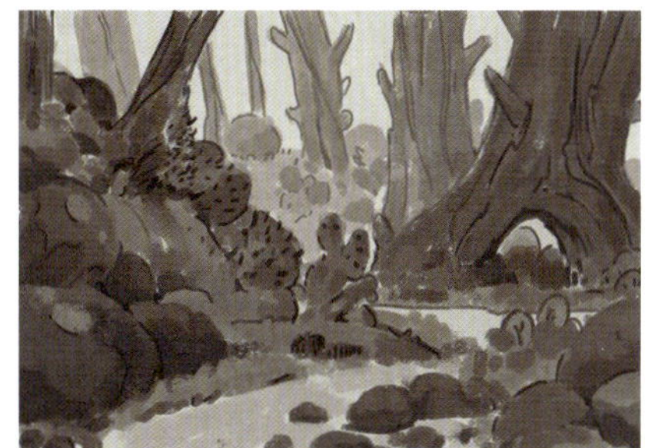

10 LANDSCAPE THUMBNAILS

I stay in the thumbnailing mindset for a little longer, creating several different potential settings for the illustration. This stage can be done in 2D or 3D – I use a mix of both. My goal is to stick to the idea of having Goldilocks stealing bowls of food using the Pied Piper's flute, but I need to answer more questions. Where is she leading the bowls? Where does she store all that stolen food? After some initial 3D sketches, I decide that a hollow fallen tree will be perfect storage for the bowls. To make the scene a little more sinister, the bowls could even be imprisoned there by Goldilocks.

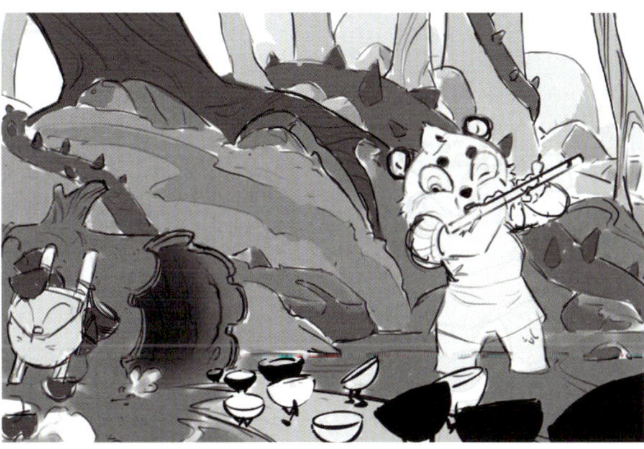

▲ **It doesn't matter whether you use 2D or 3D for your thumbnails. The subject you are creating is much more important!**

11 FULL SCENE SKETCH

Now that I have answered the most pressing questions, I choose the thumbnail that tells the story best. The environment Goldilocks lives in must be treated like a fourth character in the scene, as it's equally important for telling this tale. This means that every single asset in the environment must serve a purpose. If something is purely decorative, it should be erased from the illustration. For example, I put thorny vines around Goldilocks' log hideout, to visually show the character's troubling intentions toward the stolen bowls. A beautiful green forest with bright sunlight, mixed with dangerous thorny vines, will help portray Goldilocks as a cheerful young character with some negative traits.

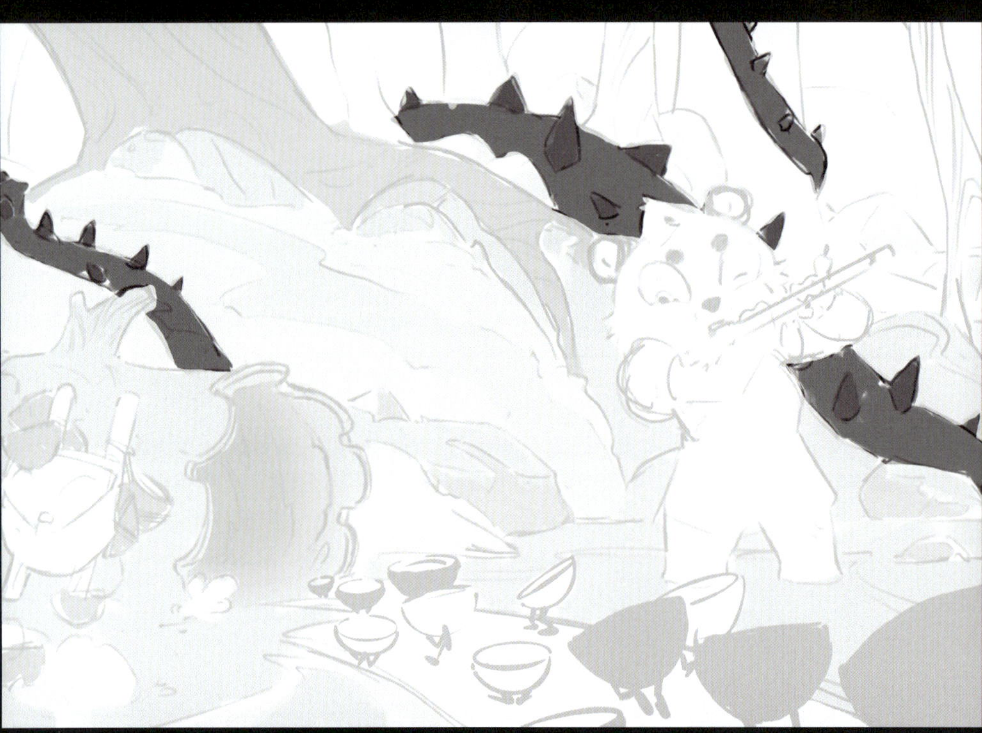

◀ **Using the environment to emphasize Goldilocks' story and characteristics**

12 QUICK 3D BLOCKOUT

Next I block out the environment. In the spirit of a children's fairy tale, I want it to be stylized rather than realistic. It does not matter if you use 2D line art to draw over your thumbnail, or jump into 3D to block out a scene. I choose 3D, creating a partial landscape with rough character placements. Using 3D can help you experiment with perspective and lighting very easily, while 2D can create different iterations very fast.

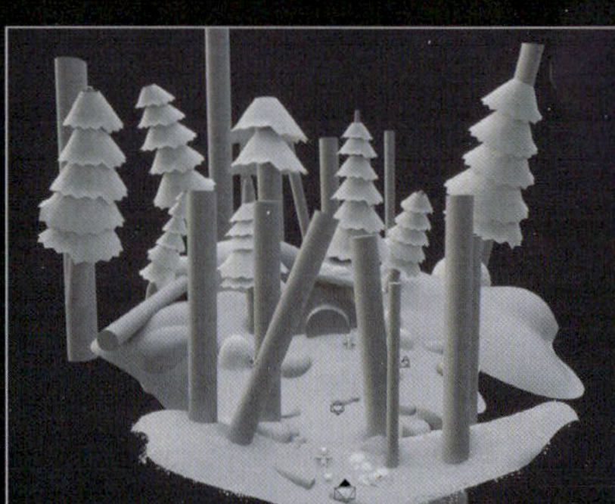

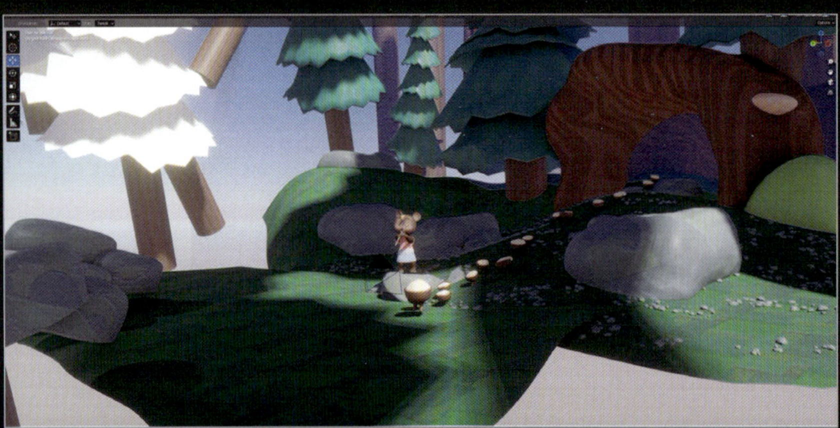

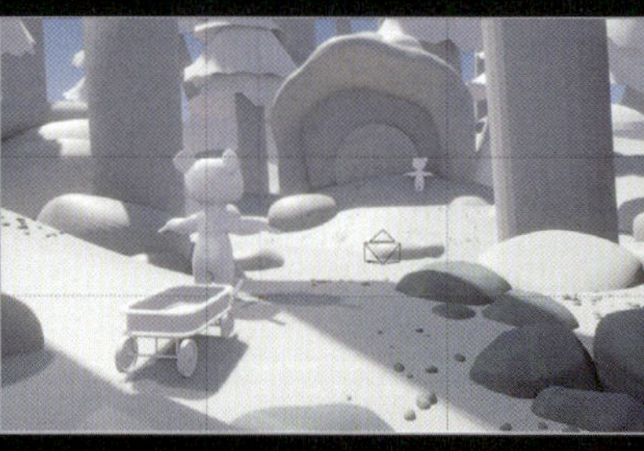

▲ **Bringing the thumbnail to the next level to make the setting more refined and believable**

13 LIGHTING AND CONTRAST

Lighting is used to guide the viewer's eye as well as tell the story. I test a few lighting options, each one emphasizing a different element of the scene. I decide to go with C, where Goldilocks is brightly lit and the background is almost entirely in shadow. It has the most value contrast, focusing the viewer straight onto the bear. The sunlight creates bright lines across the landscape, dividing the foreground from the middle and background, and casting the bowls' shadows so they point toward Goldilocks.

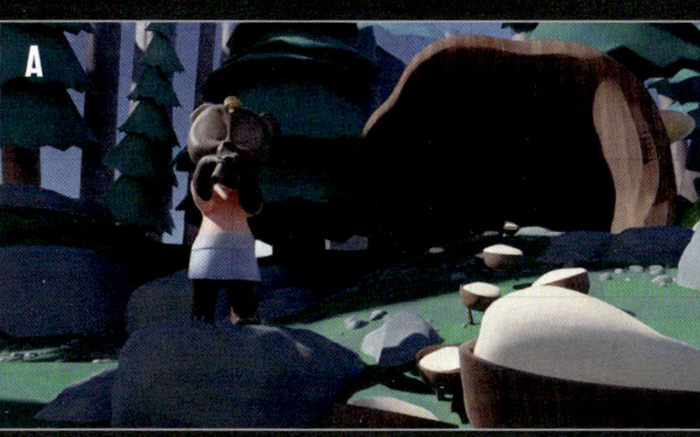

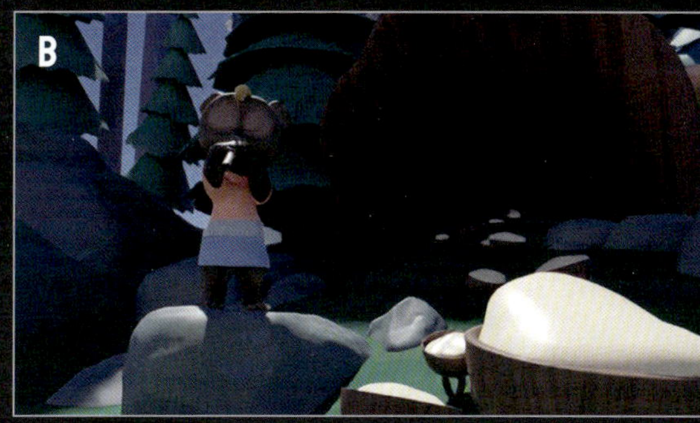

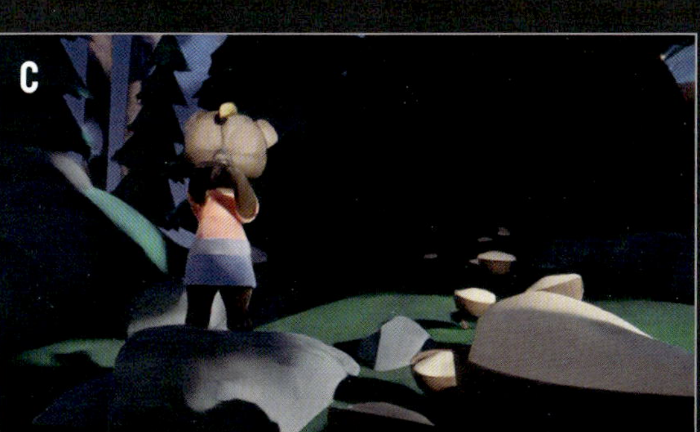

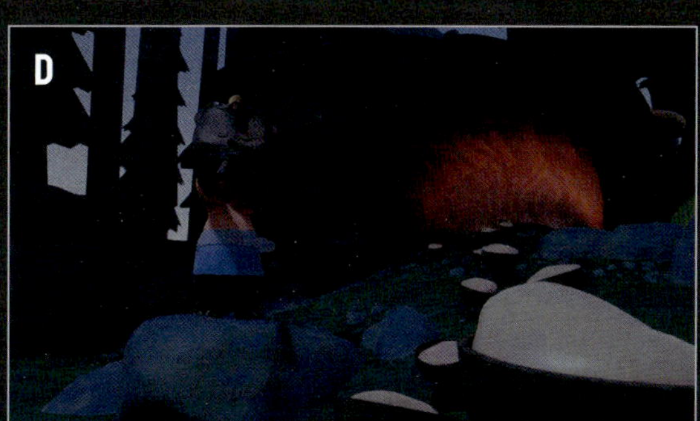

▲ Always try to find contrast on a macro as well as a micro scale

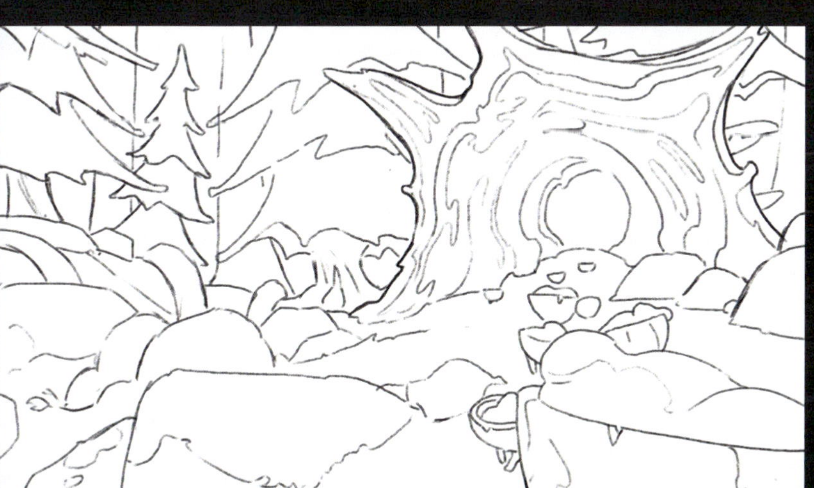

14 STARTING THE FINAL DRAWING

Now I can make the jump into preparations for the final illustration. I simply grab a screenshot of my 3D scene and enlarge it in Adobe Photoshop as a guide for my painting. I need to make adjustments to that raw image to add more life and story to it, as those 3D objects were just placeholders. I start by redrawing the hollow tree's shape to make it feel more dangerous, making the edges more spiky and triangular. Soft, round shapes feel welcoming and cute, while pointed shapes feel more sinister.

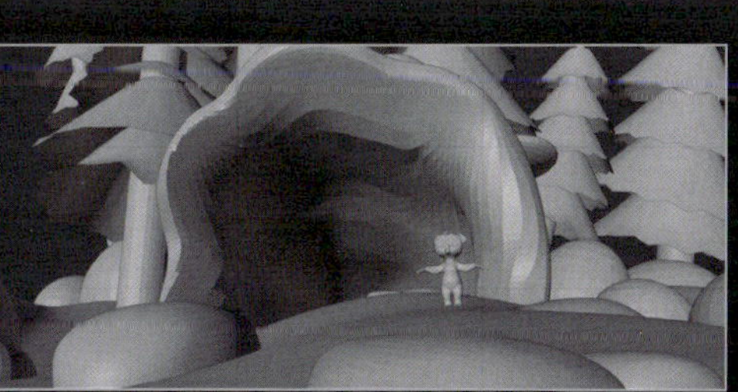

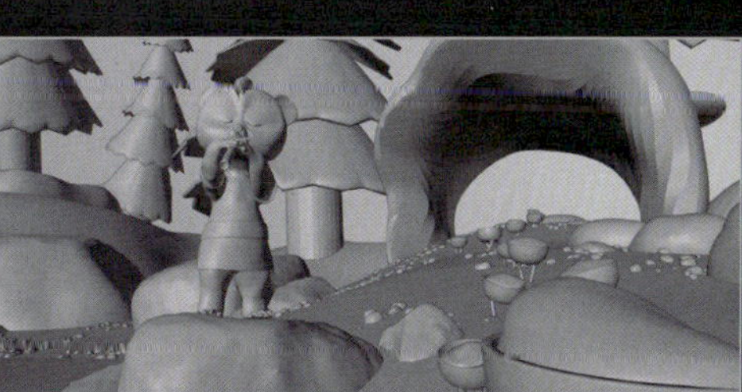

◀ Making a new line drawing using the rough 3D draft as a guide

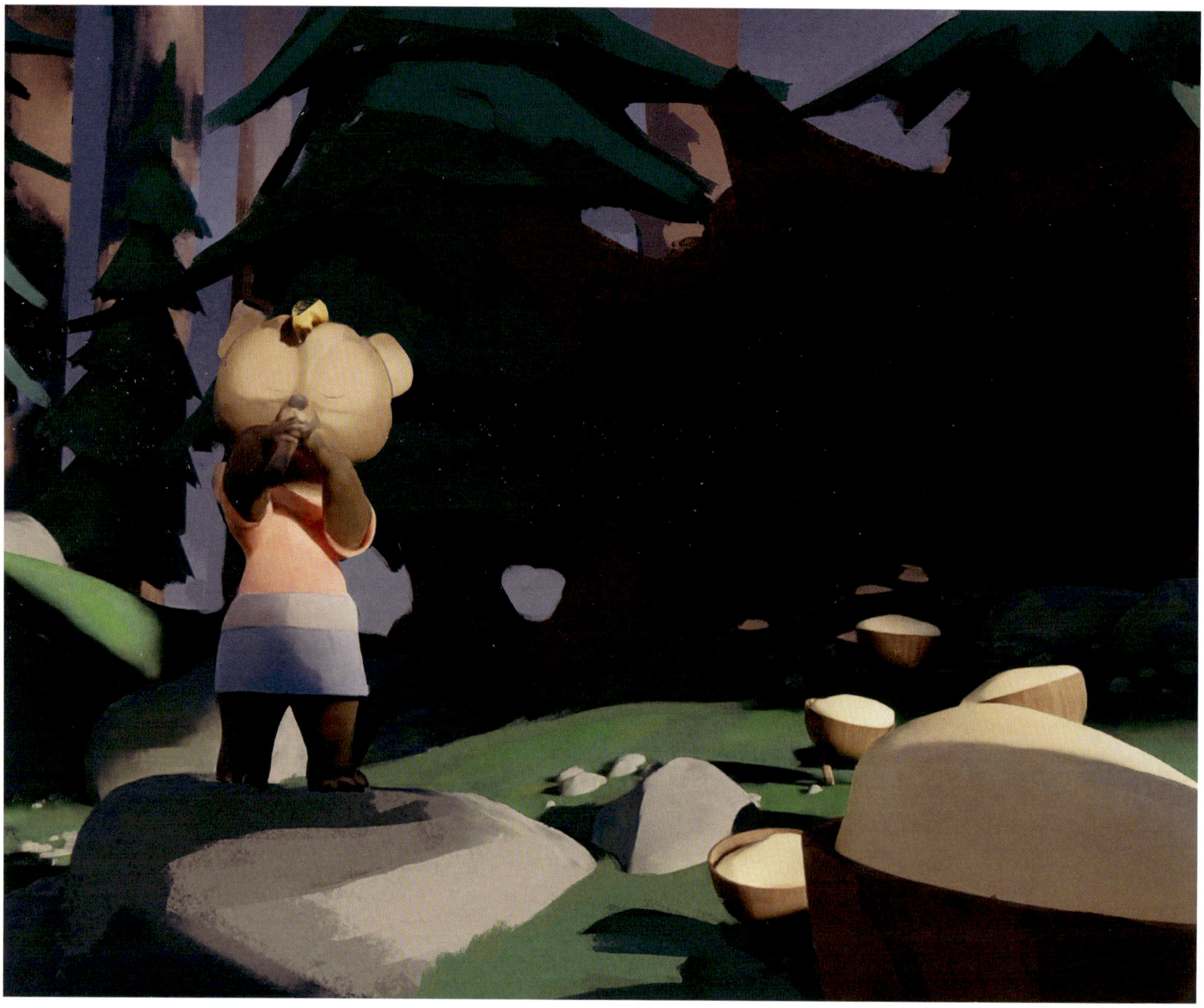

15 SKETCHING GOLDILOCKS

So far I have used a 3D placeholder for Goldilocks, which I will replace with a painted version to breathe more life into her. I change her pose to a more confident stance, as if she has been using the flute for some time. The flute not only guides the viewer toward Goldilocks, but also shows her superiority over her victims (the bowls) through her confident, upright pose. I also begin to add character-design elements that will enhance my storytelling, such as the bundles of empty bowls that Goldilocks carries. They help to show that she is up to something sketchy or strange, with the living bowls as her pawns or captives.

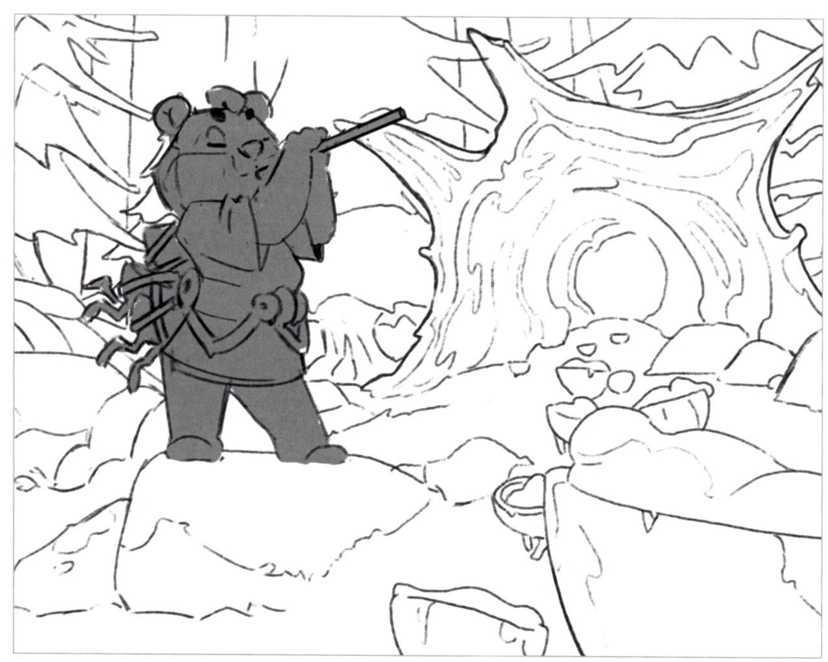

▲ Sketching a pose that carries the story through to the viewer

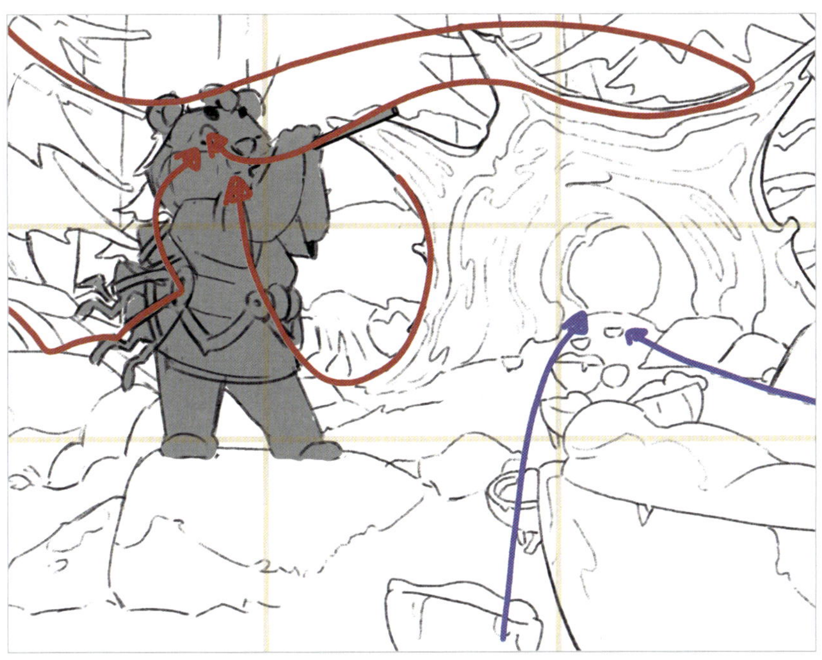

▲ Checking the composition for areas that need fixing

16 COMPOSITION CHECK

I analyze my line drawing to see if the composition could be improved. What changes would help guide the viewer to the focal points that tell my three-point story? Composition is about making elements work together to emphasize the focal point.

Check your image once in a while by zooming out or flipping it horizontally – these tricks will help you get a fresh look at it and see the areas that need work. For example, I notice that I need to change one of the pointy bits of the log, as it's currently intersecting with the flute. The same goes for the feet of the empty bowls Goldilocks is carrying – they "merge" with the underlying line art, which might lead to confusion. My goal is to have the focal points read as clearly as possible, so that the viewer can tell in an instant what's going on.

17 DETAILING THE TREE

Once I am happy with the line art, composition, and storytelling elements, I can continue painting. My original idea was to have the hollow fallen tree as storage for the bowls. However, looking at the current stage of the illustration, it feels strange not to have something placed inside the tree. The red/orange light within the tree makes it feels sinister, which helps tell the story of this greedy character and her doomed porridge bowls, but the area still looks too empty.

I use my 3D scene to test out a couple of solutions. First I add some bars shaped like a claw to imprison the bowls, but this feels totally out of place. Next I try adding some wooden cages to trap the bowls, which works much better. Do not be afraid to change elements in your illustration if you feel like the message is not carried through to the viewer clearly enough!

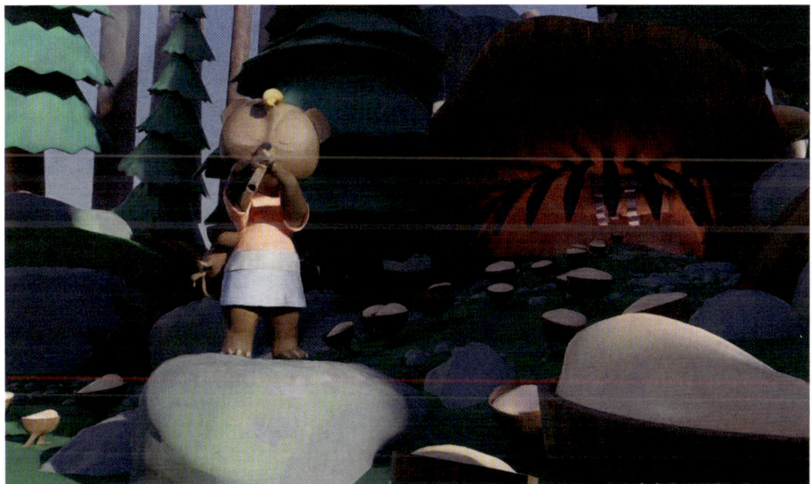

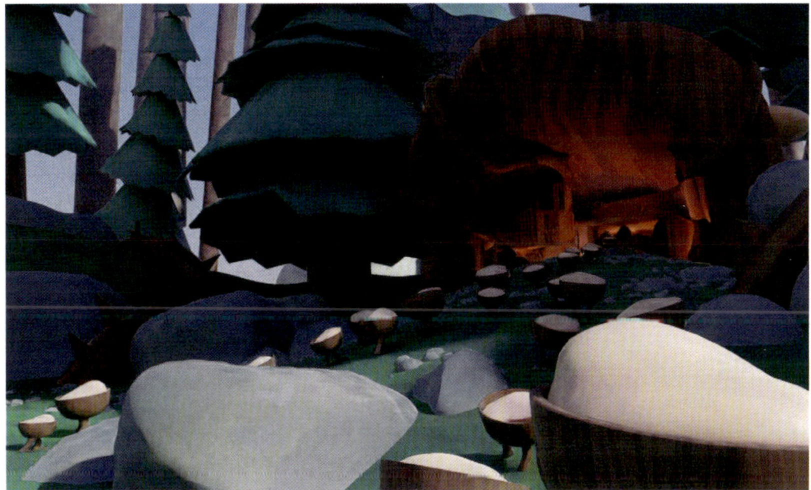

► Trying two different ideas to flesh out the hollow tree

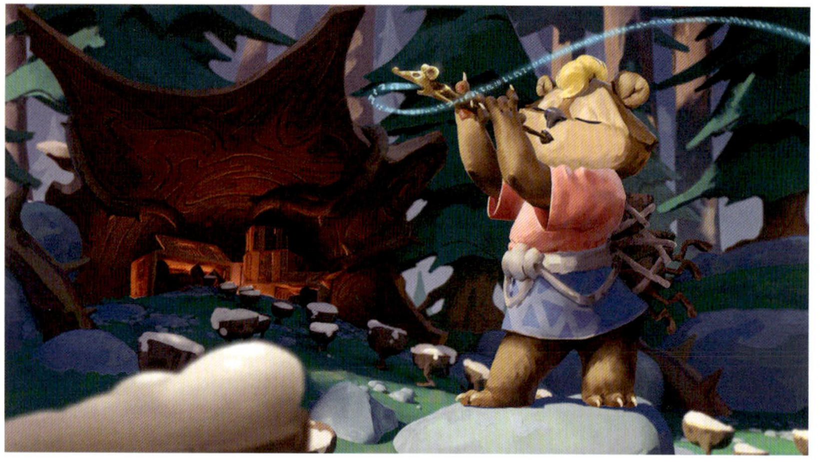

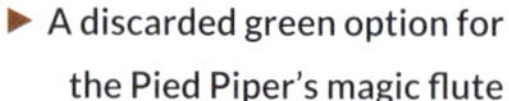

▲ Building up more detail in Goldilocks and the environment

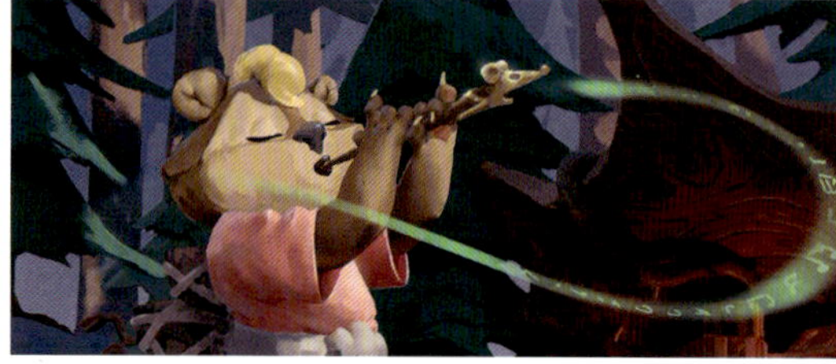

► A discarded green option for the Pied Piper's magic flute

18 PAINTING UP THE SCENE

I add the wooden cages to my painted image, merging them into the environment so the whole image looks more cohesive. The storytelling is more rounded, too, as adding the cages shows *what* Goldilocks does with the bowls after eating all their contents. Goldilocks herself is taking shape, wearing pastel hues that suggest her young age, and with a curl of golden hair that references the original tale. Trying to show the flute's "magic" visually, I add a glowing ribbon of musical notes flowing out of it, both in blue and green; the green option is flowy and exciting to look at, but I find it draws too much focus. There definitely needs to be a magical element that brings a little bit of the fantastical to the illustration, but the focus should still be on Goldilocks, the flute, the bowls, and the hollow tree. This leads me to opt for the blue version that is more discreet.

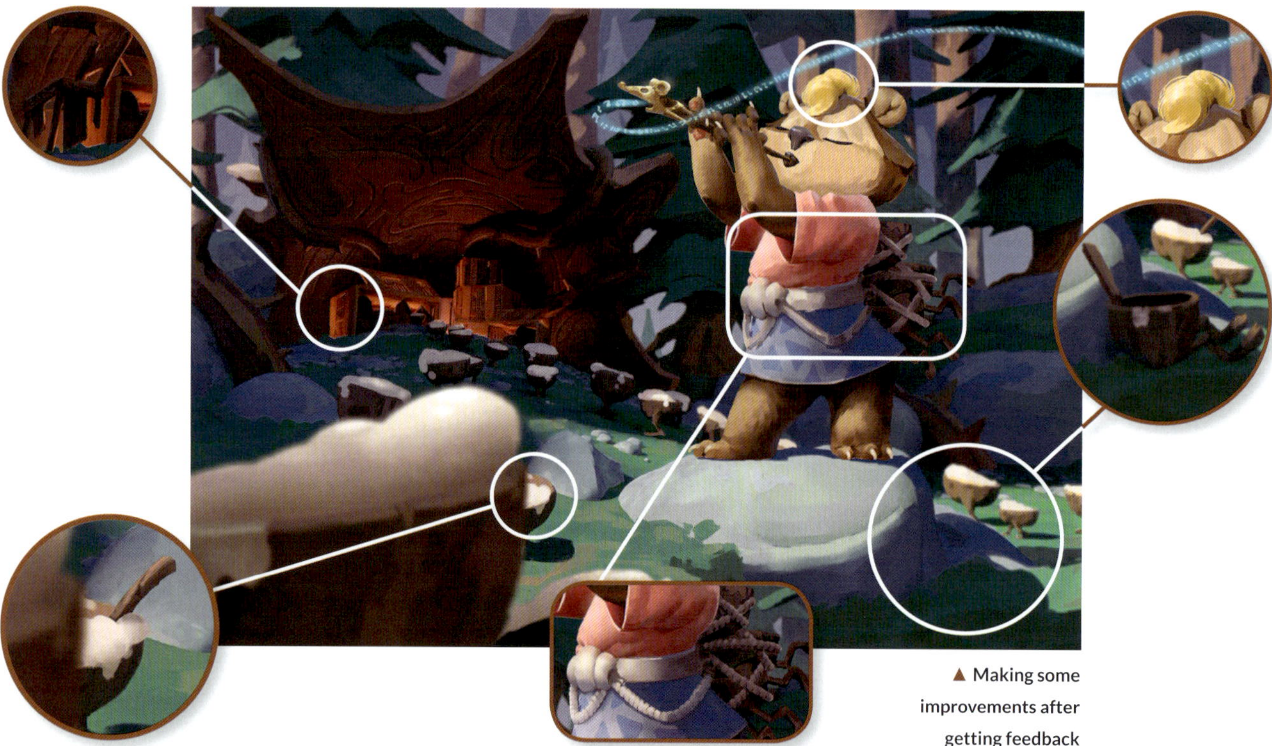

▲ Making some improvements after getting feedback

19 EXTRA DETAILS AND POLISH

At this point, it's good to ask for feedback, preferably from someone who understands a bit about art. Always try to look at constructive feedback as a way to improve your image rather than taking it personally. This is essential to being a professional artist, where you have to deal with feedback daily! I want to get away from the 3D look while maintaining the energy of the 2D drawing, so I get some other opinions on things that I can adjust, polish, or add to achieve that – furniture for the log den, more bowl details, and cleaning up Goldilocks' outfit.

20 FINISHING TOUCHES

After getting those second opinions on how to wrap up the image, I add some small details to polish the illustration and emphasize the connections between my version of Goldilocks and the original fairy tale. The broken chair next to the wooden cages is a nod to the little bear's chair in the original story. Extra highlights and strands to Goldilocks' blonde curl make it pop more, and cleaning up the detailing on her belt and ropes clarifies their material. To help characterize the bowls and make their contents clearer, I add a few wooden spoons and little spillages of oatmeal, and two emptied bowls lying near Goldilocks' feet.

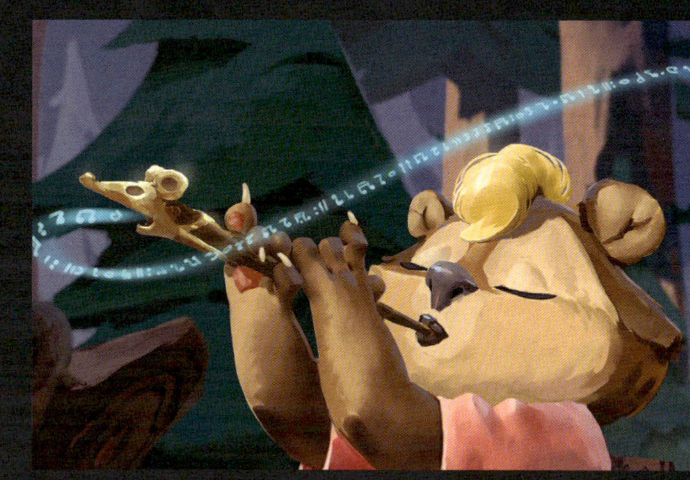

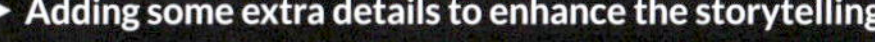

▶ **Adding some extra details to enhance the storytelling**

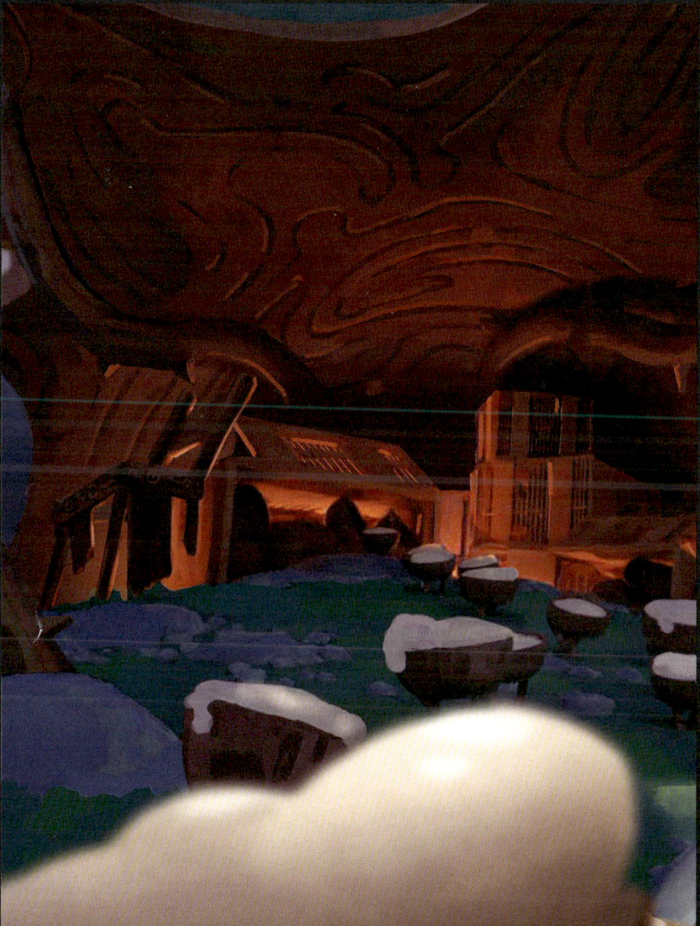

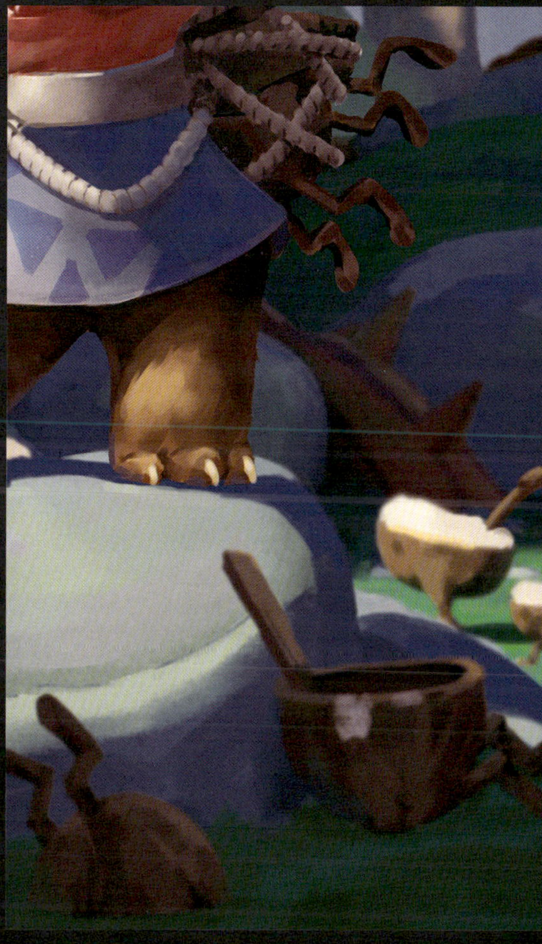

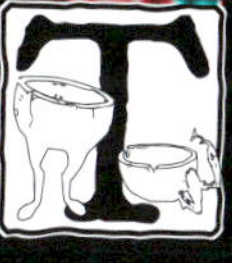

The most important, valuable skill I want to convey with this project is to *ask yourself questions* and act according to your answers. Decision-making is a crucial skill for any artist. Nothing in this illustration is there by accident, and throughout all these steps I was able to eliminate the elements that didn't work to tell my story. The result takes a classic fairy tale and makes it different by adding a twist to the story, turning Goldilocks into a bear stealing food from humans, as well as adding meta references to another tale. I succeeded in the main goal I discussed at the beginning, which was to show Goldilocks' greediness and selfishness in a playful, stylized illustration. Try using some of the tips and methods I have shown here to help with your own illustrations later on – and don't be a greedy, selfish person like Goldilocks!

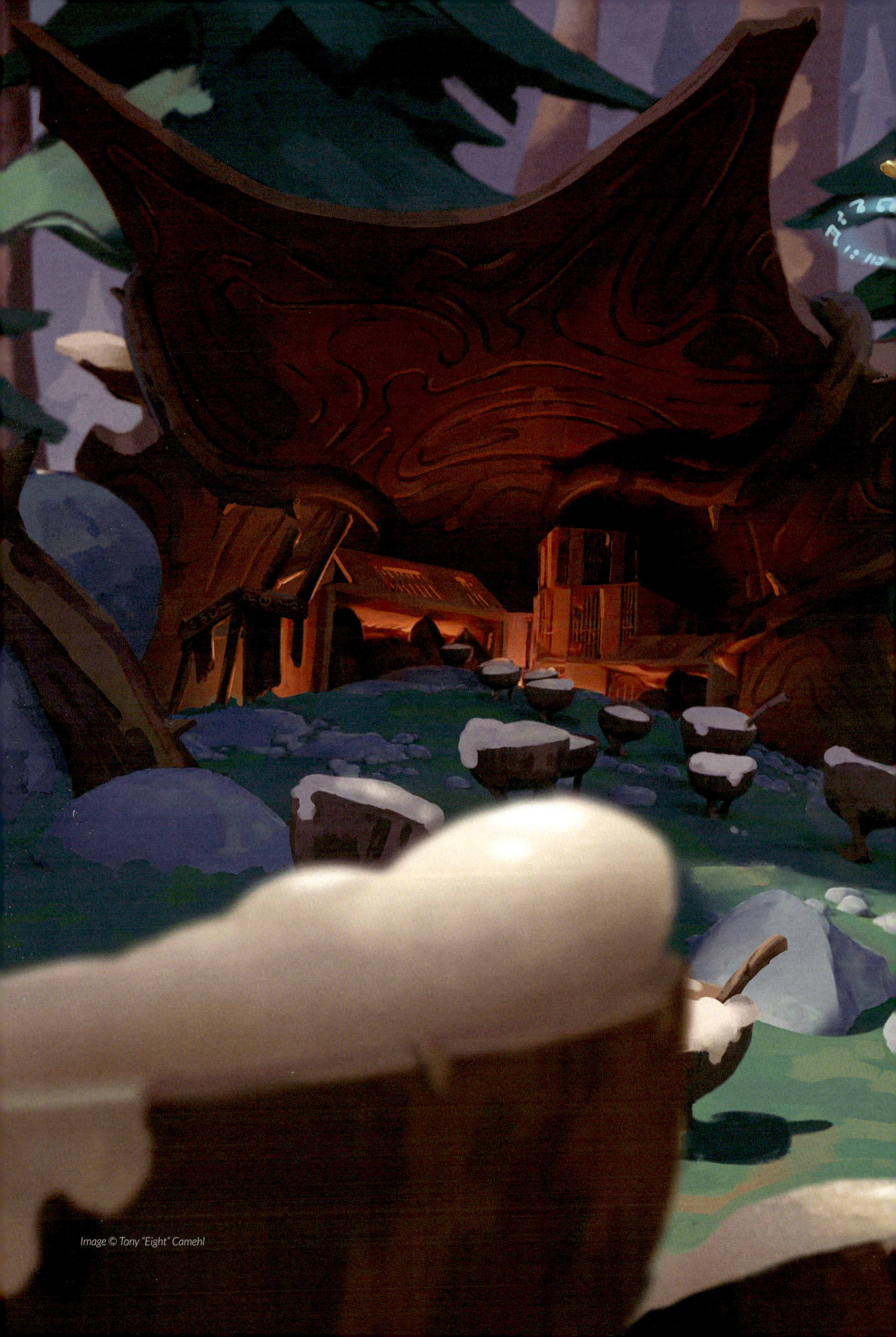

Image © Tony "Eight" Camehl

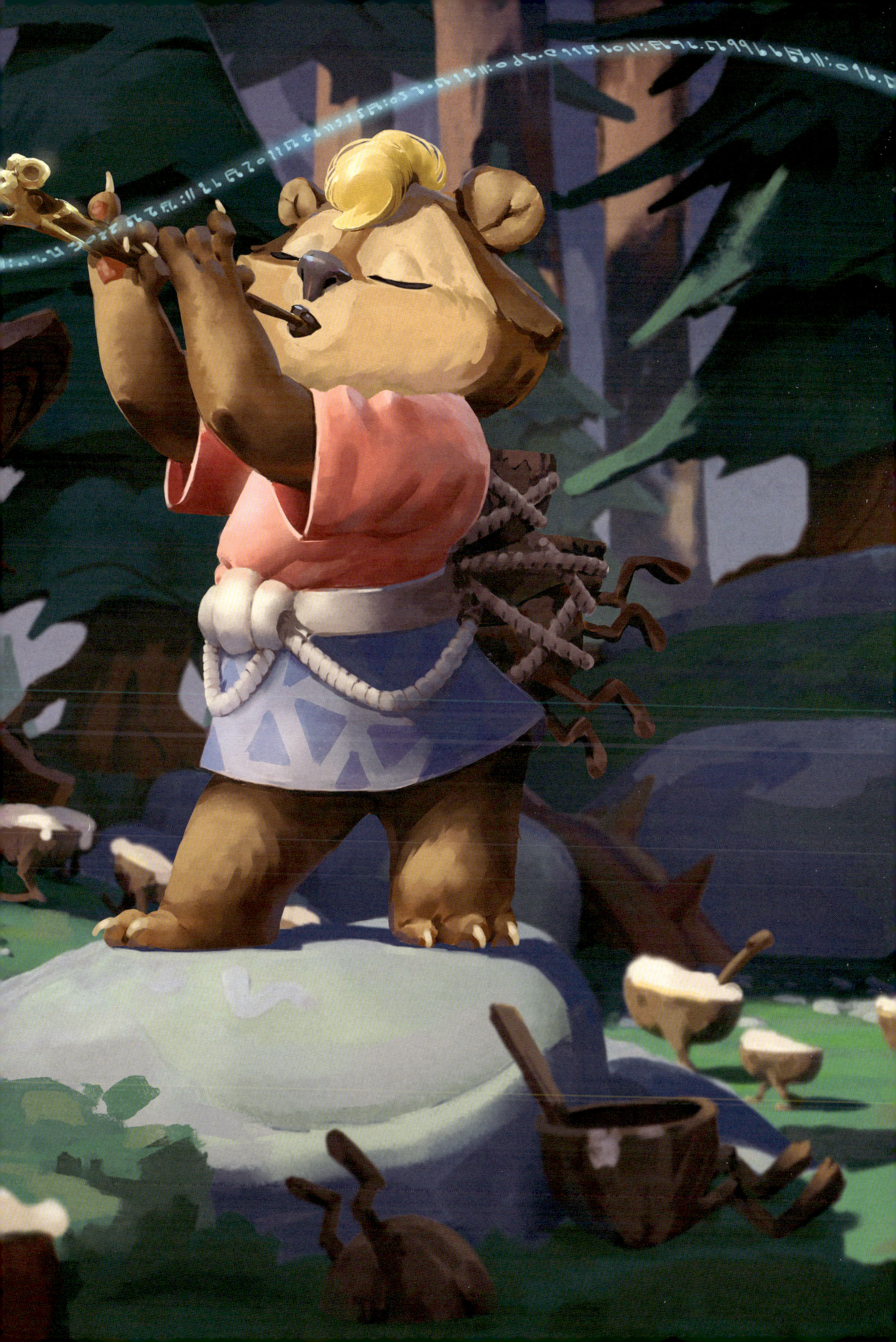

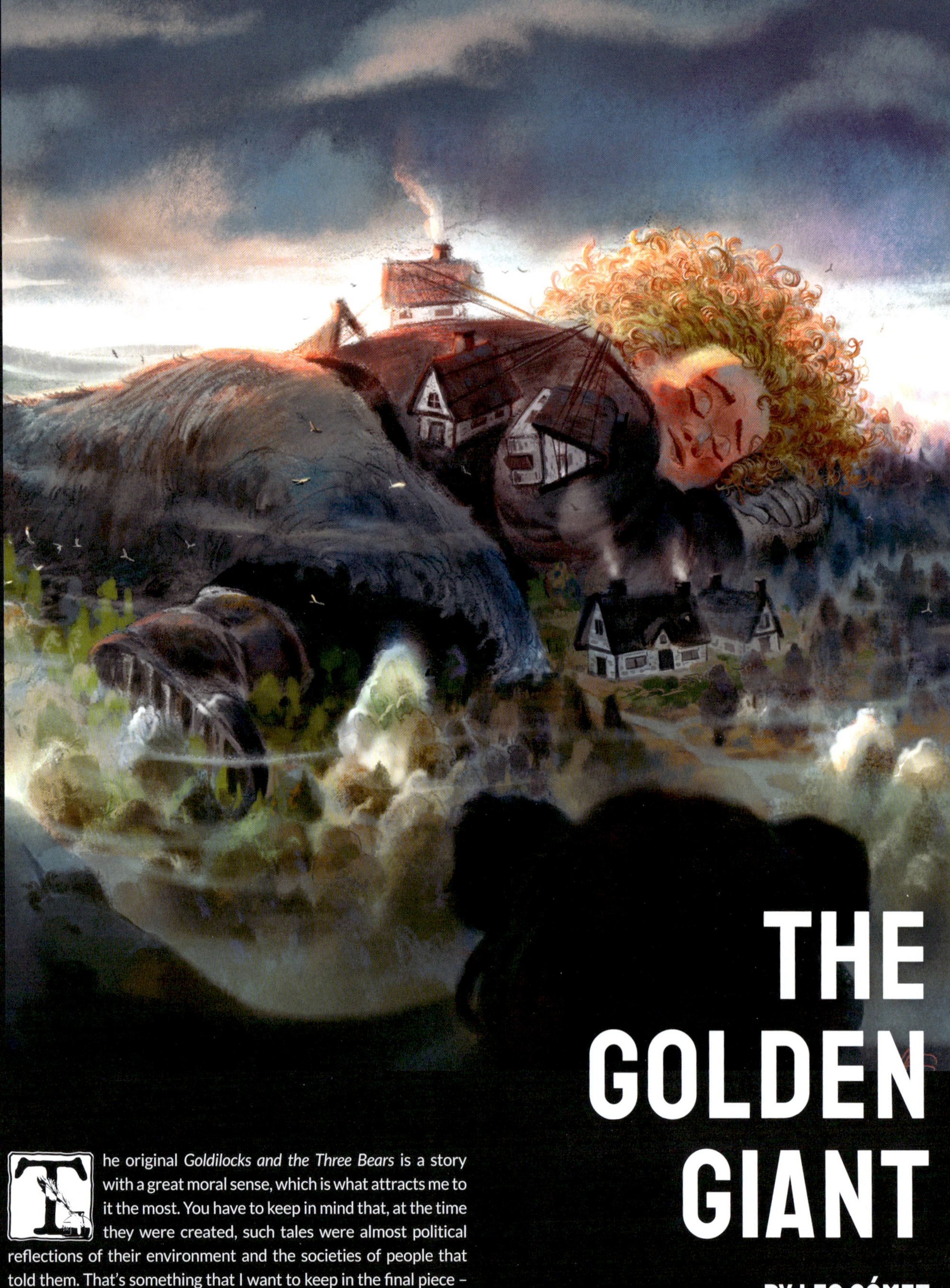

THE GOLDEN GIANT

BY LEO GÓMEZ

The original *Goldilocks and the Three Bears* is a story with a great moral sense, which is what attracts me to it the most. You have to keep in mind that, at the time they were created, such tales were almost political reflections of their environment and the societies of people that told them. That's something that I want to keep in the final piece – something that represents the universal nature of a small society.

01 FINDING AN IDEA

This first stage is a time to explore all your ideas and use all your resources. Do not limit your imagination and creativity. Making a new version of a classic story, or any other, doesn't mean that you have to stay fully attached to its original nature. Many classics have been modified over time but still retain the identity of the original story. Look at *Dracula*, *Frankenstein*, the Roman and Greek epics, or even just the story of a hero who defeats a dragon. How many versions have we seen of these events? The main thing is to maintain a sense of that original, creating a link that may be very subtle but definitely exists. Eventually I settle on a rough idea for this project: making Goldilocks an exploring giant. Like the Goldilocks of the original story, she is curious and nosy, especially about people's homes.

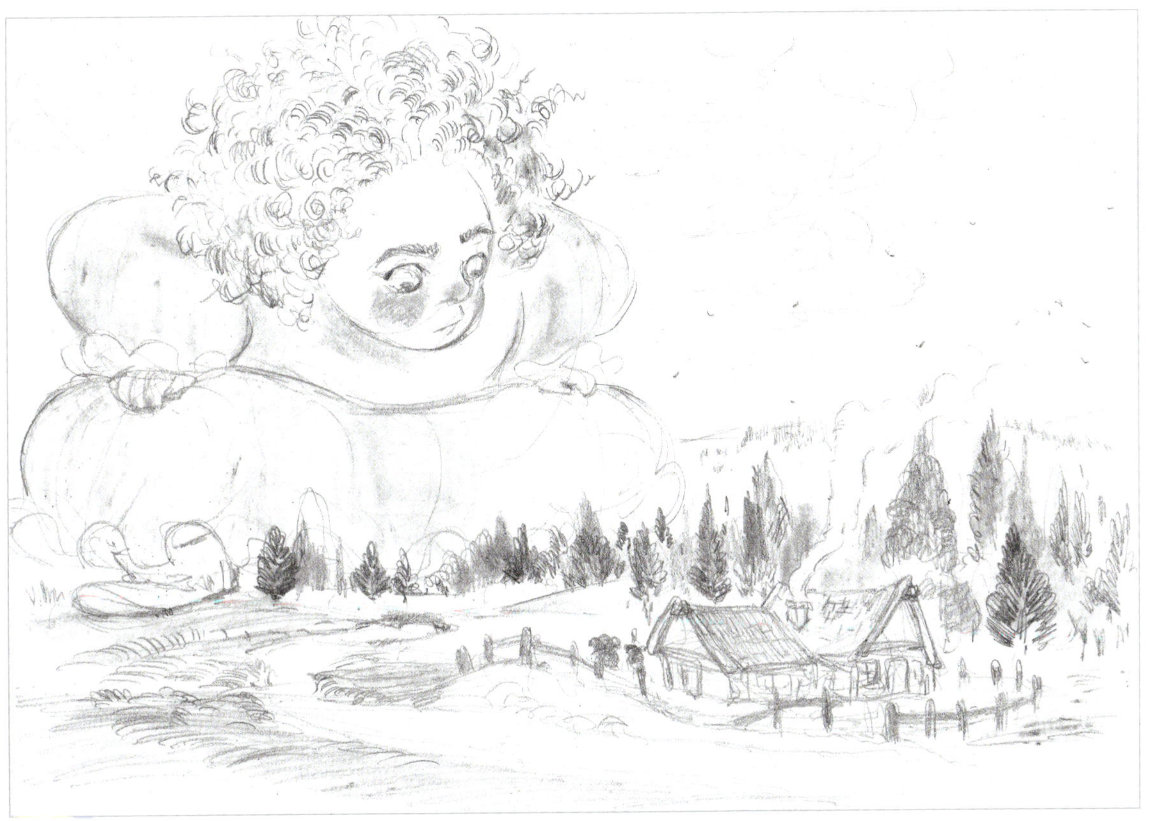

▲ The spark of an idea: Goldilocks as a curious giant

02 WORLDBUILDING

Before jumping into an illustration with a myriad of details, it's important for me to build up the story's universe. This can be a series of sketches, maps, or even texts that help me imagine where the story takes place. Researching documents about a precise period will make your story more credible – for example, if a tale is set in the Middle Ages, or among the Vikings, those people were not always the same throughout their history. Neither were the samurai; most people imagine them wielding swords, but there came a time when they used gunpowder weapons. All this extra context will make a simple sketch strong enough to tell the viewer what is going on in your story and world. In my case, I sketch a rough map of a fantasy land, including small towns and geographic features that might appear in my illustration.

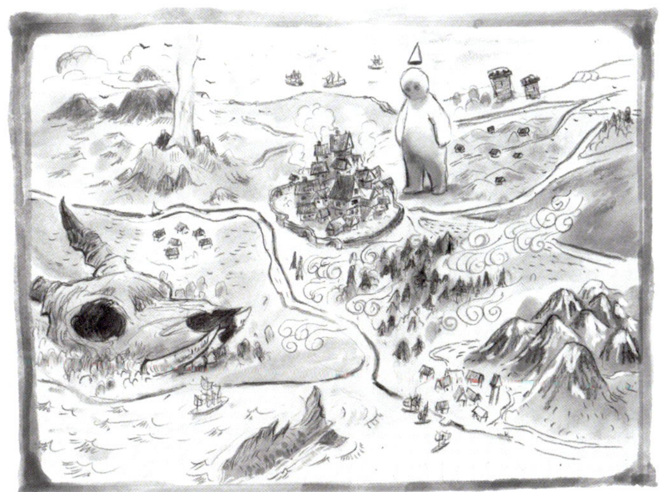

▲ Sketching your worldbuilding ideas creates valuable context

03 THE THREE "BEARS"

Every tale needs a hero, a villain, or a little mouse who will save the day – characters where we can use our creative freedom to make a unique mark. My version of the story will reverse the roles somewhat, with Goldilocks being a playful giant. Inquisitive and quite greedy, she unwittingly inflicts harm on small villages. The "three bears" of the tale could be giant-hunters wearing bear pelts for warmth, which I explore here. If you do not have a clear idea of your final goal yet, don't forget that this is still the exploration stage. Do not rush. Enjoy the process and learn from it! Your growth and learning are more important than simply making a finished piece.

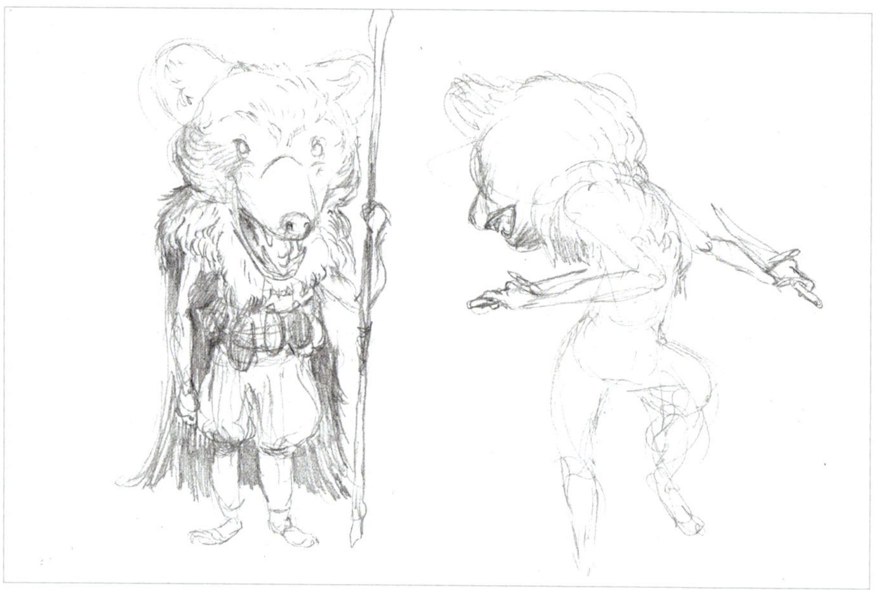

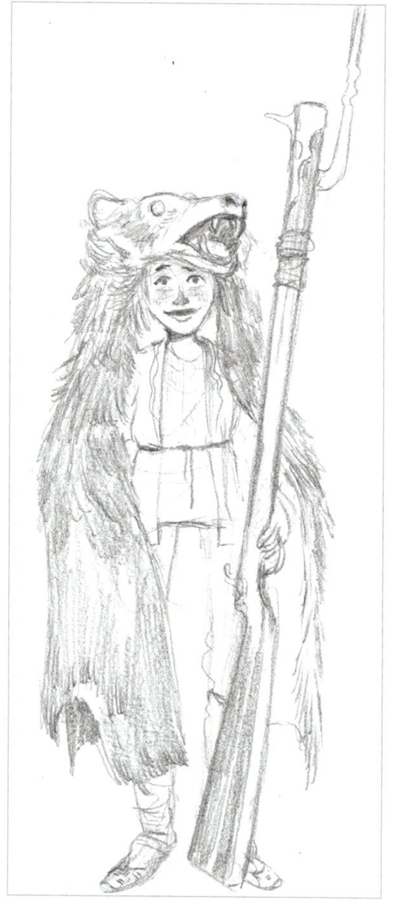

▲ Sketching ideas for the three bears

04 GOLDILOCKS THE GIANT

Now that I have a better idea of my main characters and their setting, I can delve deeper into character design. I imagine my Goldilocks picking up and collecting things she likes, such as people's houses. Like in the original tale, she is not really aware of the harm she causes. She steals entire houses and wears them like jewelry!

Allow time for your ideas to grow and don't rush. Usually, it's not until my third sketch that my concepts begin taking shape. After four or more, they begin to form a more solid idea, or strong elements will appear that can be combined. I want my designs for this project to be a mix of the traditional and the fantastic, placing the viewer somewhere that feels familiar somehow.

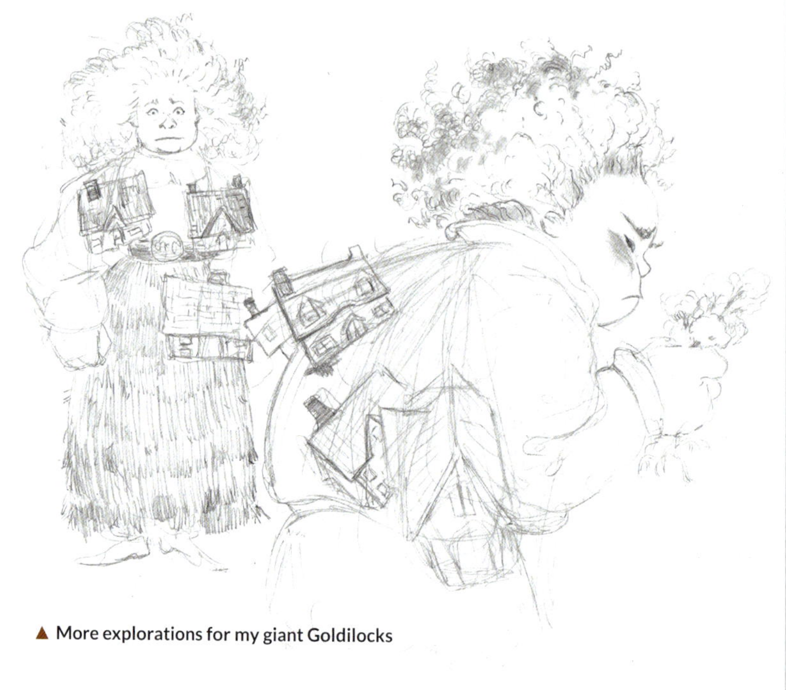

▲ More explorations for my giant Goldilocks

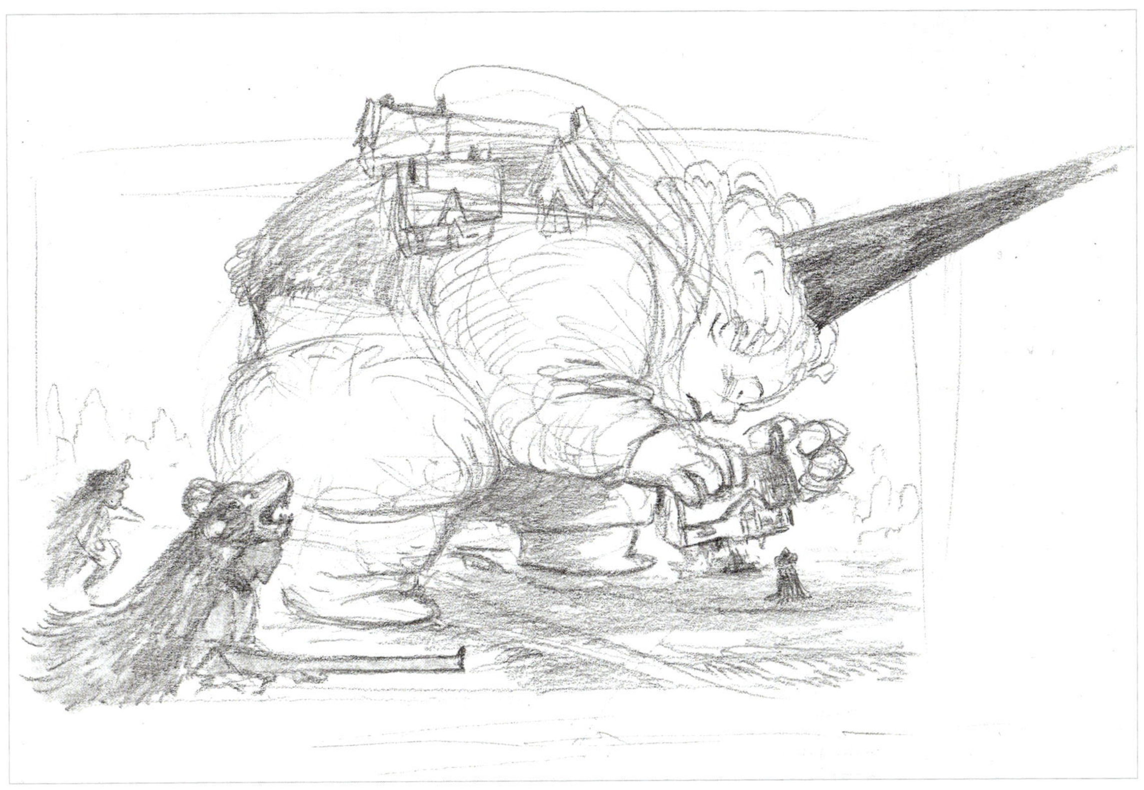

▲ Starting to consider fuller scenes with my characters

05 EXPLORING COMPOSITIONS

I begin exploring the story in the form of small thumbnail sketches, incorporating the bear characters and landscape elements. I am still very exploratory at this stage, using all my freedom to express myself. Whether an idea is simple or bizarre, it's important to keep exploring. You can combine several ideas, or take fragments of them and create something new. Even if you throw an idea away in the end, it will have shone new light on a thought that wasn't lit before. This first exploration is a sort of wizard, perhaps as a nod to the type of magical fantasy genre this story falls within. The character has an almost ridiculous pointed hat, which takes the viewer back to an era far removed from the present, but in this universe it works without a problem.

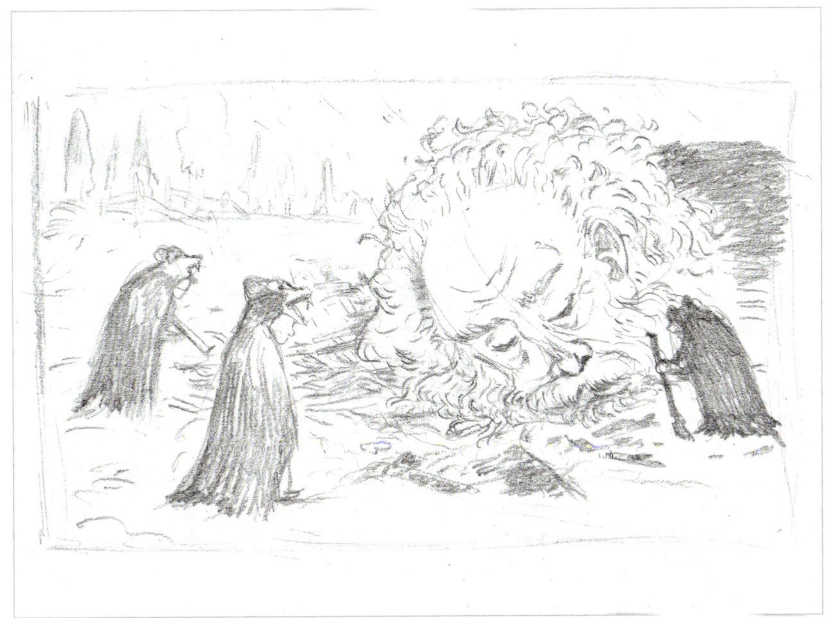

06 A SLEEPING GIANT

What if the giant was an exhausted old man, or a tired drunk? We will never know because I discarded this idea. It was one of the first I had, but never assume that your first option is the definitive one. There are an infinite number of other paths that might suit you better – you won't know until you have explored more ideas and worked through the clichés. Whether they are used or not, all these little concepts help to enrich the universe.

◀ An early idea where the giant is a slumbering old man

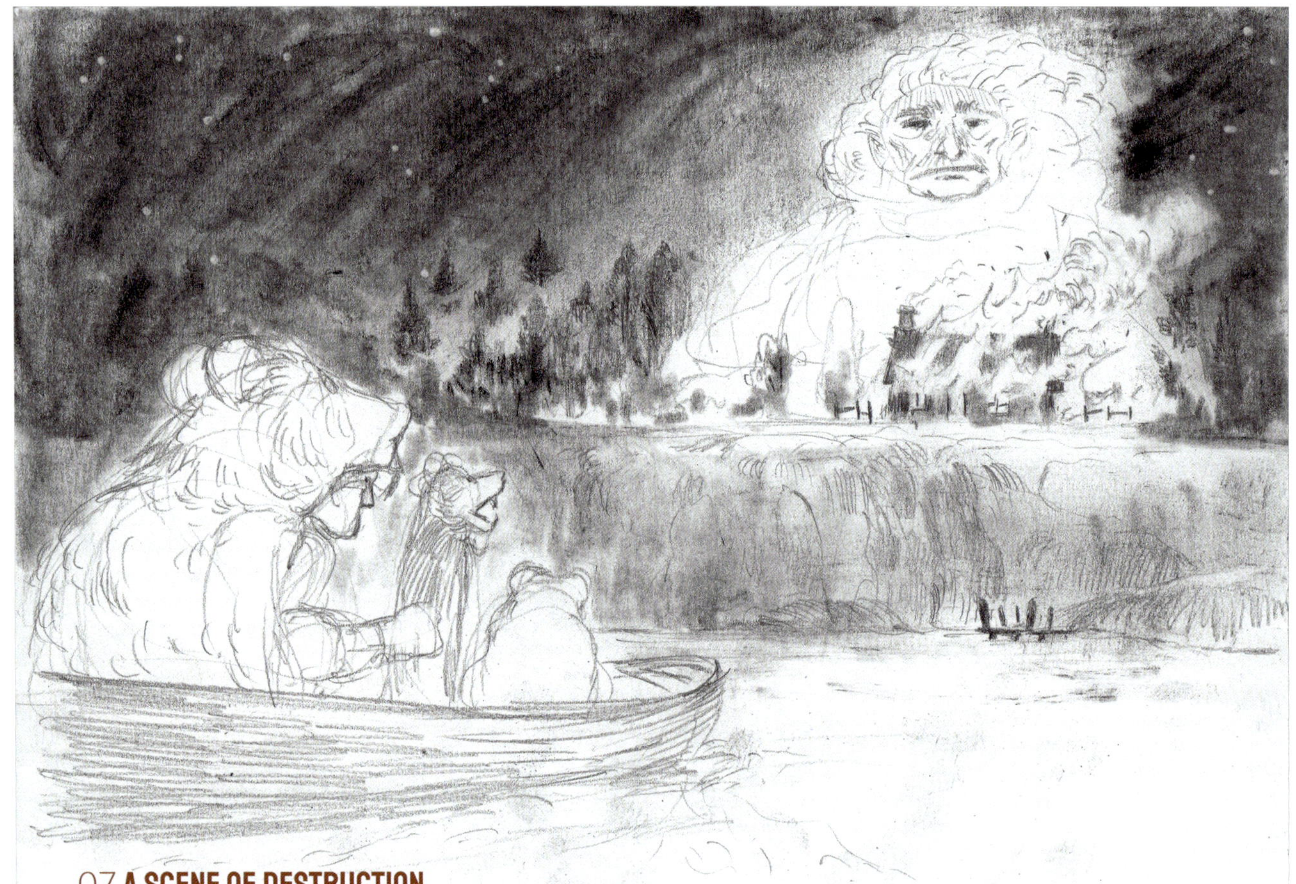

07 A SCENE OF DESTRUCTION

I continue sketching compositions, using my basic idea of a giant versus three small bears as the common foundation. These sketches have the core elements of a house in the distance, the giant, and a group of bear heroes (or even victims). They show a narrative with a winner and a loser, and an open setting where any type of landscape or season could fit. The bears look on, too late, as the house burns and the giant looms in the distance. An image can evoke intimate emotions, personal anguish, or political fears, without being direct; the viewer may not fully recognize them, but those feelings can be used to create beautiful and unpredictable pieces. We have seen a hero slaying an enemy a hundred times; it attracts us in the first few seconds, but shortly after, we will forget it forever. A scene like this one, showing a moment before or after the big event, can engage the viewer's curiosity, thoughts, and emotions for longer. Try to tell your story in another way, rather than grabbing the obvious solution.

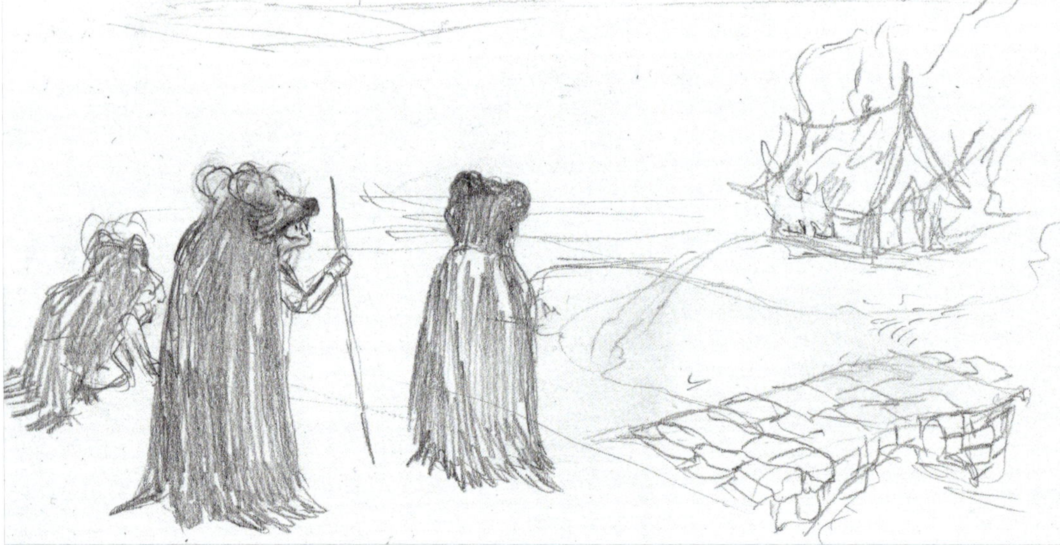

▲ Exploring a rather dark scene of a burning house

08 DEVELOPING THE SETTING

I decide to focus on the concept touched on in steps 01 and 05: a curious giant exploring mountains and villages. If you want to give your characters a natural, authentic quality, look at photos, videos, and books that are relevant to them, to the time and environment in which the story is set, and so on. For example, this story is set in a cold location, which we can see from the giant's clothing. She is able to travel with ease along the roads; these roads create gaps in the dark forests, leading to houses or villages where humans might live. I like this idea of the bears watching from a vantage point as the giant steals a house from the valley below.

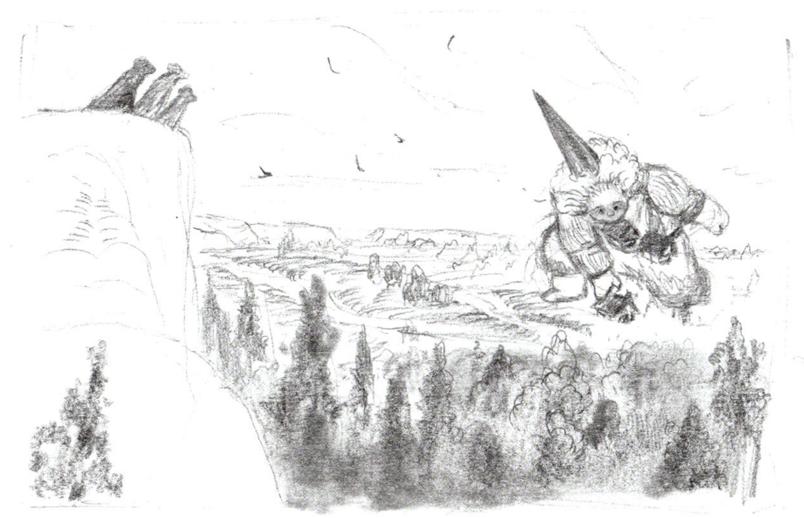

▲ The bear hunters looking out over a forest valley

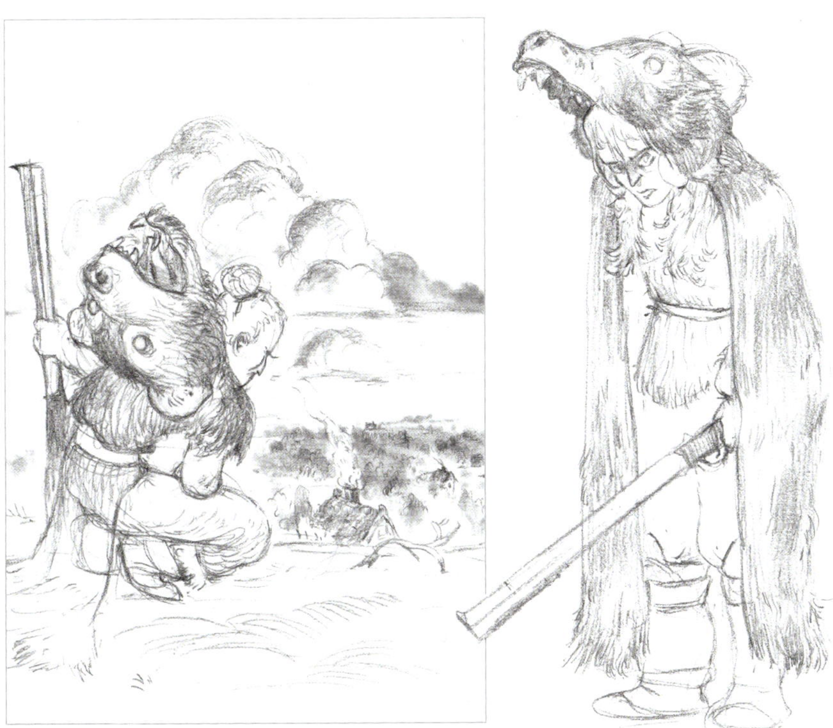

09 DESIGNING THE HUNTERS

I return to the secondary characters of the hunter "bears" to get a better sense of their actions. I think about how they would react when looking down at the scene, almost from a bird's-eye view. Before a battle, there is always a moment of calm, and I would like my final image to portray that. It could be a moment of planning or anticipation, rather than a direct conflict, with both the hunters and the viewer wondering what will happen next.

You don't have to show everything in pure action – leaving an idea open to different readings is storytelling's strongest weapon. When a story opens doors for your (and the viewer's) creativity, rather than telling everything, it can become something unique and personal.

◀ Sketches exploring one of the "bear" characters

FINDING CLARITY

When trying to create the basis for my final piece, I aim to eliminate artistic references to other artists and their images. This gives me clarity on what I truly know or don't know. Be honest with yourself about the knowledge you have at your disposal. Have you really researched and practiced everything you need to execute your idea, or are you actually imitating another artist's solutions? Being clear on this will help you explore new opportunities with more clarity and fewer doubts.

10 SLEEPING GOLDILOCKS

Now I am almost at the final stage of exploration. This sketch is a mixture of all of the previous ideas, joining all the parts that have worked well so far, and it achieves several of my aims. It avoids the cliché of relying only on action as the axis of the scene. Everyone is a protagonist here – there are no "good guys" or "bad guys," but an ambiguous scene that provokes curiosity. It refers to the original story's idea of a little girl falling asleep in one of the bears' beds, but puts it in a new light: how would a giant sleep on the open fields after a long day of travel and happily stealing people's homes?

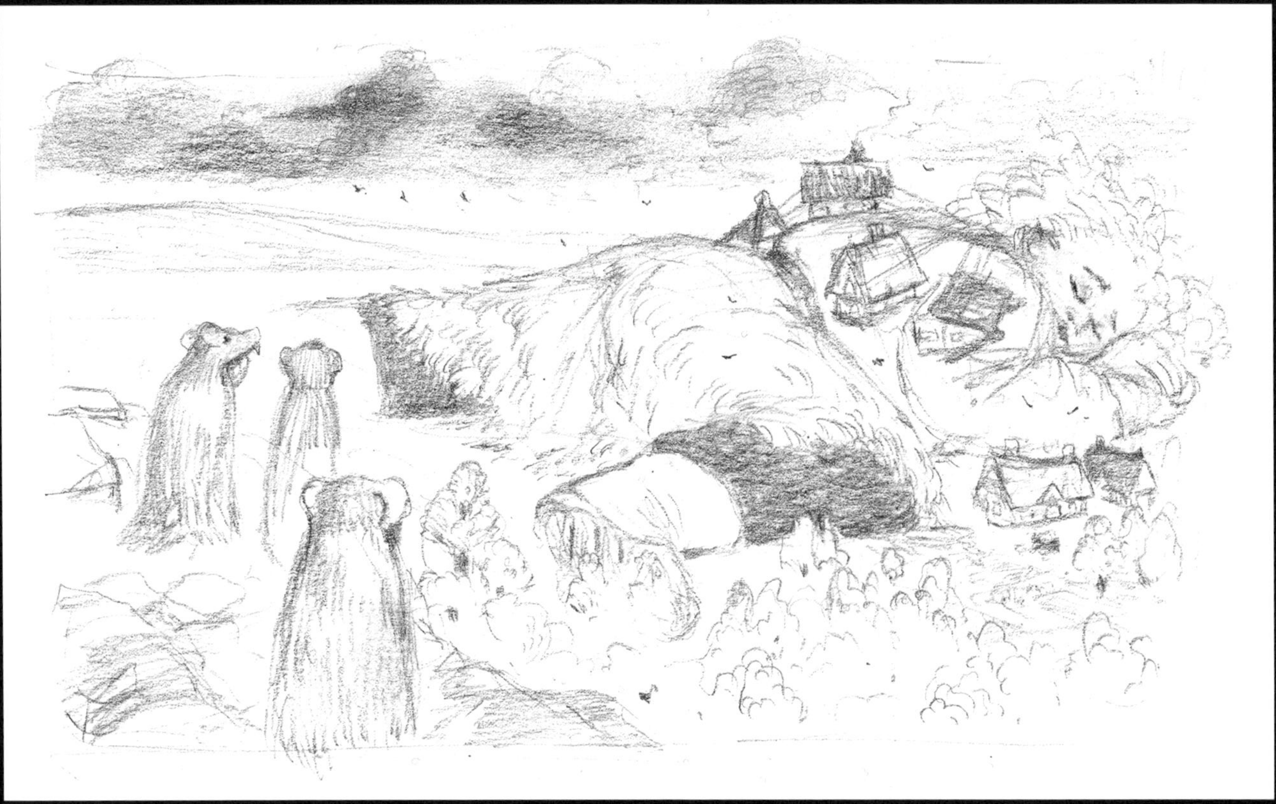

▲ A strong idea that I may take forward to the final illustration

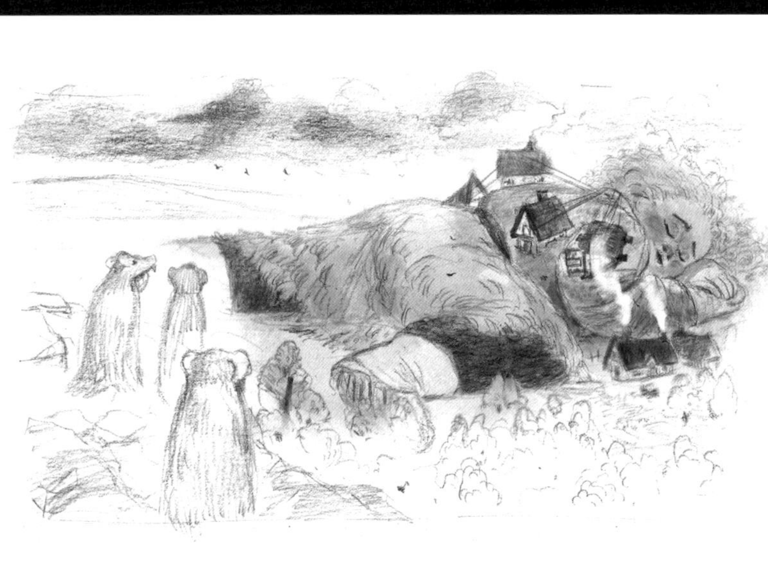

▲ Adding some base gray values to the sketch

11 STARTING THE VALUES

A little more volume will take the sketch to the next level. I use a base shade of gray, so I don't get tangled up with colors too soon – it's basic but effective. The sketch is still loose and open to experimentation, but from this point I must begin to focus everything on the mood of the final piece. I add gray values to the sketch as if I'm applying washes of ink. When your aim is to create an important, key scene, it's easy to get carried away, making the color and light effects too strong. Those effects may be striking, but they often do not help to convey the true emotion of the piece. So, even though I don't need to be precise yet, I still try to be smart. The decisions I make now will continue to be sculpted until the last moments of the illustration process.

12 SETTING THE MOOD

This image shows a young girl sleeping peacefully on a slightly cloudy day. I want there to be enough values present in the sky that clouds and colors will be visible, but they must not be too intense, or the sky will look dark, stormy, or nocturnal. If I use lighting that is too high-contrast, that feeling of tranquility will be lost. When we think of someone sleeping, two main lighting ideas usually come to mind: moonlight at night or sunlight in the morning. You may even think of an afternoon nap on a lazy day. These are ideas we can all relate to. In this case, I want to go with the soft light of morning, as if the sun has just risen and revealed the slumbering Goldilocks to the bears. The sunrise will create some striking colors and shapes in the sky, which will have a misty twilight feel, but the overall effect will not be too dark.

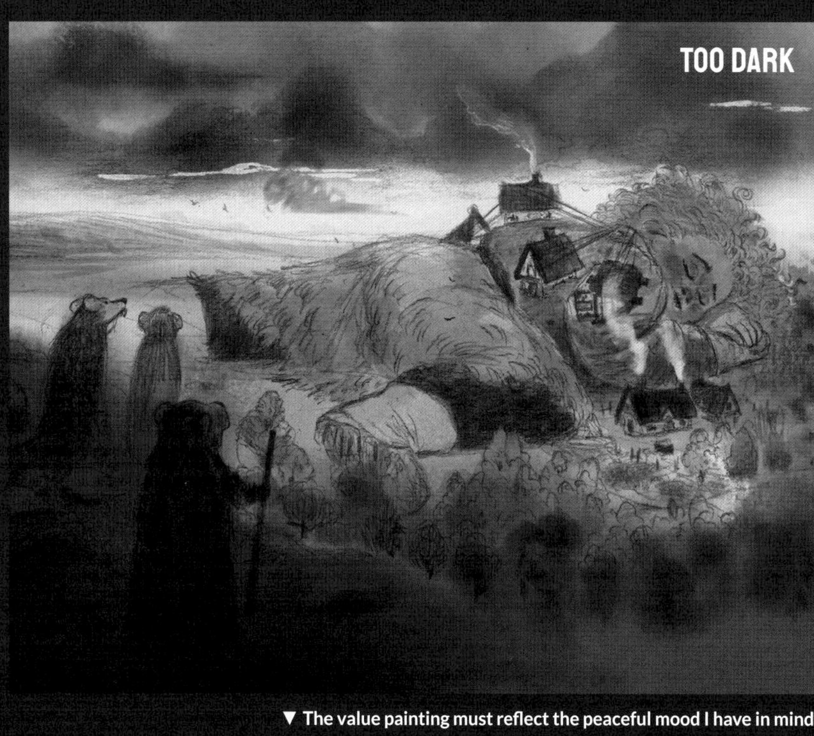

▼ The value painting must reflect the peaceful mood I have in mind

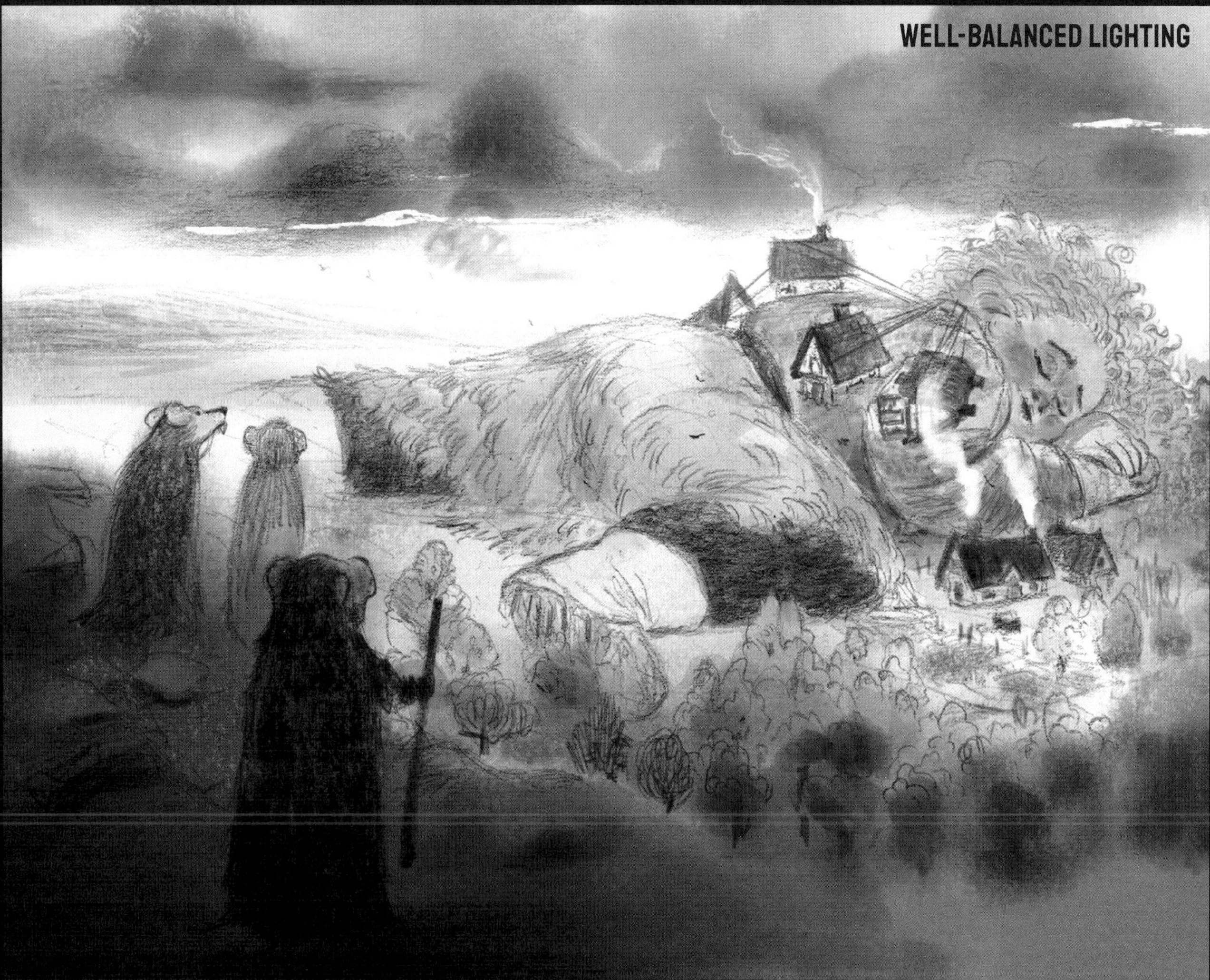

WELL-BALANCED LIGHTING

13 IMPROVING THE COMPOSITION

I take another look at the overall lighting and composition, testing a second round of values to see where I can improve the storytelling. I decide to mix a small drawing from step 09 with my main image, which gives the scene new life and solidity. The composition and visual impact are now much stronger. The desire to finish something in a hurry will always play against you when making decisions. Take your time, test different compositions and structures, or even start the drawing again until you find the option that best suits your story. Whether you are adding a new character, new object, or changing the lighting, everything is welcome. Even the old masters had several versions of their paintings, reworking as they went along!

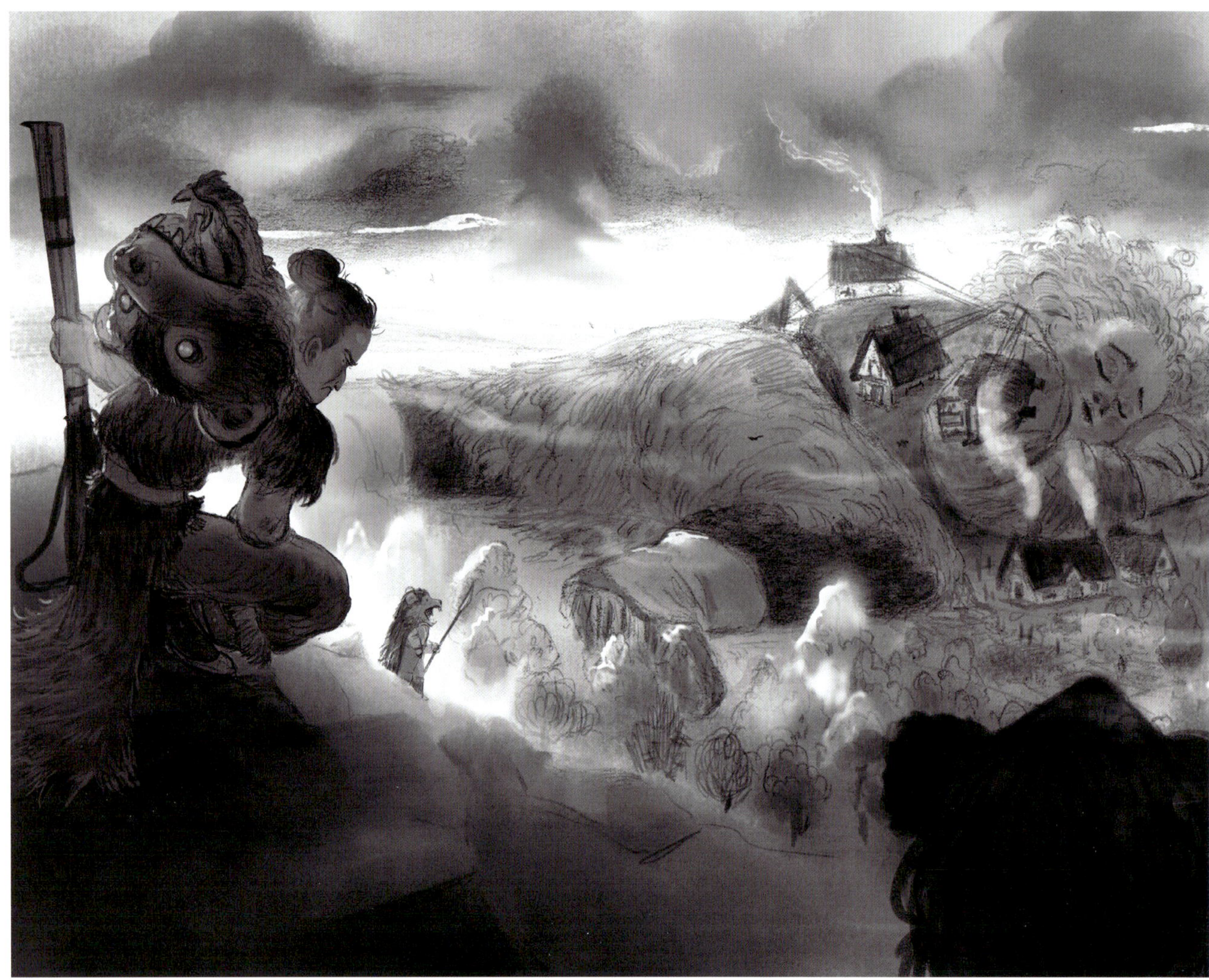

▲ Collaging in a character from a previous sketch gives the scene a boost

TESTING COLOR PALETTES

When trying to get to grips with color, a helpful exercise is sticking with a limited palette. For example, try blocking out mostly with red. Then repeat the process from scratch with a different color, such as blues or purples. Once you feel comfortable with those, why not try mixing the two ideas into one? Don't feel tied to rules – try to find your own way. There are tricks and methods for painting, but no established rule that will enable you to paint. Practice is the key!

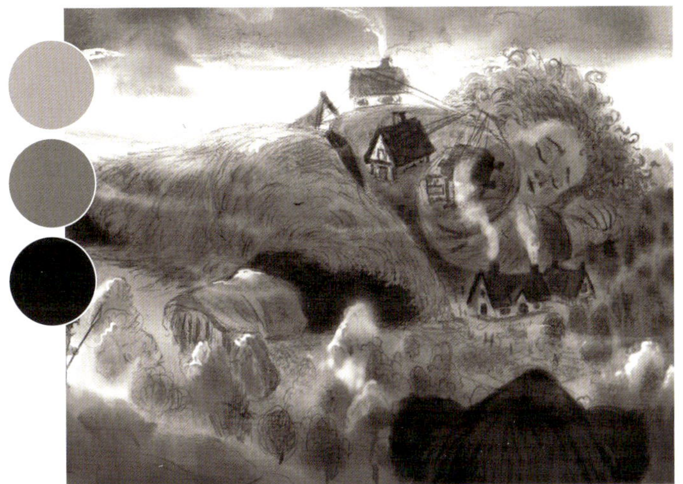

14 CHOOSING A COLOR PALETTE

Taking the first steps into color can be intimidating if you don't have much experience in that area. Choose a palette to play with and don't be afraid of making mistakes. However, no matter what palette you choose, "respect" the feeling you are trying to express. For example, if I were to add a dazzling summer sun to this scene, just because it's beautiful, it would detract from the image by prioritizing beauty over narrative and mood. The bottom left version is too cold and blue, so the warmth of the sun doesn't come through. I decide on a mix of warm and cool hues to fully capture the sunrise, golden hair, cold climate, and green forest. With this palette, I have a wide range of possible ways to add more details, and my chosen narrative is maintained.

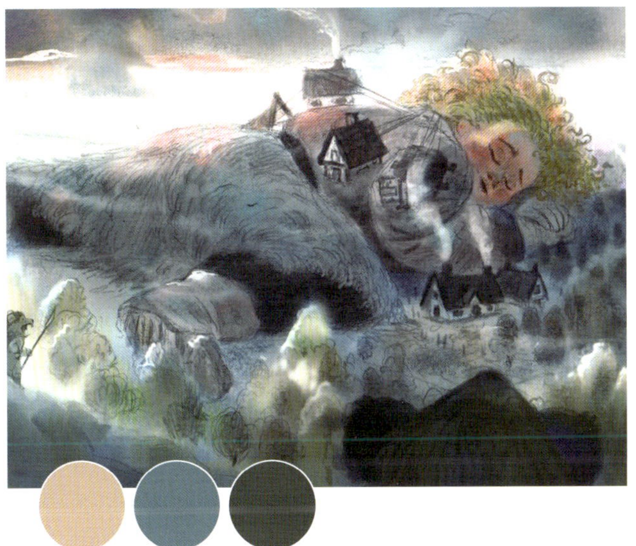

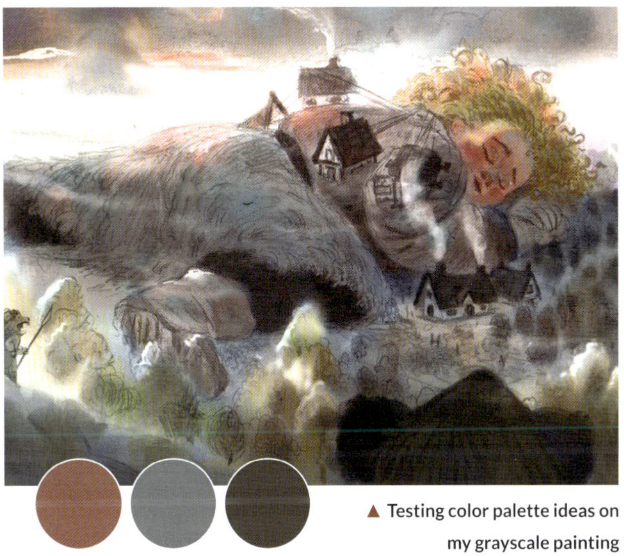

▲ Testing color palette ideas on my grayscale painting

15 FINAL COLOR PALETTE

I roughly paint up the whole scene, making sure to enrich it with color variations that add interest and subtlety to my chosen palette. The dawn sky includes grays, blues, pinks, purples, and peaches. The forest contains blues, greens, and browns. The strongest values and sharpest details are focused in the foreground, especially on the main hunter, whose bear pelt is a more saturated red-brown that makes him stand out from his misty surroundings.

► This is the base color painting that I will build upon for the final

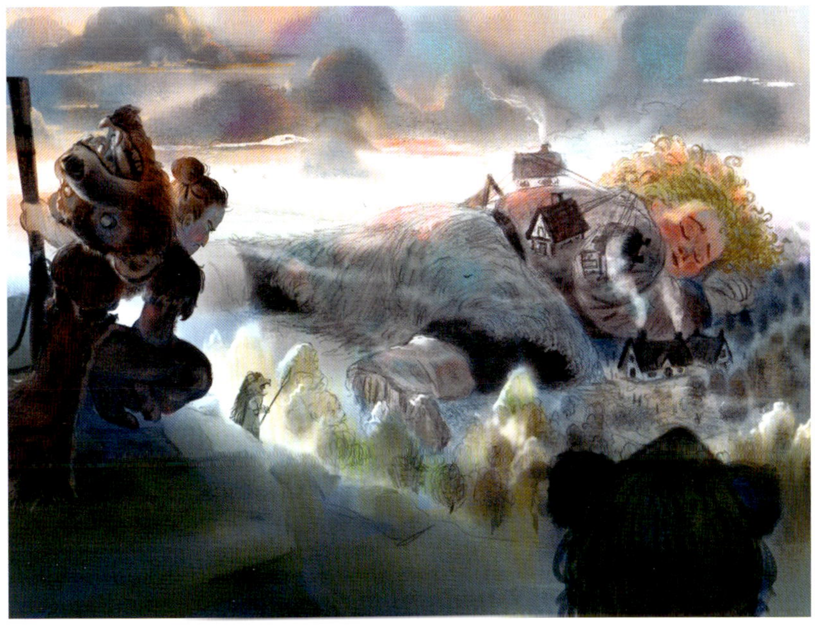

16 MAKING CORRECTIONS

Even at this stage of painting, you can add, modify, or adjust whatever is necessary. Color can give us a new vision of what we saw in the pencil and grayscale sketches; something that seemed functional before might suddenly no longer work. Each stage of the process brings its potential problems and solutions.

Here I eliminate the right bear's snout, as it didn't work with the perspective, even though it helped as a visual narrative element by pointing toward the sleeping giant. I replace it with subtle lines of light and shadow, using the forest paths to guide the eye instead. Light and dark can be applied in an infinite number of ways to suit your scene. If you ever feel stuck for a solution, I recommend looking at old film noir cinema – there you will find the best visual examples to enjoy and learn from.

▶ Building up the painting and finding areas that need revision

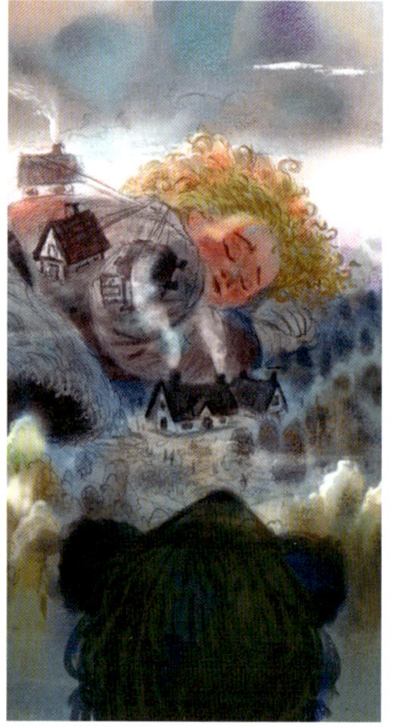

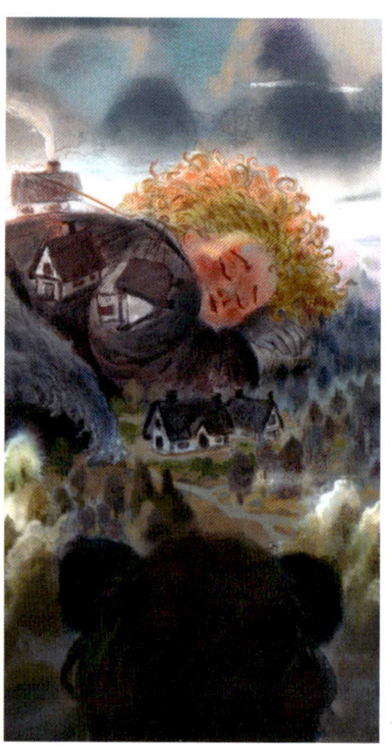

STYLE VERSUS CONTENT

There is no one way to finish an illustration, painting, sculpture, or drawing – it all depends on your style. However, there is no one style to follow, either! It's something you must keep consciously finding each step of the way. If you want a final image that has a precise style, but you keep placing things randomly on the page, your result will be confusing, frustrating, and not what you hoped for. All your decisions must aim toward clearly telling the story. In this case, we're almost doing the opposite, taking a well-known classic and twisting it into something different and less obvious, but even so the connection between the new and old versions must be coherent. The content of your illustration is most important and will lead your style decisions.

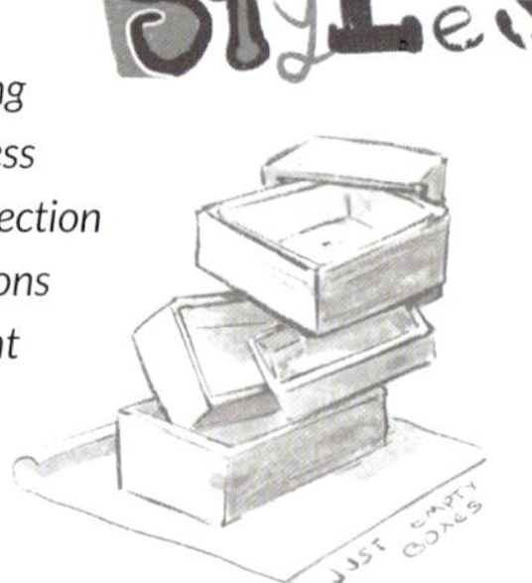

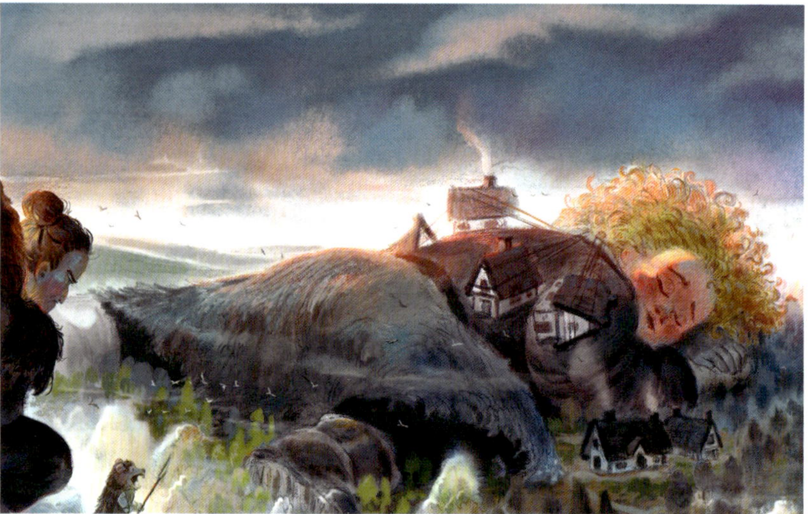

17 REFINING THE ATMOSPHERE

The cloud shapes are looking a little too busy, so I smooth over the upper sky with the same blue-gray, peach, and purple hues. This creates better contrast with the warm light on the horizon, where the sunrise is chasing away the dark sky. I add more atmospheric effects to the rest of the image, such as morning mist threading through the forest, flocks of tiny birds that help show Goldilocks' scale, and smoke coming from the chimneys of the houses. The finished image is taking shape.

◀ Revising the sky and adding small atmospheric details

18 FINISHING TOUCHES

For the final stage, I raise the contrast a little – it's like the finishing touch of varnish on a painting. I make sure the textures, lighting tones, and value separation are all clear. A layer of mist in the forest helps the silhouette of the right bear to stand out from the dark trees. Some extra refinements to Goldilocks' face, curly hair, and houses around her help to support that area as the key focal point of the illustration.

► **Final refinements for a clearer read of the characters**

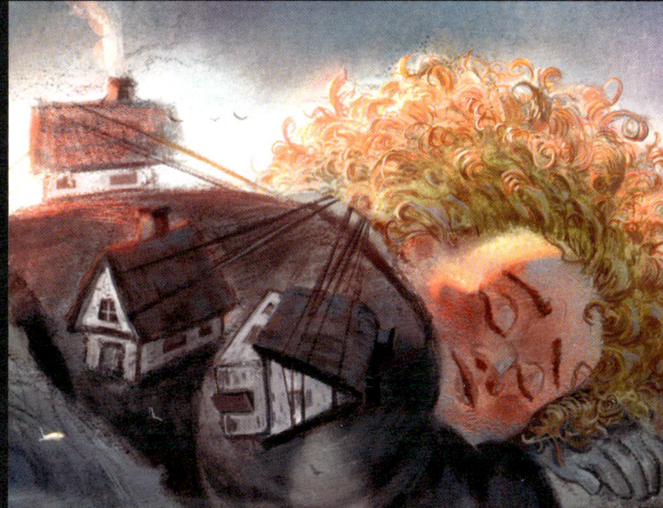

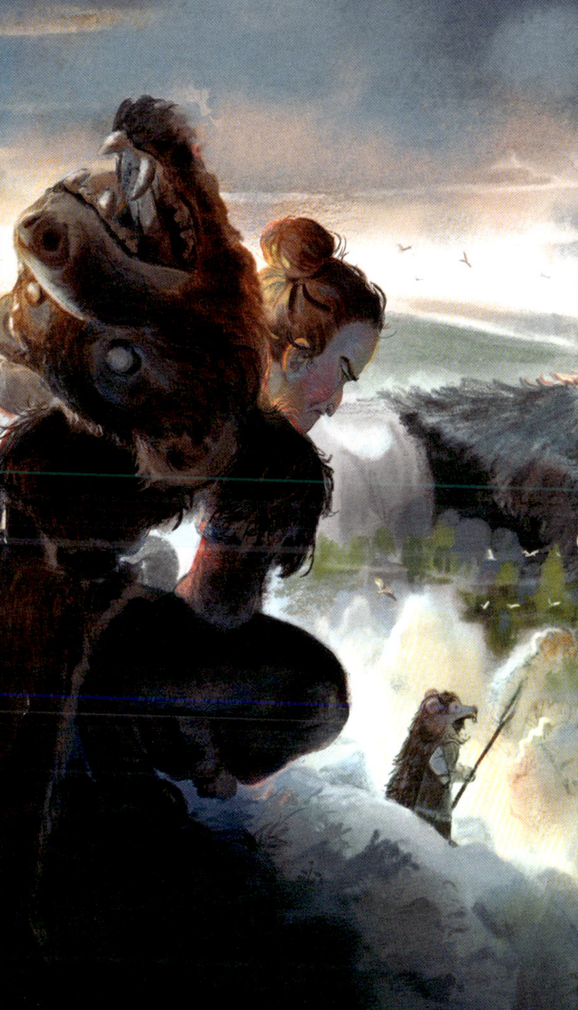

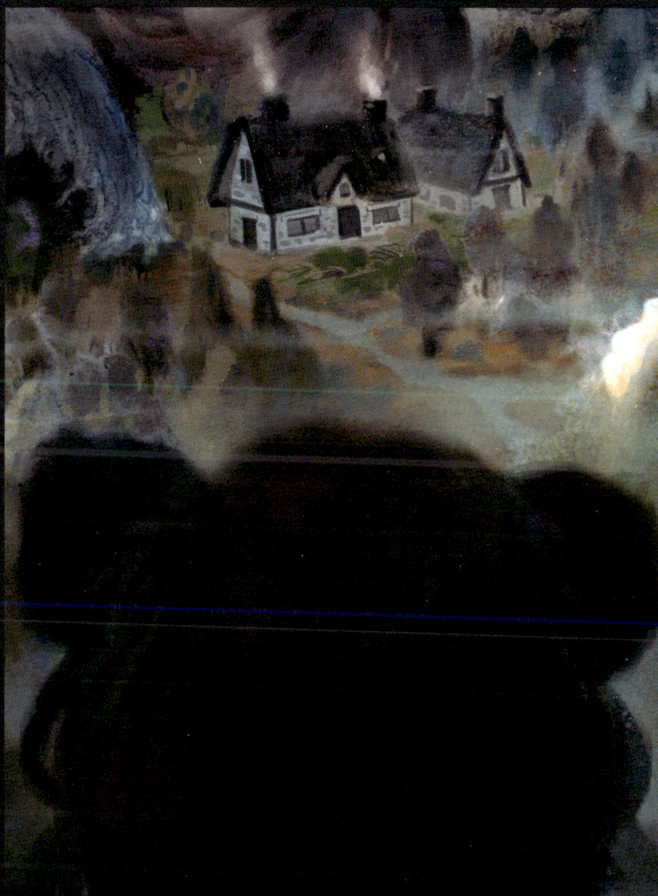

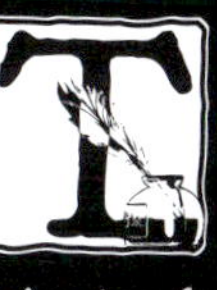

This little adventure is a process to be repeated over and over again, every time you want to go down a new path with a new image. I kept some layers of the original story, but gave it a fresh twist without going too far. The connection between the original tale and my version is still clear and coherent – the idea of an innocent giant who steals people's homes isn't too far removed from a little girl who breaks into houses. The bears are still the wronged party in this story, even though other aspects of their role and appearance have changed. When telling a story that we all know, finding a personal point of view to tell it from is what will make your version unique. Now take another classic and give it a stir!

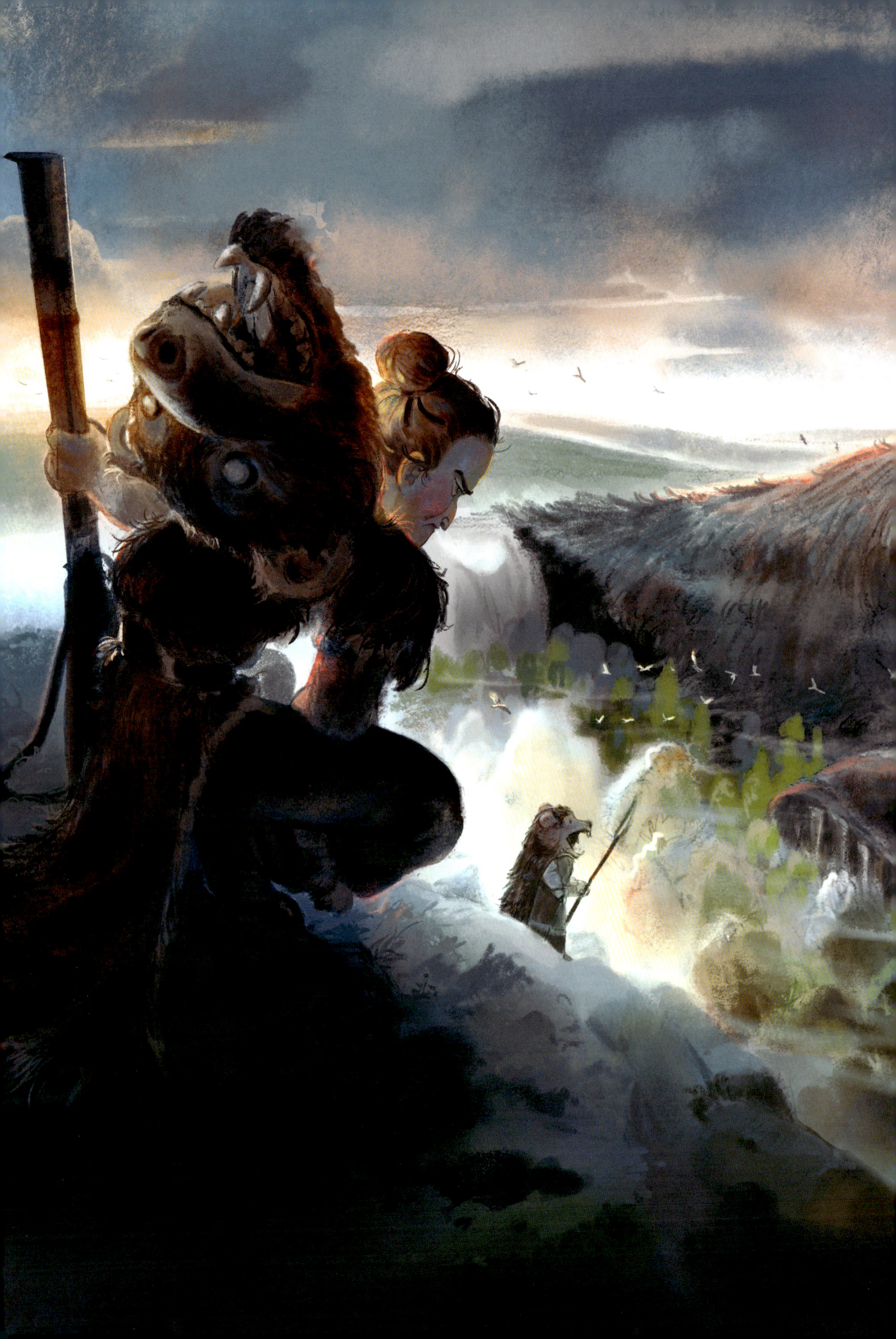

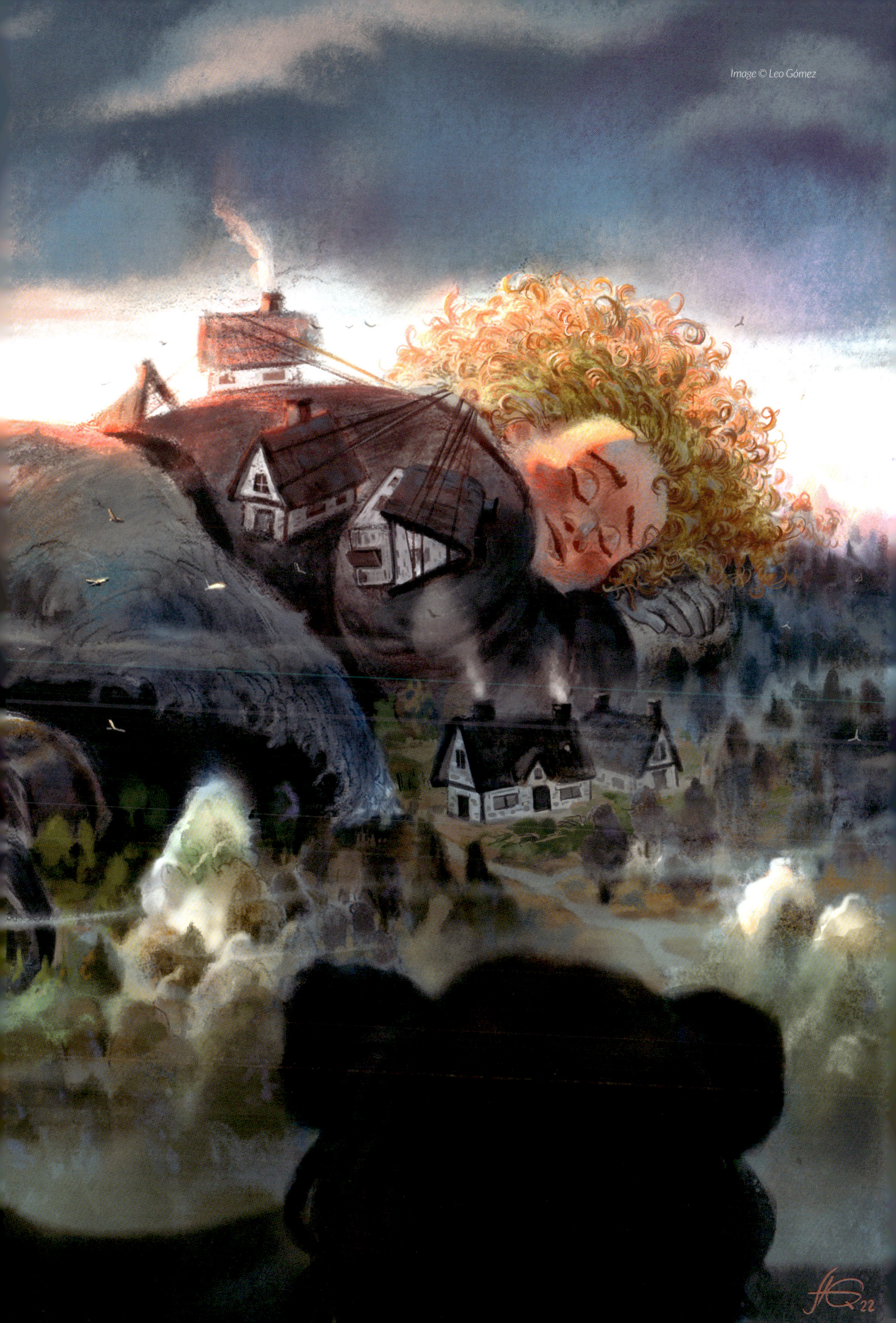

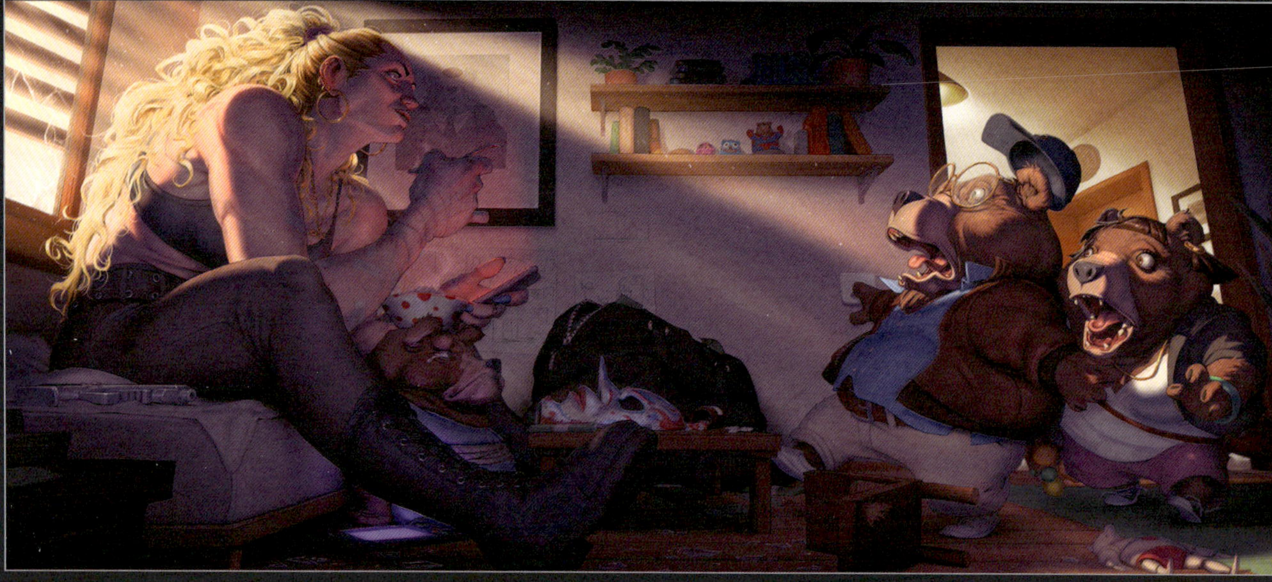

"Goldi the Gangster." Image © Leroy Steinmann

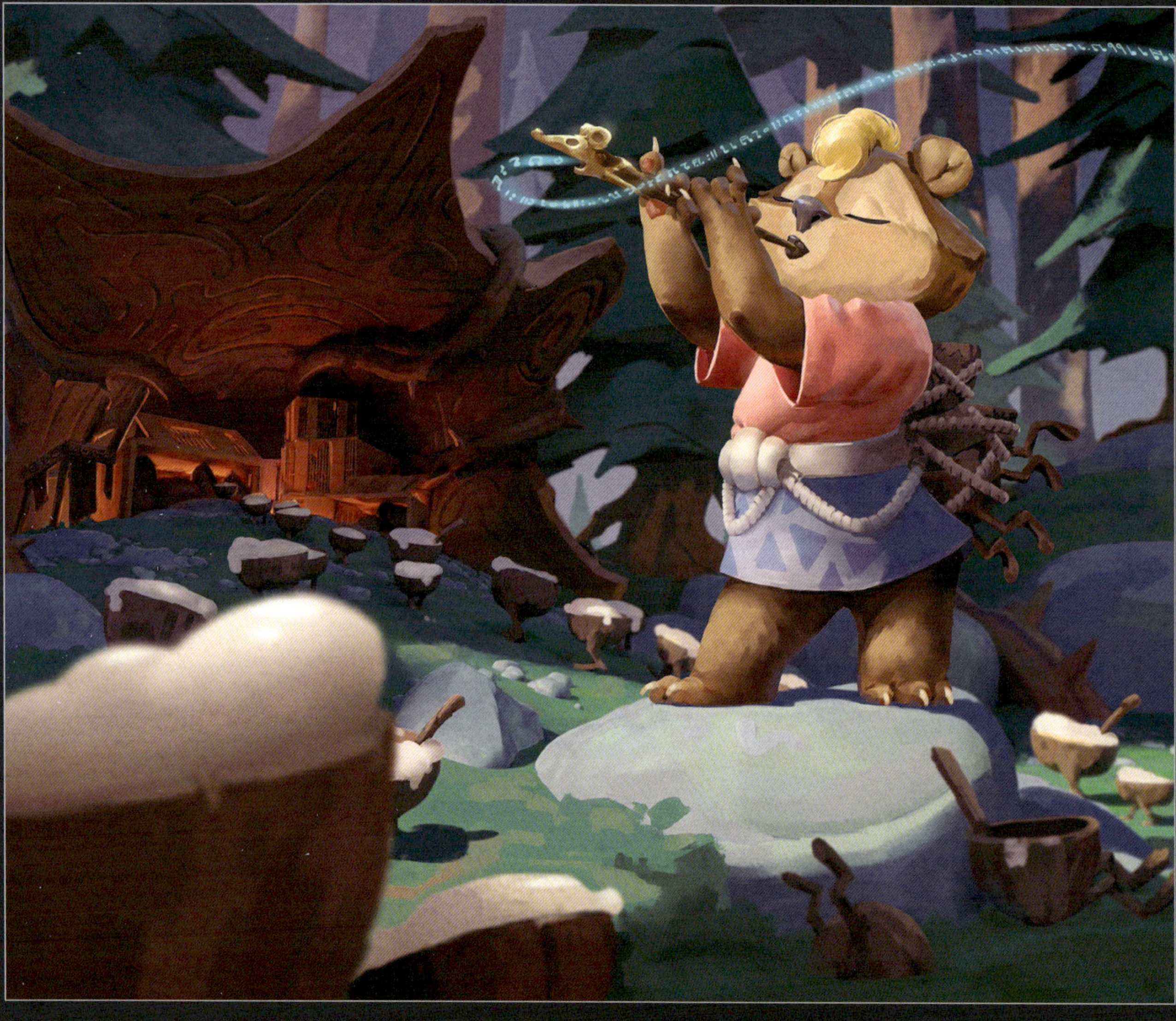

"Goldilocks the Greedy Bear." Image © Tony "Eight" Camehl

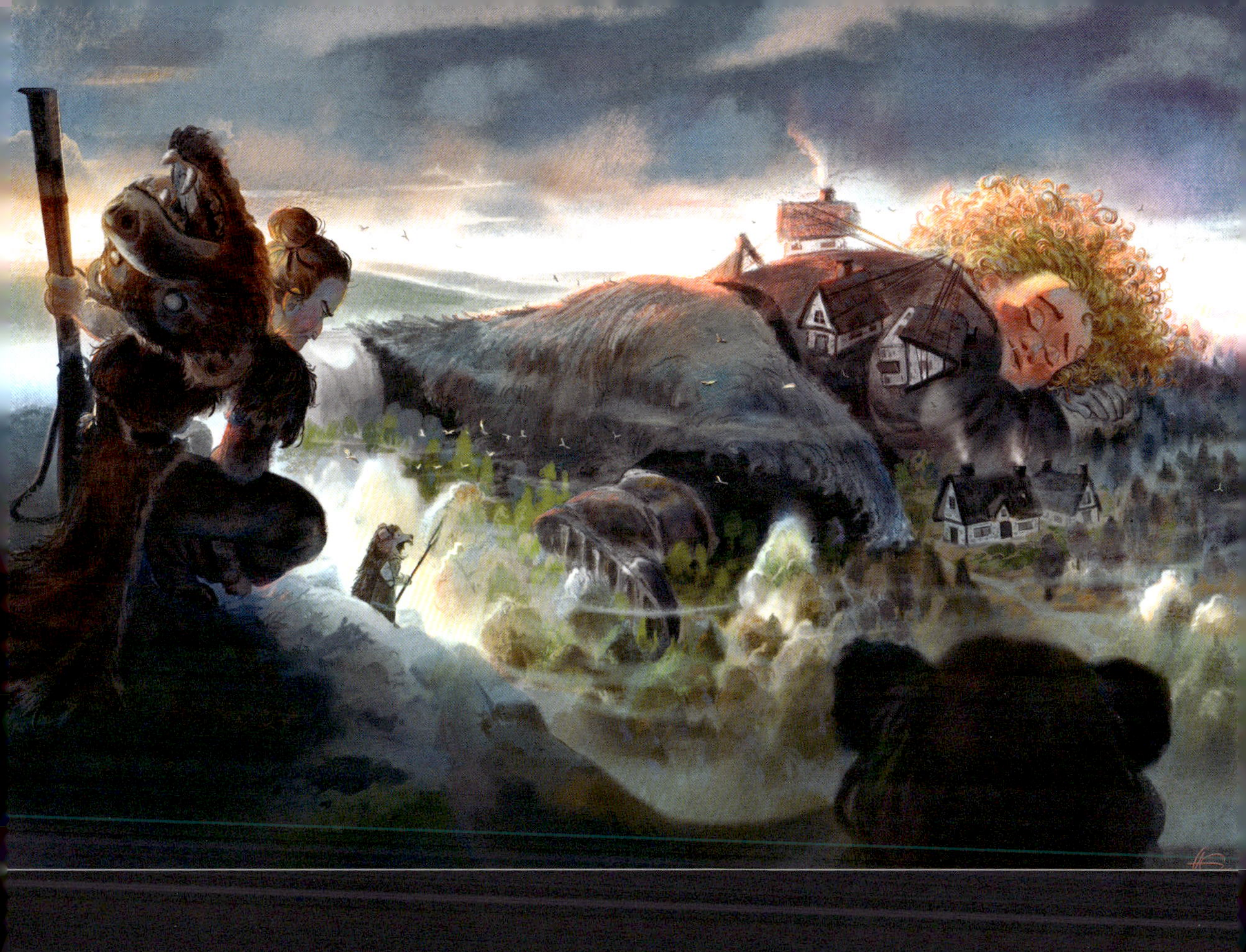

GOLDILOCKS AND THE THREE BEARS

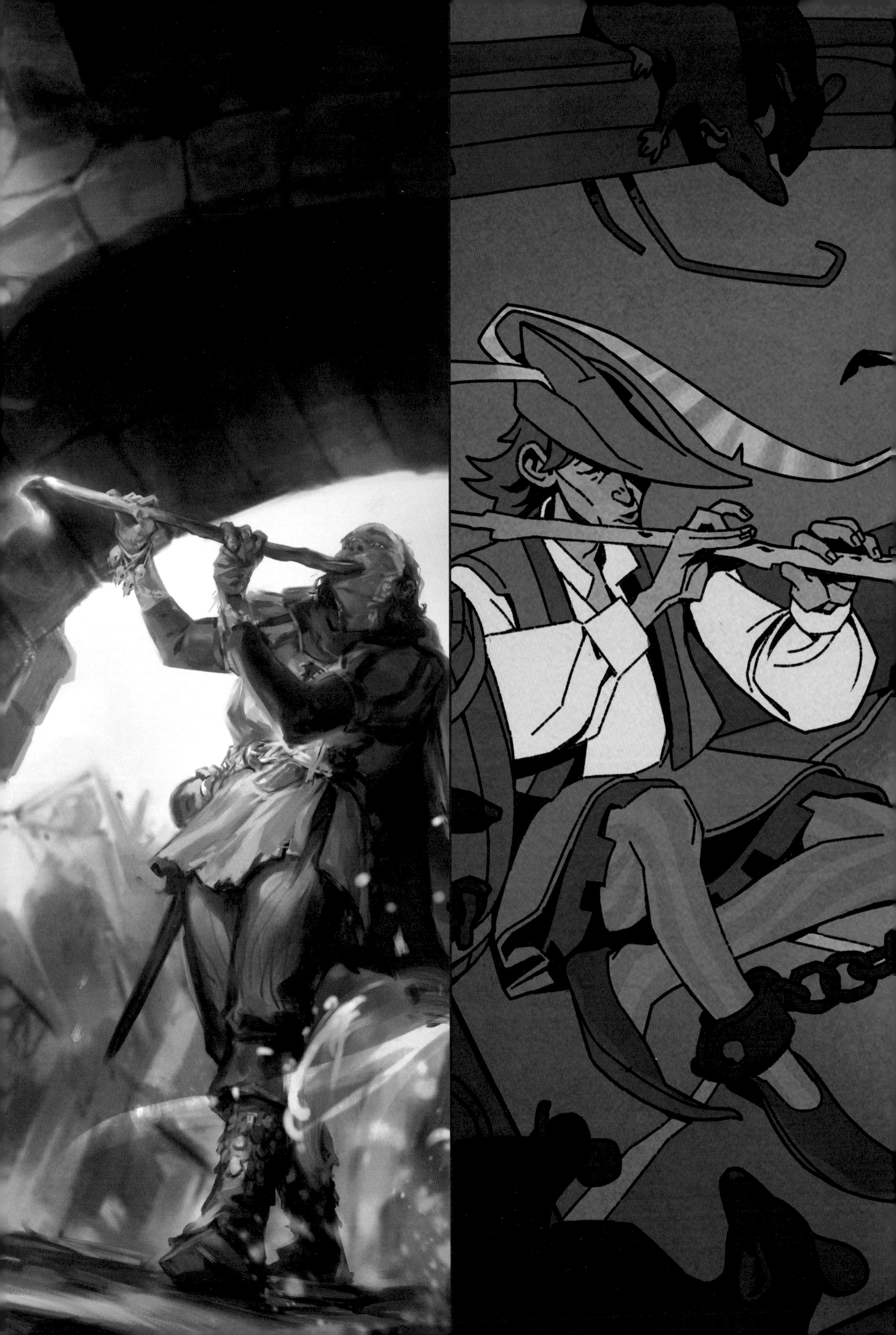

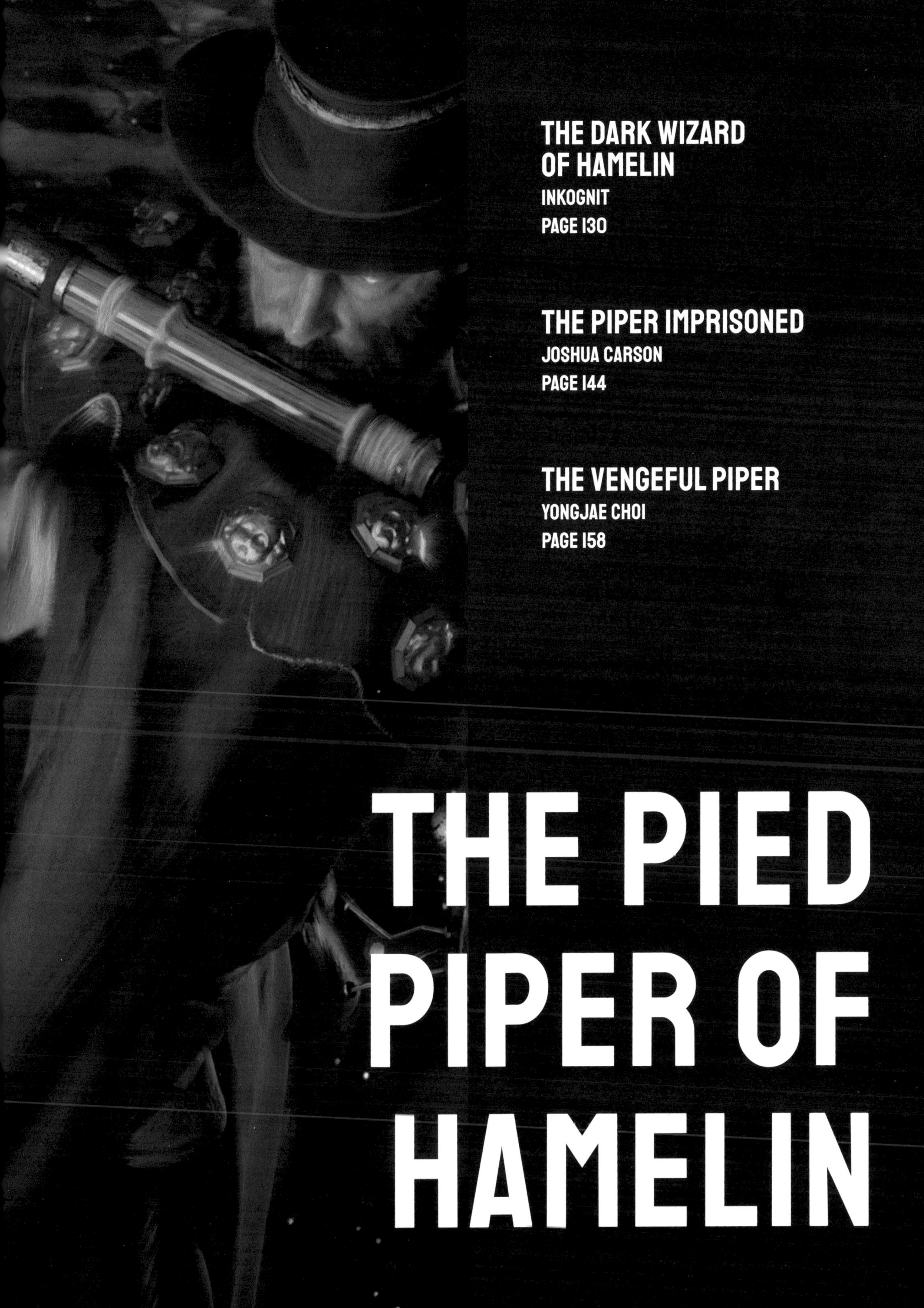

THE PIED PIPER OF HAMELIN

THE DARK WIZARD OF HAMELIN

BY INKOGNIT

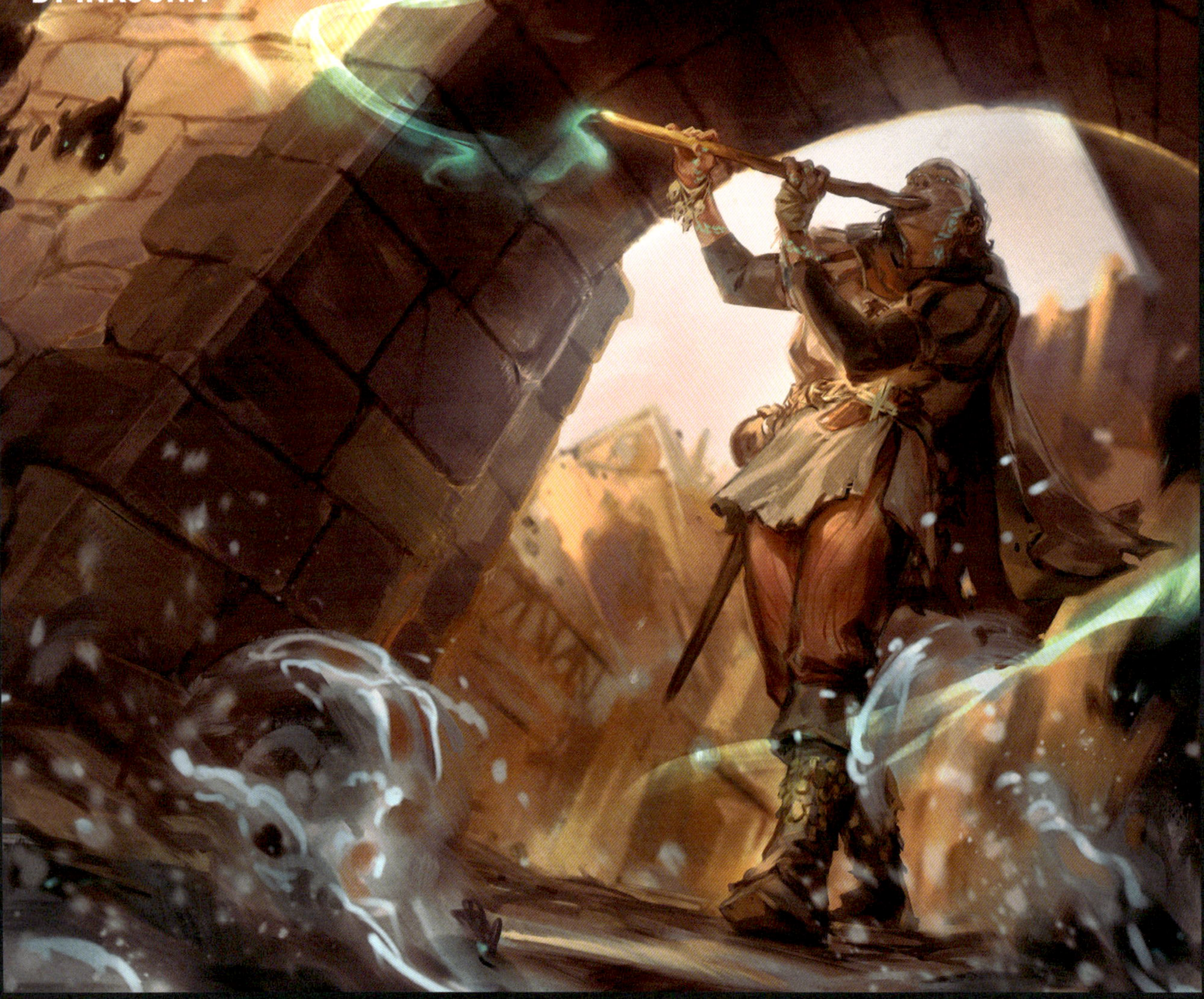

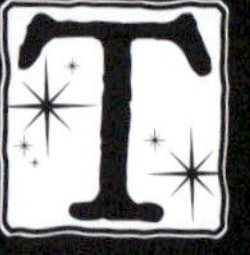

The Pied Piper of Hamelin is an iconic character of German legend and one open to many interpretations. Some versions of the tale paint the piper as quite a sympathetic character: a helpful wanderer in jolly clothes who saves the town of Hamelin but is cheated out of fair payment, causing him to teach the selfish townsfolk a lesson. He does this in quite a horrifying fashion: leading the town's children away and into a mountain, which closes forever behind them. This has led some to interpret the piper as a metaphor for death, illness, or emigration, visiting a town and taking away its children. It is this more serious tone that we will explore in this chapter, focusing on the dark powers of this mysterious stranger who can seemingly bend hundreds of minds to his will.

▼ More very early, quick idea sketches

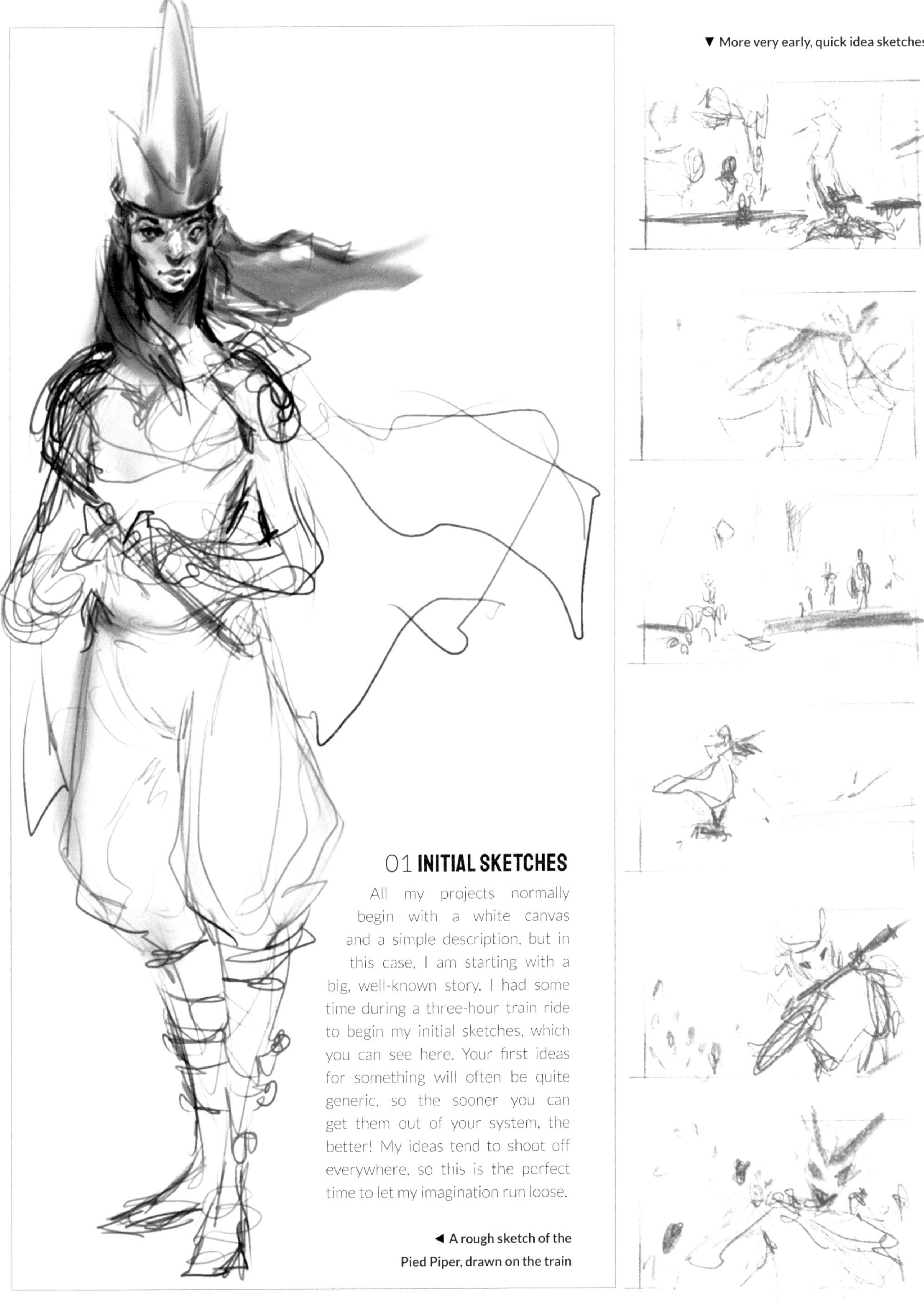

01 INITIAL SKETCHES

All my projects normally begin with a white canvas and a simple description, but in this case, I am starting with a big, well-known story. I had some time during a three-hour train ride to begin my initial sketches, which you can see here. Your first ideas for something will often be quite generic, so the sooner you can get them out of your system, the better! My ideas tend to shoot off everywhere, so this is the perfect time to let my imagination run loose.

◀ A rough sketch of the Pied Piper, drawn on the train

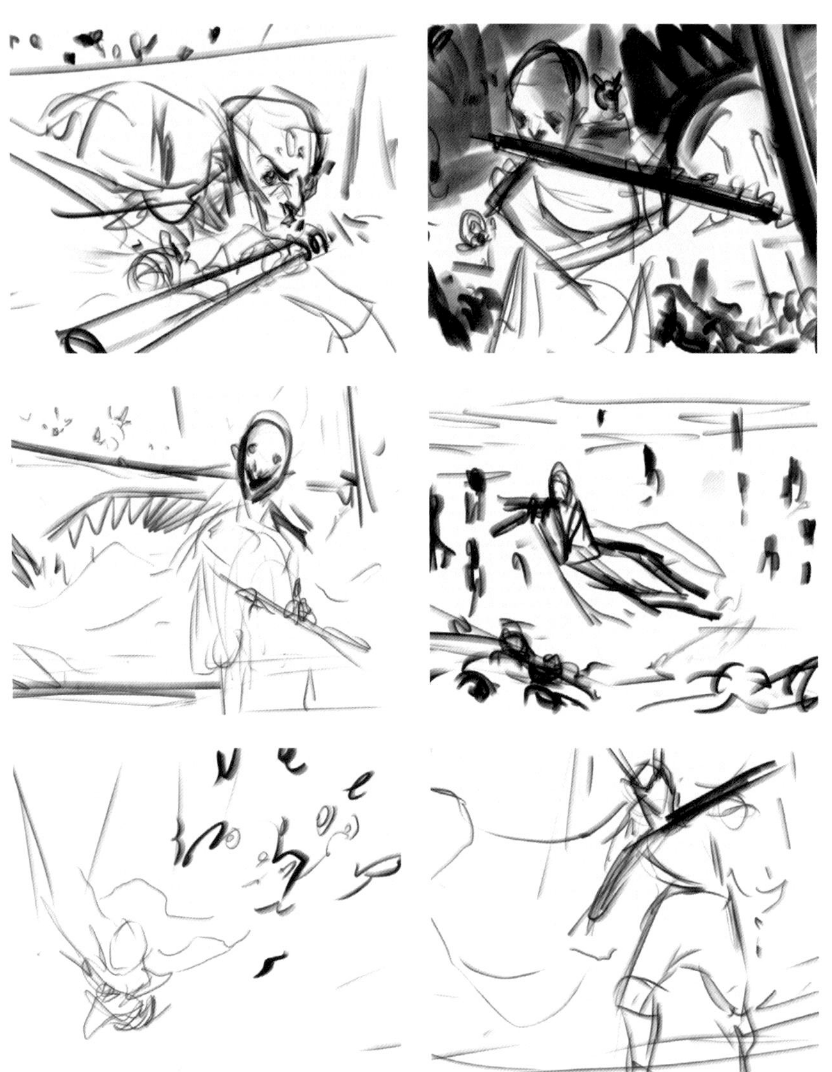

02 CHOOSING A MOMENT

I toy with some amusing ideas, such as a piper who plays so badly that Hamelin's windows crack, but there is one main part of the story that stands out to me: when the piper leads the rats to drown in the river. Even after reading through the story once more, that moment stands out as having potential for a powerful illustration. Though it is usually only mentioned in passing, glossing over the morbid details, it's a dark and dramatic event that establishes the piper's irresistible power.

I typically draw between six and nine composition sketches to generate ideas for an image, so I do that here, all of them focused on the piper guiding the rats to their death. Some of them are still quite generic, though there is one at the bottom-left where the piper is underwater, controlling the rats' undead bodies – though that's maybe a bit *too* dark!

◀ Loosely sketching more ideas and story moments

03 QUICK 3D BASE

I am keen to explore the idea of a scene with an arched bridge by a river, and the quickest way for me to do that is with some 3D. I used to use 3D tools frequently, but over time began to focus on a more painterly approach. It is only recently that I began to give 3D another shot, and this is a perfect occasion to use it, though you can achieve similar results with 2D techniques, or even by making and photographing your own miniature scene for reference. The free, open-source 3D software Blender is a powerhouse that does a bit of everything, allowing me to build a really simple scene that will help me find my composition. I want something dramatic, which leads me to this low camera angle.

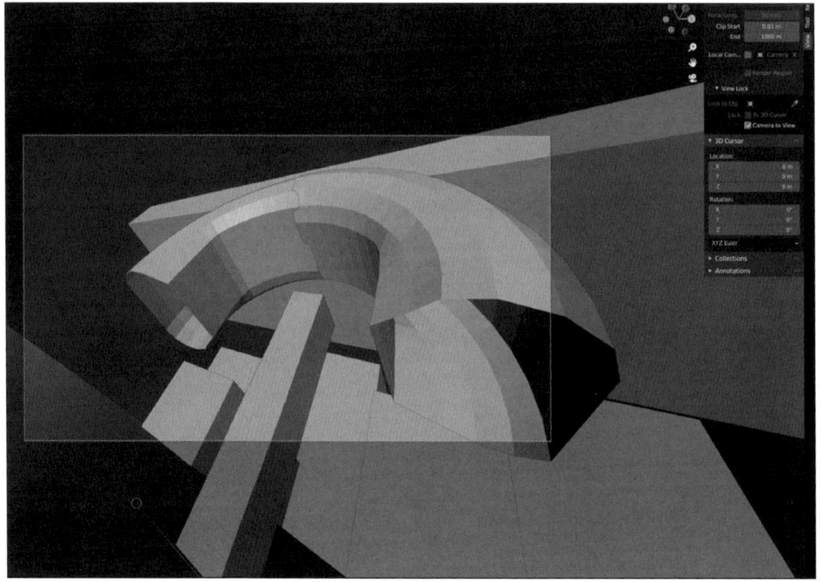

▲ Modeling a simple 3D scene and finding the best angle

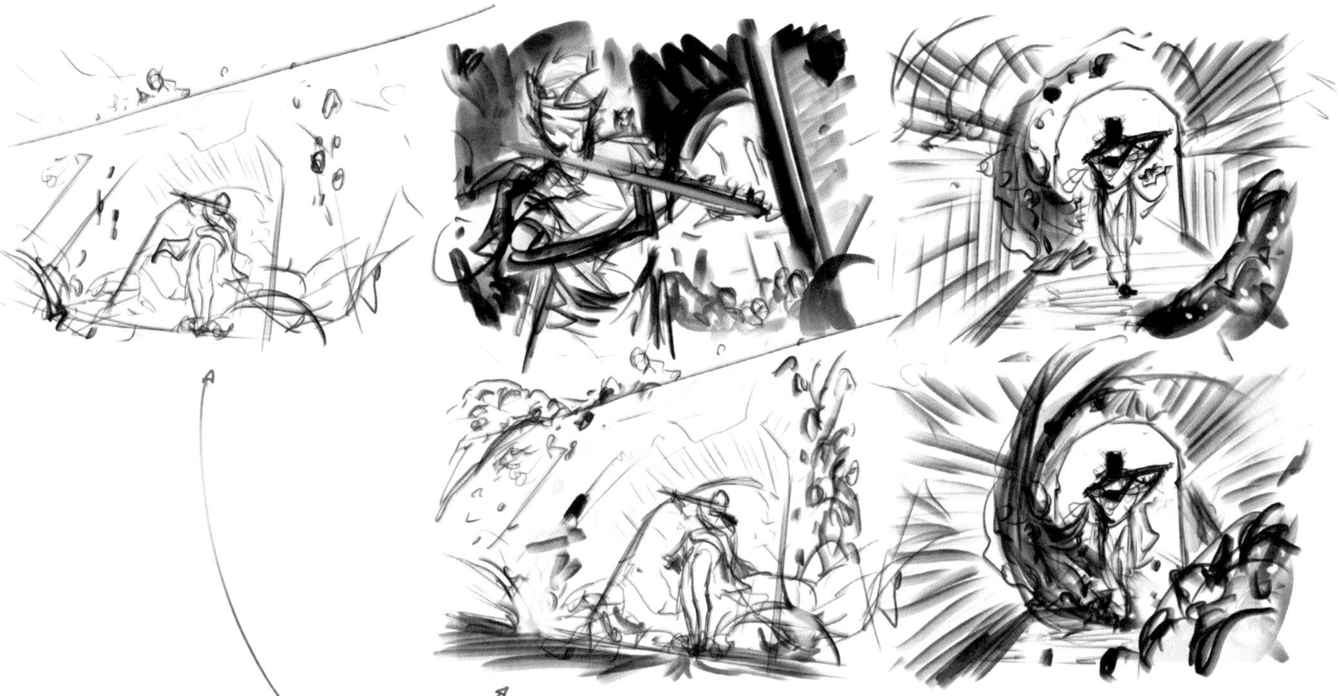

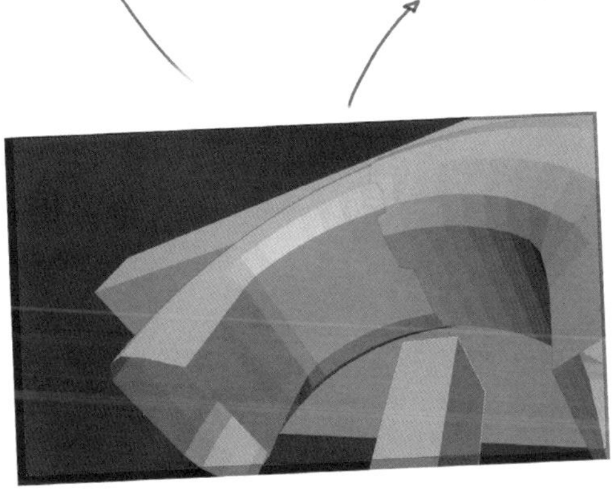

▲ Revising my composition ideas with the dramatic arch in mind

04 FRAMING THE SCENE

After Blender, I return to the composition sketches I made earlier, as I want to further develop the Pied Piper's story. In the original tale, he is a mysterious, wandering figure whose mesmerizing power is not really explained, but I like the idea of him being a mage or wizard. This wizard piper could lure massive numbers of rats, and eventually children, out of town with the power of his musical spells. The framing of the scene will be key, as I want to place the character somewhere that will allow for high contrast and a strong silhouette. This very low angle will enable me to frame the piper beneath the arch and against the sky.

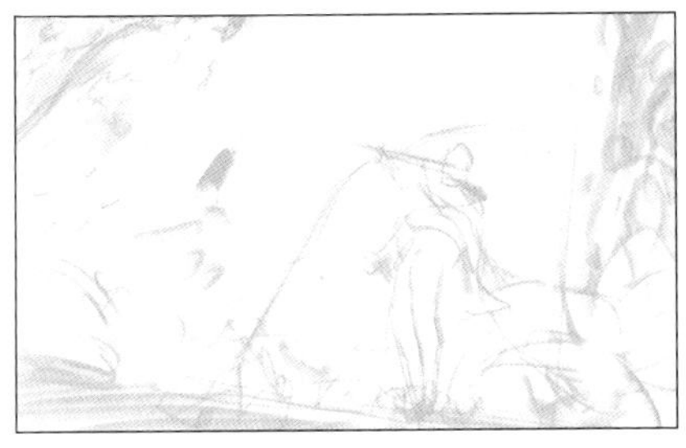

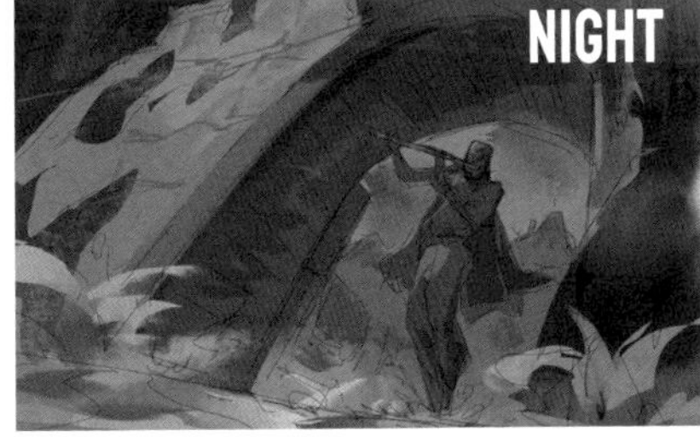

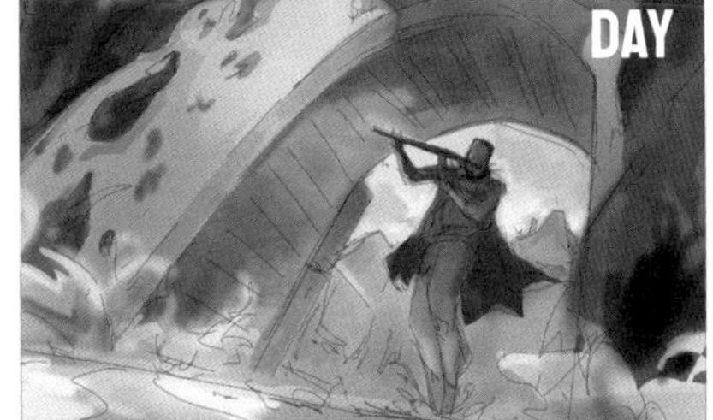

05 DAY OR NIGHT?

In my mind's eye, I have formed the idea of an epic final image requiring dramatic lighting, so I test two versions to find the right lighting for the story. The original tale is a dark one, and has been interpreted as a metaphor for deadly plagues, so a nighttime scene could really suit this tone. However, once I actually compare the lighting tests, it is clear that a daytime scene creates much better visual contrast for the character. I should discard the nighttime idea, even though its mood is fitting, because the darkness lessens the impact of the character.

▲ Comparing the effectiveness of the scene with night and day lighting

06 SUNSET LIGHTING

I'm still attached to the idea of a nocturnal scene! I make color tests comparing day and night. Night is often portrayed in blues and purples, but I have a soft spot for green lighting. Green often symbolizes poison and sickness, which would fit the story. Daytime, with the blue sky and sunshine, is too bright, almost cheerful. I realize that a sunset version, halfway between the two, speaks more to me. It's lighter than night, but still dramatic. The way the light bounces off the stone wall, framed by the dark rats on either side, functions perfectly for my concept.

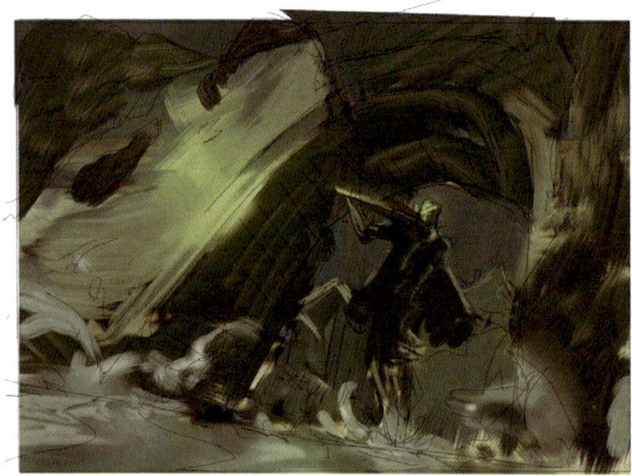

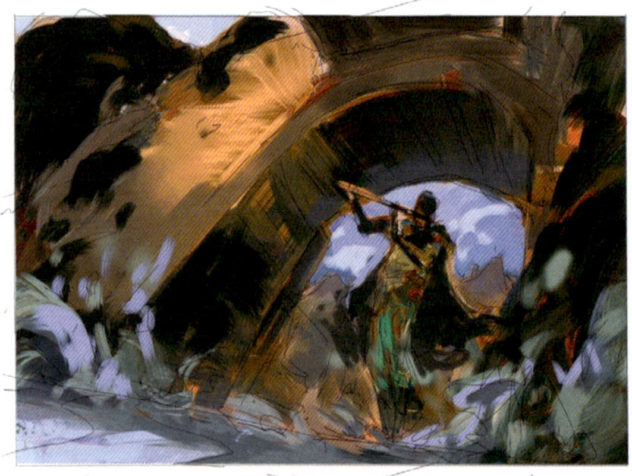

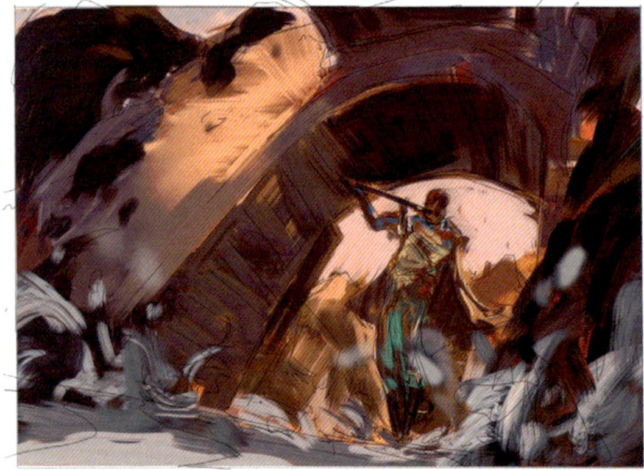

▲ A sunset scene is a perfect compromise between night and day

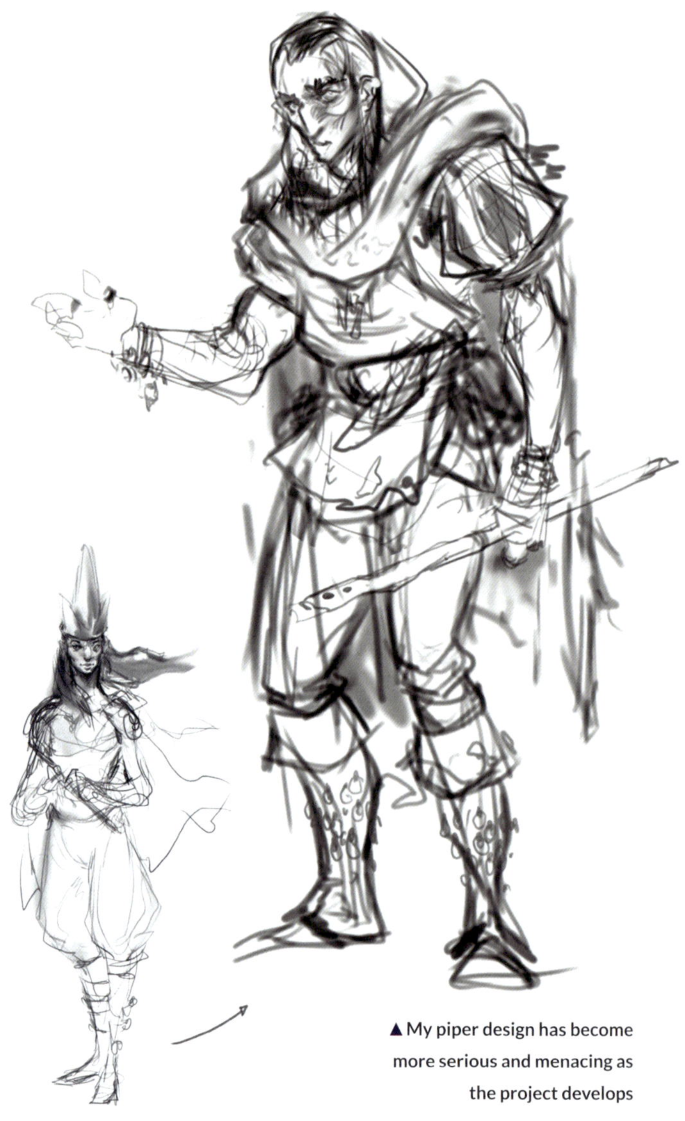

▲ My piper design has become more serious and menacing as the project develops

07 THE PIPER'S DESIGN

Now that I have decided the overall mood for the piece, I return to the main character and dig deeper into the concept of him. I am torn between the piper being a wizard or mage, and being a magical shapeshifter with rat-like features. Perhaps he could actually transform into a mass of rats, leading Hamelin's infestation out of town from within the pack, like a horde of lemmings. But I decide that the image of a human piper, with his iconic "pied" clothing, is too essential to the story to miss!

Many traditional illustrations of the piper depict him with a slightly comical appearance, but I give my piper more of a shady, suspicious look. His clothes are tattered and bitten by the masses of rats he has charmed. His boots are decorated with coins that jingle as he goes around playing his flute and collecting his payments. The flute is a simple instrument that looks like a rough wooden wand. Comparing this with my very first sketch of the piper, you can see how deciding on a darker story has influenced my design of the character.

08 POSE REFERENCE

Another thing I try to apply to my workflow is really taking the time to study what I want from an image and find the proper references for it. Reference is key to making a better piece. If you cannot find the perfect reference material for a pose, you can always make some yourself, like the photo I have taken of myself here. When taking reference photos of yourself, they will most often look silly, but I assure you that they will help throughout the whole process. In this case, my reference photos will help me with the perspective, volumes, and values of the character, as well as with drawing his face.

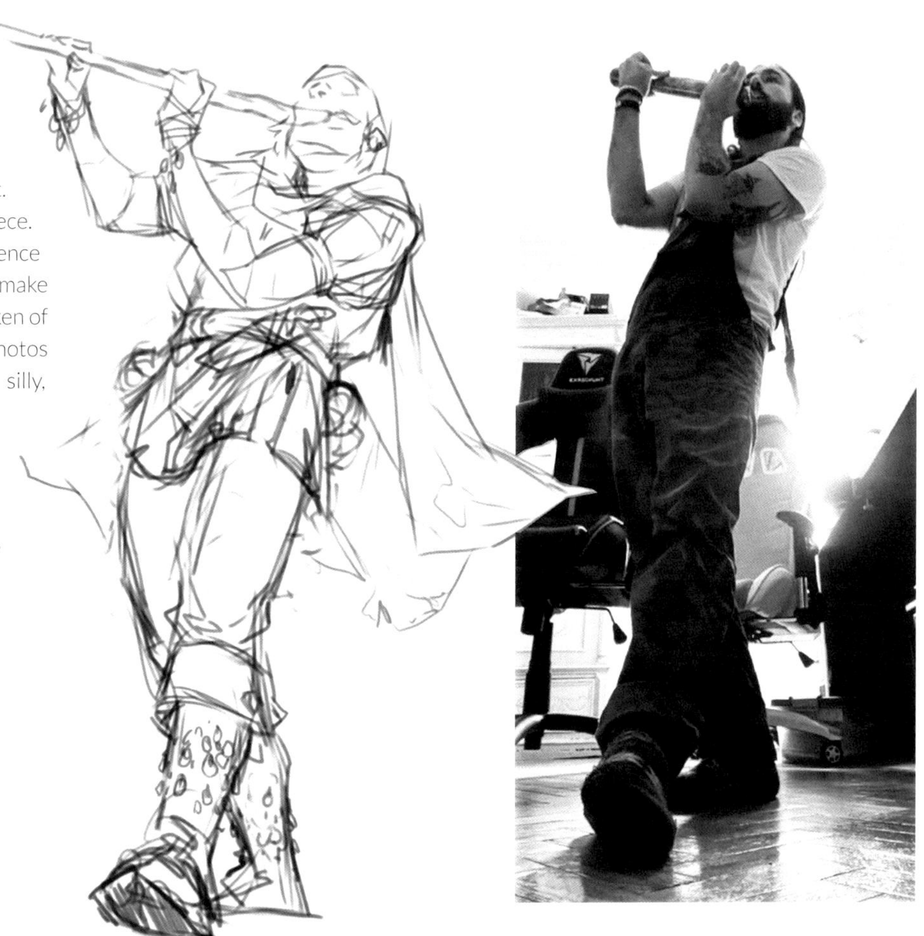

► Taking a reference photo of myself to help with the piper's pose

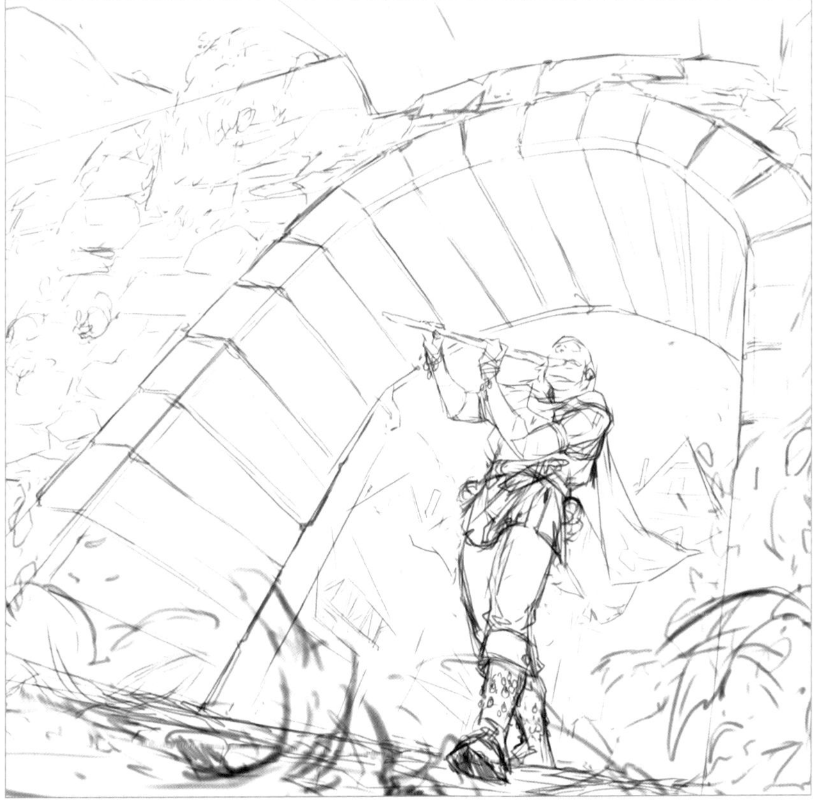

09 PLANNING THE SCENE

With the character perspective more or less solved, I can now focus on sketching out the final scene with the help of my 3D and photo references. I would usually draw a clearer version on top of this, but since I am aiming for a more painterly final piece, I just plan out the major shapes. This sketch is enough to help me figure out the background, middle ground, foreground, rats, and character. Most depictions of the story show the piper walking with the rats following obediently on the ground behind him, but I want this scene to emphasize the drama, action, and even horror of the rats plunging into the water.

◄ Sketching out the full scene, ready for painting

A DARK CANVAS

I often use dark borders when painting, as you can see from the rough edges on these pages. This margin makes it easier to adjust the image's framing or proportions. If a new composition idea comes to me, or a revision needs to be made, I can simply extend the painting outward. It's only at the final stages of painting, when the scene's composition is fully locked in, that I crop out the borders.

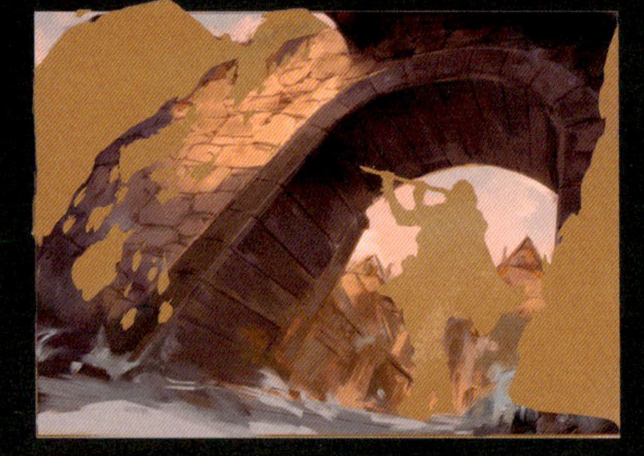

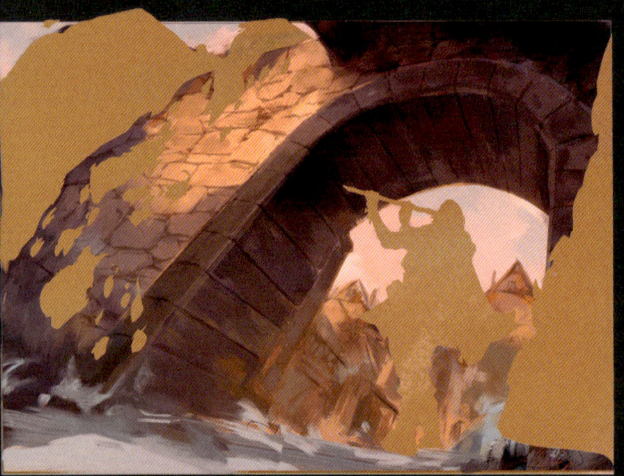

10 LOOSE BACKGROUND PAINTING

I work on each part of the image individually. You can see that the background already has some structure, though I keep my brushwork slightly loose so that it remains blurred and distant. I paint the wall and arch, building up the crevices and separate stones. The bricks, sky, and overall lighting have a warm tone that immediately establishes the "golden hour" time of day, showing the viewer that this scene takes place during sunset. Once these background parts are laid down, I can focus more easily on the piper and rats that drive the scene's narrative.

◀ Painting the backdrop first will allow me to focus on the character and action later

11 THE HYPNOTIZED RATS

From the start of this illustration, I knew I wanted to keep it as painterly as possible. I have no intention of detailing each rat and making them stand out one by one. It would be impractical to paint and distracting for the viewer, pulling attention away from the piper. Instead, I want the rats to look like a rushing mass – hundreds, even thousands of frenzied rats, jumping mindlessly and at full speed! In the background, I even depict them as one solid wave, blocking out the sky in their numbers. Picking out a few individual rats nearer to the viewer helps establish the animals without needing to detail each one. To ensure the action is legible, it's key to separate the rats from the wall, so I have them cast a cold shadow onto the warm stone to create some contrast.

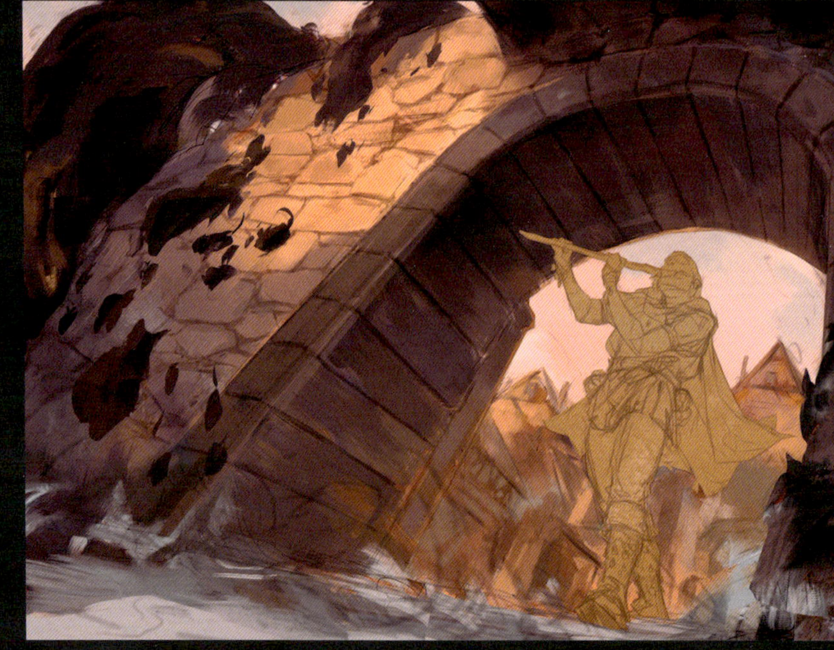

▲ The rats cascade down from the bridge, almost as one solid mass

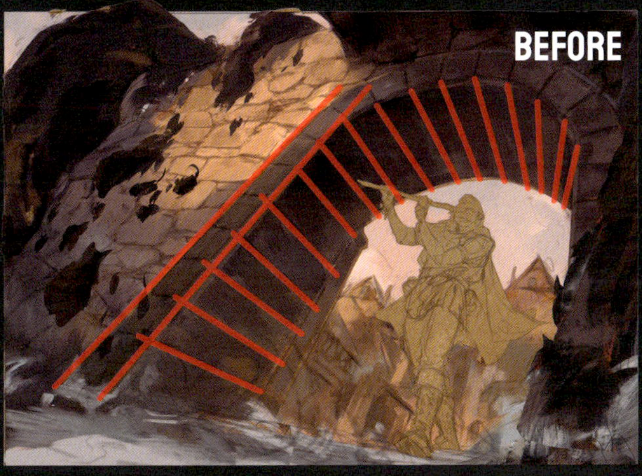

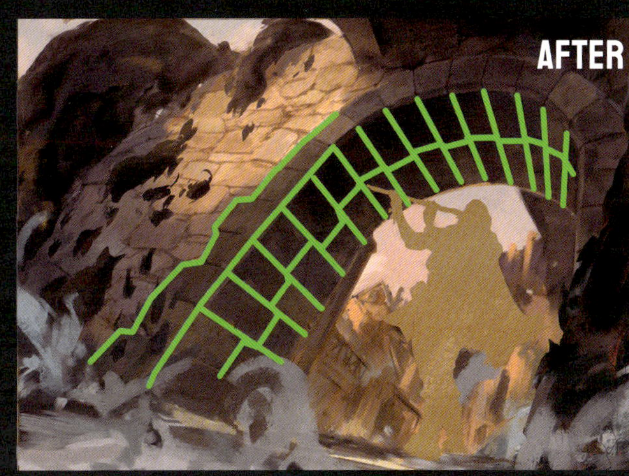

12 WEATHERED BRICKWORK

Every once in a while I stop working on an illustration, take a step back, and do a quick paintover on top of the image to test potential revisions. The first thing I notice is that the arch lacks structure behind it – it's too perfect and leaves a lot of unfocused, empty space around the piper. I add more structure to the architecture behind the bridge, helping to guide the viewer toward the piper's face. It also bothers me that the arch is so straight from top to bottom, using single stones that look too clean and perfect for this medieval town. I add variation by painting cracks and smaller individual bricks to break up the straight lines. The result feels far more authentic for the story's setting and makes the composition look more natural.

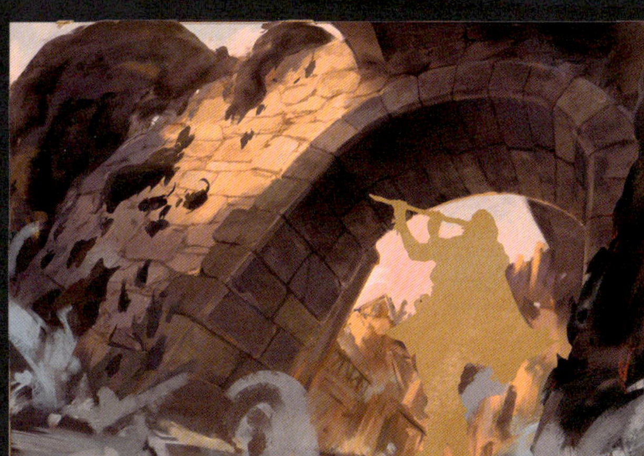

▲ Revising the bridge to make it more weathered and believable

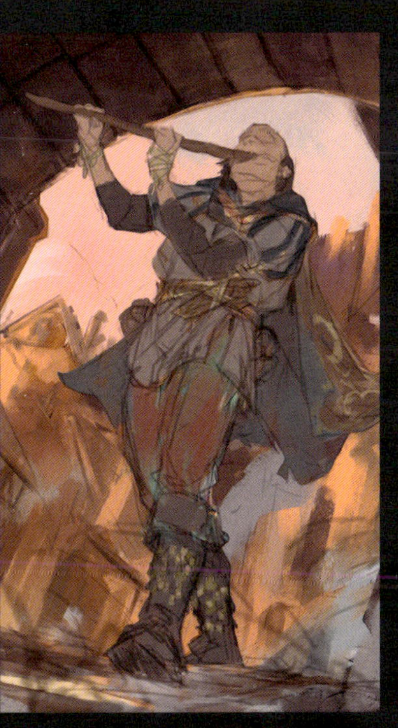

▲ Blocking out the basic colors of the piper's "pied" costume

13 THE PIPER'S COLORS

I tend to save my favorite part of an image for last, usually the character, which is not always the best way to work! However, since the piper is such a key element, I want to have all the color information needed to paint and light him later. The Pied Piper is named for his "pied" clothing, meaning multicolored. Most depictions have bright stripes, colorful robes, and big hats that make him look slightly clownish. I want to be true to his "pied" description while giving a darker, muted tone to the character, fitting the seriousness of the story's events. I pick from my color tests and apply base hues to each part of the character, contrasting dark and light areas to create a simple pied pattern; I avoid going too white or dark, to fit the sunset atmosphere of the scene. This piper does not appear bright and comical, but humbly dressed, probably worn and dusty from weeks on the road.

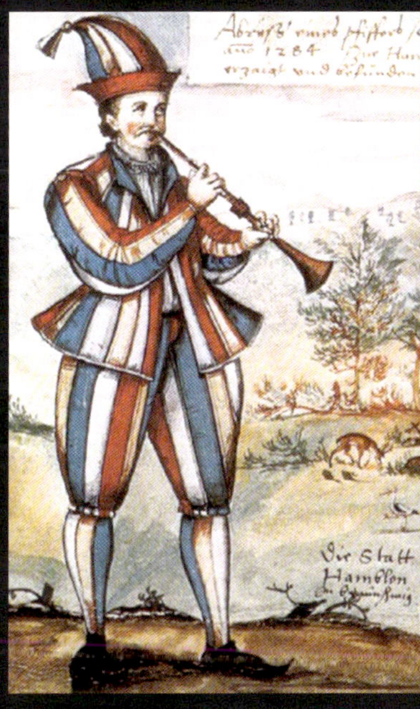

▲ *The Pied Piper of Hamelin* (1592) by Augustin von Mörsperg. This painting of the piper, one of the earliest, depicts him with a colorful, jester-like outfit

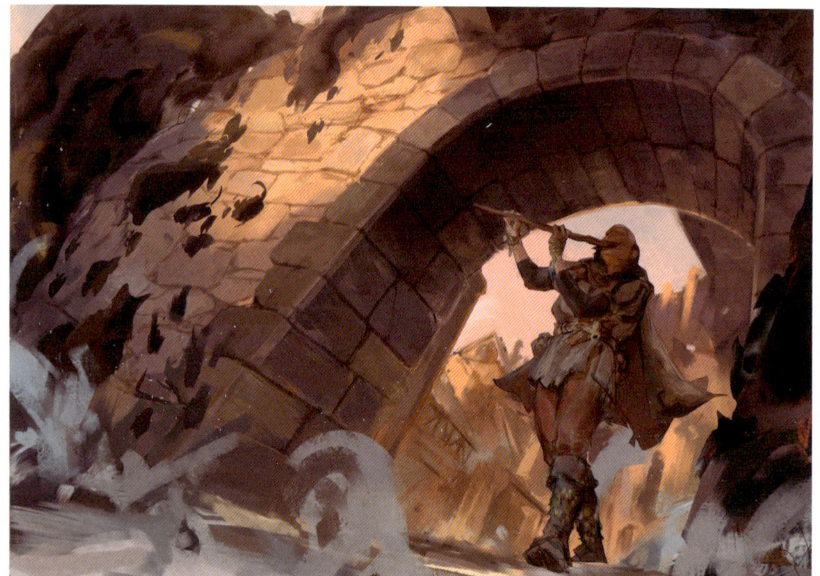

14 A STRONG SILHOUETTE

I begin adding the main shadows to the character, fitting him into the environment. This scene has very strong light and dark areas, with the warm sunset casting deep shadows. The figure of the piper is ominously shaded as he passes through the arch, creating a commanding silhouette within its frame. This is another stage where my reference photos are really helpful – I find myself going back to them constantly to observe how the light bounces and affects the planes of the face.

◀ Giving the focal character a clear, striking silhouette framed by the archway

15 DEPTH AND CHARACTER DETAIL

The image at this stage is quite balanced, and I begin to refine each part of it, but most of my attention is still on the piper. I add finer details to his face and clothes, and some light to the flute, so it really stands out against the shadowed arch. These areas of detail create contrasts that attract and guide the viewer.

Costume elements such as the tattered cape, bandaged hand, and bracelet of rat skulls emphasize the tougher, darker nature of my take on the piper. I revise one side of the character to remove a section of fabric and replace it with a sheathed sword, further pushing the feeling that this is a hardened character who can look out for himself. I also slightly blur the brickwork in the background, so the wall feels softer and farther away than the focal character.

▶ Refining the piper's accessories, shabby clothes, and other fine details

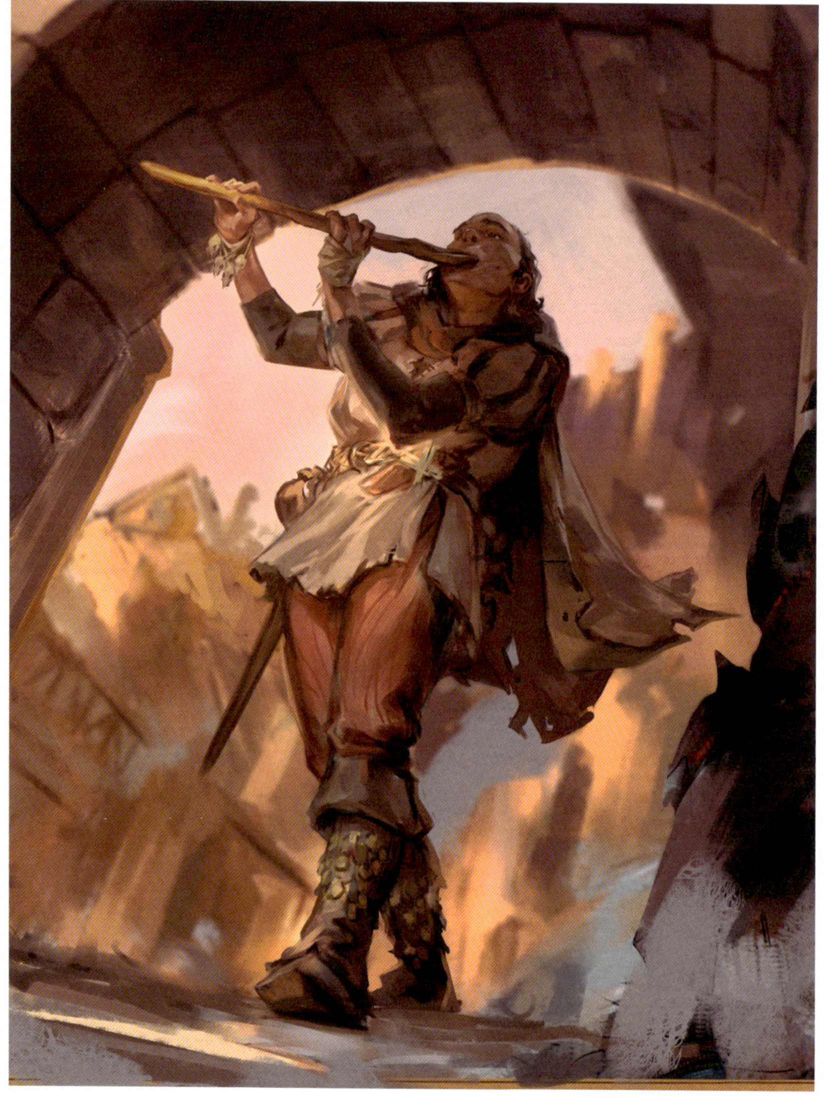

16 THE SPLASHING RIVER

The river is the most challenging part of this image to paint – another area where having proper references is useful. I even paint some studies to help me understand how to portray moving water. I want the water to look dramatic but not distracting, so I keep the painting slightly loose and focus mainly on capturing the right sense of movement. The resulting foreground is more blurry and less detailed than the piper, whose high detail and relatively still pose make him the focus in the midst of all the action. I want the viewer to almost hear the river as it rushes below the bridge, with the rats sending up great splashes of water as they plunge into it.

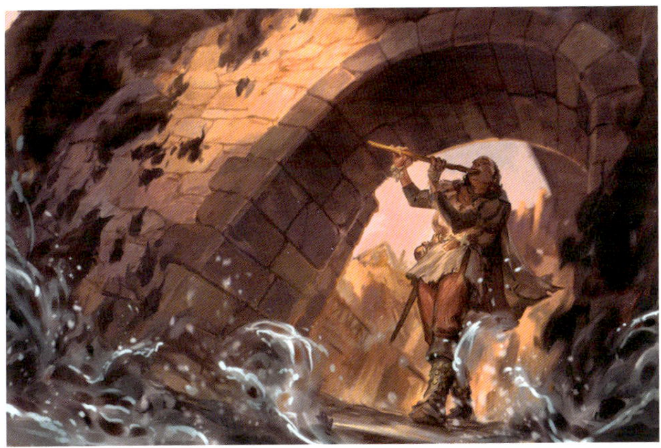

▲ Adding dramatic splashes of water to the river in the foreground

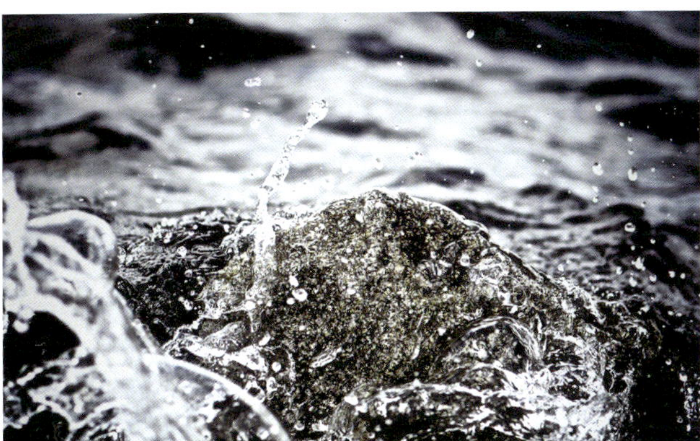

▲ Studying reference photos of water captured in motion, where it almost appears frozen in midair *Photo by Simon Caspersen on Unsplash*

17 ADJUSTING THE FOCAL AREA

Looking at the value of the sky near the rats on the top left, I notice that it's the same as the sky value behind the piper's head. This feels like a missed opportunity to enhance the image's focus and framing. I add a brighter aura around the piper, enhancing the contrast behind him without breaking the balance of colors or altering the appearance of the sky too much. This seems like a really small change, but when you need to guide the viewer's eye toward an illustration's focal point, you have to use all the tricks in the book!

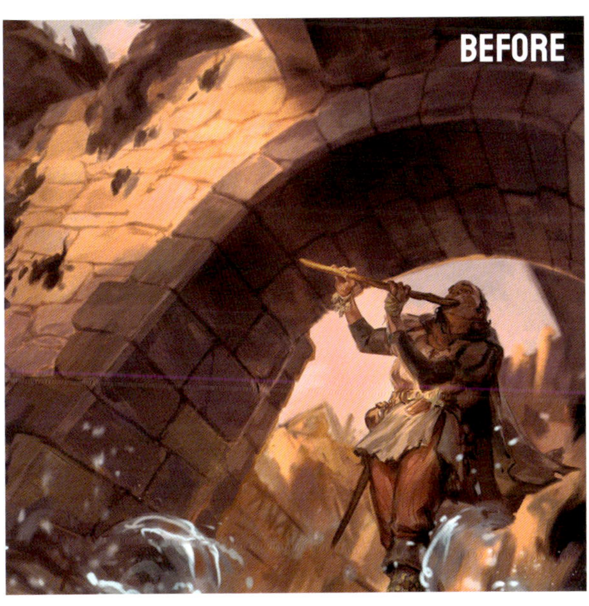

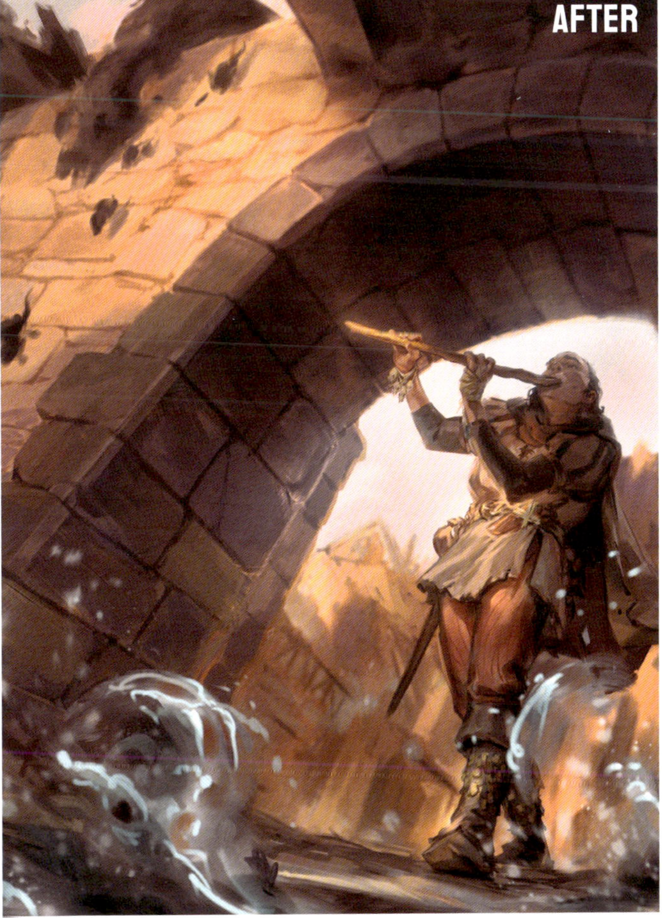

▲ A minor contrast boost goes a long way to enhancing the scene's focal point

18 INTRODUCING THE MAGIC

Now comes the fun part: adding the special effects, glows, and details. I am happy with how the image looks so far, but thinking back on my original plans, my wizard Pied Piper is missing a key ingredient: magic. Painting swirls of magic around the scene creates a visual depiction of the piper's entrancing music, as well as adding a new layer of interesting light effects to the image. The magic itself seems to swirl like water, echoing the fluid shapes and splashes of the river in the foreground.

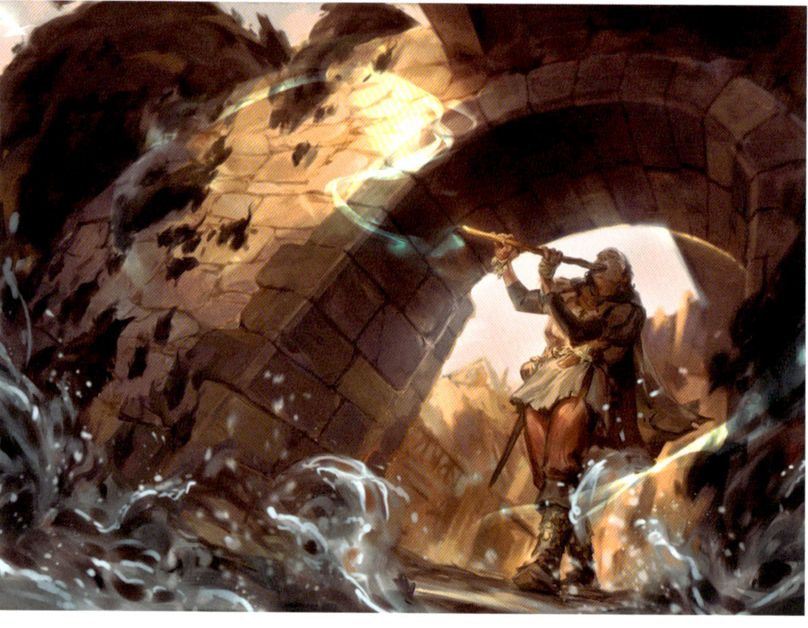

▶ **Adding swirls of magic coming from the piper's flute**

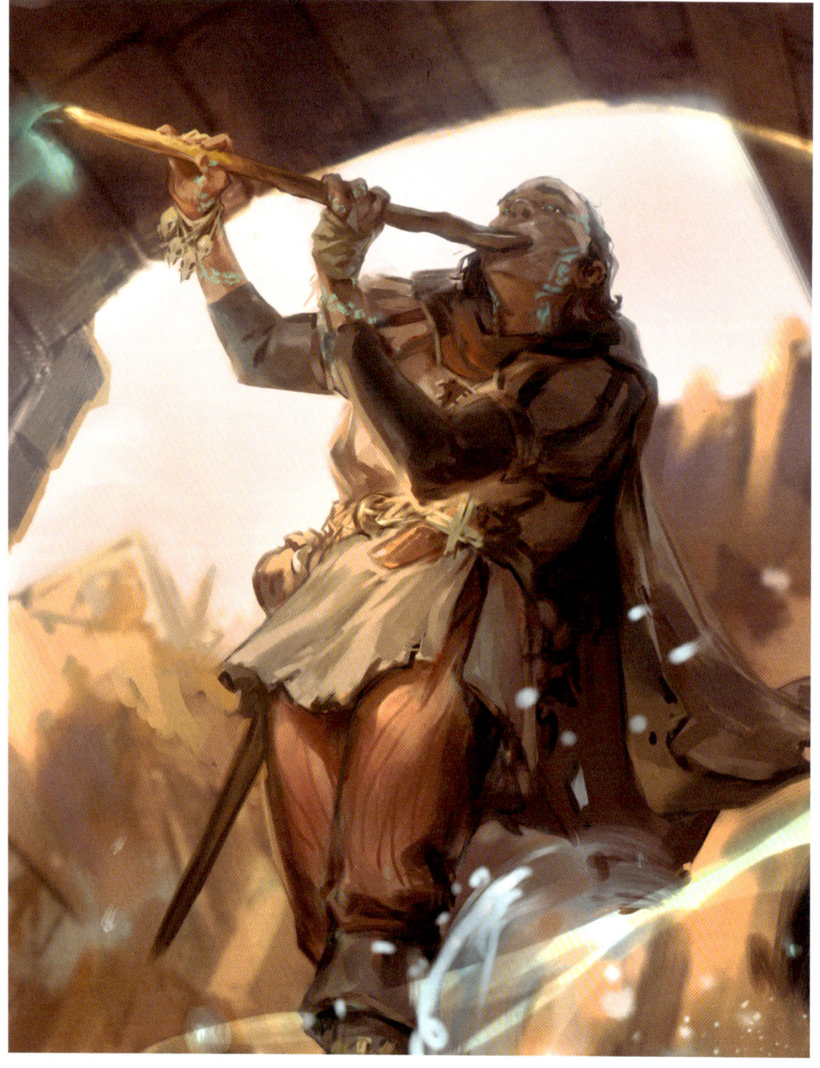

19 GLOWING EYES AND TATTOOS

I want to push that touch of magic even further to emphasize the piper's powers. I can do this by adding a glow to the rats' eyes and the tattoos snaking up the piper's face and arms, using the same color as the light from his flute. The viewer can only see a hint of these markings, but it's enough to wonder whether those strange runes cover his whole body. Perhaps they only glow when casting a spell, and otherwise appear like ordinary ink, or even become invisible. His eyes glow like the rats', suggesting some kind of mind-control spell that he is casting on them with his music. There are pipers and then there are *mind pipers* – beware of the latter!

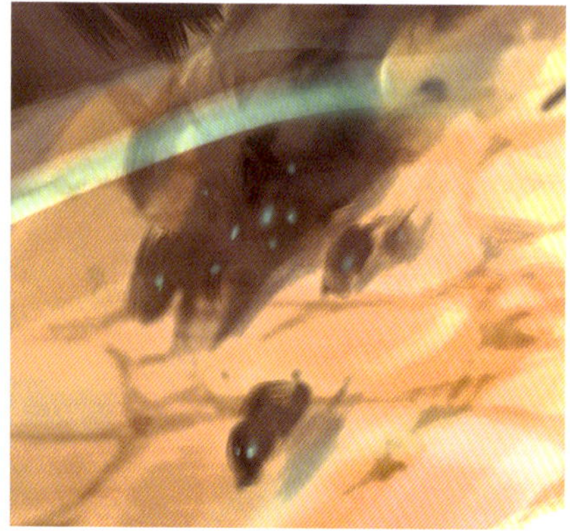

◀ **Glowing details emphasize the piper's mind-controlling powers**

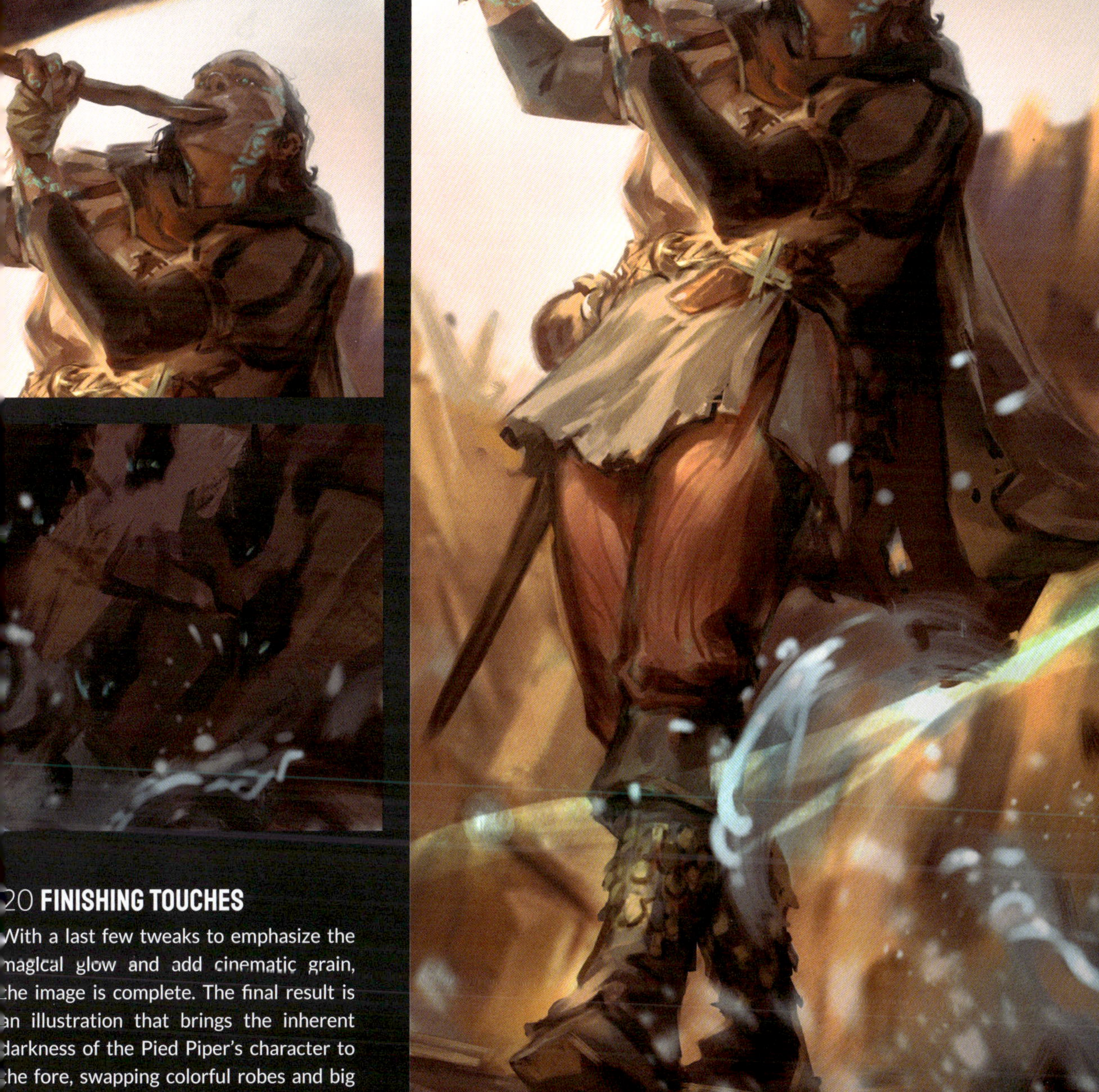

20 FINISHING TOUCHES

With a last few tweaks to emphasize the magical glow and add cinematic grain, the image is complete. The final result is an illustration that brings the inherent darkness of the Pied Piper's character to the fore, swapping colorful robes and big hats for a dramatic scene of destruction that is still true to the original tale. At this stage, I finally crop out the black margins mentioned on page 136, confident that my finished composition is strong.

▲ Adding a few cinematic effects to complete the illustration

My final illustration is one that keeps close to an event in the original tale – a moment that is dark and chilling – and delves deeper into the enigmatic character of the piper, giving him some grit and showing the mind-manipulating spell that is the source of his power. My piper is an ominous figure that the people of Hamelin dare to cross at their peril, perhaps out of fear of his suspicious, ragged appearance. Along the way, I used elements of 3D and my own photography for reference. Ultimately, I think that each artist's process is unique, and the most important thing is to never limit yourself to preconceptions of what is "right" or "professional." Take reference photos, even if they look silly. Use cardboard to create your own miniatures, even. The possibilities are limitless – the most important thing is to have fun.

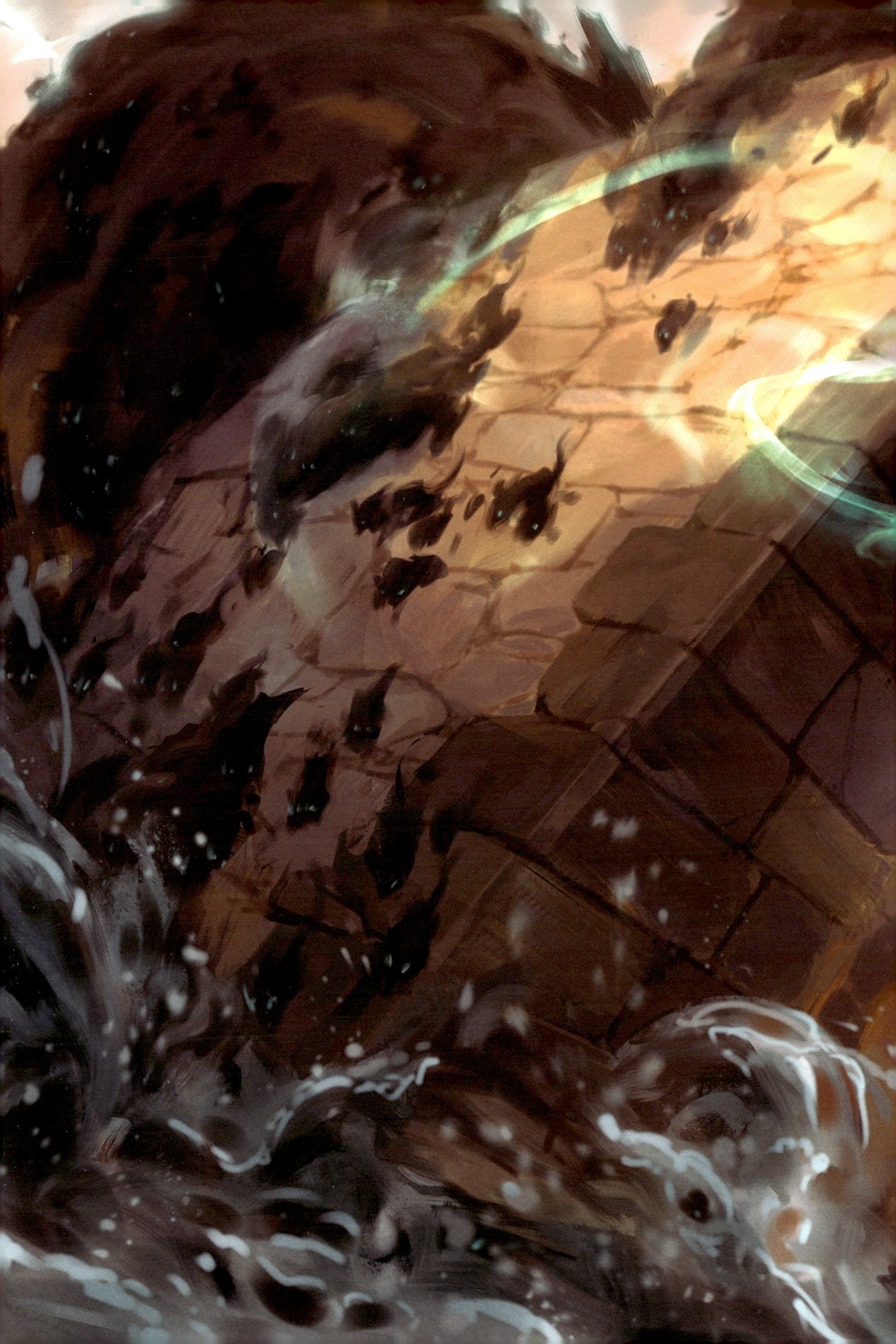

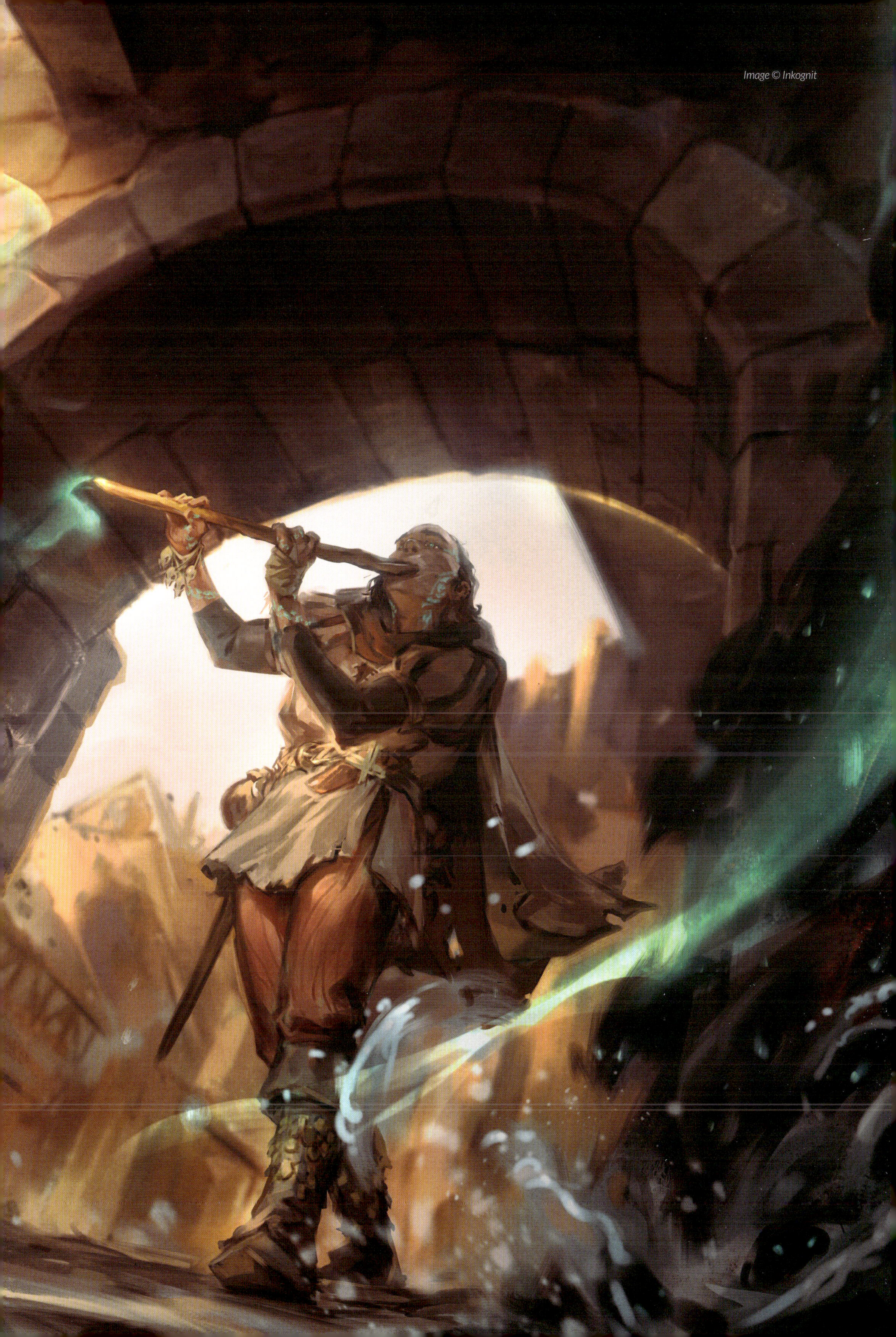

THE PIPER IMPRISONED

BY JOSHUA CARSON

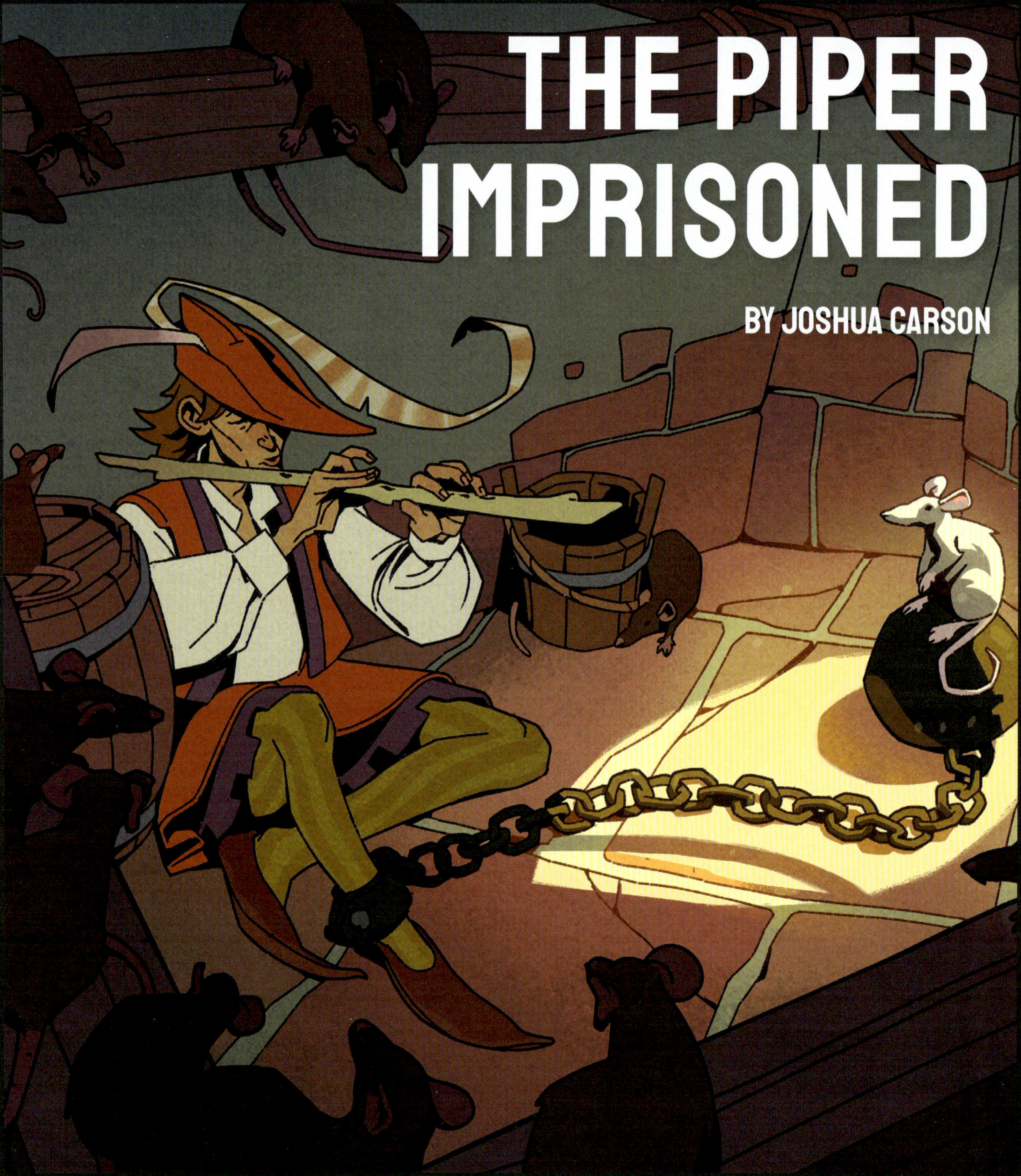

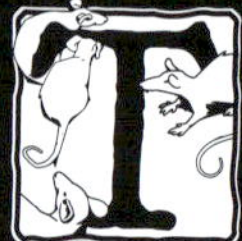

The original version of *The Pied Piper of Hamelin* is a bit too dark for my taste, containing plagues and the eventual abduction of children. The world can already be a bit too bleak at times, so instead I decide that my twist will have the piper in a kind of partnership with the rats, sharing a friendship in a time of need. The prompt I give myself is this: what if the piper is down on his luck, imprisoned for debts he has racked up with the mayor or the town, and while in prison discovers that the rats are receptive to his music? What would that quiet moment look like? What kind of audience would the piper have?

01 FINDING REFERENCES

The first thing I do when receiving any kind of prompt is put together a moodboard of images that will inspire the visual direction of my designs. Usually these moodboards will have images that are directly relevant to the idea, such as historical costumes or anatomical reference pictures for difficult posing. They also sometimes have art from other artists I find inspirational. It can really vary! I think the most important thing when making a moodboard is to not have *too* many reference pictures. If you limit yourself to a few inspirational images that resonate with you the most, it distills your inspiration down to a stronger direction.

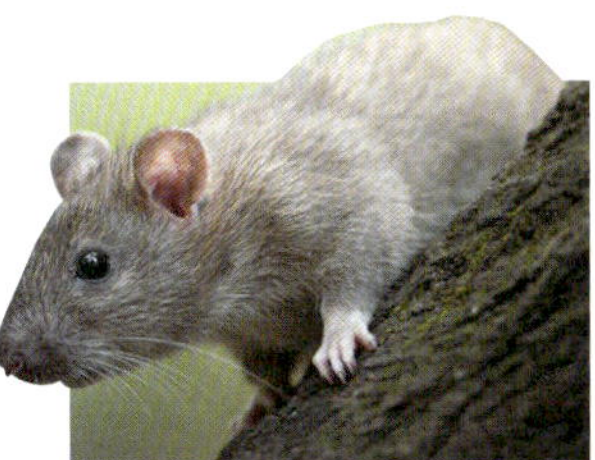

▲ Reference image of a rat

Photo by Daniil Komov on Unsplash

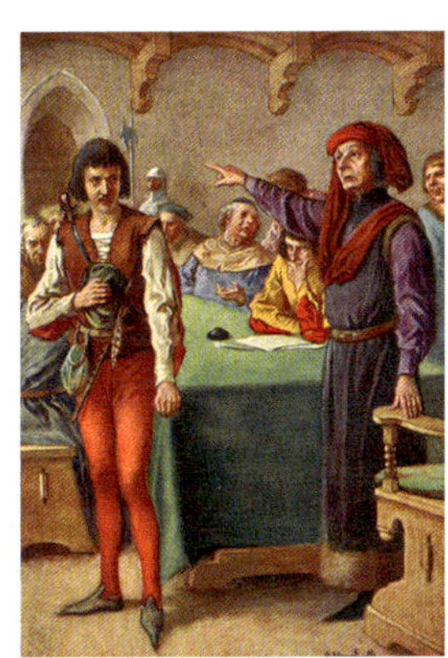

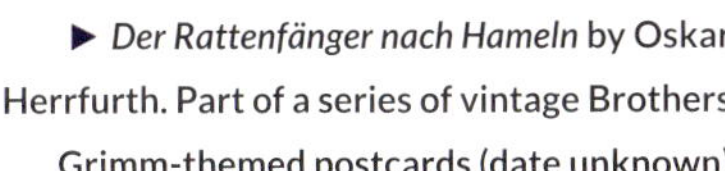

► *Der Rattenfänger nach Hameln* by Oskar Herrfurth. Part of a series of vintage Brothers Grimm-themed postcards (date unknown)

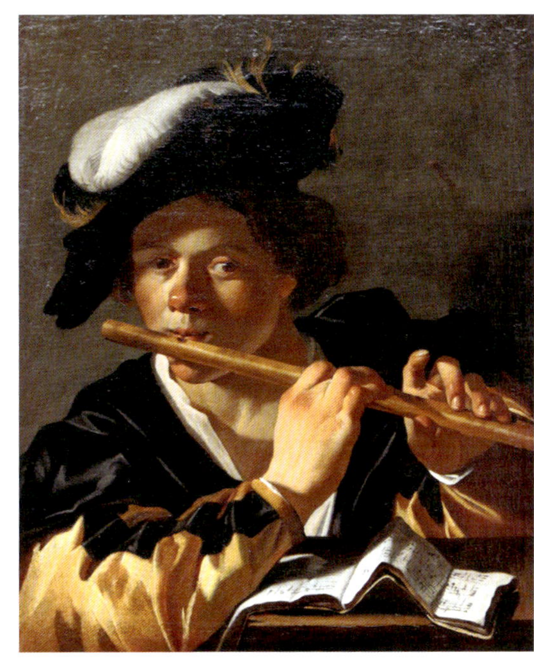

▲ *Der Flötenspieler (The Flute Player)* by Dirck van Baburen (c. 1620)

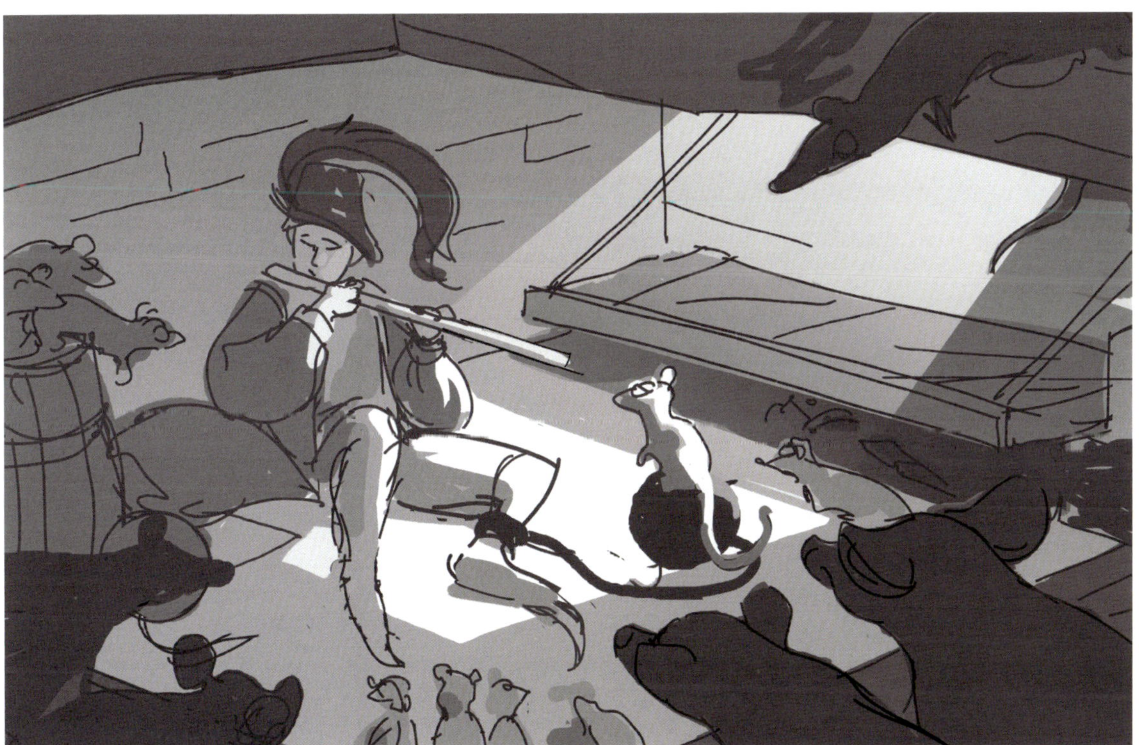

▲ Thumbnail drawing of the piper in his cell with an audience of rats resting on the beams above

02 THUMBNAIL SKETCHING

After I put together the moodboard, I begin sketching loose thumbnails for the idea. I used to get really caught up on the perspective in these beginning sketches, making sure that everything was accurate. However, I have since found that the looser I sketch, the less inhibited I feel creatively when coming up with a composition. The specifics and structure of the drawing can be figured out later! For now I just try to throw out an idea.

03 IN THE SEWER

Usually I like to draw a few thumbnails, so I am not just settling on my first idea. It's always good to try to push yourself creatively to come up with just one more idea, even if you think you have run out and can't come up with anything else. When I seem to run out of ideas for a design, I fall back on looking at more reference material and other visual media for inspiration. For this sketch, I explore the idea of the piper first encountering the rats in a sewer and beginning to play his music to them.

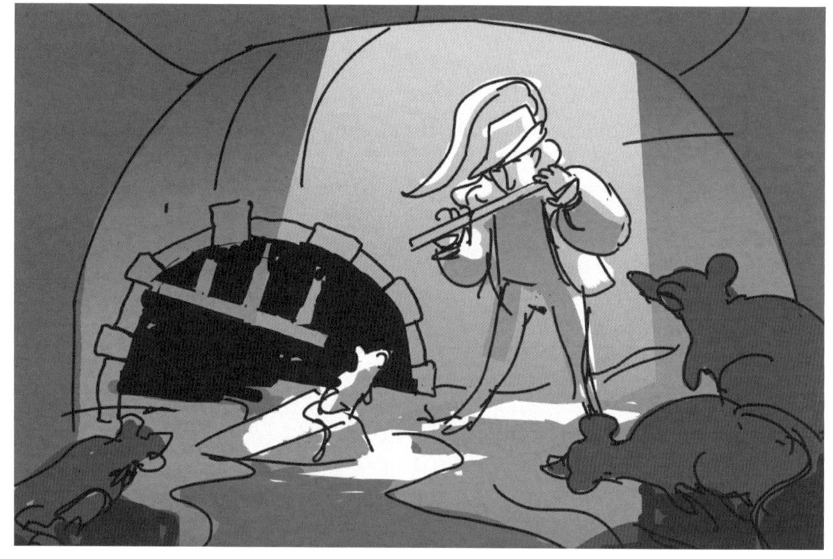

► The piper playing to the rats in the sewers

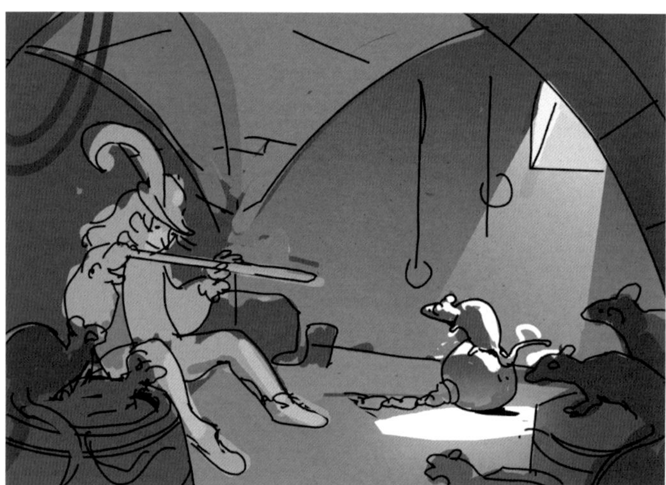

04 IN THE DUNGEON

This is another iteration of the piper being in a prison of some sort. I thought it would be interesting to have vaulted ceilings and a high window to signify that he's in some sort of subterranean basement dungeon. The gestures of the ceiling would guide the eye toward the piper, his flute would lead to the rat, and the light streaming through the window would allow for some strong contrast to further strengthen the composition.

◄ The piper playing music to a rat in his cell with vaulted ceilings

05 THE CHOSEN SCENE

Sometimes it does work out that the first idea you had was the strongest, and your creative intuition was correct! This was the case for me, but I always like to explore a few designs just in case that initial idea is not love at first sight. Pushing yourself to explore designs in different ways is a bit like creative "exercise," and you don't want to skimp on that. So I return to my first idea, with the imprisoned piper playing to a quiet audience of inquisitive rats, and begin making revisions to clarify the values and framing. The camera being positioned above the piper, looking down on him, further solidifies the idea that he is at a low point in his story. We, as the audience, are positioned among the rats like we are part of the crowd.

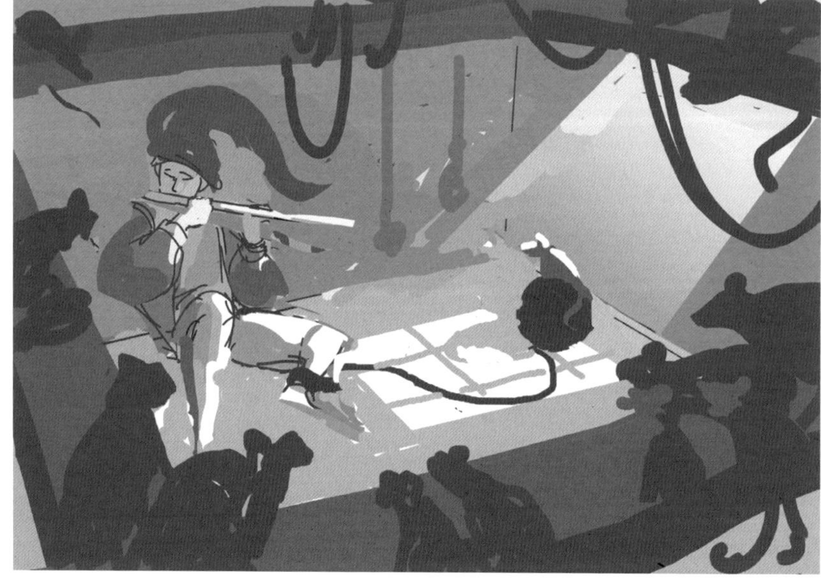

▲ Returning to my strongest idea: the piper viewed from the ceiling beams of his cell

06 LOOSE LINE DRAWING

After deciding to push that first thumbnail further, I begin a very rough sketch of the specifics to make sure the drawing can work in perspective and will structurally make sense. I lay down a three-point perspective grid, as the camera is positioned up in the rafters looking down at the piper, to help me with this process. The shapes and specifics of the drawing begin to form here, though the linework is still very loose.

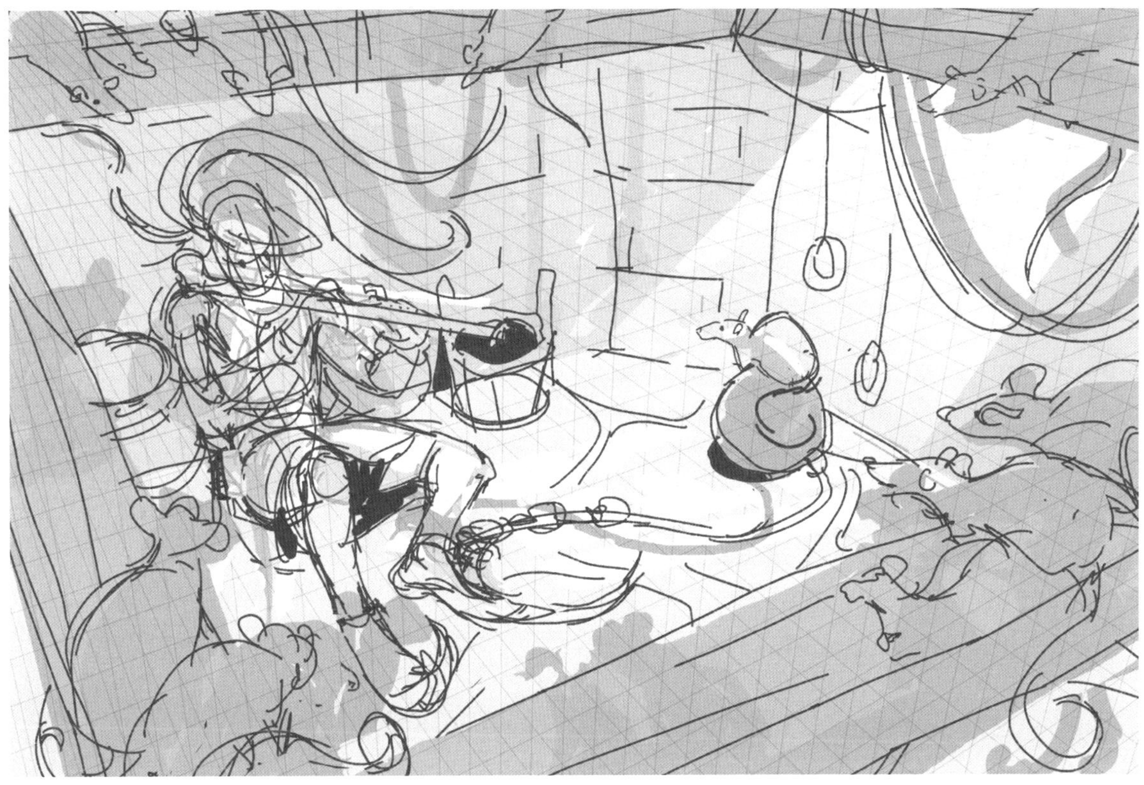

▲ Building up a loose line drawing of the piper in his cell

07 THE WOODEN RAFTERS

Here I begin to draw out the final shapes, starting with the rafters. You can see that they are not particularly straight, nor do they follow the perspective grid perfectly. Completely straight lines that totally adhere to perspective guides can feel a bit lifeless, and very long lines like these are a perfect opportunity to introduce some gestures. I love adding wonkiness to shapes, so I give the beams very subtle "S" curves to make them more appealing. The beams also act as a "frame within a frame"-style composition, containing the important parts of the image within them. On a symbolic level, having the piper be contained within the frame of the beams further sells the idea that he is contained in a prison, not free to roam around outside the bounds of his cell.

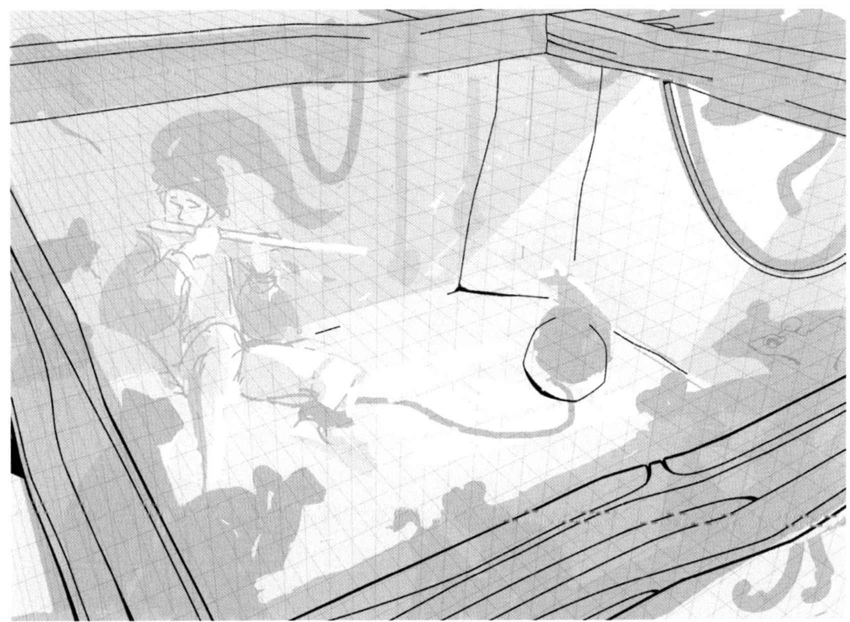

▲ Refining the line drawing, starting with the ceiling beams

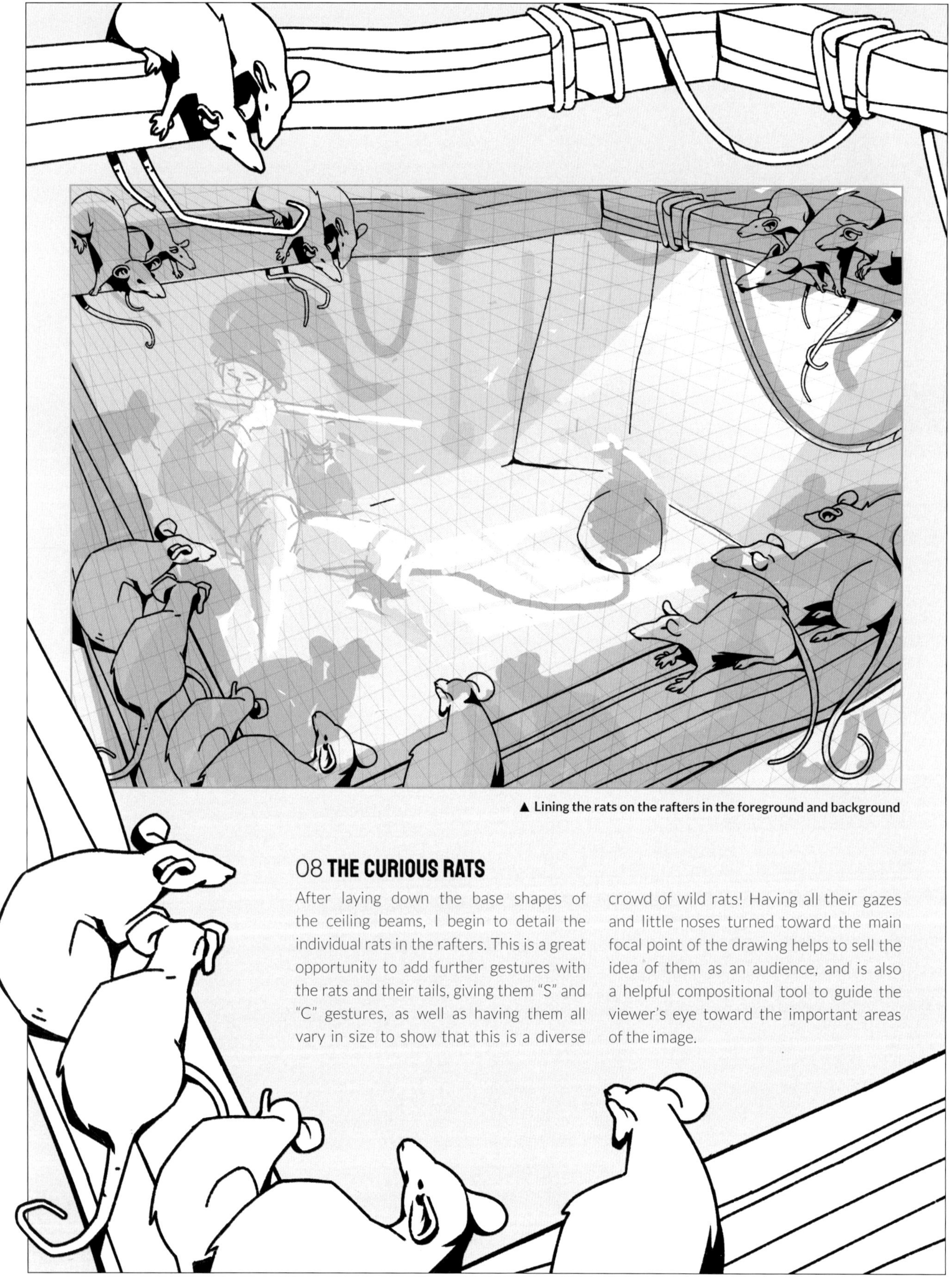

▲ Lining the rats on the rafters in the foreground and background

08 THE CURIOUS RATS

After laying down the base shapes of the ceiling beams, I begin to detail the individual rats in the rafters. This is a great opportunity to add further gestures with the rats and their tails, giving them "S" and "C" gestures, as well as having them all vary in size to show that this is a diverse crowd of wild rats! Having all their gazes and little noses turned toward the main focal point of the drawing helps to sell the idea of them as an audience, and is also a helpful compositional tool to guide the viewer's eye toward the important areas of the image.

09 THE PIED PIPER

After drawing the rats up above, I move on to the most important part of the drawing – the piper himself. I usually begin illustrating a character with a very messy, loose sketch to figure out gestures and posing. In this scene, I want the piper's flute to be pointing to the single rat in the center of his cell, leading the viewer's gaze between the participants in this story. The piper will be leaning against a barrel in one corner of the room while the rat perches on the end of his ball and chain, so I draw in these two props – the flute and the barrel – first.

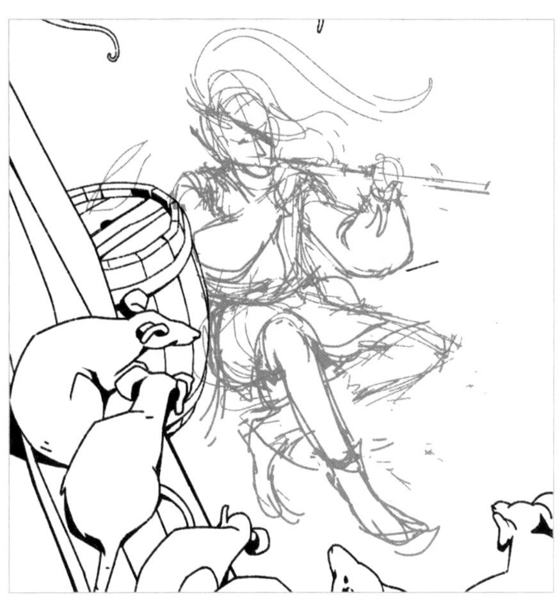

▶ Making a loose sketch of the piper's gesture

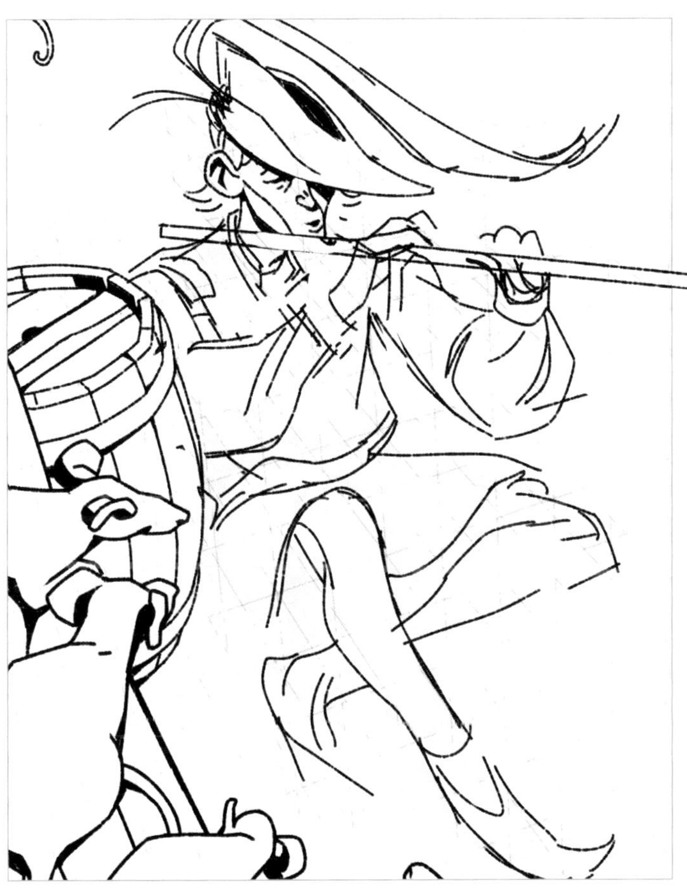

10 THE PIPER'S APPEARANCE

Using the loose sketch as a base drawing, I begin to solidify the shapes of the piper. I give him his iconic feathered cap, pied tunic, tights, and pointy shoes, wanting to keep him familiar and instantly recognizable even in this different context. I make his face thin and his nose pointy, as well as giving him very large ears – I want his character to subtly share some physical aspects with the rats themselves, in order to emphasize their connection!

◀ Developing the piper further – his face and hat shapes begin to take form

11 AN INQUISITIVE RAT

Here I further the drawing of the piper, lengthening his nose even more and adding in a little rat sitting atop the barrel he is leaning against. With this addition, both ends of the flute are now pointing to focal points and areas of interest in the illustration. The scene shows that the rats are curious about the piper, daring to come closer to listen to his music. I also continue fleshing out the piper's outfit, based on clothing I found in photos and paintings in my research.

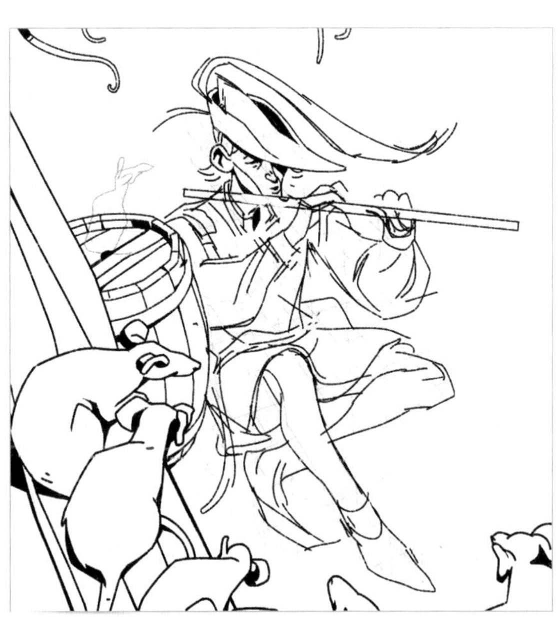

▶ Building up the piper and adding a rat to the barrel beside him

12 FINISHING THE PIPER

Now I finalize the drawing of the piper, adding his ball and chain prominently in the middle of the drawing. It should be immediately clear to the viewer that the piper is a prisoner, creating intrigue as to how he has ended up here.

The feathers in his cap reinforce the focal points and have strong gestures; for example, the largest feather has a fun, curved gesture adjacent to the straight flute. I am looking for a good balance of curves versus straights to create appeal. Like the wooden beams above, the flute isn't perfectly straight, having organic bumps and imperfections that give it more detail and personality. The piper's clothing has a dagged hem based on my research, which helps gives the scene a sense of historical time and place.

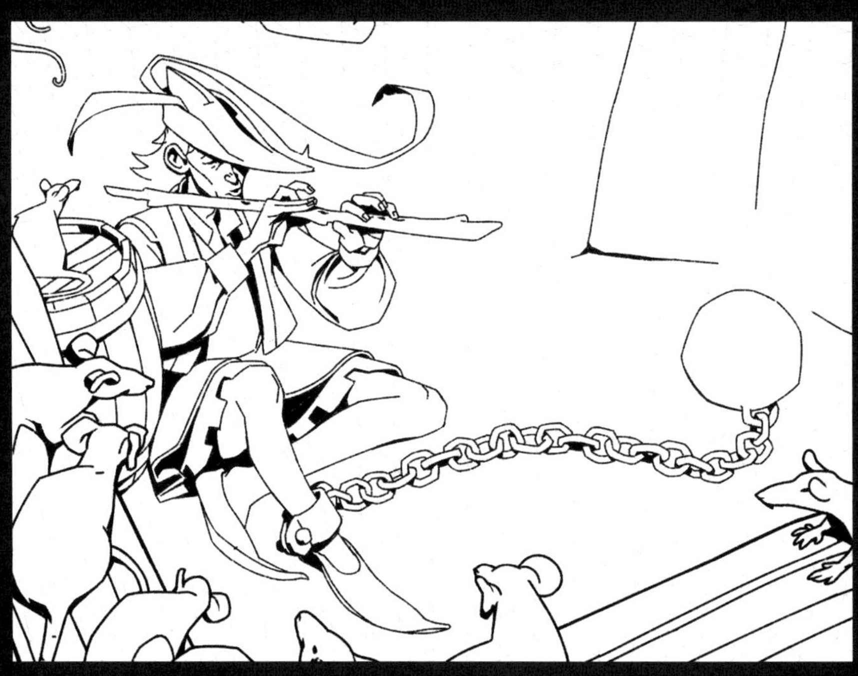

▲ Detailing the piper's accessories and shackles

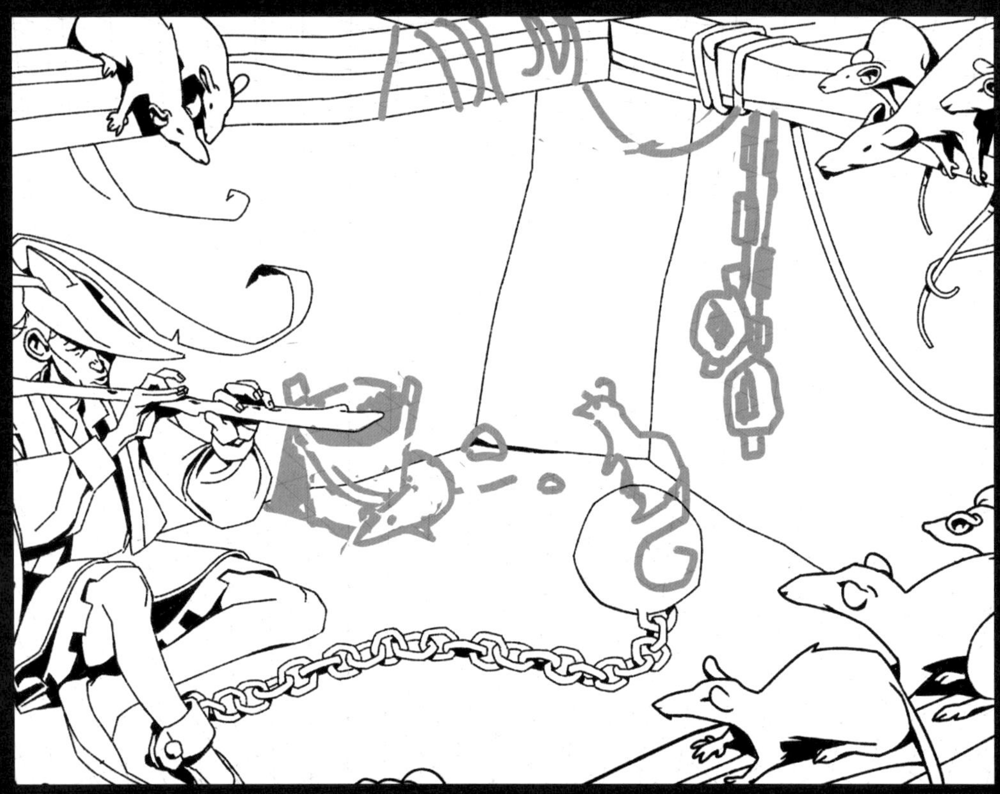

◄ Adding more objects to flesh out the setting

13 CONSIDERING MORE PROPS

After finishing the line art for some of the most important subjects, I go on to loosely sketch more props, as well as the single rat the piper appears to be playing music to. Adding a bucket and hanging chains helps to make the room feel squalid without introducing too many props – it's a jail cell, after all, so needs to be mostly bare! An apprehensive rat peeking out from behind the bucket is another fun detail that adds life to the room.

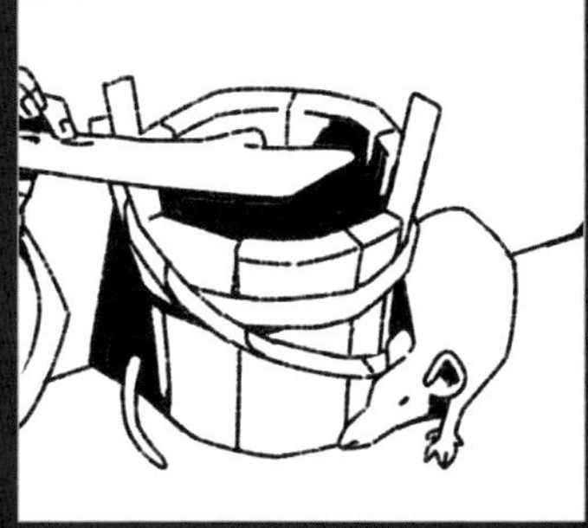

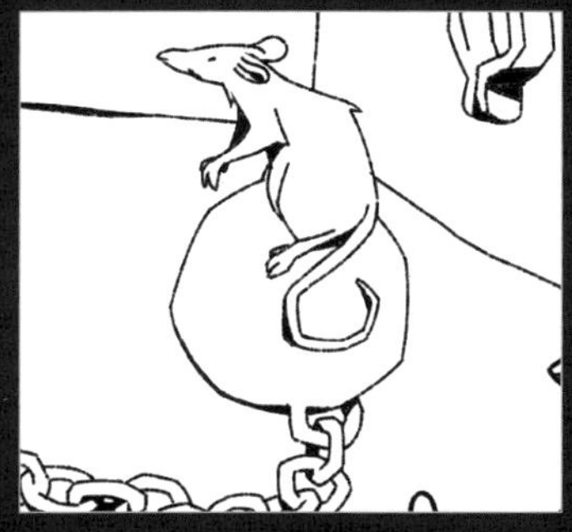

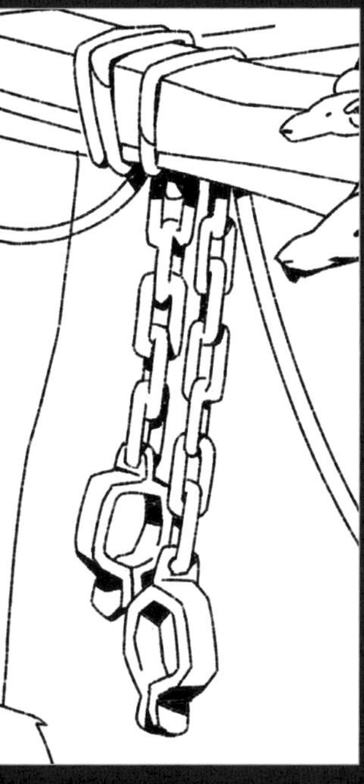

14 ADDING VISUAL INTEREST

I continue to solidify the line art of those newest details, drawing the rat on the ball and chain quietly listening to the piper playing his flute, and another rat peering curiously around the bucket. However, I think I still need to populate the cell with a few more areas of visual interest to draw the viewer in and help guide their eye through the illustration. The mostly empty walls and floor would be a good opportunity to introduce more detail to the room – I will look closer at those in the next step.

◄ **Additional rats and props add life to the scene**

15 REVISING A FLAT RAT

I realize my initial drawing of the rat on the ball and chain is flattening the image a little – it's not quite in the pose and perspective that I would like. I redraw it in a stronger pose that has more depth, with its head and body angled toward the piper's position, rather than being in profile like before. This looks much better and more three-dimensional. I also begin loosely sketching in some bricks and flagstones to add detail to the room. By saving this stage until now, I can design the shapes of the floor and walls around the most important parts of the drawing. If I had drawn them first, before the piper and all the other elements, I might have had to redraw them over and over. Work smarter, not harder!

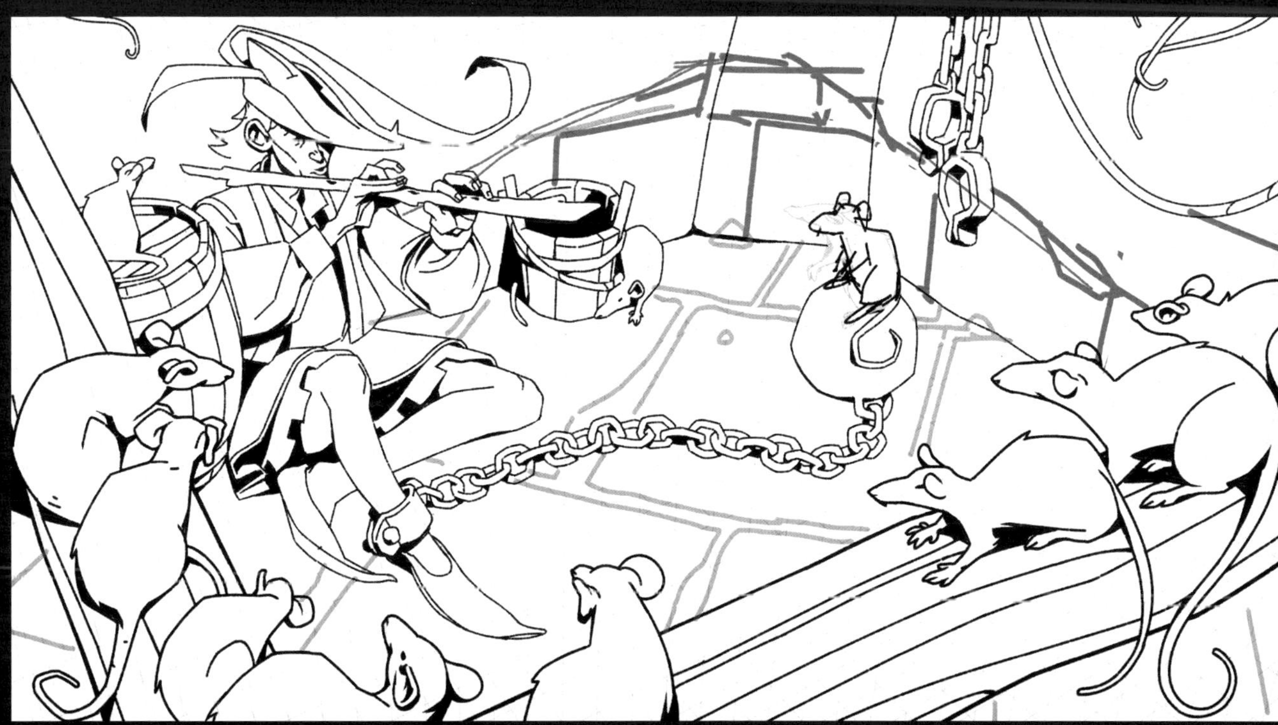

▲ **Adding the floor and wall stones and revising the rat**

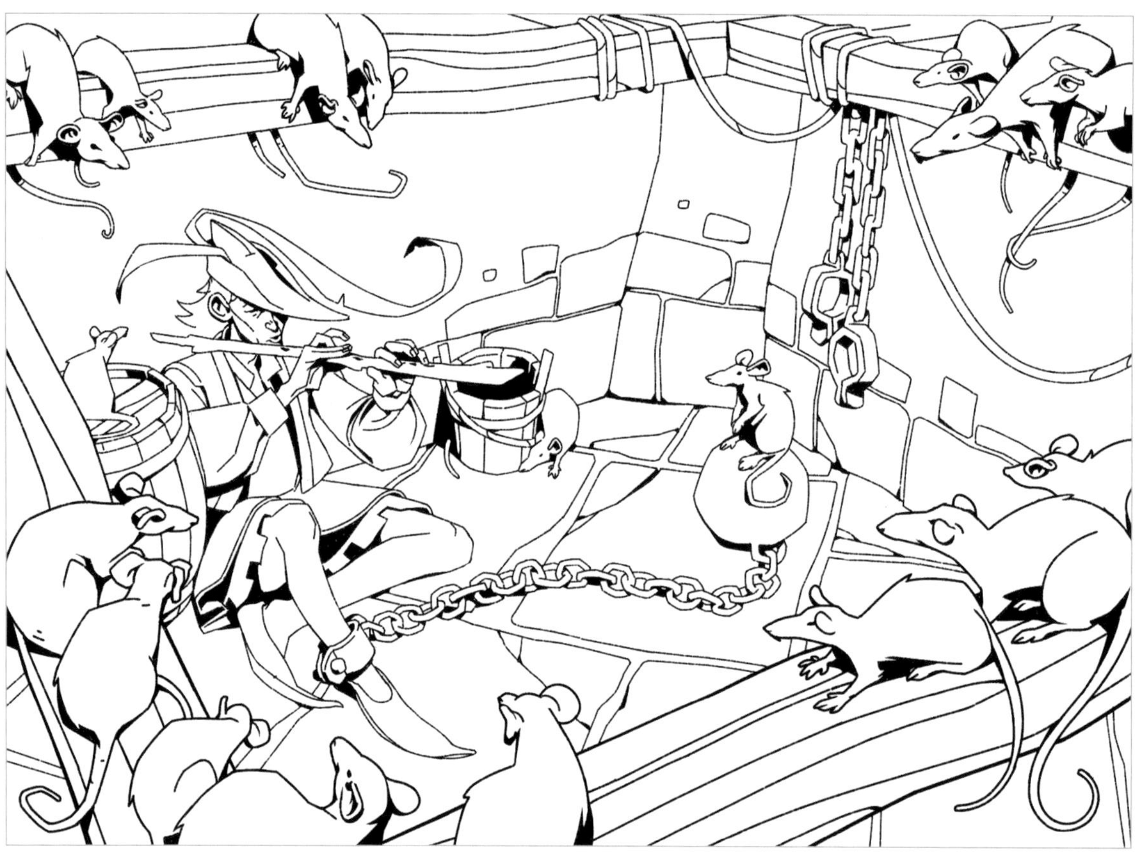

▲ Completing the linework for the scene

16 DETAILING THE ROOM

I finalize the line art by adding wonkiness and gestures within the stonework, always thinking about how to direct the viewer to the important details. The walls are a mix of stonework and stucco to balance out the illustration and create contrast between areas of interest and areas of rest. If the upper walls were more detailed, they would become a distraction, so they stay plain and simple. Nearer the floor, the brickwork helps create another connecting path between the piper and the rat.

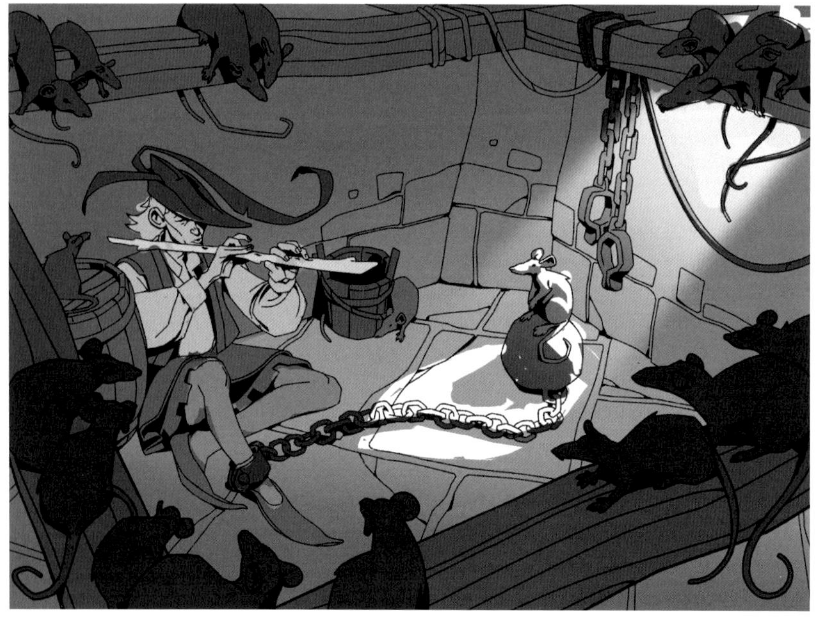

17 REVISING VALUES

After finishing the line art, I need to resolve the value scheme of the illustration. The initial thumbnail laid out the general idea, but I need to revise the values to make sure they work properly with all the new elements I have added since. It is easiest to do this step in black and white, rather than trying to figure out both the color and value schemes at the same time. I take the time to work out the values of details such as the bucket, chains, and the piper's pied clothes. I use value contrast to reinforce the two main focal points that tell the story: the piper and the main rat sitting in the light.

◄ Applying some cleaner values to fit the finished line art

18 INTRODUCING COLOR

After figuring out the values of the image, I move on to laying down harmonious flat colors with no shadows or light. The exceptions to this are the rats and ceiling beams, which I know will be darker as they are above the light source, hidden near the shadowy ceiling. Though the piper is locked in a shabby cell, I don't want the overall mood to be too cold and bleak. Instead I want a feeling of warmth, almost coziness, to come through – something that fits this lighter story of an unlucky character discovering new friends. Focusing on warm oranges, greens, and browns helps me set this warmer mood. The rat perched on the ball is a lighter color than the others, which will distinguish it as being one of the main "characters" in this narrative.

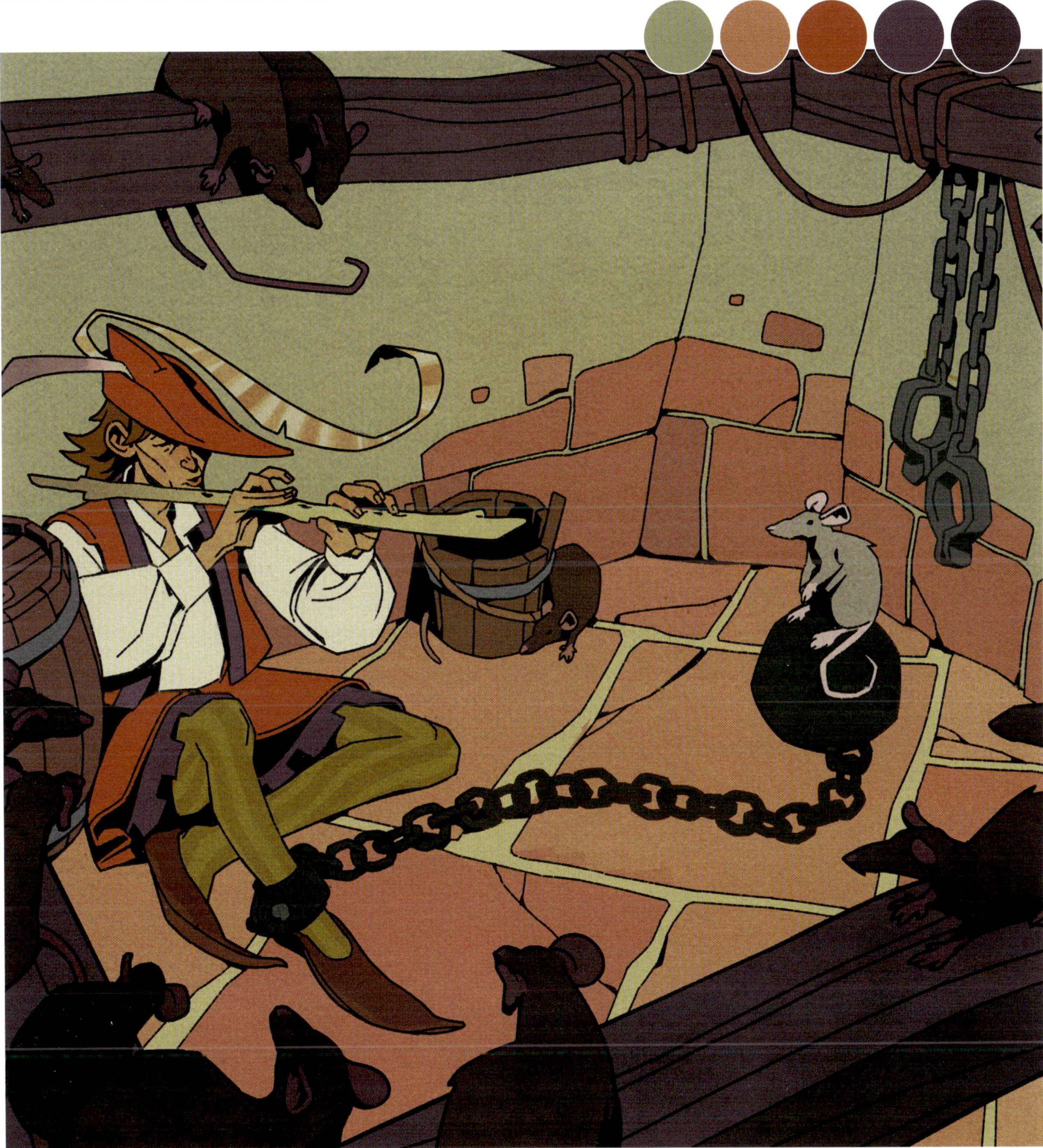

▲ Choosing a warm color palette for the scene

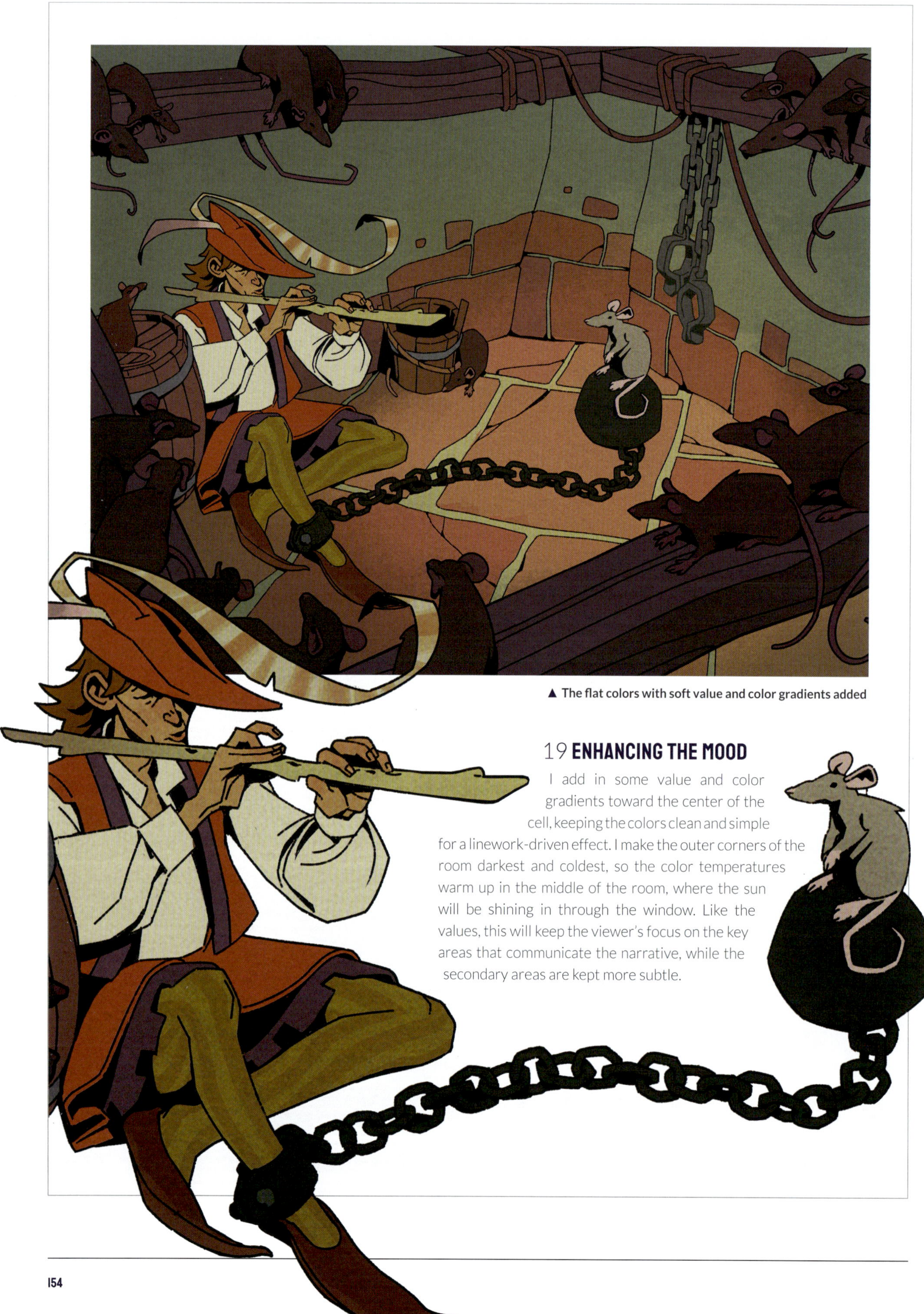

▲ The flat colors with soft value and color gradients added

19 ENHANCING THE MOOD

I add in some value and color gradients toward the center of the cell, keeping the colors clean and simple for a linework-driven effect. I make the outer corners of the room darkest and coldest, so the color temperatures warm up in the middle of the room, where the sun will be shining in through the window. Like the values, this will keep the viewer's focus on the key areas that communicate the narrative, while the secondary areas are kept more subtle.

20 FINISHING TOUCHES

I add in the final details of the image, such as the light source coming through the unseen window. The light shaft streams down into the cell and onto the floor in the center of the illustration, acting as a bright spotlight for the rat sitting on the ball. The corners of the image are subtly but visibly darker and colder, emphasizing the warm sunbeam and cheerful pied colors of the piper. A few dust motes floating in the light help create a tranquil, indoor atmosphere that suits this friendly encounter. I also color the linework itself, so that instead of being a harsh black in some areas, it's a warmer color that helps the overall color harmony and cozy mood.

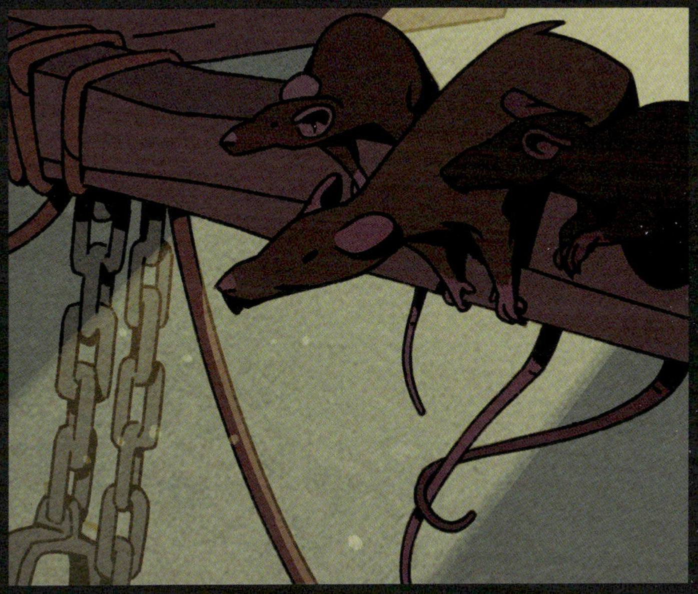

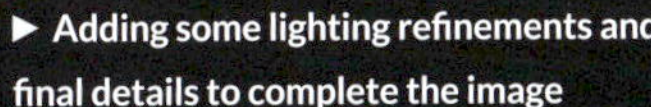

► Adding some lighting refinements and final details to complete the image

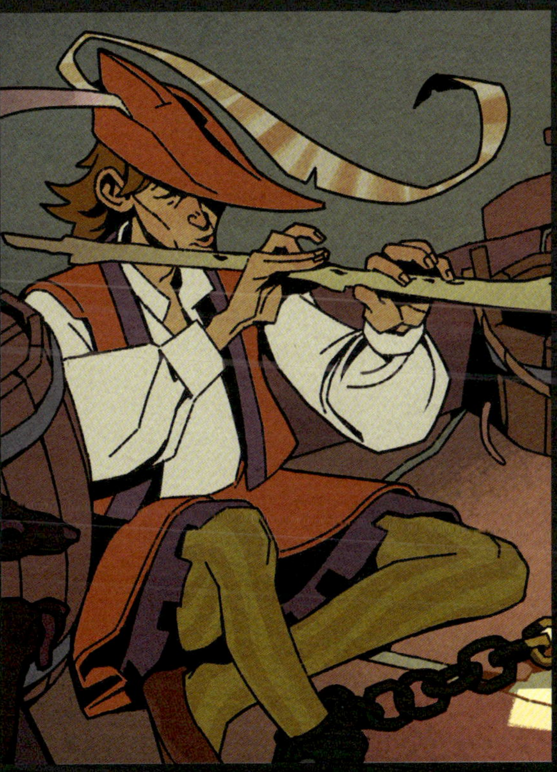

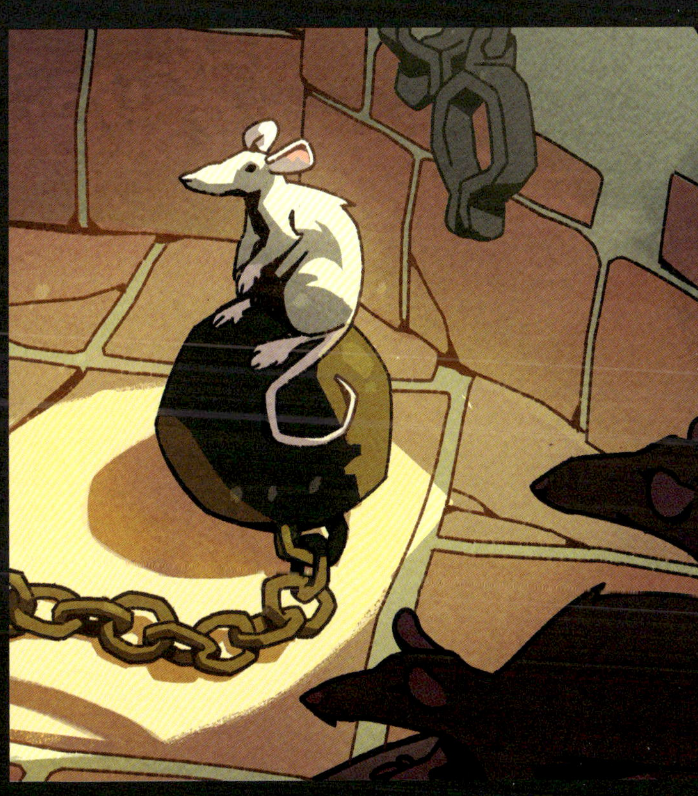

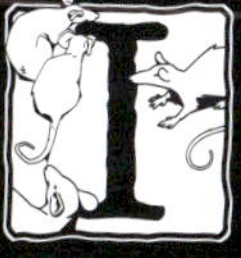

I am very satisfied with how this illustration has turned out! When you are working on an image, keep in mind how intentional decisions within your composition – whether related to character, environment, lighting, or color – can further serve the story you are trying to tell. I think the warm color palette reflects the lighter mood I wanted to capture at the beginning: a peaceful moment as the piper plays his flute. I'm glad I managed to take a cold and disturbing tale and turn it into something warmer and brighter. It shows a softer side to the piper's character that is quite distant from the sinister events of the original story, and makes us wonder about his relationship with the rats. Perhaps they become his faithful helpers, popping up in small towns so the piper can earn his living – not really a "plague" at all!

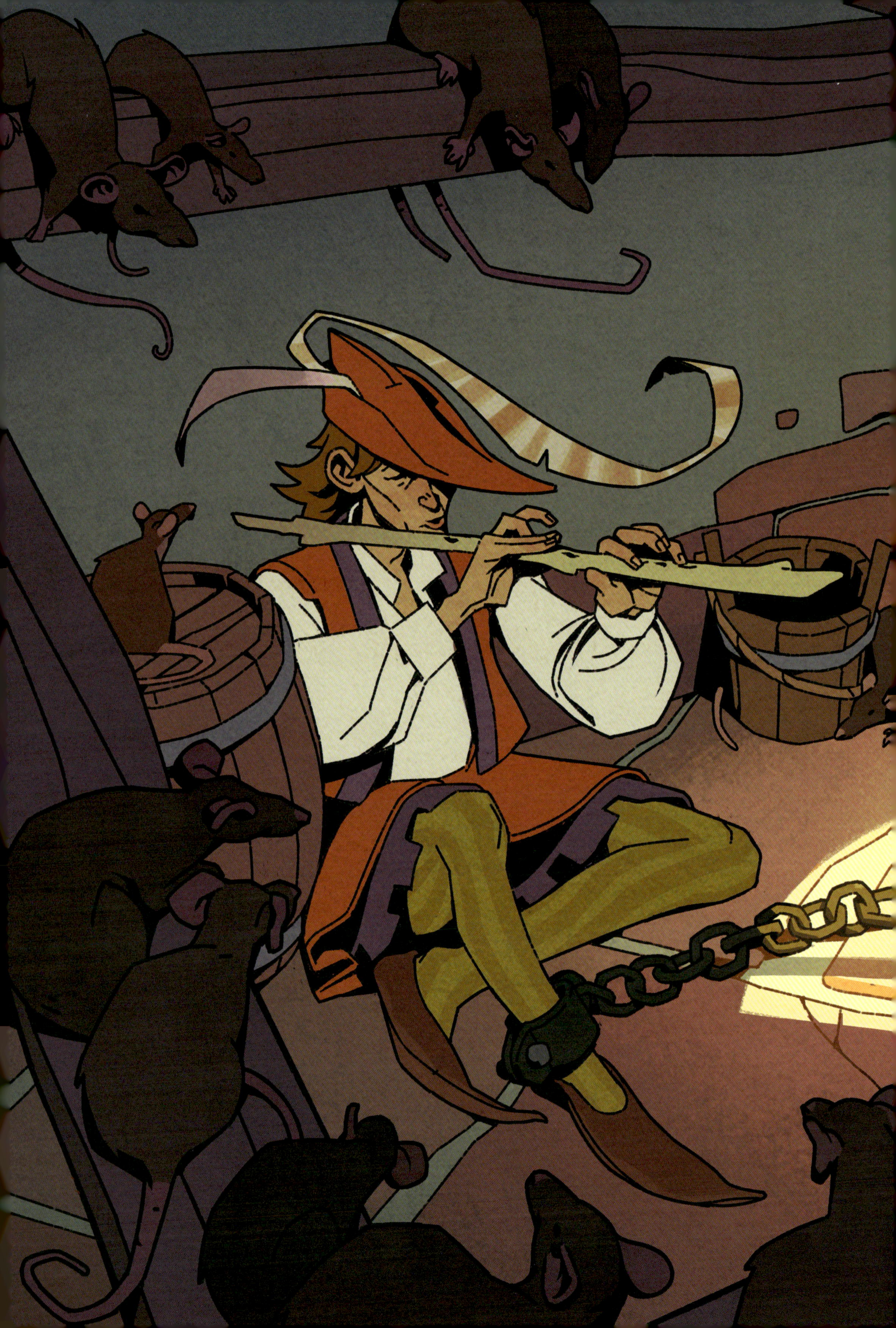

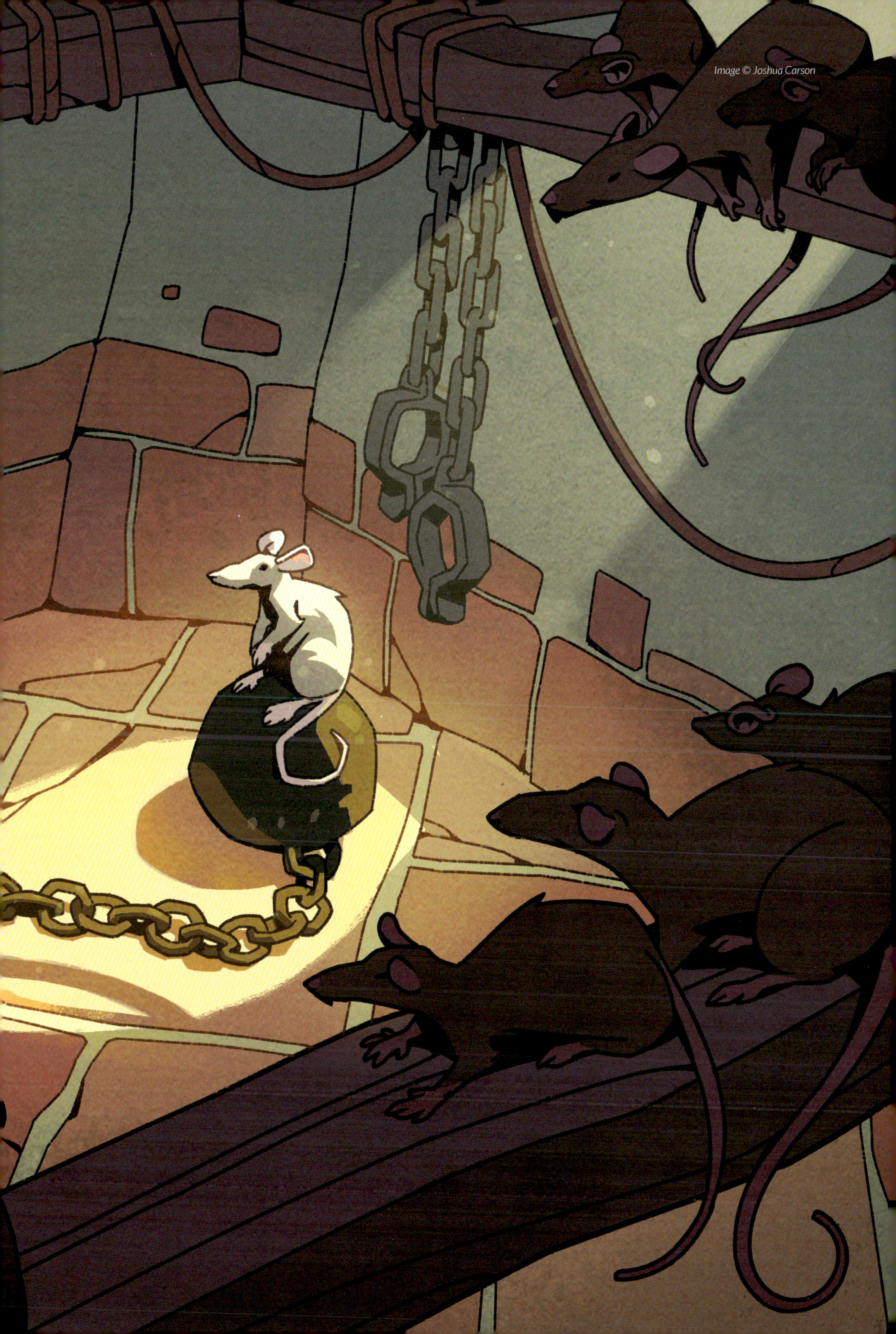

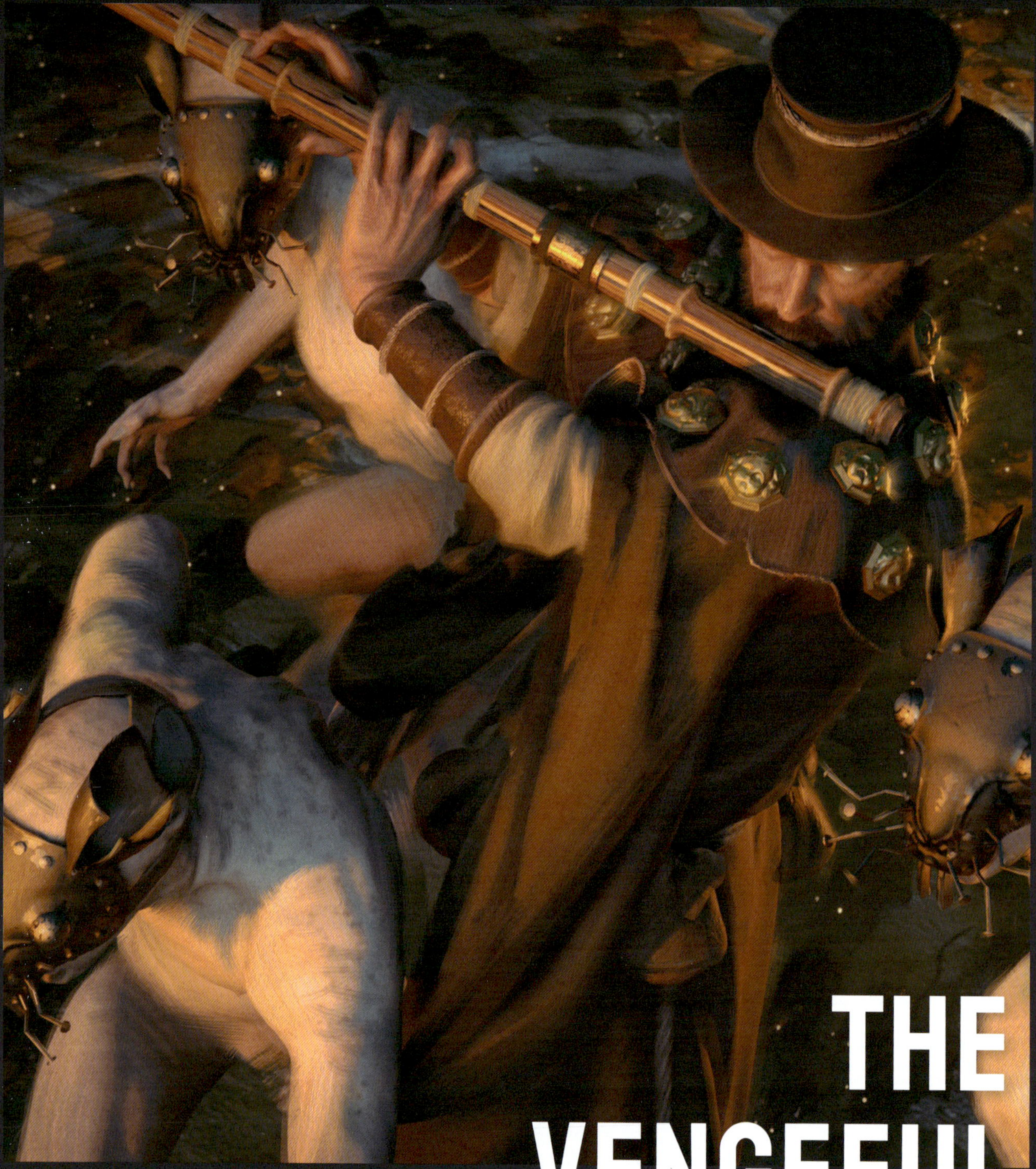

THE VENGEFUL PIPER

BY YONGJAE CHOI

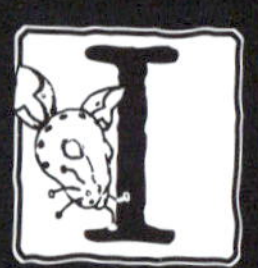
I really like the mystery of the original *Pied Piper of Hamelin* story. I am especially drawn to the creepiness of the pied man, the central character of the tale, who uses his music to punish the town of Hamelin. How could I illustrate a more direct expression of this character's revenge? I would like to make an image that hints at more "behind the scenes" stories to come.

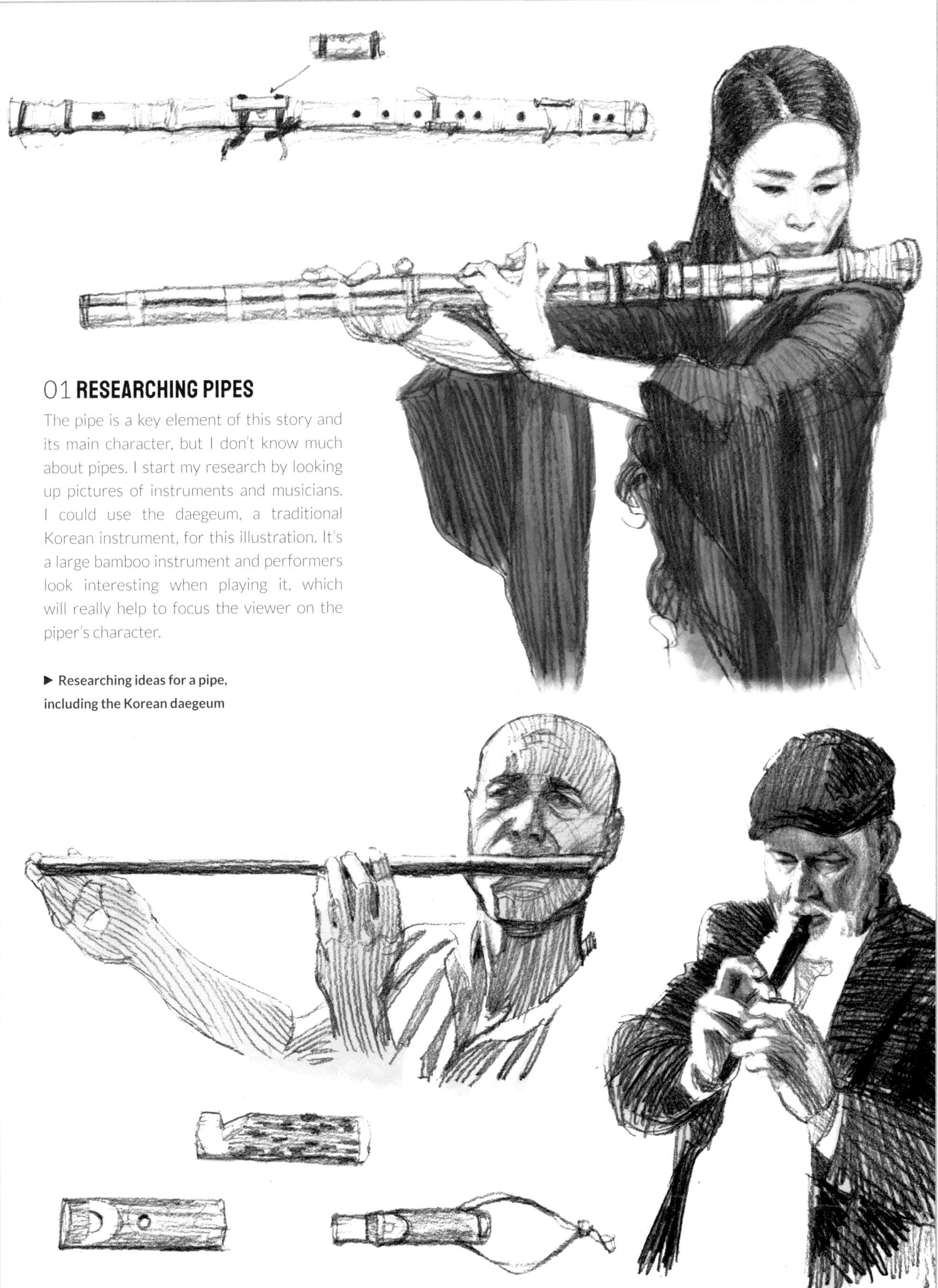

01 RESEARCHING PIPES

The pipe is a key element of this story and its main character, but I don't know much about pipes. I start my research by looking up pictures of instruments and musicians. I could use the daegeum, a traditional Korean instrument, for this illustration. It's a large bamboo instrument and performers look interesting when playing it, which will really help to focus the viewer on the piper's character.

▶ Researching ideas for a pipe, including the Korean daegeum

02 **RESEARCHING MASKS**

I personally do not want to express the "missing children" as they are in the story. Instead, I want to use something more subtle to symbolize them, such as an object in the scene. I decide that masks would be a good device for this, so I research a few different ideas – Greek theater masks are excellent expressive references. Perhaps the children could be referenced in the piper's costume, with tragic faces appearing on his costume or among his accessories.

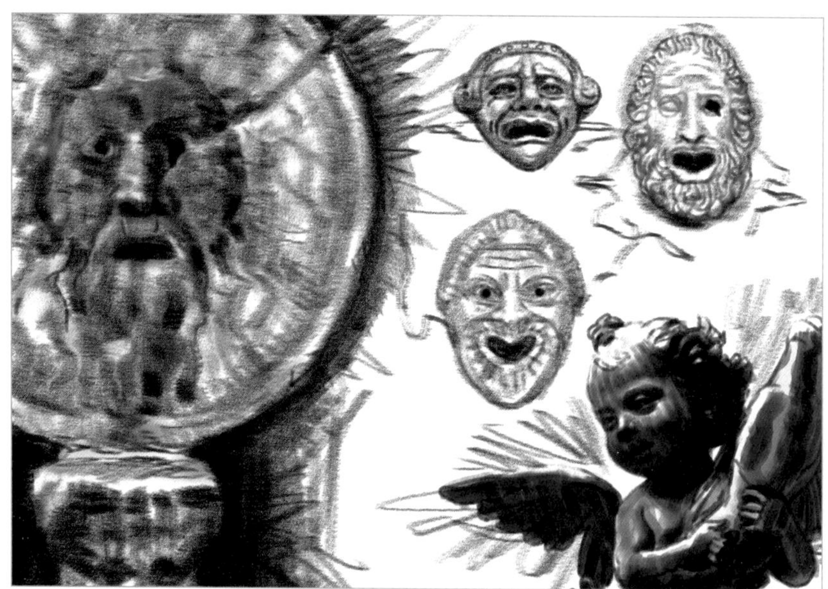

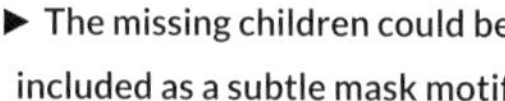

► The missing children could be included as a subtle mask motif

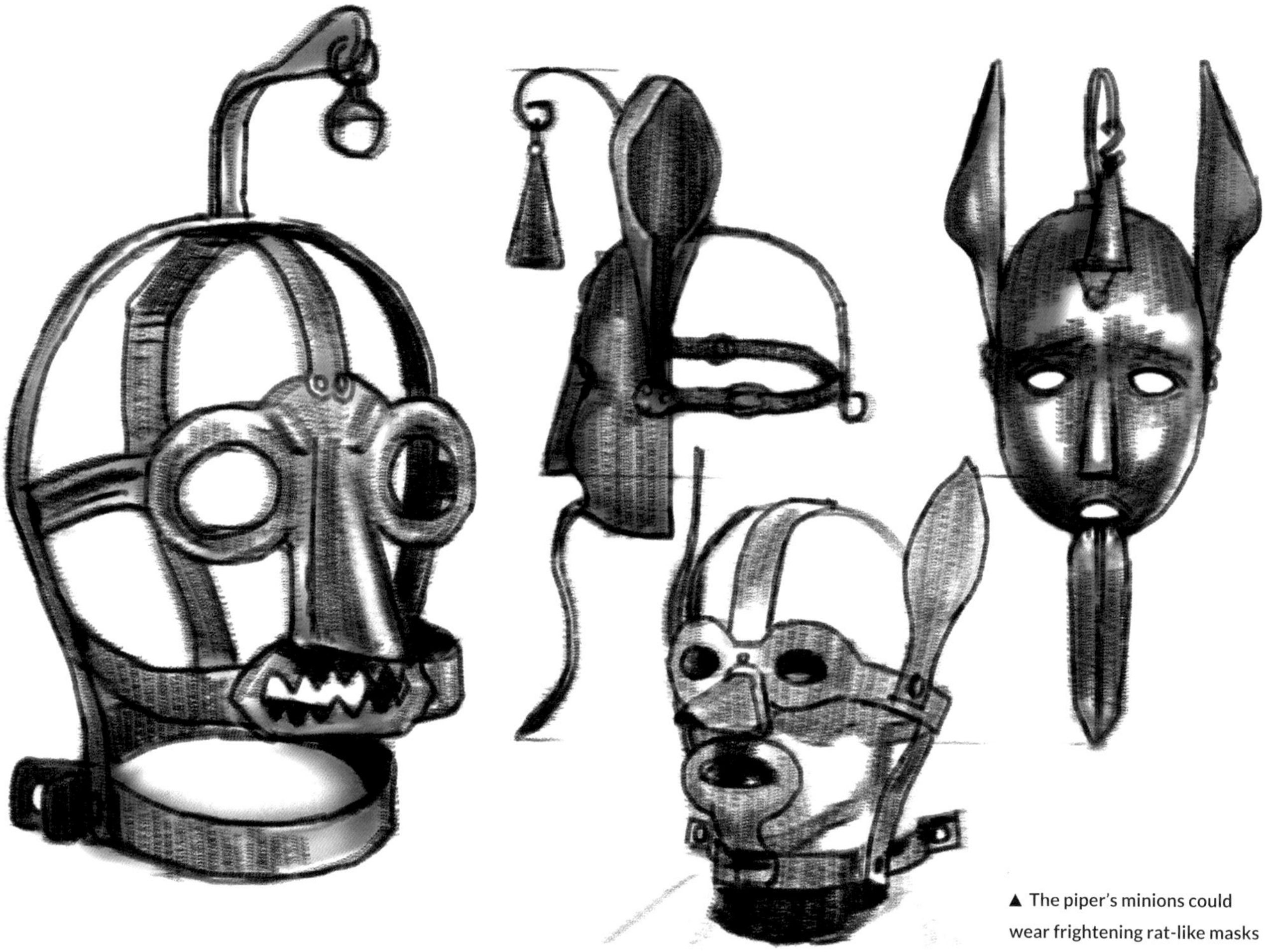

▲ The piper's minions could wear frightening rat-like masks

03 **MORE MASKS**

In my scene, I imagine the piper returning to town for vengeance, supported by menacing thugs with a rat-like appearance. Their faces could be hidden by masks to make them more mysterious and frightening, continuing my current research into masks. I am intrigued by a type of mask called a scold's bridle, an iron device worn historically as a punishment for gossip. These masks often had an ugly, threatening appearance, sometimes including a bell that would ring to draw attention to the wearer. I sketch a few design ideas and play with adding rat-like features to the masks, such as pointed snouts and large ears.

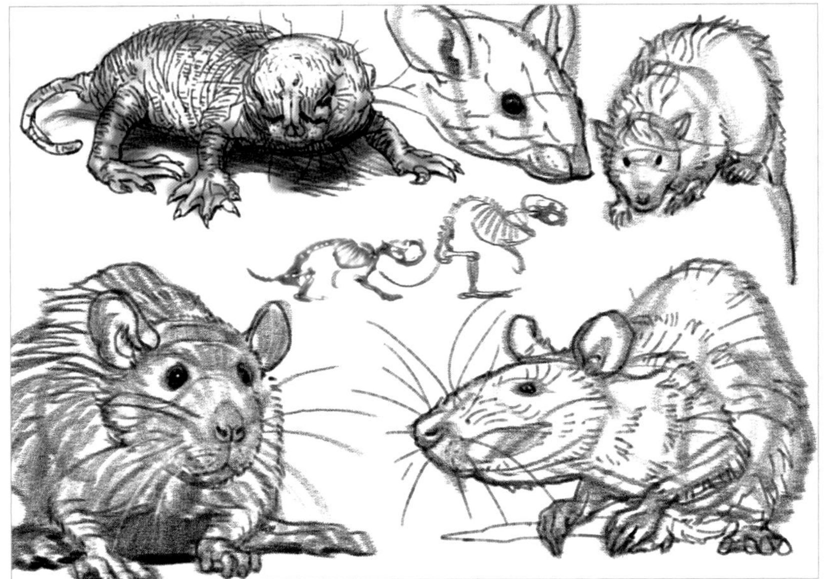

04 RESEARCHING RATS

I also don't know much about rats, so I research them too, looking up plenty of pictures and sketching studies of different types. I include some skeleton sketches to help understand their posture and structure, and even sketch a naked mole-rat for a completely different kind of rat. These bald, subterranean rats are not the type traditionally associated with this story, but they have a strange appearance that could work well for a scary scene!

◀ Sketching some studies of different rats

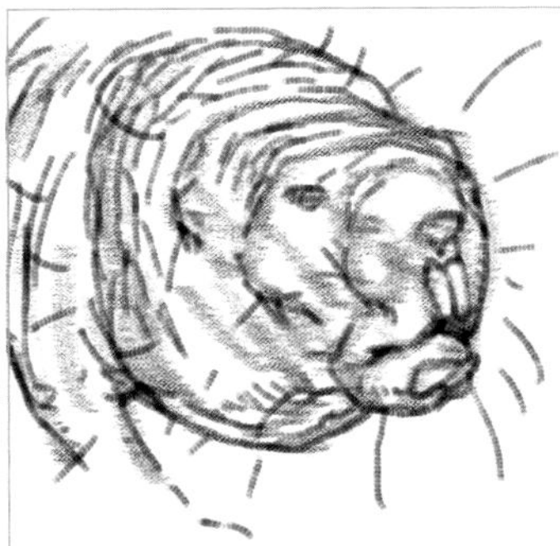

05 MORE RATS

The naked mole-rat really appeals to me, so I explore further with a few more studies. These rodents have pale, wrinkled skin; small, weak eyes; and very long teeth that grow outside their lips. I would like to use them in some way, but they have to be right for the story and setting. I haven't decided yet, so will continue sketching.

▲ The naked mole-rat is an intriguing animal that could help me create an unusual take on the story

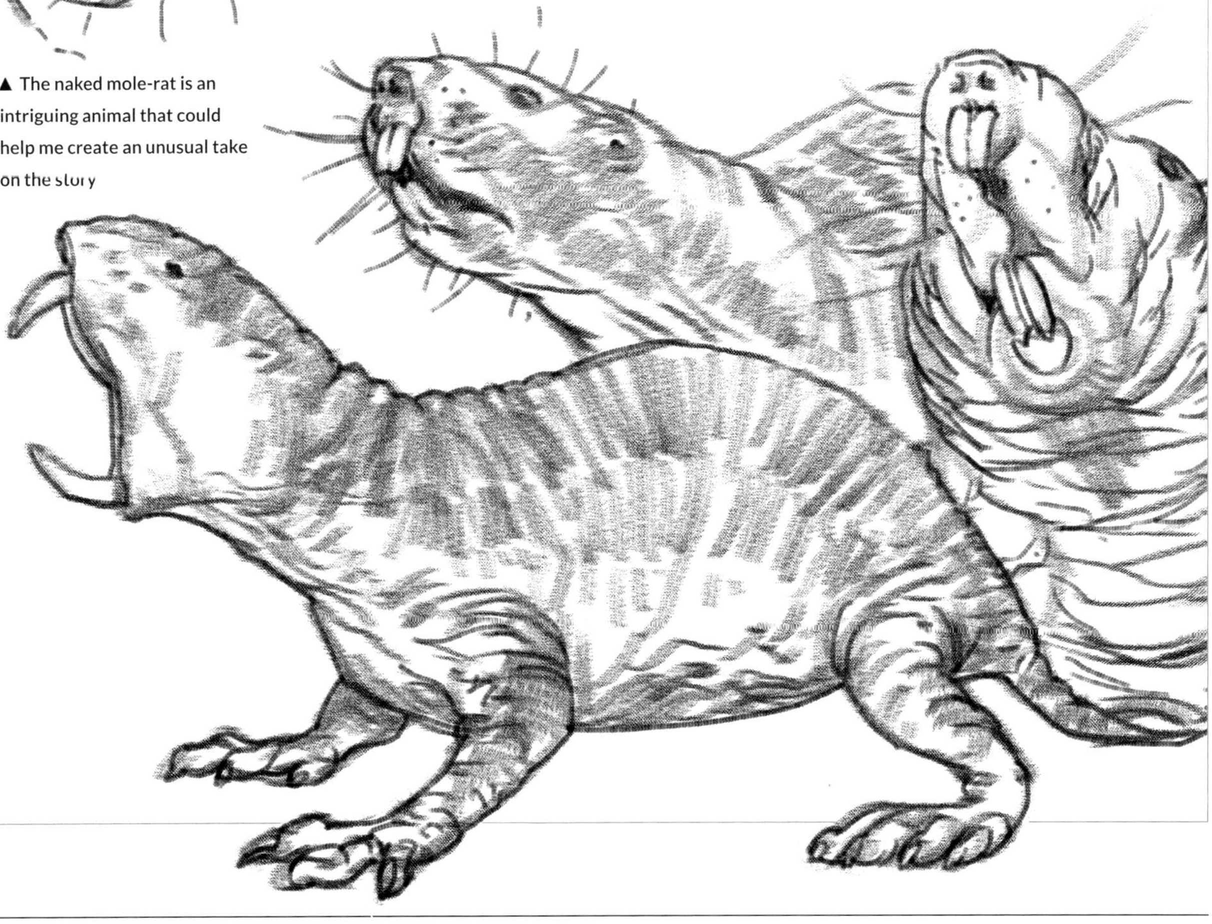

06 CREATURE DESIGNS

I debate on whether the rats will simply be rats or more like fantasy creatures. It could be interesting if the piper's followers are rat-like humanoid creatures that move in groups with the real rats. Perhaps they would help command the rats and intimidate the townspeople of Hamelin. In these sketches, I try combining the rat features from my studies with more humanoid posture and anatomy.

► Combining human and rat anatomy to make a creature design

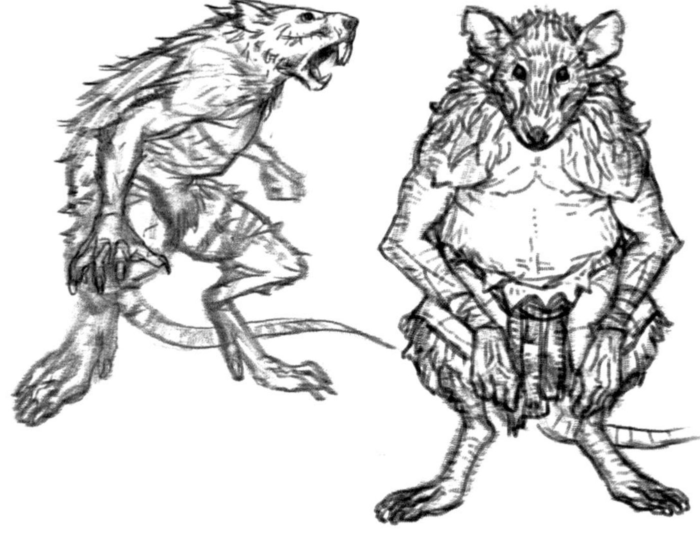

07 MOLE-RAT HYBRID

I find myself really engaged by the idea of these large, humanoid rats moving among the hordes of normal rats being led by the piper. I develop the creature into an even larger, scarier monster based on the naked mole-rat, with huge, exposed teeth and a hairless body covered in scars. I am still not fully decided on the type of creature I want to use in the scene, but I feel comfortable leaving this idea here and moving on to explore some other characters.

◄ Incorporating some mole-rat influence into the creature design

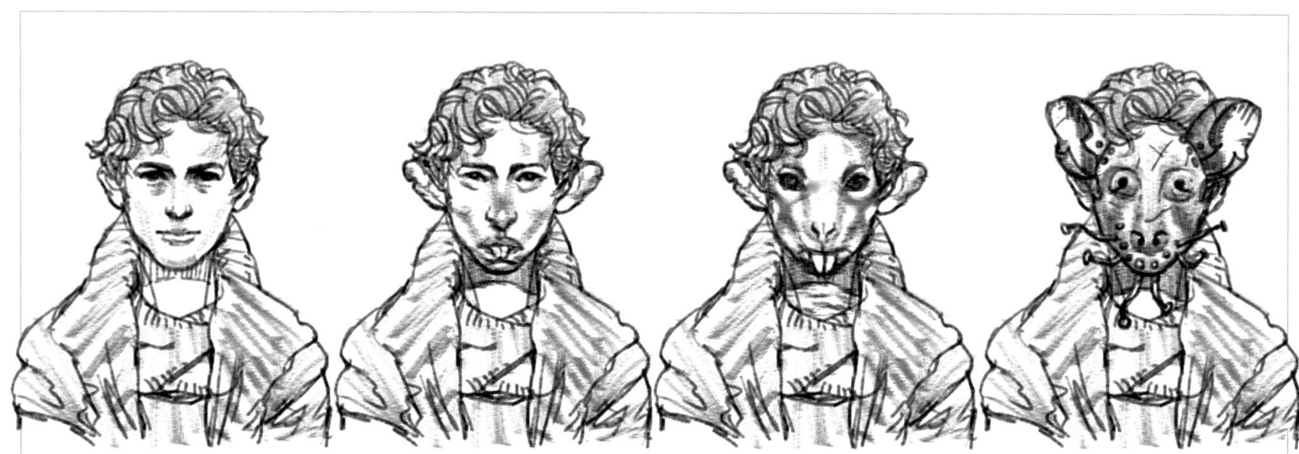

▲ Trying out some ideas for a partially transformed rat-child

08 THE MISSING CHILDREN

Perhaps Hamelin's missing children could return as allies of the Pied Piper. They could be wearing masks like I explored in step 03, or even be partially transformed into rats themselves. The latter could be a powerful indicator of the piper's influence. I sketch a few different ideas with varying levels of "ratness."

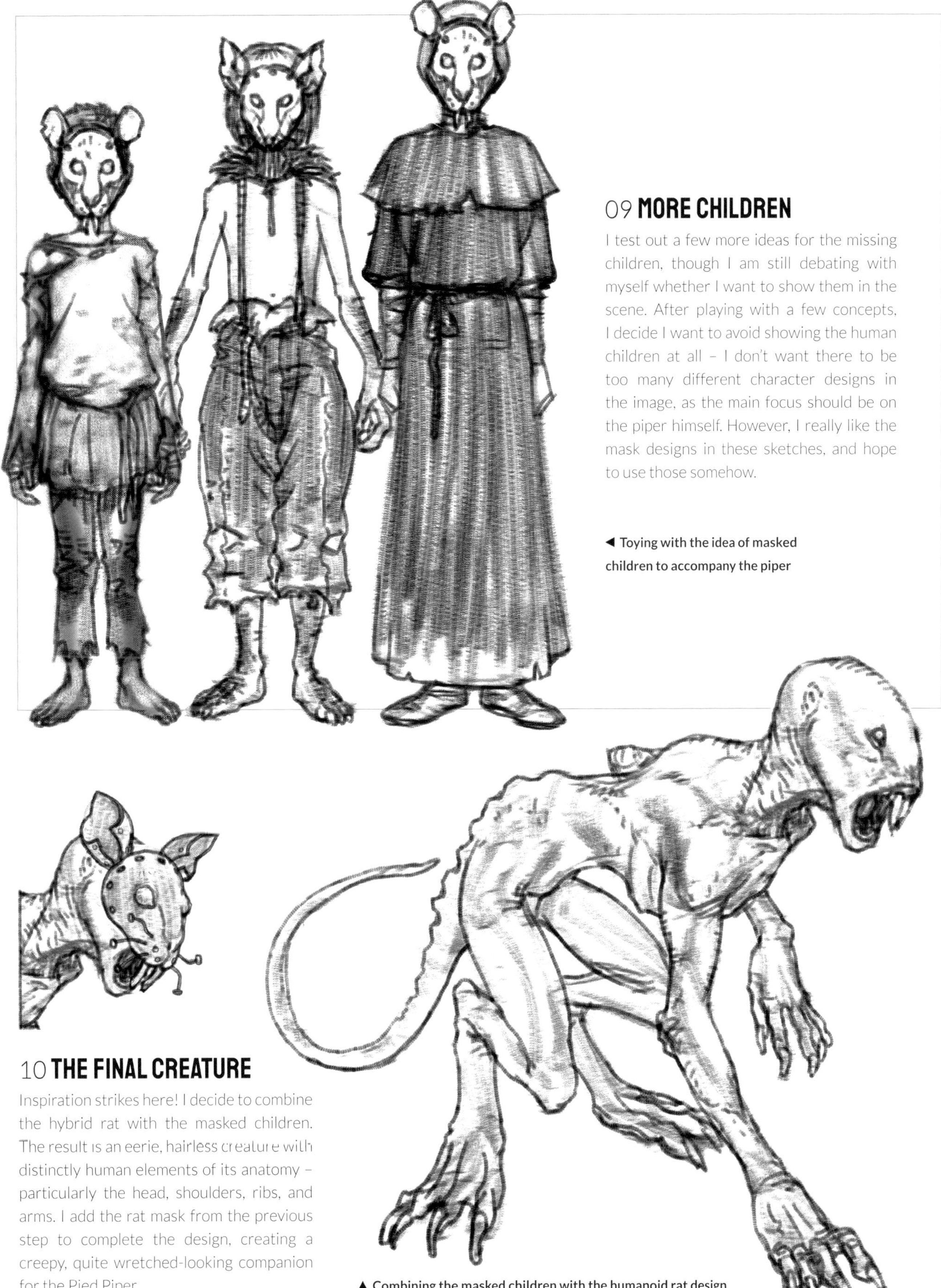

09 MORE CHILDREN

I test out a few more ideas for the missing children, though I am still debating with myself whether I want to show them in the scene. After playing with a few concepts, I decide I want to avoid showing the human children at all – I don't want there to be too many different character designs in the image, as the main focus should be on the piper himself. However, I really like the mask designs in these sketches, and hope to use those somehow.

◀ Toying with the idea of masked children to accompany the piper

10 THE FINAL CREATURE

Inspiration strikes here! I decide to combine the hybrid rat with the masked children. The result is an eerie, hairless creature with distinctly human elements of its anatomy – particularly the head, shoulders, ribs, and arms. I add the rat mask from the previous step to complete the design, creating a creepy, quite wretched-looking companion for the Pied Piper.

▲ Combining the masked children with the humanoid rat design

11 PIPER SKETCHES

Now I am ready to explore the Pied Piper himself. I do this with pen on paper to get my ideas out quickly and simply. Wandering hunters, secret necromancers, and dark missionaries come to mind. My thumbnails range from bow-wielding warriors to monastic figures – all powerful designs with commanding silhouettes. I decide to explore a few different options next, based on these rough thumbnails.

▼ Turning to my sketchbook to draw out some quick character ideas

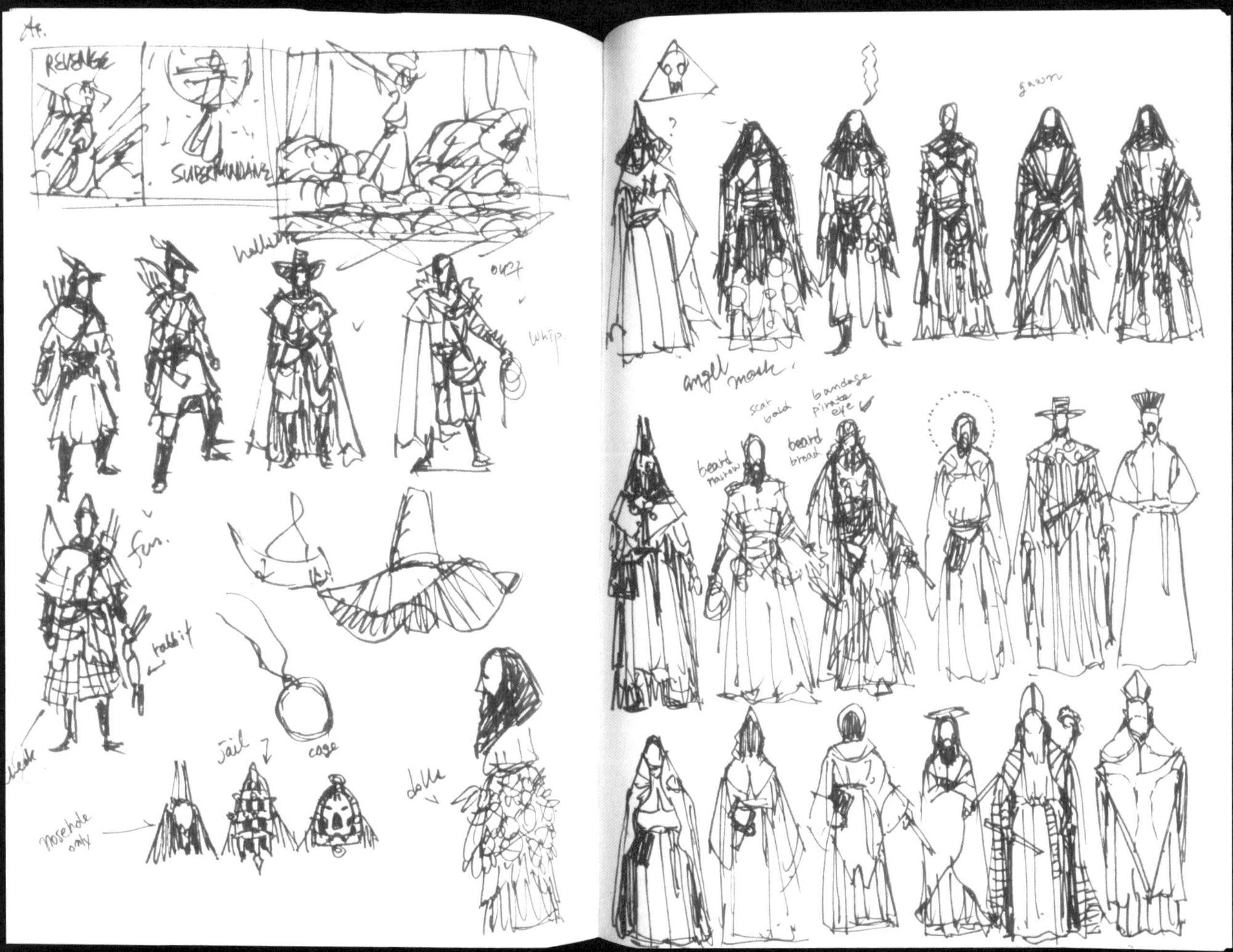

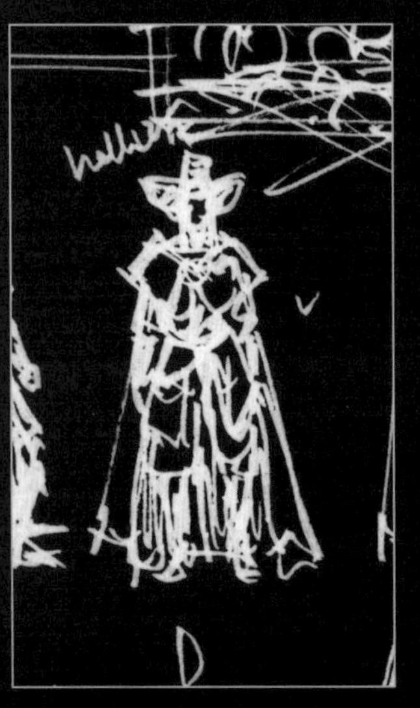

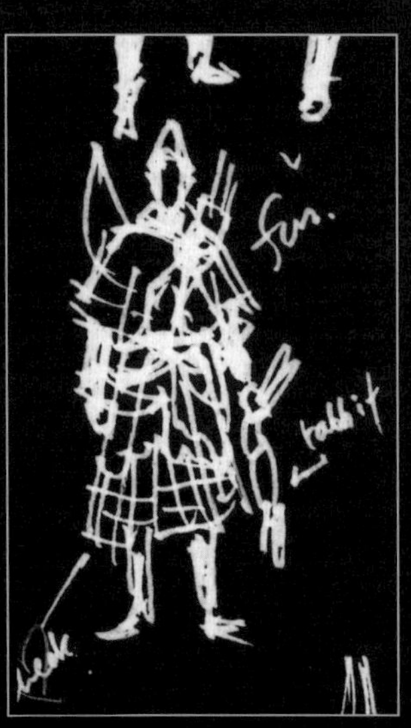

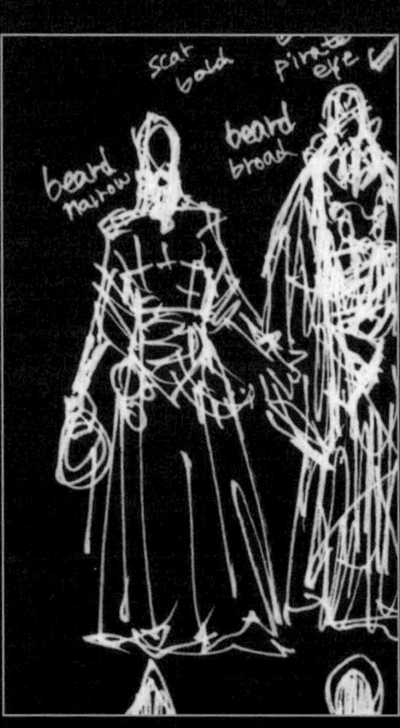

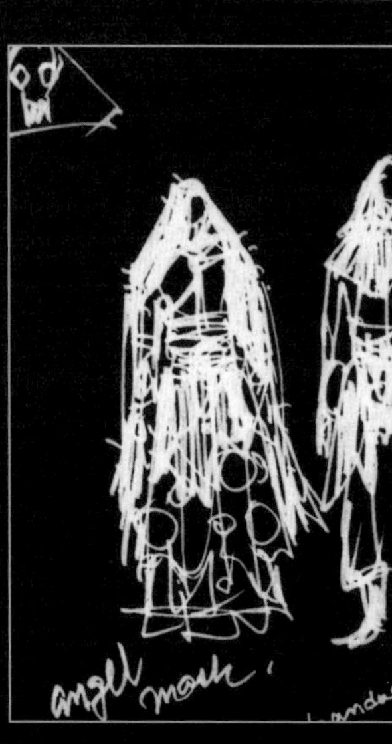

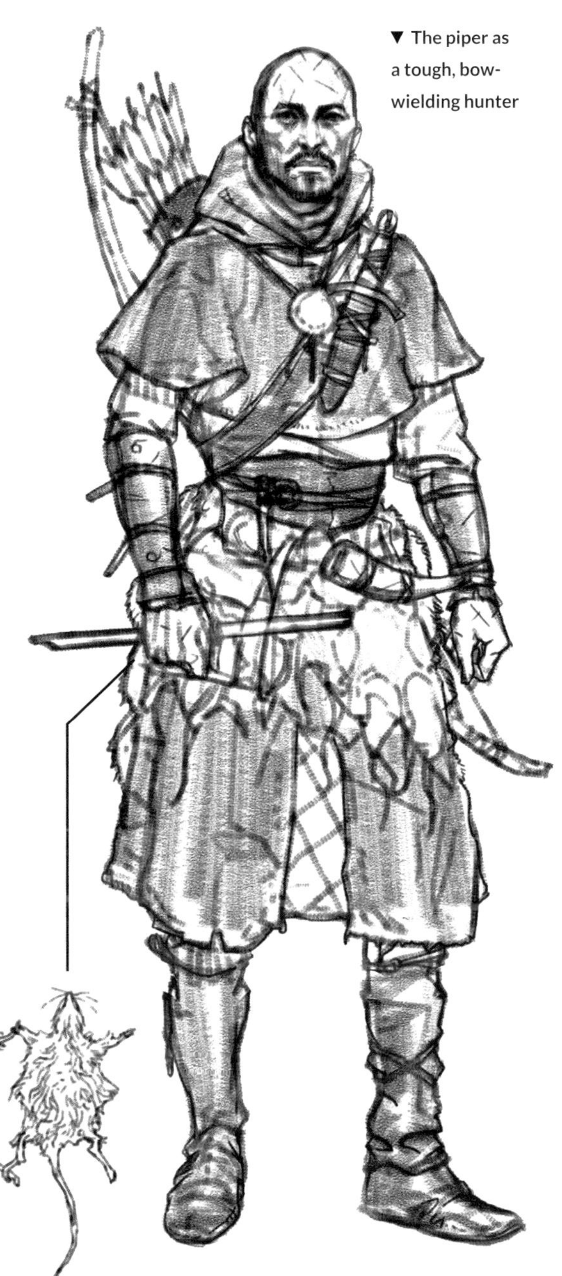

▼ The piper as a tough, bow-wielding hunter

12 THE HUNTER-WARRIOR

My first version of the piper is a skilled hunter who has no hesitation in catching rats. He carries a knife and bow for when his pipe is insufficient, and he wears a protective kilt of rat hides tied around his waist. He looks weathered and well-prepared – a character who is ready for a tough livelihood of traveling around. He feels very grounded and practical, but I would like my piper to have a little more magic.

13 THE WANDERING ARCHER

This is another take on the idea of a bow-wielding piper. Though he also appears to be a tough old fighter, ready for life on the road, he is friendly with the rats and controls them without difficulty. Therefore his whole appearance is softer and less armored than the previous concept. His wide-brimmed hat protects him from the elements and adds a bit of mystery that I like. His beard and long cloak give him a wise, almost wizardly look, but overall he looks a little too kind for the dark story I have in mind.

▼ A weathered but friendly piper who befriends rats

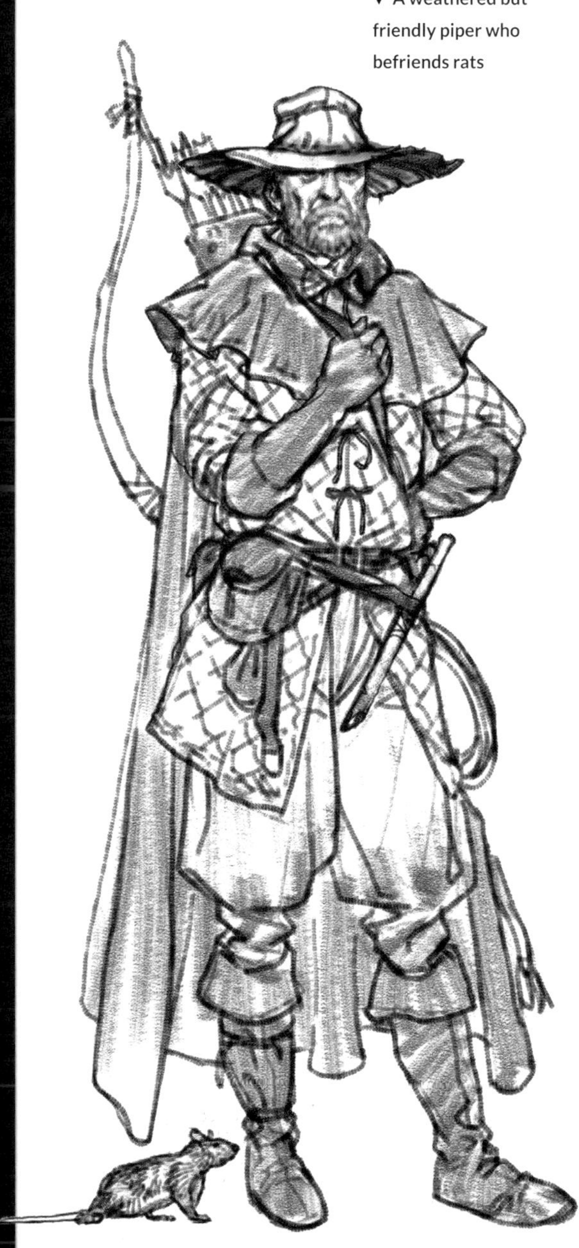

14 THE DARK WARLOCK

This third version is a dark wizard who summons rats to do his bidding. His appearance is menacing and gothic, covered with rags, straps, and scars. His belt is adorned with masks symbolizes the missing children. His whole appearance is malevolent and dangerous, but the pipe has become a bit of an afterthought, as if he does not really need it to cast his spells.

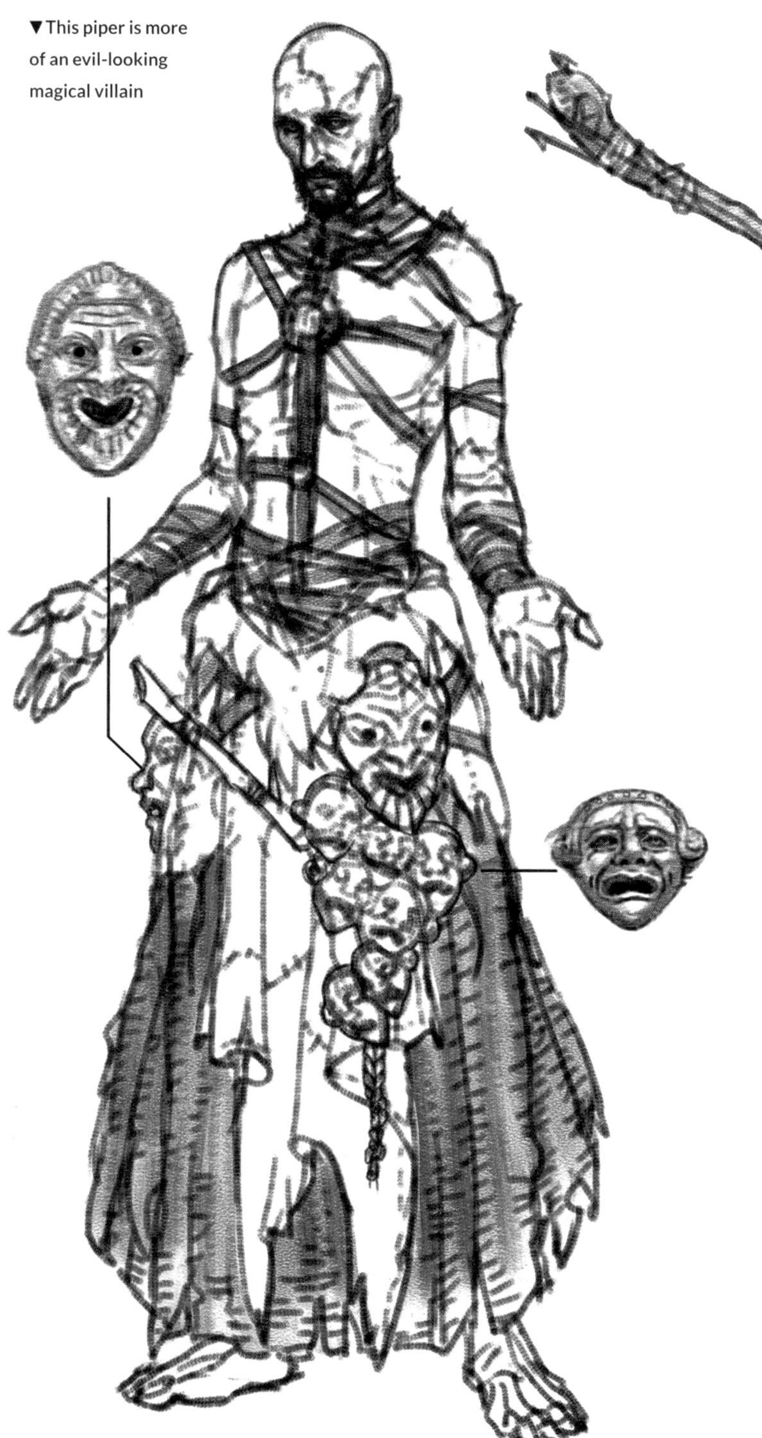

▼ This piper is more of an evil-looking magical villain

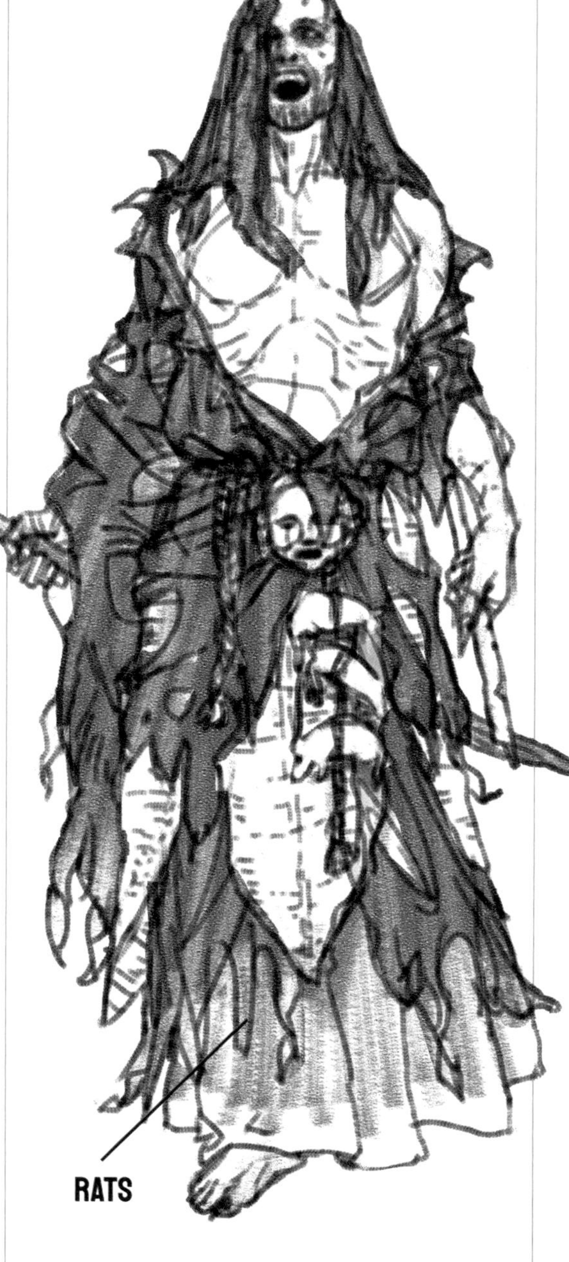

▲ Another attempt at a malevolent piper-magician

15 THE CURSED NECROMANCER

I try a second warlock idea with a less extreme costume. This version has dead rats hanging from his waist and a reference to the missing children in the mask ornament on his belt. He also carries a wooden staff for his spells, but again, his overall appearance draws too much attention away from his pipe.

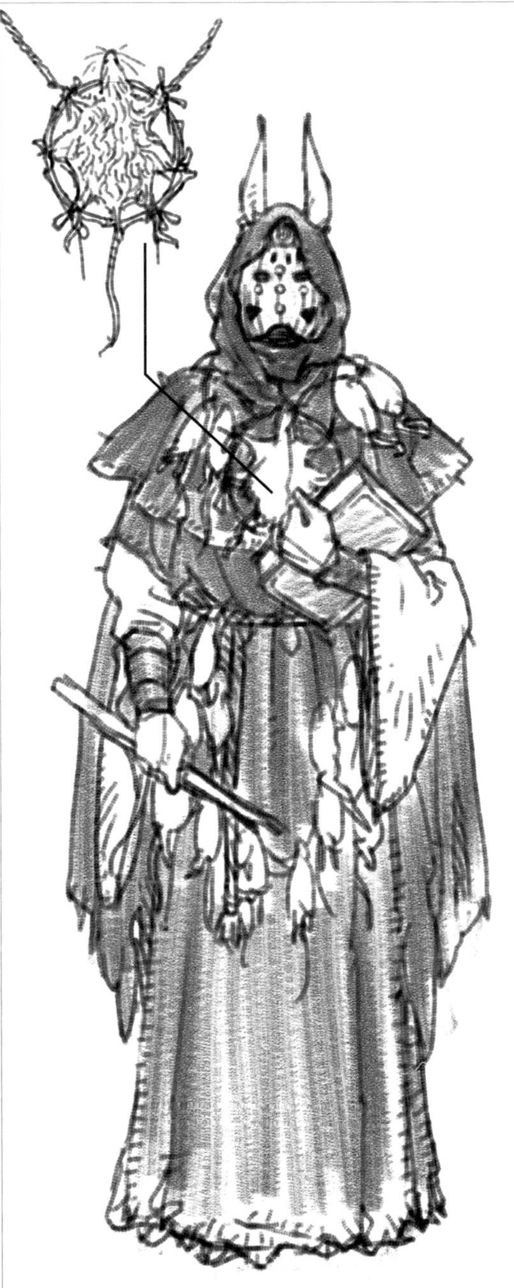

▲ A masked, monk-like piper

16 THE HOLY SLAYER

This dark missionary hides his face under a mask inspired by the scold's bridles in my research. A pipe and book are his main accessories, and his belt and neck are adorned with rat bodies. His long robes, sleeves, and cloak give him an authoritative silhouette. However, as the piper is my main character and will be the focus of the scene, it would be a shame not to see his face.

17 THE FINAL PIPER

This final version strikes a good balance between all the different aspects explored so far. This piper is well-equipped for wandering, with a wide-brimmed hat and many pouches on his belt. The hat shades his face, giving him a mysterious, menacing air. His long robe and sleeves subtly give him the look of a monk or wizard, but his overall appearance is more practical than some of my other ideas. The pipe is his sole instrument and the sorrowful faces of missing children decorate his cowl. There is almost a "Wild West villain" look to him, which suits the idea of this character arriving in town to cause trouble or enact a violent feud. The only thing I will change is his pipe, which is still quite small, instead opting for the large bamboo daegeum from my research.

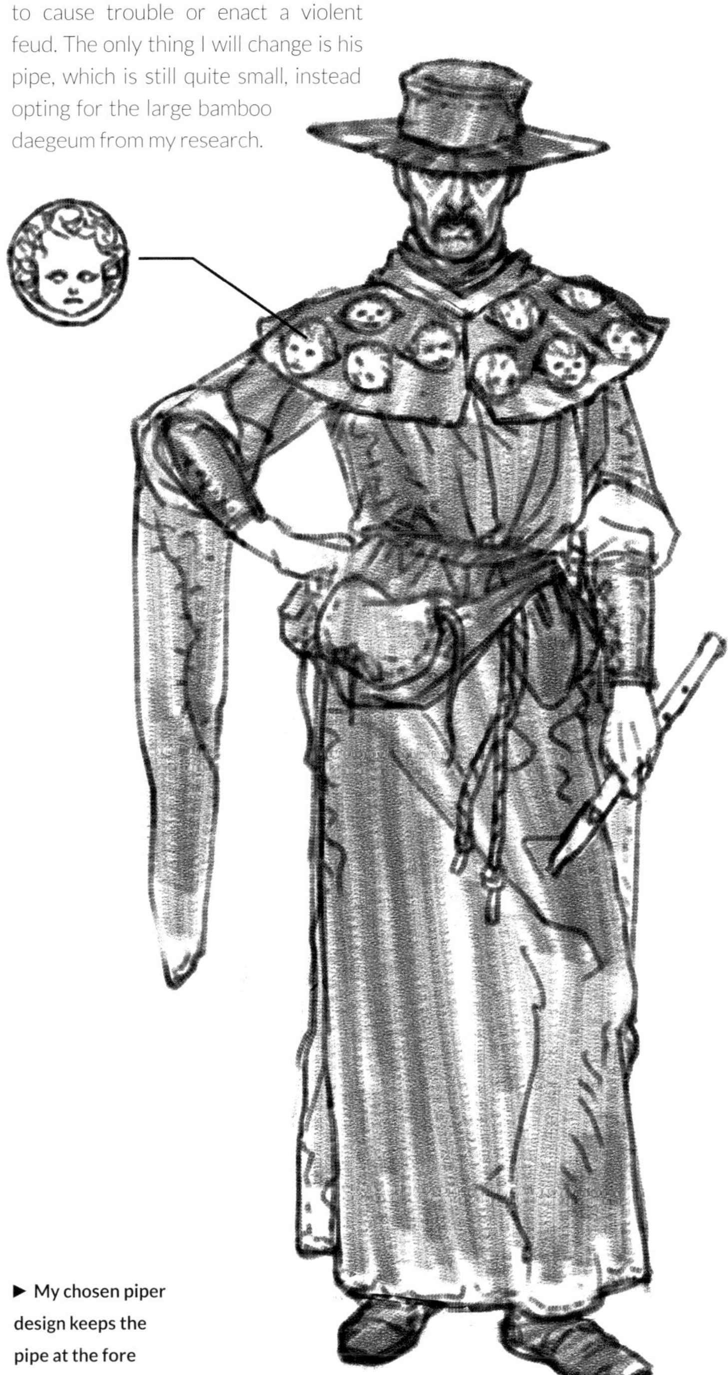

► My chosen piper design keeps the pipe at the fore

18 ILLUSTRATION THUMBNAILS

I return to my sketchbook to map out ideas for the final illustration. In my version of the tale, I imagine the Pied Piper returning to Hamelin with a horde of rats to avenge himself on the town. Large rat creatures would be mixed in with the swarm – the townsfolk won't realize that these are transformed children, perhaps from another unfortunate town. I also explore a few ideas where the piper makes rats rain from the sky, which would be fun, but I decide to go with a more readable option. I select two strong thumbnails and draw them in a more legible way. In one, the piper leads a horde of rats, including massive mole-rat beasts. In the other, the piper and his masked minions stand surrounded by the rushing swarm.

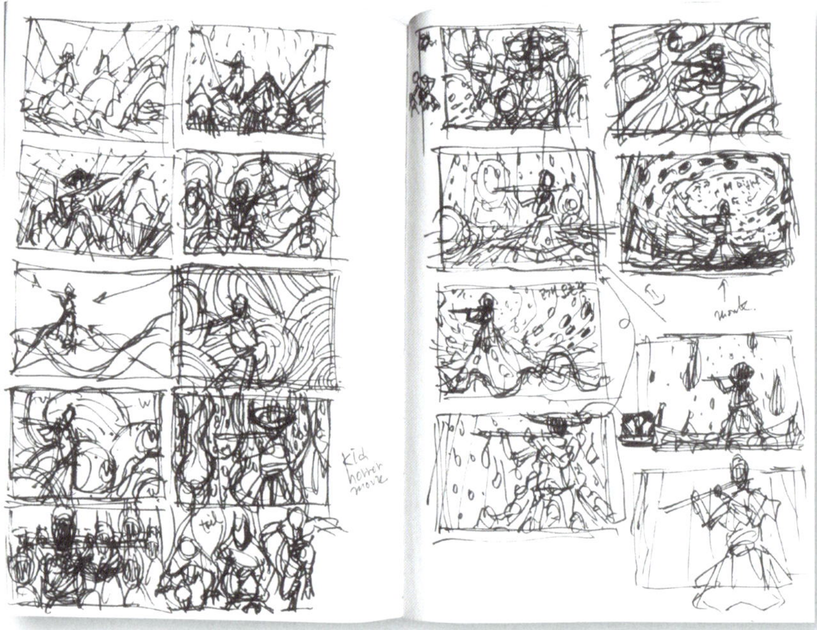

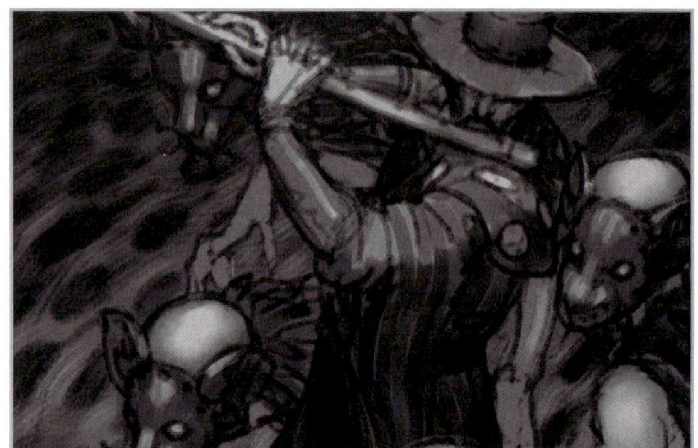

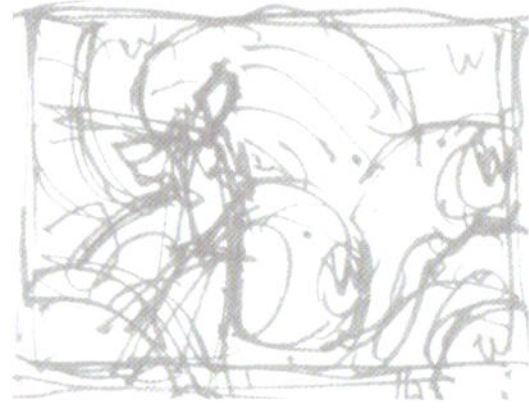

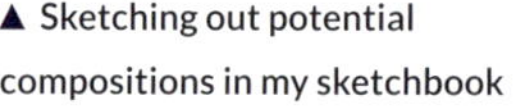

▲ Sketching out potential compositions in my sketchbook

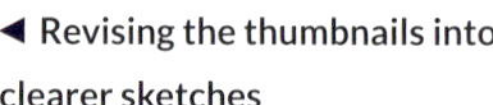

◄ Revising the thumbnails into clearer sketches

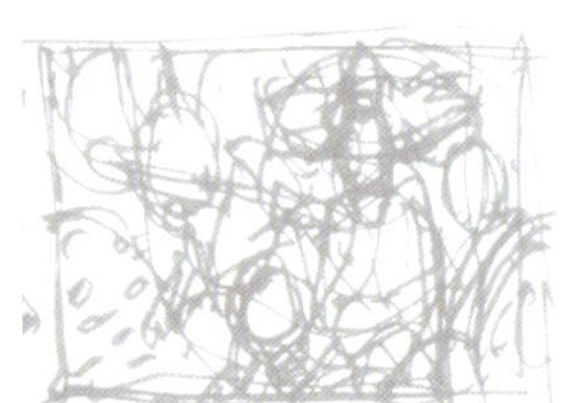

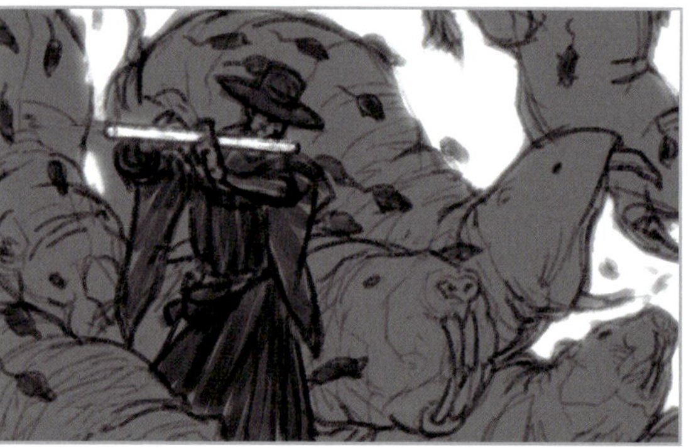

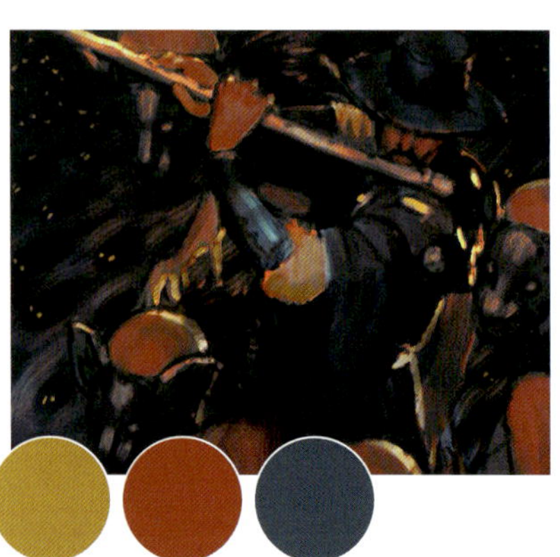

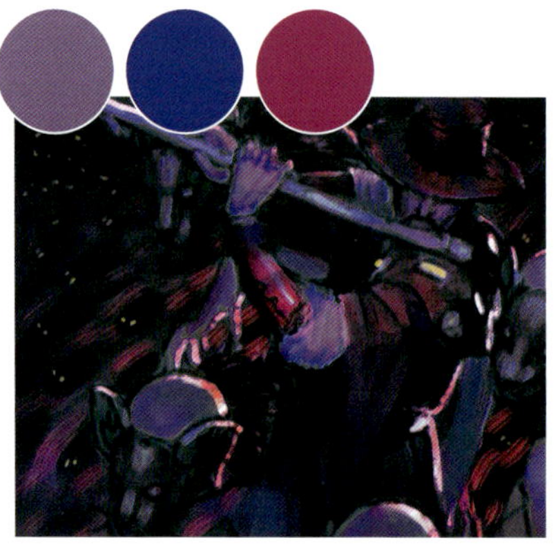

▲ Testing potential color and lighting palettes

19 COLOR AND LIGHTING

I choose the composition that is the most intriguing, because it uses a more dramatic angle and includes the additional characters of the piper's minions. I use the sketch as a base to test some simple color and lighting scenarios: one is warmer and based around orange and green, while the other is colder and driven by blues and reds. The latter is eerie and dramatic, but I decide to go with the former. It will work better to show the humanoid skins of the masked creatures.

20 THE FINAL IMAGE

The finished scene shows the mysterious piper and his masked thugs standing in the street, as his army of rats rushes over the paving stones below. The piper is playing a large daegeum that gives him a commanding pose in the composition. He is modestly dressed in the practical brown clothes of a wanderer, unlike the classic multicolored piper, but his role and story are still unmistakable. His masked minions seem human at first, but on closer inspection, the viewer is not so sure, creating some fear and unease about what is concealed beneath those masks.

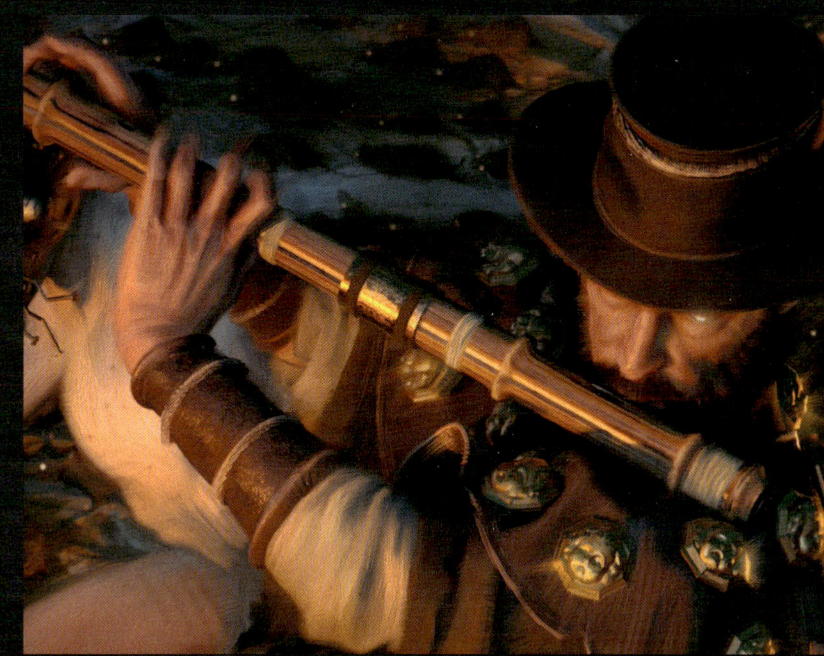

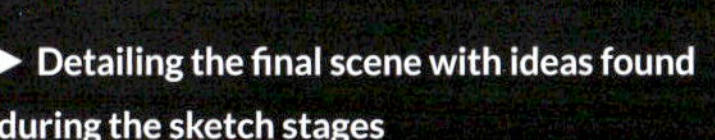

▶ Detailing the final scene with ideas found during the sketch stages

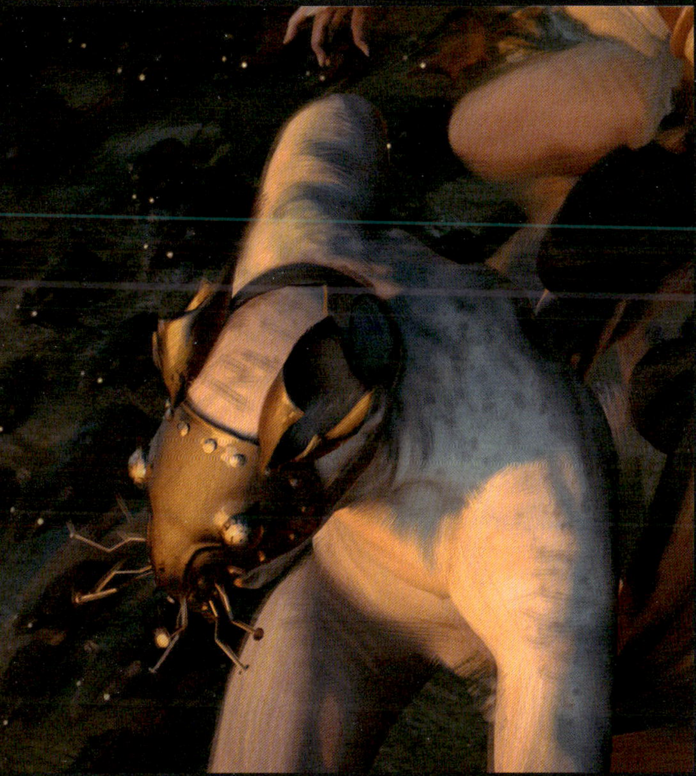

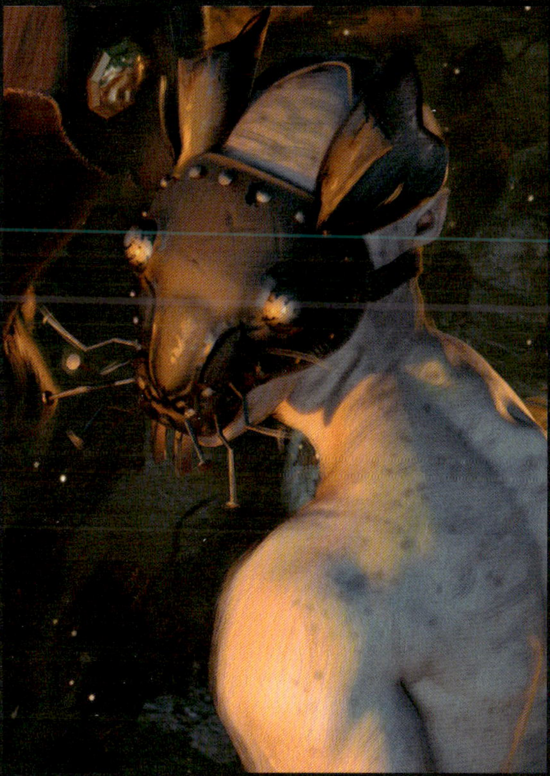

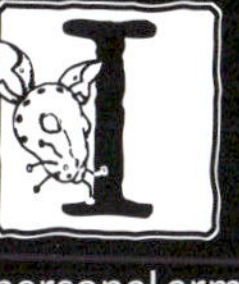

I wanted to put a twist on the typical *Pied Piper of Hamelin* story by almost reversing it. Instead of the piper leading a plague of rats away from Hamelin, he is commanding them toward it like his own personal army. His wide-brimmed hat and plain-colored traveling robes are not the typical colorful attire of the Pied Piper, but between the pipe and the rats, the connection to the original tale is unmistakable. The humanoid creatures that accompany him further emphasize the character of my piper – a mysterious, threatening figure with a gang of masked minions. The missing children of the original story are a subtle reference contained in the piper's costume.

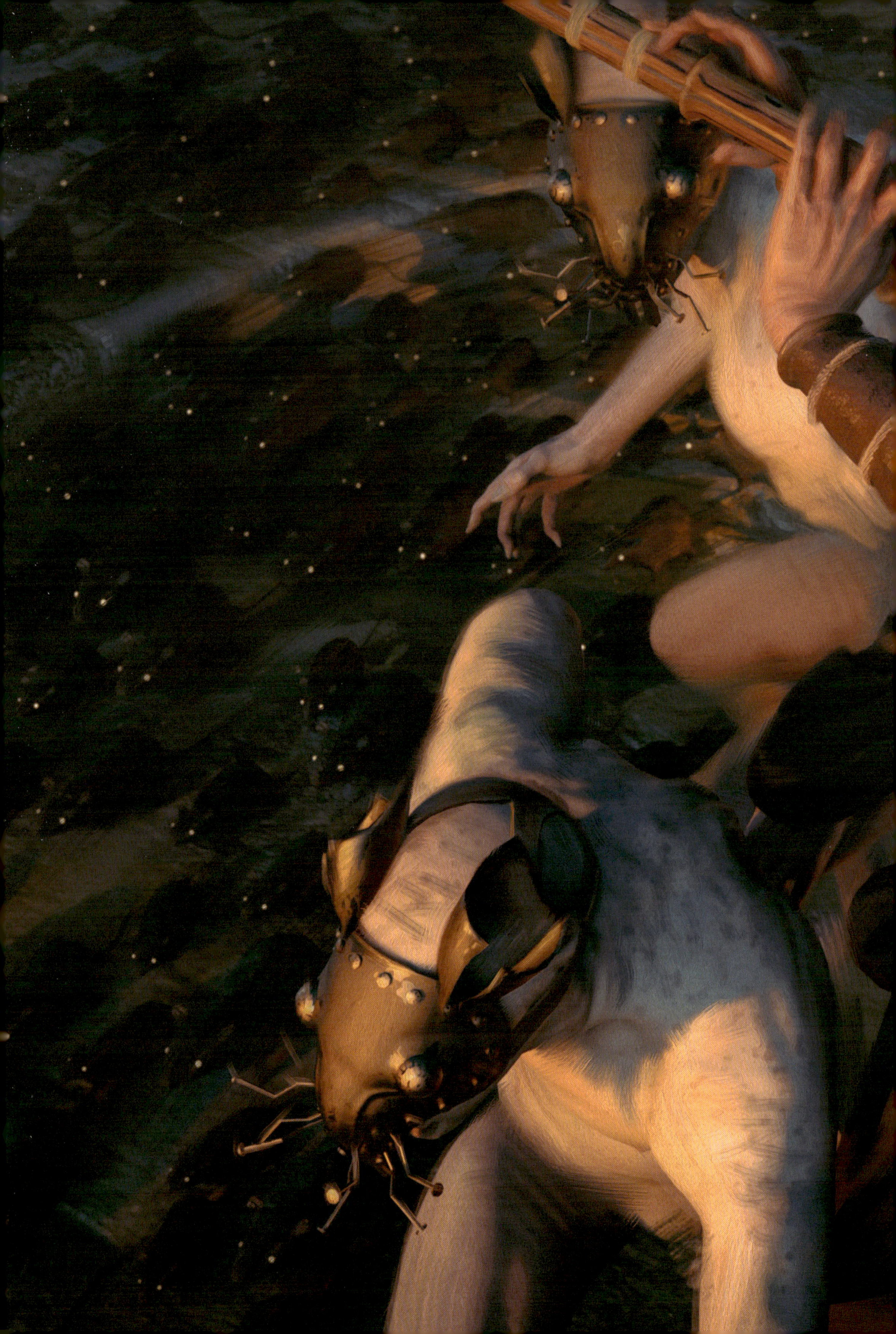

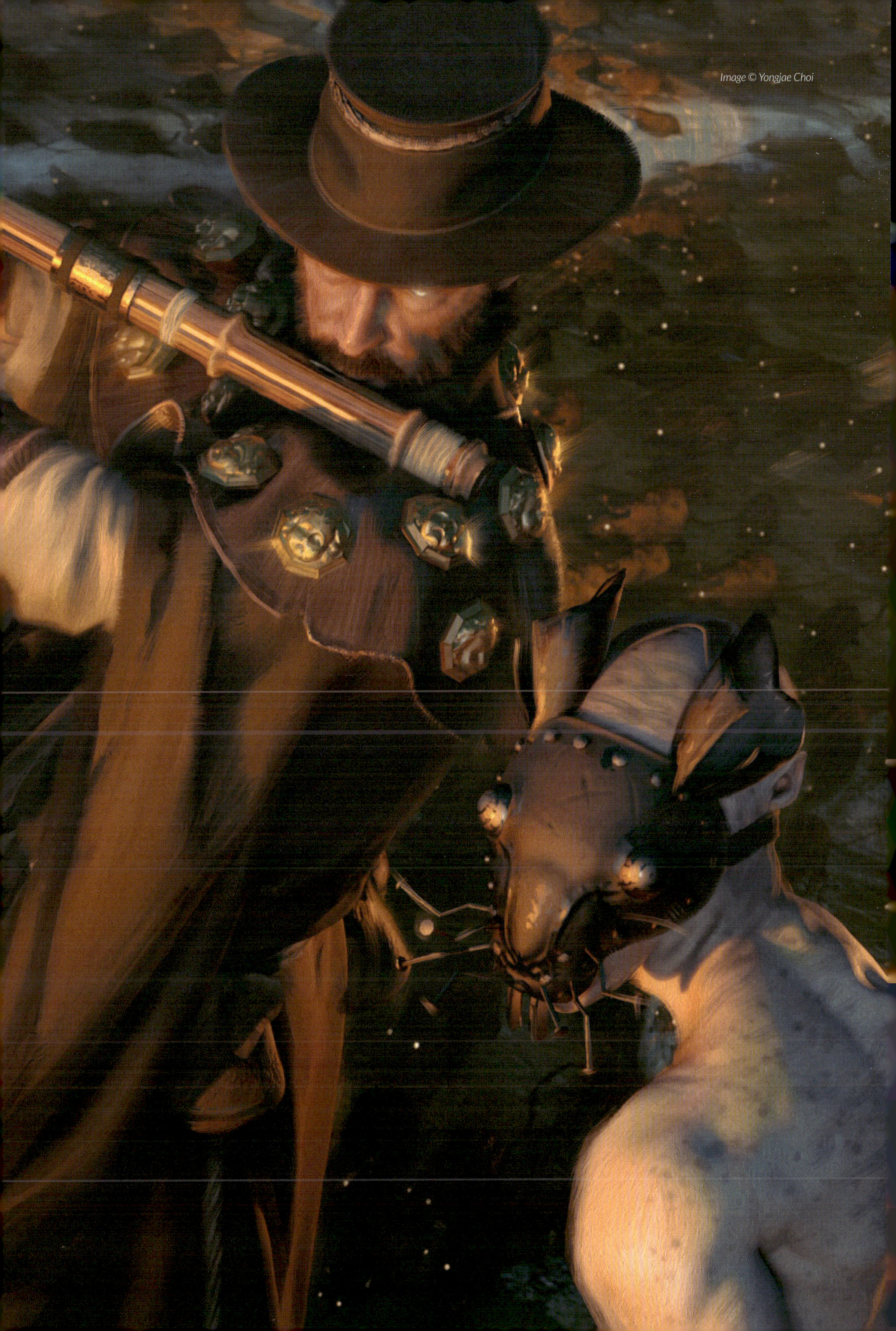

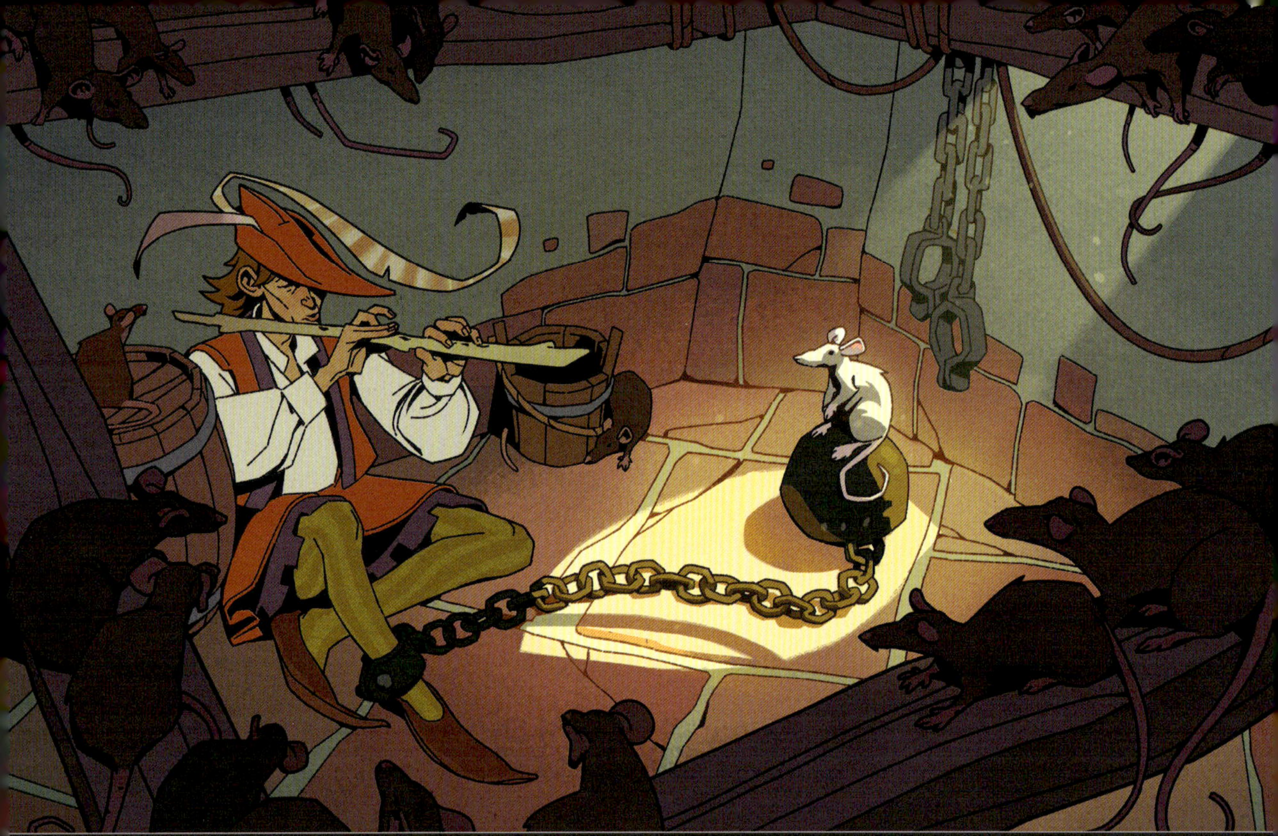

"The Piper Imprisoned." Image © Joshua Carsor

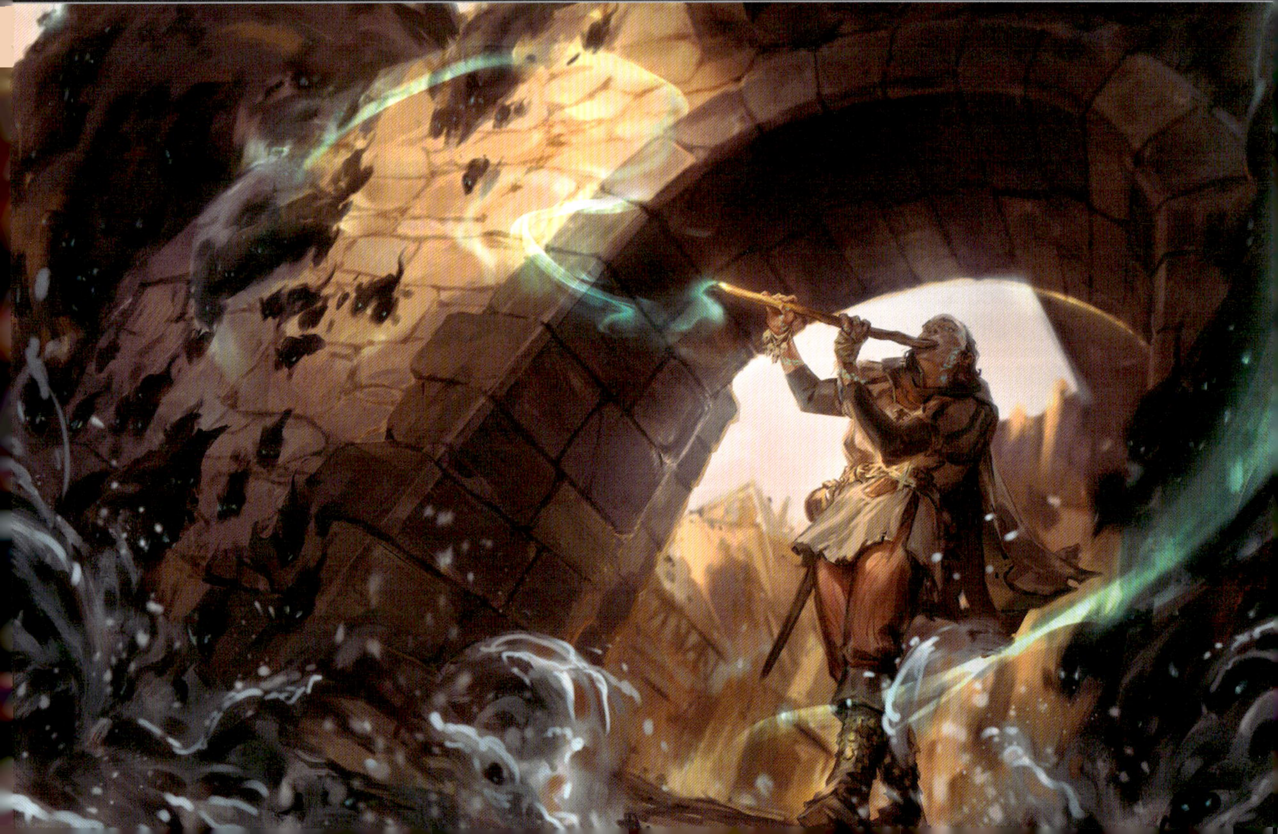

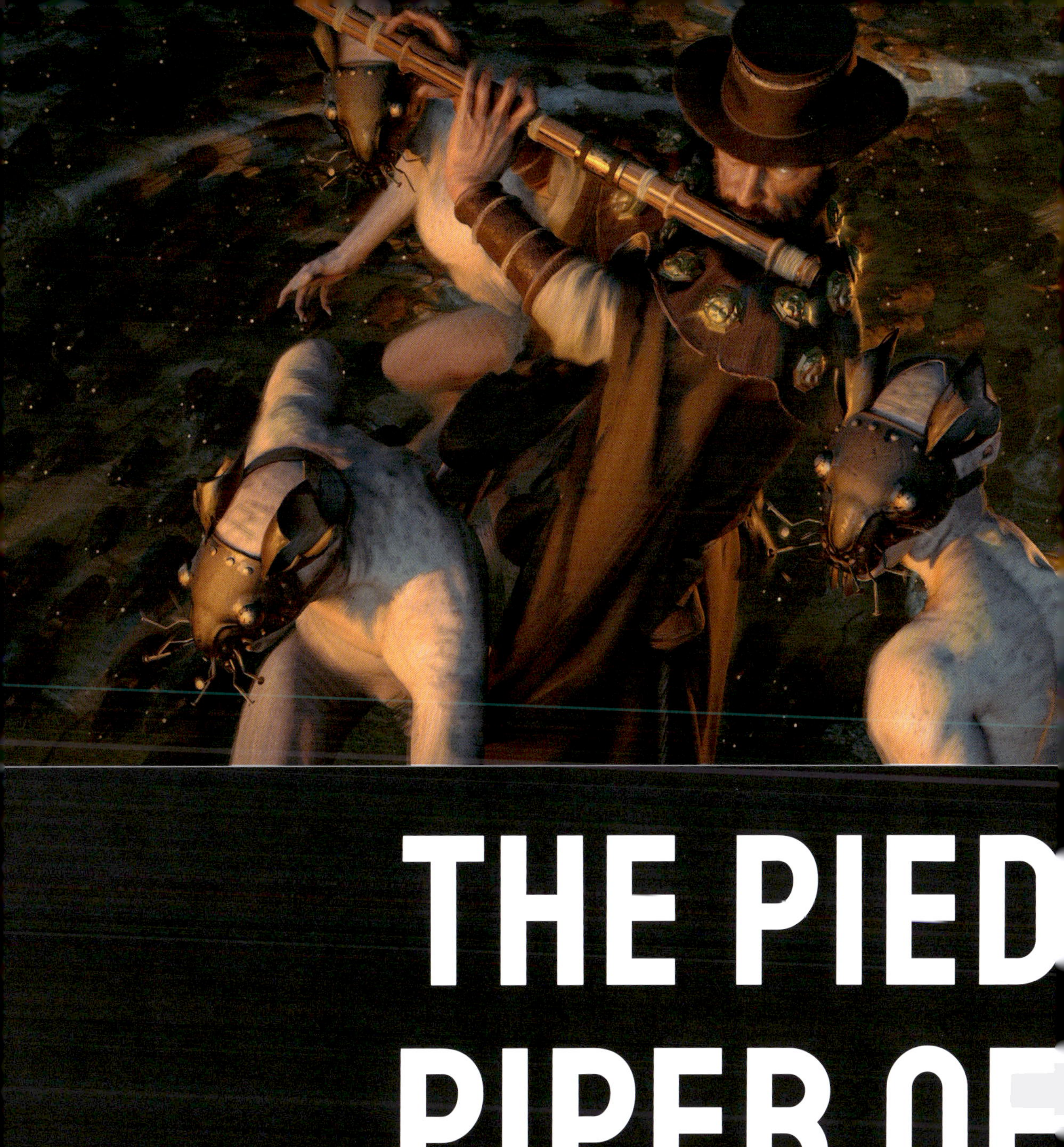

THE PIED PIPER OF HAMELIN

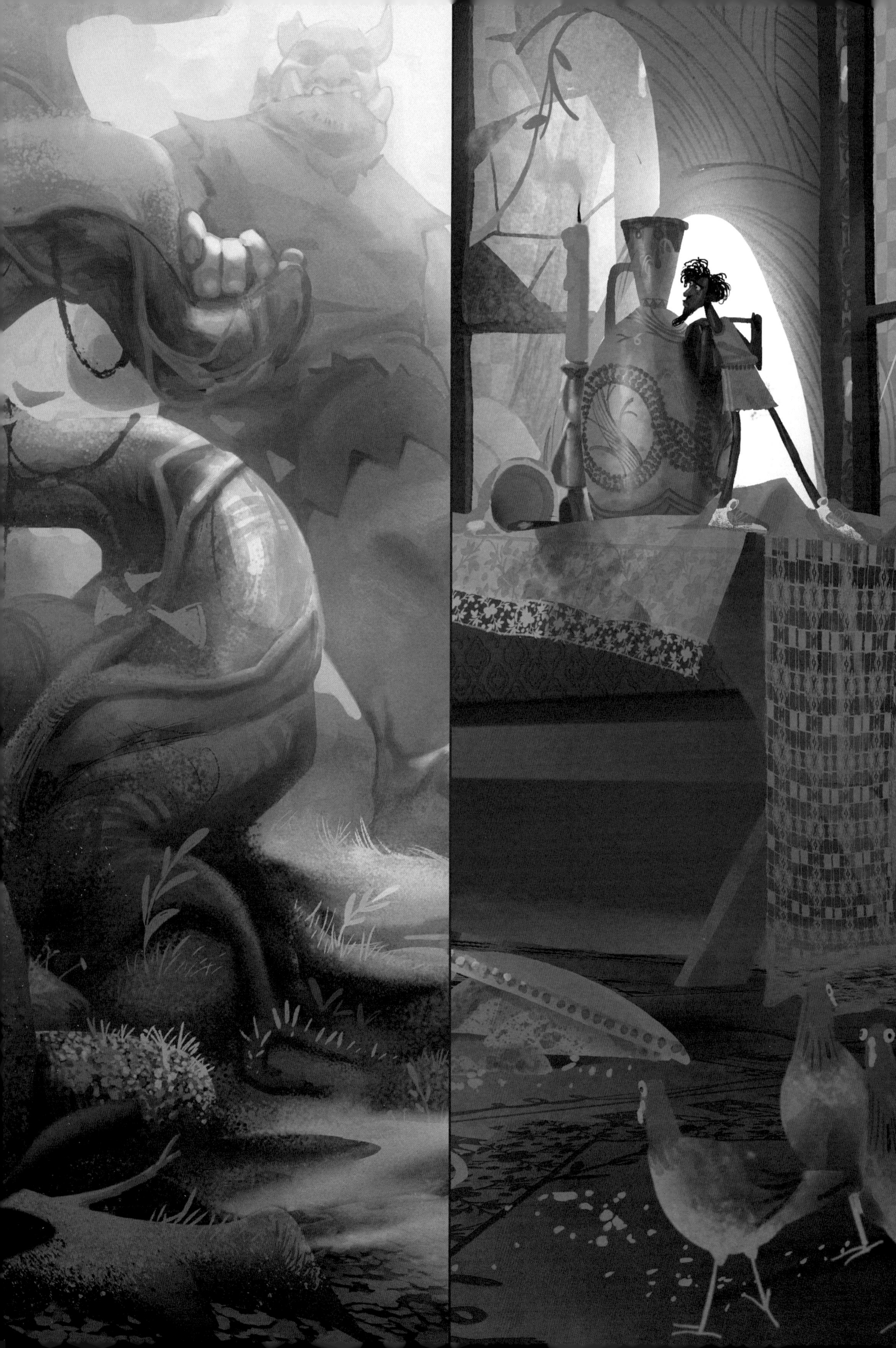

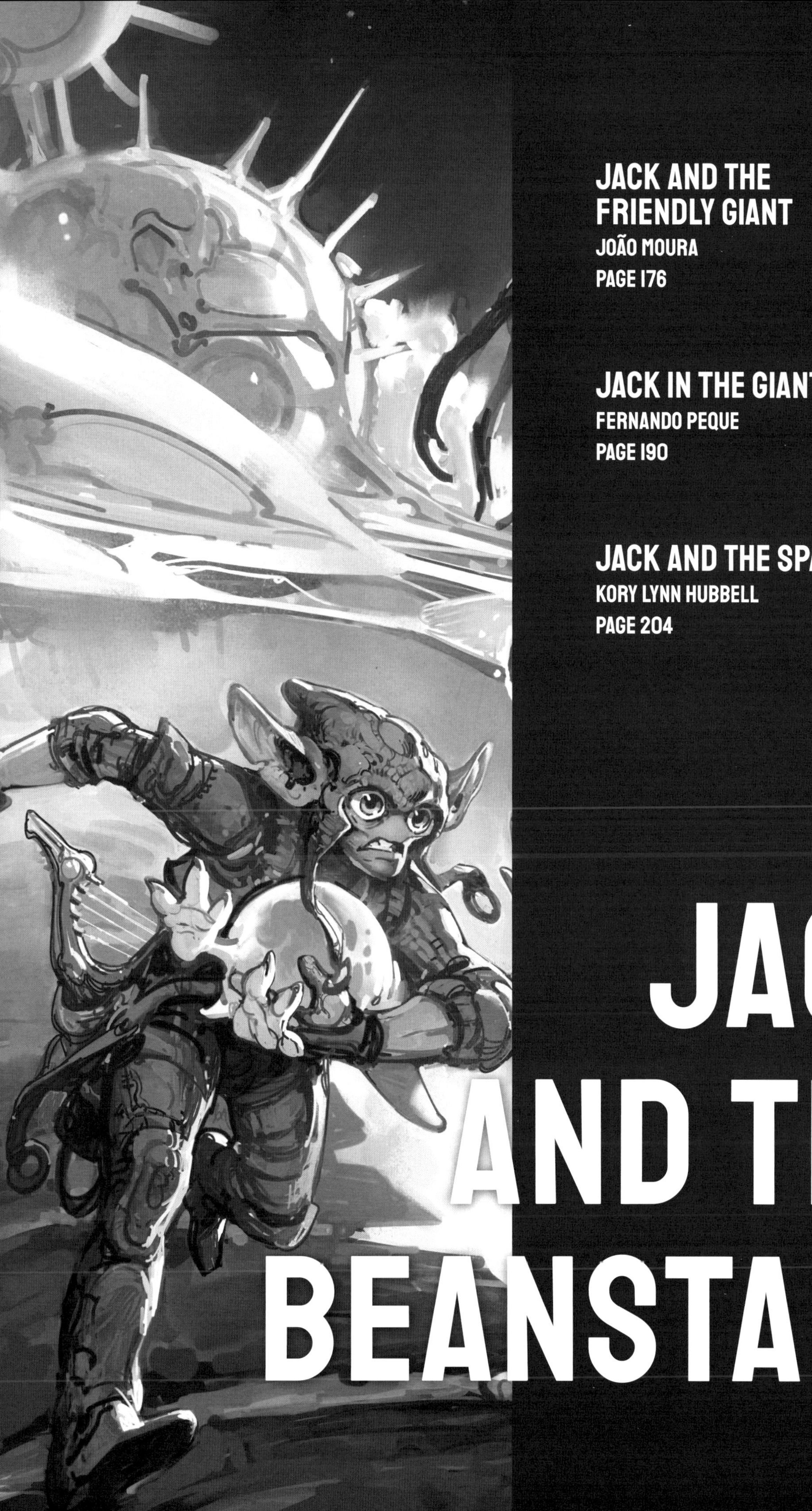

JACK AND THE BEANSTALK

JACK AND THE FRIENDLY GIANT

BY JOÃO MOURA

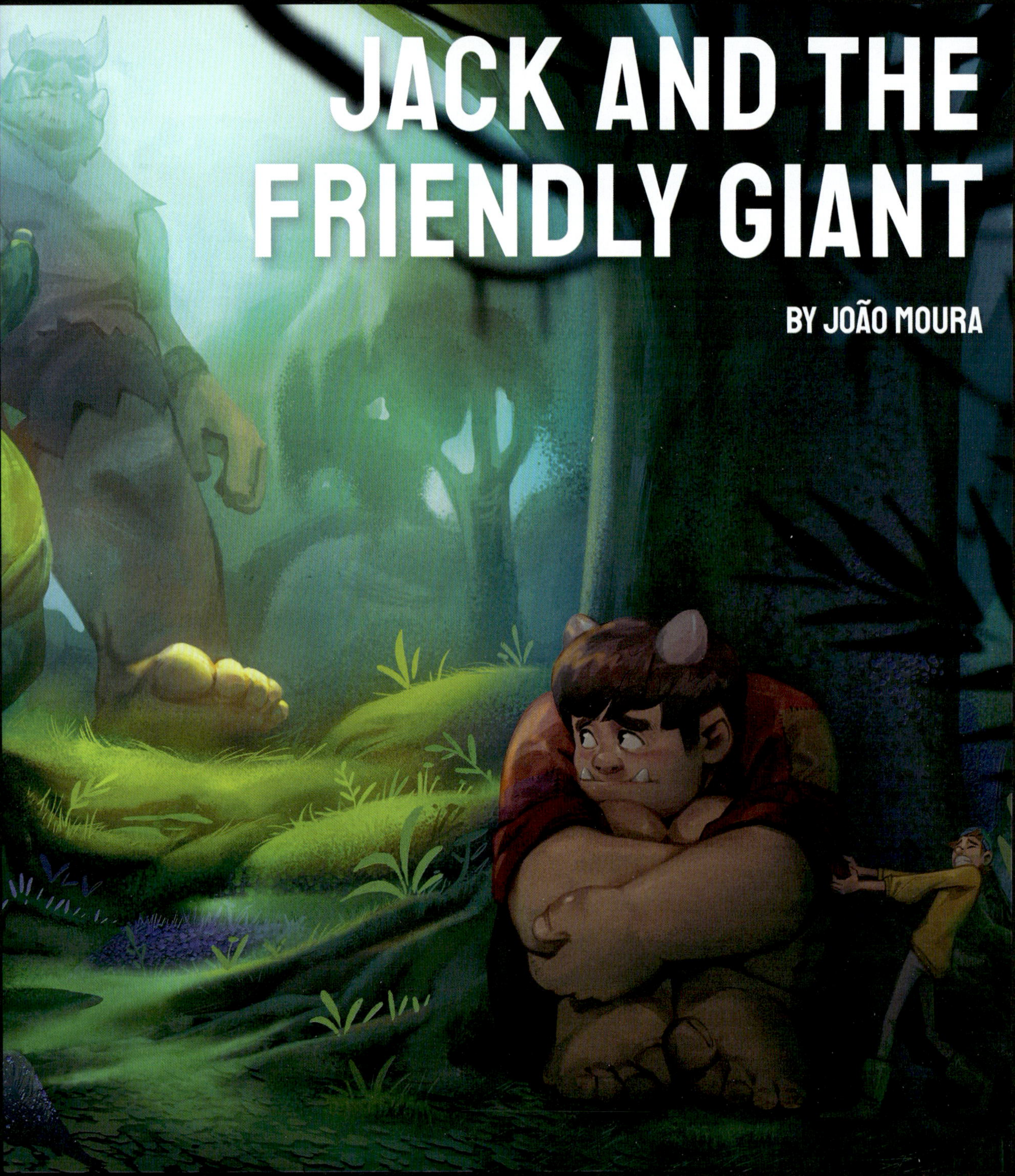

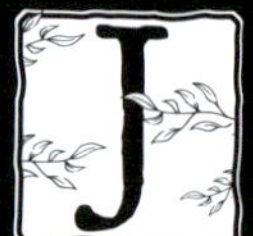

Jack and the Beanstalk is an interesting story to me because it puts a human character in front of something with vast scale: a giant. In the traditional fairy tale, Jack ends up being chased by the giant, who is the villain of the story, even though Jack is an intruder in the giant's world and has stolen from him. For my rendition, I want Jack, a spoiled human teenager, to meet Zug, a sweet and friendly giant who is the smallest of his kind. Although different in size, they both feel like they don't belong in their worlds, leading to an unlikely friendship. I think this version will lend the story and world more depth by giving Jack a character arc and showing a sympathetic side to the giants.

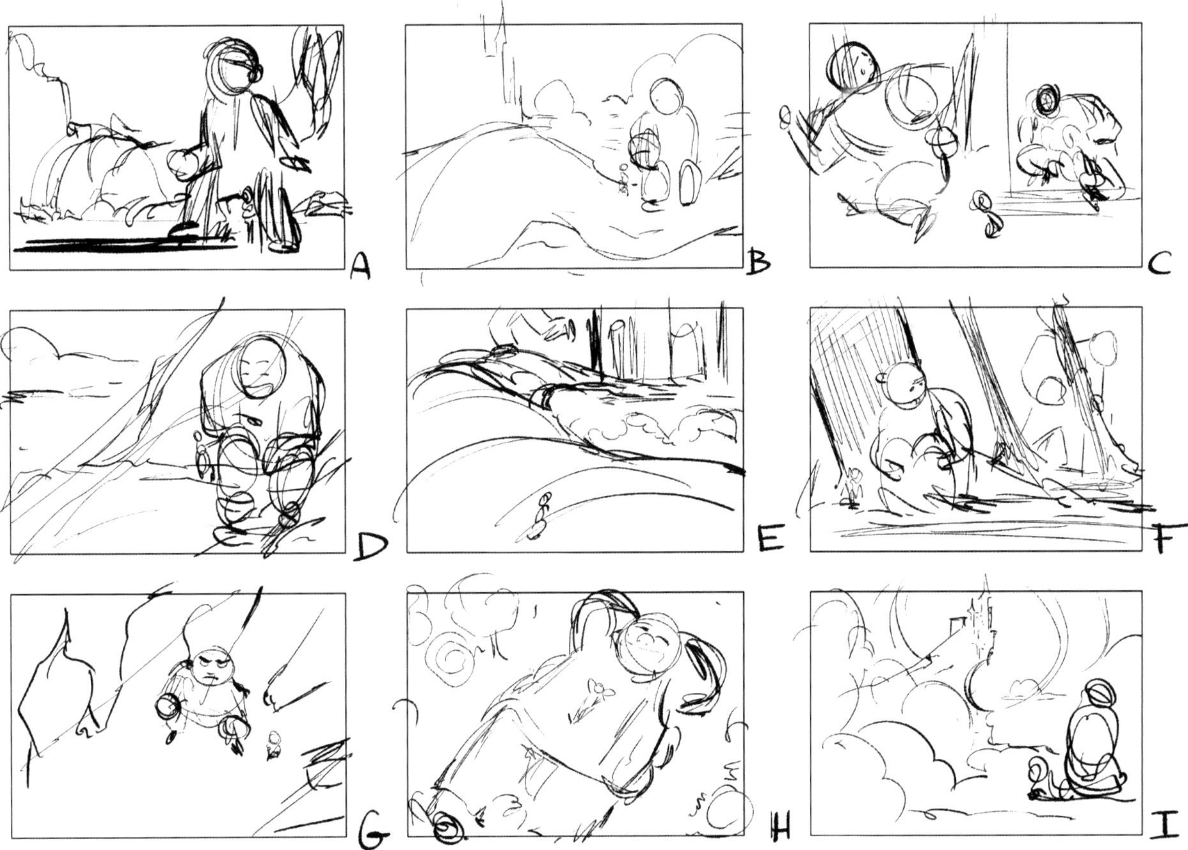

▲ Using loose thumbnail sketches to find the key moment from my story

01 BRAINSTORMING

My main concern when starting an image is story. My premise for this image will be: "What if Jack and a giant became good friends?" Jack wants to teach his new friend, Zug, to be more confident and face his worst bully, his father. In the process, Jack ultimately learns to be a better and kinder person. I start making very rough, small doodles, trying to find a key moment of the story that is already developing in my head. As you can see, I am not too concerned about these sketches being "good." They are just for getting thoughts out of my head and onto the page.

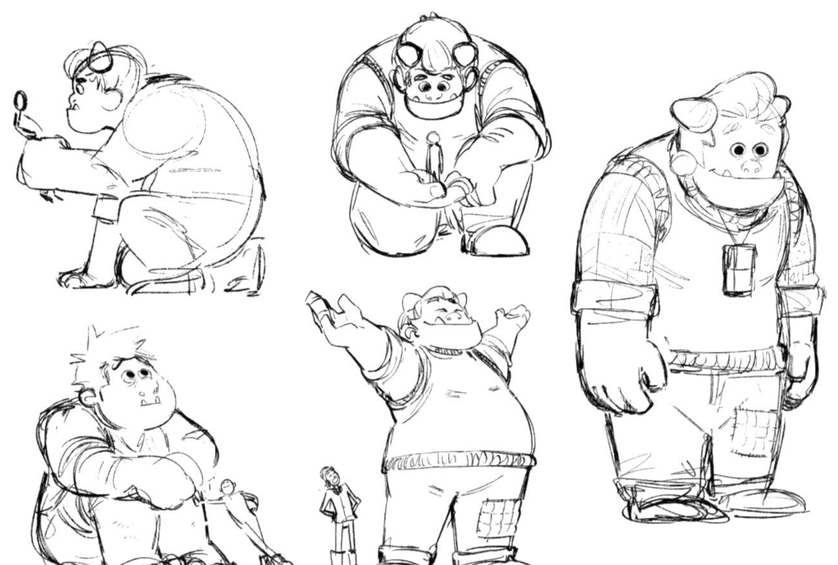

02 SKETCHING ZUG

To help realize the new character, the giant Zug, I develop his personality and physical traits by imagining him in different situations and interacting with Jack. Zug is a gentle soul and collects human items that he proudly wears around his neck. He is bullied by other giants, especially by his father, for being tiny, weirdly dressed, and having peculiar tastes. He secretly fantasizes about having a big brother that would guide him and protect him.

◀ Initial sketches of Zug to flesh out his design and personality

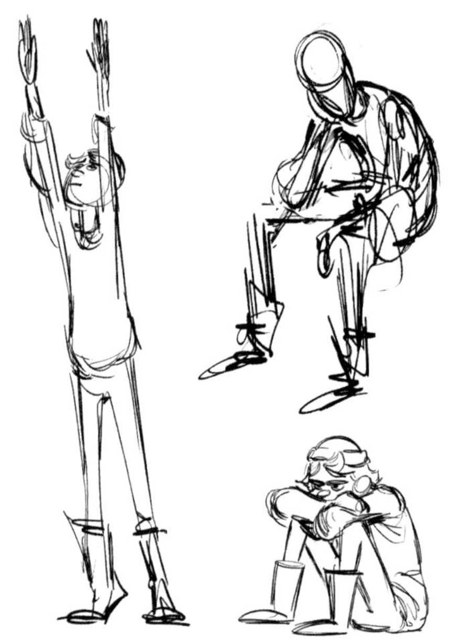

03 SKETCHING JACK

I spend less time developing Jack's character, as he is already established by the original fairy tale, but I also want him to have some new layers to his personality. My version of Jack is a spoiled, entitled teenager who doesn't help his hard-working mother in the least. When she asks him to pawn off one of their last family heirlooms, he messes up by trading it for some beans. He loses the beans on the way back, arriving home to a furious mother. The next day, Jack goes back to try to find the beans, and is surprised to find they have grown into a huge beanstalk. This is his big opportunity to climb into a new world and bring back riches to prove his mother wrong.

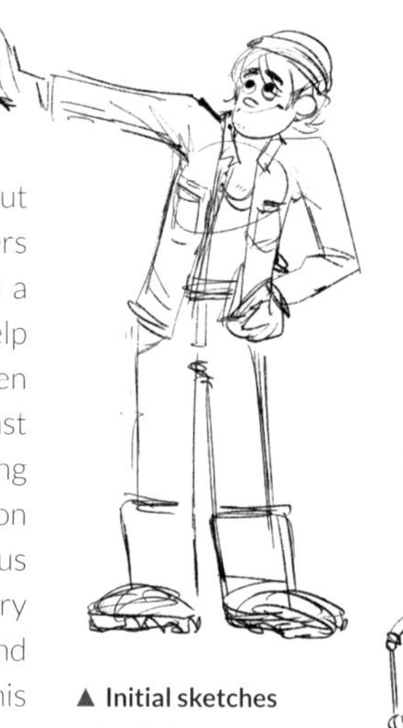

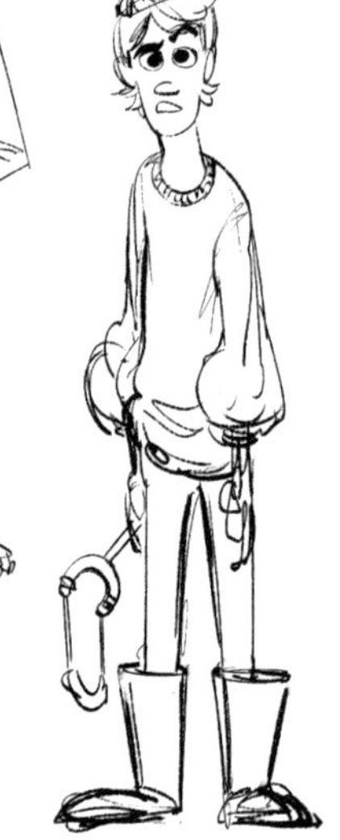

▲ Initial sketches of Jack, focused on capturing his general attitude

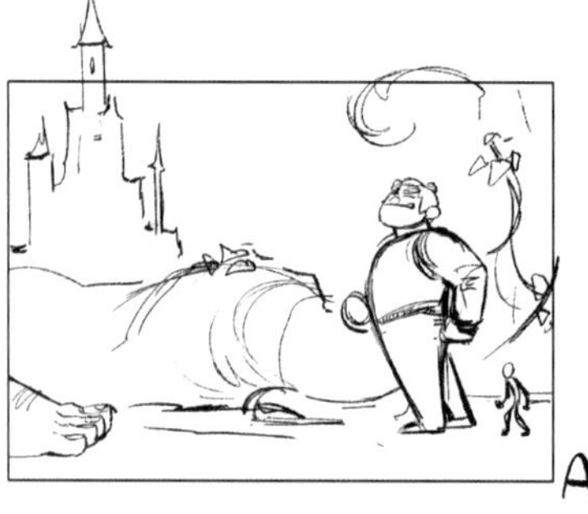

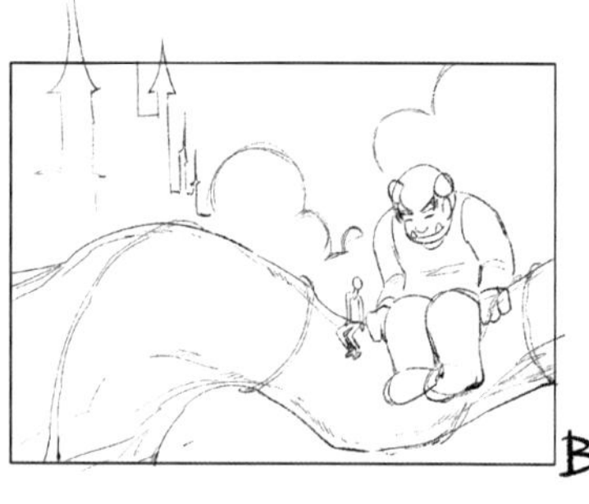

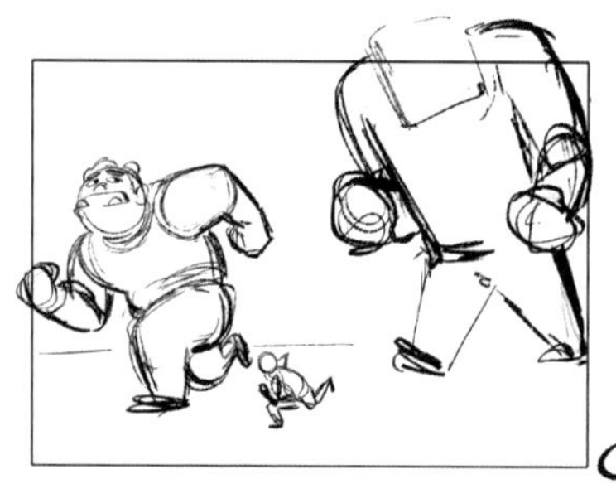

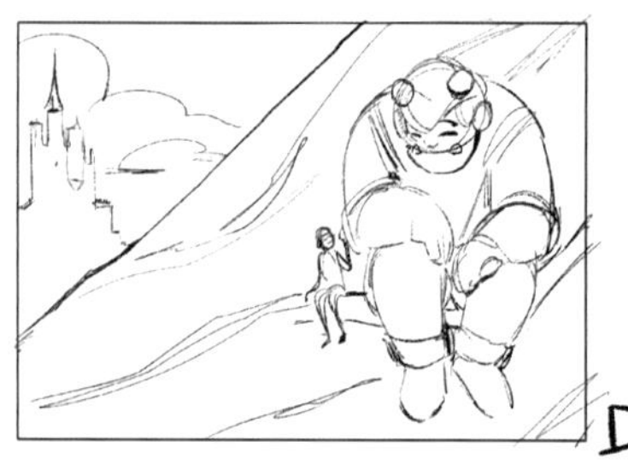

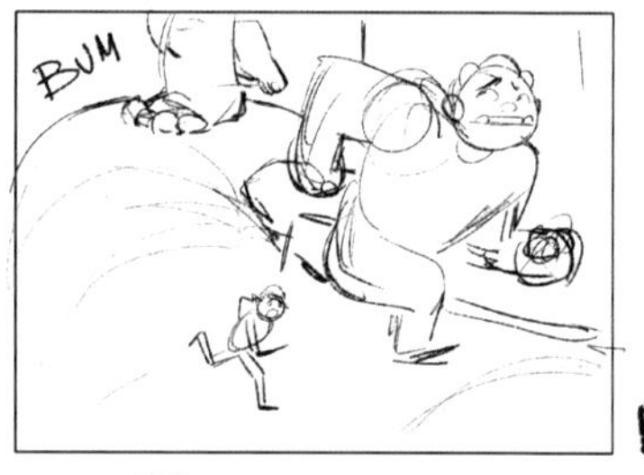

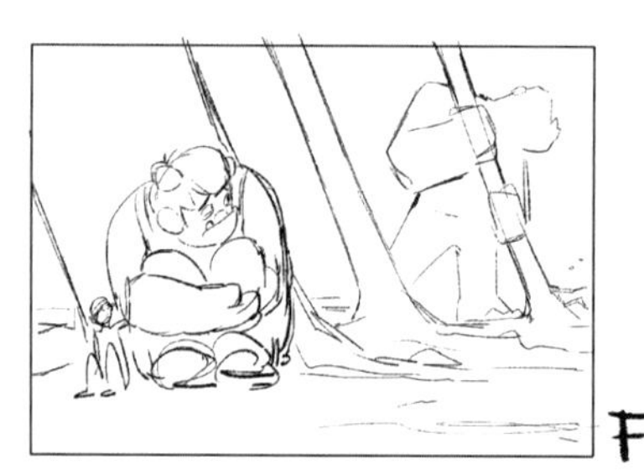

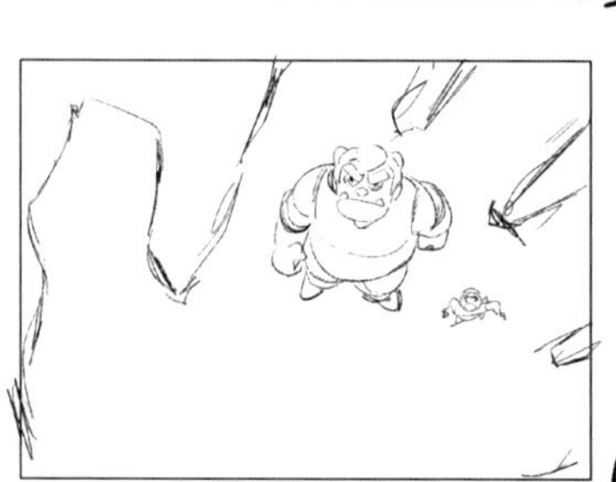

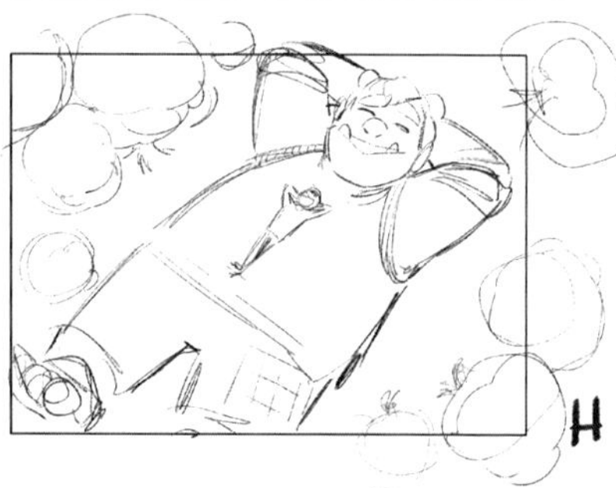

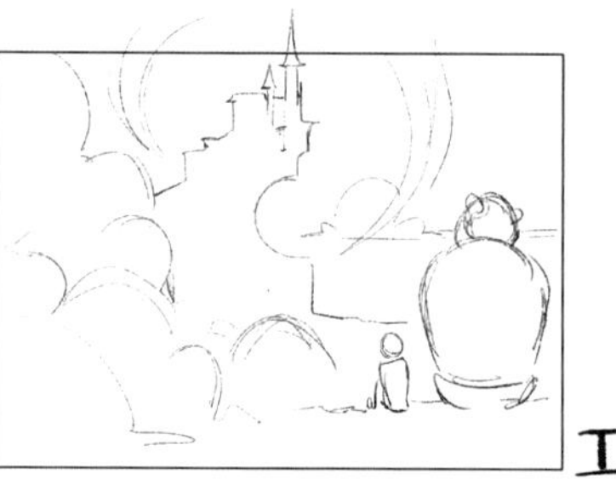

▲ Further development of the key-moment thumbnails

04 DEVELOPING THE KEY SCENES

After developing the main characters a little, I go back to my "key moment" thumbnails and try to add more information and elements of the character designs. At this point, I think my composition ideas are a bit weak and flat, but the story is still coming through. I'm torn between depicting a friendly moment between the two characters and a dramatic moment where Zug is finally facing his father.

05 ZUG AND JACK INTERACTIONS

This step is not strictly necessary, but let's call it a guilty pleasure! Zug is my favorite character in this project, and I want to polish the drawings of him and focus on his interactions with Jack. Since this small giant is a collector, I try to include different items that he would wear on his necklace. The strangeness of these object choices shows his innocent personality – such as wearing a toilet or a fridge like a pendant! Zug also dresses like a human, showing his admiration for these people.

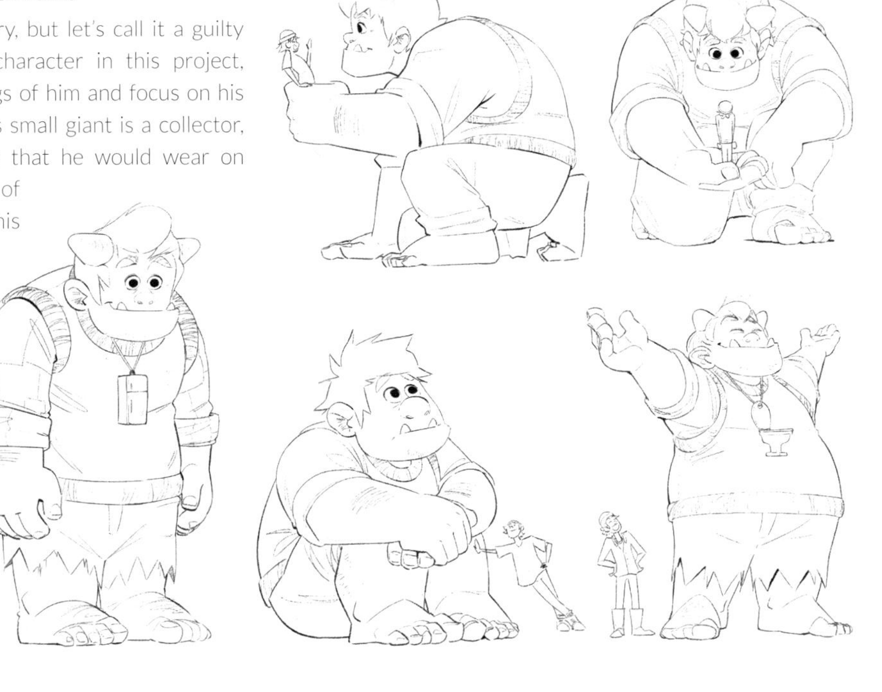

▶ Sketching interactions between the characters and exploring Zug's accessories

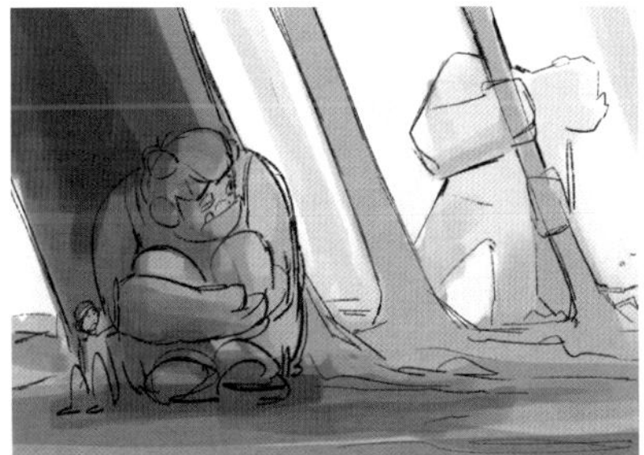

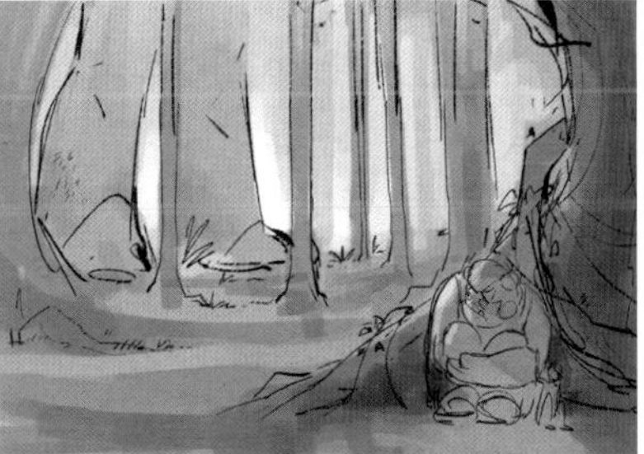

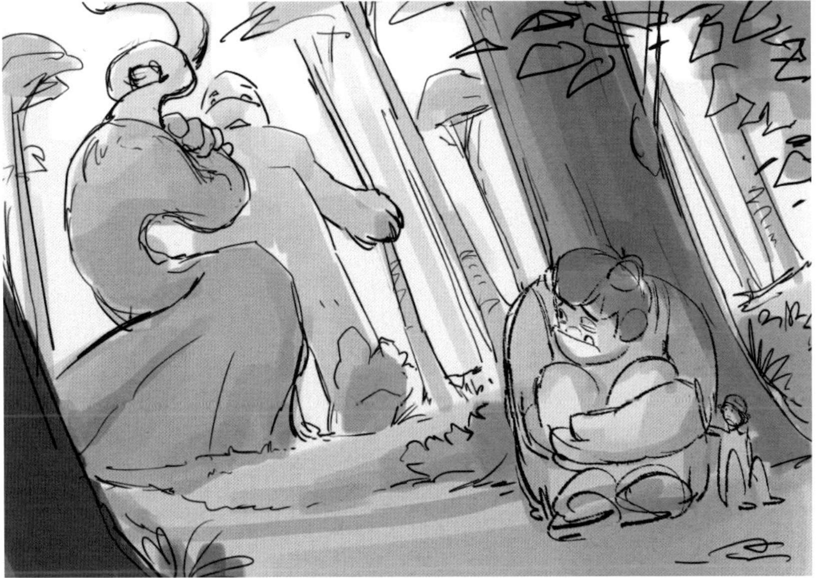

06 CHOOSING A MOMENT

Looking back on step 04, the key moment that speaks to me the most is F. In this scene, we can see all the characters' personalities very clearly. Zug is very nervous and scared to face his father. Jack is trying to urge him to move and do something. The father giant is a massive figure looking for his son and Jack with the intent to do harm.

I still feel that the composition is a bit too flat for this particular moment, so I sketch two more variations to choose from, and introduce some black-and-white value information for depth. Out of these three options, I go with the third, as it's more dynamic. The composition makes the viewer feel small and trapped, like Zug and Jack, as the huge giant approaches.

◀ Creating small value studies that build on the key-moment thumbnail

07 FIRST COLOR THUMBNAIL

My first attempt at a color thumbnail focuses on a cold, blue atmosphere. I choose these colors to show the characters' fear and dread, and it partly works, but feels a bit too cold and grim! I still want the image to have a warm, fantasy feeling to it, as if this forest was a beautiful place to be before it was invaded by a massive, murderous giant. Introducing more green and yellow could achieve this.

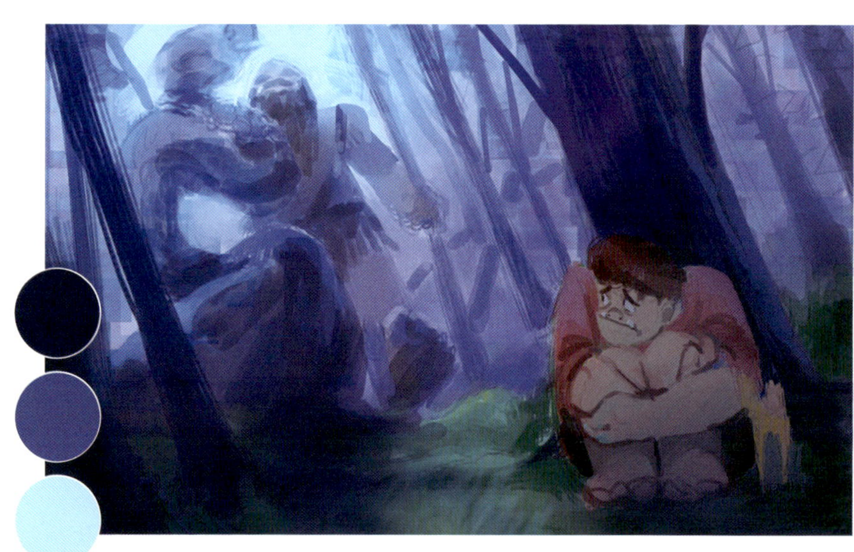

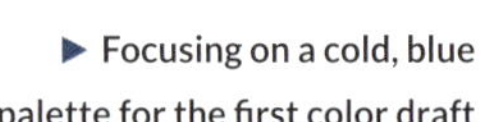

▶ Focusing on a cold, blue palette for the first color draft

▲ The second color attempt has a claustrophobic green atmosphere

08 SECOND COLOR THUMBNAIL

My second color thumbnail is much greener and has some strong attributes that work very well for the story I am trying to tell. The viewer can almost feel the thick atmosphere that traps you in the image, with one dramatic beam of light showing the humongous giant entering the scene. The only issue is that the scene now feels *too* warm and green, almost like it's set in a jungle, due to all the saturated, atmospheric greens. I want to make the forest more playful and fantastical, so I move on to the next idea.

09 THIRD COLOR THUMBNAIL

By the third color thumbnail, I feel much more confident! I introduce some blue-greens to achieve that dense, smothering atmosphere while still feeling luscious and magical. I add the beam of light from the previous color draft, as it worked very well to highlight the massive giant and create anticipation. From the start, I imagined Zug having a red shirt; red contrasts well with green and has some warmth to it, which feels fitting for this character.

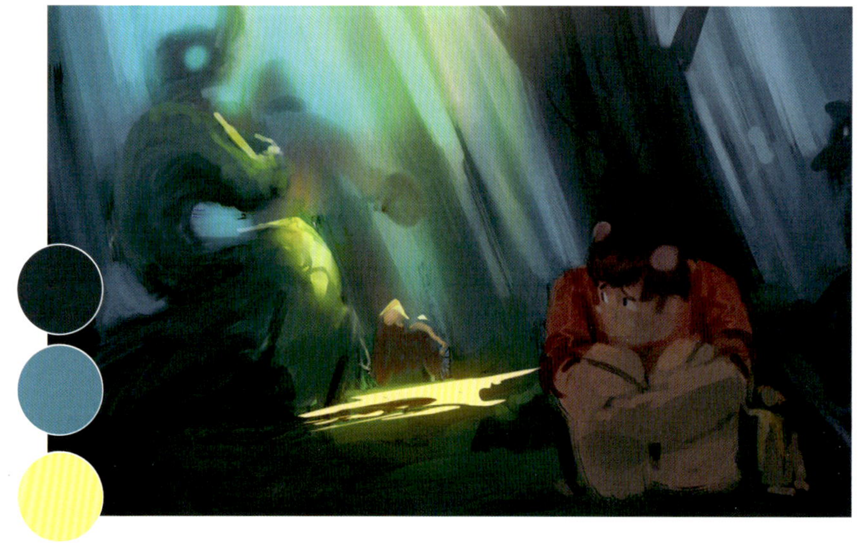

▶ The third and final color thumbnail with a bluish-green atmosphere

▼ **Good references are important. Try taking your own photos!** *Photography © João Moura*

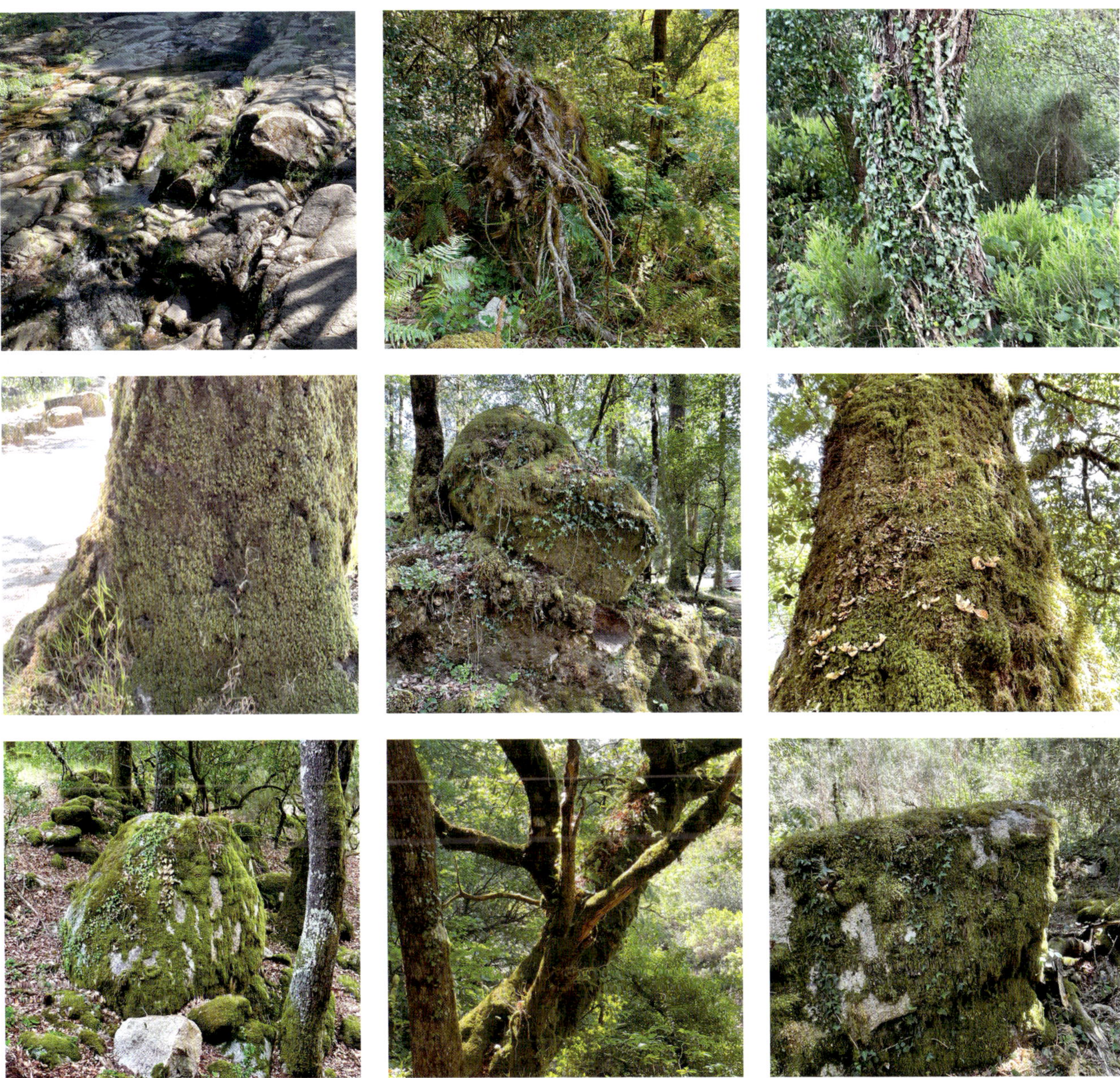

10 A WEEKEND IN THE WOODS

One important element of any project is the use of good references. I was lucky enough to have a weekend in the woods planned with friends, in a place called Gerês, in my home country of Portugal. It is a wondrous place filled with trees, plants, waterfalls, and wildlife. I took the opportunity to photograph anything that could inspire me for this image. I noticed how weeds and moss took hold of every surface they could reach, which I loved and wanted to bring to my painting!

COLLECT ARTISTIC REFERENCES

As well as photographs, try gathering references of artwork by other artists. These could be references for the stylization of shapes, a great mood, a color palette, or even just some interesting textures. This might be a habit you eventually lose, if you lock in on a strong personal style that you really like, but it's good to have some art references that are your standard to aspire to. Just be careful not to let yourself simply copy!

11 BEGINNING TO RENDER

Now I can proceed to the rendering. I start by scaling up the thumbnail, then work very broadly and loosely from that. Working "from big to small" works wonders for me. Some artists are amazing at working immediately in detail, but I am not one of them! So at this stage, I start to create the large volumes and shapes that will set the base for the rest of the image.

The rough details of the environment and the characters' appearances begin to take shape, especially the bigger giant, whose design I only begin to pin down at this stage. He and Zug have horns, tusks, and similar clothing, suggesting that they are from the same setting, even the same family. Jack's pose has changed from crouching to pulling urgently on Zug's arm, showing us more about these two characters and their relationship.

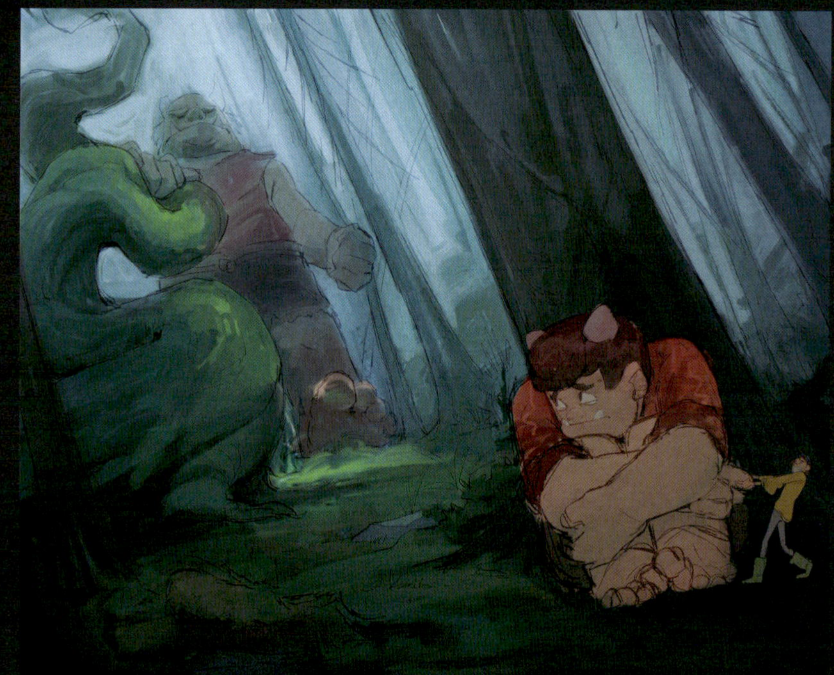

▲ Starting to render, beginning with broad colors and shapes to set the base

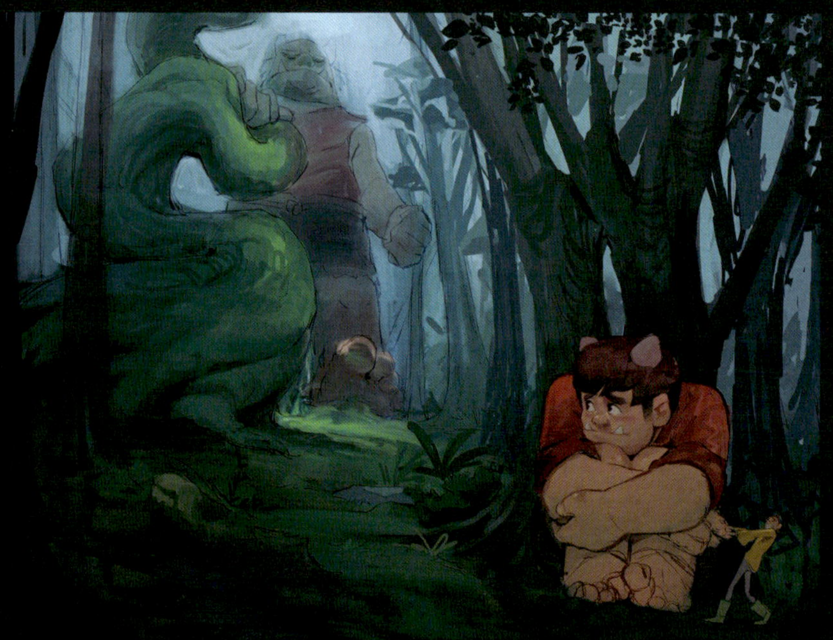

REST IS KEY

Take some time off from the image you are working on. You have probably heard this advice before, but it really is important! If you find you have been struggling for a while, it's good to take a break, go out, or work on something else for a while. You will come back with a fresher view of things.

◀ Taking a small break and making terrible decisions – all part of the process!

12 MAKING MISTAKES!

At this point I take a break from the image for one or two days, to see if the composition and scale of the elements still work for me with fresh eyes. Unfortunately, when I re-open the image I realize I was trying to make something too cinematic and had lost my sense of scale. I attempt to revise the composition, using fewer diagonals and dramatic angles. I want the forest to be part of the human world, so I change the big tree behind which Zug and Jack are hiding, replacing it with a bunch of smaller, messier trees. But this loses some of the scene's readability, and I regret the decision immediately! At least Zug is successfully starting to take shape, with large eyes and worried brows that make him look young and afraid. His curled-up pose makes him look even smaller than he already is compared to his father.

13 REVISING, AGAIN

I try to get back some elements from step 11, where the trees were taller and had some tilt to them. I think this works better to guide the eye toward the threatening element: the big giant. Though I regretted changing the trees in step 12, I try changing them again to improve the sense of scale, adding more branches to make the setting feel more like a human-sized forest. It works much better this time! I also start thinking of a few foreground elements that could help guide the eye, and lightly sketch them in. I enlarge Jack slightly, so that he and Zug feel closer to the viewer, and we can see his expression better.

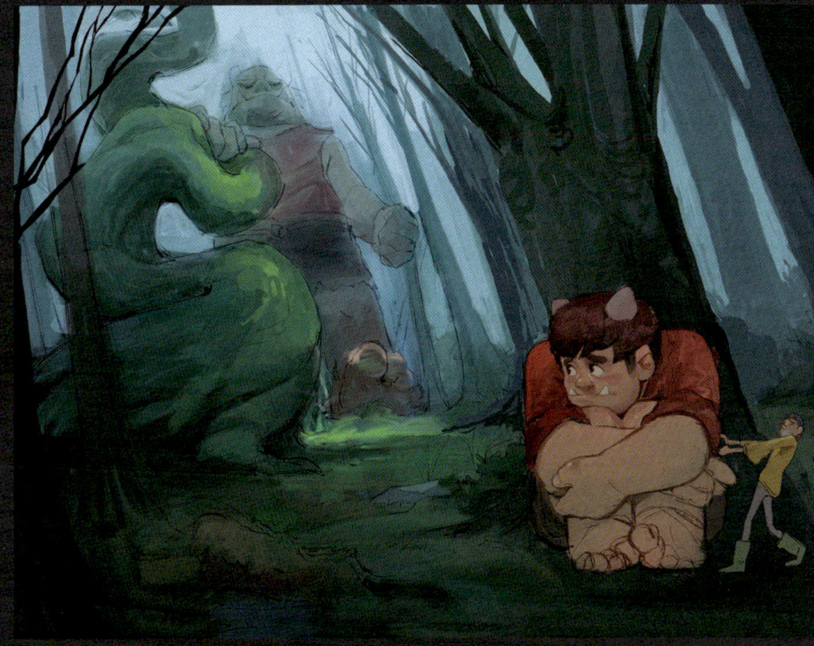

▶ Going back on some decisions and trying to make better choices

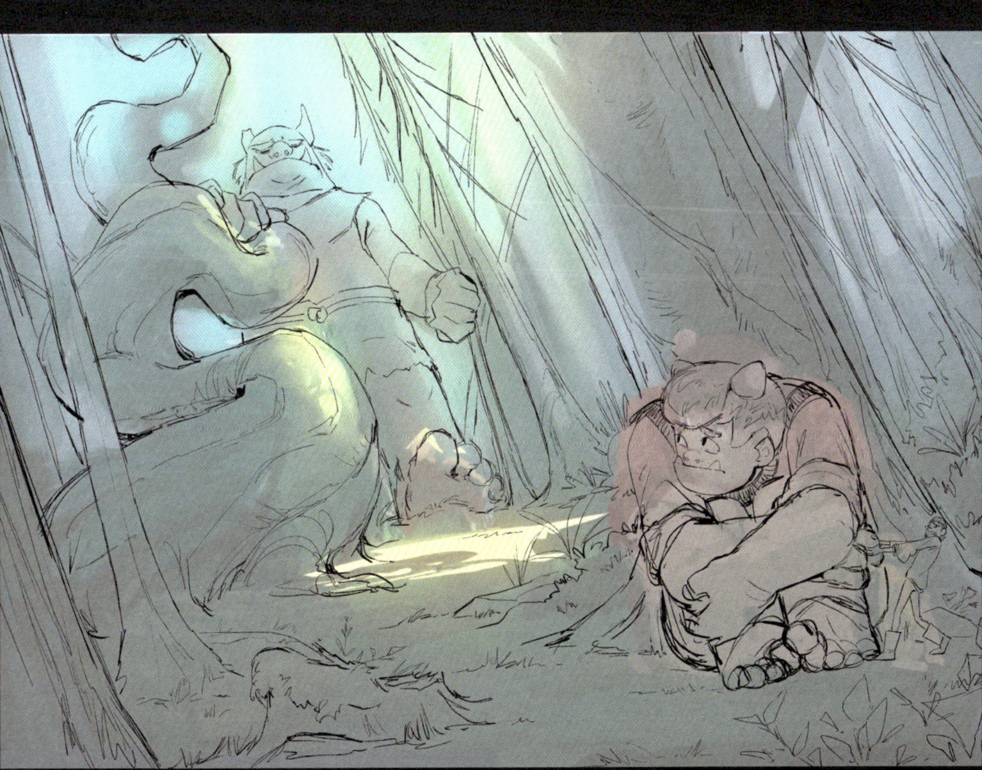

◀ Back to line drawing. The struggle is real at this point!

14 CHECKING THE LINE DRAWING

At this point, with all these structural changes, I feel the need to stop painting for a while and go back to thinking about shapes and volumes. I do this with the help of the line drawing I made earlier. I use a semi-transparent white layer to help see the drawing better, and go over the lines to clarify some of my decisions. Again, I contemplate going back to tall, monolithic tree shapes, with no branches, since the current ones are a bit messy and work against the image's readability. But I also don't want to lose that feeling of being enclosed under the canopy of a forest, with the massive giant towering above the treetops. I will have to find a balance of shapes and scales in the environment that fits the characters and story.

15 REVISING THE STALK AND GIANT

I am still not satisfied with the main tree – I try adding some leaves to the top again, which could potentially work toward a clear reading of the composition. I'm unsure, so I move on for now. I am also uncertain about the beanstalk. At first, I really liked the idea of a very thick beanstalk, but after a while it began to feel like it was taking too much attention away from the giant. In this step, I try to find a slimmer, better design for it, but I feel like I am failing horribly! I come up with the design you see here, which I really don't like, and end up discarding. However, I am successfully finding a better pose for the father giant, making him less stiff and more scary.

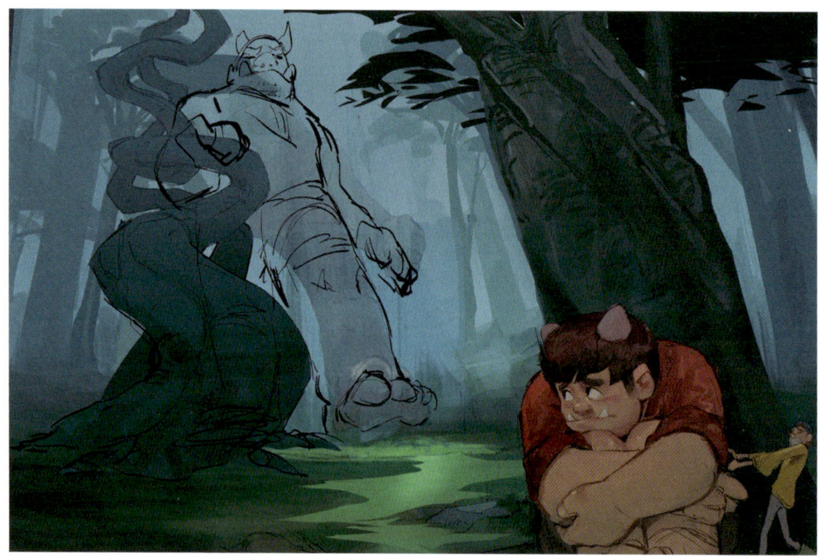

▲ Trying to do something different and regretting it (again)!

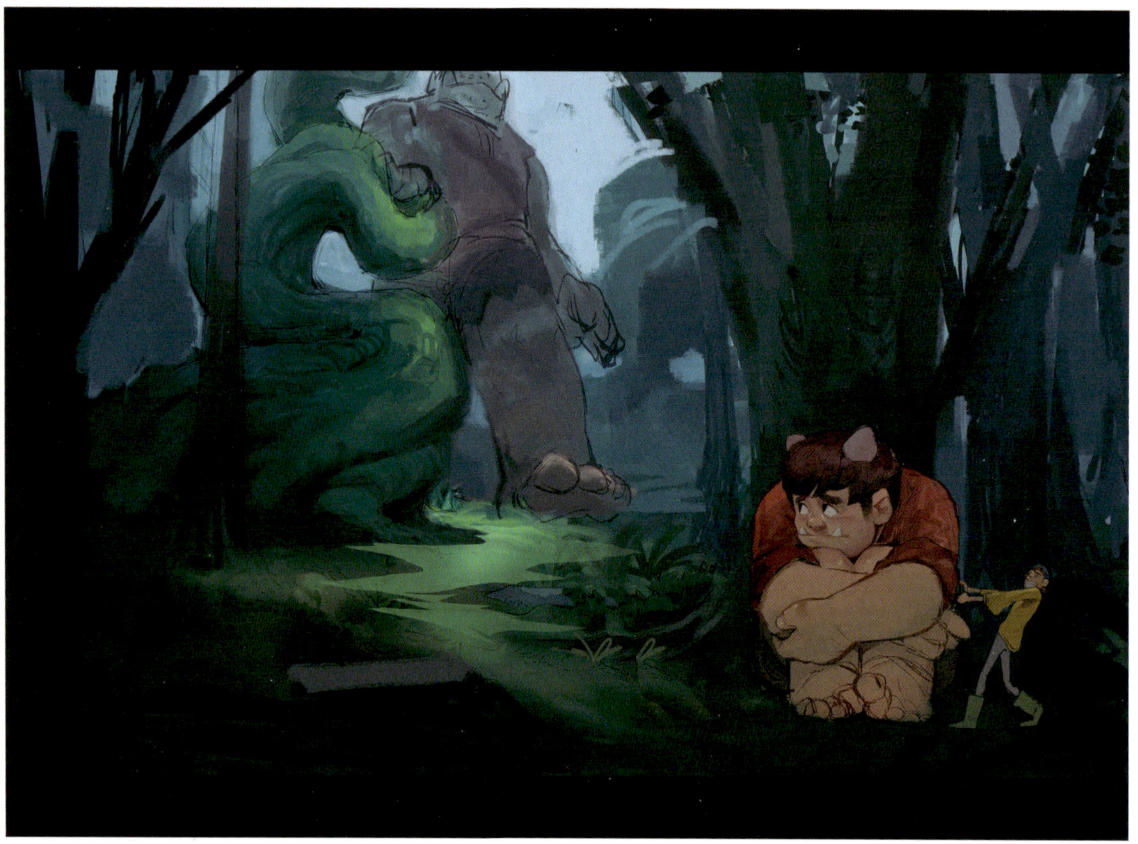

▲ The image improves after changing to a widescreen ratio

16 A CHANGE OF RATIO

I decide to add two black bars to the top and bottom of the image, making the illustration more of a widescreen ratio. This helps the composition to breathe, allowing me to create bigger, clearer negative spaces between the giant and the trees. The wider ratio also allows for a clearer diagonal line of action between the giant and the two smaller characters. I play around with making the giant so big that he's partially cropped from the image, but although there is some appeal to the idea, I decide that he has more impact when surrounded by negative space.

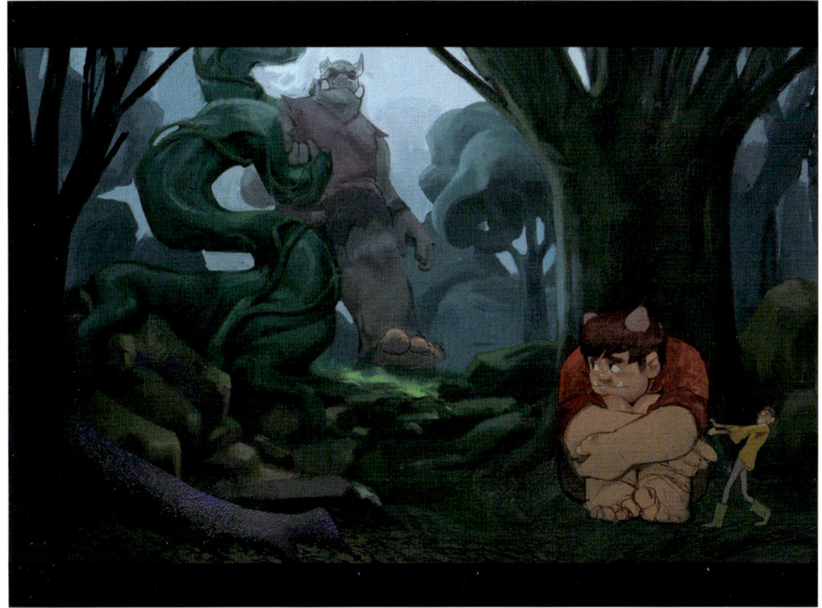

▲ Using a bit of photobashing to refine the environment

17 REFINING THE SCENE

Now I am getting to somewhere that I like, composition-wise, I start fleshing out more of the scene. The flat green path through the forest needs work – I want the setting to feel wild and enchanted, covered with rocks, plants, and moss. This is where the photos that I took in the forest are very useful. I pay close attention to detail and try to insert elements that help tell the story. I don't use "photobashing" very often, but I do a little of it here, to create the terrain under the big giant's foot. I paint over the photo texture with broad strokes to remove unnecessary information, leaving behind painterly organic shapes that form the rocks and undergrowth. This technique allows me to quickly flesh out the scene with smaller natural shapes that I may not have considered before.

18 ADDING MORE ATMOSPHERE

I continue to polish the details and separate the image into foreground, middle ground, and background areas. This enables me to zone out the unnecessary information and focus purely on each section. In the middle ground, I use more photobashing for the tree roots, painting over the photos to fit the mood of my scene; in the foreground, the terrain and characters are the most detailed, so they feel close to the viewer. These separate planes will also be helpful for creating an atmospheric ambience, which is one of my goals for this image, by painting "fog" over each layer to create depth.

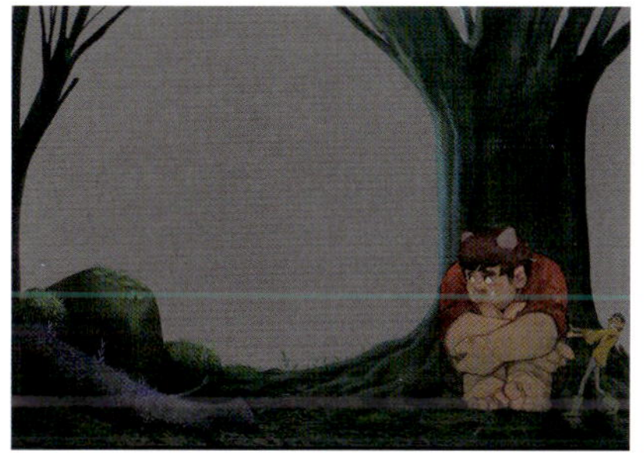

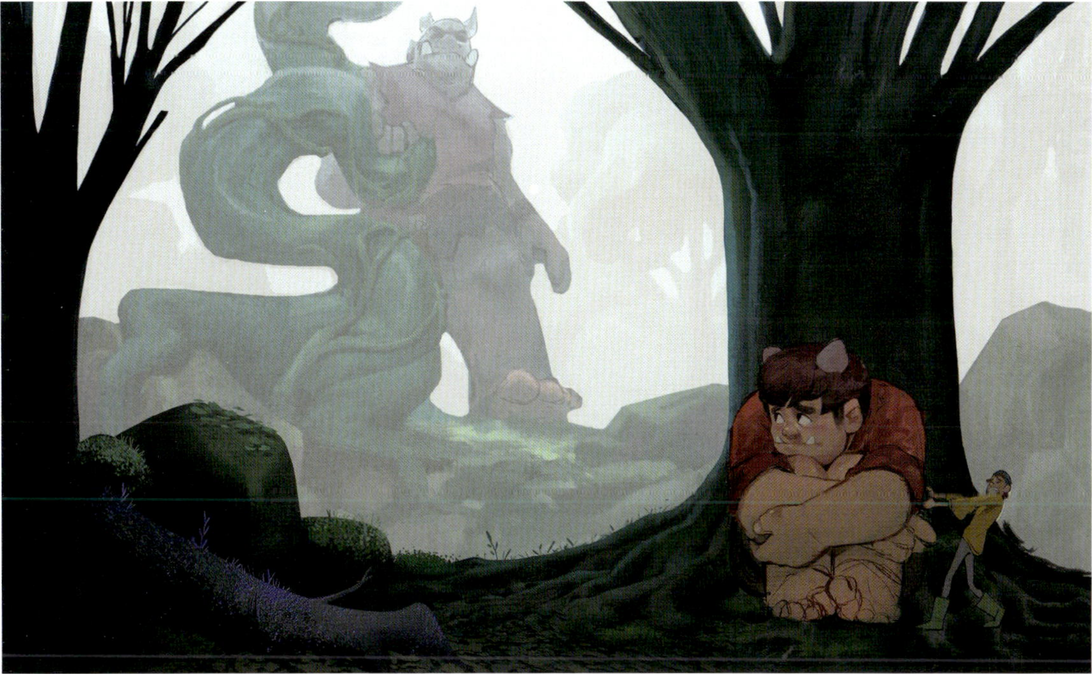

◀ Just as an example, you can see here how my scene splits into a clear foreground (shown isolated above), middle ground, and background

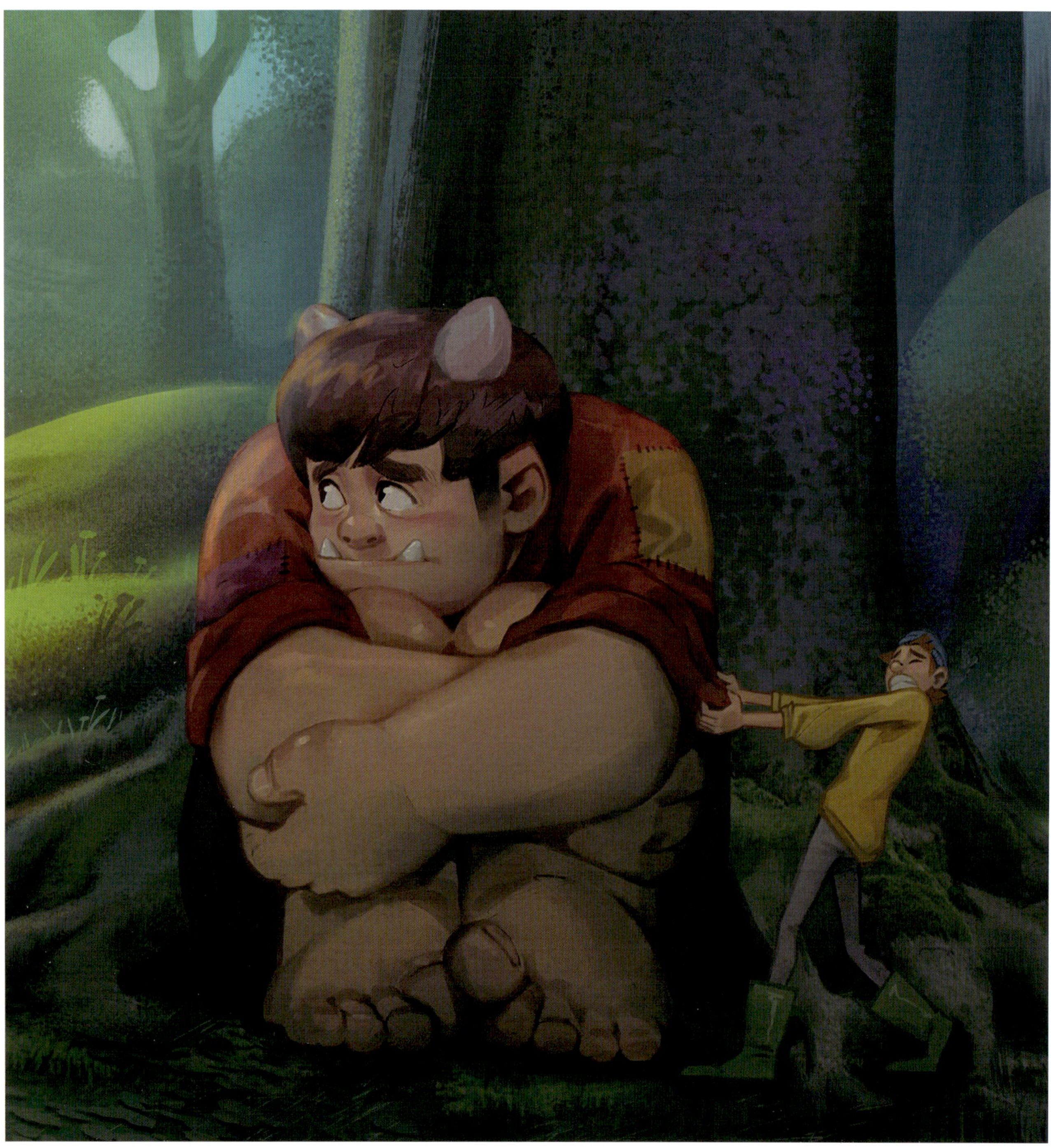

19 FINISHING ZUG AND JACK

Now it's time to give more attention to the main characters. I paint over their sketchy lines and try to think volumetrically about how to make Zug and Jack belong more to this scene. It's a difficult balance to achieve because I have some graphic-looking background elements and the characters need to match this style. I decide to make them a bit more cartoony than the background, with rounder shapes and smoother shading, as I quite like the effect that this creates. The characters feel like they blend in with the scene's atmosphere, but stand out from their surroundings at the same time, as if they are in an animated film. This helps keep the viewer's focus on them and the moment of emotional tension that is currently unfolding.

▲ Detailing the characters and blending them in with the environment

20 FINISHING TOUCHES

For this final step, I go over everything, adding more information or removing unnecessary details. I add more foreground elements, such as plants and vines, which will help guide the viewer's eye, frame the image, and increase the feeling of depth.

I also work on the beam of sunlight coming down from above the giant – this is a fun element that highlights the tension and menace of the approaching villain. The patch of light makes the forest floor glow with warmth, which makes the surrounding purples and blue-greens feel even more cold and ominous. The giant is so tall that his head fades into the light and fog above the treetops. Finally, I add more graphical elements, such as weeds, ivy, and small plants, which help give life to the scene and emphasize its fantasy look.

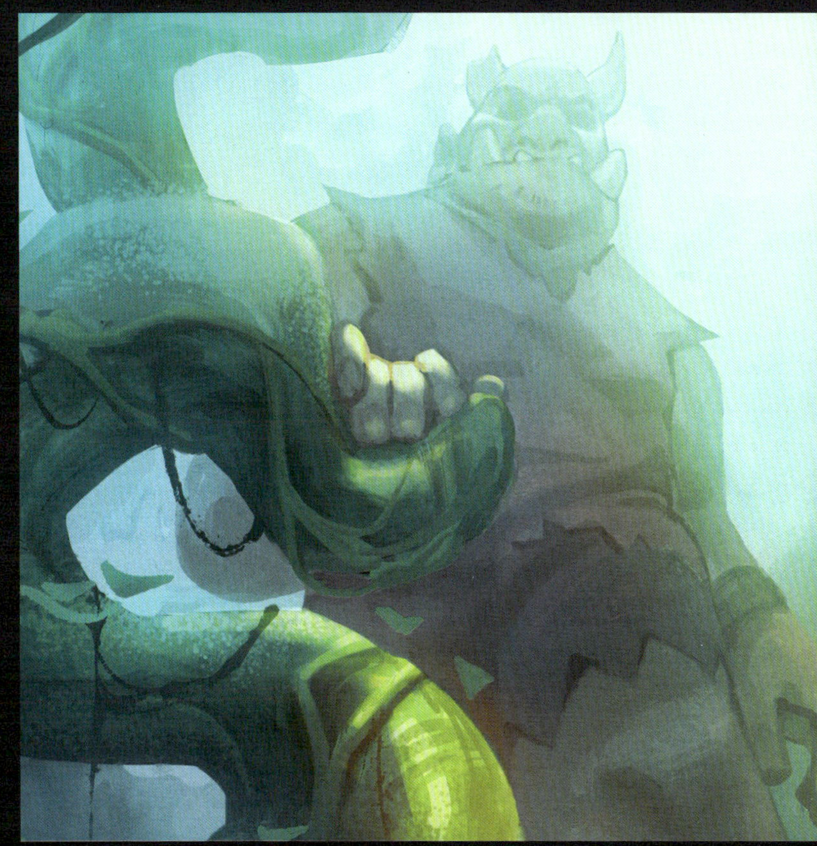

► **Adding little plant details, painting the light beam, and refining the foreground**

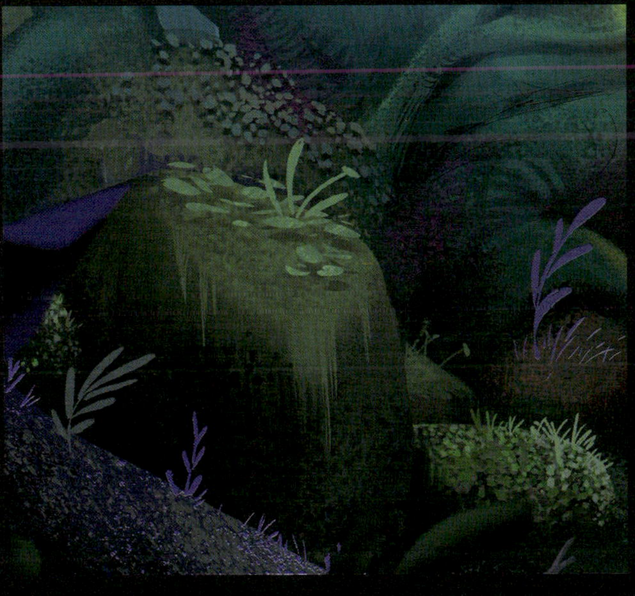

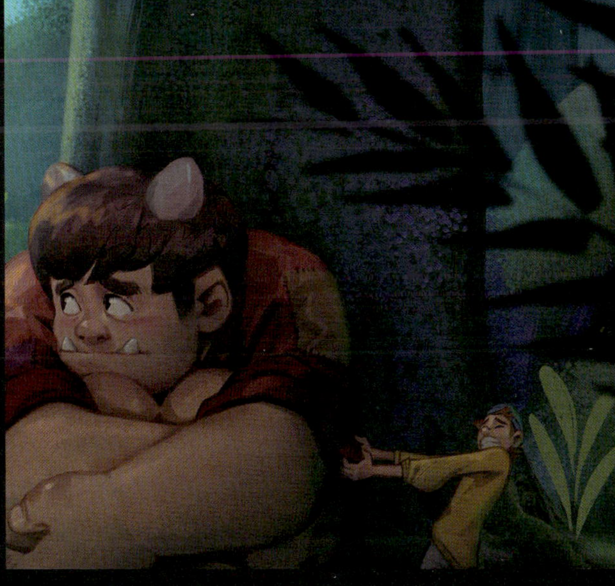

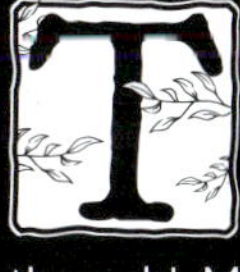

This project was loads of fun, as well as a big challenge. In the end, I am happy with the result, which doesn't show all the difficulties and revisions that the illustration went through! My goal was to tell the viewer a whole new story with one image, and I feel that I ultimately achieved that. The fairy-tale imagery of the huge beanstalk and menacing giant is immediately familiar; it provides context that helps us intuitively grasp the backstory of the new character, Zug, and his friendship with the human, Jack. Even in just one image, the viewer has an insight into the sympathetic side of these characters, which they might not have considered before.

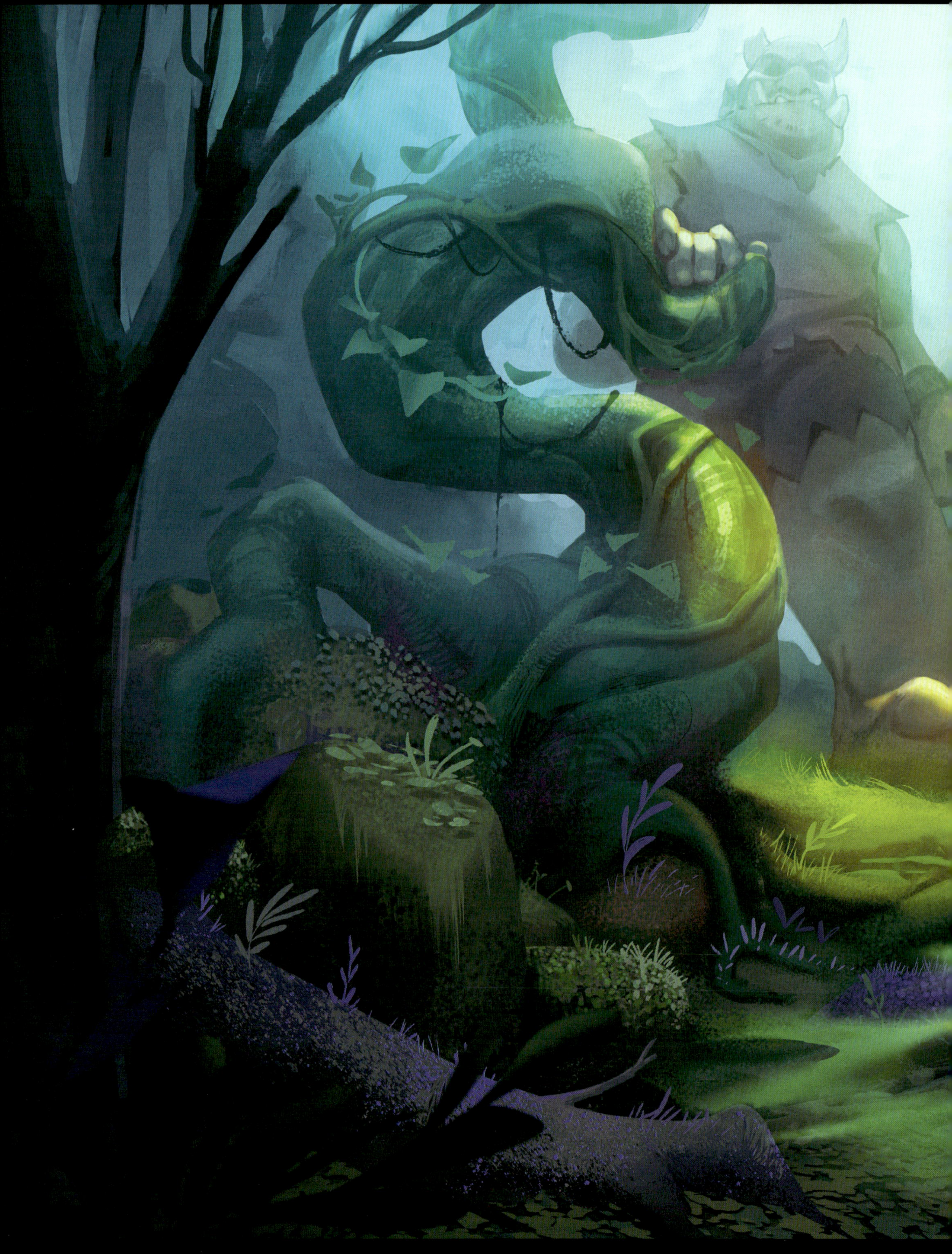

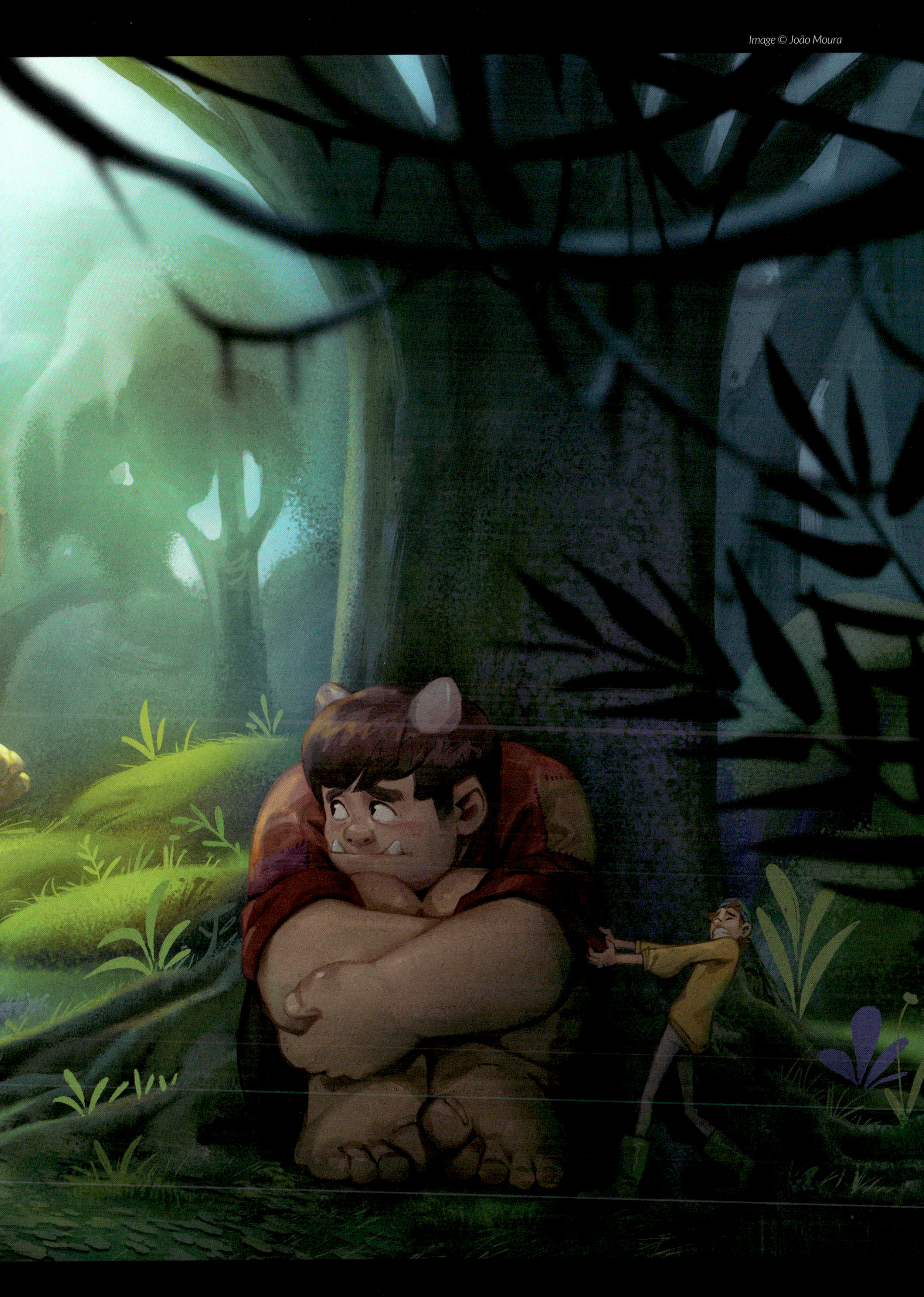

Image © João Moura

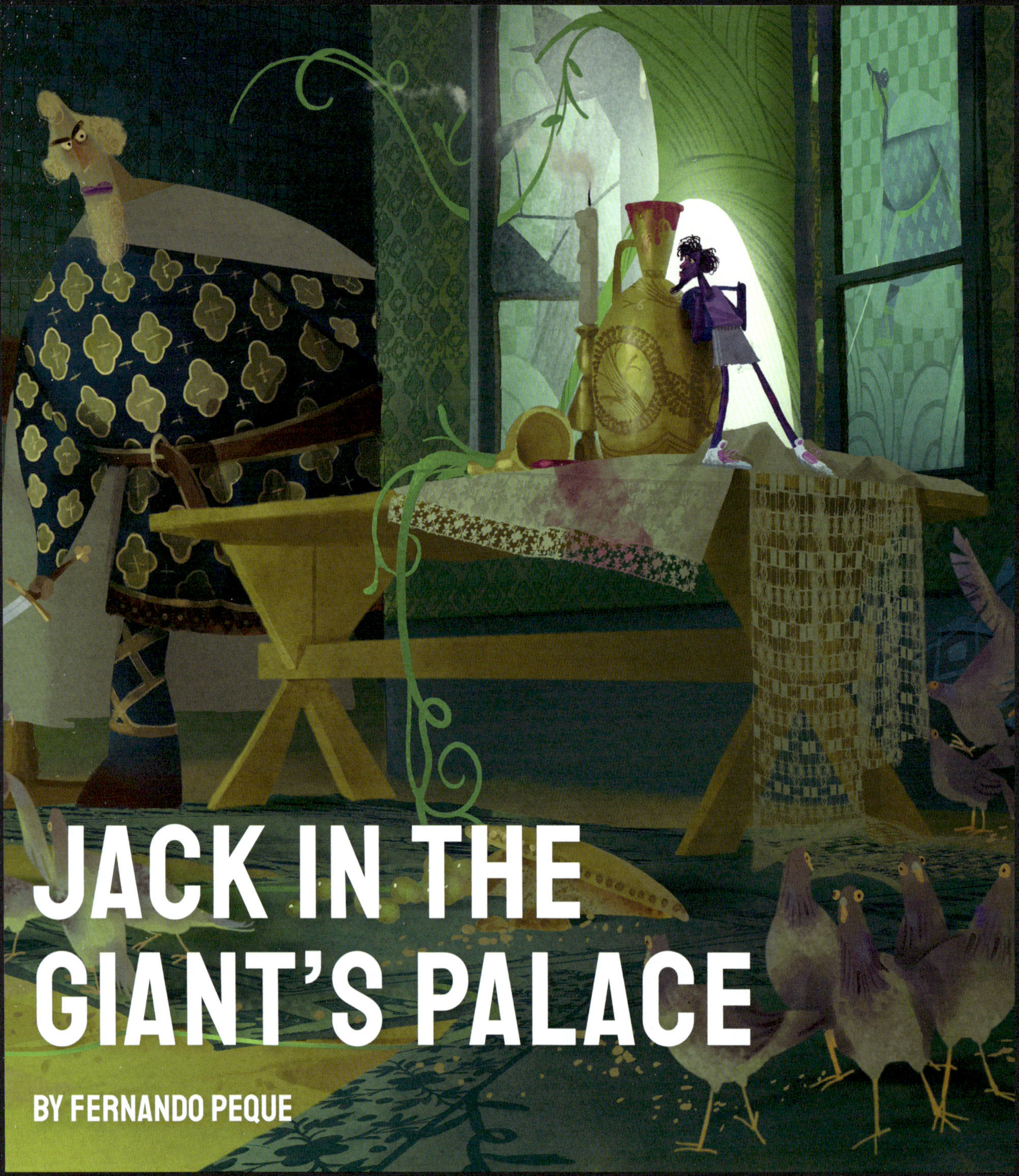

JACK IN THE GIANT'S PALACE

BY FERNANDO PEQUE

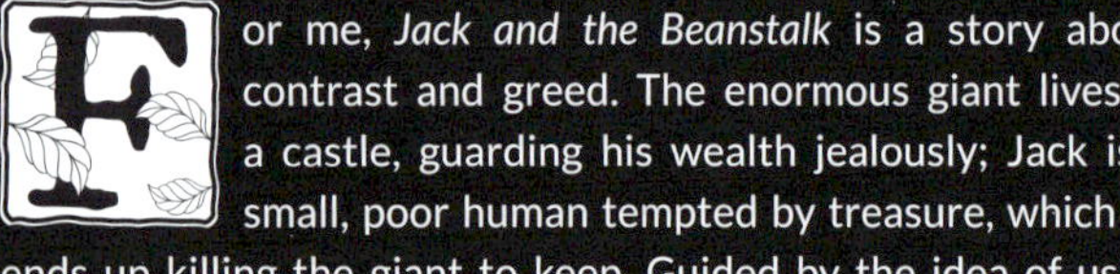

For me, *Jack and the Beanstalk* is a story about contrast and greed. The enormous giant lives in a castle, guarding his wealth jealously; Jack is a small, poor human tempted by treasure, which he ends up killing the giant to keep. Guided by the idea of using luxury and detail to create contrast, I want to show the giant's grand castle contrasted with the simplicity of Jack, portraying the story's social inequality in a subtle way. I can use colors, textures, and design details to help tell this story. In the original story, a golden harp and a goose that lays golden eggs are among the giant's treasures, putting shiny golds and opulent yellows in my mind for this image.

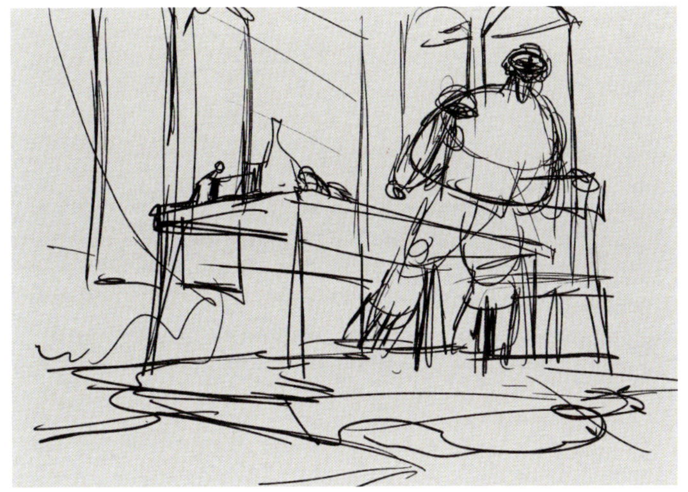

01 ROUGH THUMBNAIL

I imagine a moment in the story where the beanstalk breaks straight into the giant's room, and Jack hides behind a wine jug on the table. The scene would take place in a castle with medieval decoration and furniture. This first small sketch is loosely laying down that idea without worrying about it too much – I will refine the drawing and composition as I go. It's useful to do some research at this stage, to know where you are going, but the most important thing, for me, is to leave room for changes. I know lots of things will still change, but the basic idea and main composition will be there.

◀ Sketching a quick, rough thumbnail to capture the basics of my idea

02 BASIC 3D BLOCK-IN

Next I jump into a 3D block-in, as I am trying to incorporate it more in my process. I don't know too much 3D, and do not want to be stuck with what the block-in gives me, but I use just enough to visualize the light, values, and composition of the scene. If you do not use 3D, you can simply block out the values in 2D, but 3D offers a good way to play with the camera angle and lens, if you want. If a composition did not work at this stage, I would try something new, but I find something that works well and keeps close to my original thumbnail. The room will be lit by a large window, with the giant's table and chair in prominent focus, and the giant himself looming around the corner.

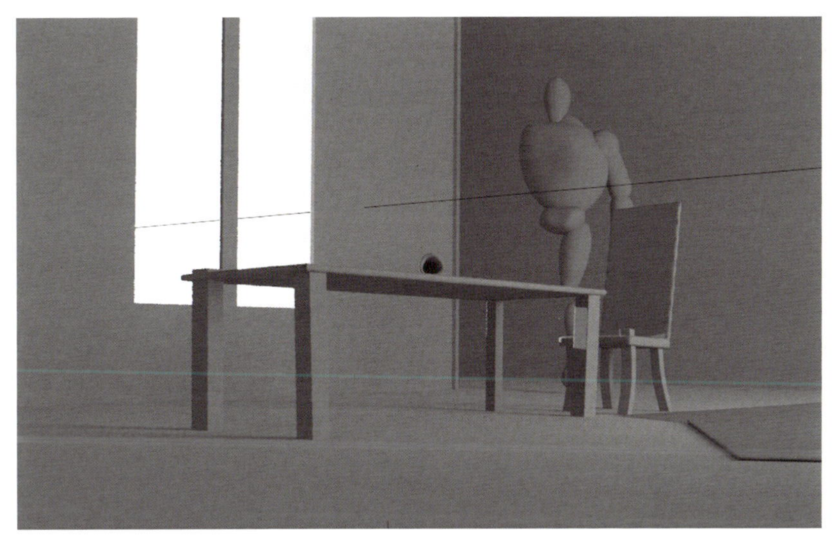

▲ Using some basic 3D can be a helpful way to plan a scene

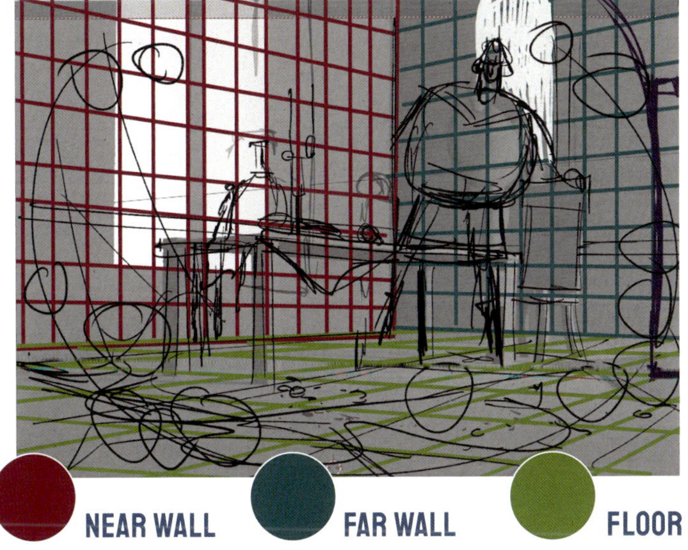

03 BUILDING UP THE SCENE

I start to sketch over the image of my block-in, visualizing the shapes and overall composition. I also add some perspective lines, just so it is easier to sketch the objects and elements I need. At this stage, I am thinking about how I want the image to read, and what I can add to enhance the story and help the composition. Some elements are already clear in my mind, and some I am unsure of, so I just put some placeholder scribbles in. For example, I love to use birds in my images, so these rough circles might become birds. The window will be the area with the highest contrast, creating a good opportunity to place my focal points against the light. A second window behind the giant could work well to frame his head as he appears menacingly around the corner.

◀ Continuing to sketch roughly over the 3D block-in

04 **SKETCHING THE BIRDS**

As I sketch, I start to develop the image's storytelling. I like to leave room for what the image tells me. As strange as it might sound, the illustration is a dialog between me and the story I am trying to tell, so I'm always open to adding, removing, or changing things. In the previous step, I sketched rough circles that might become birds, so I develop that idea further.

I like the idea of the beanstalk breaking through the castle's window, allowing birds to fly into the room and eat the bread that has fallen on the floor. This type of small interaction, though it isn't essential to the story, will make the image's world feel more alive. The viewer might initially be confused by the birds being indoors, until they look at the broken window and piece together the previous events in their imagination. This creates a dialog between my illustration and the audience, too!

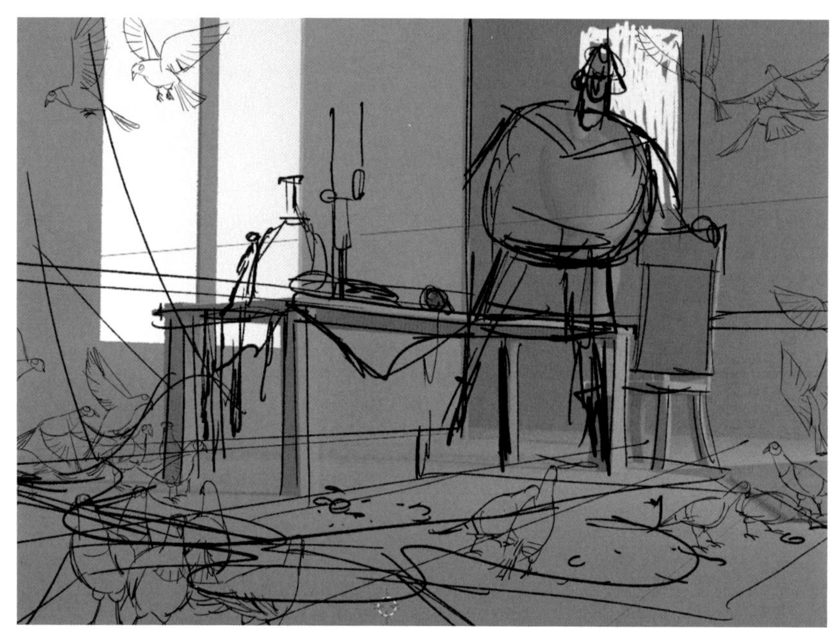

▲ Bringing more life and storytelling into the scene with some birds

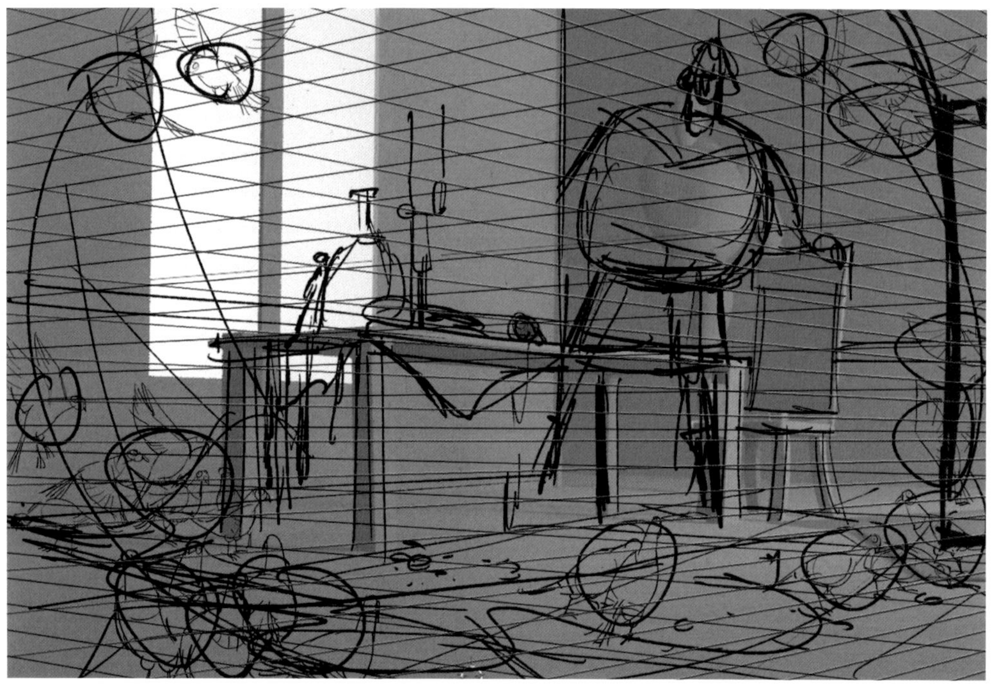

◀ The composition is in a strong place to begin rendering

05 **FINALIZING THE SKETCH**

This image shows the previous two steps combined: my rough sketch, perspective grids, and added birds. The composition and story are already working well, but I decide that the second, smaller window might become too distracting. Instead, I will keep just one area, the large window, as the zone of highest contrast. I will place Jack there so the viewer will notice him straight away. The hardest part of the illustration process is this early stage of making big decisions, but now I am comfortable and confident with my idea. My new goal is to make everything more interesting – getting the shapes right and making the scene appealing!

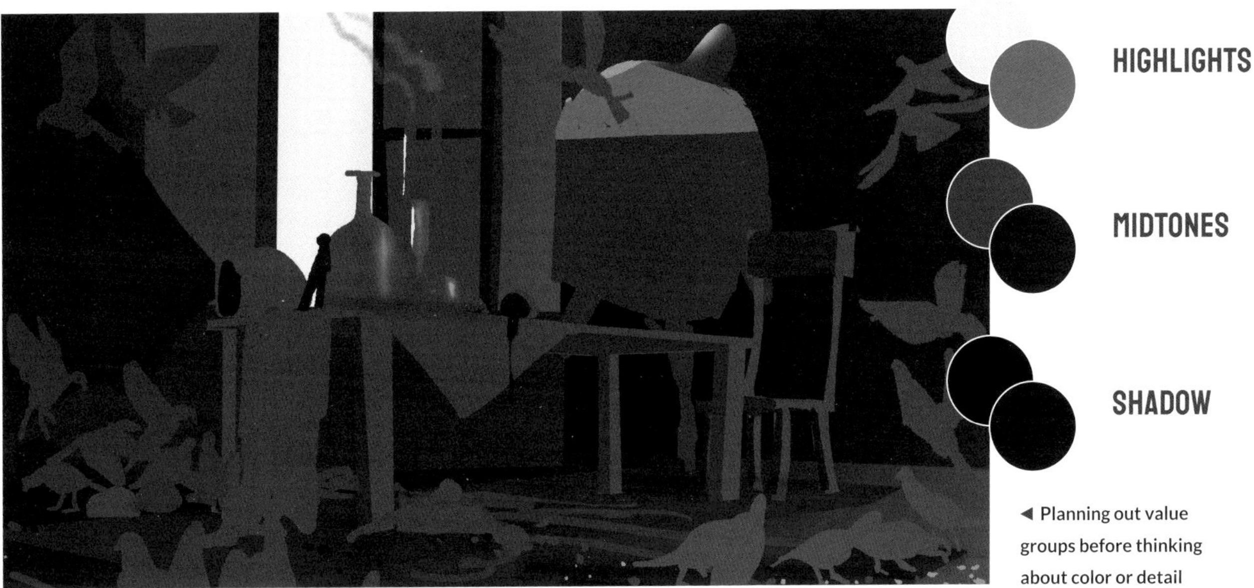

◀ Planning out value groups before thinking about color or detail

06 VALUE GROUPING

Before I can get to painting, I need to plan out and group the values. I always like to experiment with values before I even start polishing the drawing, because it helps me work out how to design groups of elements in my image. I think about every element the way I think about characters. For example, an object needs to have an interesting silhouette, which I can then break down into smaller elements. A character's face can be broken down into shapes for the eyes, nose, and mouth; each one in relation to each other, and in relation to the head shape, should be interesting. The same principle goes for the entire image – it needs to be engaging as a whole, while consisting of smaller elements that are still individually interesting and work in relation to each other. I don't think of specific small details here, just the "big, medium, small" masses and areas of contrast.

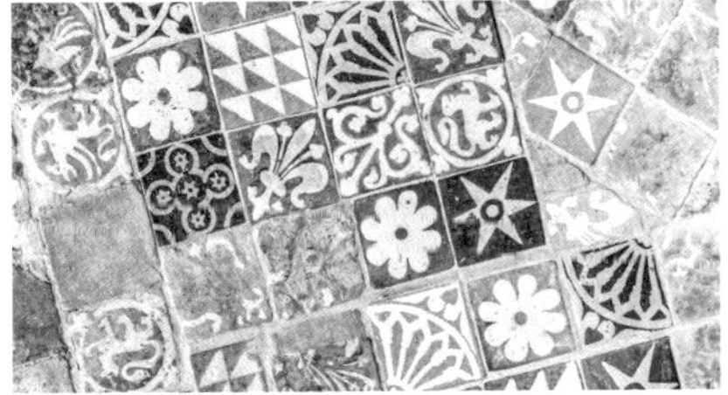

▲ Patterned medieval tiles are a big inspiration for the ornamentation in this room

Image © Steve Mann / Adobe Stock

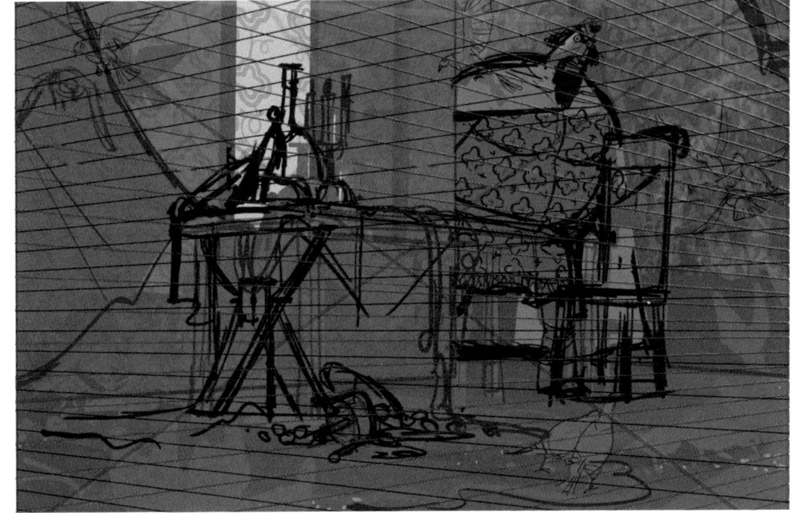

▲ Sketching and testing out details, patterns, and object shapes

07 SKETCHING DETAIL IDEAS

With the important value groups all laid out, it's now a matter of trying to make things look interesting. I work on top of my value sketch, planning where I will use textures and patterns, and sketching out clearer shapes. My mind is still open to changing anything that doesn't work. At this stage, I also research more references to help flesh out the objects in the scene, such as interesting table shapes and decoration. Adding elements such as a curtain and some items on the ground will help enhance the mood, perspective, and composition. I sketch each new object in a different color so I can see all the different components of the scene. The giant's design takes shape with a scowling face, severe beard, and patterned fabric that matches his ornate furnishings. This stage is still a sketch, so I am still experimenting and not yet fully committed – it's like talking to the image, expecting to hear a "yes" or "no" back from my computer screen!

08 DEVELOPING THE DETAILS

By now I am making good progress toward a final composition, sketching out almost everything that will be in the scene. Here you can see how I use my value sketch as a guide for grouping objects. Look at Jack, the wine jug, the candle holder, and the goblet, for example. When I draw them, I am not looking at just the interior lines of each object, but at the outside lines and how the group reads as an overall shape. I do this for each and every element of the image, such as the birds and objects on the ground. Grouping is such an important tool for composition – make sure to use it if you feel comfortable doing so.

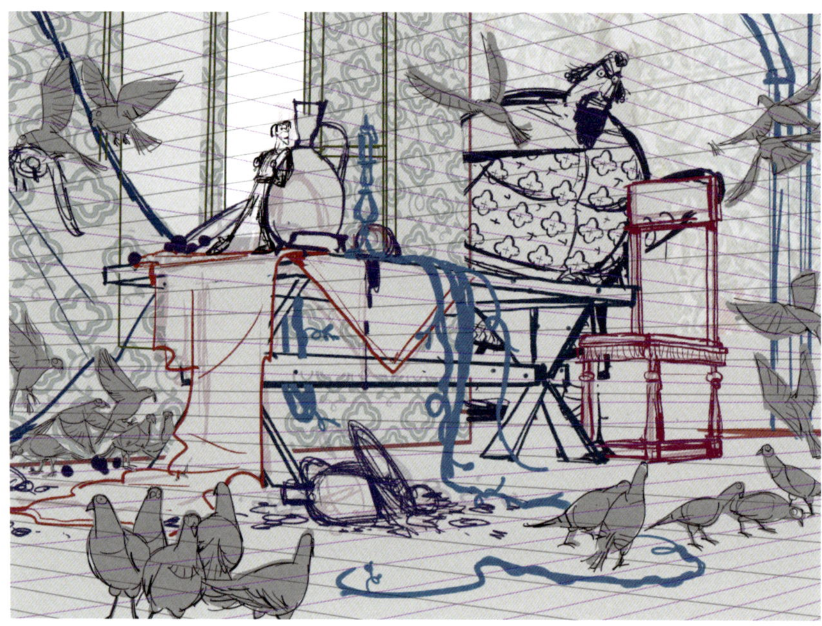

▶ The scene and all its contents are beginning to come together

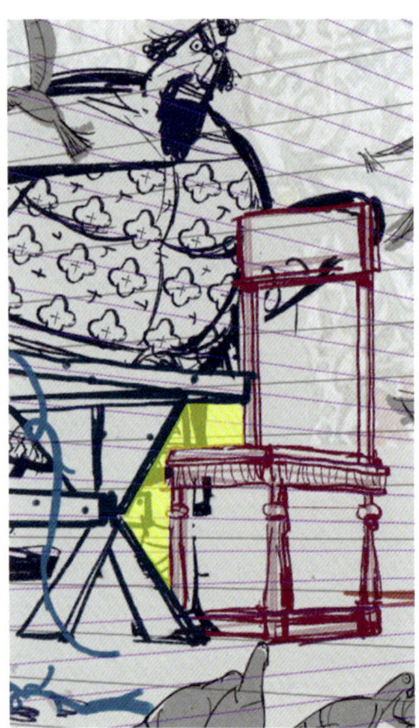

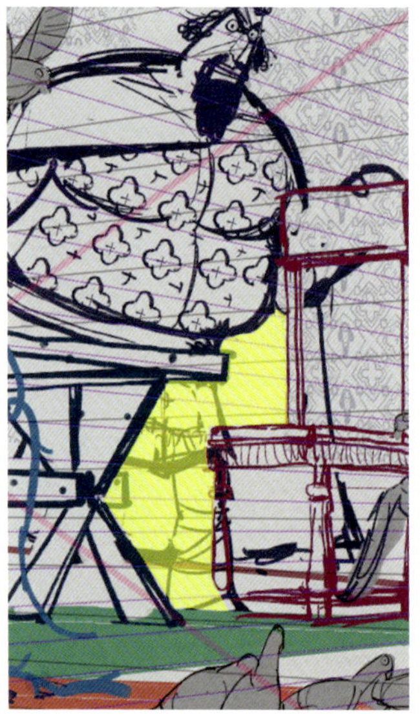

09 TIDYING UP THE FLOOR

Next I move the giant's chair slightly over to the right, creating more separation and depth (highlighted in yellow on the left). The giant's legs were previously hidden by the table, but now we can clearly see his menacing stance as he approaches Jack's hiding place.

One area that has been challenging me is the floor, which I am finding very unclear. I will lay a heavy pattern on many areas of the image, such as the walls, but it would be too much to put the same one on the floor as well. To achieve a more pleasing balance, I add some rugs on the floor. They will help show the room's perspective, include a more subtle pattern for interest, and help the viewer's eyes to travel through the image from foreground to background.

◀ Moving the giant's chair gives his design more room to breathe

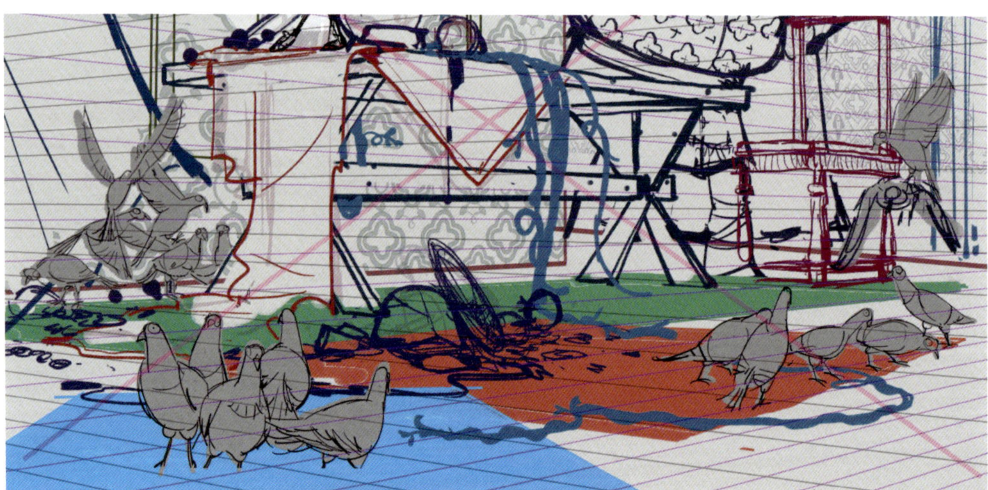

▶ Blocking out the placement of some rugs on the floor

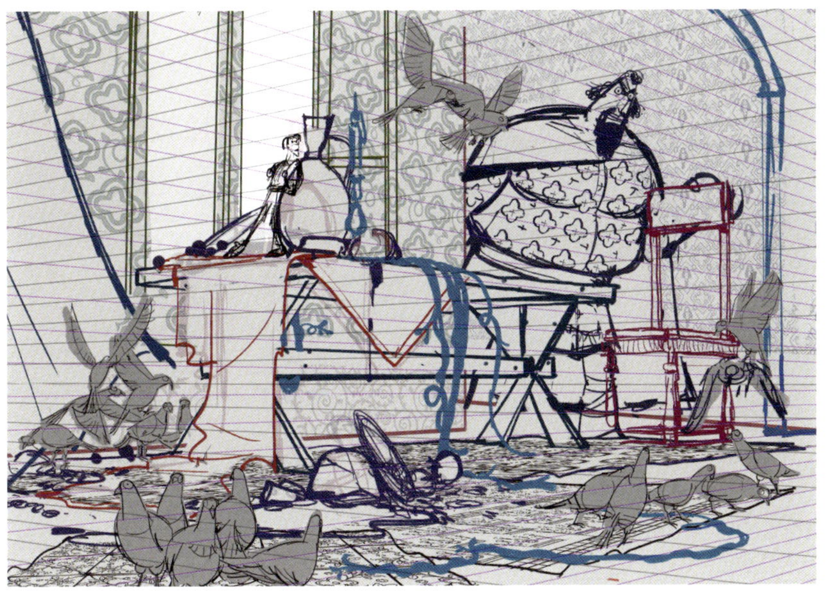

▲ Wrapping up the sketch phase of the illustration process

10 EVALUATING THE SKETCH

Happy with where the scene is going, I can now call the sketch stage finished. The image so far is strong and interesting. The focal point against the window will work very well; the birds will help us travel through the image; the flowing shapes of the curtain and beanstalk will draw the viewer's eye through the action of the story. I am still unsure about some shapes, such as the broken wine jug on the floor. Perhaps I will replace it with food fallen from the giant's table. This leads me to wonder, "What would this giant normally eat for lunch? Apples, salad, bread?" I can finalize this later. For now, I am ready to move on to the next step, which is the last and most important setup decision I will make: choosing a color palette.

DON'T GET TOO ATTACHED

Avoid getting too attached to your drawing. For example, if you love a part of your sketch so much that you try to work around it to keep it, even if it doesn't work well with the entire piece, the final illustration will really suffer. The overall look and feel is always more important than details, so be patient and remember that you can always redraw something. As you can see so far, I sketch very roughly and am open to changing anything to find what works. The story is the most important part of the illustration and everything else needs to favor it.

11 ROUGH COLOR STUDY

As I mentioned before, I like to leave room for change in all stages of the process. My goal here is to experiment quickly with color and see if the values are working well, like the value study in step 06, just as a rough guide for the final painting. I want green to be the core of the color palette. I imagine the giant as a king or prince, very rich, and green is commonly the color of money, as well as often signifying something toxic or poisonous. This palette would allow me to play with some deeper symbolism and the theme of social inequality. I feel I have found an overall mood, but I know it isn't completely there yet – I will move forward and see if the next step brings me closer to what I want.

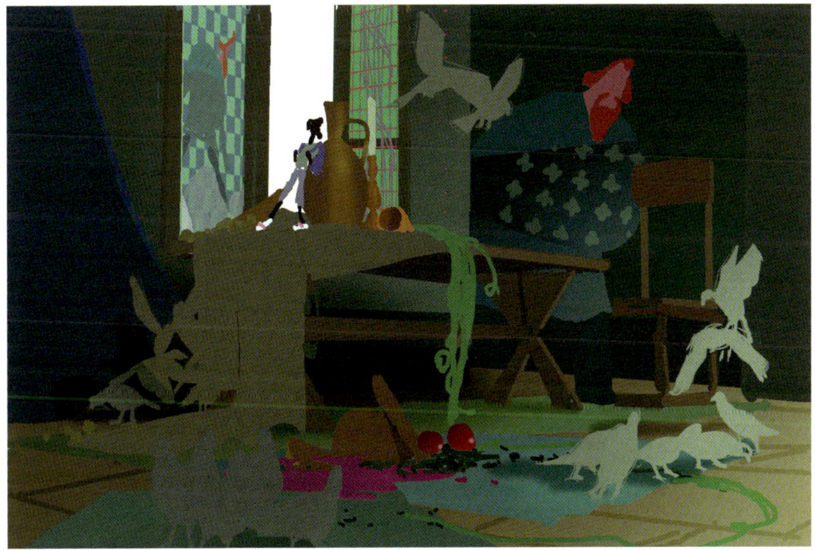

▲ Testing a possible palette with a rough color thumbnail

12 SETTING A BASE MOOD

I start to block out a kind of underpainting. I am not paying attention to any details here, but to the overall value structure and light direction. My main goal here is to have a feeling of unity in the painting, which I can achieve by building up from the same hue. This yellow-green base will make it easier to maintain the illustration's overall harmony as it develops. I am still keeping the shape design of all the objects in mind, and I make sure to flip the image from time to time to make sure everything is still working. In this view, you can clearly see the two areas of the image with the highest value contrast and definition: the jug in front of the window, where Jack will be hiding, and the shape of the giant's head against the dark wall. These are the two focal points that the viewer will immediately look toward and between.

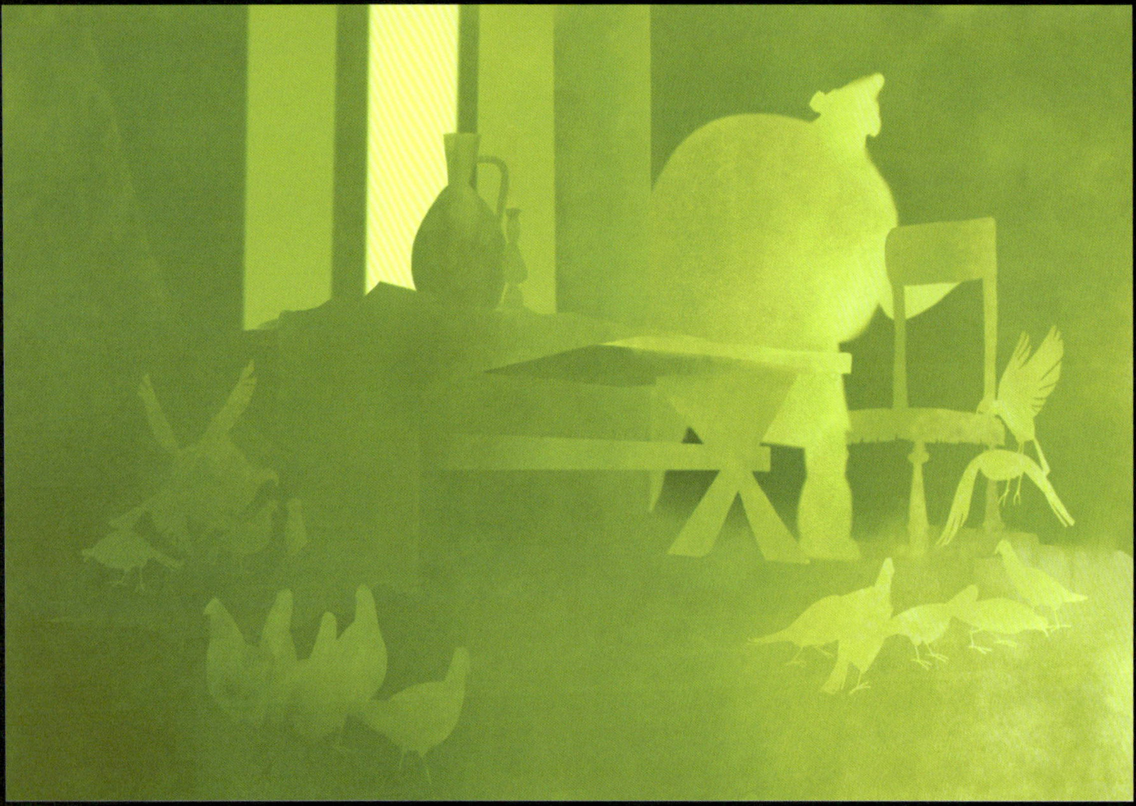

▲ Using a green underpainting as a base for the final color palette

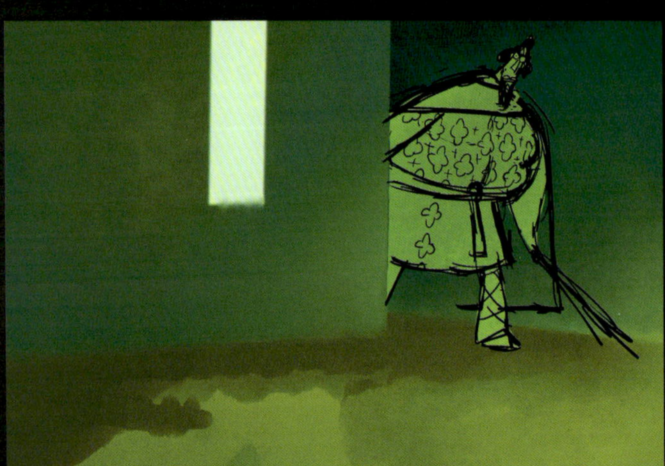

▲ A few more enhancements before starting to finalize the painting

13 PUSHING COLORS AND SHAPES

As with all the visual features so far, color can be pushed and exaggerated. As I start laying down my intended final colors, I feel that I could push the saturation a little more, creating a range of rich greens. As I continue to paint, I also decide that the giant could have a more exaggerated silhouette and more interesting shapes. Looking at the medieval patterns from my research, I realize I can incorporate some of those forms into the shape of the giant's head. Instead of him just pulling out the chair, giving the giant a sword will work well to balance the image's focal points, introducing another element with high values. As you can see, I am still making decisions and finding improvements that can enhance the image – it's the ongoing "dialog" I mentioned before!

14 PATTERNS AND TEXTURES

Now I start to refine the elements, adding patterns as planned, trying to keep my values close to what I mapped out in my studies. Each prop is on a separate layer, so that I can control the silhouette and placement of each one, and hide objects when I want to work on something underneath. I block out the base color of the giant, choosing a dark blue-green against which his fancy embroidery and lighter head color will stand out. I haven't yet added the detail of the sword in his hand – it would be a distraction at this stage, so I will add it last. The Pixar animator Ricky Nierva coined the term "simplexity" for the art of capturing the simple shape of a subject and maintaining it, even after applying complex textures and details on top; I keep that in mind throughout the whole detailing process.

TIME AND PATIENCE

Something that I am also learning is how to recognize when I am avoiding a part of the process out of fear of "ruining" the image, or simply because I don't know what to do. When I hit those moments, I try to put the image aside for a couple of hours, if I have time, and start researching things related to whatever I am afraid of or unsure about. I do not get lost in this research, but try to learn just enough to get my brain working again. This helps me look at my piece with fresh eyes when I return to it. Taking that bit of time is important.

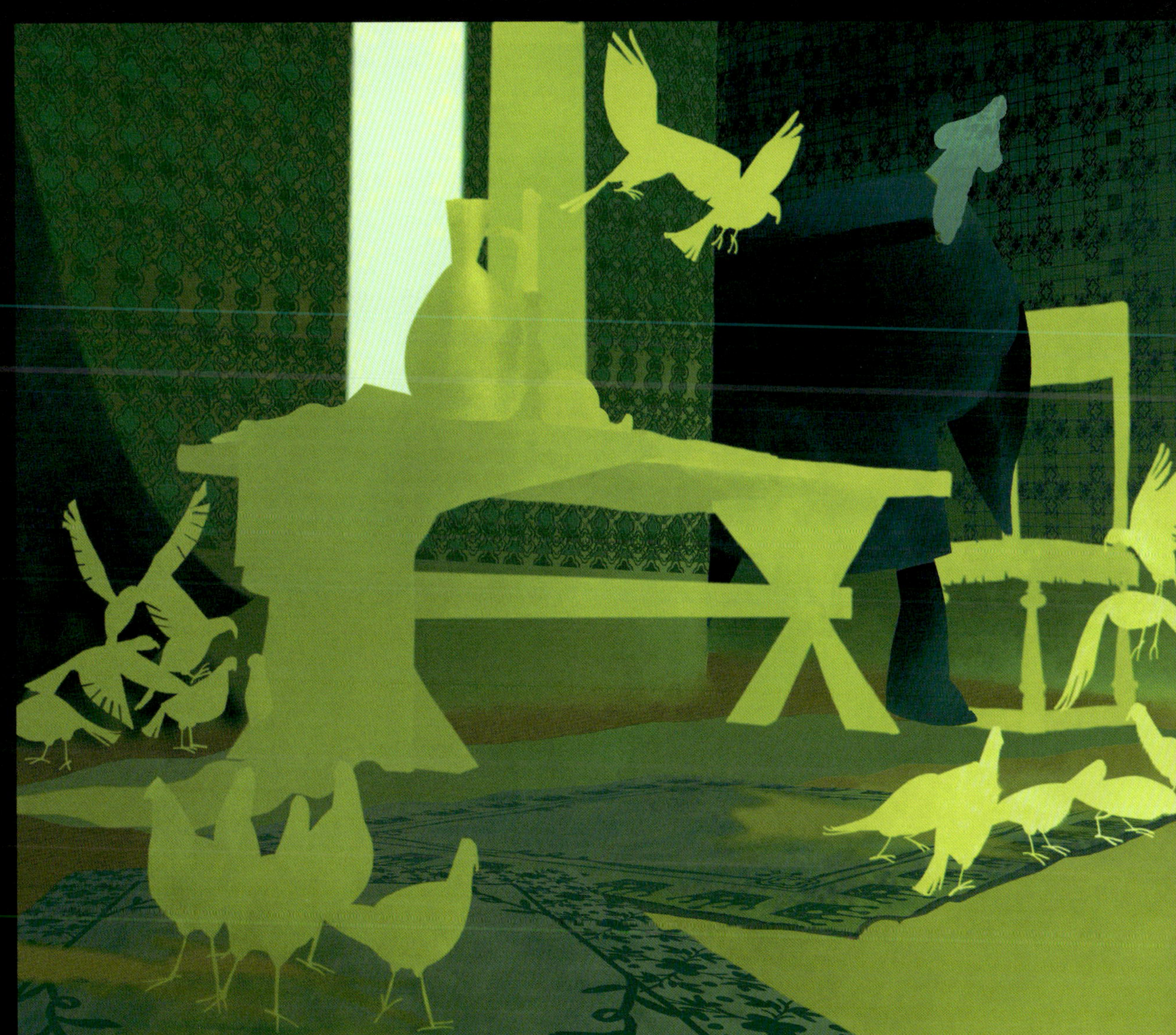

▲ The setting starts to feel more rich and luxurious once I begin adding patterns

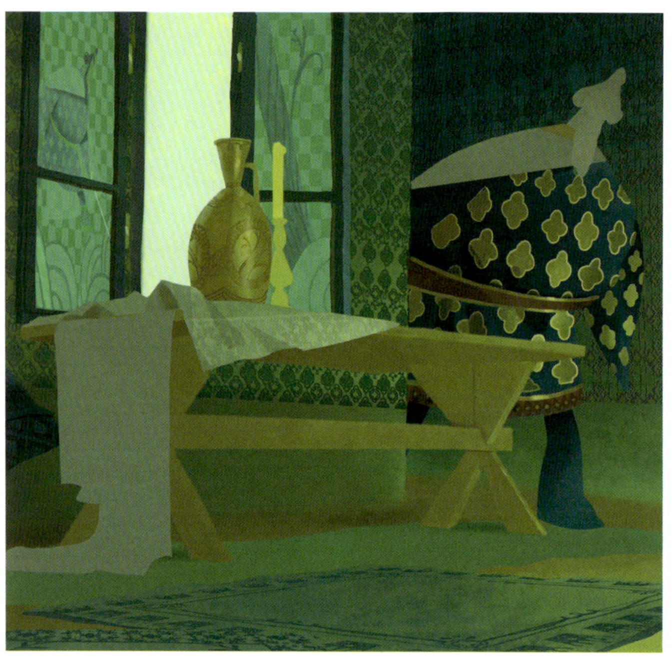

▲ Bringing the scene to life with more textures and subtle details

15 GLASS AND GOLD

I start to add details to the window panes, which I can use as an opportunity to add more intrigue to the story. One window has a design of the giant himself on it, holding a sword and looking down at Jack's hiding place. It will be a subtle detail that entertains the viewer while also showing the giant's vanity – spending his wealth on stained-glass windows of himself! I notice that the patterns on the nearby wall are a little too busy, so I make them slightly simpler and larger, while still looking lavish and ornate.

By now I have drifted away from the color study I made in step 11. In that draft, I made the objects on the table brown or bronze, but I now feel that adding more gold will help to represent the opulence of the setting. Golden treasures were the giant's most prized possessions in the original tale, so gold should be more prominent. During my research, I also found many examples of historical clothing with golden embroidery, so I incorporate that into the giant's clothing. This enables me to create more contrast in his costume, drawing more attention to him.

16 BRINGING IN THE BEANSTALK

My original color draft included shades of green, blue, and yellow, with some areas of orange, pink, and purple for contrast. However, I now realize that I should limit the palette more, making the giant and the giant's room look more cohesive by using fewer colors. This would help create better contrast with Jack. I want the viewer to feel that Jack doesn't belong here, with a costume and color palette that stands out in the giant's domain. I also use a pop of purple wine on the jug and table, where Jack will be hiding, to appeal to the viewer's eye with extra color contrast.

At this stage, I also give the beanstalk a stronger presence in the scene, showing it growing in through the window. I break the glass of one window to show that the beanstalk has burst through with some force. This inspires me to blow out the candle, with a puff of smoke drifting away, as if the window broke just a few moments before the scene we are now seeing.

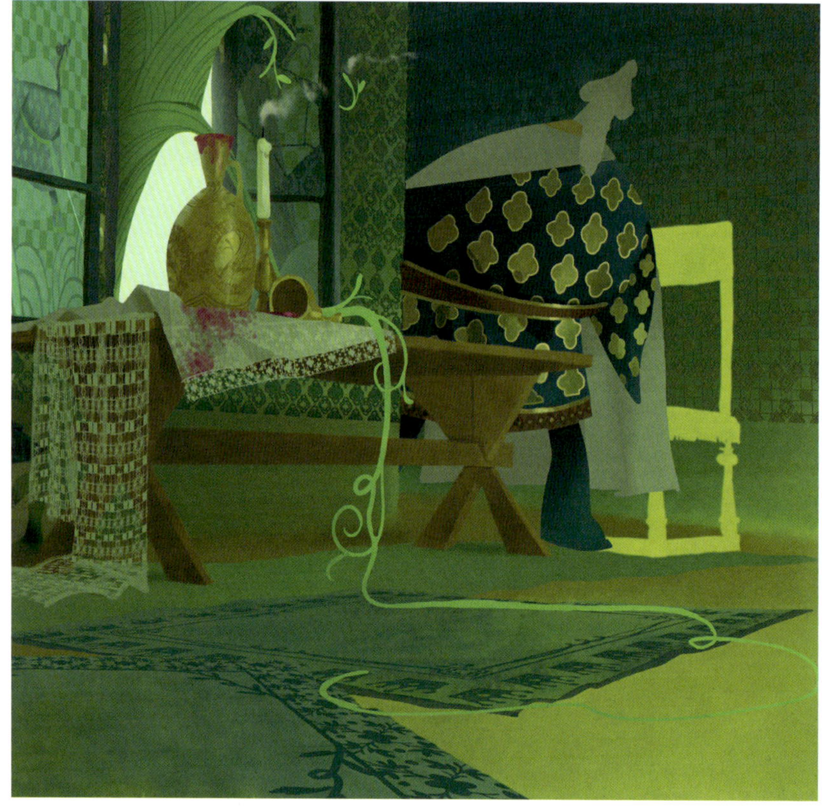

▲ Focusing the color palette and adding the beanstalk bursting through the window

The beanstalk's long tendrils help the composition by trailing down onto the floor, leading the viewer down to where the pigeons will be gathered. The cloths on the table are now made from fine lace – another reflection of the giant's character and lifestyle. It is now very evident that he is not a typical monstrous fairy-tale giant, but a wealthy figure with refined, expensive tastes. In some ways, this will make him more menacing than a giant who is simply a brute.

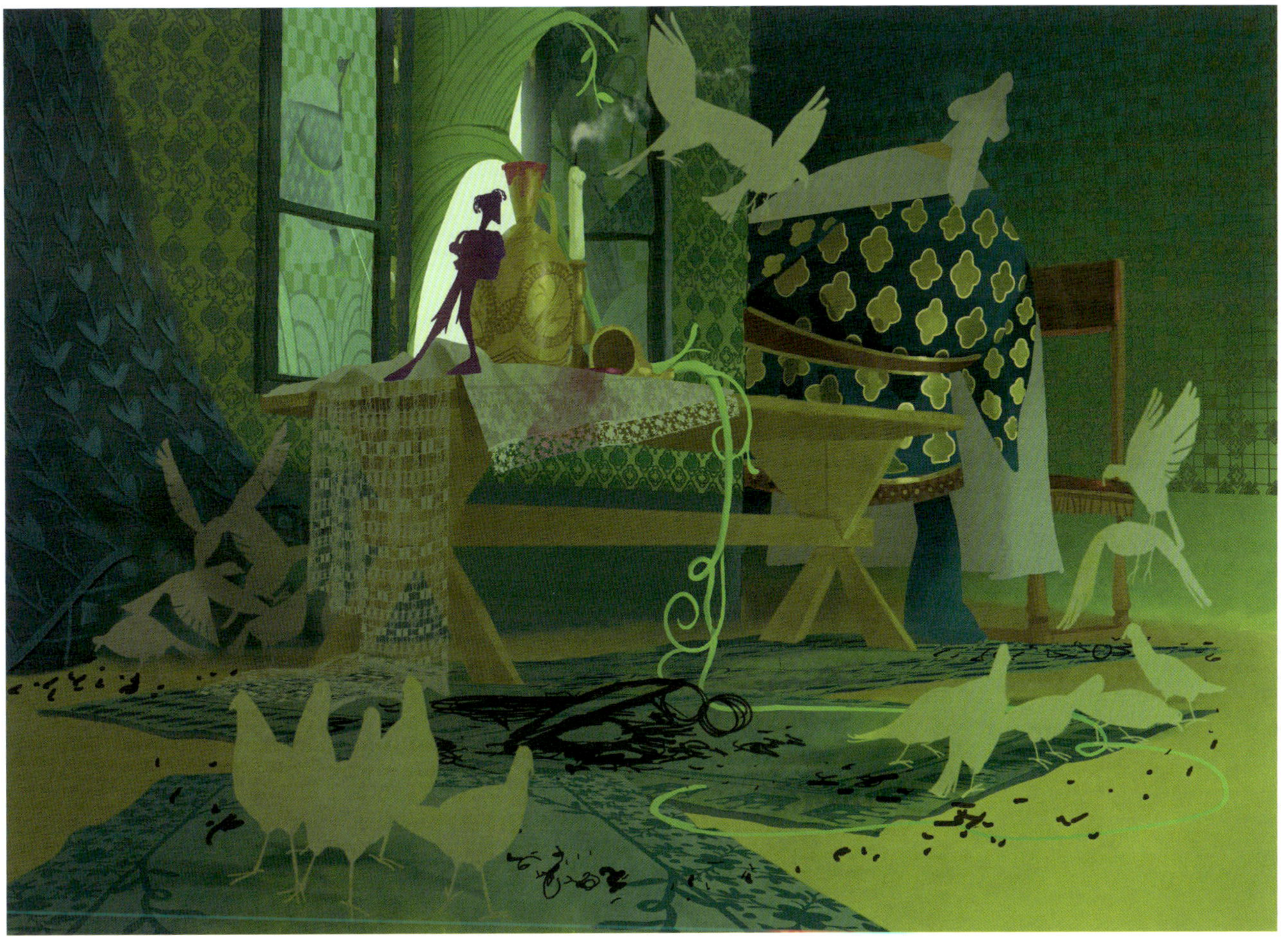

17 INTRODUCING JACK

I am beginning to think about how all the final elements will look together, in terms of their color, shape, and texture. There are still some parts that need adding and defining, but I don't want the finished scene to look too busy. For example, I am still deciding what food will be spilled on the ground, because it's a good story detail, but I do not want to draw too much attention to it. I also block out a color for Jack, using a purple base that is complementary to his green and yellow surroundings.

HAVE FUN WITH DETAILS

My favorite thing about these later stages is that I can add little story details to the props in a scene. If you look closely at the golden jug, you can see it's decorated with a beanstalk design, rewarding observant viewers with an amusing connection to the story's events. I always try to put as much thought and story as I can into these tiny details.

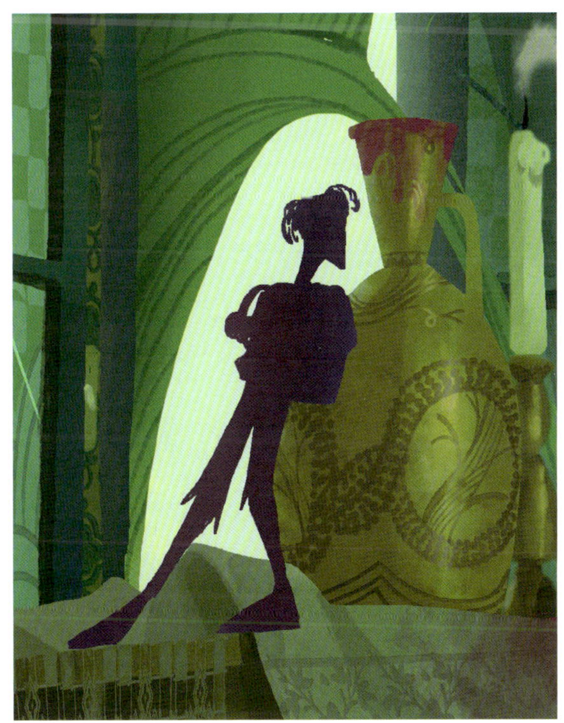

▲ Jack's purple base color will provide an eye-catching contrast with his environment

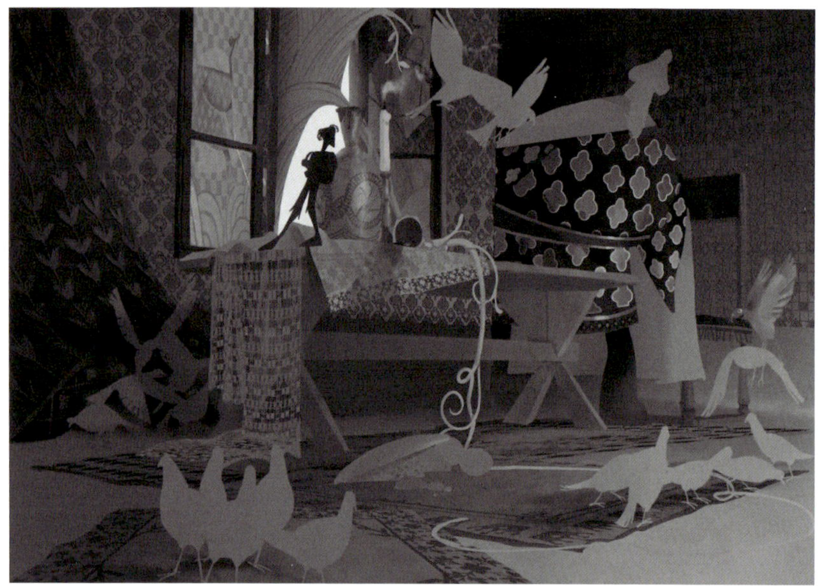

18 GRAYSCALE VALUE CHECK

Checking your values is always important. When I am trying to feel the balance of the image and don't want to be distracted by color, I check the image in grayscale to see if I need to fix anything or adjust the lighting of any elements. Looking at the image now, I realize that there are too many elements between Jack and the giant. There needs to be a cleaner read between the two main characters, so I will try taking out those two flying birds and see if the image works better. The rest of the image works well.

◀ **Checking an image in grayscale can help you pinpoint weaknesses in your composition or values**

19 THE FINAL COMPOSITION

The image works much better without those birds between Jack and the giant! In their place, I use a green tendril to help support the composition and flow in a more subtle way. When flipping the image to check the composition, I find it works better that way around, with the viewer following the giant's gaze from left to right, toward Jack's hiding place. The whole composition works as a series of connecting points that lead us around the scene and tell the story. The viewer won't literally see a line, but it is subtly formed by the composition, props, and characters.

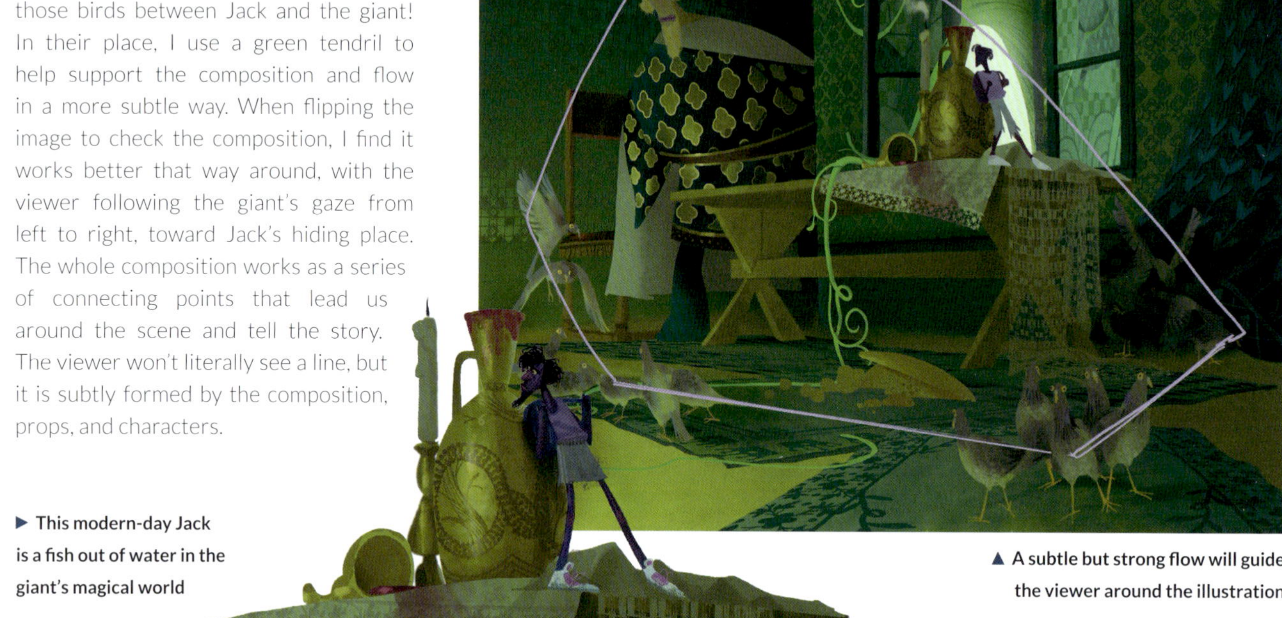

▶ **This modern-day Jack is a fish out of water in the giant's magical world**

▲ **A subtle but strong flow will guide the viewer around the illustration**

I also add more detail to the pigeons and the giant's face. The pigeons are of secondary importance to Jack and the giant, so they are more muted in color and contrast. The giant has a blond beard and hair, so his head stands out distinctly against the dark background, and his purple lips add some color contrast within his design. Jack's design is also taking shape, with ragged, modern clothing that makes him look like a total outsider in the giant's world.

20 FINISHING TOUCHES

I finish detailing Jack and the giant, then add the sword to the giant's hand, moving two of the pigeons slightly to help it fit in the composition. The giant's beady eyes create tension in the scene as he comes around the corner, armed and ready to confront an intruder, seeing the pigeons but not yet suspecting Jack's presence. Jack fearfully takes cover behind the golden jug, clearly framed and silhouetted in the window for the viewer, but hidden from the giant's sight. On the floor, I detail the fallen plate, deciding that the food should be bread and a bunch of grapes – classic medieval-looking food that also fits the image's palette, much better than the wine and salad I sketched earlier. I scatter more crumbs on the ground, completing the story of the food being knocked from the table. Finally, I boost the contrast and blue/purple tones so they are not lost among the greens.

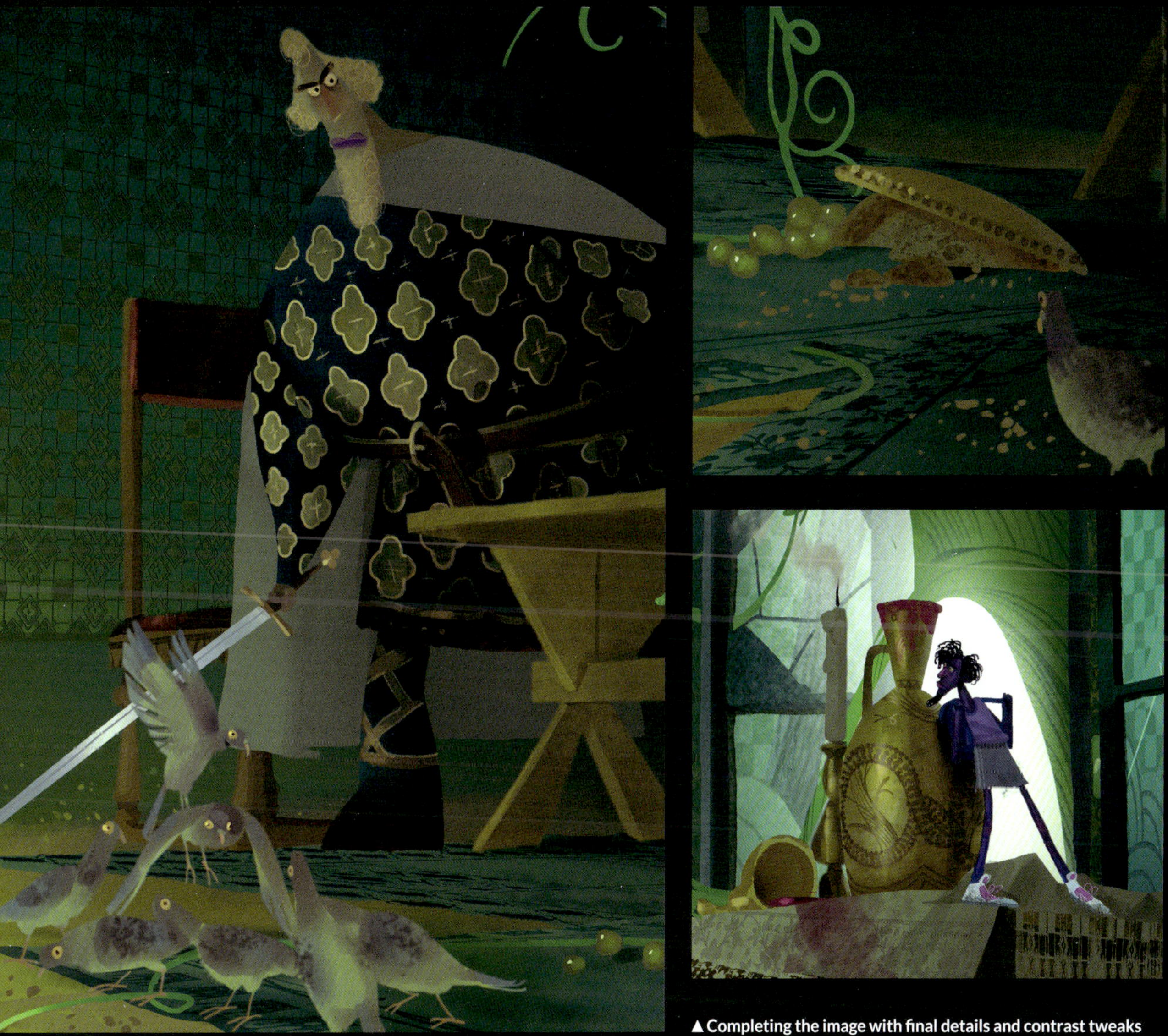

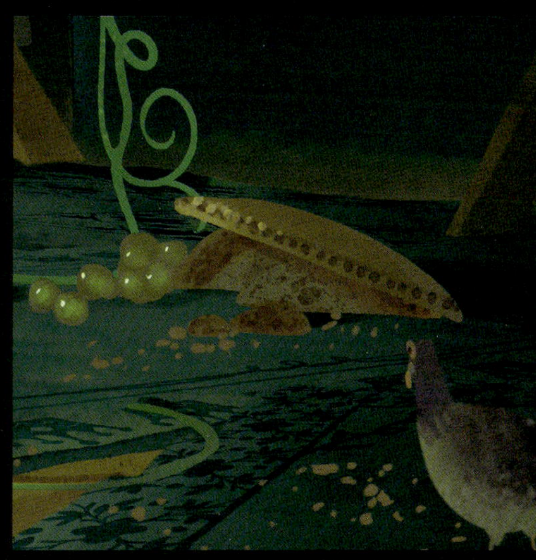

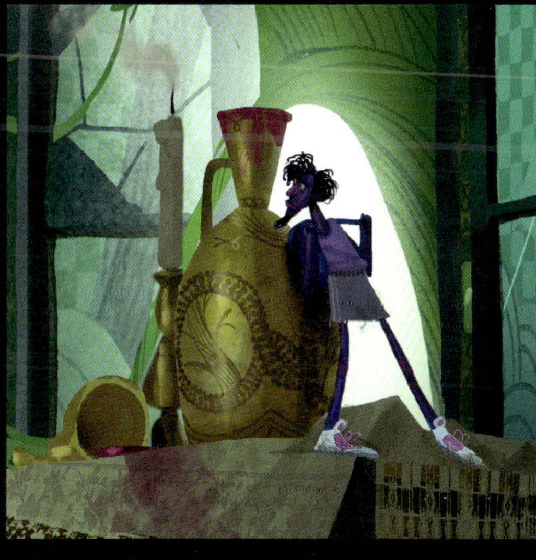

▲ Completing the image with final details and contrast tweaks

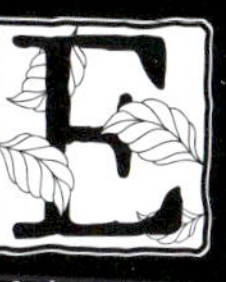

very piece has its own challenges. I personally try to get as far as I can in my head before I sketch anything, and then as far as I can with my sketch before I paint anything! I wanted to keep the key elements of the story – the beanstalk, the giant, and Jack – but present the story in my own way. The giant here isn't a brutish ogre, but more like a prince or king, and Jack is just a normal man. My main goal was to emphasize these contrasts by having social inequality and greed as backstories. To exaggerate the vast difference and distance between the characters, I made Jack more modern and the giant more medieval, as if the magic beanstalk connects two very different worlds.

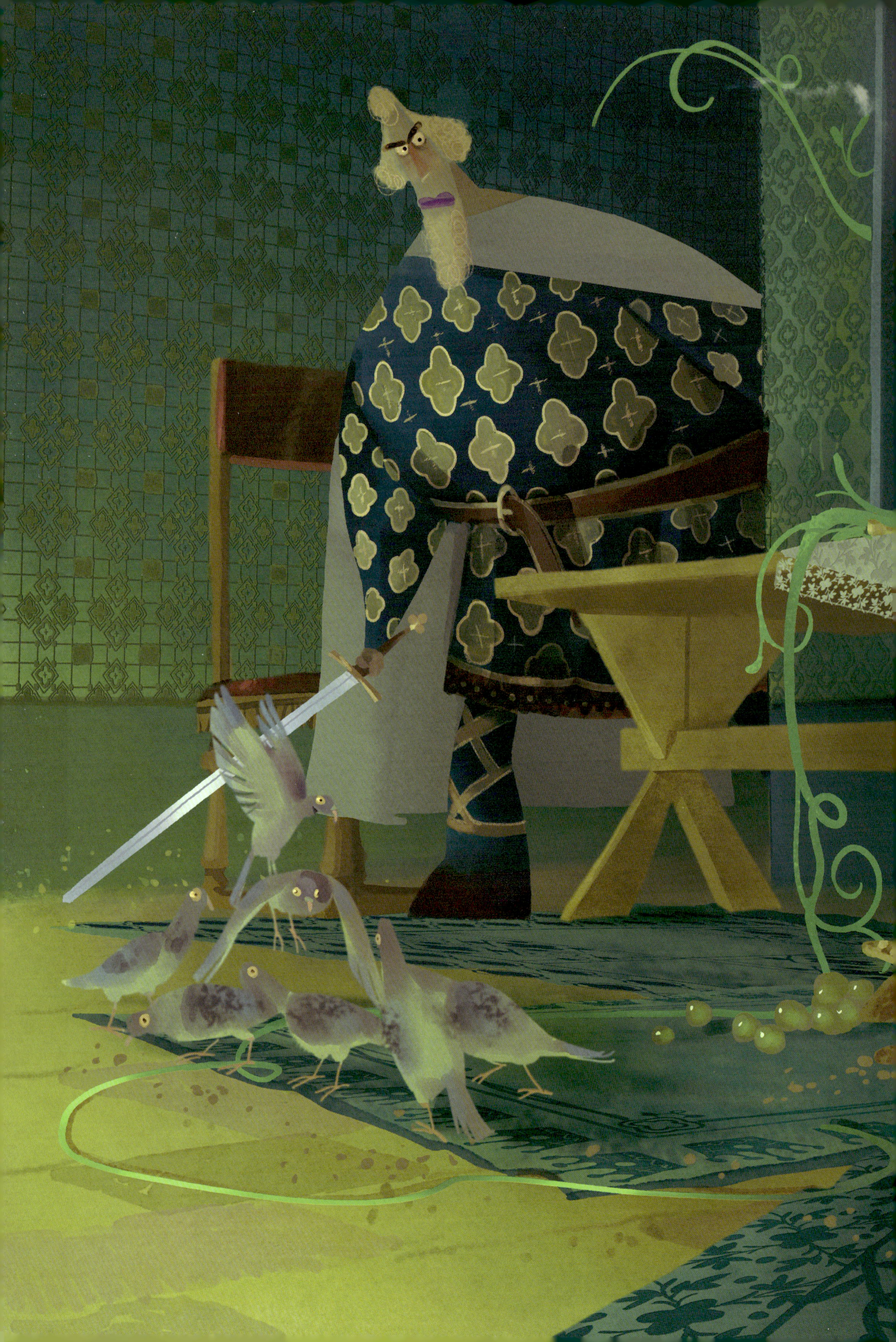

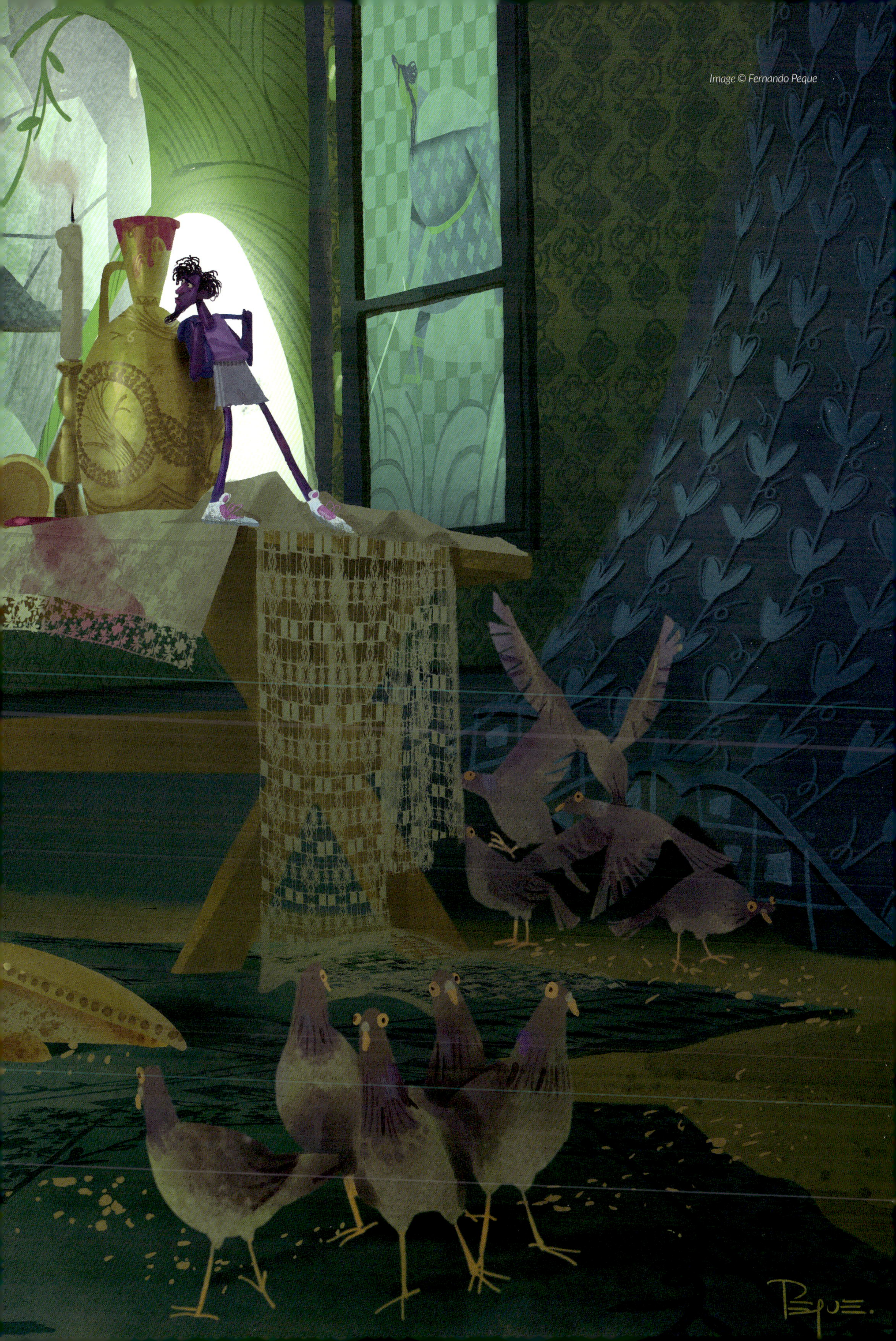
PEQUE.

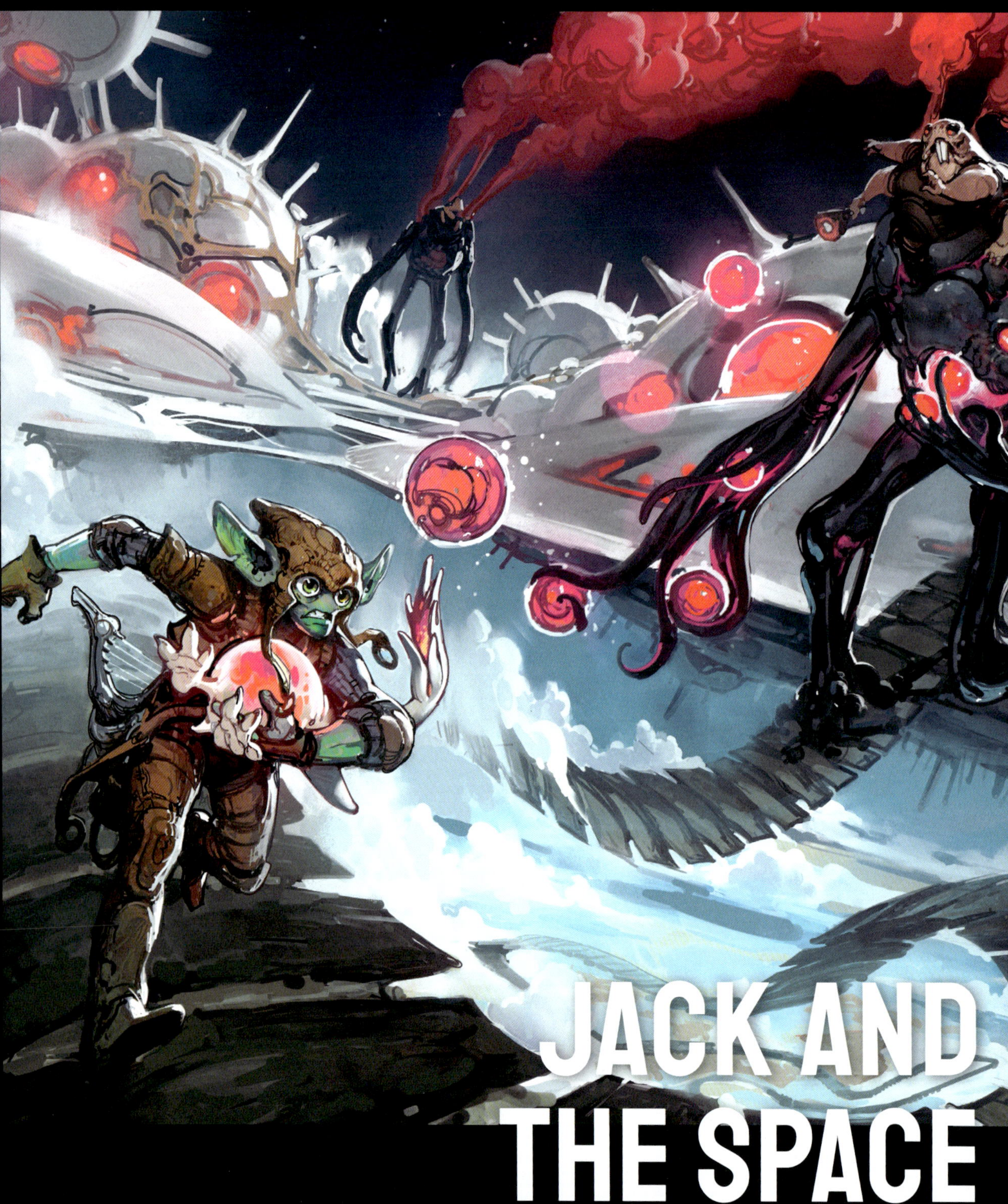

JACK AND THE SPACE GIANTS

BY KORY LYNN HUBBELL

I have always loved *Jack and the Beanstalk*. The idea that someday we might find a magic pathway to a better life is a fantasy shared by many, and the story highlights the vast differences in wealth between those who may as well dwell in floating castles and... the rest of us. I wanted to show how alien the world of a giant living in the sky could be, as well as illustrate the greed of those who would hoard limitless wealth away from those who could use it to survive.

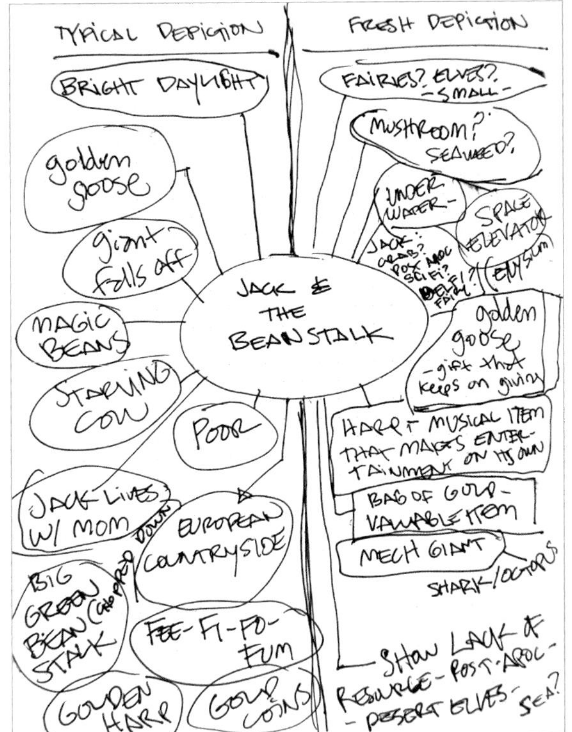

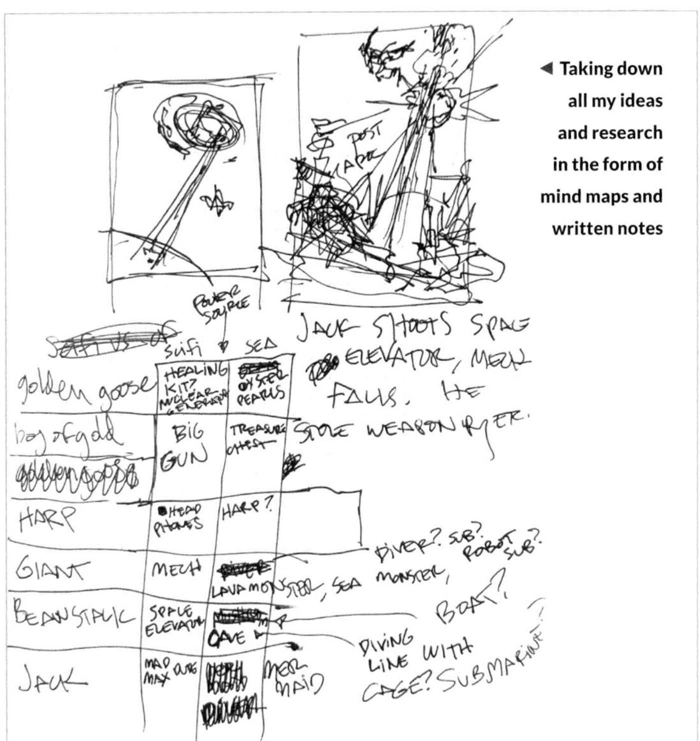

◀ **Taking down all my ideas and research in the form of mind maps and written notes**

01 BRAINSTORMING

The first step of every painting I make might surprise you: I do a lot of writing and reading. I like to make a brainstorm web and get out all of my initial thoughts on paper. From there I can start to sort through the elements and decide what to do next. I don't think too hard about it or care much about how it looks – it is just an exercise to loosen up and think through the story. I take time to read through a few versions of the story and refresh my memory of the events, characters, locations, and objects in it. Once I have my brain wrapped around the story, I can break down its elements and try to think of different ways to look at it.

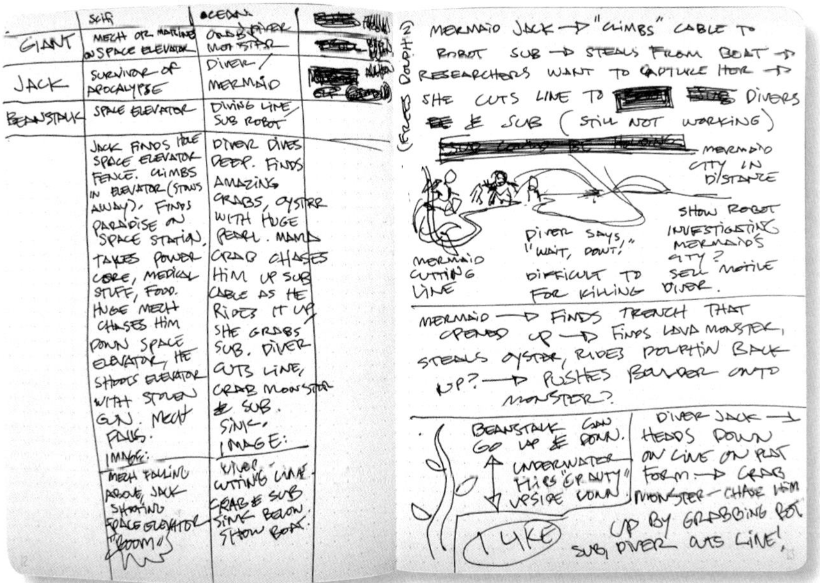

▲ **Don't worry if you can't read any of this chicken scratch – it's just me getting my brain on paper and thinking through all the decisions I need to make!**

02 NARROWING DOWN

I begin to explore further into the ideas generated with my initial brainstorm. My problem at this point is usually an over-abundance of ideas and directions to take – choosing a path is fairly difficult for me! My first instinct is to turn it all upside down and put the story underwater. Down becomes up and up becomes down, in a way, thanks to the nullification of gravity and the introduction of buoyancy. I think about some deep-sea versions, perhaps where the Jack character is a mermaid cutting the line of a deep-sea diver, or where Jack is a diver escaping from a crab monster. These prove to be difficult ideas to match well with the story, so I opt for a sci-fi scenario set on an alien planet, where the residents are suffering and struggling to survive as the giants drain their planet of resources from orbit.

03 FIRST SKETCHES

I begin sketching very rough ideas for what this illustration could be. The moments where Jack is running from the giant or chopping down the beanstalk are what stand out most in my mind. I imagine Jack firing a rocket launcher at the alien beanstalk from the ground, causing a giant robot to fall to its doom, or perhaps Jack could have been given keys to a ship instead of magic beans, allowing him to fly up to the floating castle in the sky. However, I decide to focus on something simpler in the end – many of these ideas are quite abstract, and I don't want to pile on too many weird elements onto the story and confuse the viewer. I am not yet sure if I've succeeded!

▼ Sketching an initial, very rough idea for a story moment

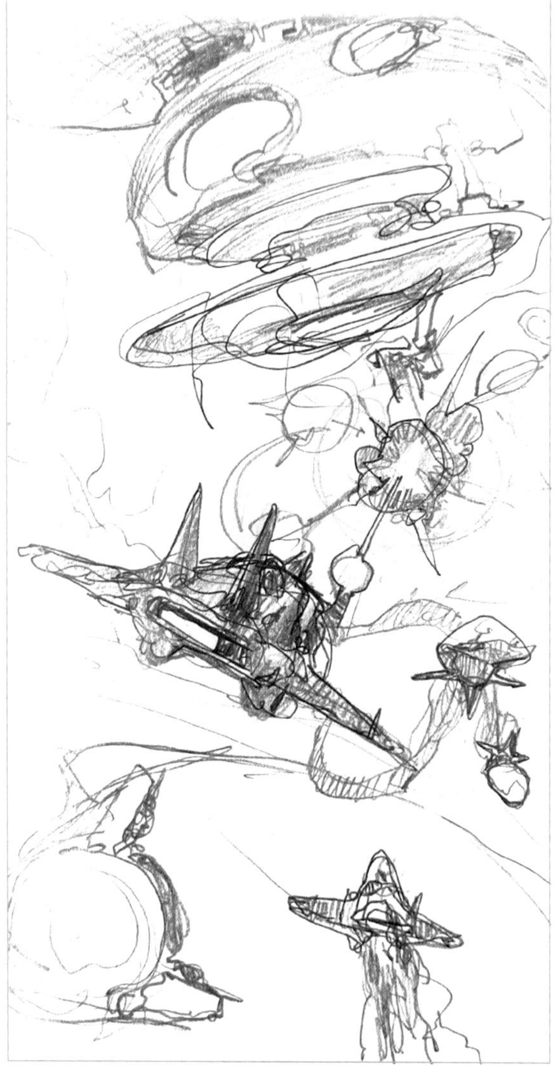

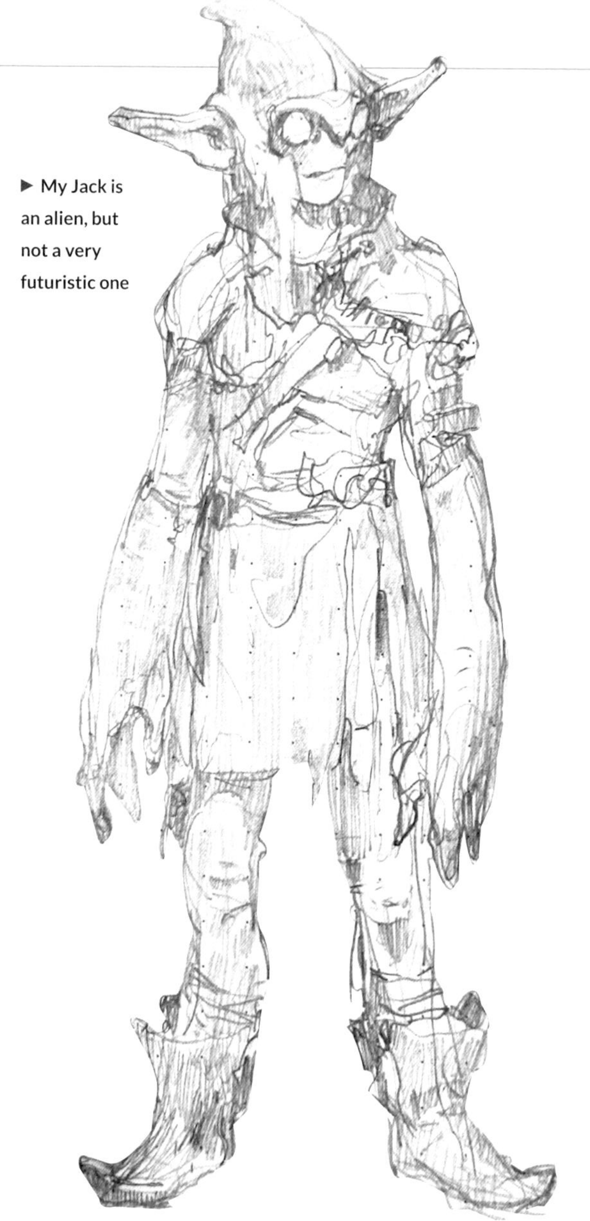

► My Jack is an alien, but not a very futuristic one

04 AN ALIEN JACK

I turn my thoughts to Jack and what he would look like. I know I want Jack to be an alien, but I also want him to maintain a bit of a fantasy look, as though he's an alien who lives in an agrarian society with medieval levels of technology. I give him elf-like ears and some stretched proportions to move him away from being human. He is meant to look a bit scrapped together, as if he's surviving in a harsh world and has a bit of armor to defend against attackers. His costume is practical and simple, but clearly mended and modified many times over, as if it doesn't get changed very often. His hat is inspired by my memory of *Jack and the Beanstalk* illustrations in an attempt to win recognition from the viewer and, again, to tie him to a medieval setting. My goal here is to think about the costuming and how that tells a story outside the illustration so I can focus on other things in the final painting.

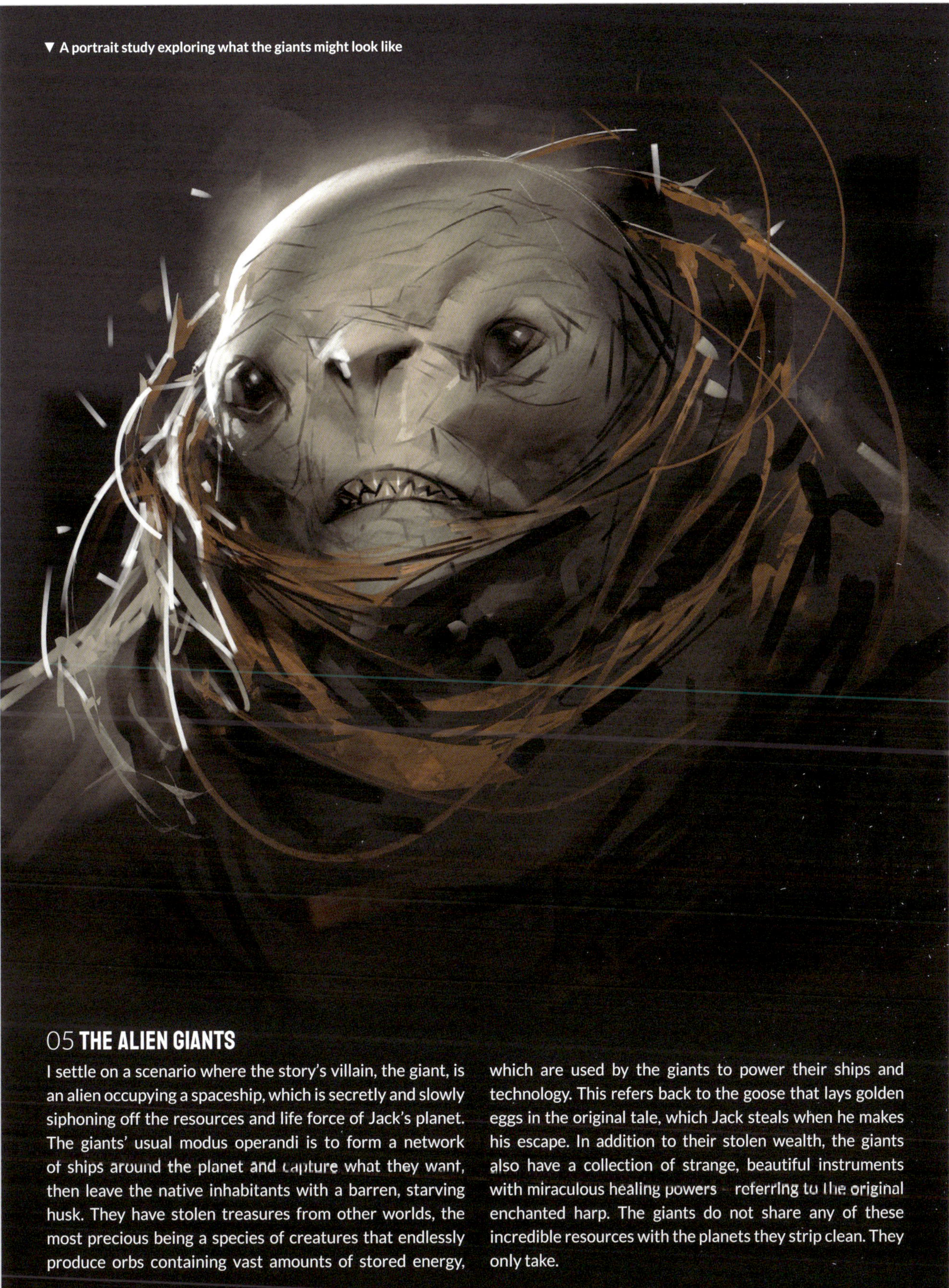

▼ A portrait study exploring what the giants might look like

05 THE ALIEN GIANTS

I settle on a scenario where the story's villain, the giant, is an alien occupying a spaceship, which is secretly and slowly siphoning off the resources and life force of Jack's planet. The giants' usual modus operandi is to form a network of ships around the planet and capture what they want, then leave the native inhabitants with a barren, starving husk. They have stolen treasures from other worlds, the most precious being a species of creatures that endlessly produce orbs containing vast amounts of stored energy, which are used by the giants to power their ships and technology. This refers back to the goose that lays golden eggs in the original tale, which Jack steals when he makes his escape. In addition to their stolen wealth, the giants also have a collection of strange, beautiful instruments with miraculous healing powers – referring to the original enchanted harp. The giants do not share any of these incredible resources with the planets they strip clean. They only take.

06 SPACESHIPS AND ENERGY ORBS

I was originally going to have Jack take a spaceship to the giant aliens' orbital castle, and the result would be the giant grabbing onto the ship as Jack flees. Here are a few spaceship sketches to explore the idea, but I decide that it would be more recognizable to show something more beanstalk-like.

I also continue exploring what the villains might look like. On the bottom right of my sketchbook page is an exploration of a more ethereal, energy-based life-form that would tower above Jack. The idea is that this villain produces the "golden egg" orbs from his own body. I decide that something less elegant and more brutal or slovenly would be better for this particular type of being, but I might keep the egg idea for later use.

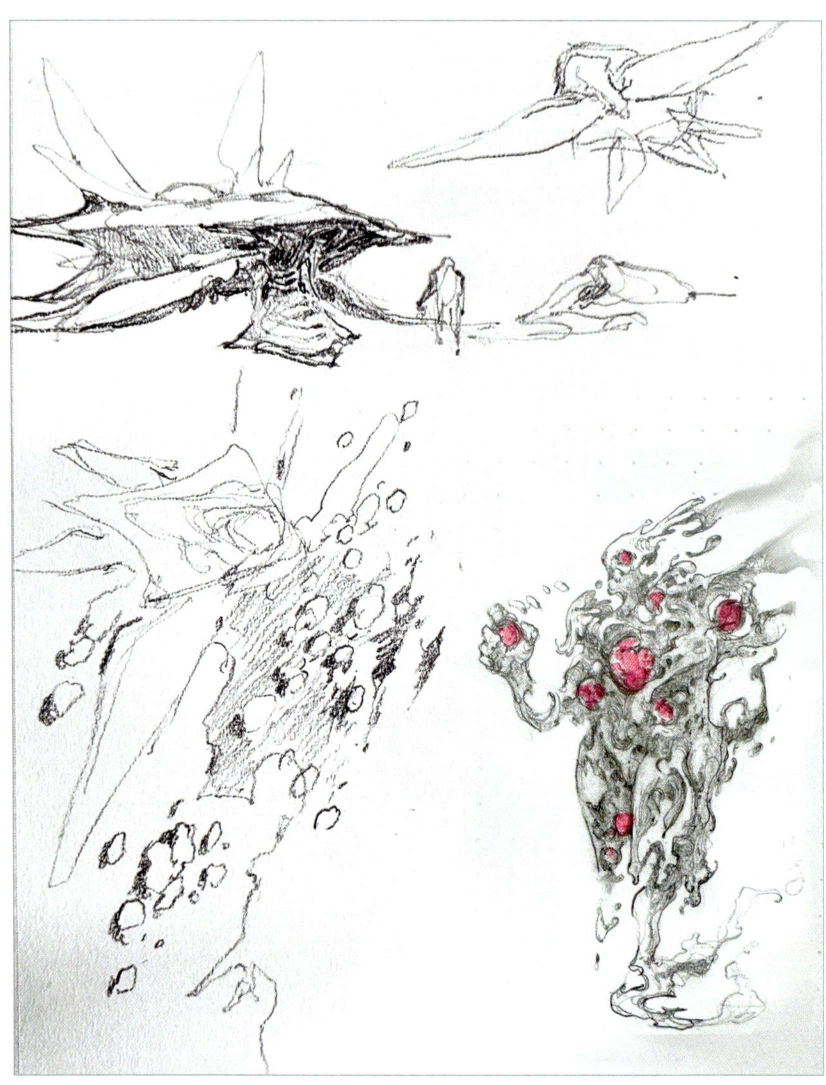

► Further sketchbook explorations that I eventually discard

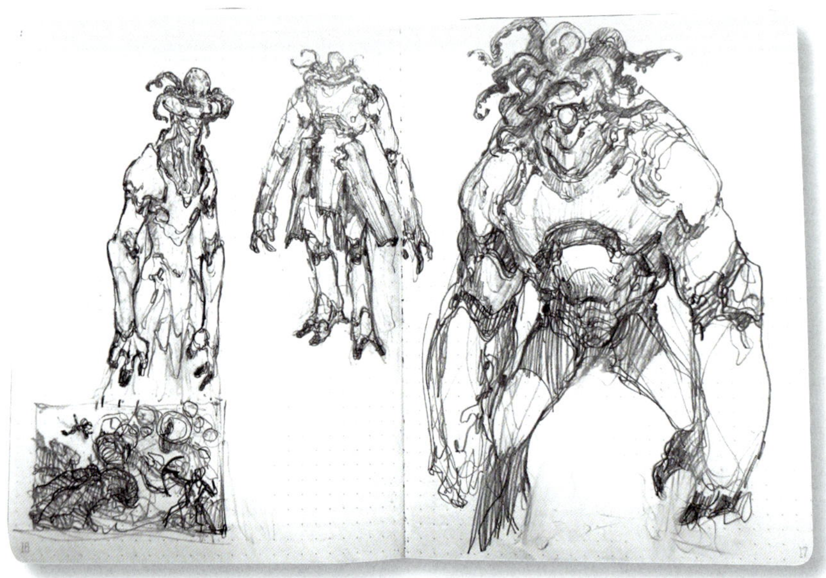

▲ Playing around with some different shapes and formats for a mech design

07 A GIANT MECH?

I decide that I really like the idea of the giant being a slimy, grotesque creature riding around in a mech – a huge robotic suit. I am drawn to the idea of a lazy ruling class of giants who harness stolen technology to make their lives easier in every way. These villains would not use their own legs – they would use a machine of convenience stripped from another world. These giants wouldn't be bothered to move their bodies around of their own volition because, in their minds, walking is for planet-dwelling peasants. This habit of riding around in these strange, massive vehicles is consequently what makes them into "giants." They like the fear it produces in those who are unlucky enough to encounter them.

08 HUMANOID MECHS

I explore the direction of the alien invaders having a slightly more humanoid silhouette, still keeping the idea of them riding around in huge, creepy mechs. I feel that with such a vast departure from the look and genre of the source material, I need to ground my designs in a humanoid shape. I like the idea of the alien giant's silhouette being somewhat representative of a traditional giant, even if their appearances are overall quite different. I consider the general idea behind how their ships would circle a planet for resource extraction. I begin to think of their overall behavior as that of a virus, using the cores of innocent worlds as factories to produce resources the giants need until the planets collapse. Those resources are turned into more ships and machines to extract even more resources. It's never enough.

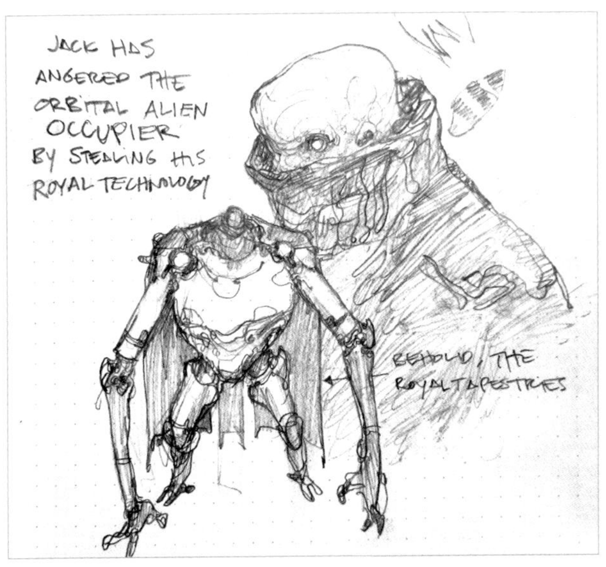

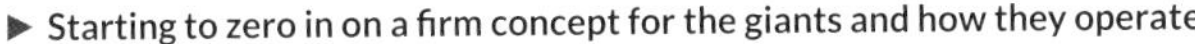

▶ Starting to zero in on a firm concept for the giants and how they operate

09 THE TYRANNICAL GIANT

I take another crack at the mech and develop it further, stretching out the limbs and refining the general body layout. I experiment with a long, flowing cape – for some reason, tyrants seem to love banners and capes and flowing tapestries! Red would be an impactful color for this. People associate red with power and strength, but it can also represent fire, destruction, and tyranny. For those reasons I feel it's important to make red a strong presence in the giant's color scheme. The design may change further in the later painting process, but for now, I like this idea.

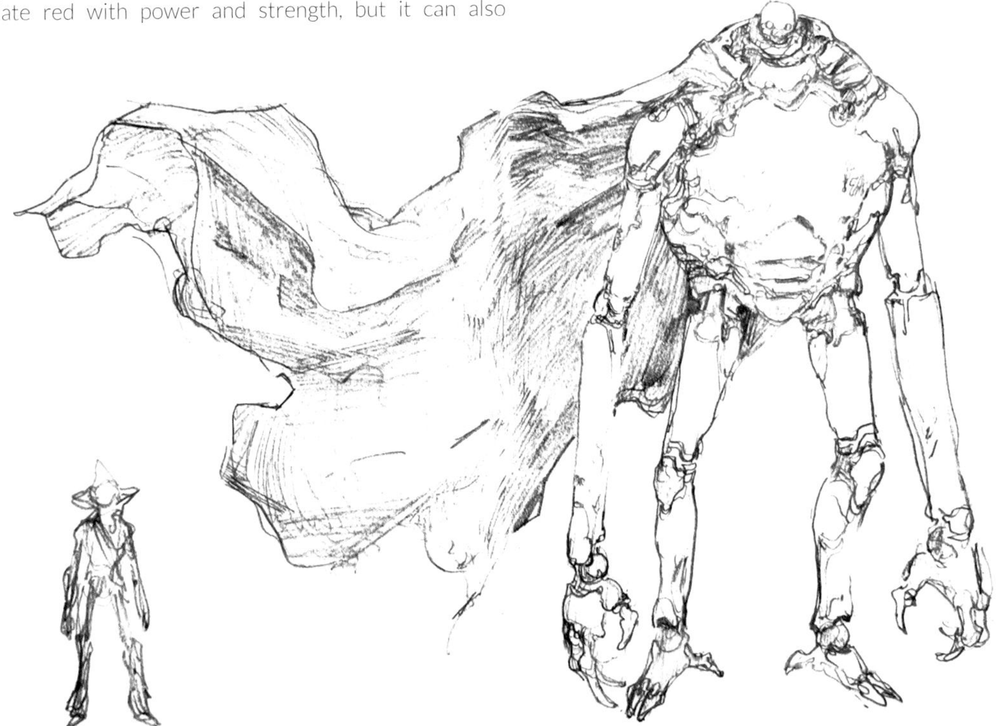

▲ A flowing red cape would make the mech look grand, powerful – and villainous

10 SKETCHING THE SCENE

This is my drawing of the scene on paper, after a few sloppy thumbnails that were unfortunately destroyed in a spill! I originally wanted to show Jack chopping down the beanstalk in whatever form it had taken, but I decide that the scene needs to show the giant more clearly and give the viewer a glimpse of the castle in the sky. I explore the nature of the giants and hint at viral forms with the shape of their machinery. In general, I feel like a virus is a good analog for the giants and their harmful influence in my version of the tale. My idea for the beanstalk develops into a giant worm, flat and tape-like so Jack can run along it.

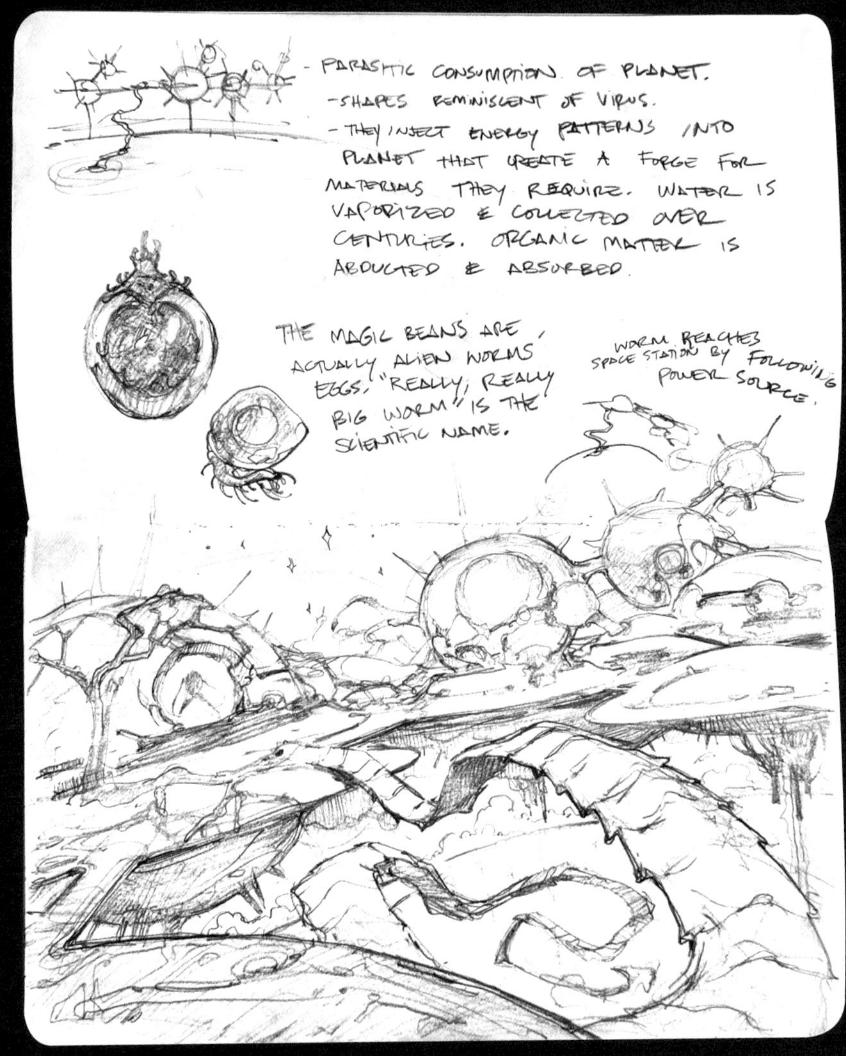

► **Sketching the environment where the scene will take place**

DON'T NEGLECT THE BACKSTORY

In my version of the tale, Jack's "magic beans" are actually eggs from a mysterious bean salesman who is a former prisoner of the giants, kidnapped from another world. The prisoner stole the eggs as he escaped and began using them for trade on the planet below, hoping that people would discover the giants and either drive them away with superior numbers or steal their technology. He kept his identity secret because he knew the idea of an alien invader wasn't even in this society's zeitgeist, and he would likely be accused of some medieval crime! I know this is a lot of thought for a character who won't appear in the final illustration, but it's important to think your story through from start to finish, because all those decisions will inform the image in one way or another.

11 ROUGH COLOR DRAFT

I feel ready to bring my pencil sketch into Procreate and make a color rough. I want the scene to feel high up in the sky, maybe even near the edge of the planet's atmosphere. I imagine there is some sort of breathable air surrounding the ship, allowing Jack to run along the plant-like "beanstalk" worm. He is holding a strange, goose-like alien creature – a homage to my favorite artist, Mœbius.

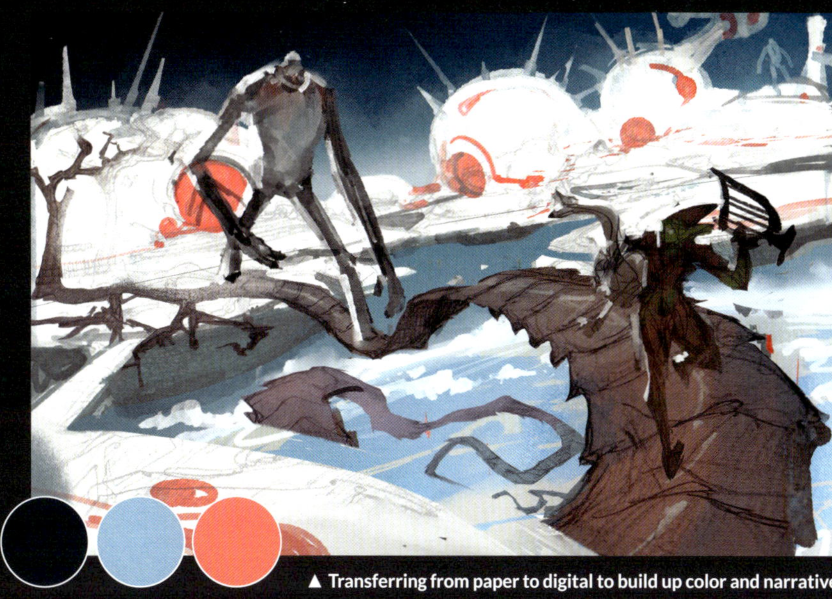

▲ Transferring from paper to digital to build up color and narrative

I make the giants' structures white, because it feels like they would consider themselves holy and clean. Perhaps you have heard of the term "the ivory tower," a metaphorical place where the wealthy and privileged live completely safe and separated from any strife in the world around them. The term is often applied to nobility and the educated and monied upper classes, so I think the structure being an ivory white is very fitting. An insidious red color punctuates the white to show that they are powering their ships and systems with the energy source produced by the "golden geese." The giants rely on limitless egg production and have engineered the goose species to have this one purpose. Even though they have plenty of these creatures, this giant is enraged at Jack for taking one of them.

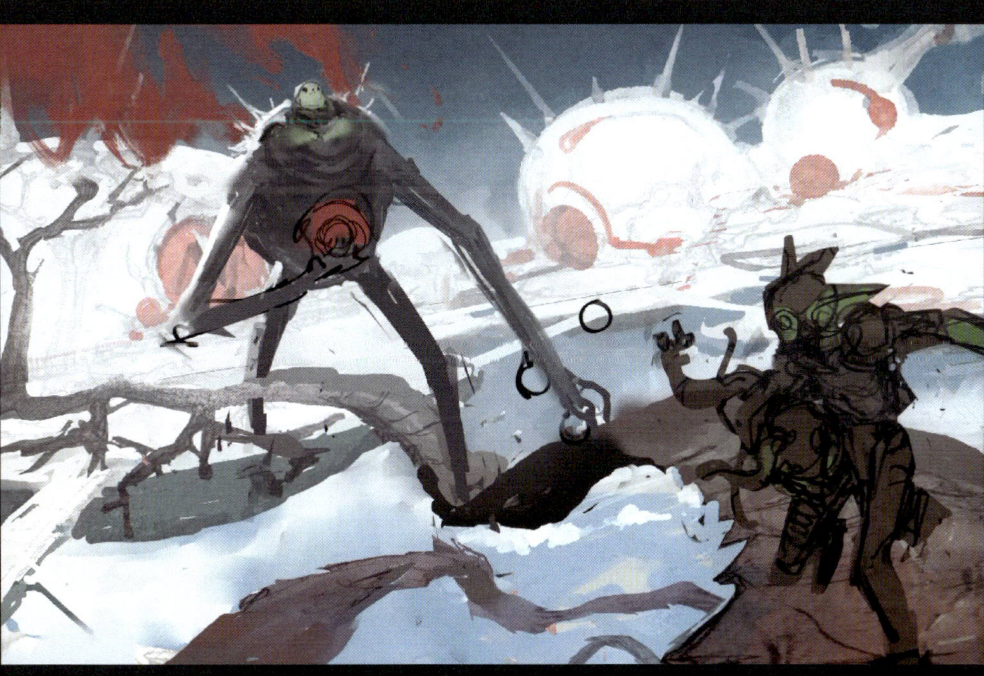

◀ Jack and the giant are taking clearer shape

12 BUILDING UP THE DRAFT

Here you can see Jack becoming more fleshed out. Bringing him closer to the viewer will help show his design and expression. He has a fairly whimsical feel, as I said before, with elf-like fantasy elements in his design. I want to hint that his culture is quite in tune with nature, giving him clothes that suggest this. Despite his more low-tech fantasy look, he is still clearly an alien, to sell the idea that this is a sci-fi version of *Jack and the Beanstalk*. As for the giant, the cape felt out of place but the design looked incomplete without the red, so I give him toxic red smoke coming out of his back. This reinforces the idea that the mech is powered by burning the energy of the red orbs. I even play around with the idea of the giant stuffing fallen "eggs" directly into his belly as he chases Jack.

13 DEVELOPING THE GIANT

Up until now, I have spent more time on the giant's general silhouette and design, and how the giants operate as a species, but I haven't thought much about the individual inside the suit. Here I explore the idea of him drinking a cocktail and nonchalantly allowing his robot body to do all the work. This might be an interesting comedic element, but I decide that it lacks the drama I want. I also experiment with the robot's anatomy, adding some abstraction to the limbs. I think it may be more unique if the aliens have some kind of liquid form, which then turns into the idea that this "mech" is actually a living being that has been subjugated to carry its ruler. Making this creature look dark and slick, like oil, fits the theme of being a vehicle for the extravagantly wealthy.

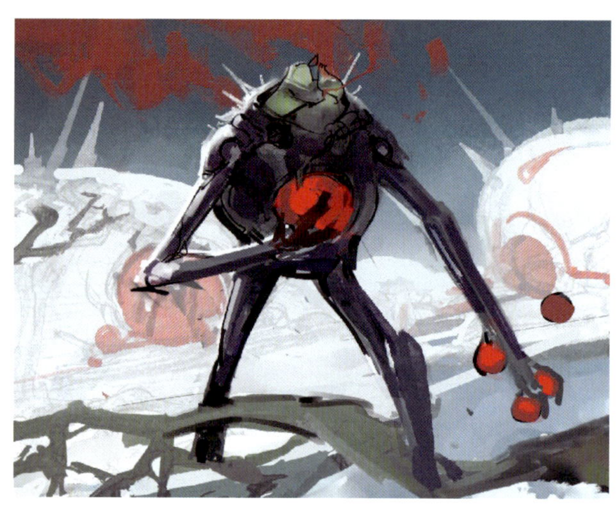

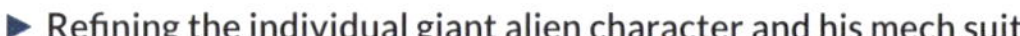

▶ **Refining the individual giant alien character and his mech suit**

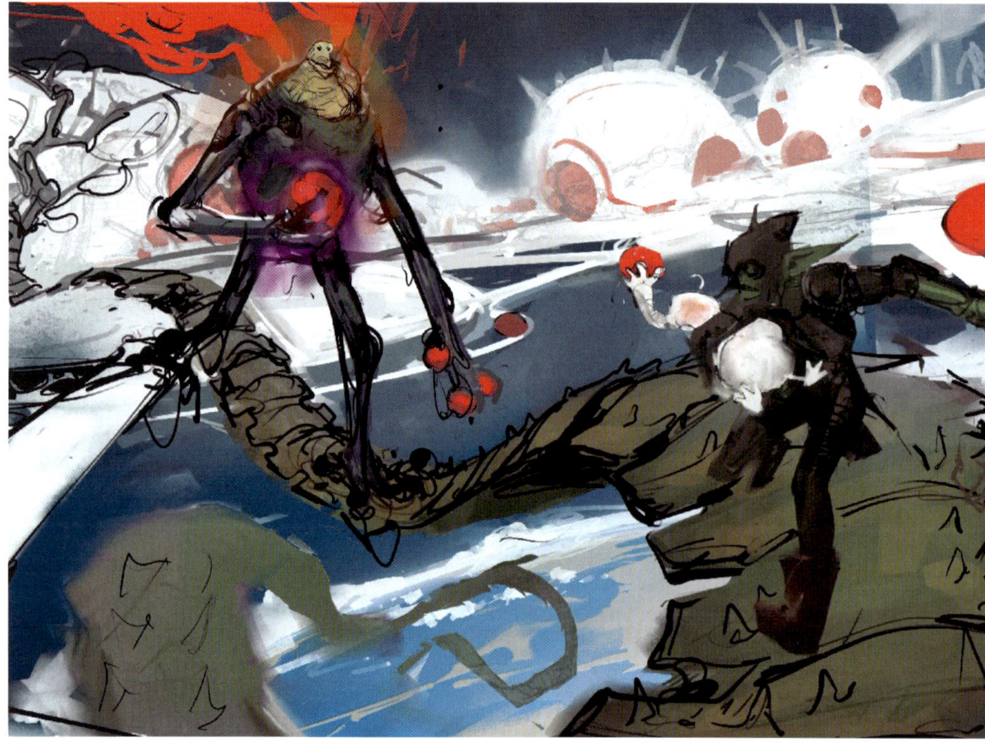

◀ **My daughter provides some valuable ideas when I get stuck with the image**

14 OVERCOMING A STUMBLING BLOCK

At this point I'm not sure if I am happy with my decisions, but the painting is quite far along already! I really like to work on paper for as long as possible, because I find it more intuitive, and perhaps I should have stayed on paper for longer. But every work of art is an experiment, and we can save those lessons for the next painting!

I decide to let my daughter take a crack at giving me a paintover. I strongly value the input of others and I try not to finish any piece without letting somebody give me a critique or a paintover somewhere in the middle of the process. I tend to want to make art in a vacuum, but it really isn't the best way. The best way to make art is to immerse yourself in the study of people and places, through experience if possible, and to get feedback along the way. Anybody can give good advice to an artist humble enough to ask.

My daughter changes the villainous alien to be much more angry and focused on Jack, and she adds glowing effects, spikes, and other dangerous elements to the piece. I pull a lot of inspiration from the enraged face she has drawn, and with her permission incorporate some of her glowing energy effects into the piece. I also love the addition of spikes, but the worm should be friendly and I don't want it to appear potentially dangerous to Jack.

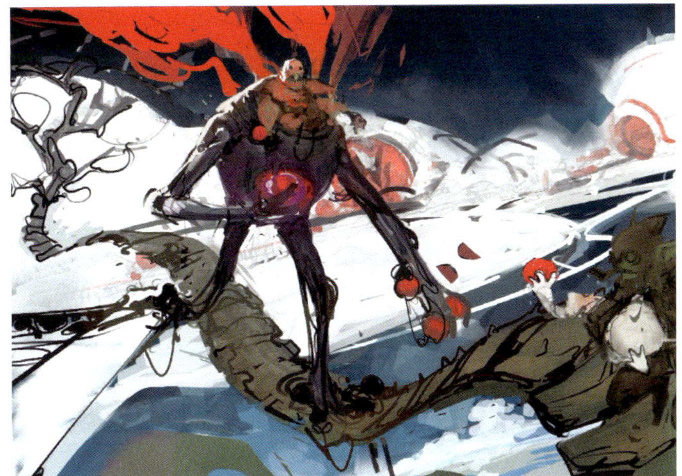

15 MAKING THE REVISIONS

Taking inspiration and motivation from my daughter's paintover, I change the giant alien to look more vicious and greedy. Whereas before he seemed to be nonplussed, now he is furious with Jack for *daring* to enter his palace, with his filthy surface-dweller clothing, taking his forty-third highest-producing goose! I give him six little arms to emphasize his grabby nature, as well as exaggerating the goopy alien limbs. I also experiment with the castle in the background; the castle is meant to look somewhat fungal or viral, so I play around with various structures to get the right feel for the ship's construction. Spikes and spheres subtly reinforce that viral look.

◀ **Incorporating the new ideas into the painting**

16 ATMOSPHERE AND FOCUS

By this stage of the process I have made most of my creative decisions and can begin executing the final render. I add in some atmosphere and light to make the setting feel surreal, and stylize the clouds and characters to give more of a fairy-tale look. I also want it to feel like the ship is lower in altitude, not in outer space, so I lighten up the atmosphere and add more clouds. The clouds also help to make Jack more readable and to frame him as the main focus of the piece.

▶ **Simplifying some areas and lightening the atmosphere**

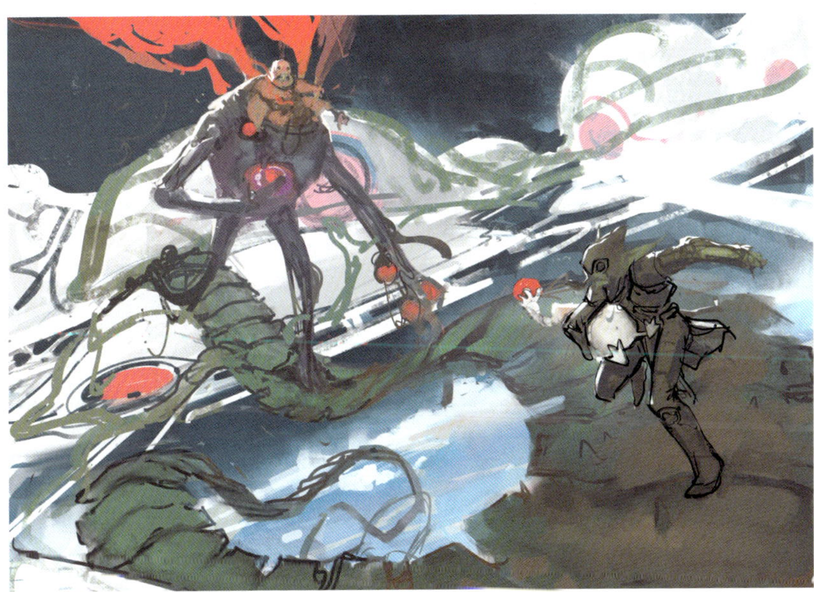

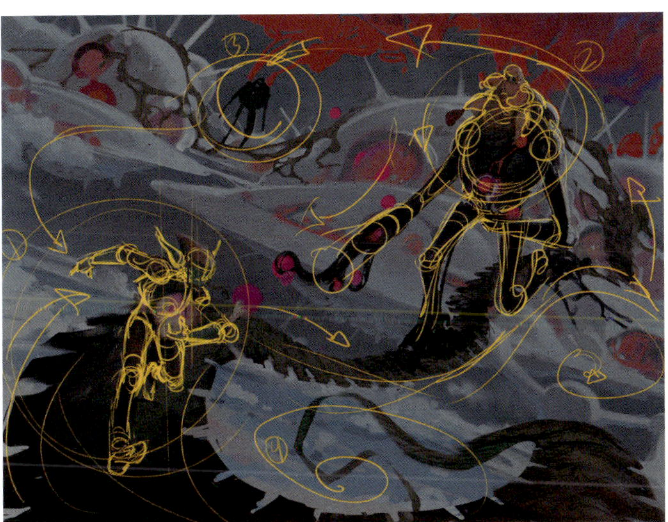

17 COMPOSITION CHECKS

I feel that the drawing has shifted as I have rendered, which happens to me all the time. As you paint over a drawing, the structure and energy of the initial sketch can be lost or changed. In order to get back on track, I draw over the image with highly visible lines, adjusting poses and silhouettes and making sure the eye has a strong path through the image. We want the viewer's gaze to find its way onto the canvas, then follow a story through the scene that has been arranged to keep their eye looping back inside the frame, rather than shooting outside it. There should be visual guides to pull the eye back in for another walk through the painting. I find that drawing the "flow" of the painting, tracing the path I'd like the eye to follow, helps a lot with readjusting the composition.

◀ **Making sure the composition stays focused as it develops**

18 REFINING THE BACKGROUND

Once I am happy with the draw-over, I implement my composition changes and begin to render. I give the clouds more attention to create a more magical feel, evoking a "fairy-tale" vibe through stylization. The realistic clouds that I was moving toward felt too stiff, so this change helps keep the image on track. I detail Jack a little further, but mostly focus on the giant, as I tend to render paintings from background to foreground – it's easier to build the layers of the scene that way. The giant's arms become much more tentacle-like as it scoops up energy orbs, my analog for the golden eggs. The legs bubble and ooze over the surfaces they touch, leaving damage behind on the plant-like worm.

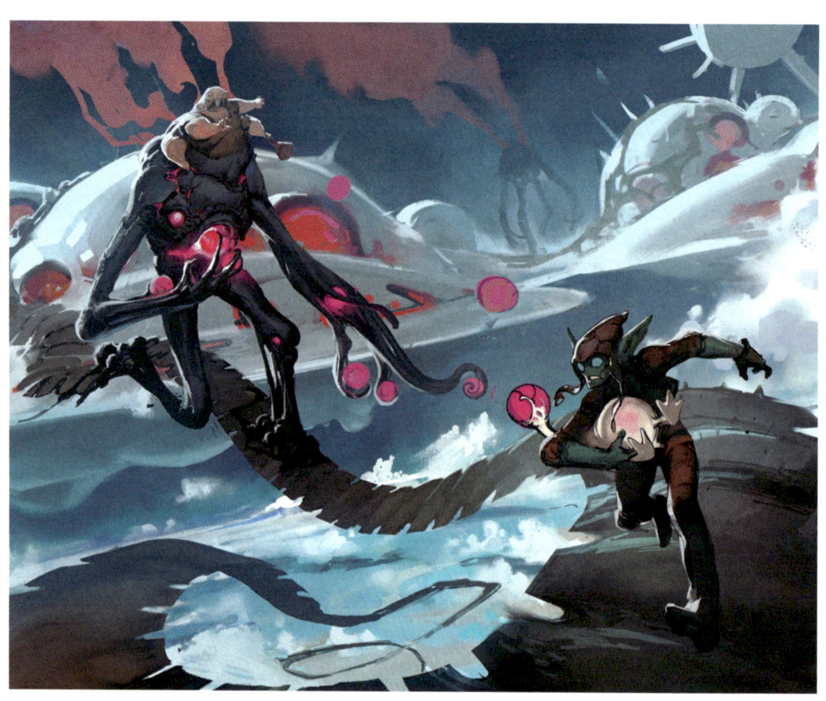

▶ Building up the scene from background to foreground

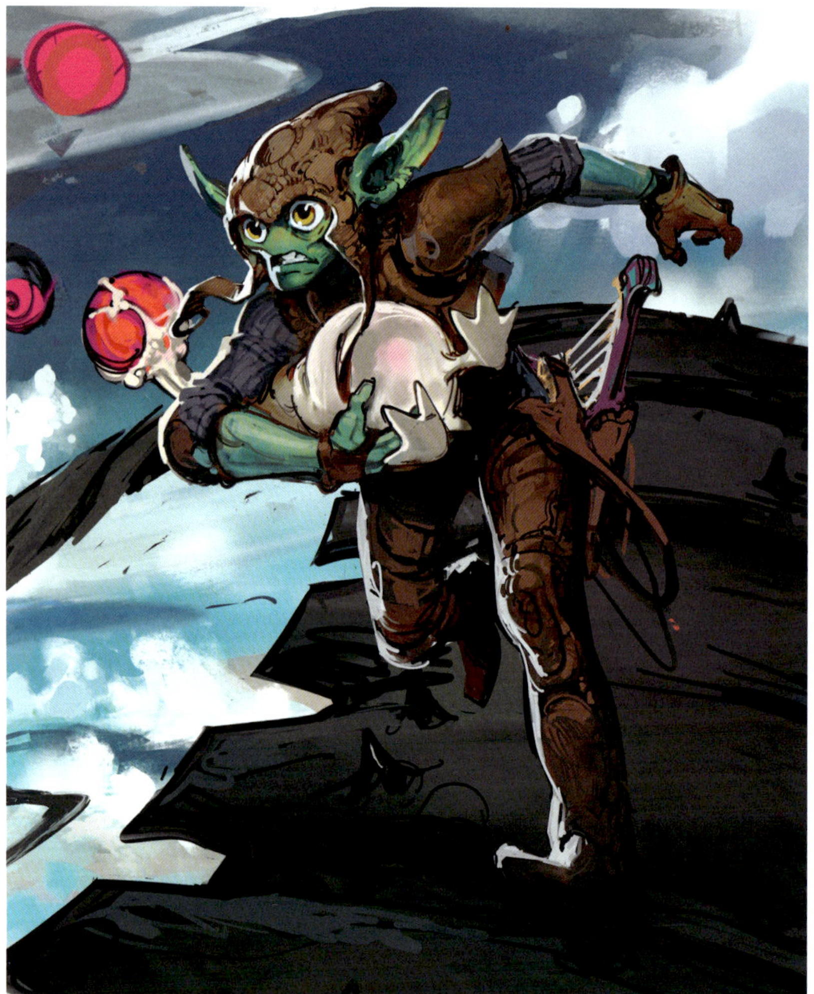

19 DETAILING JACK

Jack finally comes into view as I render and detail his face and clothes. I want him to look frightened but determined to escape, as well as confused by what is happening. He needs to look appropriately overwhelmed as he drags a magical space-goose away from a rabid alien riding a glorified scooter down a giant plant-worm – a worm Jack thought would be a cute little pet in a fishbowl on his windowsill. One moment he was at home living a simple rustic life, and the next he's being stalked in low orbit! It is important to put yourself in the shoes of your subjects and paint them with that perspective in mind.

At this stage I also push the background colors closer to the hue and value of the foreground, as well as deepening the opacity of that bluish color. Instead of the pale, misty blue, I find this deeper color helps emphasize Jack's brown and green palette, making him pop more.

◀ Rendering Jack and capturing the fear and panic in his expression

20 THE FINAL IMAGE

To wrap up the image, I intensify the rendering in the focal areas, and play with the background clouds to make sure the characters read well against the background. I clarify planes and shapes by making sure my values are clearly grouped. I ensure the silhouettes have plenty of dynamic energy, even though it's impossible to keep the full energy of the original rough sketch. I adjust the design of the "golden goose" to make it seem more like a creature, giving it a more beak-like head. It's still quite abstract, but it's weird and alien and I like it! The giant rider has become rather like a centipede mixed with a naked mole-rat. Jack is terrified as he runs away down the space worm and toward the viewer.

▶ **Adjusting the values, characters, and composition to finish the image**

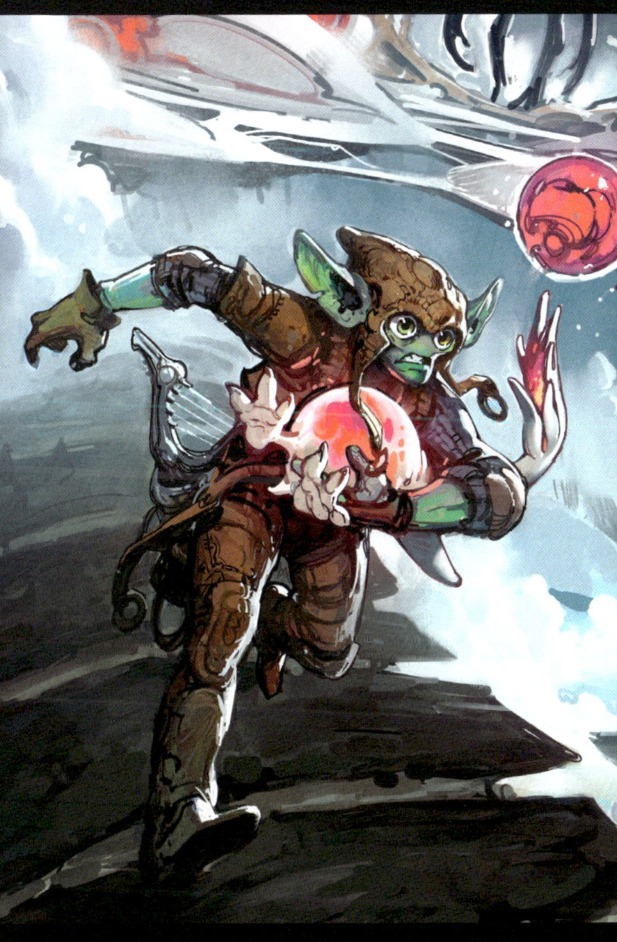

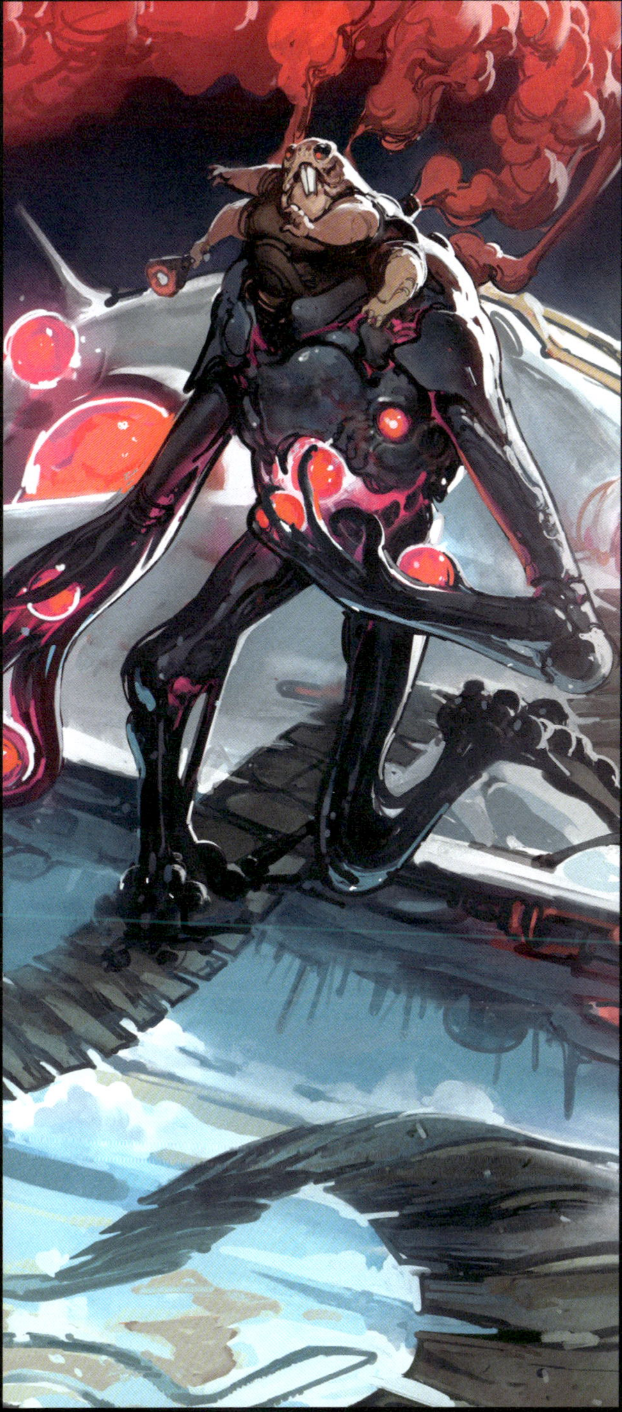

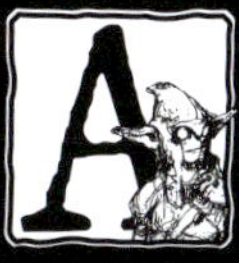

And thus we arrive at the strangest version of *Jack and the Beanstalk* I could reasonably present to you! The basic idea remains the same: an obscenely wealthy sky-dwelling ruler encounters a tiny intruder in his floating palace, and descends to terrorize the land below. To me, the story has always been about the fantasy of getting a small taste of wealth, while depicting those who hoard it as cruel, greedy ogres. I wanted my illustration to capture that spirit, showing an average citizen defying the destructive powers that are ruthlessly pillaging his starving planet. Those who dwell in floating castles can afford to share a few golden eggs!

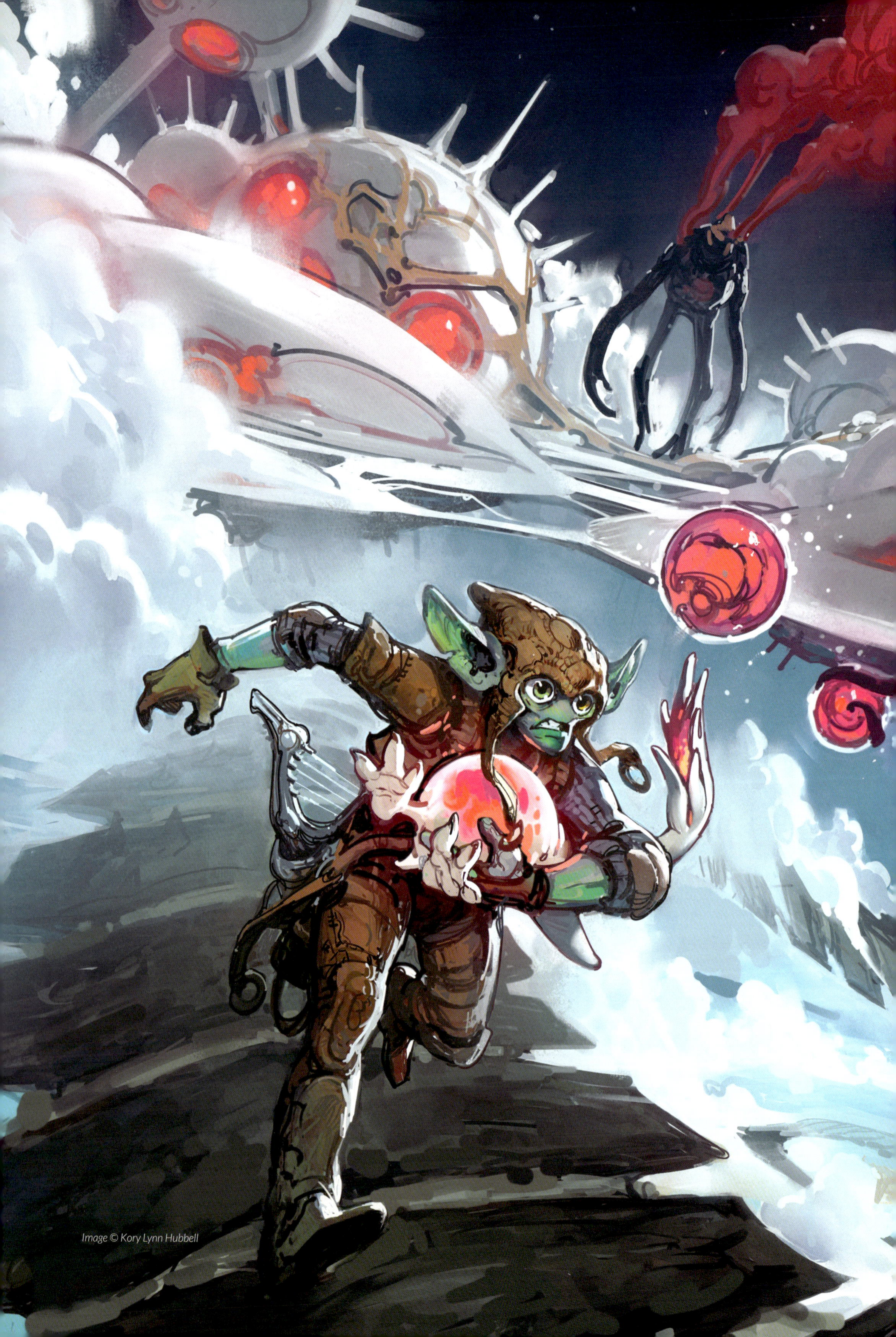

Image © Kory Lynn Hubbell

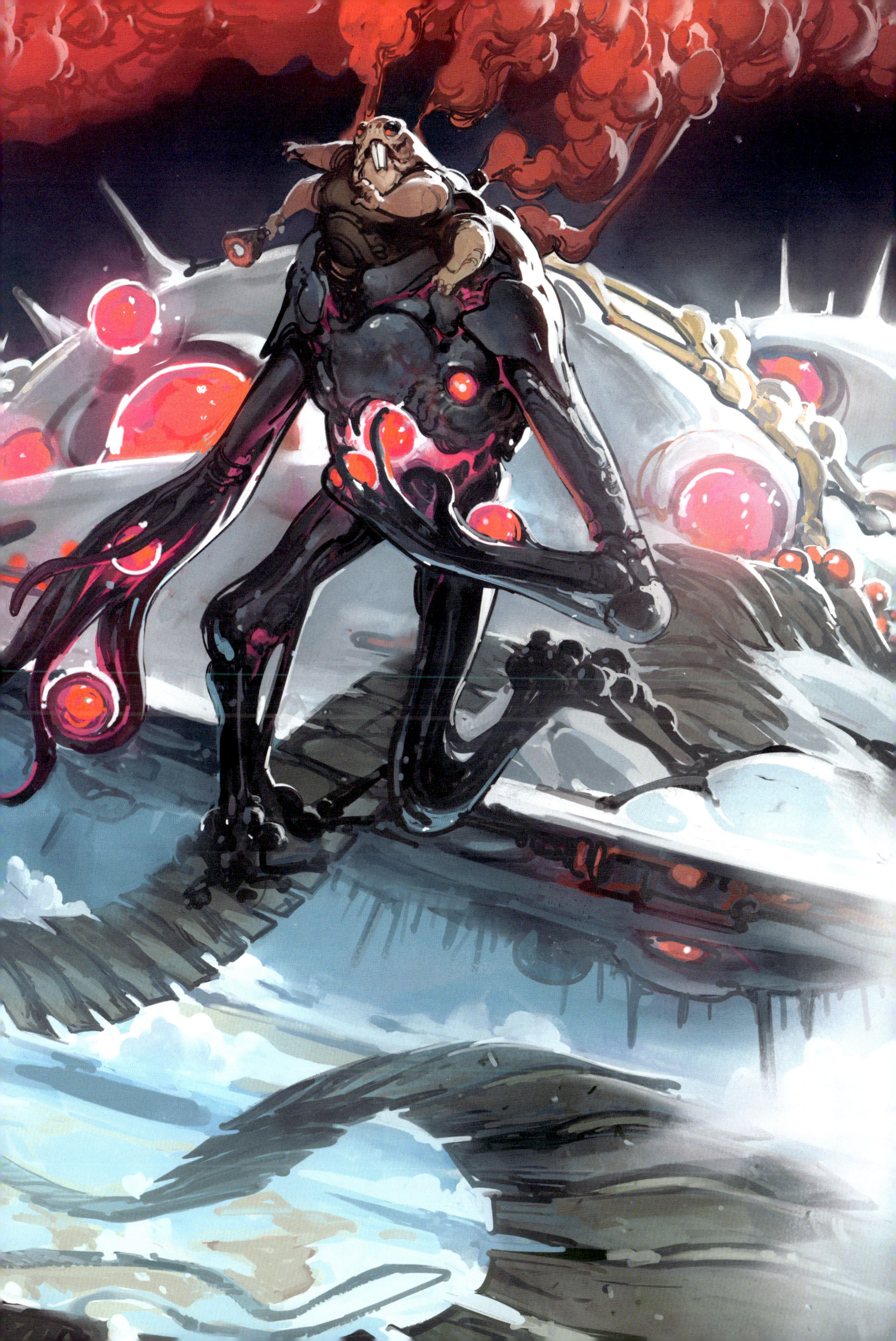

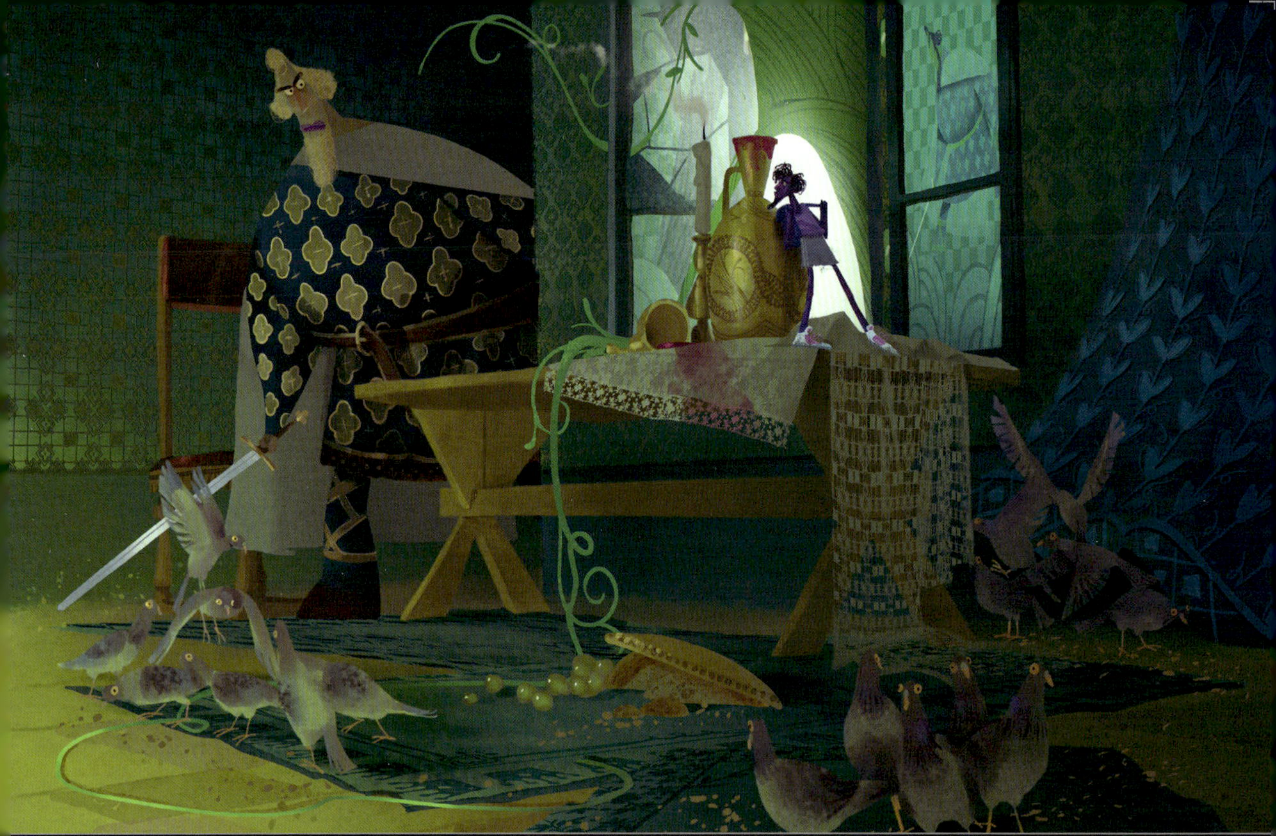

"Jack in the Giant's Palace." Image © Fernando Peque

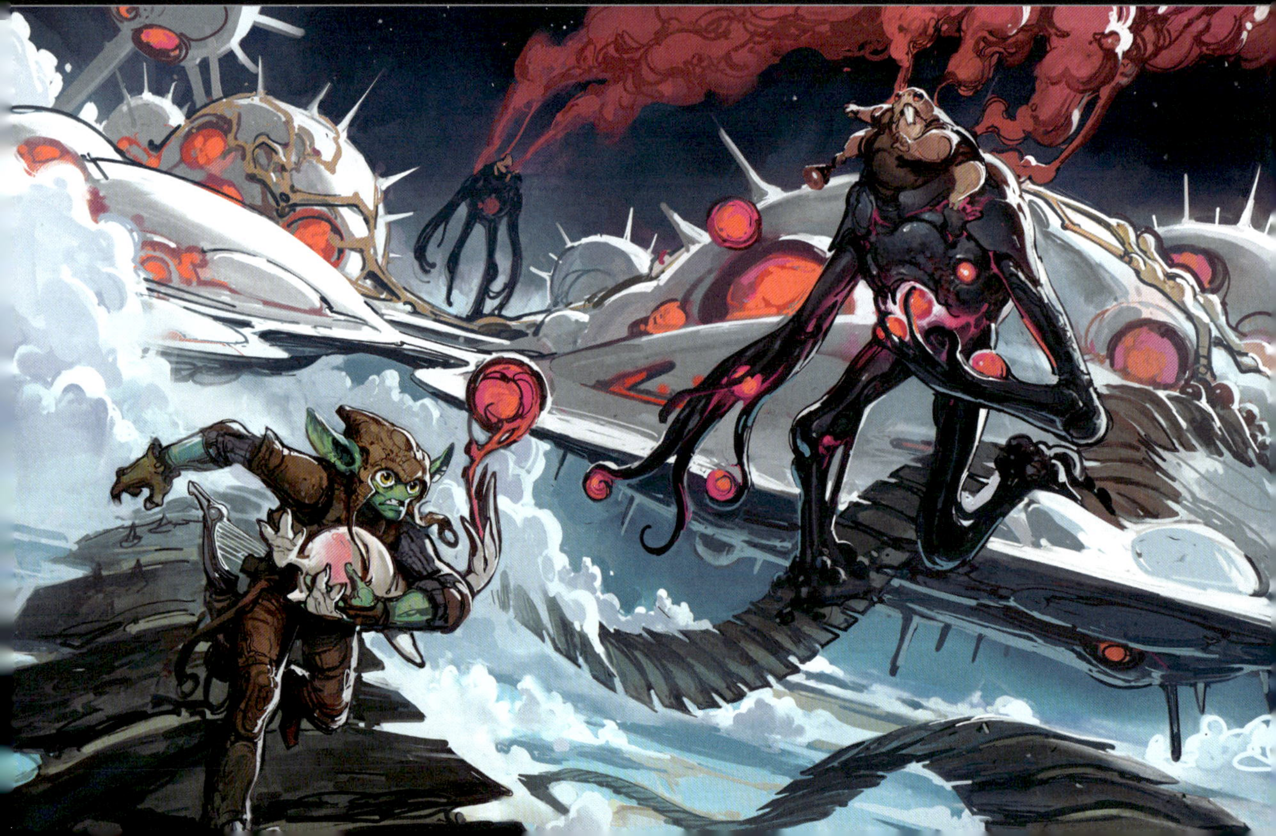

"Jack and the Friendly Giant." Image © João Moura

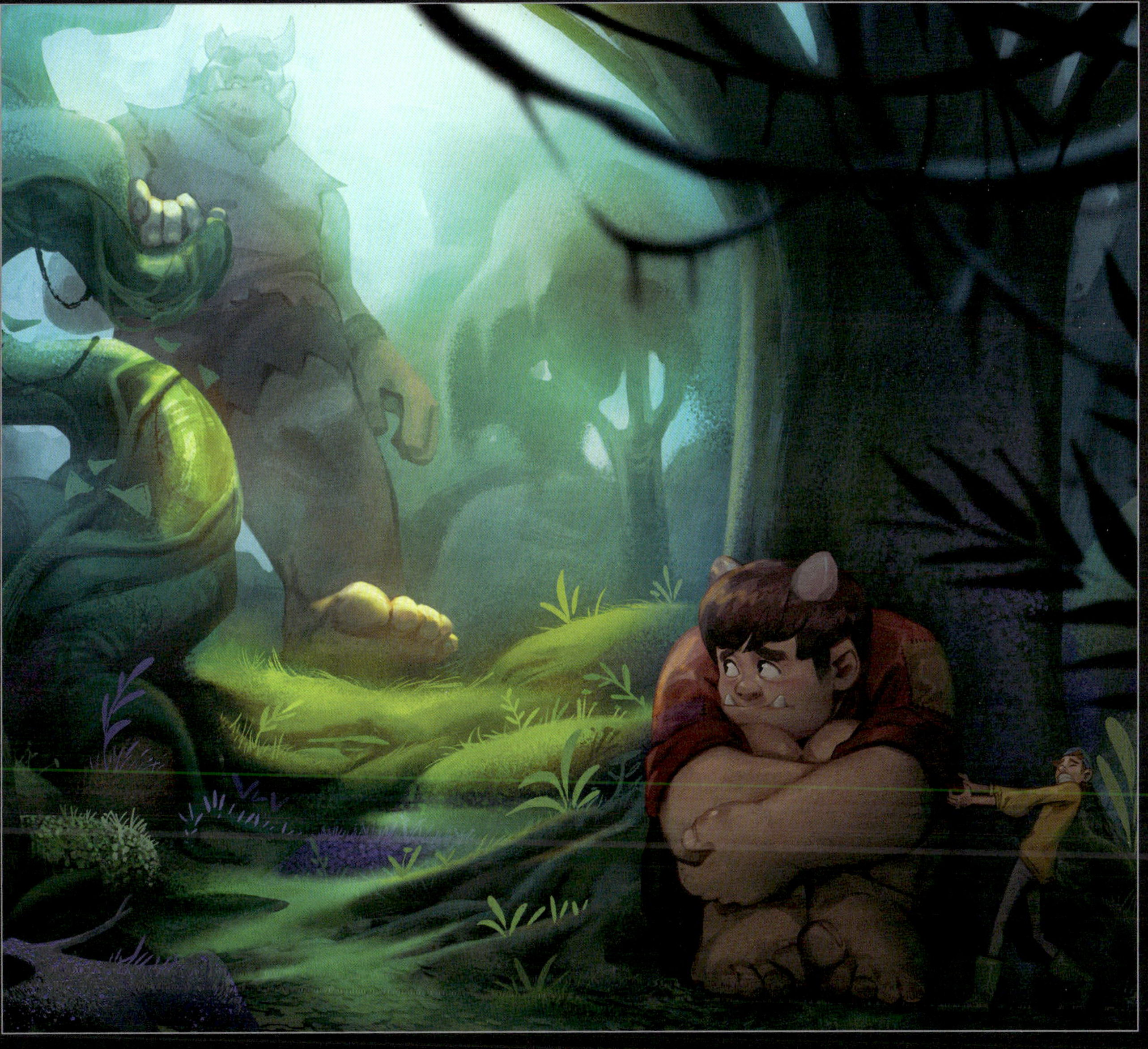

JACK AND THE BEANSTALK

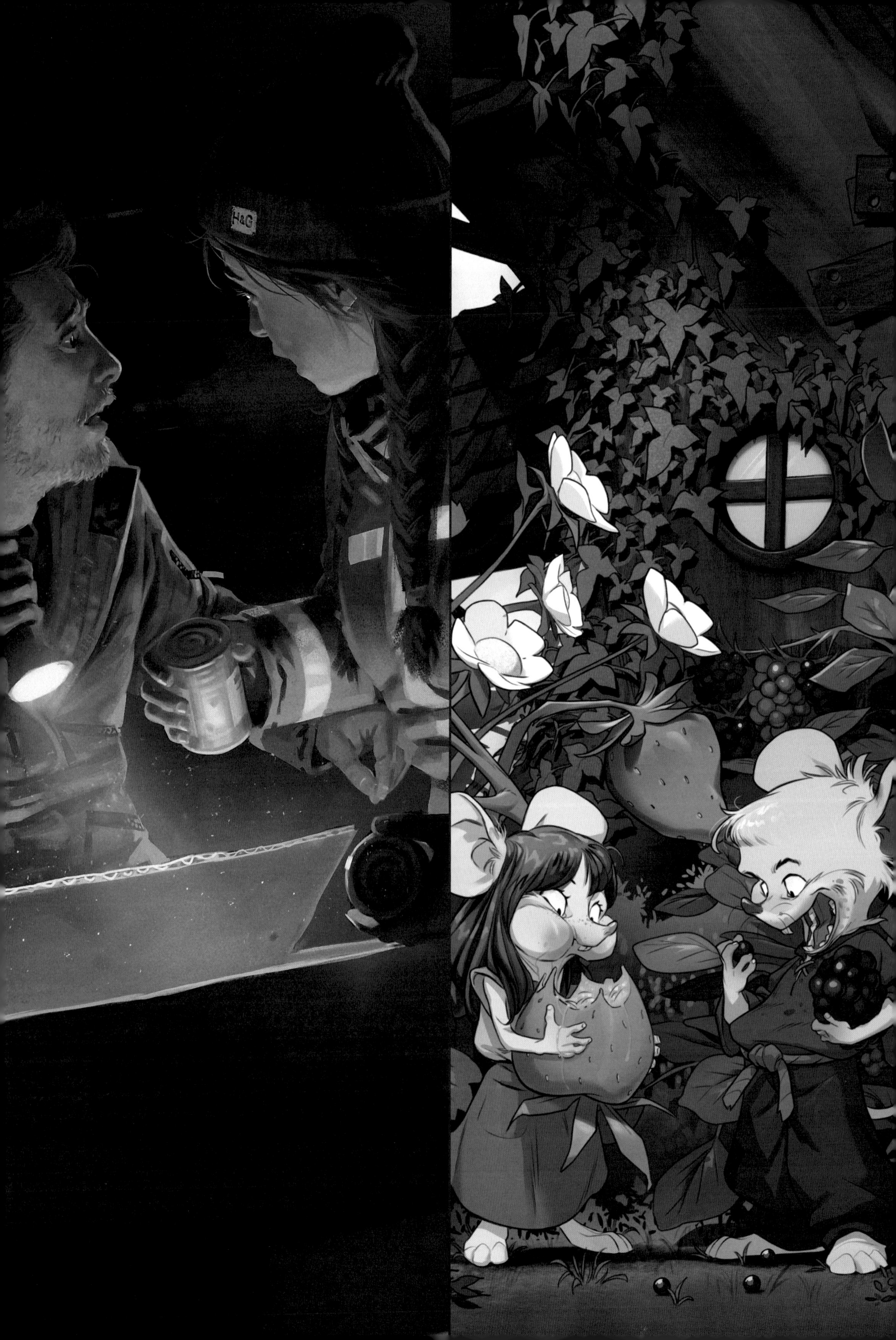
H&G

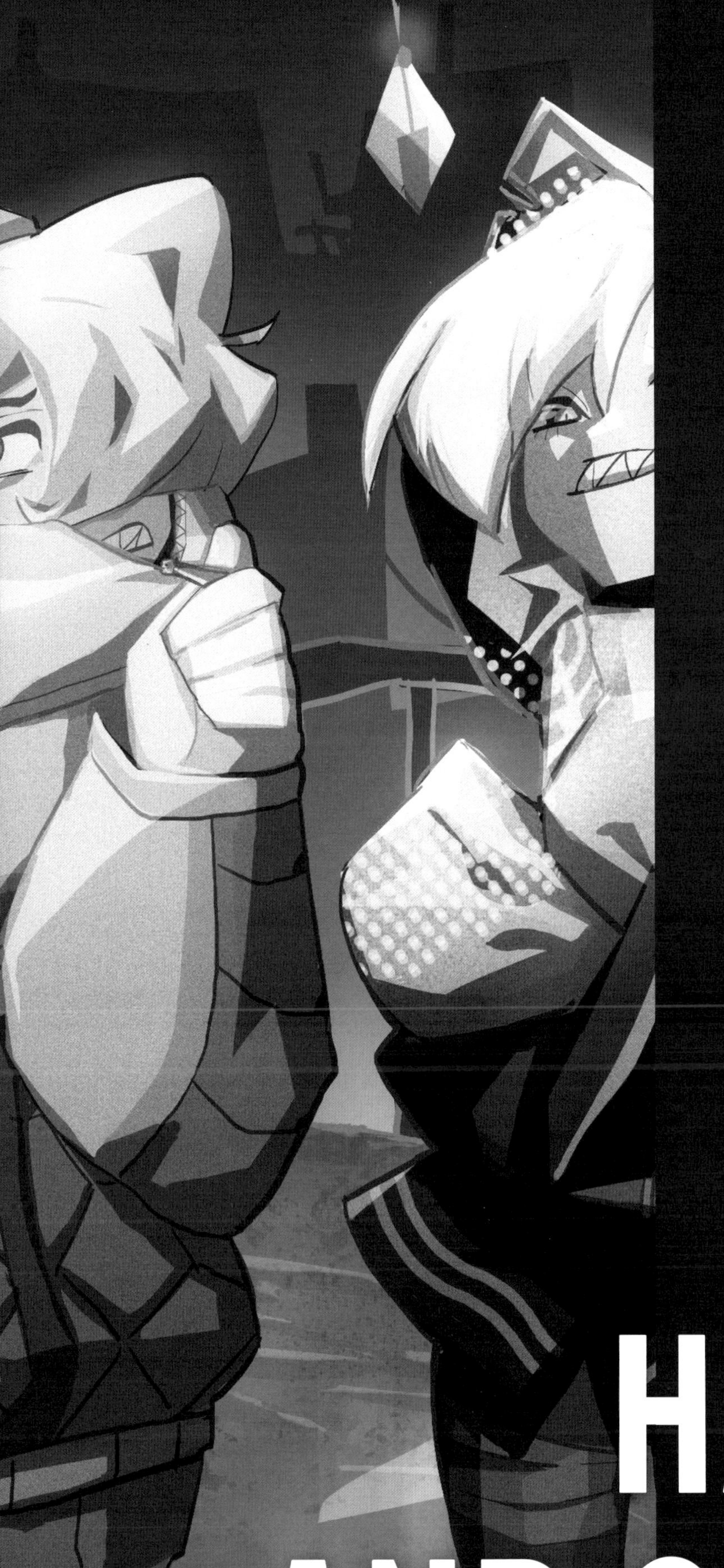

HANSEL AND GRETEL

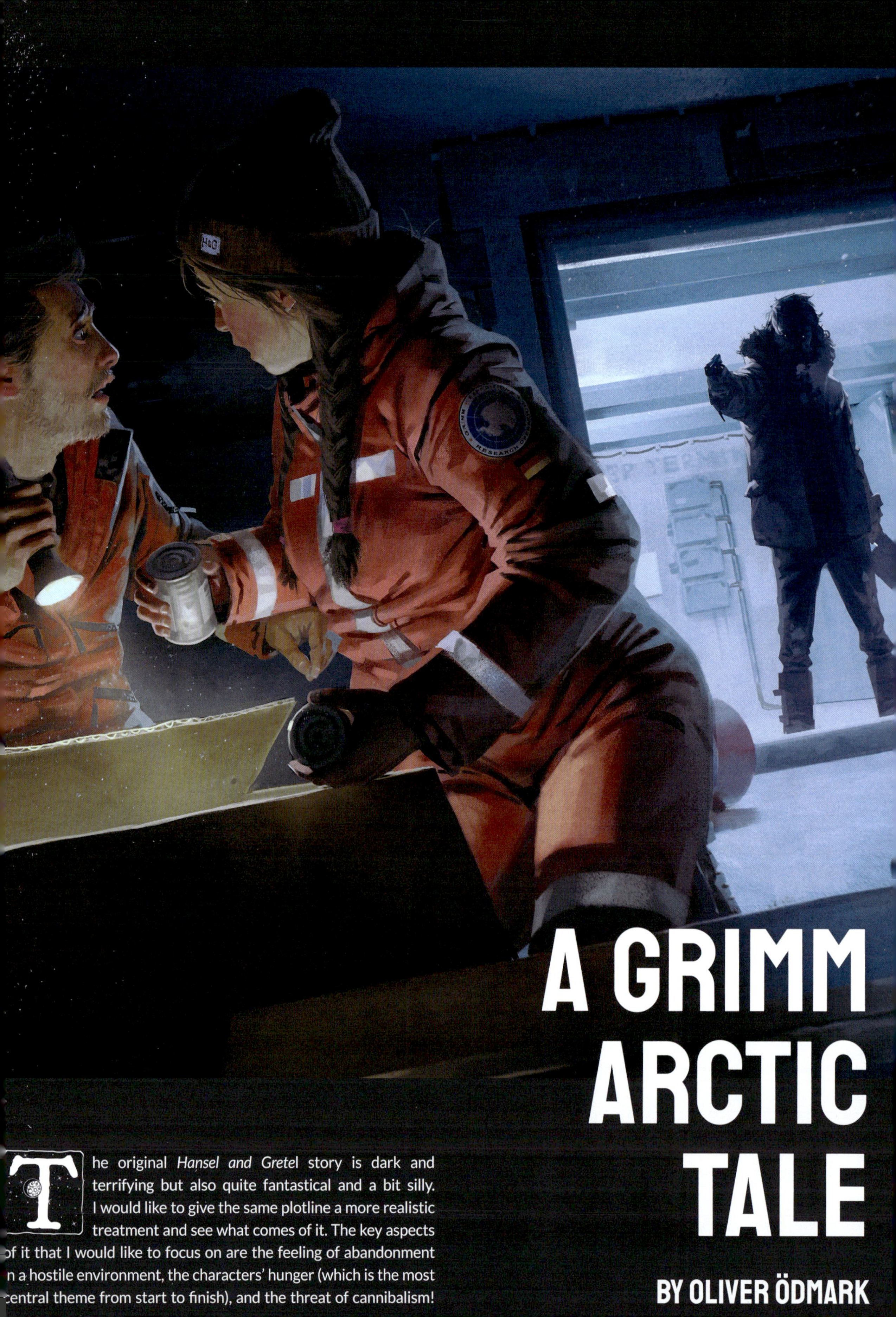

A GRIMM ARCTIC TALE

BY OLIVER ÖDMARK

The original *Hansel and Gretel* story is dark and terrifying but also quite fantastical and a bit silly. I would like to give the same plotline a more realistic treatment and see what comes of it. The key aspects of it that I would like to focus on are the feeling of abandonment in a hostile environment, the characters' hunger (which is the most central theme from start to finish), and the threat of cannibalism!

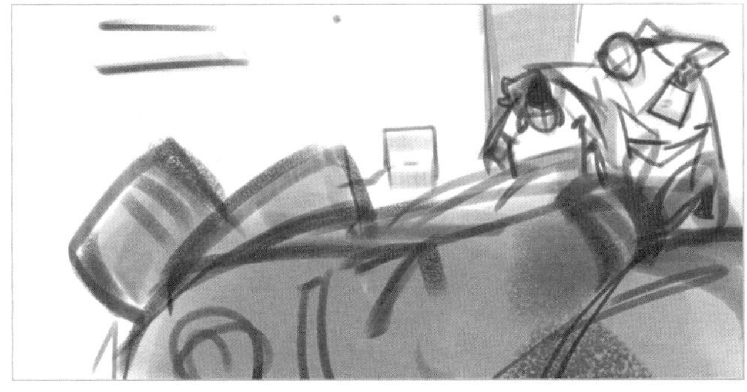

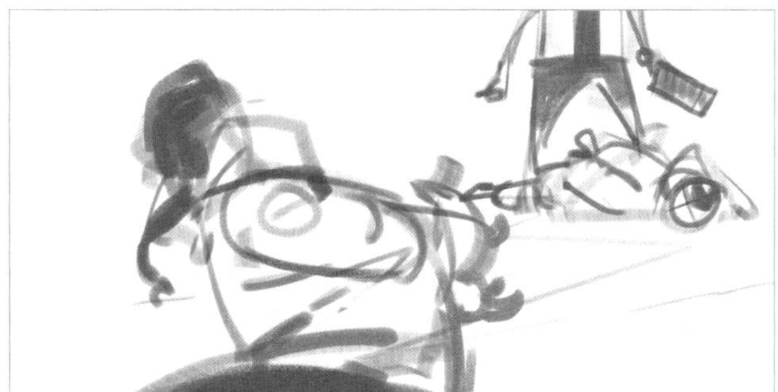

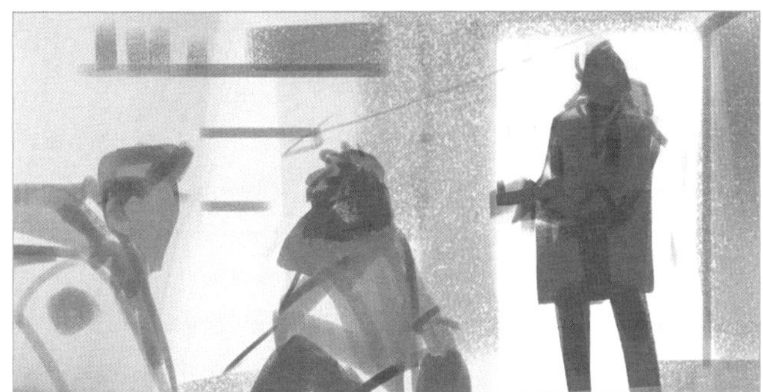

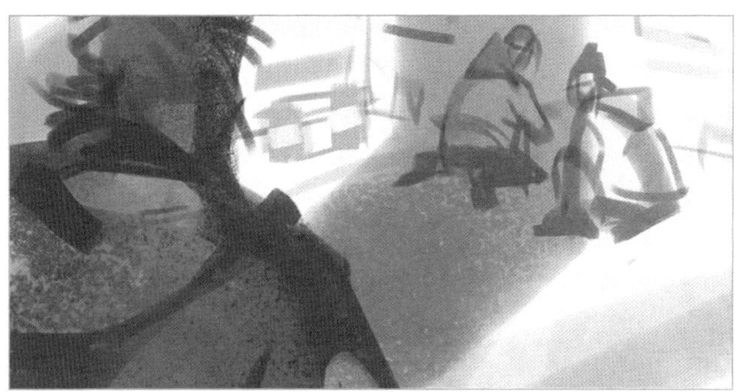

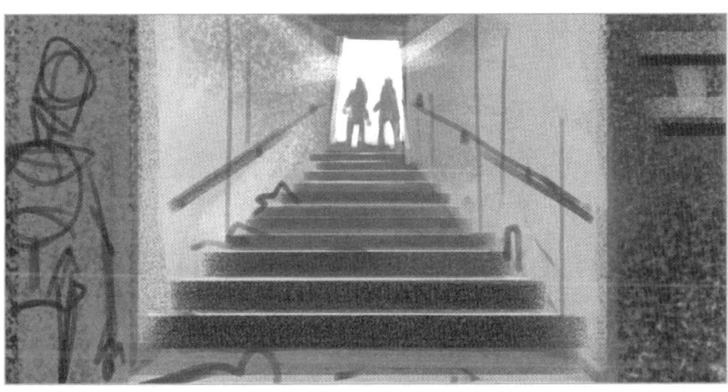

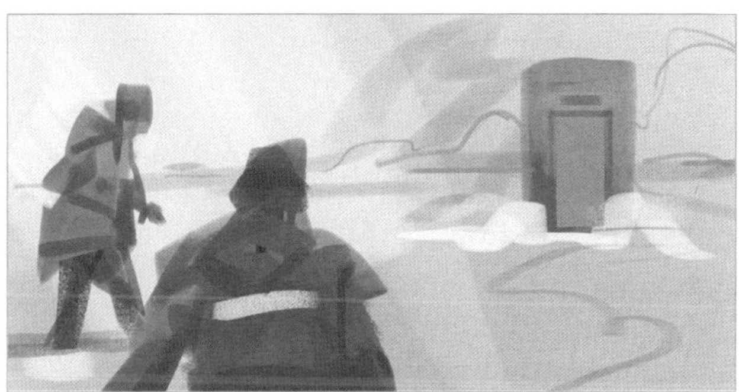

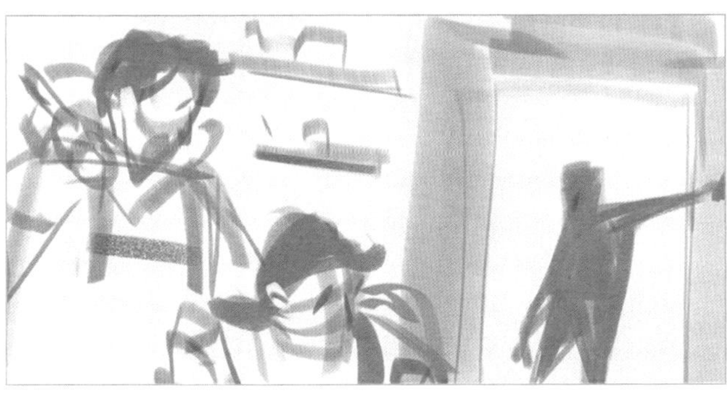

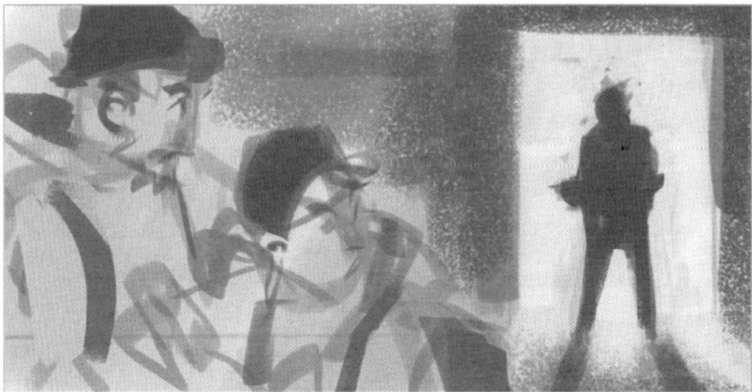

▲ Starting off with really rough thumbnails to help activate my brain

01 FIRST THUMBNAILS

My idea is for Hansel and Gretel to be adult scientists – perhaps still brother and sister – from the same Arctic expedition. They get cut off and abandoned by their team after a crisis, leaving them without food. They drift around the endless snowy wastes for a long time before coming across what seems to be a hidden, abandoned research bunker. Inside, however, is one lone survivor who has almost run out of food supplies. He has long since lost his mind and sees Hansel and Gretel as fresh meat to stock up his larder.

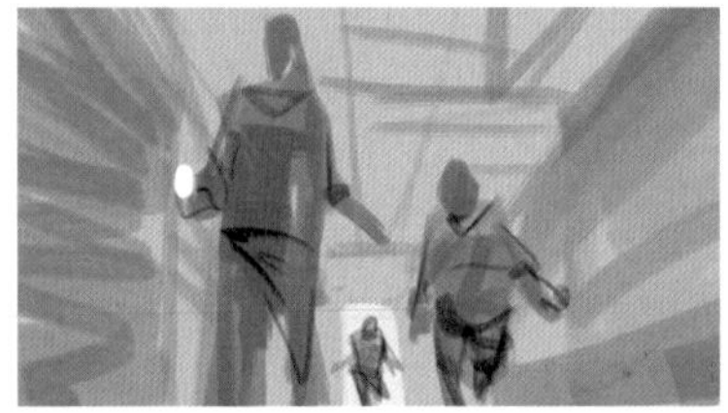
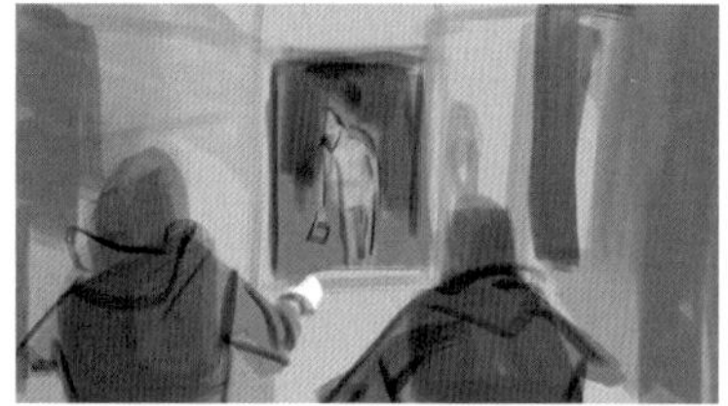
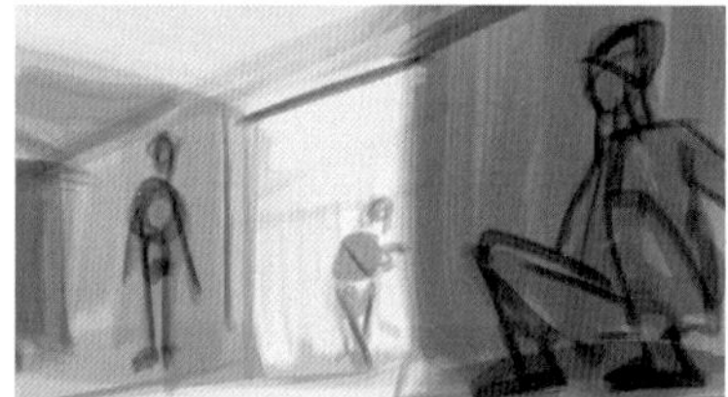
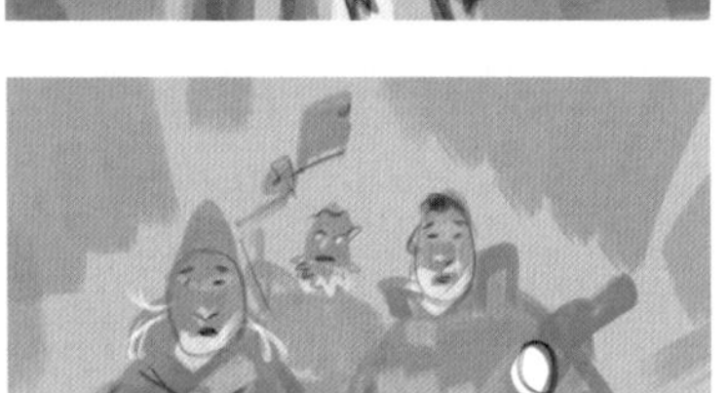
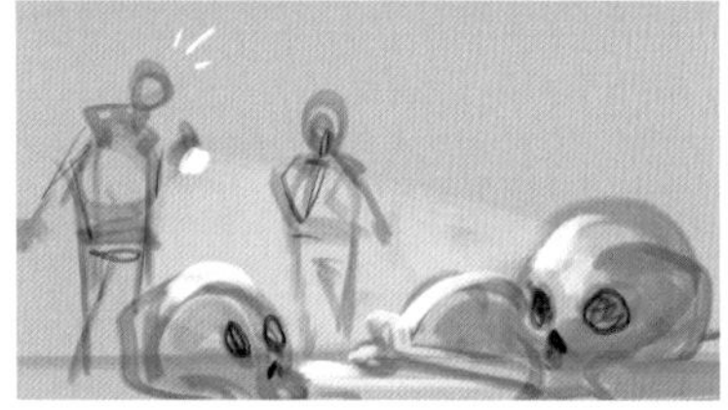
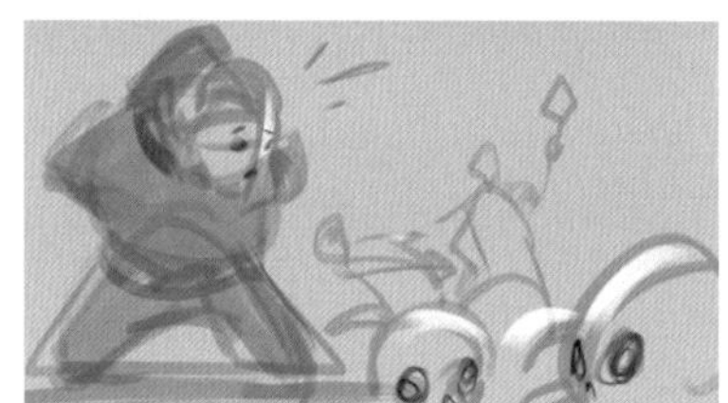
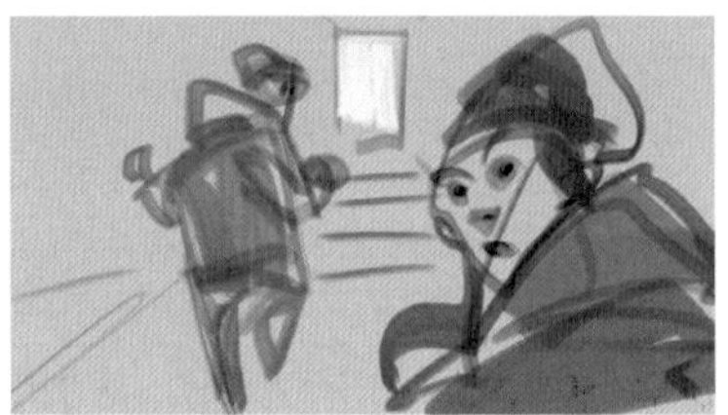
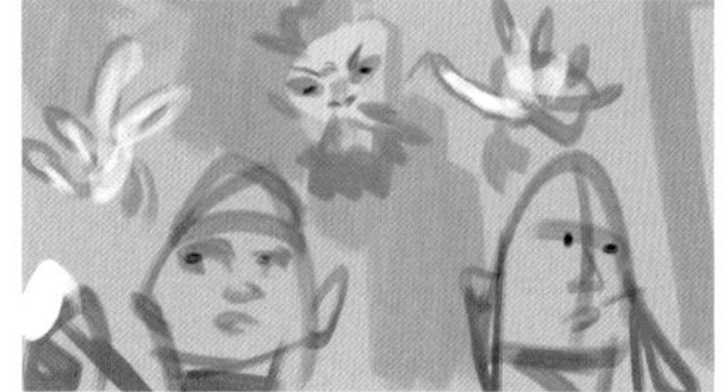
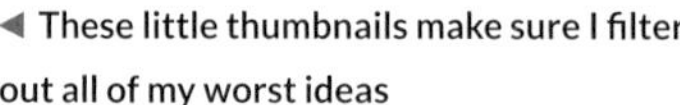

◀ These little thumbnails make sure I filter out all of my worst ideas

02 SECOND THUMBNAILS

Most of this second batch of thumbnails have some good qualities and tell parts of the narrative well enough, but I want this illustration to encompass as many key elements of the story as possible. There is strength in veiling parts of the story in mystery and keeping some things vague and suggestive, but for this example, I want to show the value of using contrast and composition to tell a story in the most effective and clear way.

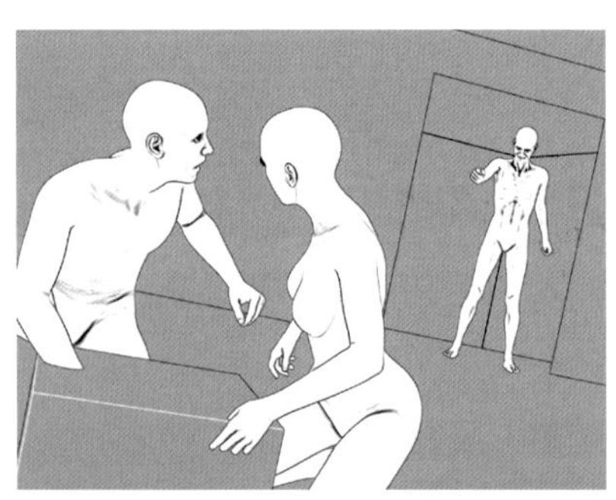
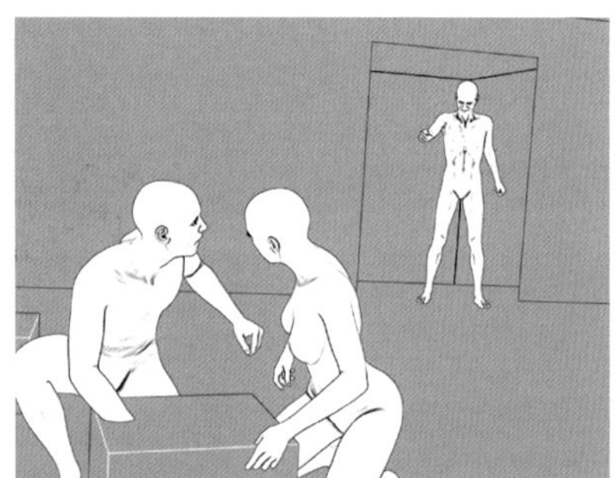
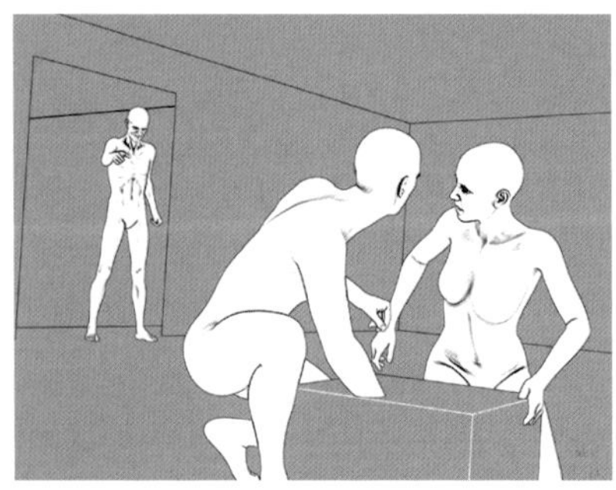
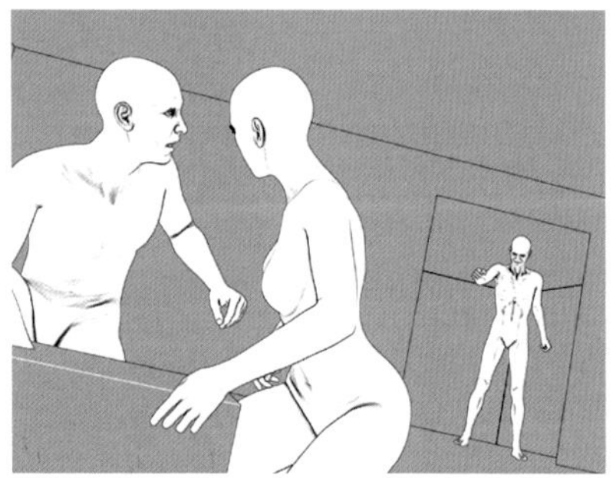

03 "NIBBLE, NIBBLE..."

One of the most memorable scenes in *Hansel and Gretel* is the "Nibble, nibble, little mouse!" scene, where the children are caught gnawing on the witch's gingerbread house. This is the scene I interpret here, where the villain – the lone survivor – catches Hansel and Gretel going through his last boxes of food. In this first batch of compositions, using basic human models in Daz Studio, I place the camera in front of the siblings, showing what is approaching from behind them. It's a perfect angle to get all the characters in the scene fully on display. We see the villain in all his glory, as well as the frightened faces of Hansel and Gretel.

◀ Simple 3D programs such as Daz Studio are great for iterating an idea you like

▶ Continuing to play with different angles in Daz Studio – 3D lets me do this without having to redraw!

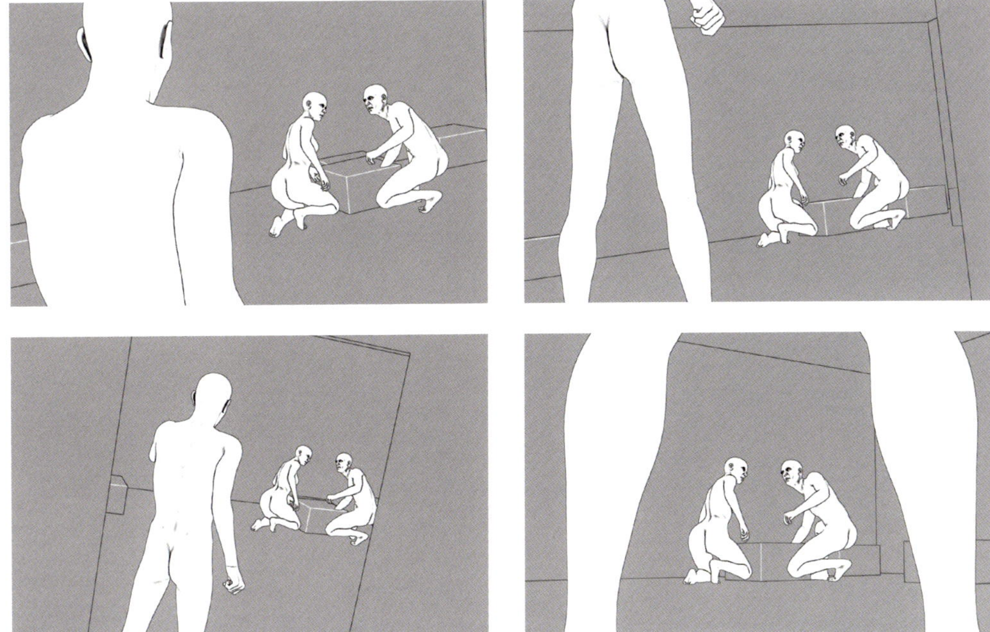

04 TESTING MORE LAYOUTS

Happy with the first batch of layouts, I want to make sure I'm not settling too early and missing something better. This is the most important, foundational part of the illustration, so I want to ensure I'm making the right decision. Putting the camera behind the madman, with the siblings in the background, is also a great option. It shrouds the villain in mystery, but we can tell from the expressions on the siblings' faces that what they are seeing is terrifying. This is also a good opportunity to make the siblings look weak and exposed by having the camera look down on them over the stranger's shoulder.

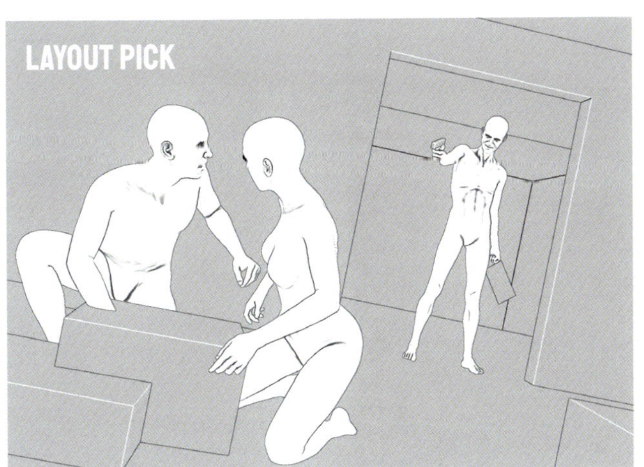

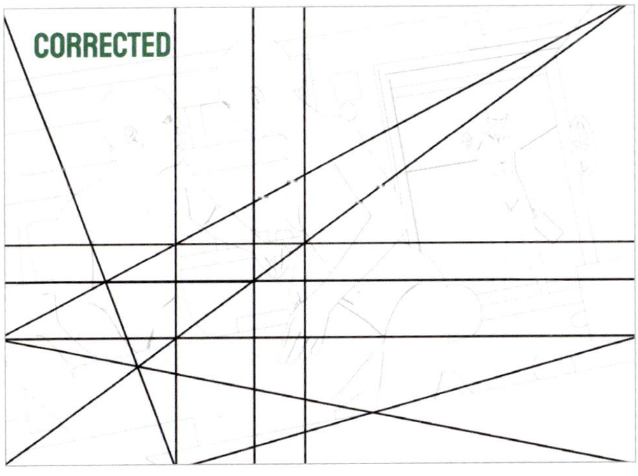

▲ Testing my composition with Andrew Loomis' informal subdivision guides

05 INFORMAL SUBDIVISION

One step I almost always add to my illustrations is "informal subdivision" by Andrew Loomis. His books have been the most useful resource in my career as an artist. After I have a layout and composition I'm happy with, I run it through this set of guidelines created by Loomis, which are intended to help you divide a picture "unequally and interestingly." I always find some lines that suggest an even better composition if I nudge my layout a tiny bit. So, after putting my sketch through this treatment, I find a better, more pleasing placement for the models and camera. I also realize that the weight of the image isn't quite right. Instead, I want the big, closeup characters to tilt the camera, as if the scene is on a weighing scale where the far-away smaller, secondary character is tipped upward because he is "lighter."

06 FINAL COMPOSITION

This composition and angle are best because we are up close and personal with the main characters. I want the story to be very clear from this one image: Hansel and Gretel are desperately looting old food storage and find themselves trapped by a villain with a gun and a cleaver. This angle immediately lets us see what they are holding as they pick up canned food from the cardboard box. The meat cleaver really pulls its weight in this image, as it implies the madman's intentions of chopping them up like animals, showing that he sees them as nothing but meat. These are all aspects of the story I want to put on display in this illustration.

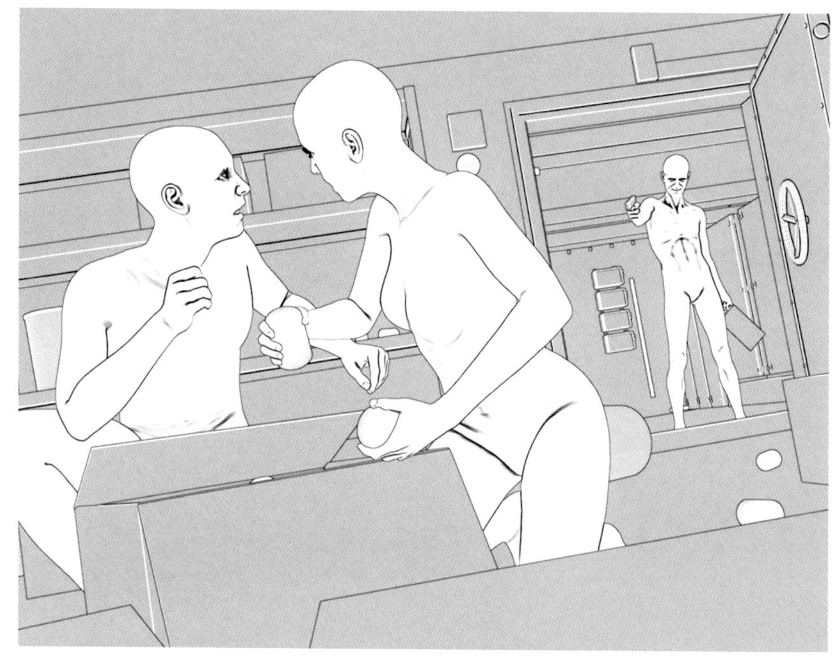

▶ **Depending on what I'm working on, I sometimes take the 3D stage into much more detail**

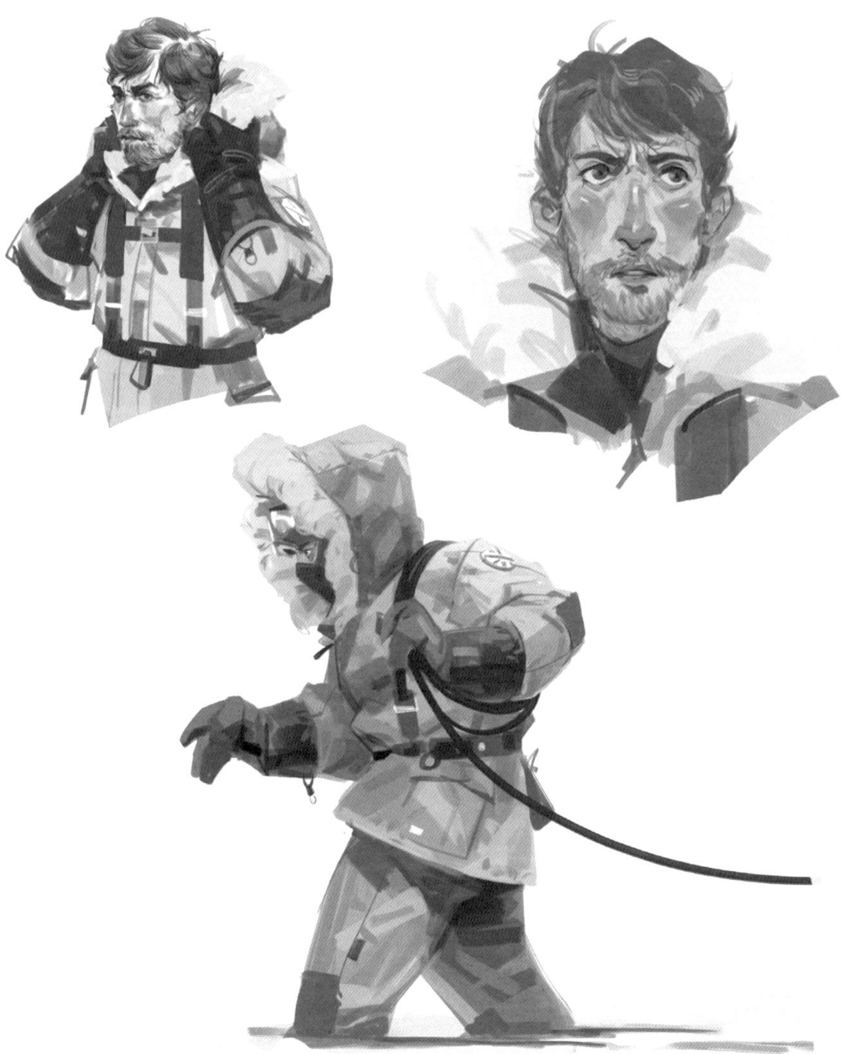

07 INITIAL HANSEL IDEAS

Now that I have my idea worked out, I start to flesh out the characters, starting with Hansel. One of the reasons I really like the Arctic as a setting for this story, instead of the woods, is that it lets me dress the main characters in puffy jackets, thick gloves, and overalls. All these big outdoor clothes make even an adult look like a child! Even their cheeks, rosy from the cold, will make for a childish look.

The original Hansel and Gretel are quite resourceful and clever, even though they fall for the witch's gingerbread house trap, but they are still children under threat. Even though these are fully grown adults in a different time and setting, I want them to have the same vulnerable quality that inspires the audience's sympathy.

◀ **Getting a good feel for the characters before starting to work on the final image is crucial**

08 MORE HANSEL SKETCHES

When designing a character, it's important to know their story. The goal is not making the best-looking character but the character that best fits their role. Continuing my thought process from the previous step, I really want Hansel to have quite a boyish look. I imagine his hair to be tousled and not too trim. His cheeks are red and his beard is quite sparse. There is a balance I need to be mindful of here, where the contrast needs to be obvious between the main characters and the villain. Hansel and Gretel are both in a desperate situation, hungry and unkempt. However, the villain is beyond that, driven insane from isolation and starvation. So, even though Hansel can have a bit of a scraggly beard, and perhaps some bags under his eyes, I do not want him to be too gaunt or too haggard. I want the cannibal to own that look.

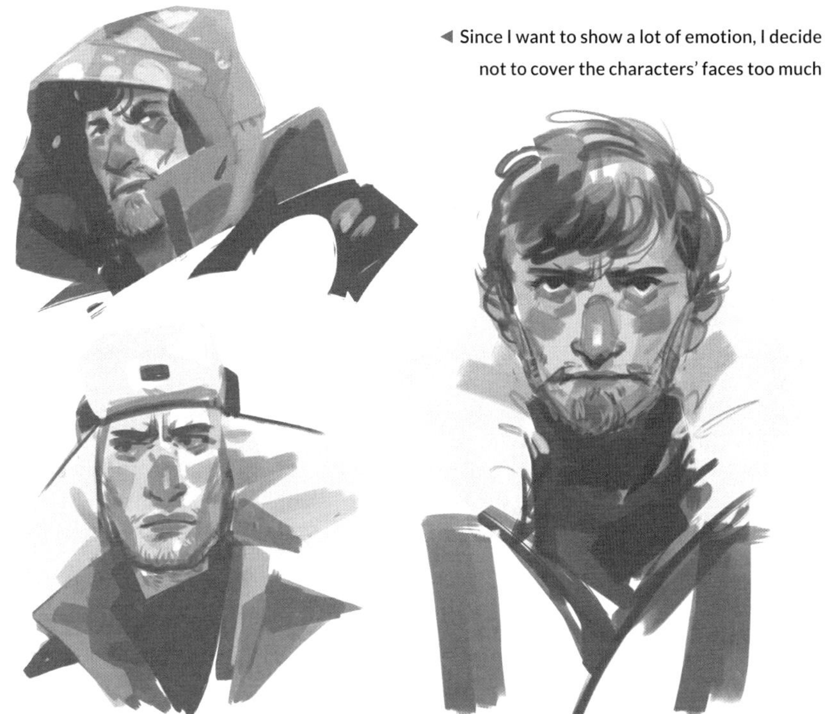

◀ Since I want to show a lot of emotion, I decide not to cover the characters' faces too much

09 GRETEL SKETCHES

I start sketching Gretel while thinking further about storytelling and design opportunities. Every little aspect of this image needs to help tell the story. The outfits of both Gretel and Hansel will be similar, as I want them to look like a team and a family. For example, if Hansel had a blue jacket, Gretel a red jacket, and the villain a green jacket, you could still tell the story with the composition and character positions, but you would have missed an opportunity to visually connect the two siblings. If Hansel and Gretel are wearing same-colored jackets with the same logos on them, they will be clearly portrayed as a team or related in some way.

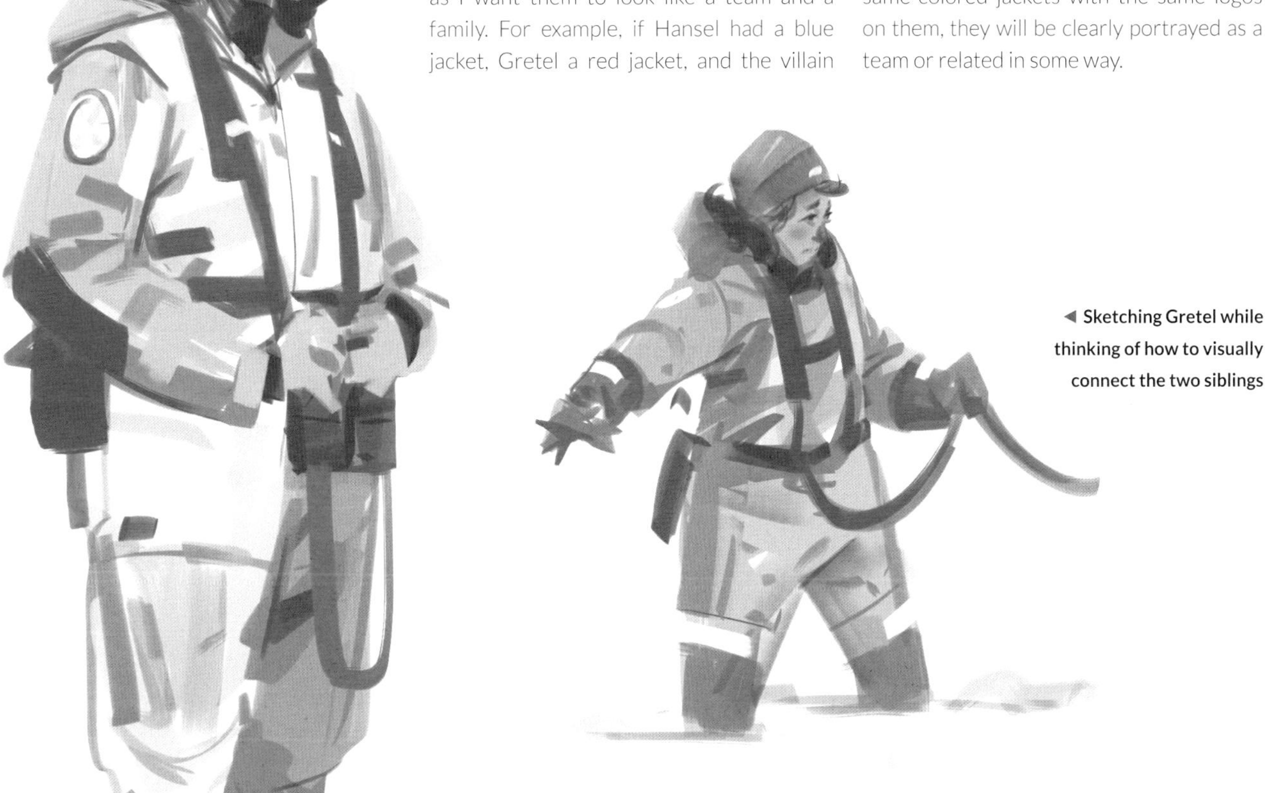

◀ Sketching Gretel while thinking of how to visually connect the two siblings

10 GRETEL DEVELOPMENT

As with Hansel, I want Gretel to have a very youthful look. Two big braids, combined with her big, puffy overalls and gloves, could be exactly what I'm looking for. Showing her face uncovered and her hair loose and visible will give her more personality. As with the matching jackets, I think I will also give both siblings the same hair color, helping to visually unite them even further.

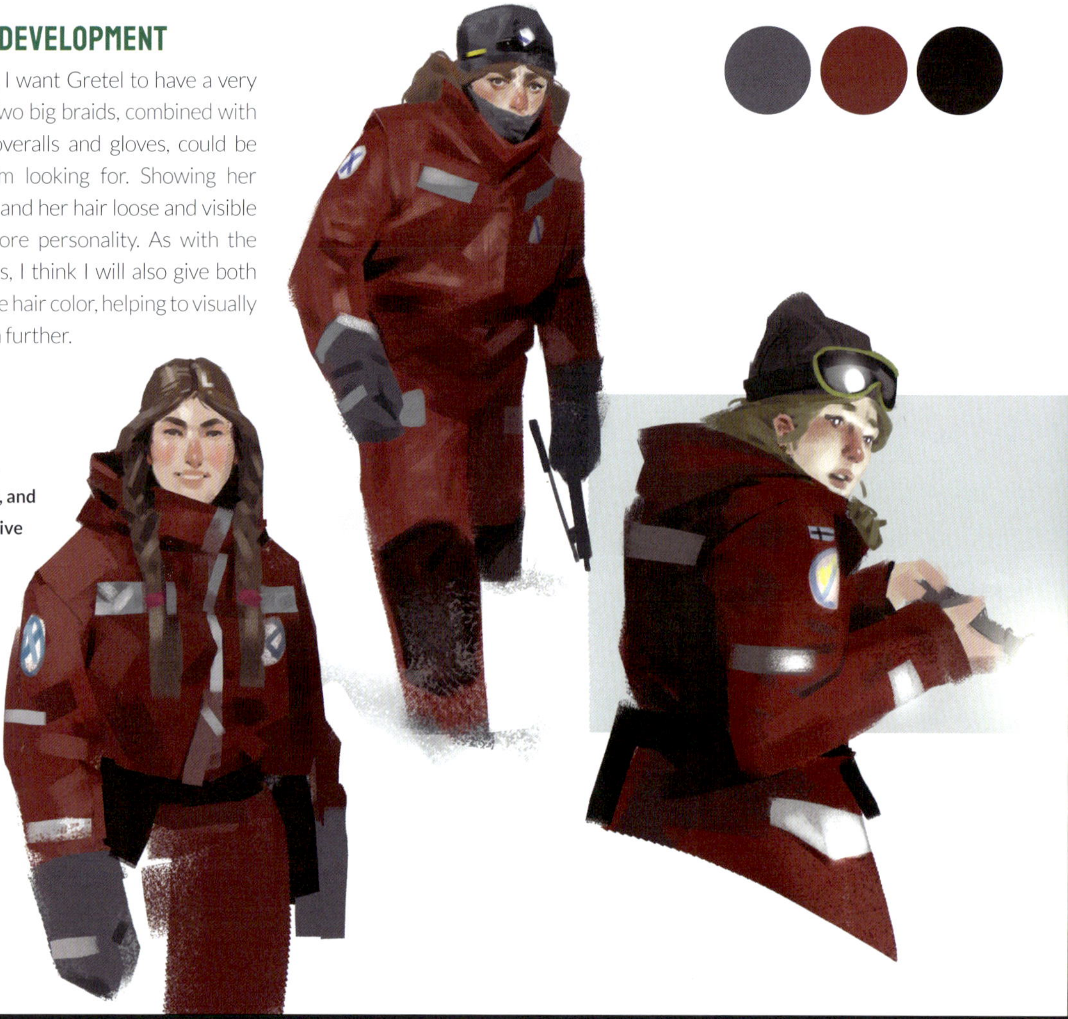

▶ Gretel's braids, oversized clothes, and rosy cheeks will give her a youthful appearance

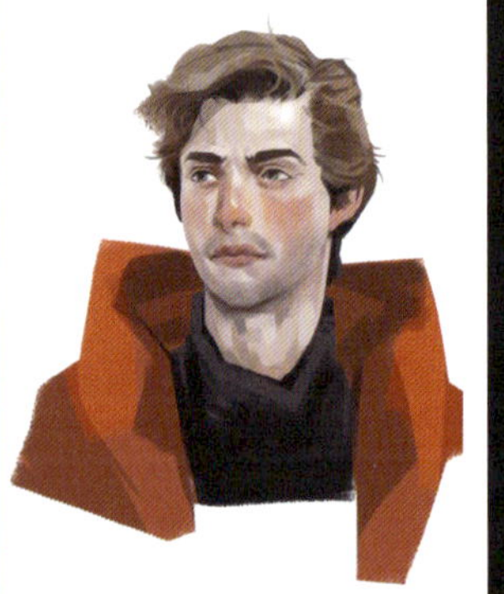
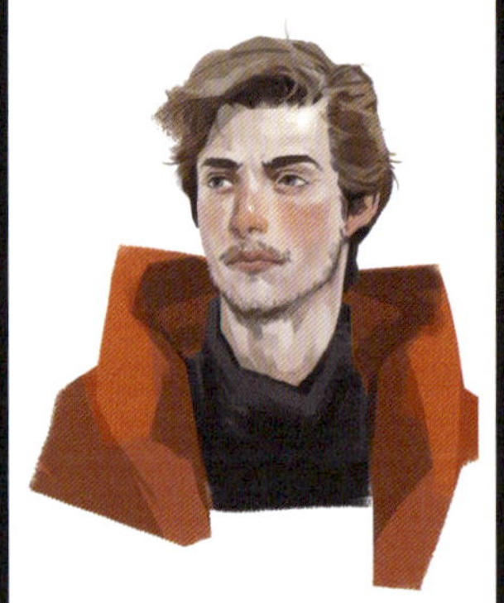
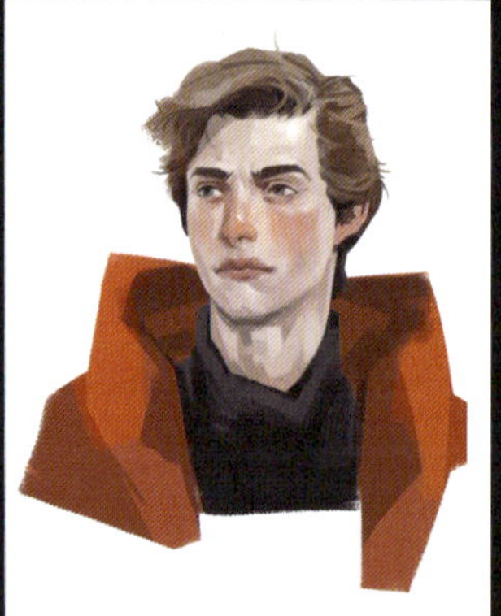
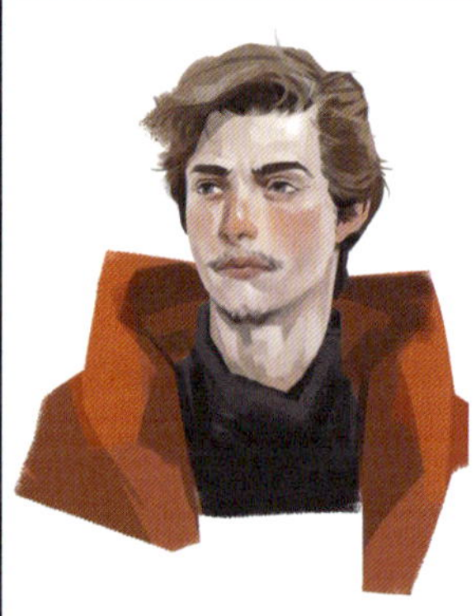

▲ The story a mustache tells!

11 REFINING HANSEL

I try out different facial hair for Hansel, still exploring that balance of distress and fresh-faced youth. I would like him to have a scraggly beard, quite poorly kept after his time in the field, but it also needs to be a young man's beard and not very thick. As I mentioned in step 08, this character's design is somewhat shaped by what the villain will look like. Even when I am working on one character, I like to keep everything else in mind, such as the other characters who will be sharing the scene.

12 THE CANNIBAL

If this was a very stylized illustration I would play much more with size and proportions, but it's supposed to be a somewhat realistic setting, so I will have to be a bit more subtle. While Hansel and Gretel are dressed in big overalls and gloves because it makes them look childish, I want the madman to have a skinnier look, emphasizing that he's gaunt and hungry. Perhaps the bunker is somewhat warmer, allowing him to shed some garments.

▶ **I would like the villain to have many differences from the main characters**

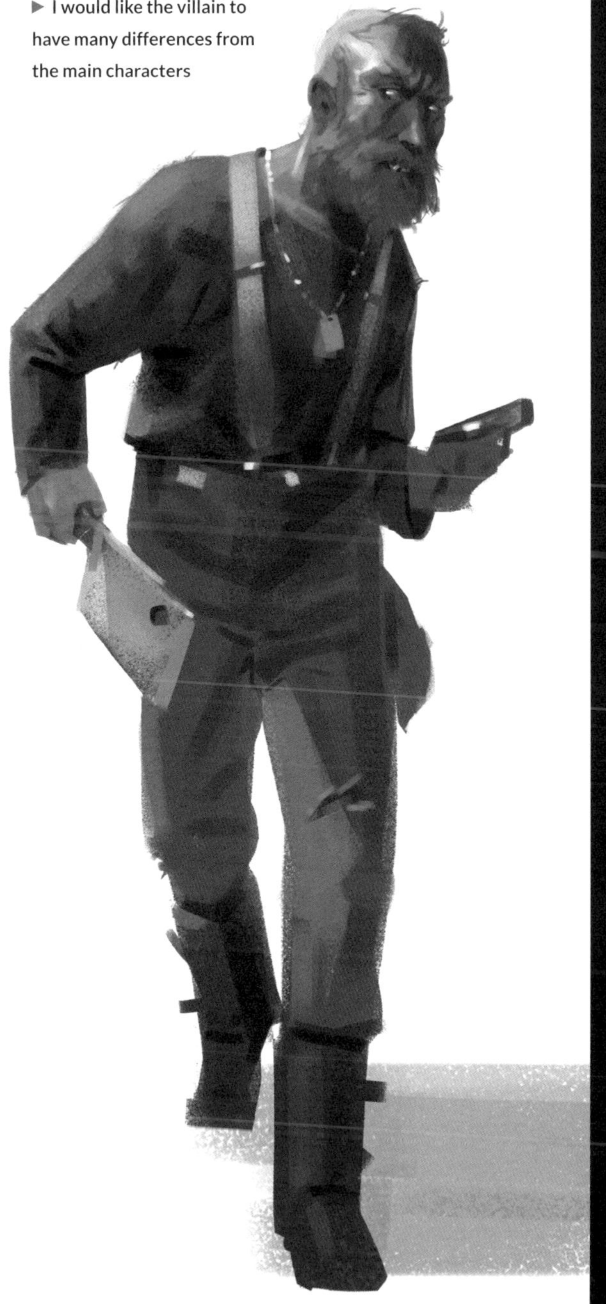

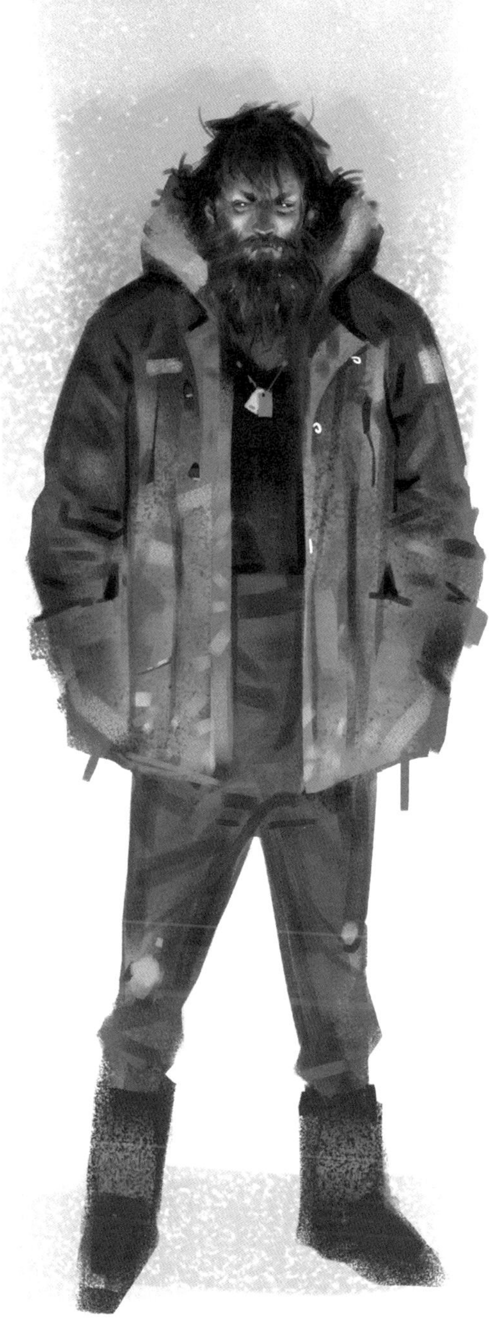

▲ **A wild, bushy beard would create a stark contrast with Hansel's patchy young-adult beard**

13 DEVELOPING THE VILLAIN

In the final illustration, I imagine the cannibal will be backlit, so that all the stray hairs will be illuminated and give him a scary silhouette. Adding the reflection of some light in his eyes will give them an eerie, almost supernatural glow, reminiscent of the witch in the original tale.

14 A CREEPY CLOSEUP

The witch in the original tale is a frightening figure. She traps children to eat, not out of desperation and hunger, but for her own unknown reasons. She is just evil like that! My "witch" is driven mad by his situation, being left alone in the frozen wastes for so long. He may not be evil per se, but I want him to be completely unreasonable. The more haggard and scruffy he looks, the better. I want him to make a shocking appearance in the illustration.

▶ Though the villain will not be seen in this much detail, I still want to explore his character

15 OUTFIT COLORS

I am certain I want a classic red Arctic outfit for both siblings, like in step 10, but I still want to explore my options. I look at reference photos from earlier expeditions for color palette ideas. I even wonder if I should set the whole story in a different era, such as the early 1900s, but I want the scene to be as relatable as possible and I am already excited by the bunker idea. I decide to stick with a modern-era setting and red outfits for strong contrast against the Arctic setting.

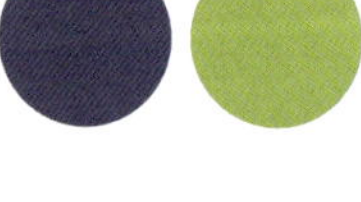

◀ Testing different color options for the siblings' expedition clothes

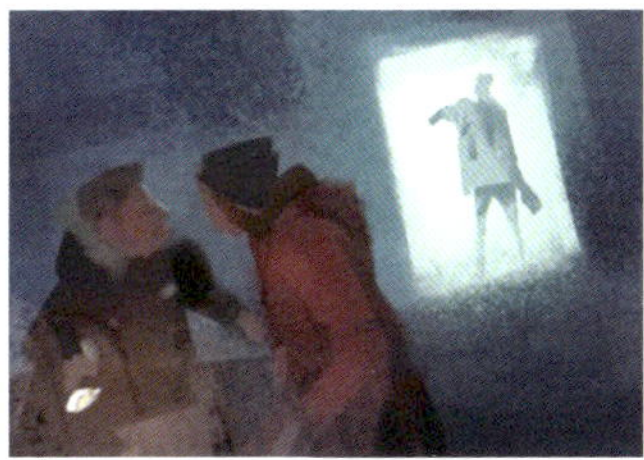
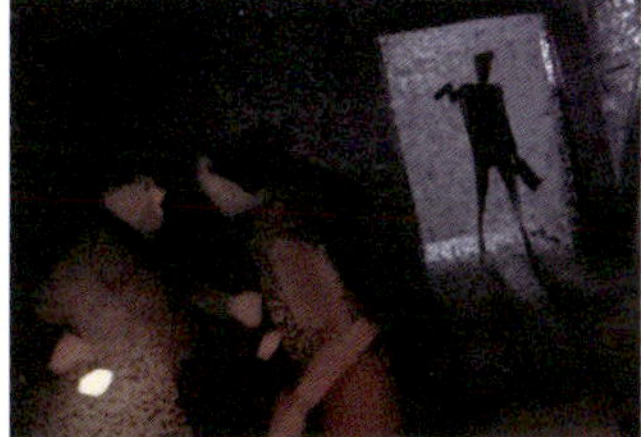
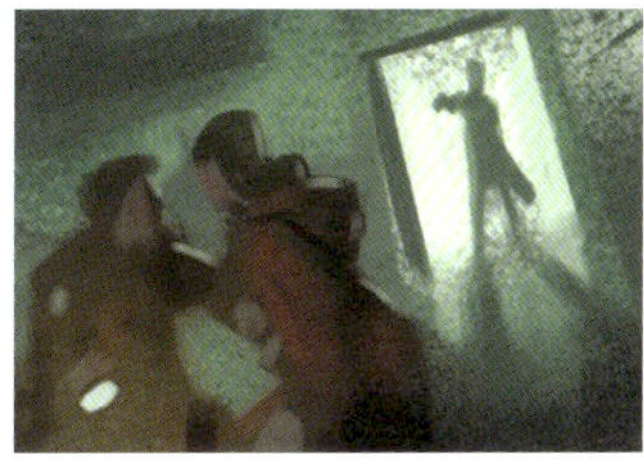
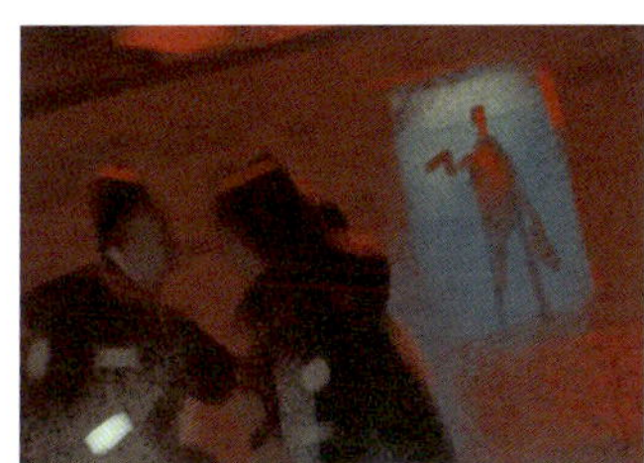

16 MOOD AND LIGHTING

The illustration will come out wildly different depending on the color and lighting I choose. I make a few color sketches to try out the lighting in thumbnail format. I think each one shows promise and I like all of them in different ways. The first one has a cool light that brings home the Arctic feel. The dark one has an especially scary feel, with the siblings lit from below by the flashlight in the dark. The green option is the weakest of them all, as it feels less relevant to the setting. The final one is very impactful and alarming, but perhaps the red is too much.

◀ Trying to decide on a color palette for the final painting

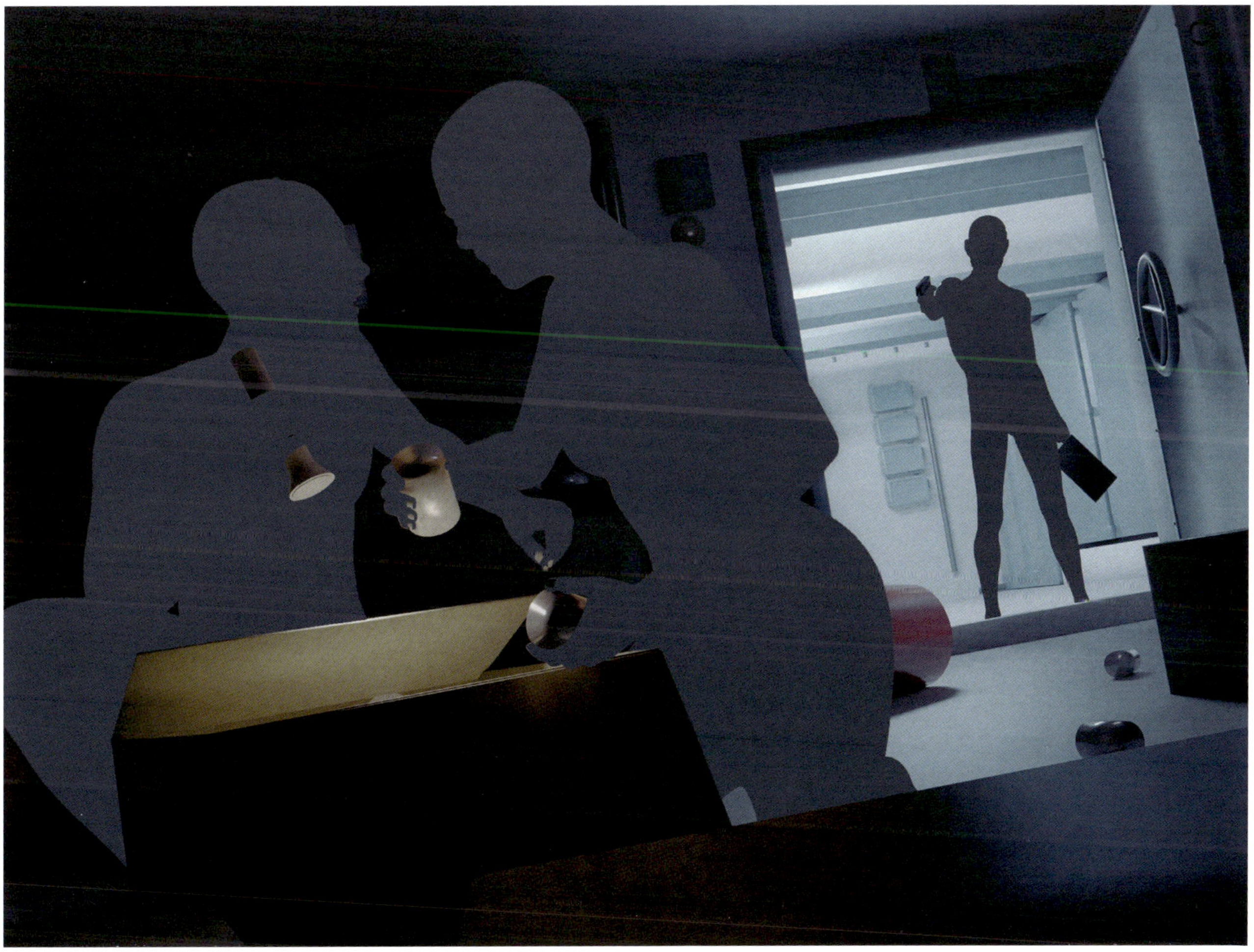

▲ Now I have everything ready to take to the next step

17 CREATING FOCUS WITH LIGHT

The human silhouette makes for a very powerful focal point. I have the light sources illuminating exactly what I want them to bring attention to – the villain and siblings – and nothing else. Lighting is a hugely important tool in storytelling; the same scene can tell different stories when lit differently. The upper-right focal point is the gun pointing the viewer toward Hansel and Gretel, and the lower-left focal point is the siblings lit by the torch, which brings attention to them scavenging for food.

18 LIGHT STUDIES

There will be a lot of dramatic lights in this scene, so I would like to quickly study some similar light situations. I want most of the image to be dark, with the focal points carved out with light for high contrast and dramatic effect. I always use several references for stages like this, to ensure I have enough information to work from.

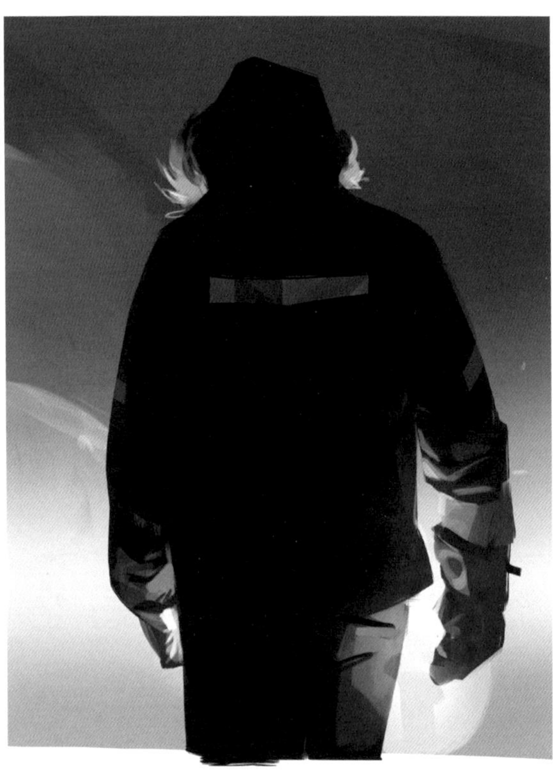

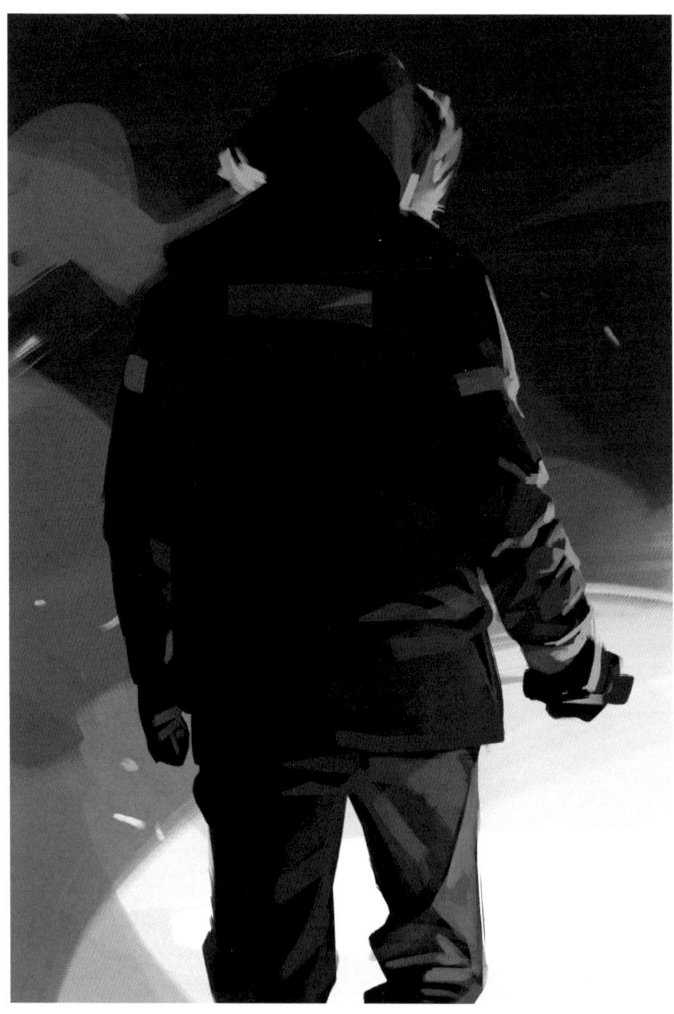

▲ Painting some quick studies for the dramatic lighting

19 BLACK-AND-WHITE CHECK

When I have everything in place and have done some work on painting the image, I like to use Adobe Photoshop's Posterize tool to generate a black-and-white version. This helps me judge if the basic lighting and values work as intended. The composition has a "yin and yang" quality to it, where the right side is predominantly light with the dark silhouette of the villain, and the left side is a dark space where the siblings are carved out with light. This is working just as I hoped, so I carry on. If the idea was not readable in this simplified state, I would have to increase the contrast in key places and lower them in the peripheral areas.

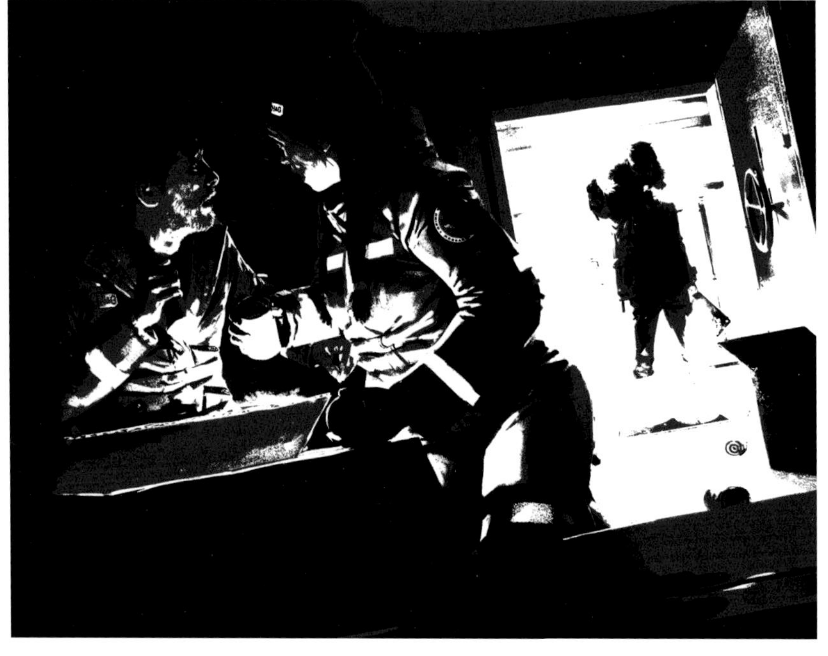

► Simplifying the values is always a good way to get a new perspective

20 FINISHING TOUCHES

Focal points are the most important for storytelling, so they are where I put most of my efforts. In this case, the siblings are the main focus, so they have a higher level of detail than their surroundings, and interesting details for viewers to take in: for example, the little flags and patches that give an extra hint at the tale's origins. An image can gain more from leaving the peripheries simple than working up the whole image to the same level of detail. You as an artist direct the viewer's attention with the use of lighting, composition, and levels of detail, so it is important to know what story you want to tell and focus on that until it reads just as intended.

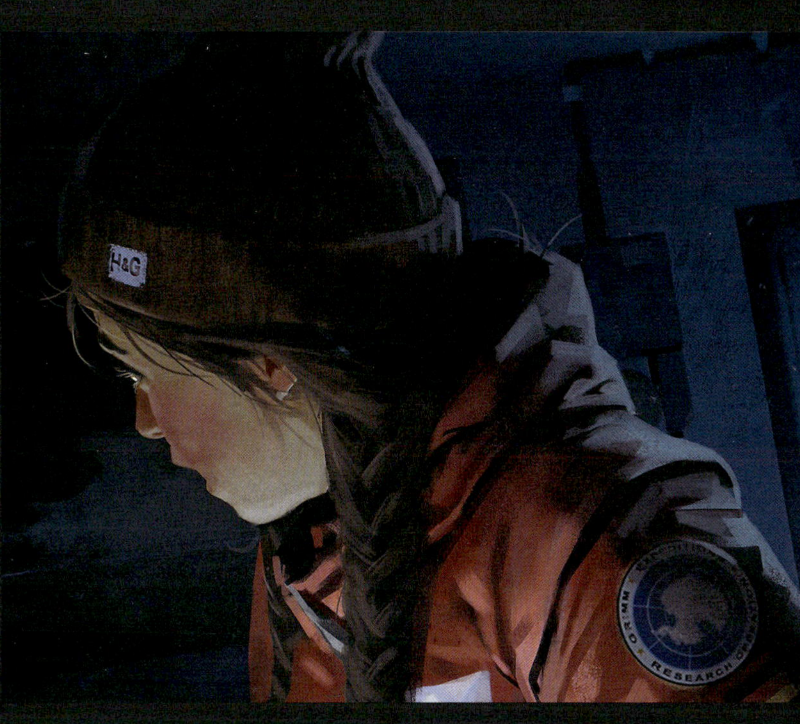

▶ **Polishing the image and adding focal details until I feel happy with the whole illustration**

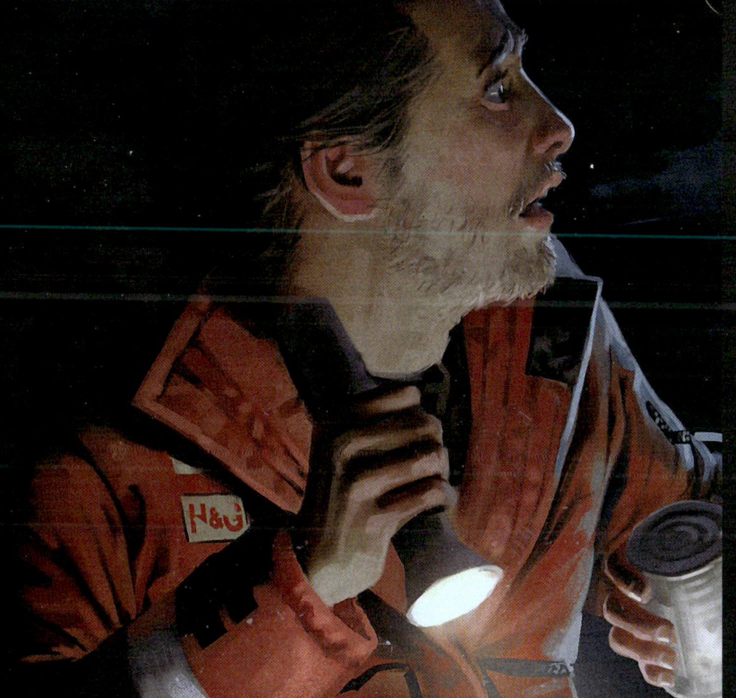

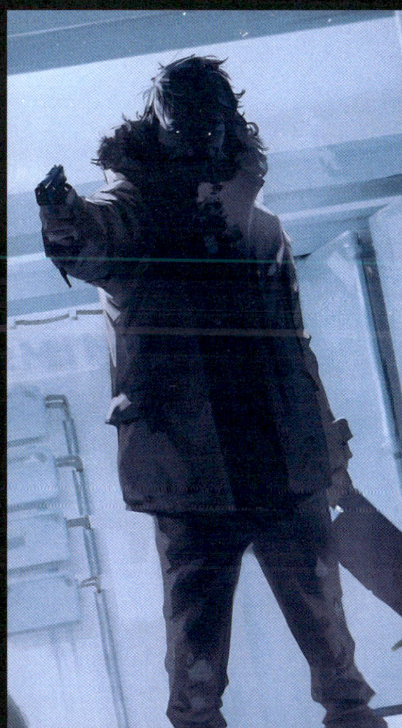

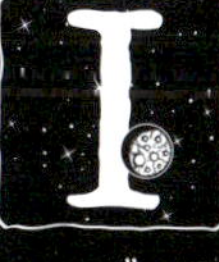

In the end, I am happy with the final image, as it shows all the aspects of the story I set out to convey in the beginning. I chose this scene very deliberately because the "nibble, nibble, little mouse" scene translates well to this scenario, creating an equally exciting and dramatic moment. Like in the original tale, the salvation of the food leads to a terrible situation and the reveal of the villain. I see a lot of beginner artists struggle to focus on the main things in their illustrations or concept art, and this tutorial shows how important it is to know exactly why you are making your piece. What are you trying to tell the observer? You are the director of your own illustrations, and you have all the tools you need to make sure the viewer's attention is drawn to the right places.

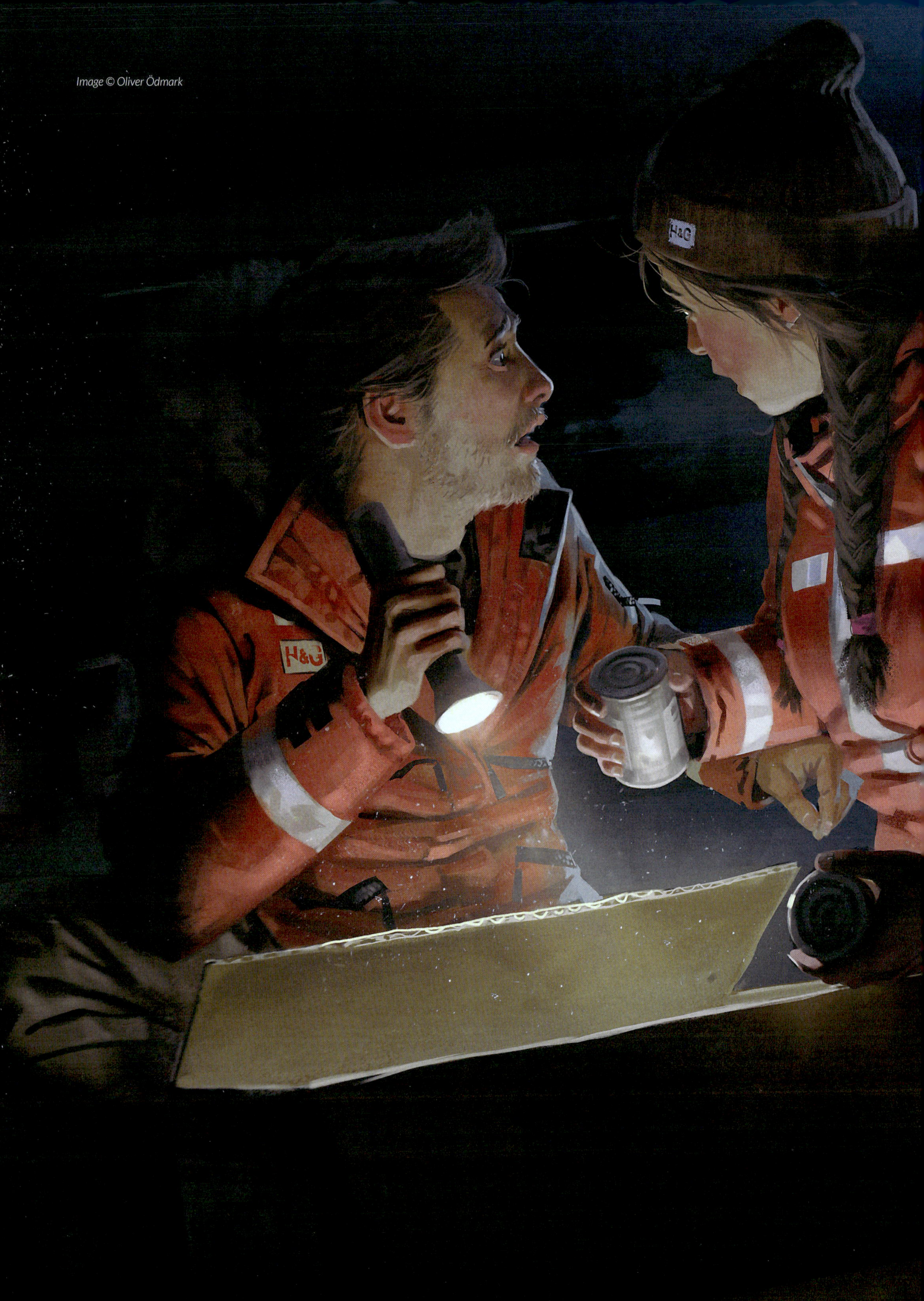
H&G
H&G

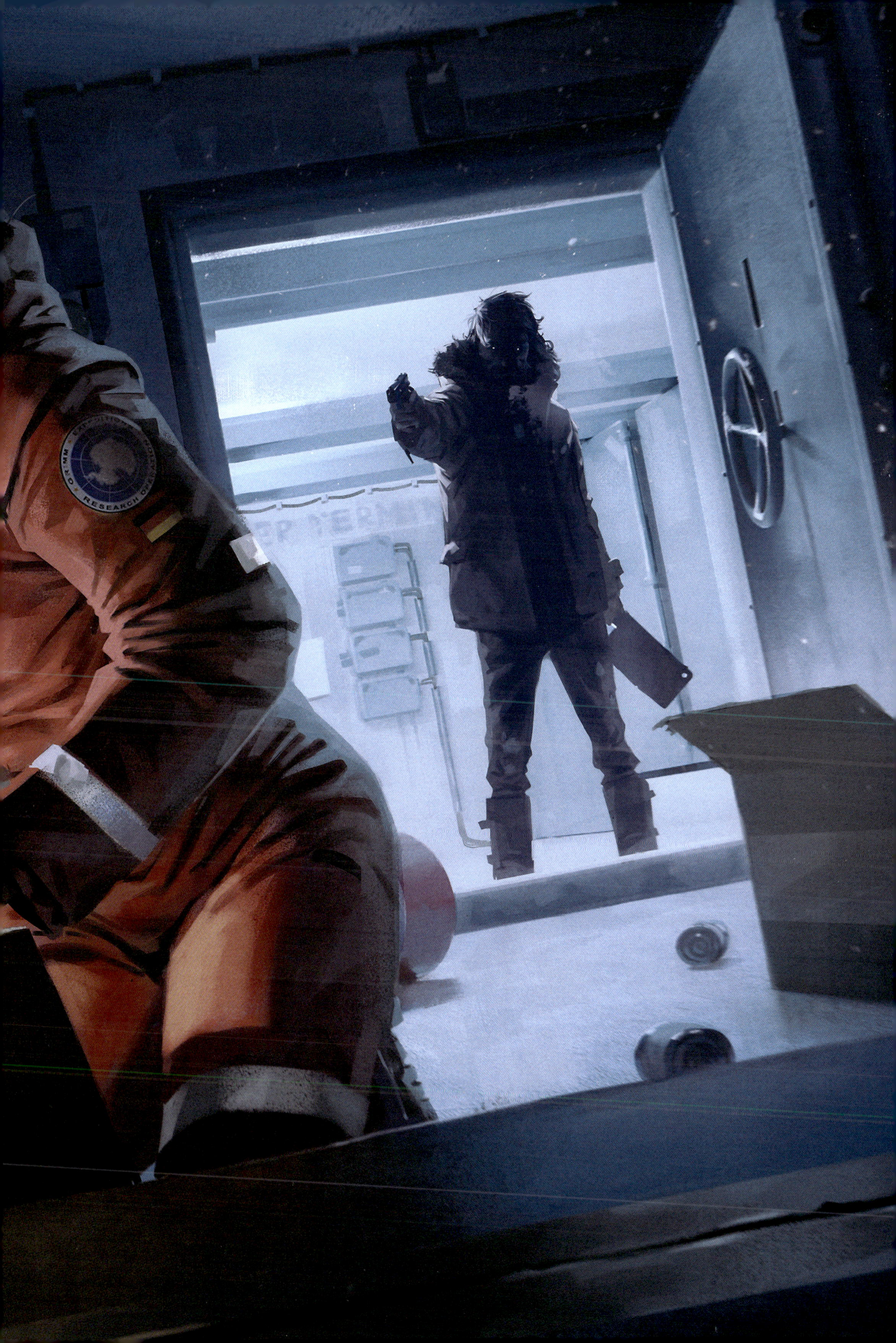
RESEARCH

THE MICE AND THE OWL

BY GABRIEL GÓMEZ ALMENZAR

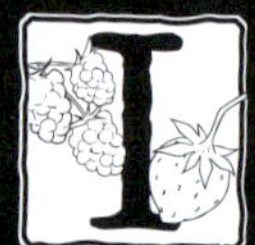

I think the original story of *Hansel and Gretel* comes in many very powerful versions, featuring many interesting elements, such as the witch, the forest, and the horror story of two children under threat of being eaten. For my project, I want to focus on the scene where the witch discovers the children outside her house. This will allow me to focus on an illustration that brings all those key elements to the foreground. I would also like to turn the characters into anthropomorphic animals, as I think this will allow me to bring even more interesting tension to the story, casting Hansel and Gretel as prey animals and the witch as one of their natural predators.

01 RESEARCH AND INSPIRATION

When faced with a project like this, where I have to illustrate a story, the first step I take is to find as much information about the original tale and its lore as possible. In this case, there are text versions of *Hansel and Gretel*, as well as some movies and shorts that can be watched online, but my greatest source of inspiration is illustrations. I find and compare many versions by different artists who have depicted the story throughout history, such as Alexander Zick, Arthur Rackham, and Frank Adams. The most interesting thing about studying the work of different artists is that you can see how each one has approached the illustration in their own way, and try to incorporate the elements that interest you most in your version.

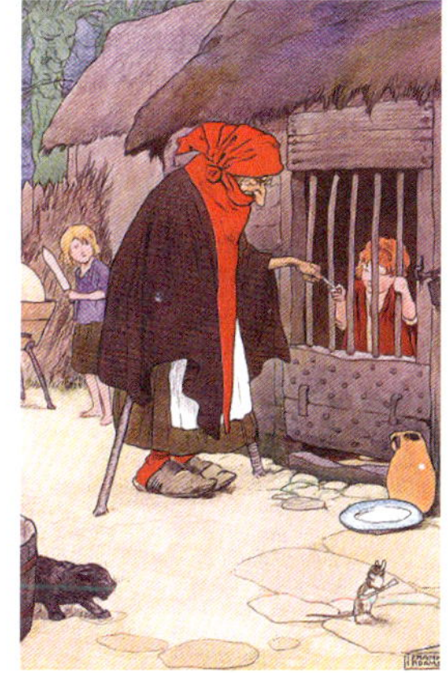

▲ Illustration by Frank Adams, c. 1925

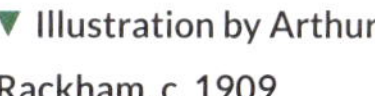

▼ Illustration by Arthur Rackham, c. 1909

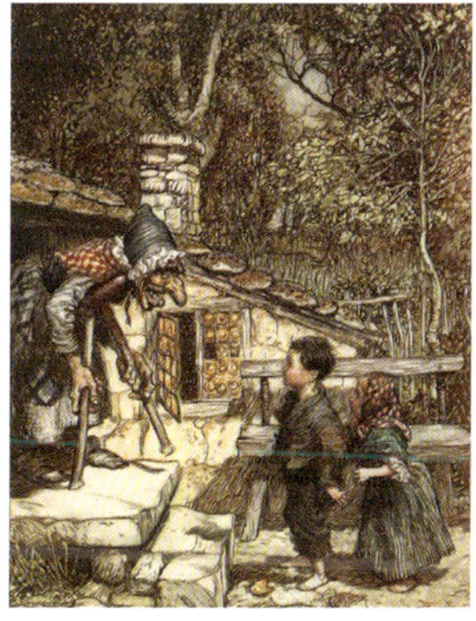

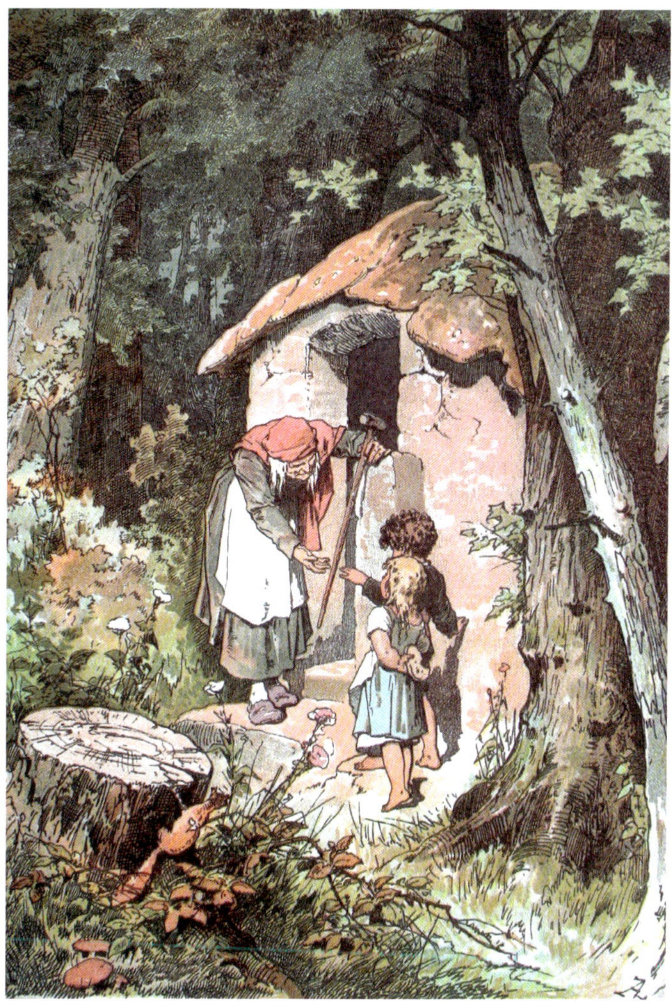

▲ Illustration by Alexander Zick, date unknown

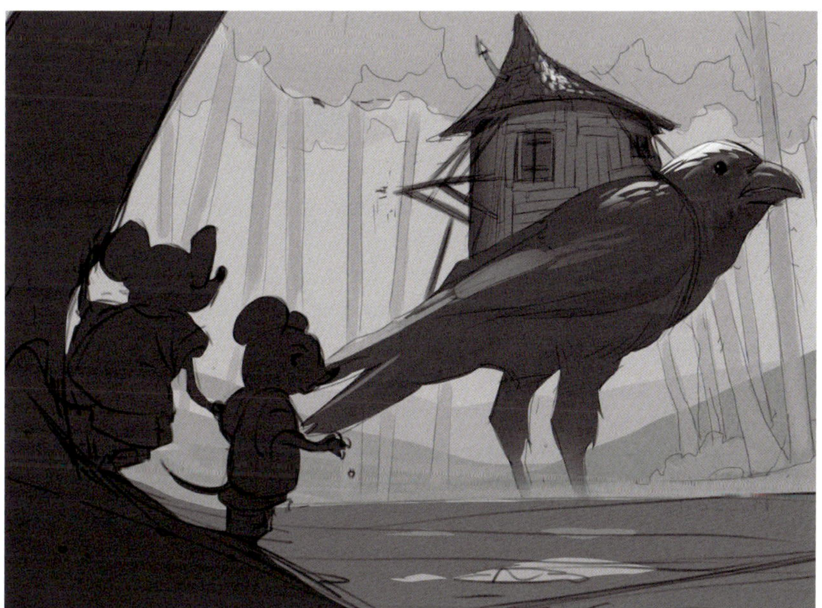

▲ The mice in the forest approaching the house of the witch Baba Yaga

02 THE MICE FIND A HUT

My next step is to brainstorm some ideas based on the information gathered from the references. The first idea that comes to my mind is to place the scene at the moment when the children arrive at a clearing in the forest and find the witch's house. I am a big fan of witches and horror stories, but I want to add a more cartoony side by changing the protagonists into animals. It also occurs to me to introduce the character of Baba Yaga, a classic forest-dwelling witch from Slavic folklore, perhaps with her house carried on the back of a giant crow. However, as interesting as this idea looks, I soon dismiss it on the grounds that two little mice would never go near such a place! The key moment of the children being tempted into danger would be lost here.

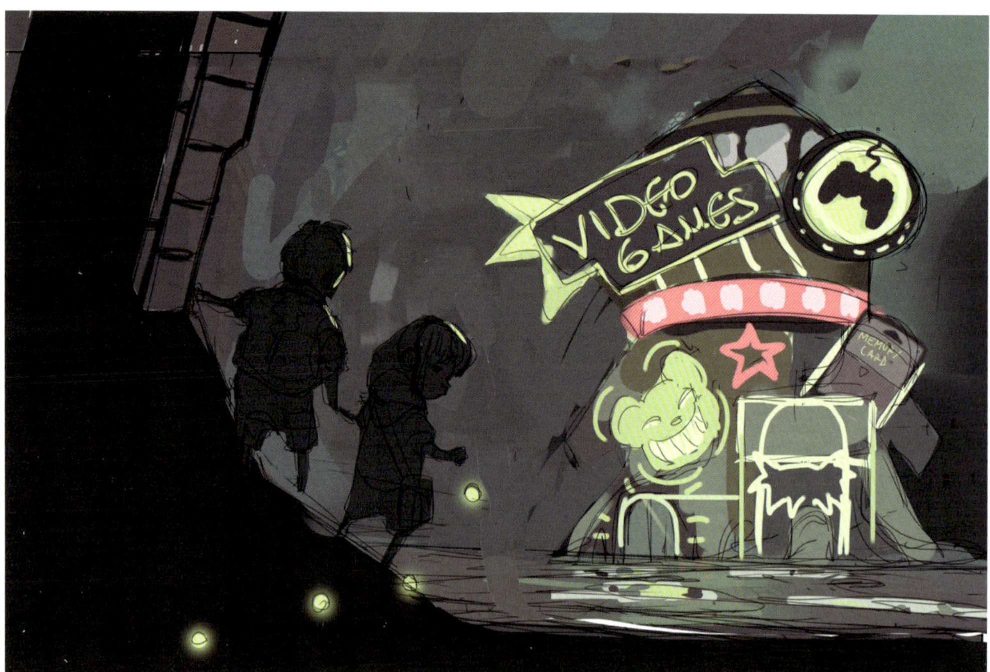

◀ Attracted by the lights, the children approach a place full of arcade machines and video games

03 TRYING A SCI-FI SCENE

I don't want to miss the opportunity to try a sci-fi version, placing the story in a dystopian future with elements that would still complement the original tale: tempting lights, deteriorating structures, and tall, dark structures that act as a "forest." References for this idea could be manga such as *Akira*, video games such as *Cyberpunk 2077*, and movies and TV shows such as *Blade Runner* and *Arcane*. The scene shows the children arriving at a place full of arcade machines and game consoles – drawn to the lights, billboards, and the idea of walking into a place where they can play and forget their worries. Having animal characters would be a change too far for this setting, so the children are human again. However, I decide the futuristic setting loses too much of the essence of a cautionary fantasy story, so I end up discarding it.

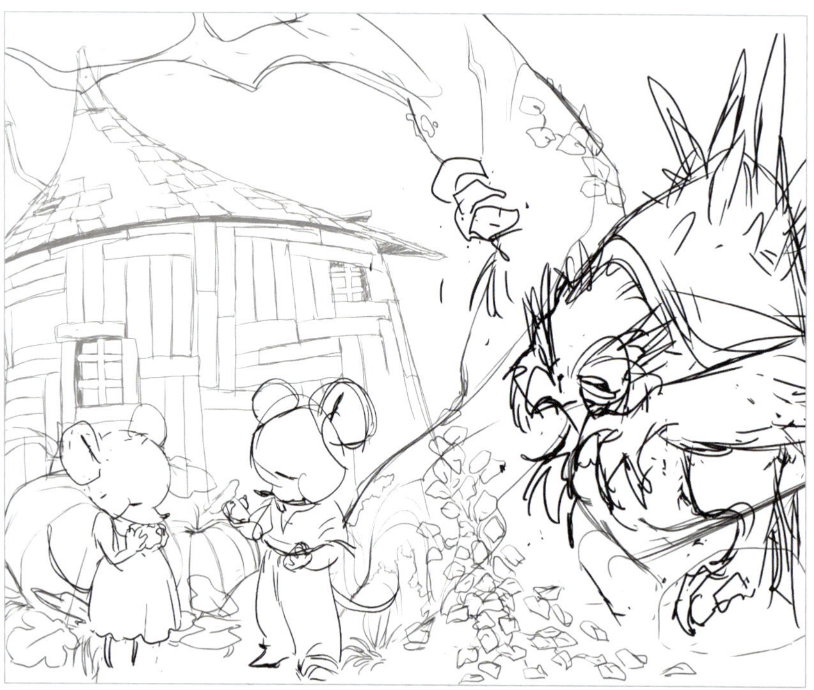

04 THE CHOSEN IDEA

I end up going with my first idea as it fits the theme more, but I make some big changes. I keep the mice as the main characters, but change the witch Baba Yaga into an owl – a character that would, in real life, be terrifying for two little mice! To get a clearer idea of the scene, I make a quick sketch showing the two mice eating pumpkins in the owl witch's garden, while the owl stalks them from behind a tree. This scene is similar to the original story, where the witch surprises the children eating from her candy house. The sketch is drawn quickly, without much regard for detail or proportion – I simply want to capture the idea so that I can develop it further.

◀ Selecting an idea where two hungry mice discover an owl's garden

05 FINDING REFERENCES

The step is one of the most important and most fun for me: collecting references. Before starting to draw, it is always advisable to make a moodboard of reference images. This is where you gather all the images that you are going to need to refer to when developing the illustration. So, if I don't know how to draw a subject – such as an old wooden house, for example – I can go to my collection of references and study those images to help me build that house. For my moodboard, I collect references of old stone houses, crooked trees, pumpkins, vegetation, and owls (especially main elements such as their plumage).

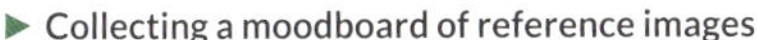

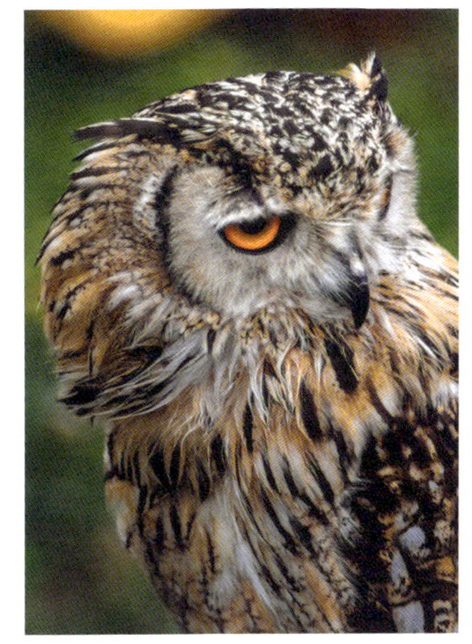

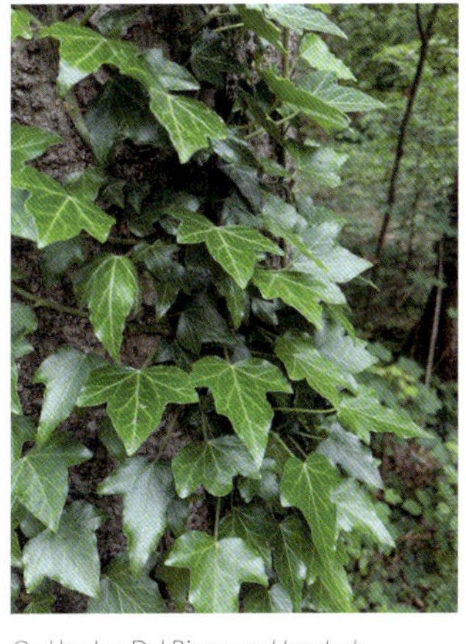

Owl by Jon Del Rivero on Unsplash
Ivy by Eloy Martinez on Unsplash

▶ Collecting a moodboard of reference images

06 INITIAL SKETCHES

After compiling references into a moodboard, I can start specifying the elements that make up the illustration. I like Tim Burton-style building designs, so I want to give the house a rickety look, with derelict wooden construction, as well as a weathered, peaked roof that feels typical of a witch's house. In the foreground, the tree will be gnarled and covered with vines, and the ground will be covered with mushrooms, creating the feeling of a wild forest environment. The mice will be in a pumpkin patch, which I surround with a wooden fence to give the impression of an orchard related to the witch's cabin. I use the sketch to make a grayscale study to test out values for each element – I want to make sure that there are clearly separated planes of depth before I begin applying color later.

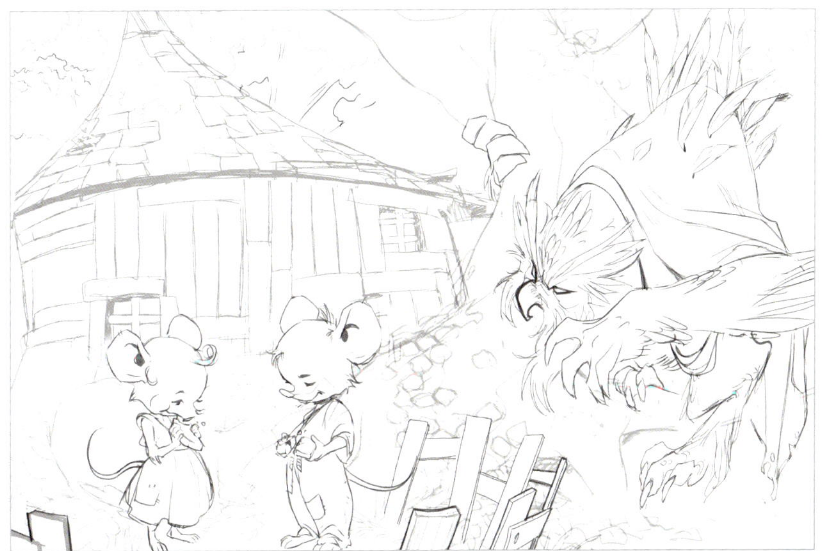

▲ Making a second sketch to clarify shapes and objects

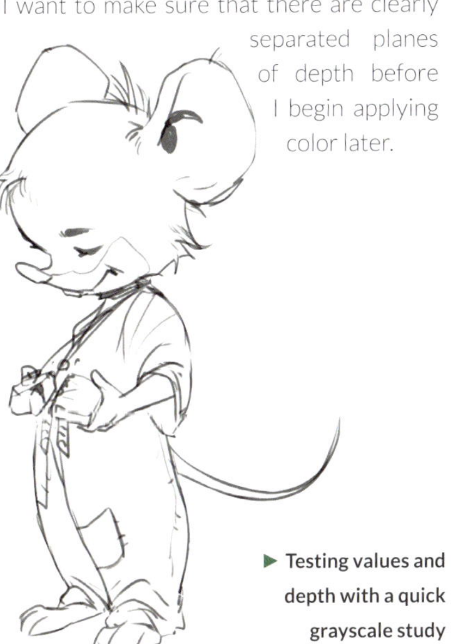

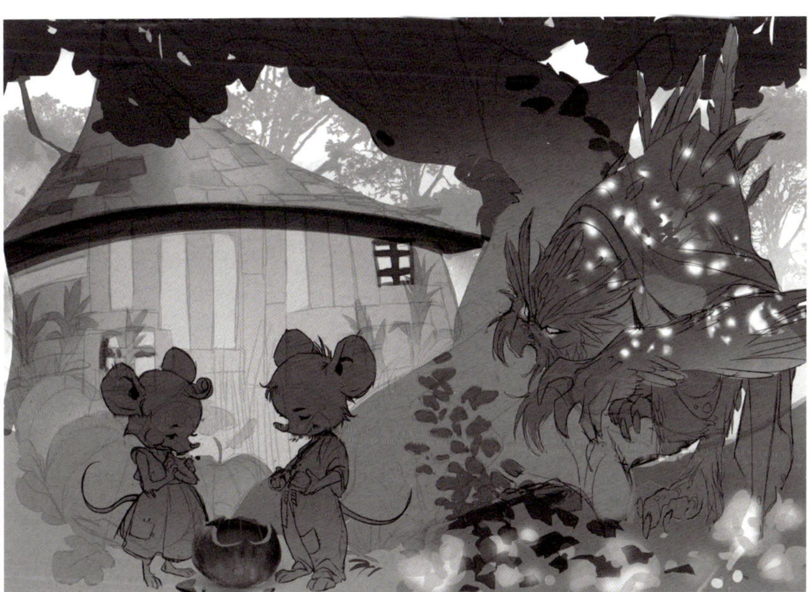

▶ Testing values and depth with a quick grayscale study

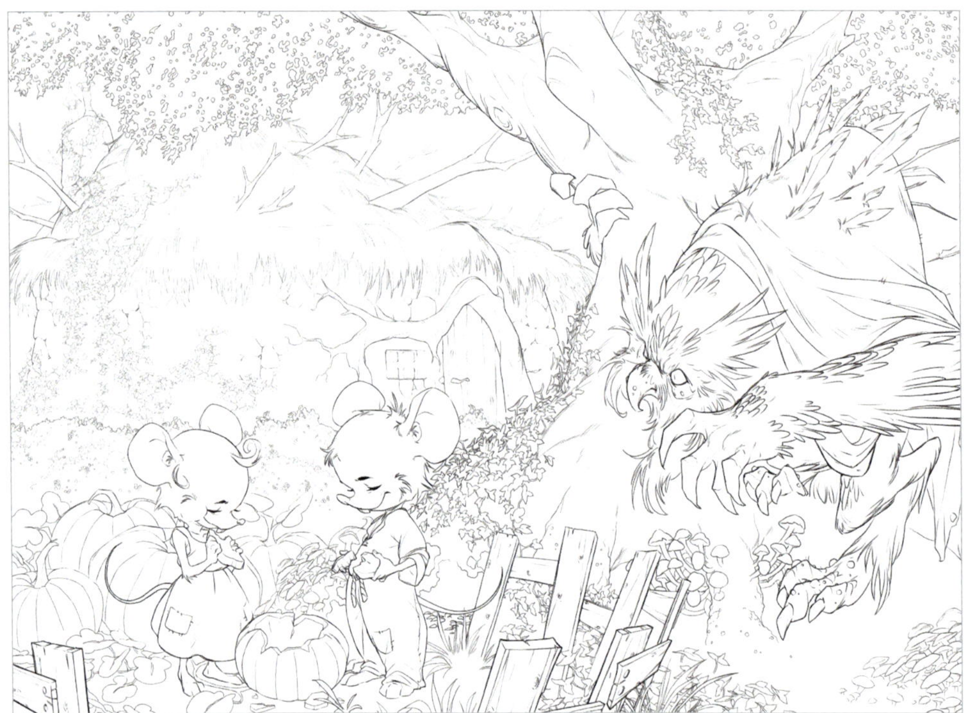

◀ Refining the drawing and ideas in preparation for the color stage

07 REFINING THE DRAWING

I refine the drawing with cleaner, clearer lines that will facilitate coloring. I make some changes that improve the scene, such as replacing the wooden roof with straw and adding branches, as if it were an owl's nest, relating it more to the witch's character. I replace the wooden planks with walls of dirt and stone, so the house looks more natural and the background is less saturated with details. I add a large root to frame the door and enhance that organic look. As for the witch herself, I like the idea of making her feathers grow out through her shawl, giving her a wild, scruffy look. Even though they are animals, I want the characters to have some human characteristics – such as posture, gestures, and clothing – to help tell the story.

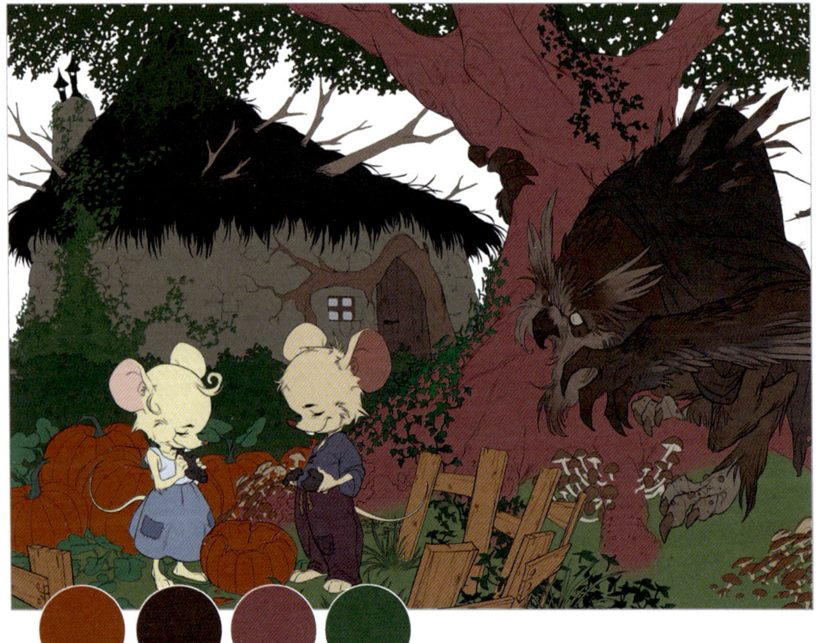

08 BASE COLOR PALETTE

Once the line art is finished, I start applying flat colors, aiming to relate the image's palette to the story's theme. Although the scene takes place in a forest, my intention is not to color everything green – I like to compose a palette from different hues to make my illustrations more interesting and unusual. All the elements that are closer to the viewer have a more saturated color than those that are farther away. This represents the atmosphere and distance of the environment, creating the sensation of depth. As for the characters, it is important to choose the colors well, since they represent the personality and role that each one has. Thus the mice have lighter, more saturated colors, while the witch's palette is darker and less saturated.

▲ Applying general colors representing the atmosphere of the setting and personalities of the characters

09 ADDING SHADOWS

I usually apply various levels of shadow to my images. First I apply general shading to set the atmosphere and represent the general volumes; then I add more detailed, darker levels of shading to specify smaller forms. Here, the light is coming from the top left, so the shadows will be cast to the right. I also take into account the reflection that objects project when the light falls on them; depending on the material, the light will be reflected with more or less intensity, creating small areas of light that will affect other objects. I want the mice to stand out as a focal point, so they are less shadowed than the surrounding areas. The witch, however, being hidden behind the tree, will have a darker level of shadow to give her a more fearsome appearance.

▶ The first level of basic, general shadows

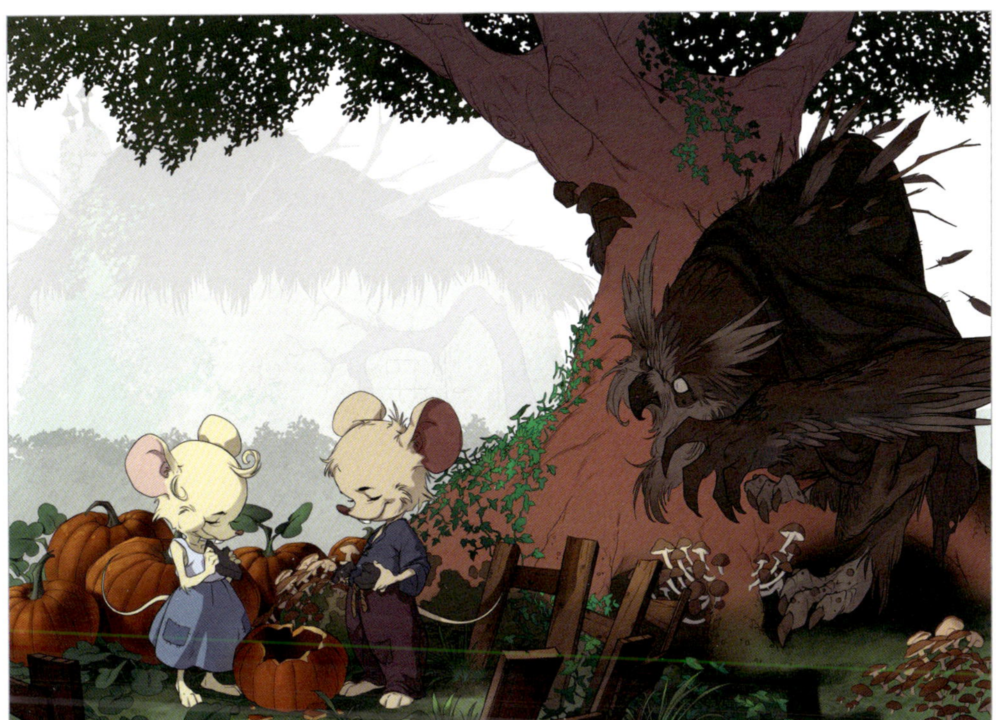

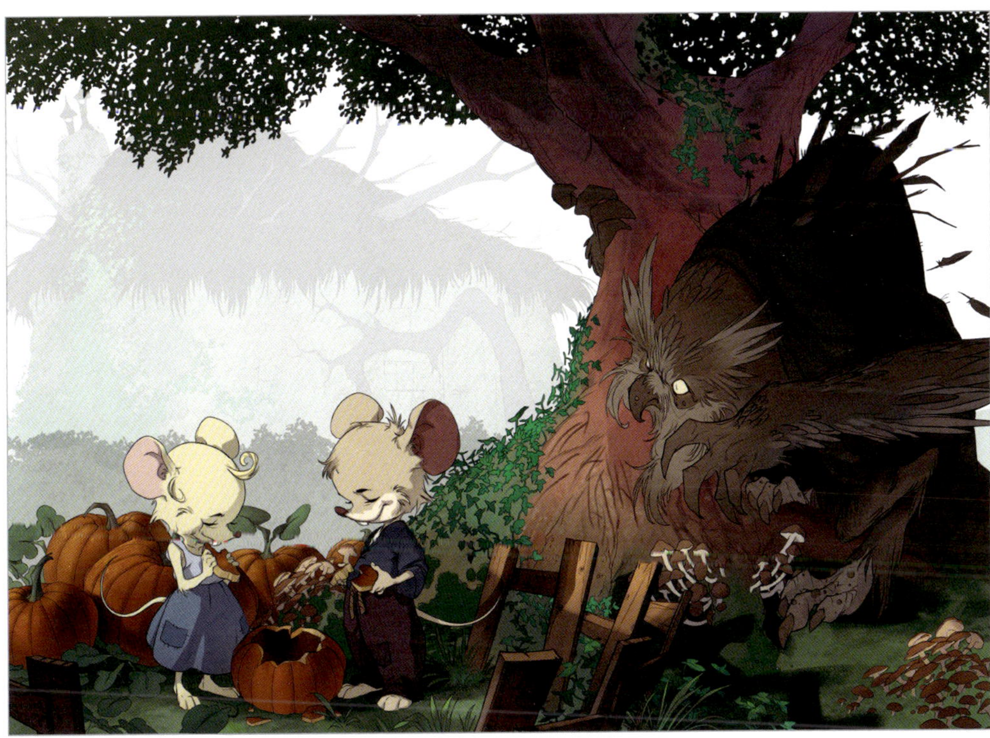

◀ The second level of more intense, detailed shadows

10 LEVELS OF DETAIL

The background is made up of three different parts: the house, the forest interior, and the bushes that separate the characters from the background plane. The bushes have more intense shading at the top, leaving the lower part with a lighter tone that makes it easier to read the outlines of the two mice. The trick is to intersperse higher-detail elements with lower-detail elements, enabling them to stand out from each other. If all the parts of the illustration had the same degree of detail, it would be far too complicated and much less interesting to look at! For the farthest areas of the background, I use the same principle, giving the treetops a darker hue than the rest. Dappled textures give the scenery an organic, natural look.

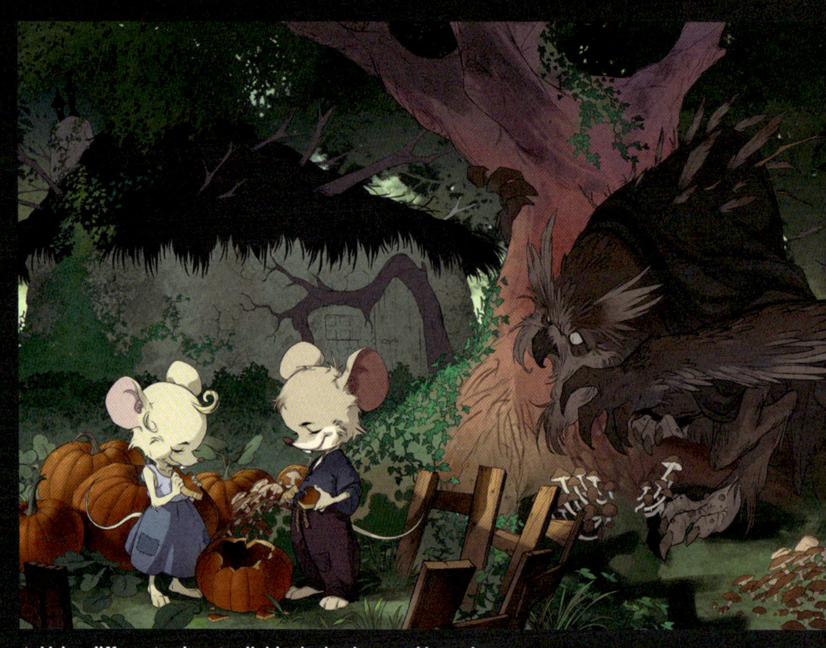

▲ Using different values to divide the background into planes

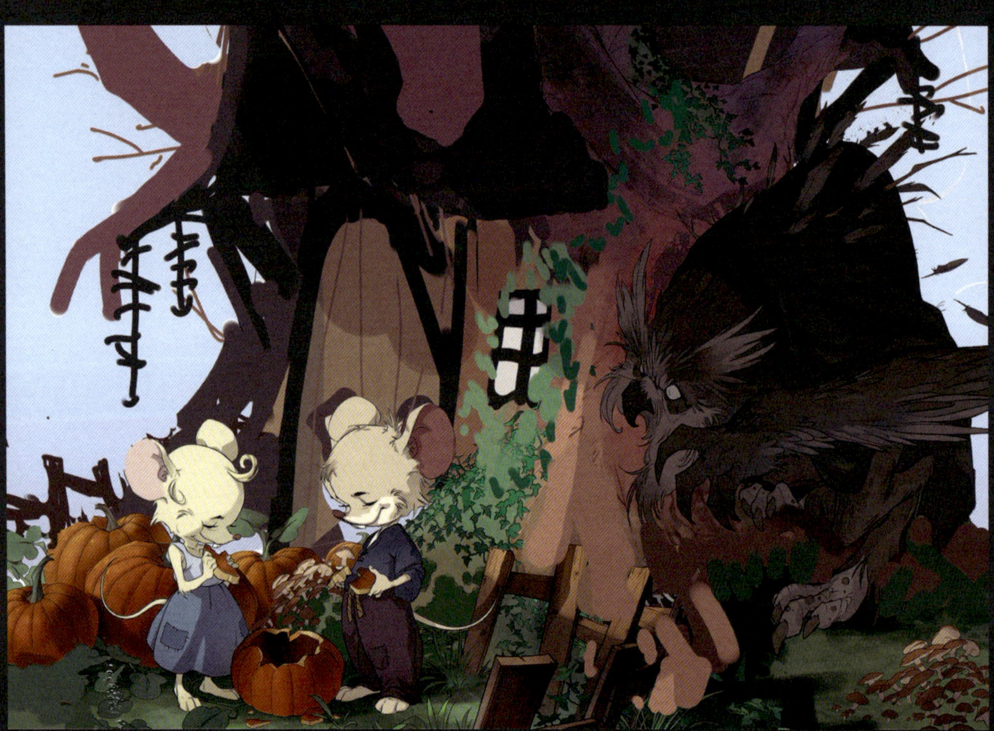

▲ Making a new sketch to redesign the structure of the illustration

11 CHANGING MY MIND

Things don't always turn out the way you want, as I discover at this stage! My idea was good, but at some point in the process, the scene began to twist into something that didn't feel "Hansel and Gretel" enough. I believe it's important to make the right decisions even when the work is well advanced, so I decide to revise until I get a result I am happy with. Don't worry if this happens to you – it is just part of the creative process. If you are not happy with your idea, it will become very hard for you to keep working on the project, and that feeling will be apparent in the final result. I make a quick sketch of my new idea to check that it could work, using elements of what I have already done, as there are still many parts that I want to keep.

12 A STRONGER DESIGN

My new composition focuses completely on the foreground, taking away the distant background. I have placed the characters next to the house, which is now closer to us, practically another protagonist in the story. As owls usually make their nests in trees, I directly use the tree as the witch's house. I rotate the house so that the door is closer to the witch, indicating that she has gone outside to see who is in her garden, rather than having the door facing the mice while the witch creeps around the back of the tree. I add more decorative elements to the tree, such as mushrooms and planks of wood. In addition to the wooden roofing, I also add a staircase with a railing to create a more interesting composition with different elevations of the ground.

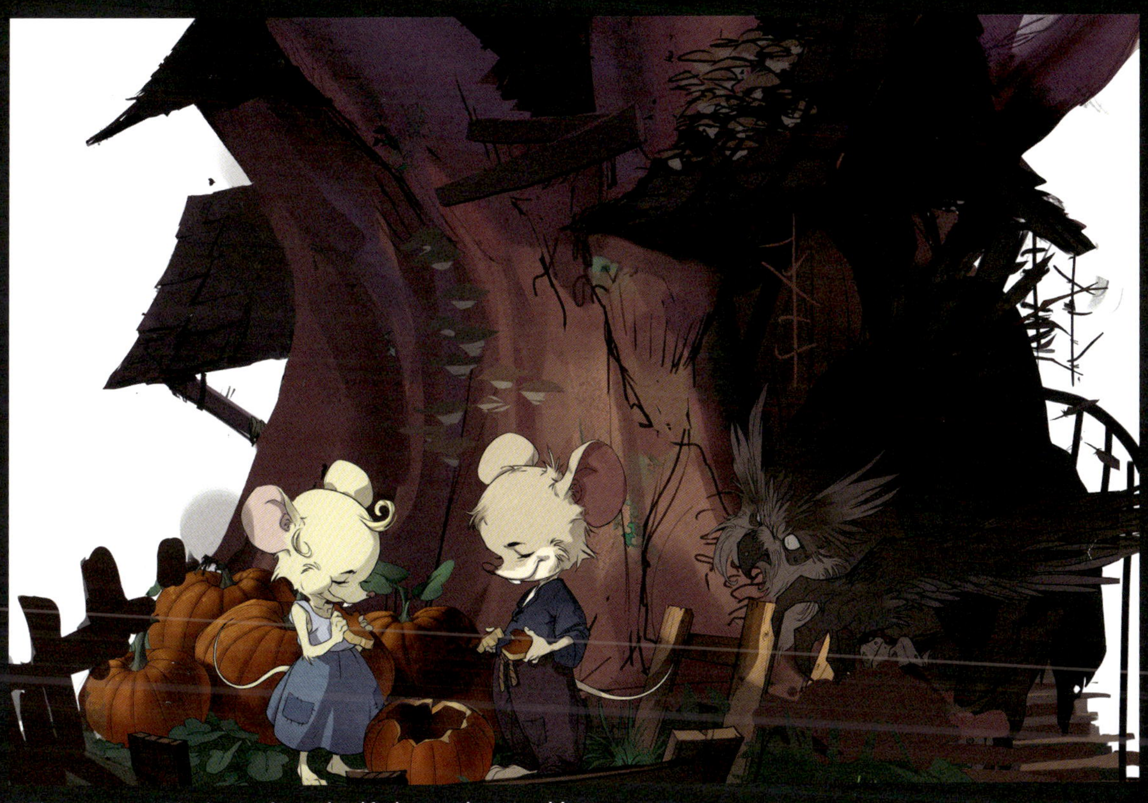

▲ The new composition is more focused and feels more character-driven

13 CHARACTER REDESIGNS

Due to the change in the composition, I also need to redesign the characters. I realized that they don't convey enough feeling or personality, which is especially obvious now that they are more strongly the focus of the scene. I have to add more expressiveness in their postures and gestures. I redraw the mice, emphasizing the way they eat, with their mouths full of food and smiling happily. Meanwhile, the witch, seeing that the mice have fallen into her trap, is smiling and licking her lips as she hides in the shadows, waiting to catch them. By lowering the opacity of the old character-design layers, I am able to build on what I had already drawn, making the redesign process easier and faster.

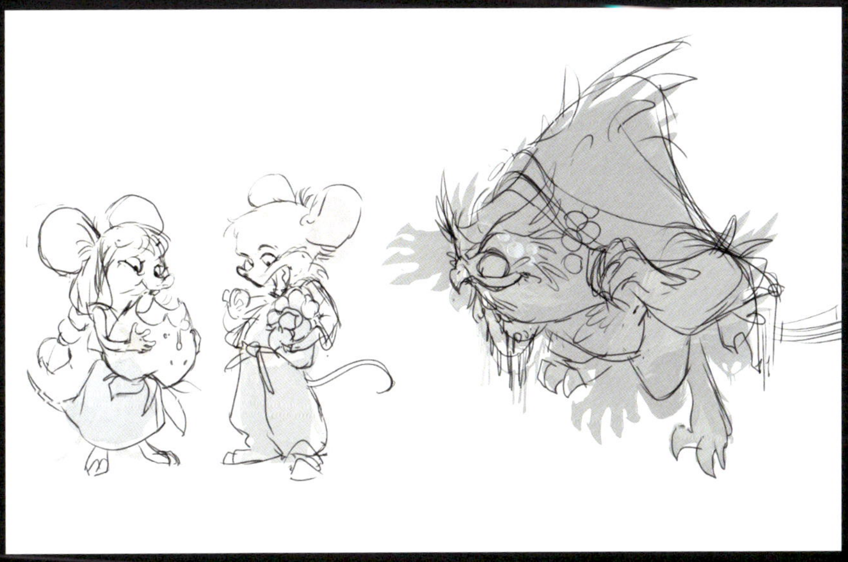

▲ Redesigning the characters and their poses according to the new scene

BE EXPRESSIVE!

Always try to be expressive, whether you are making a character design or a background. It is what will make your illustration fantastically interesting. If you are working on a character, make their expression, gesture, or movement intense and really reflect their intention. A straight and serious character is not as interesting or entertaining. Even with environments, the principle is the same – try to create fun, uneven shapes. Exaggerate and experiment without fear of doing the "wrong" thing.

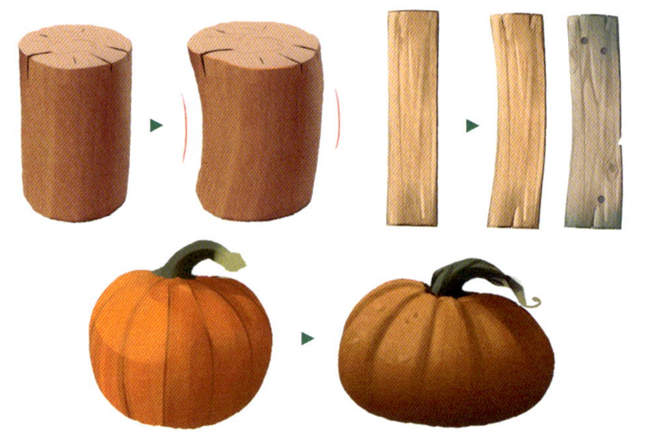

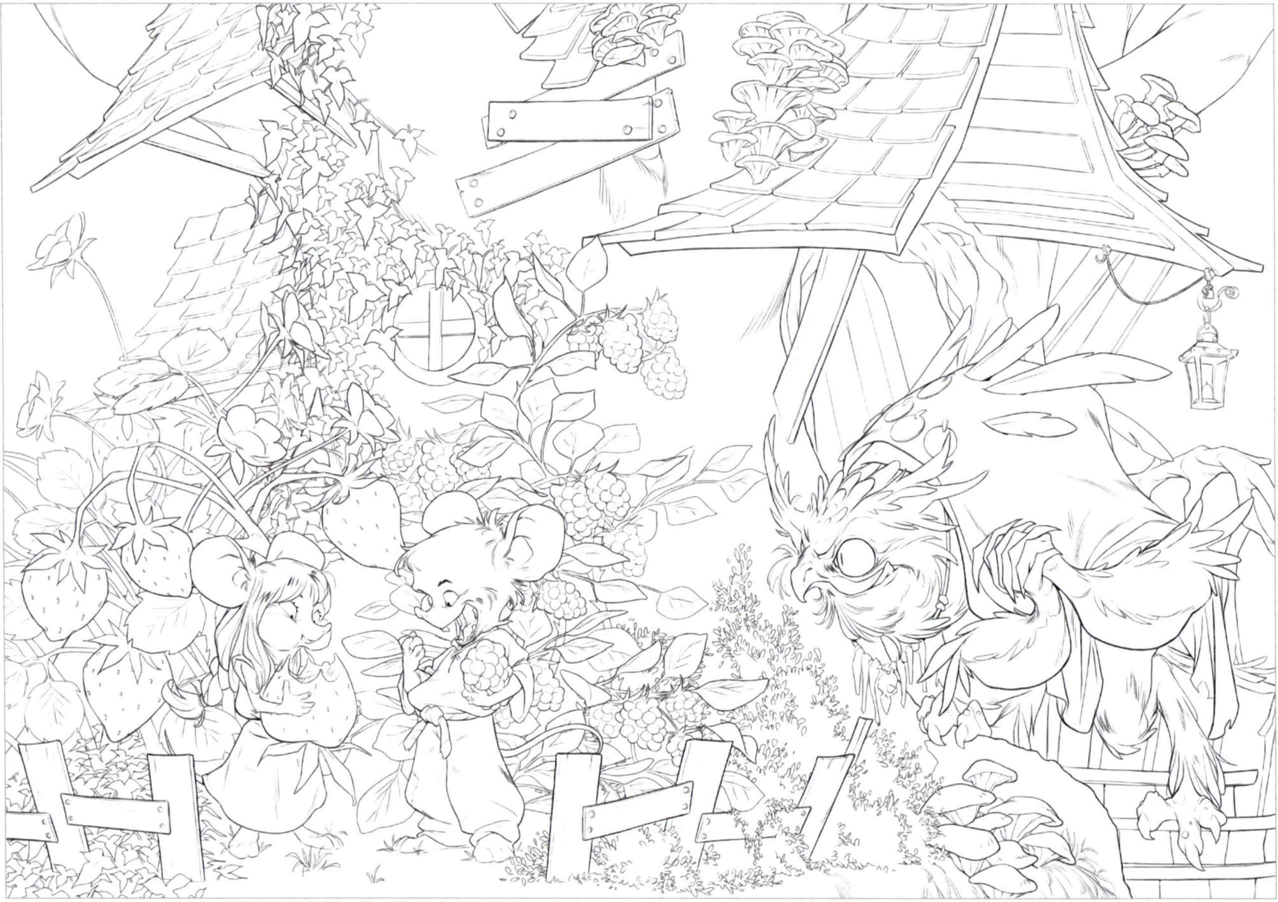

▲ The final design for the full illustration

14 NEW LINEWORK

Based around the new character designs, I make changes to the environment as well, to bring it more in line with the story and make the narrative more meaningful. Instead of a pumpkin patch, the witch's garden contains strawberries and blackberries, which look more juicy and appetizing for the mice. This gives a more realistic reason why two little mice would approach the dilapidated old house! I reduce the size of the fence and distribute the planks in such a way that they don't get between the characters and the viewer. To make the witch's home an even more attractive place for passersby, I add grass along the ground and some bushes at the base of the tree.

15 NEW GRAYSCALE PLAN

Once the design and the final linework are finished, I proceed to fill out each element with a different shade of gray, which will help speed up the coloring process in the next steps. I also use grayscale to determine the hierarchy of elements within the composition. Less-important elements, such as bushes and vegetation in the background, have subtler values to attract less attention from the viewer. The tree-house has a softer value against which the rest of the elements stand out, so the composition is uncluttered and easy to read.

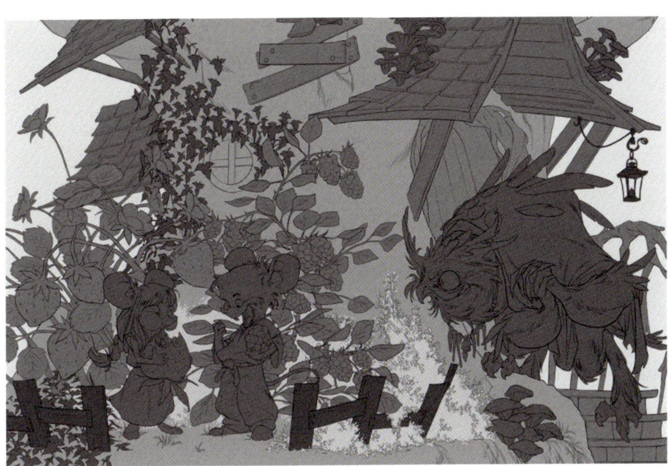

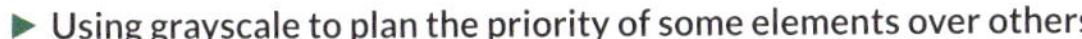

▶ Using grayscale to plan the priority of some elements over others

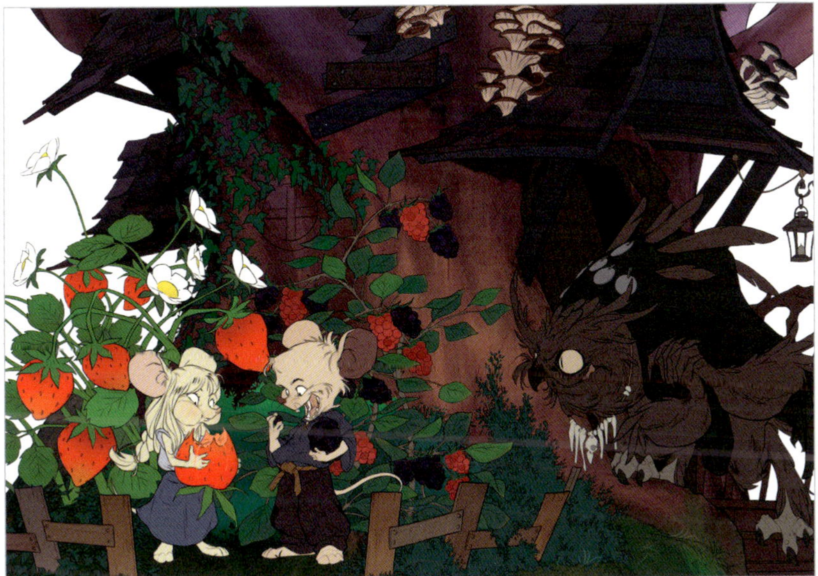

▲ Adding flat color to determine the overall tone and palette of the illustration

16 CREATING A COLOR PALETTE

I can now choose a color palette that will guide the tones I use in the rest of the process. I organize it around two main hues: brownish-purple and green. The purple and brown hues are used for the tree and roofs, creating a more attractive result than simply using brown. Each of the wooden shingles has a slightly different color, as using one single shade would look flat and uninteresting. I use different shades of green in the garden for a natural, varied touch. Those greens combine well with the vivid fruits and flowers. The resulting mood is slightly dark and mysterious, but also lush and full of variation, just like real woodland can be. It's a simple color palette, but with the help of some additional effects and tones, it will become much richer.

17 COLOR AND FIRST SHADOWS

In this step, I begin adding the first pass of shadows, which is a relatively quick process. I choose where the light is coming from and paint in the general shadows to give volume to the shapes. In this case, I choose the upper-left side as the source of the main light, so the shadows will generally fall on the right side of the subjects in the scene. This is when it's important to prioritize some elements over others, as discussed in previous steps. My grayscale plan helps me differentiate between different planes and groups of shapes, in the same way the shadows help to emphasize some shapes over others. Thus the background elements, such as the house, can be hidden with a larger shadow. This leaves the foreground elements, such as the characters and garden of delicious berries, more exposed to the light, as they are the focal points that drive the narrative.

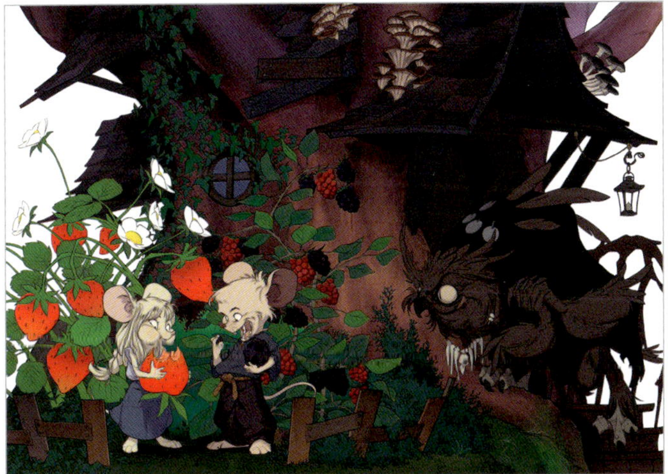

▲ General shadows enhance the volumes and show the direction of the light

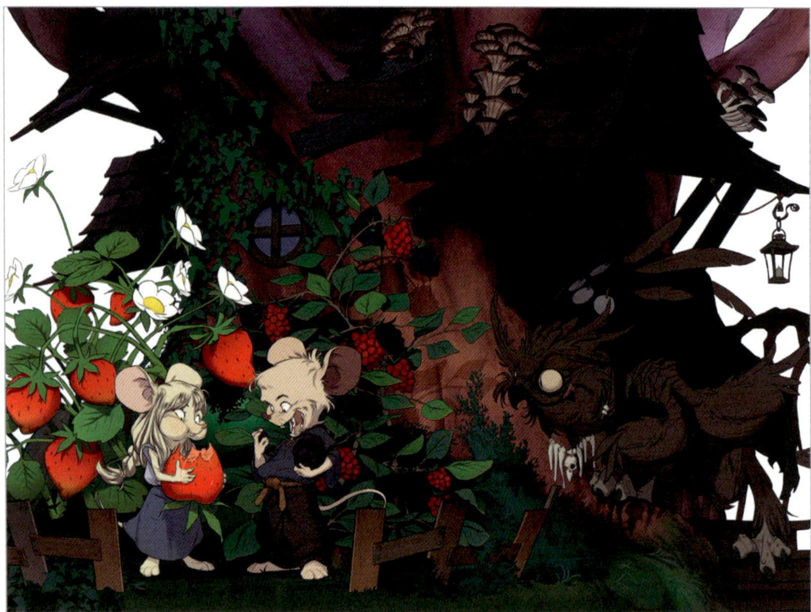

▲ Highlighting each element of the illustration with hard shadows

18 SECOND SHADOWS

I deepen the shadows with darker tones, which takes longer because it requires shading each element individually. It may seem like a monotonous process, but it makes the resulting image much more expressive and realistic. My goal is to give each element the importance it deserves, within the limits I have planned, as I want to preserve the harmony and structure of the composition. I delve into the shadows in the bushes, flowers, vines, roofs, and tiles – each element has a role to play in the composition, so the shadows help to show them clearly, without standing out too much compared to the characters. The shadows under the objects and characters are essential to situate them on the ground or other surfaces, giving them realism and a sense of weight.

19 LIGHT AND TEXTURES

I proceed to render the illustration, which usually consists of two things: adding light tones and adding texture or variety. I add some brighter tones to the roof to give it a warmer feeling, as if it's being touched by sunlight. I add varied textures and tones to the owl's plumage, studying my references to get the most out of the three brown tones I have chosen for the character. This creates some interesting shapes and features that emphasize the witch's pose and expression.

I add some highlights to the leaves and the children's hair, making them look vibrant and full of life. The mice's faces and clothes are stained with berry juice, showing their enthusiastic rush to eat. I add different textures to the fences, drawing lines that simulate wood grain and knots, and even some greenish areas as if the planks have grown mossy. These details all give the scene a higher level of finish and realism, offering the viewer a rich scene to explore.

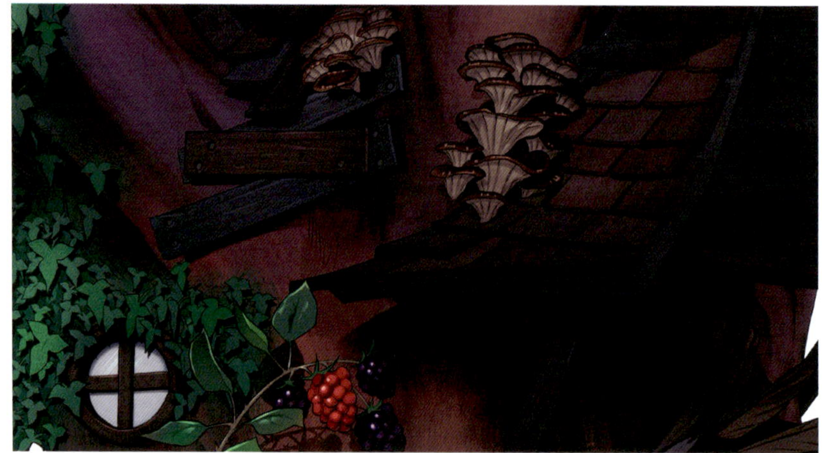

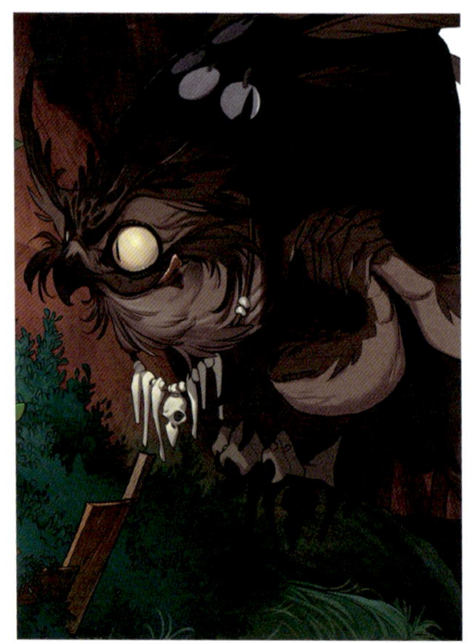

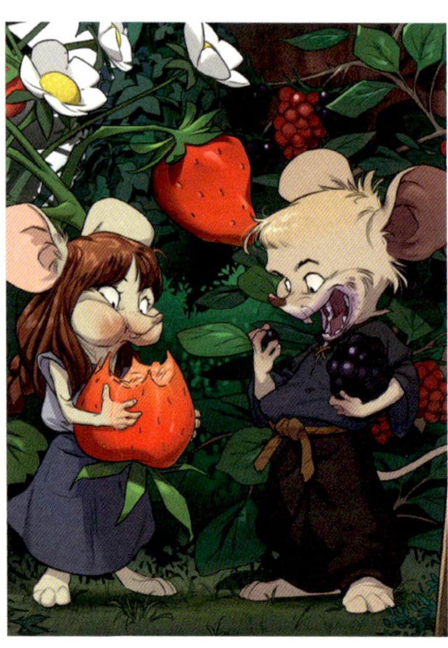

► Rendering brightness, tones, and textures

20 FINISHING TOUCHES

To finish, I apply a mixture of bluish tones for the sky and add some clouds to give the scene ambient depth. The sky is a darker blue at the top and lighter blue at the bottom, representing the atmosphere as it appears in reality. To finish off the owl witch and make her easier to read, I add some bluish highlights to her shawl and feathers, glossy highlights on her eye and beak, and some shiny drool. I use a touch of light blue to separate her from the tree and doorway behind her, creating more depth and ensuring that her outline is not lost in the shadows. Finally, some fallen berries on the ground show the children's oblivious haste to eat.

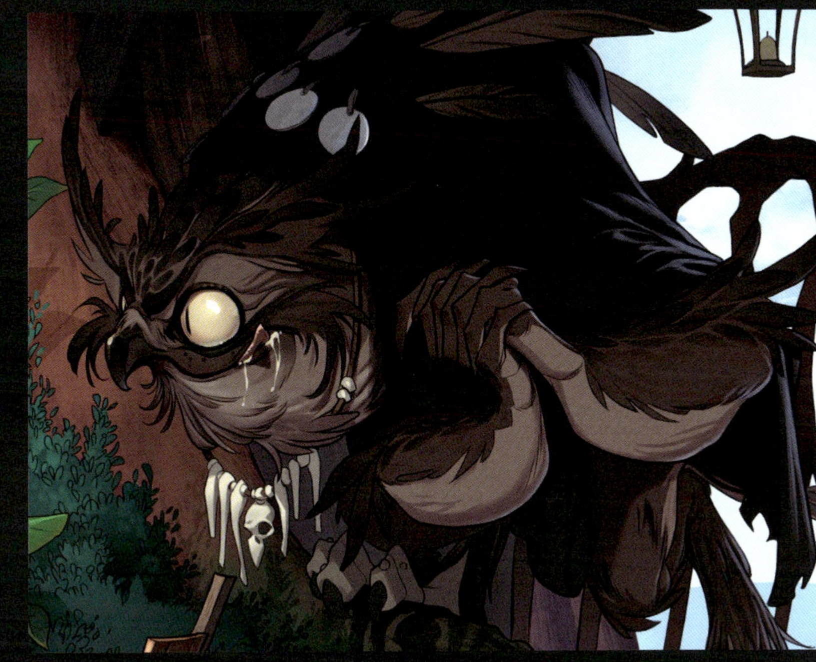

▶ **Rendering the last few details**

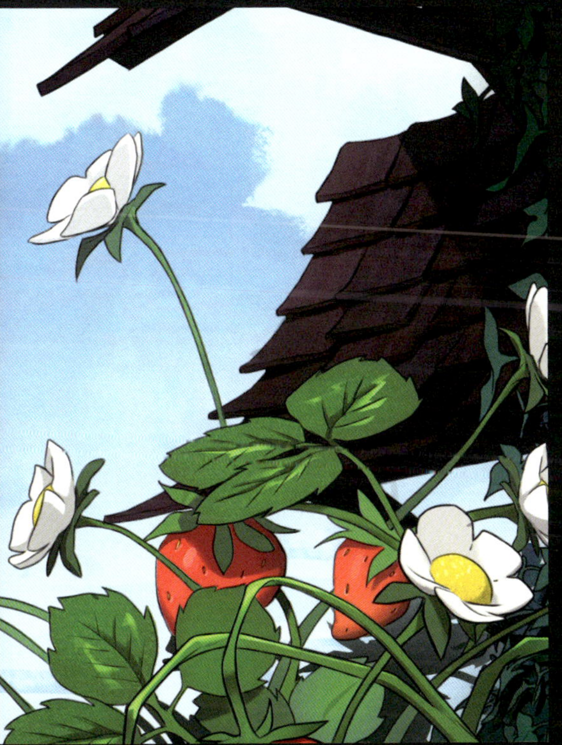

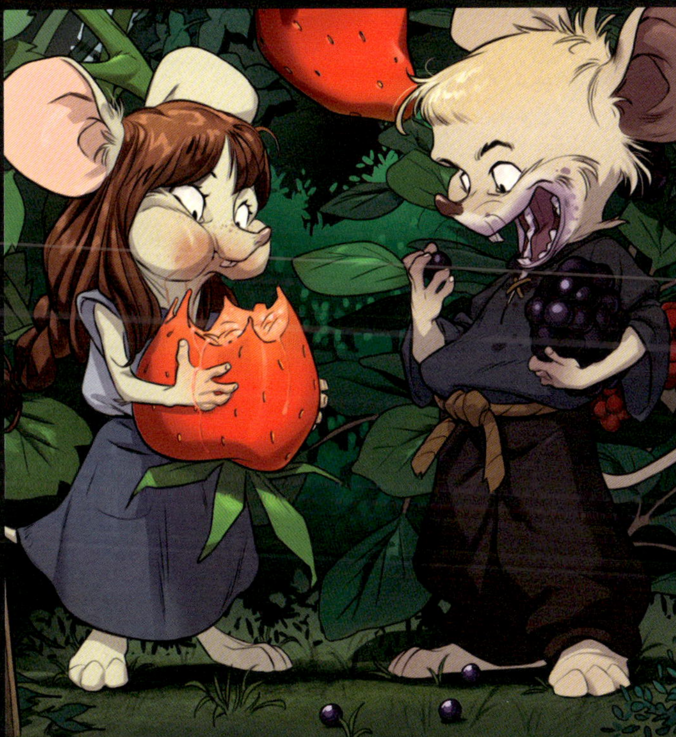

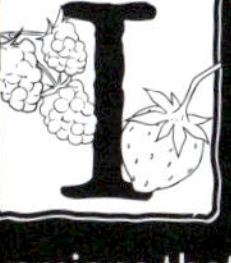

Illustrating a version of a well-known tale such as *Hansel and Gretel* is quite a challenge. Many of the ideas I had along the way ended up being scrapped, but that allowed me to experiment with other versions that were better for the story. If you have ever struggled with a project, I hope you can identify with this, and I encourage you to always look for new ideas and embrace a work process that evolves in the face of obstacles. In my final version, I have preserved the fantasy woodland theme and the classic scenario of the two children outside the witch's house – except the witch is now a cunning owl, Hansel and Gretel are two hungry mice, and the gingerbread house is an old tree with a tempting garden of delicious fruit!

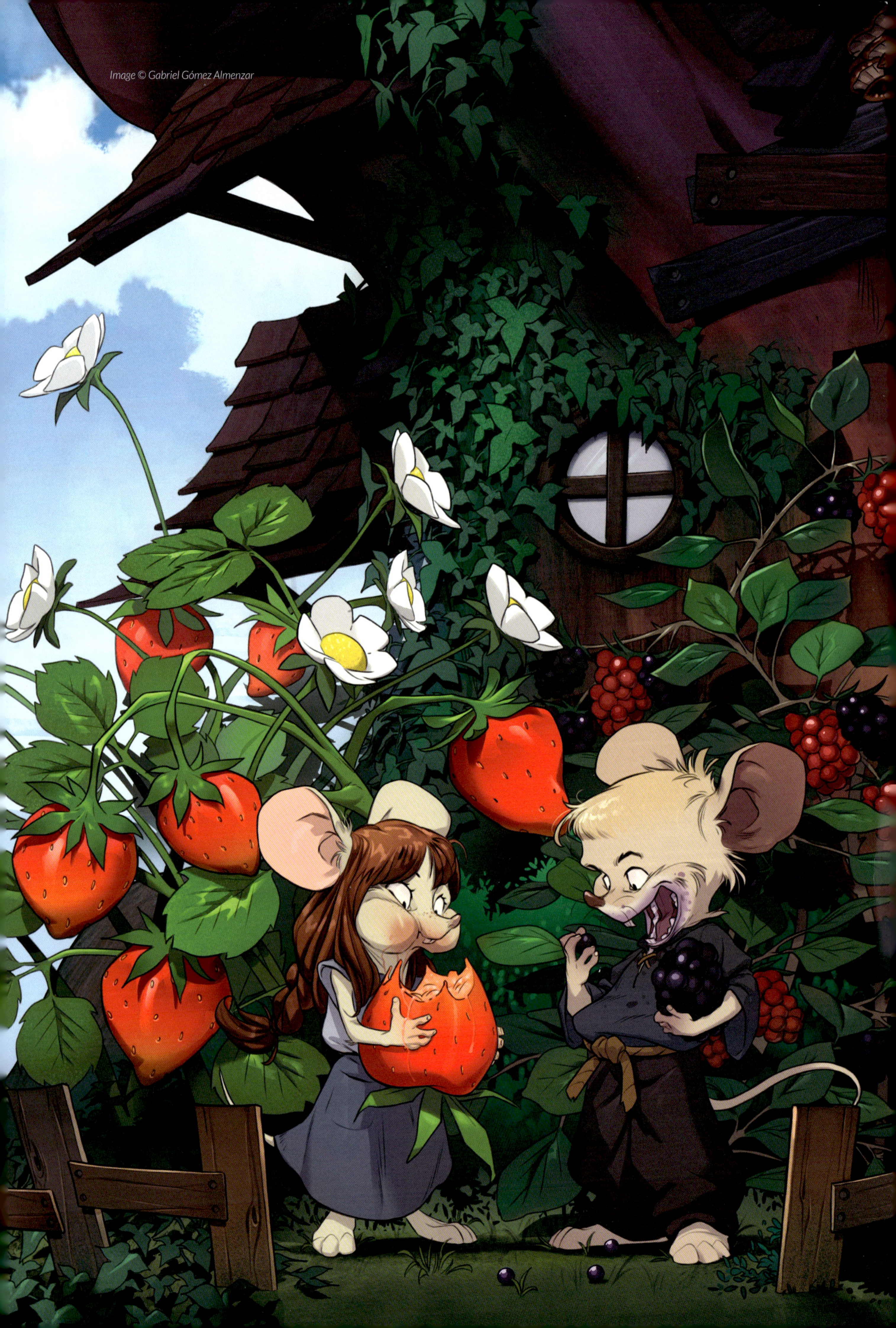

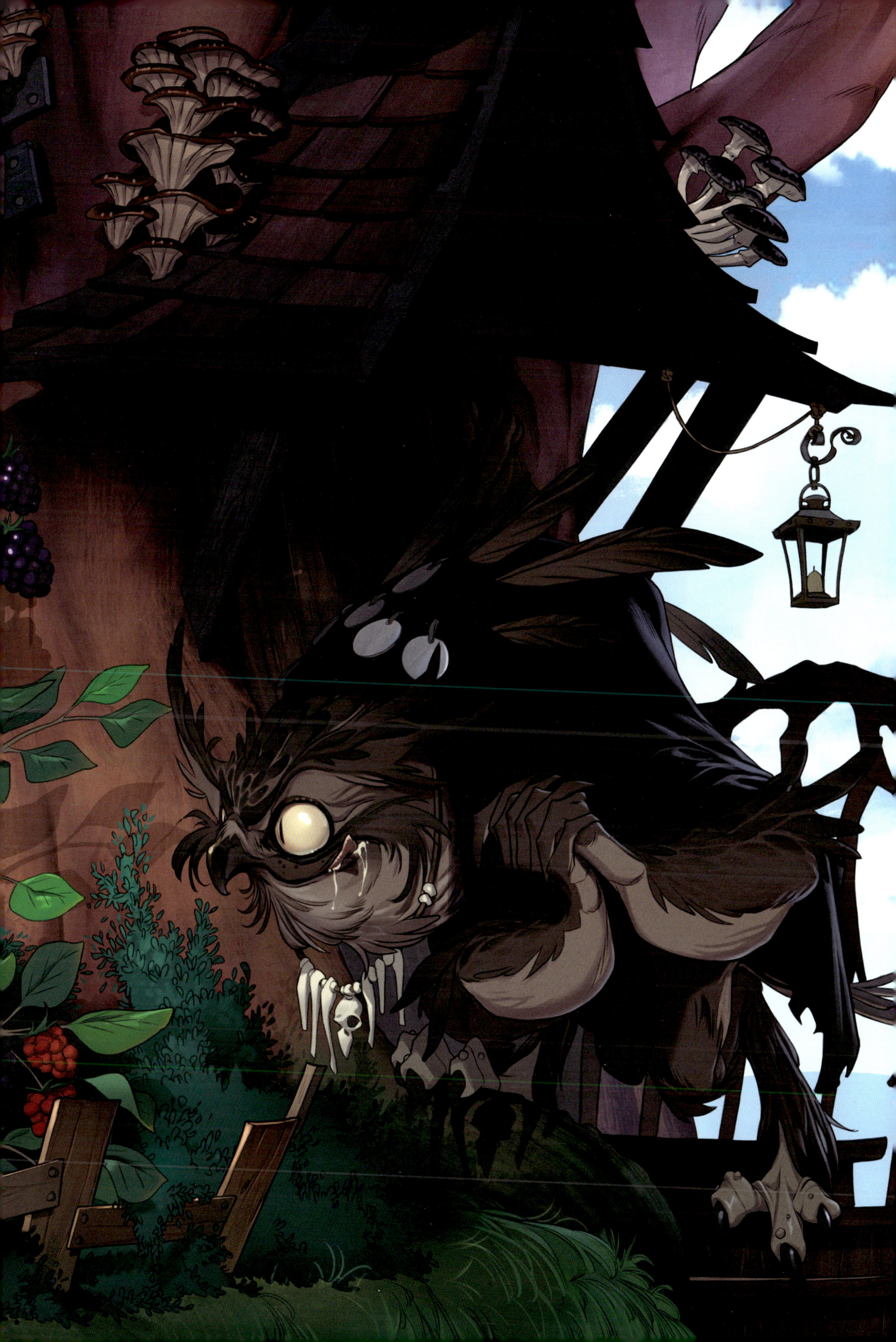

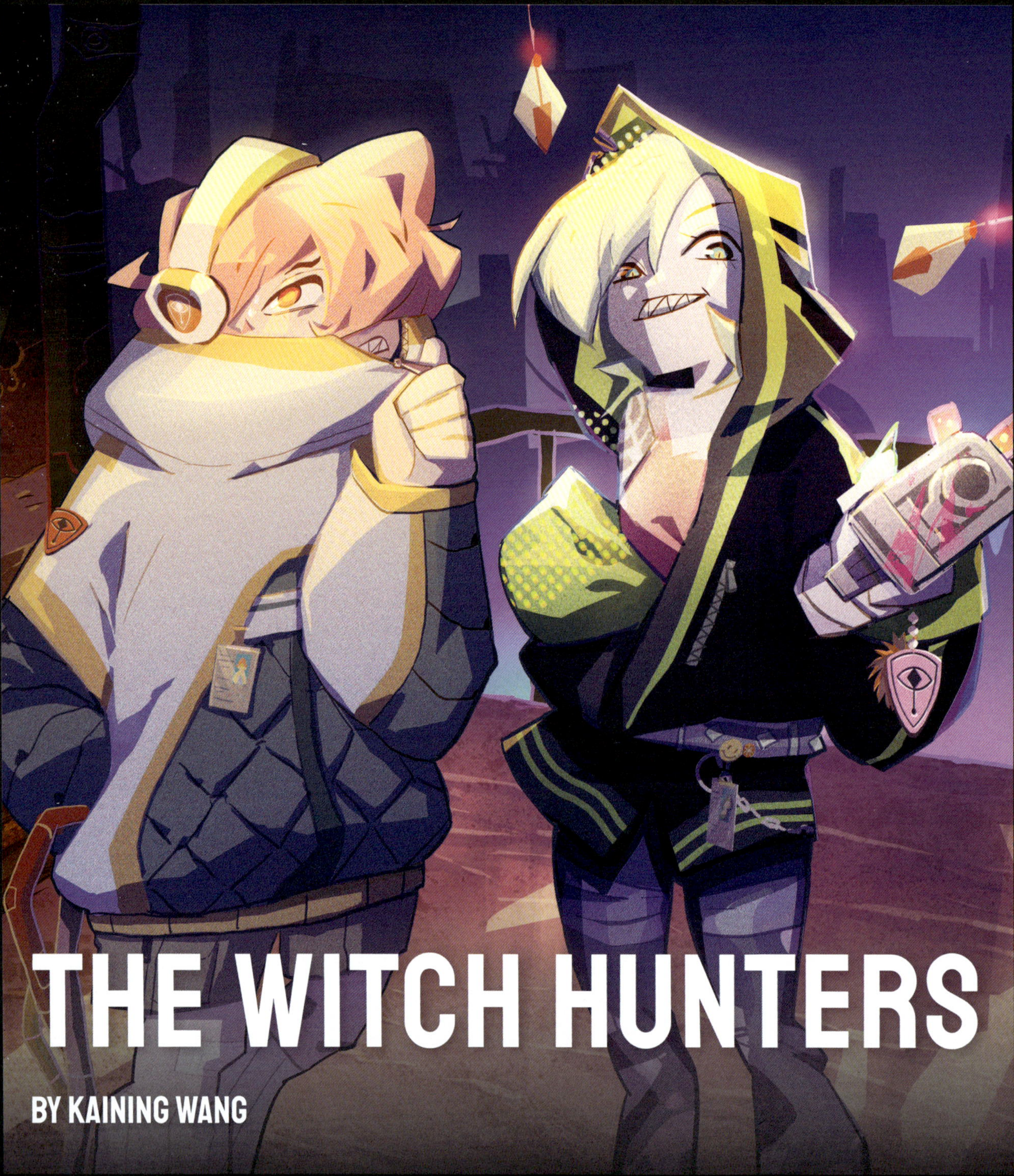

THE WITCH HUNTERS

BY KAINING WANG

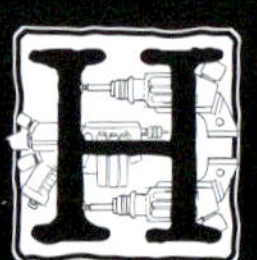

Hansel and Gretel is such an iconic, much-adapted fairy tale. The part of the story that leaves the biggest impression, for me, is when the captured children push the witch into the fire and run away. In many fairy tales, it seems that the protagonists are very innocent, getting themselves into all sorts of trouble involuntarily, and miraculously escaping at the end with their bravery and intelligence. In my version of *Hansel and Gretel*, I want to switch things up by making the children the wicked, mischievous ones – not so innocent at all! This tutorial will explore how to convey the unique personalities of these siblings and how to tell their story through character design, color, and lighting.

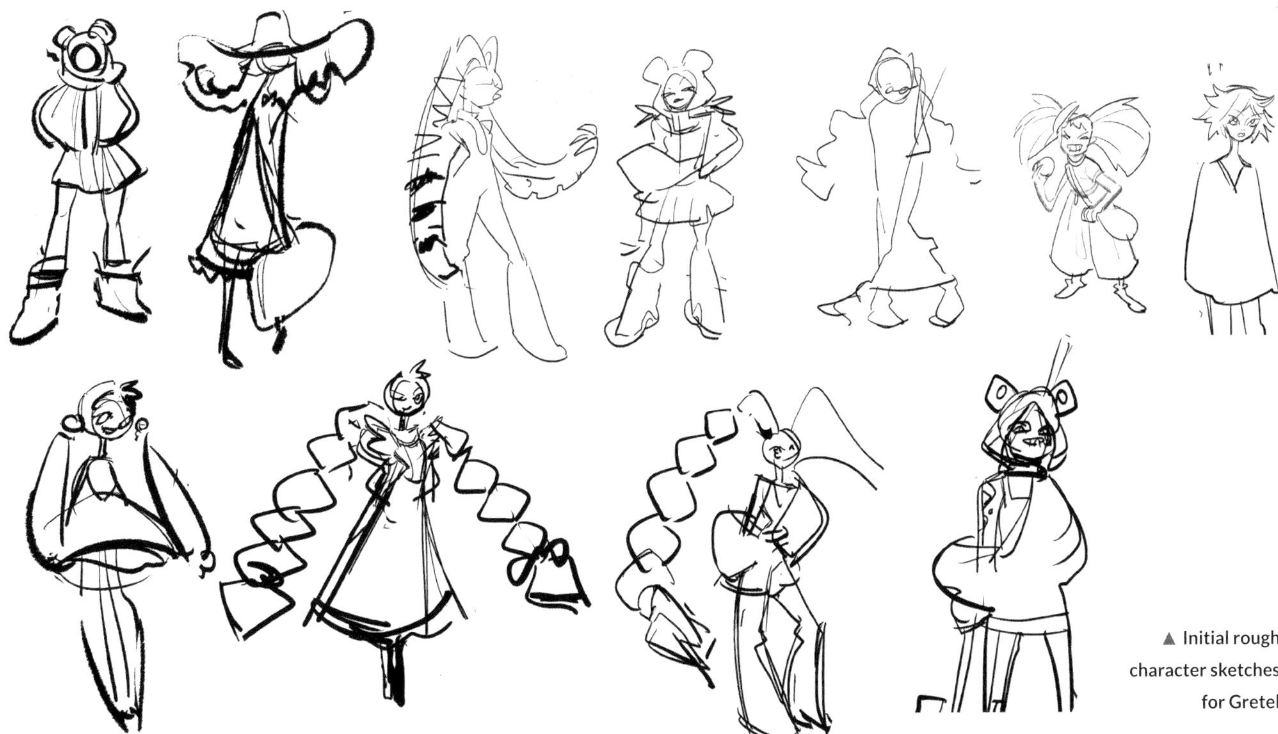

▲ Initial rough character sketches for Gretel

01 EARLY GRETEL SKETCHES

It is really important to stay loose when you are exploring different possibilities at first. I like to sketch very loosely until I am certain about the idea I want to portray. In these first explorations, I try to convey gesture, flow, and silhouette without thinking about details, pushing all kinds of possibilities for the characters in different directions. For my version of the story, I want to avoid a medieval or fantasy setting. Instead, I want to try something modern or even futuristic, with two streetwise kids who hunt and fight witches. I explore a wide range of personalities for Gretel; as the sibling who kills the witch in the original tale, it makes sense if she is the more confident child. She could pretend to be shy or innocent, with a dark undertone, or she could just be overtly mischievous. She could dress up as a maid to play along with the witch, or just dress as a stray kid on the street. Many illustrations of the story present Gretel with braided hair, which I push to extreme proportions here.

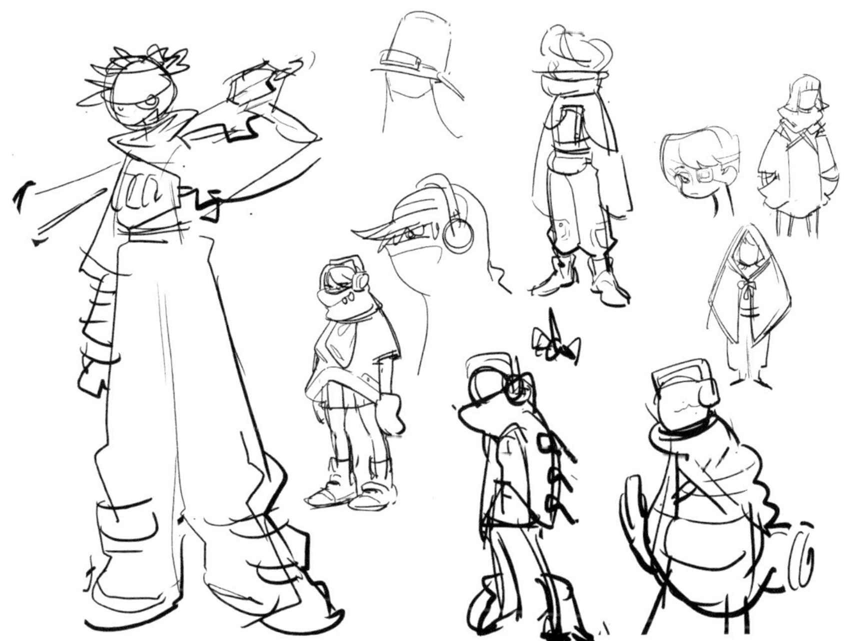

02 EARLY HANSEL SKETCHES

After exploring Gretel's character, I want to do the same for Hansel. Even though the two characters are not so innocent in my adaptation, I still want to avoid giving them personalities that are too similar. In this case, I try to contrast Hansel's personality with Gretel's – he is quite timid and unaggressive. This needs to be shown through his posture, shape language, silhouette, and color palette – but as this is such an early stage, I focus on silhouette and posture first. I give him a smooth shape that is more rounded than Gretel's, even slightly hunched or slumped.

◄ Initial rough character sketches for Hansel

03 CHARACTER CONTRASTS

When you are designing a duo, it's important to put the characters side by side early in the process. It allows you to tweak, shrink, or exaggerate their silhouettes and their shape languages to show contrast. In character design, it is crucial to make silhouettes as concise and distinctive as possible. Sometimes exaggerating certain parts is helpful to create a character's unique characteristics. In this case, Gretel is more outgoing than Hansel, so I try exaggerating her hair. Perhaps those cute, classic braids could become her hidden weapons, with blades or metal attachments. These changes indicate her bolder personality, in contrast with Hansel, who is more shy and subtle. Perhaps he doesn't attack people directly, instead using his weapons to absorb energy from his target.

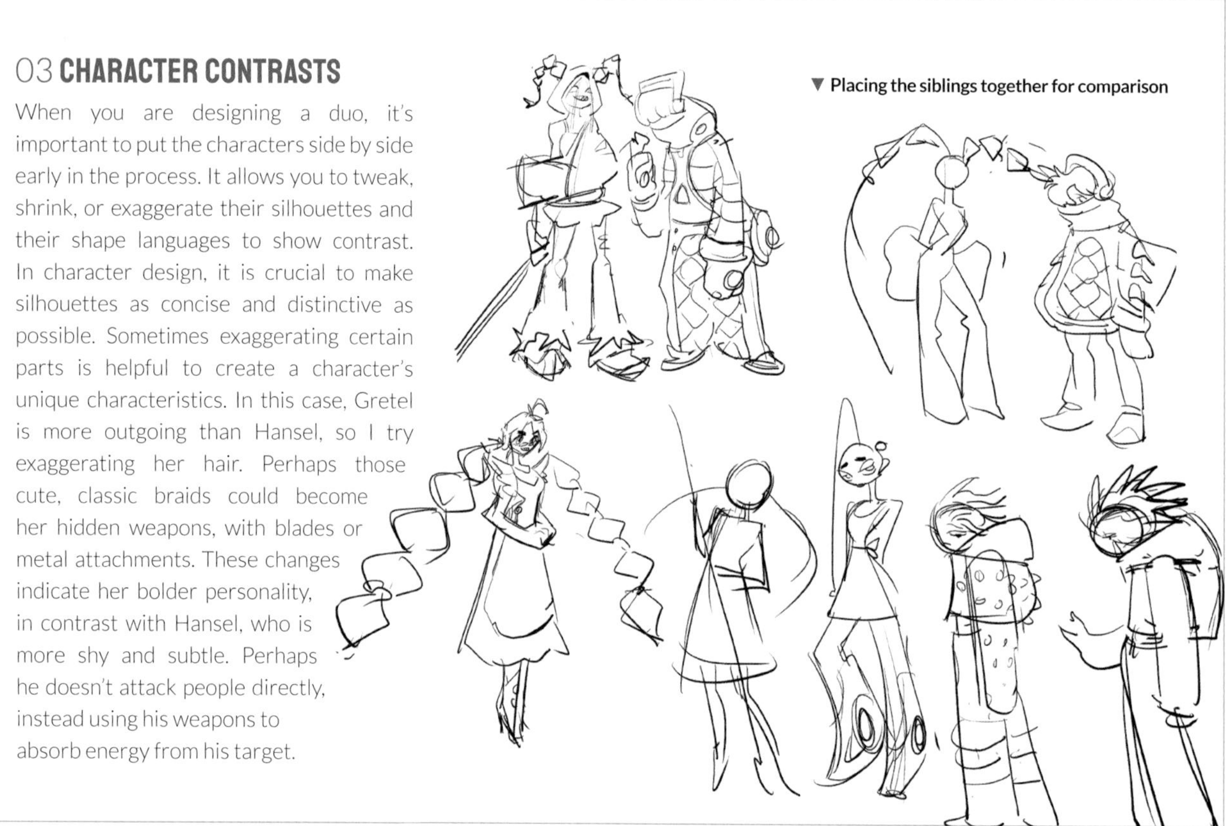

▼ Placing the siblings together for comparison

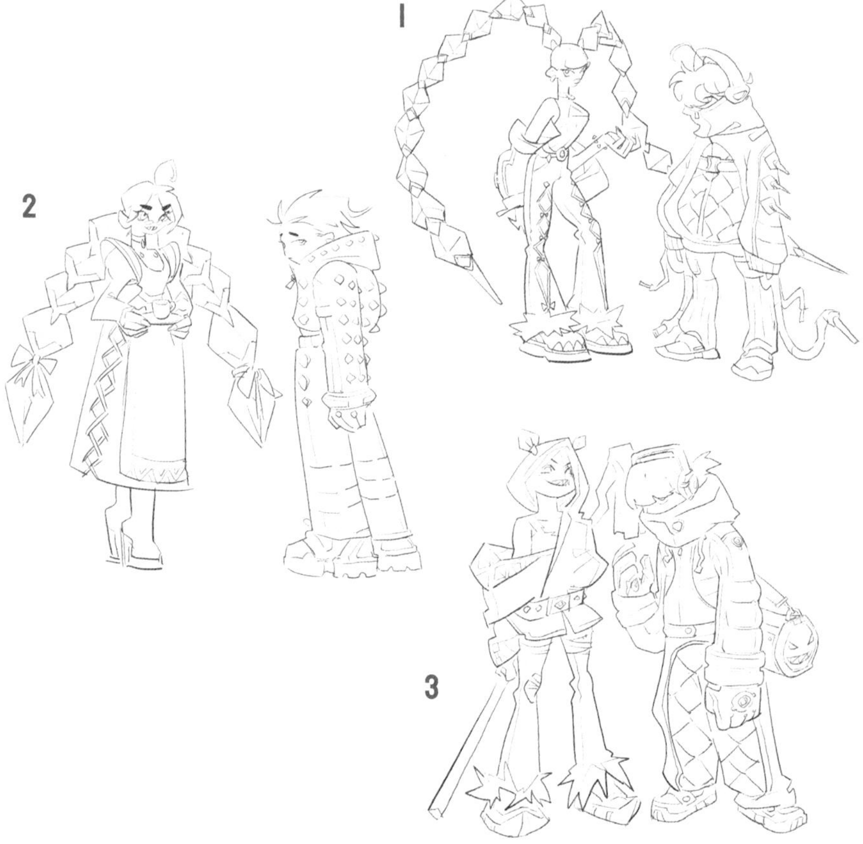

04 DUO DESIGNS

I continue to develop and clean up my paired sketches, trying to define the details and characters a little more. In my adaptation, both Hansel and Gretel are witch hunters in a futuristic city. In the backstory in my mind, they grew up as stray kids, adopted by two mysterious figures, known as "Father" and "Mother," who trained them in their witch-hunting profession. The confrontation between the siblings and the witch is their final test before becoming official hunters.

To emphasize the futuristic, urban setting, Hansel and Gretel's outfits are heavily inspired by Japanese street fashion. Baggy layers, padded shapes, and bold patterns are in vogue in this setting. Their weapons are half-hidden inside their clothes and accessories, to catch their targets unawares. Little do the witches know that the predators will soon become the prey!

◀ Developing the sketches and accessories

05 **FIRST OPTION**

I now have three strong potential versions for the characters, which I weigh up in more detail to compare their pros and cons. Let's start with this example, with the exaggerated braids. As I mentioned in step 03, my goal was to differentiate the siblings by opening up Gretel's gesture and silhouette while closing up Hansel's. Gretel's pose shows her outgoing personality, while the edginess of her ponytails indicates her aggressiveness. Her shape language is heavily based around diamonds – a sharp, dynamic shape. Her ponytail consists of diamond-shaped weapon segments; her clothes and even the negative spaces around her are diamond-shaped.

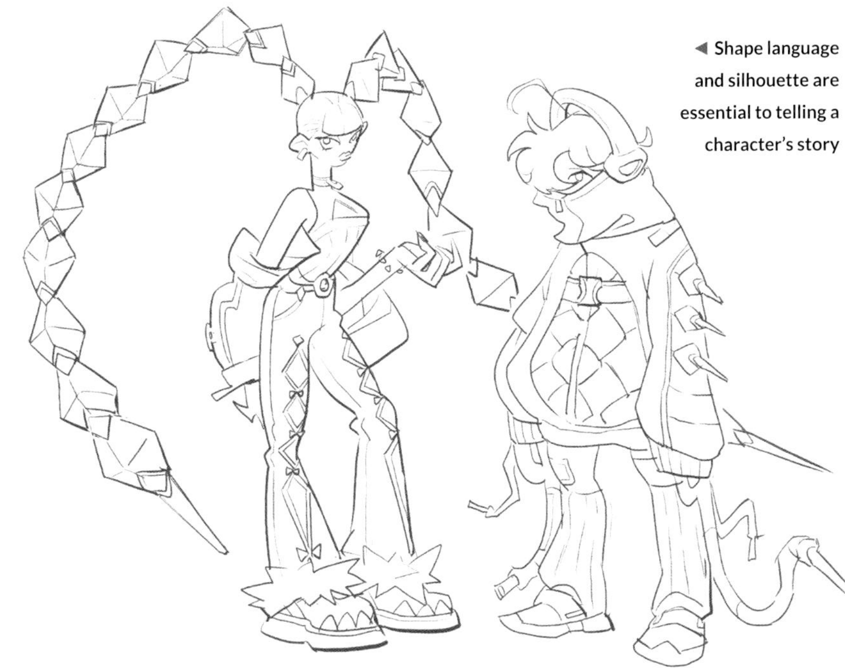

◀ **Shape language and silhouette are essential to telling a character's story**

It is essential to keep a character's shape language consistent so that their personality comes through clearly. In contrast to Gretel, Hansel is very hunched, with a big curve gesture going throughout his silhouette. His face is half covered to emphasize his shy personality. Electric wires come out of his sleeves like snakes, suggesting that he could ambush people when they put their guards down. Perhaps that is how he tricks the witch who captures him – putting wires through the bars of the cage, fooling her into believing that he is still too skinny to eat.

06 **SECOND OPTION**

This ideation is similar to the previous one, but here I imagine the siblings playing along with the witch, staying in her home and feigning innocence. Gretel would dress as a maid to do cleaning for the witch in exchange for food and shelter. Her ponytails are still the same – I imagine they would disassemble into small pieces when it is time to attack – but her long dress is more quaint and traditional, reminiscent of classic illustrations of the story. It is harder to tell her intentions or personality as a character, so her facial expression plays a bigger part – her cunning eyes and smile show the real intent behind her cute outfit.

Hansel's design here is more inspired by a puffer fish: a round creature that looks small until it's in danger, when it becomes large and threatening. I imagine that he could expand his thorny suit when he encounters danger, in order to protect himself and poison his attackers. The resulting design is still more reserved than Gretel, but he has lost some roundness.

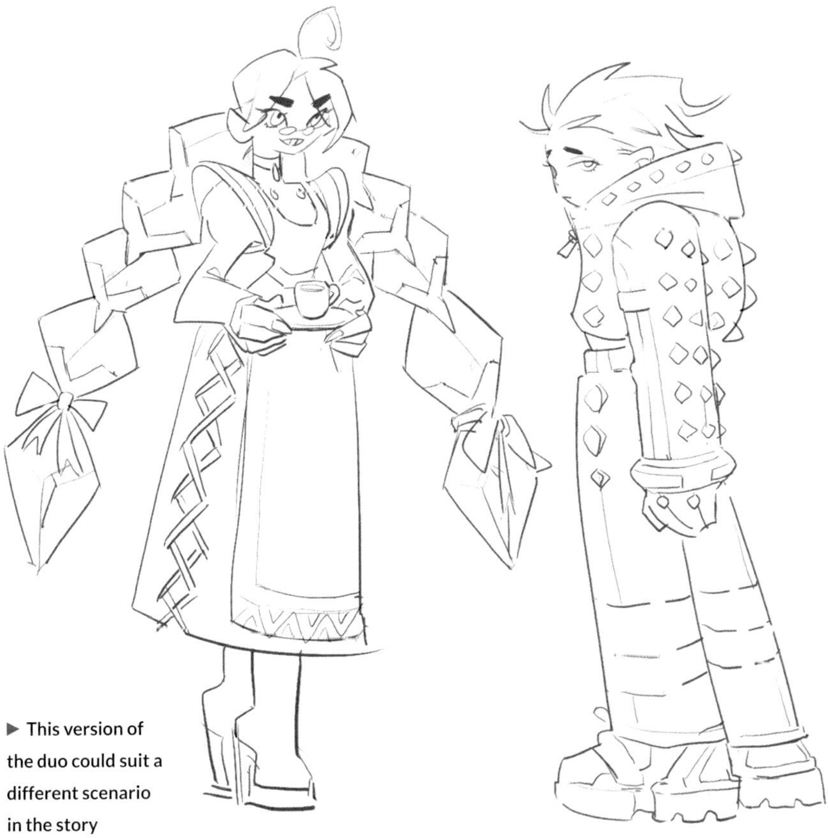

▶ **This version of the duo could suit a different scenario in the story**

07 THIRD OPTION

This version emphasizes the "stray kids" side of the characters, with layered clothes and oversized hoods that give them a more practical appearance. Their overall look is more subtle – for example, Gretel's huge pigtails have been removed in favor of a simpler, scrappier look. Continuing the cleaning idea from the previous sketch, she carries a mop on her back.

It is always fun to play with ratios between different elements and see what results you can get. In this, the proportion of "normal" to "sci-fi" elements is higher than in other examples, which makes the characters seem a little more young and relatable. Perhaps Gretel's two diamond-shaped accessories could detach from her hood, being secret laser weapons, and Hansel could use his sucker-like gloves to drain power from the witch. These are visually subtle compared to previous ideas, but they support the idea of these characters being part of a covert operation.

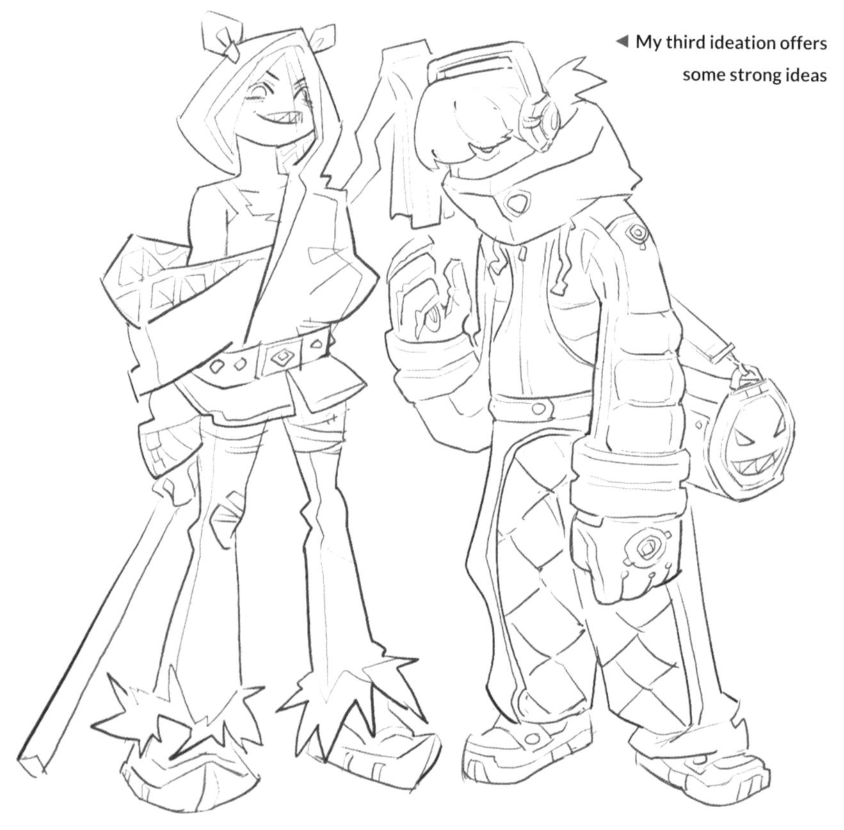

◀ My third ideation offers some strong ideas

08 CHARACTER CLOSEUPS

I decide to progress with Hansel from step 05 and Gretel from step 07. These two options pair well together: the most tough, practical Gretel with the most shy, rounded Hansel. I take some time to develop the characters' facial features, as those are where the viewer will pay the most attention. I am already satisfied with Gretel's facial expression, so I mostly play around with her hair. For Hansel, I explore different accessories that fit his timid personality. A hat would help to make him look young and shy, but I like the headphones most. He might be very sensitive to noise from his busy urban surroundings, which is why he covers his ears, and could partly be the reason for his reserved, nervous personality.

▼ Sketching character heads in more detail

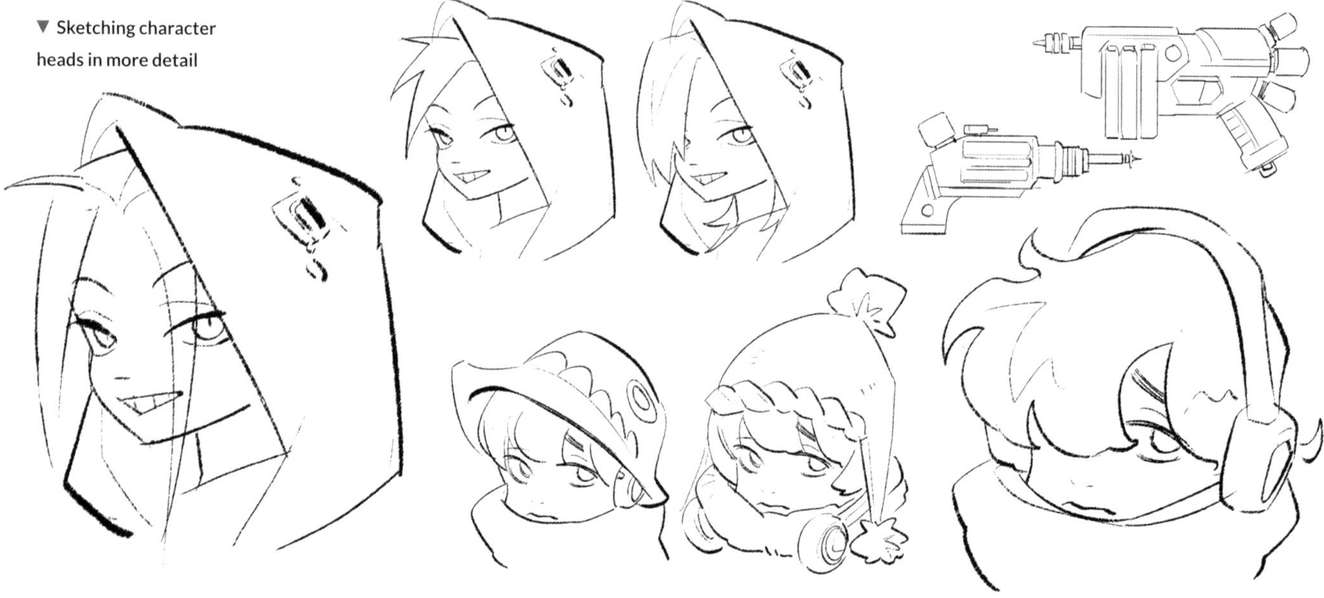

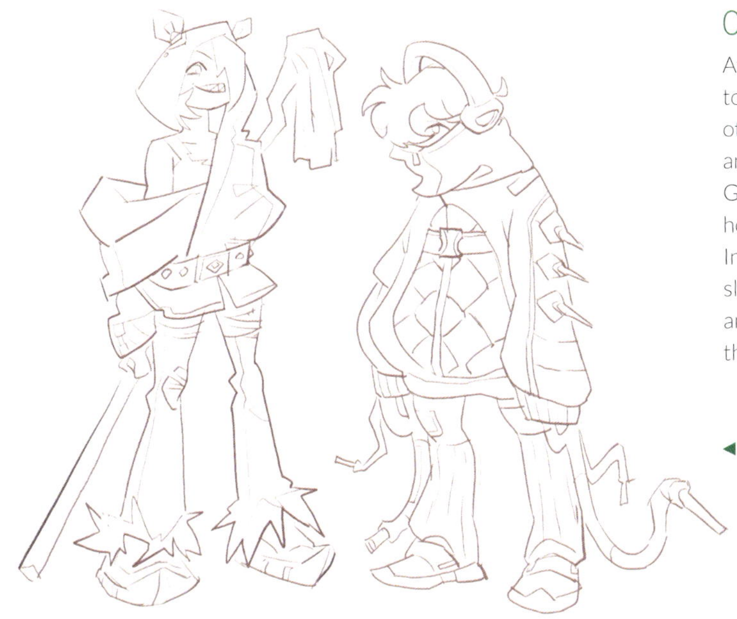

09 FINAL CHARACTER DESIGNS

After finishing those extra detail explorations, I apply them to my final character designs, making two cleaner sketches of the duo. I now have a good base to start planning color, and later to create a final scene focused on these designs. Gretel looks outgoing and aggressive, with her oversized hoodie and shoes giving her a practical, almost sporty look. In comparison, Hansel hides inside the deep neck and baggy sleeves of his clothes, his face barely visible under his hair and headphones. They both have an edge of danger, but their differing personalities are immediately clear.

◀ Revising details to make a final version of the characters

10 COLOR VARIATIONS

Next I test different color variations for the characters. It is always good to try different options and set up rules for each character. What do you want the colors to convey? What does the character represent? Value structure is very important here. I go back and forth between viewing my palettes in color and in grayscale, to make sure the focal points are emphasized with enough contrast. Gretel's focal point is her head and face, where her expression and hood are located. Her palette is darker, with bright accents creating higher contrast; the ratio of darks, midtones, and lights is something like 7:2:1. This makes her look bold and eye-catching, which suits her personality.

Hansel is the opposite: lighter and more pastel-based, giving him a softer look that emphasizes his sister as the leader. After comparing both color palettes, I choose the second. The bright green accent on Gretel's clothing adds a futuristic pop of brightness, and distinguishes her from the softer colors of Hansel's design.

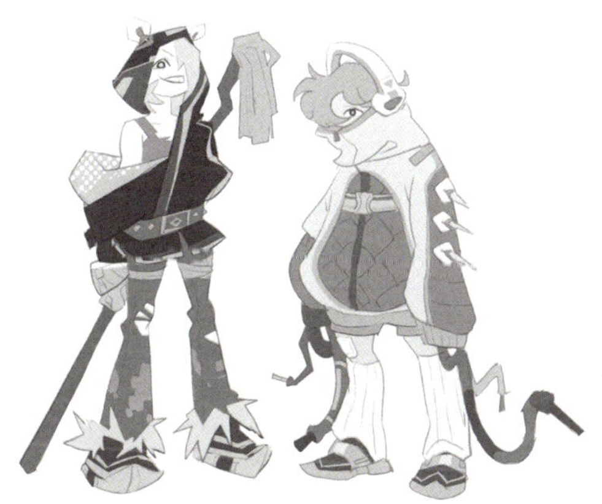

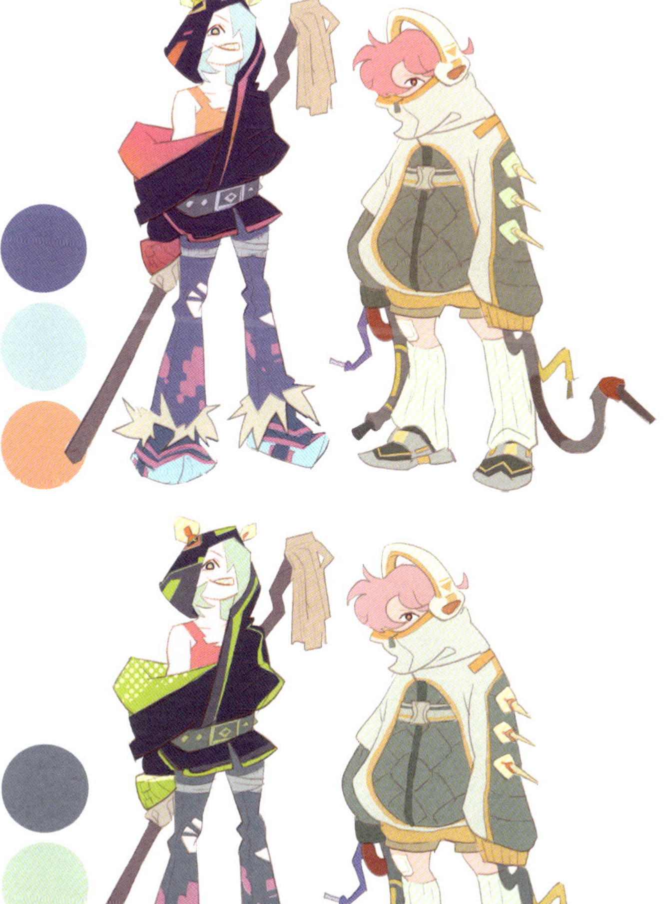

▲ Comparing color variations and checking them in grayscale

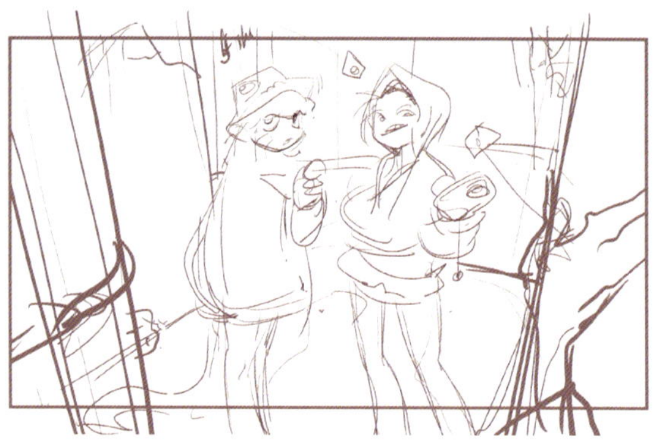

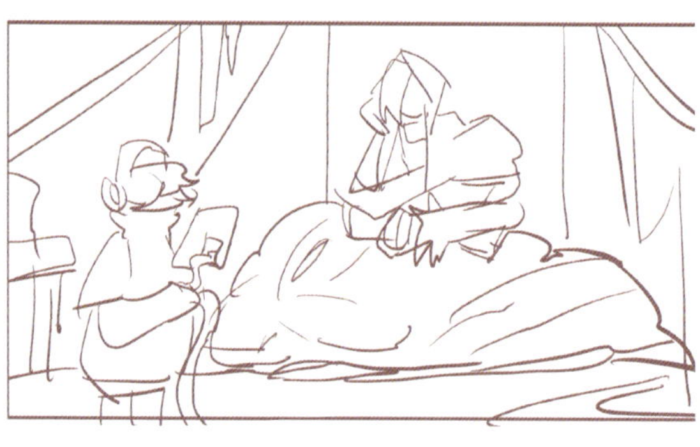

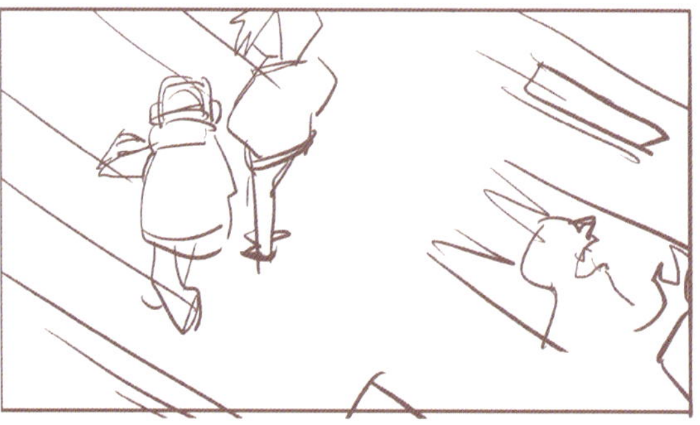

▲ Sketching different options for a full scene

11 CHOOSING A SCENE

I come up with three different scenes that could represent my story. In the first, the armed siblings confront the witch on her doorstep, in a role reversal of the original tale. The second option takes place after the action, with Gretel casually sitting on the witch's dead body while talking to Hansel. The third shows Hansel and Gretel walking away from the witch's house, which is burning down in the distance. I favor the first option, as it captures a surprising encounter for the witch as well as the audience, with two kids who were once prey now becoming the predators.

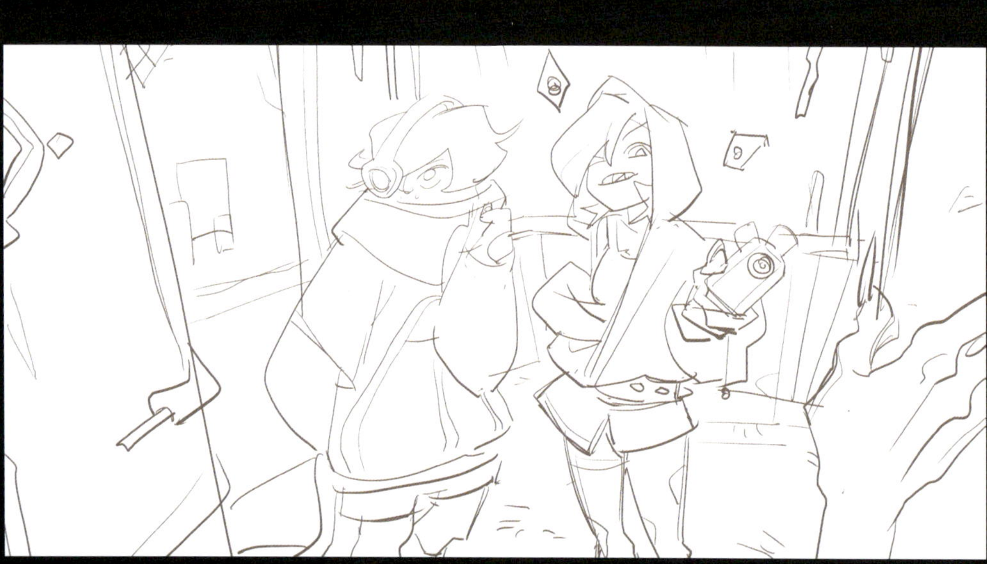

◀ Detailed linework for the final scene

12 SKETCHING THE SCENE

Now I create a cleaner drawing that figures out the details of the linework. I like to "think" with lines, but you can start the illustration however you are most comfortable; some people prefer to start with a black-and-white value sketch or to jump straight into rough colors to work out the lighting. At this stage, I try to figure out exactly what kind of environment the characters are in. I am heavily inspired by Tatsuyuki Tanaka's artwork and I really want to suggest that kind of dirty, highly industrialized setting, without adding too much distracting detail. I also consider what poses the characters should have in this shot. The viewer is seeing from the witch's point of view, so the siblings need to make a surprising, confrontational impression.

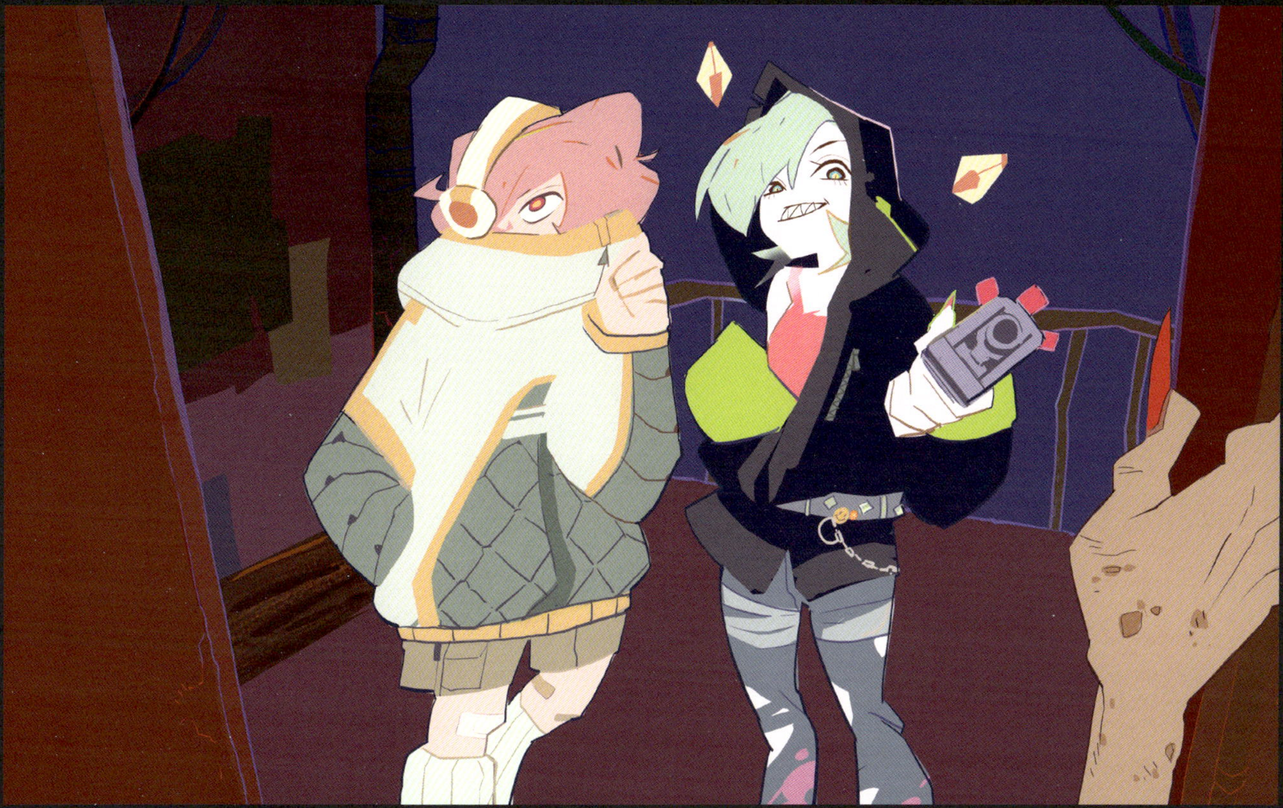

▲ Planning out the scene's base colors

13 BASE COLORS

Next, I apply a base of flat colors. I want the final illustration to have a lively, slightly grungy style that preserves a degree of looseness. Instead of over-rendering the painting, I will color some of the lines to blend them in a little more, and lighten the lines within the characters' silhouettes. I add pipes and wires to the architecture in order to frame the characters and give a run-down industrial feel to the location. A purple background will help create the atmosphere of a futuristic city at night, while the foreground colors become gradually warmer to show the light shining from the witch's open doorway. The witch is only shown as a hand, but the viewer will know it's her! You don't always have to squeeze every single character into one scene – sometimes just a small part of a character is enough to tell a story and show their role in the scene.

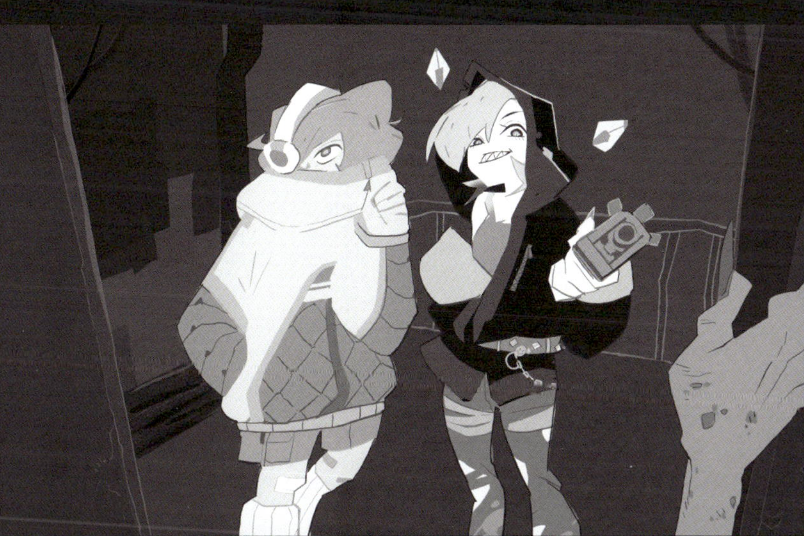

▲ Checking my flat colors in grayscale before rendering

14 GRAYSCALE CHECK

As I did with the character palettes in step 10, I frequently check the illustration in grayscale as it progresses. Here you can clearly see how Gretel is the most high-contrast area of the scene. As the main threat and the leader of the two siblings, she commands the most attention. Hansel's values are much lighter, but his overall lower contrast makes him stand out less than his sister. The siblings contrast well with the night sky behind them. The values of the witch's hand are bright enough to stand out against the door frame, but not as bright as the other characters, so the viewer arrives there last as they piece together the narrative.

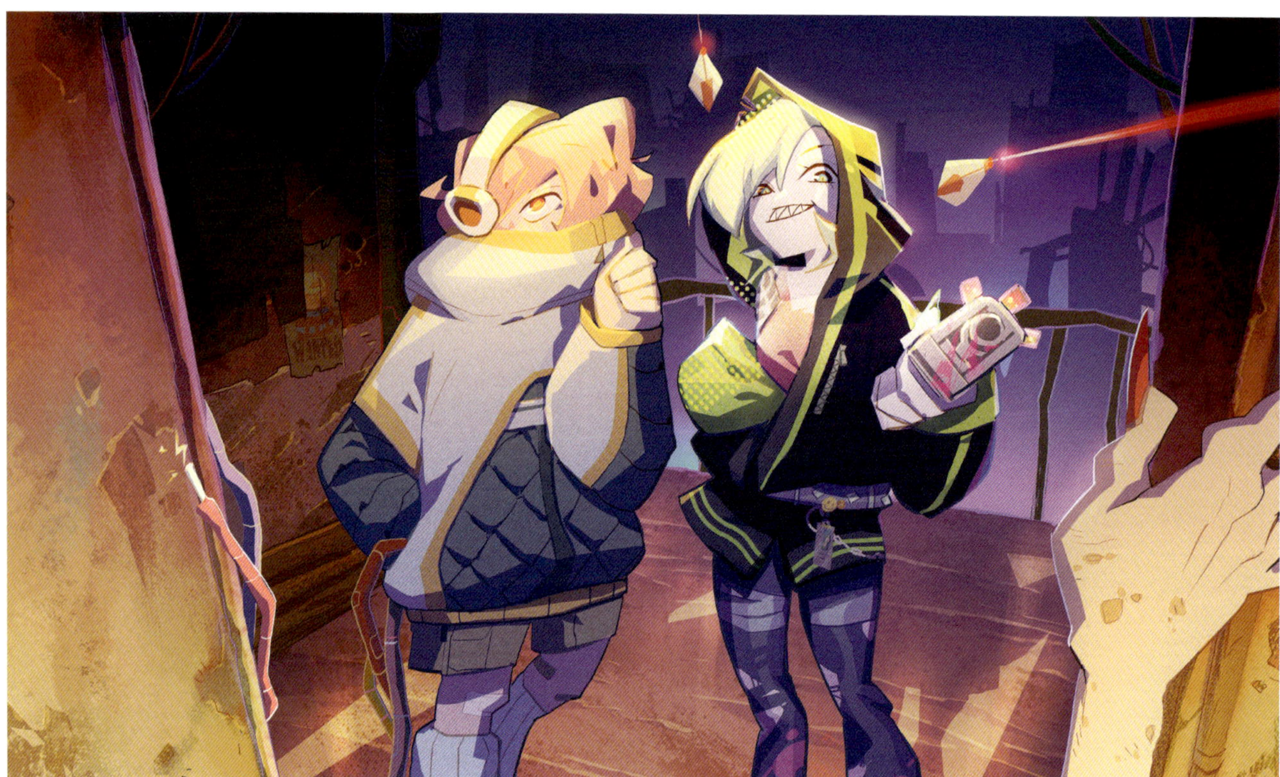

▲ Building up the lighting, details, and textures

15 LIGHTING AND TEXTURES

I develop the scene with lighting, textures, and details. The building's paintwork is rough and cracked, with more grit and texture focused on those areas. The characters have less texture to help them stand out from their environment, giving them a cleaner look as if they are in a sci-fi animation. Gretel's laser weapons are detached from her hood and directed through the doorway, directly past the witch's (and the viewer's) head in a menacing fashion. Hansel is more nervous and reserved, peeking out through his hair while his cable weapons creep up the doorframe with a life of their own. The "Wanted" poster on the wall outside hints that a witch is at large in the area – though she probably won't be for much longer!

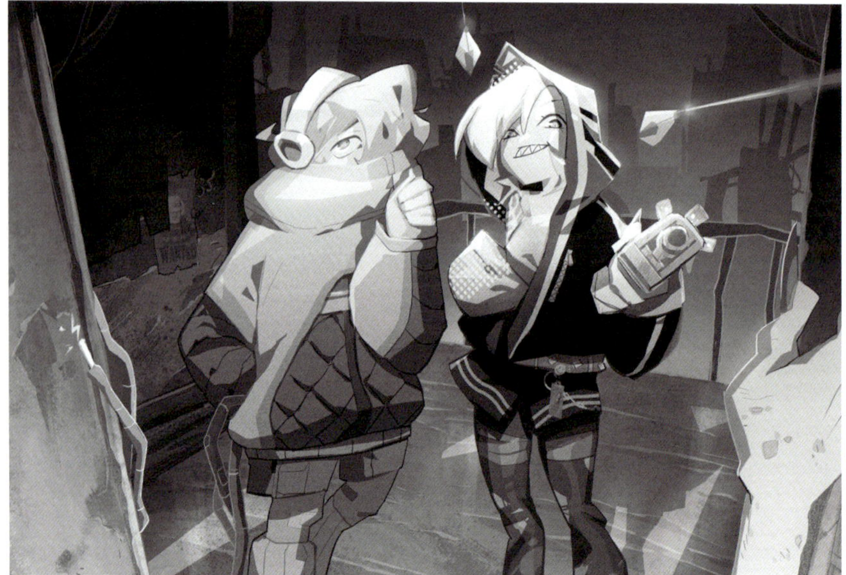

▲ Checking the value structure again as the lighting develops

16 BACKGROUND VALUE CHECK

Now that the scene's lighting is more complex and developed, I need to check that the values still hold up. I view the image in grayscale again to confirm that the structure reads well, which it does. The background is lighter now, with more value detail and layers of buildings creating depth, but that does not distract from the characters in the foreground. Hansel and Gretel stand out clearly from their surroundings, with the extra glow from the doorway helping to boost them against the background. The far left wall is a lighter value than before, but this emphasizes the warm light of the witch's home, and helps to focus the viewer in this immediate foreground area as the location for the narrative and action.

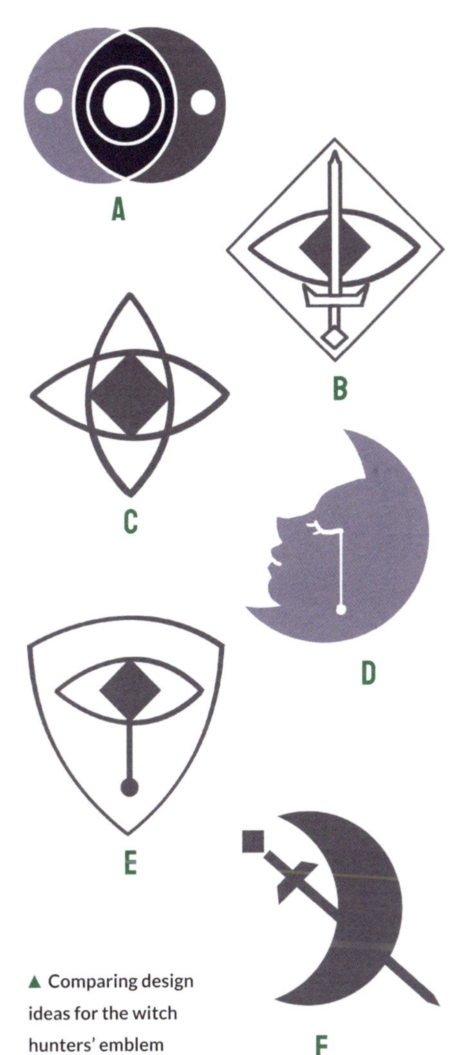

▲ Comparing design ideas for the witch hunters' emblem

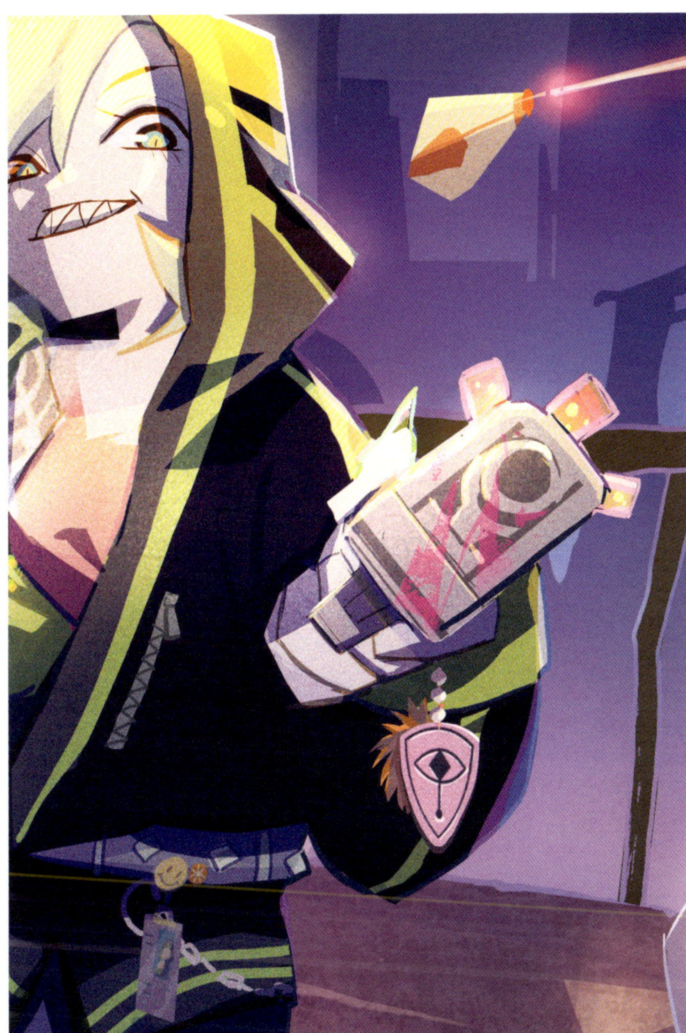

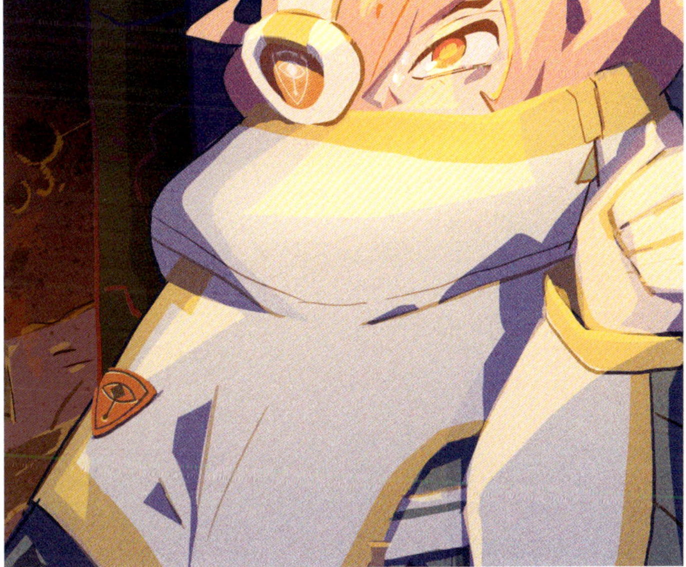

17 WITCH HUNTER BADGES

I can push the worldbuilding a little further by adding some smaller details to the scene. I'd like to include more references to the witch hunters' organization, such as a badge or logo, so I toy with a few different designs. These would not be shown very large in the illustration, so I discard some of the more complicated designs. Option E is perfect – still quite simple, but with a slightly menacing look. The combination of the shield and eye shapes suggests that these hunters view themselves as guardians keeping a watchful eye over the community.

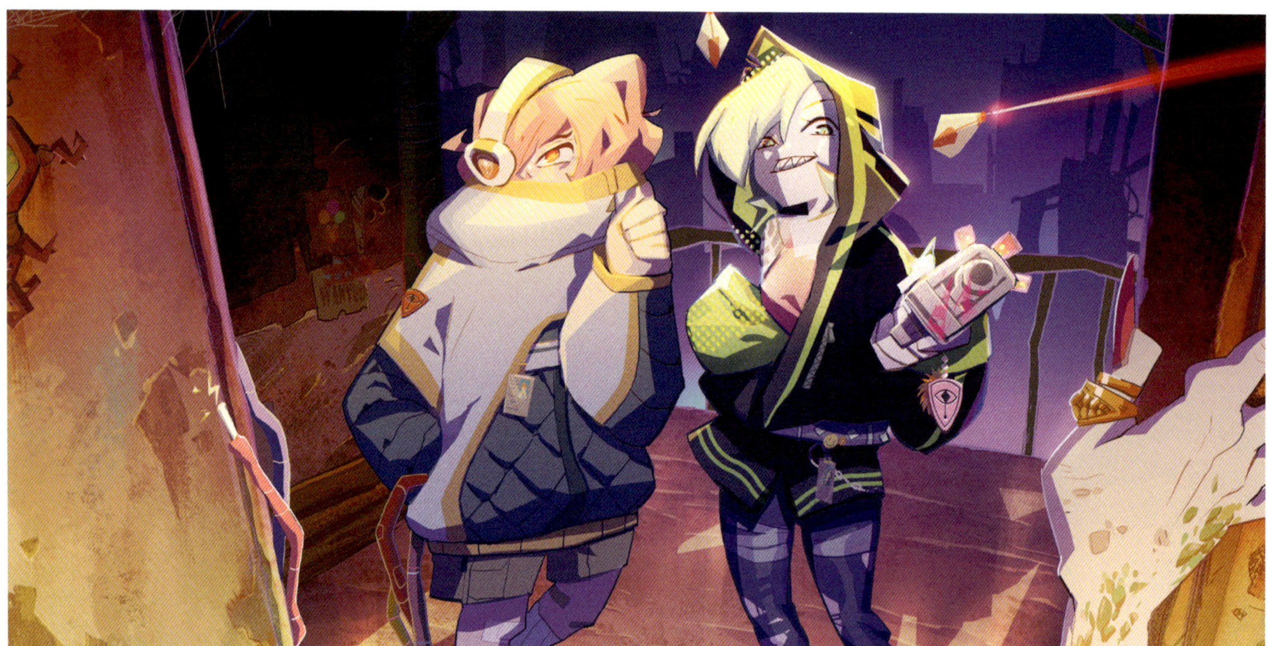

18 REVISING THE DETAILS

I continue the image, incorporating the designs from step 17. Hansel and Gretel now have matching badges among their clothes and accessories. Even if the viewer does not know exactly what that ominous eye means, they will still get the impression that these two characters belong to the same team or gang. In the foreground, I enhance the spookiness of the witch and her home by adding the wooden ornament, some cobwebs, and jewelry and greenish scales to her hand. On the wall outside, I add a poster promising free candy, as if the witch goes around surreptitiously removing or covering the "Wanted" notices.

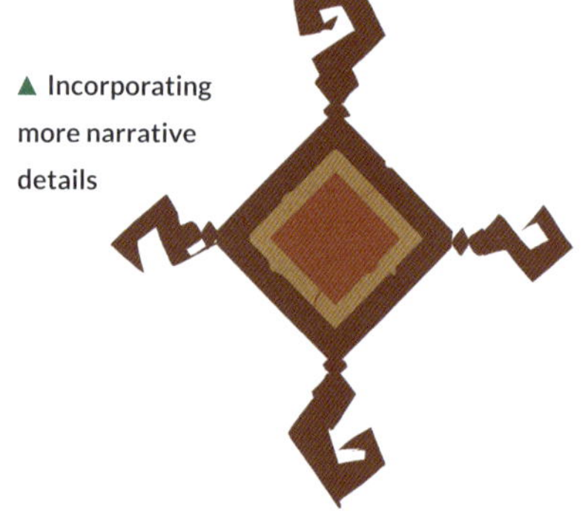

▲ Incorporating more narrative details

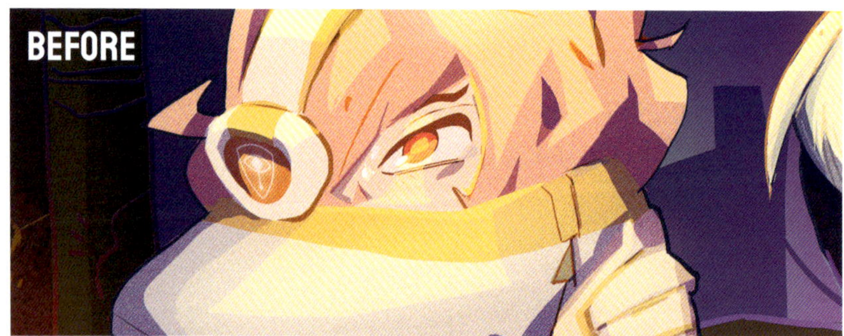

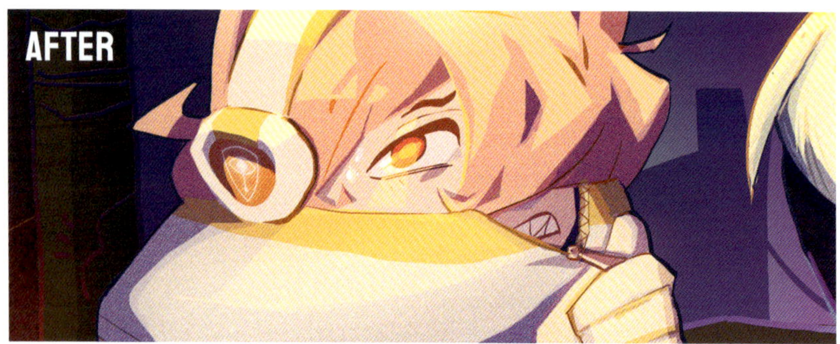

19 REVISING HANSEL'S FACE

Taking a step back from the image, I decide that Hansel could show a little more expression. Even though he is intentionally lower in contrast and gentler in personality than Gretel, I don't want the viewer to gloss over him completely. I adjust his existing pose so that he is tugging nervously on his jacket's zipper, showing a bit of his worried mouth. It's a minor change, but it adds a lot to his shy character and offers an extra bit of detail that holds the viewer's gaze on his face.

◀ Showing a little more of Hansel's face

20 FINISHING TOUCHES

Now all I have to do is polish up the strong foundations I have already placed. The shadows on Hansel's legs are not quite consistent, so I revise them to give the lighting more direction. I enlarge the poster on the wall to make "FREE CANDY" easier to read, making it slightly askew so it looks more naturally placed. I subtly add the witch hunters' logo to the "Wanted" sign, as if these warnings have been put up around the community by the hunters themselves.

The resulting image captures the feeling of a nighttime scene with unexpected intruders. The main light source is the witch's house, with a warm, cozy light contrasting with the cool darkness that Hansel and Gretel have come from. Instead of two starving children seeking shelter, the witch encounters two streetwise kids with weapons pointing at her. The futuristic, urban feel is supported by the painting style, which I have kept as graphic as possible, with clean, bold lighting and a few simple textures that fit with the stylization of the characters.

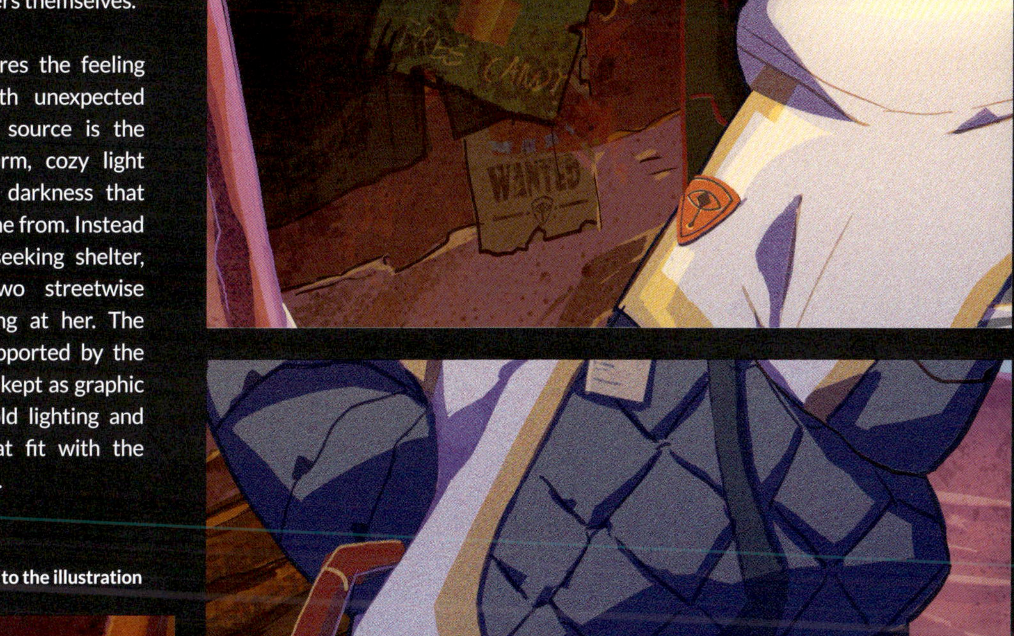

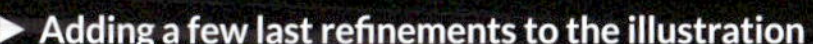

► Adding a few last refinements to the illustration

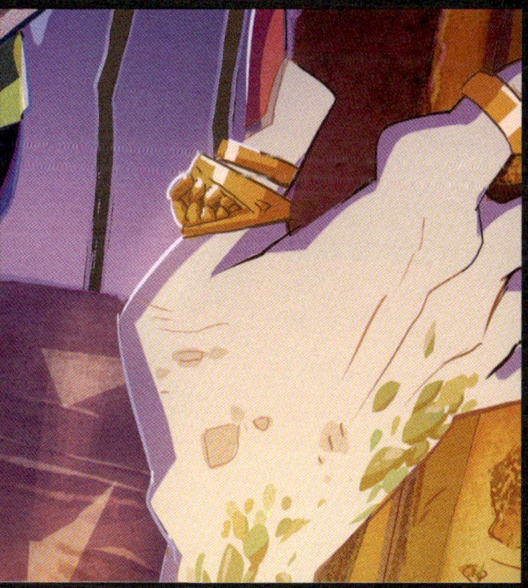

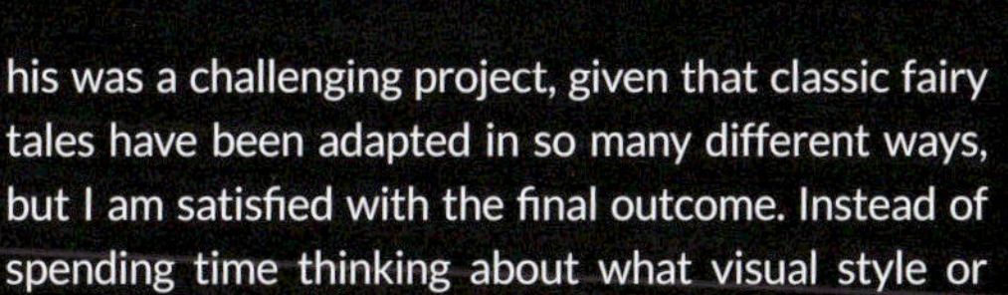

This was a challenging project, given that classic fairy tales have been adapted in so many different ways, but I am satisfied with the final outcome. Instead of spending time thinking about what visual style or kind of painting audiences may not have seen before, try to think about what kind of flavor you can add to the story itself. Can you change the narrative, or even the identities of the characters? Can you change both? When you allow yourself the freedom to go nuts, you can begin to think outside the box and come up with something unique!

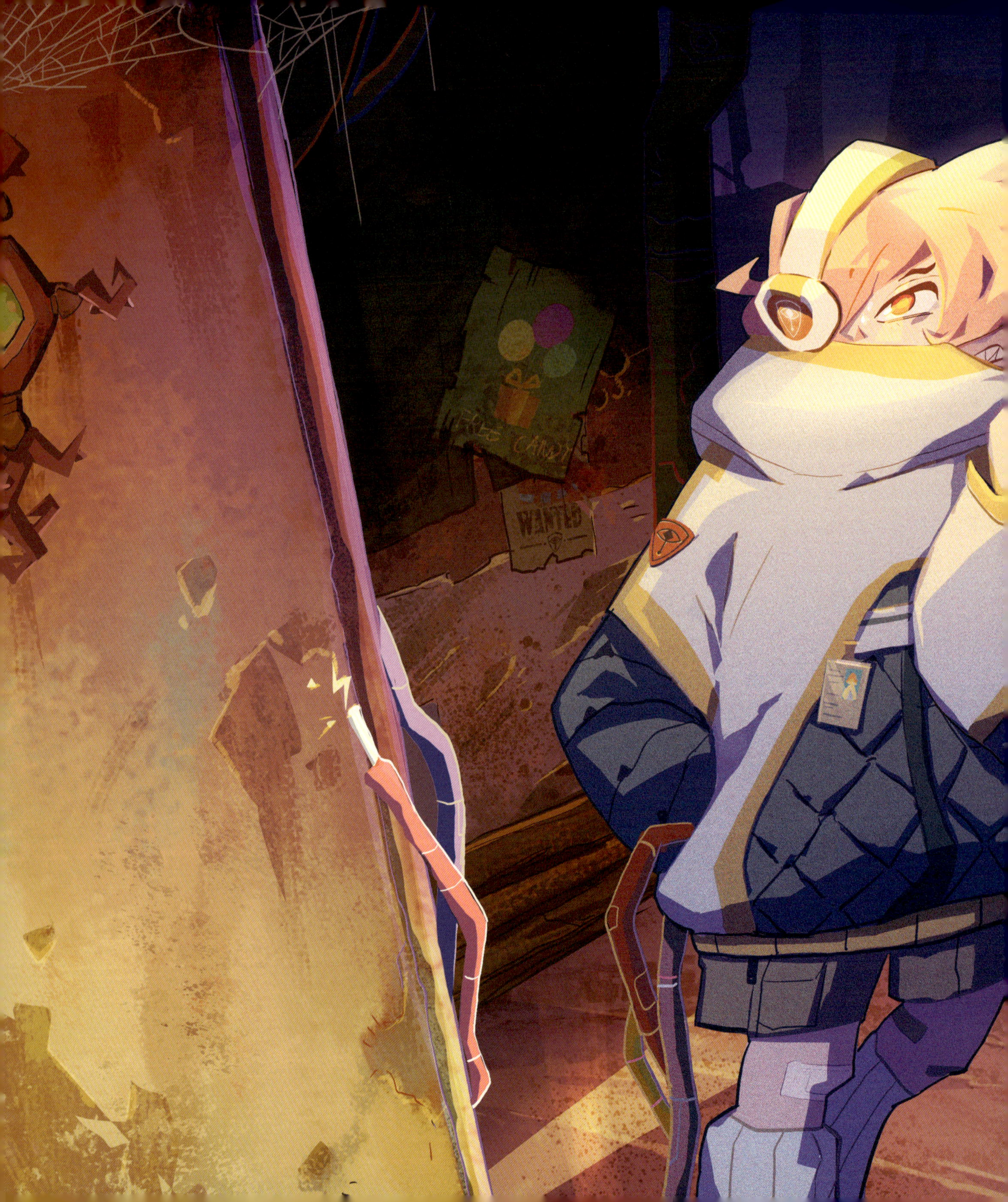
WANTED

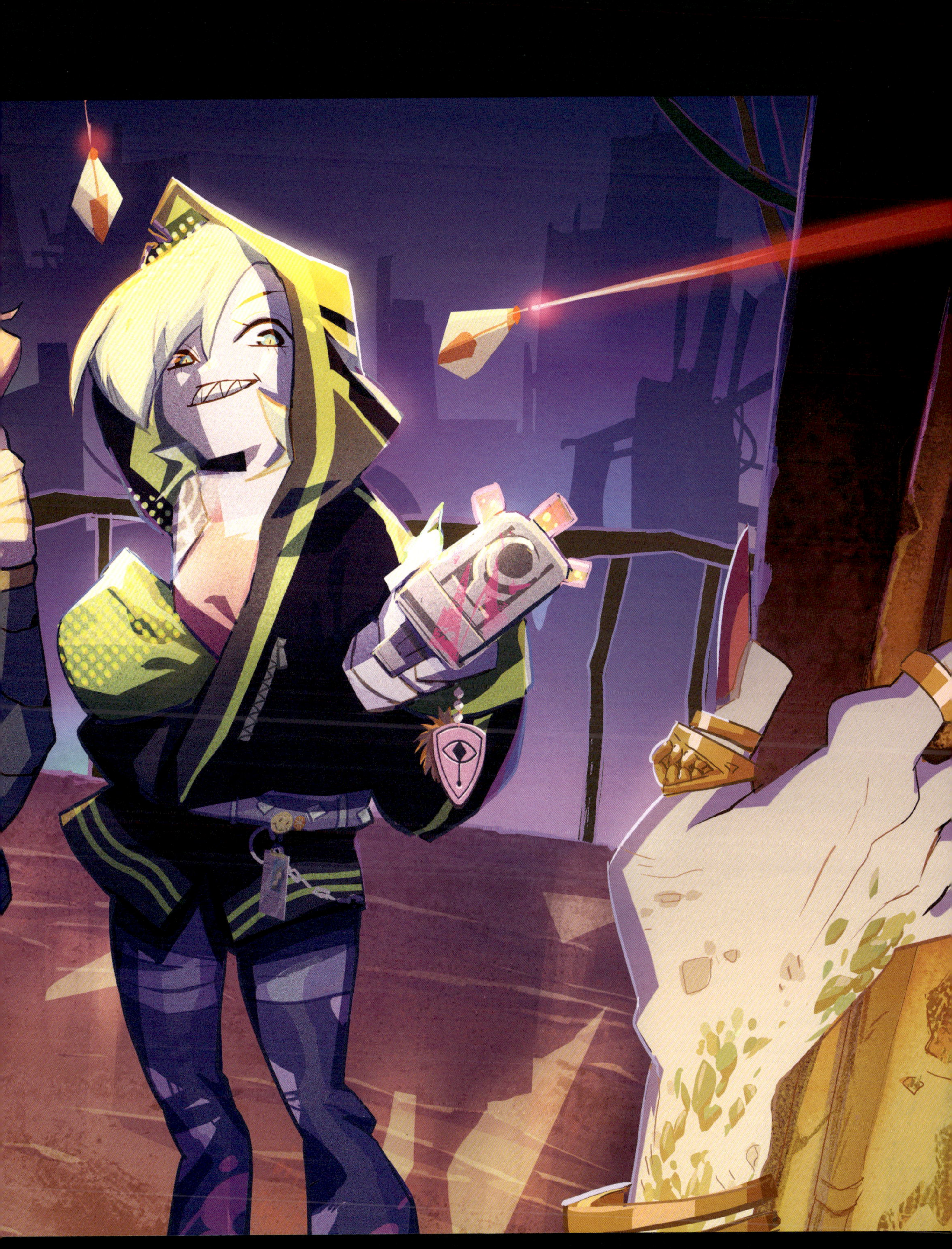

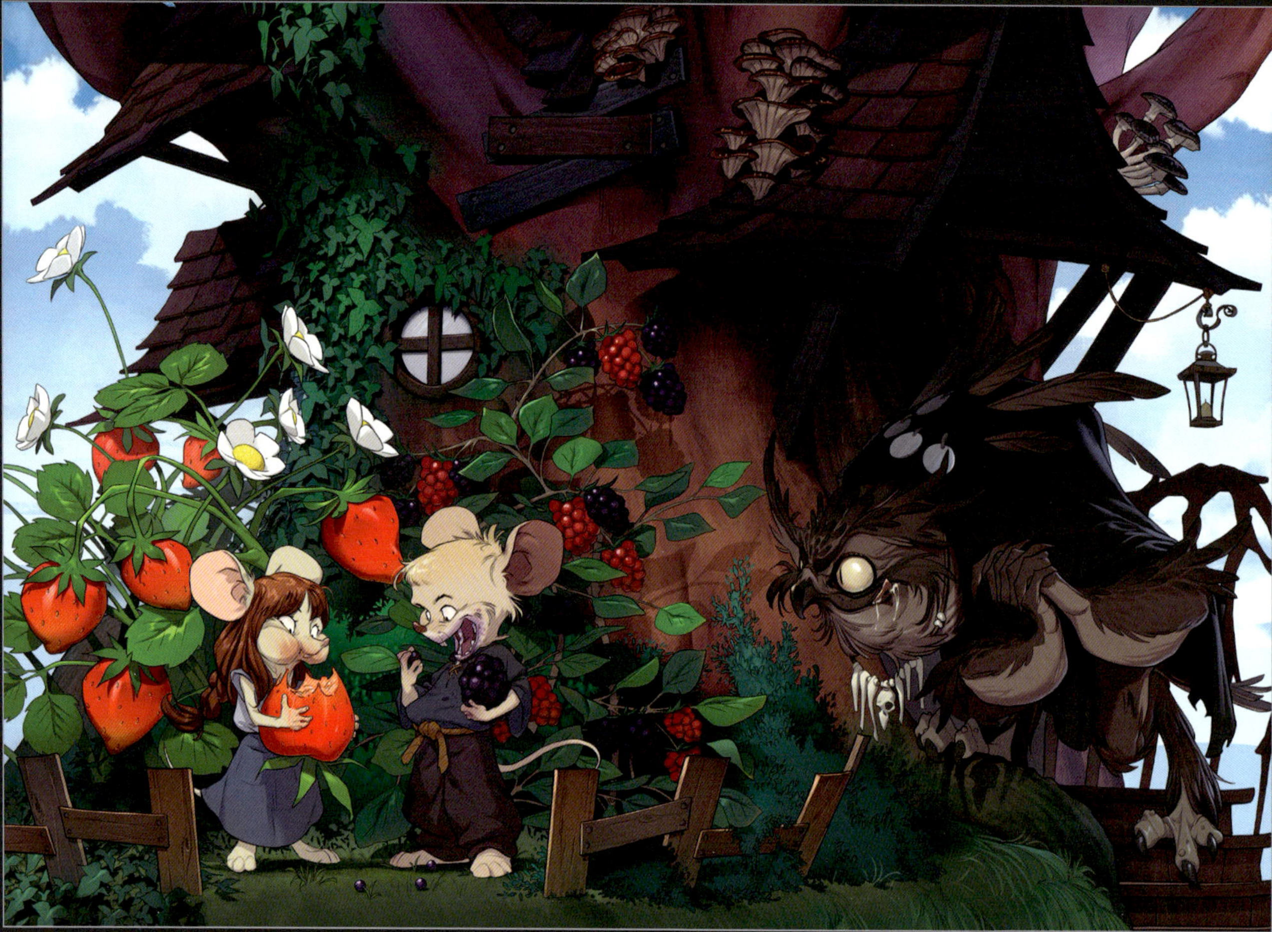

"The Mice and the Owl." Image © Gabriel Gómez Almenzar

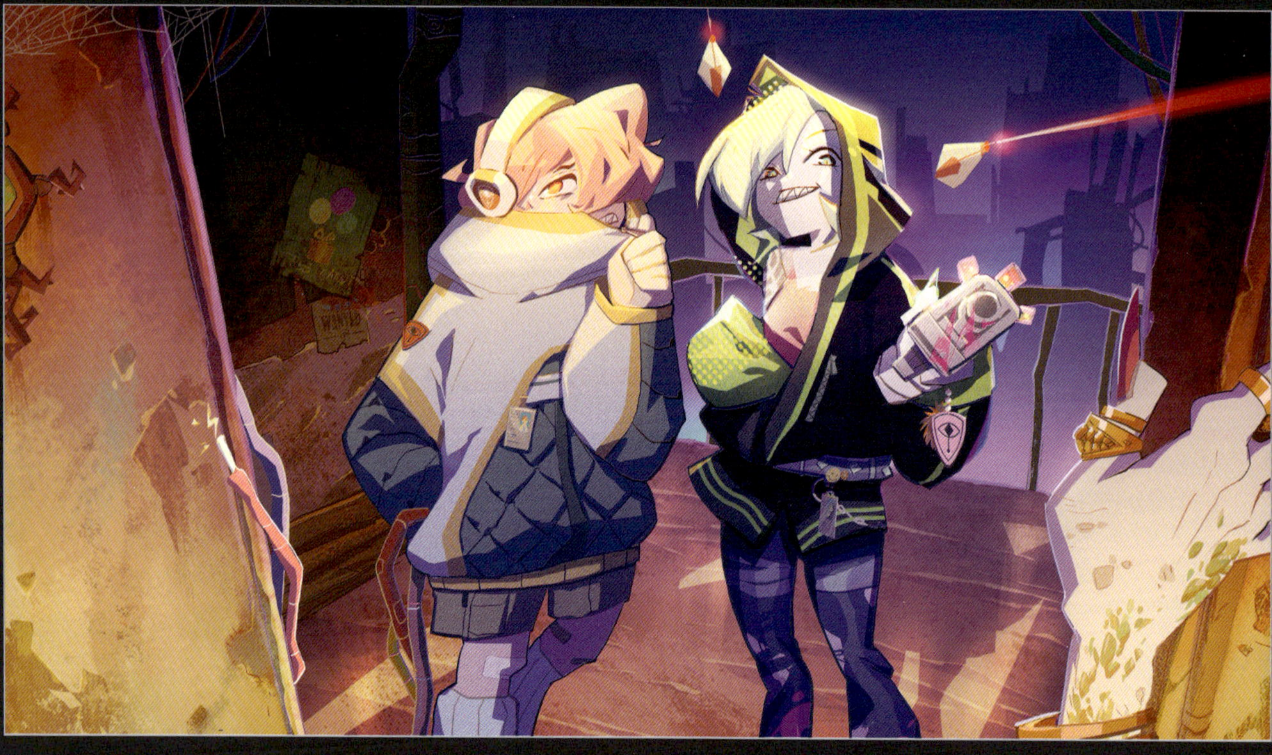

"The Witch Hunters." Image © Kaining Wang

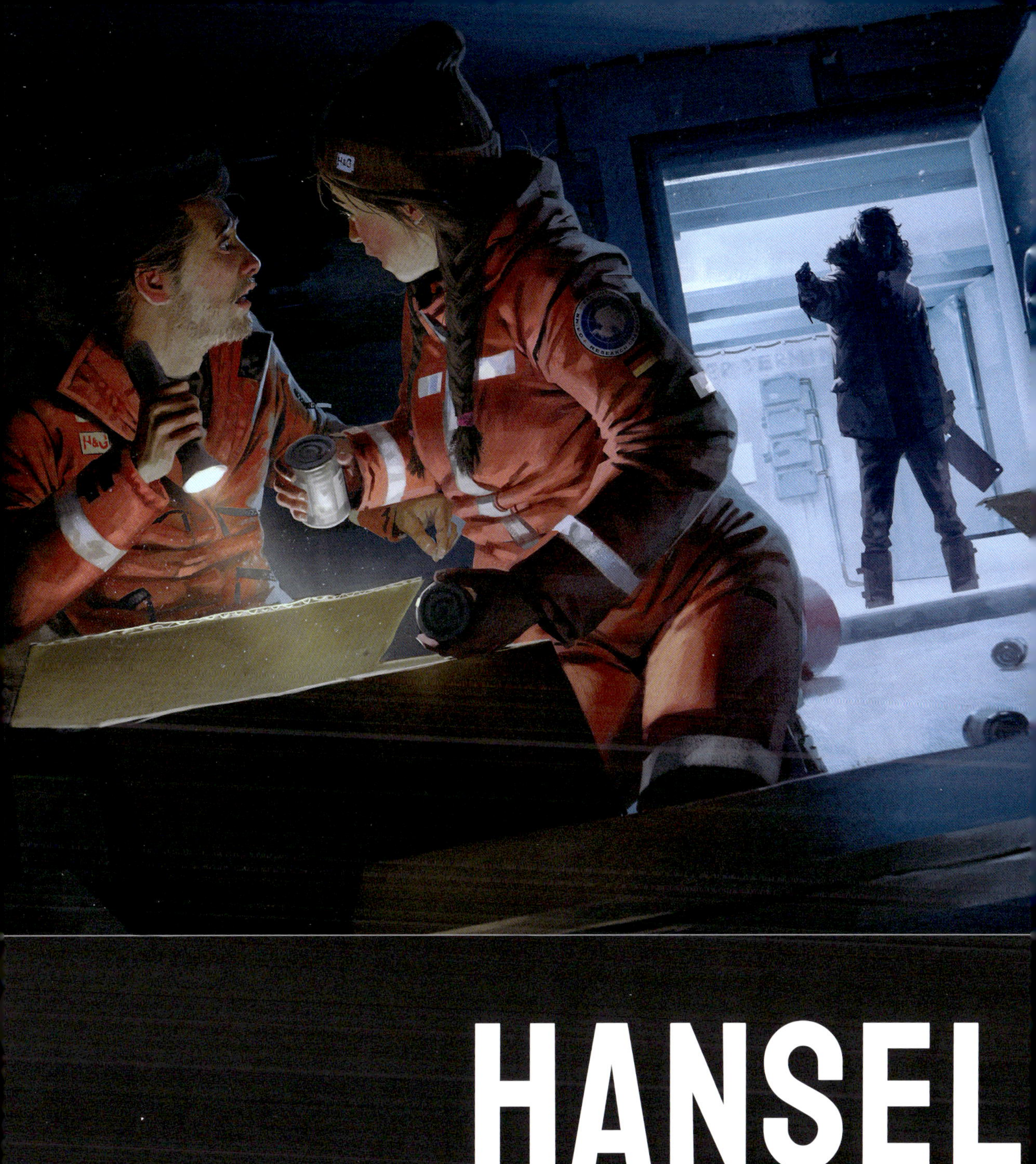

HANSEL AND GRETEL

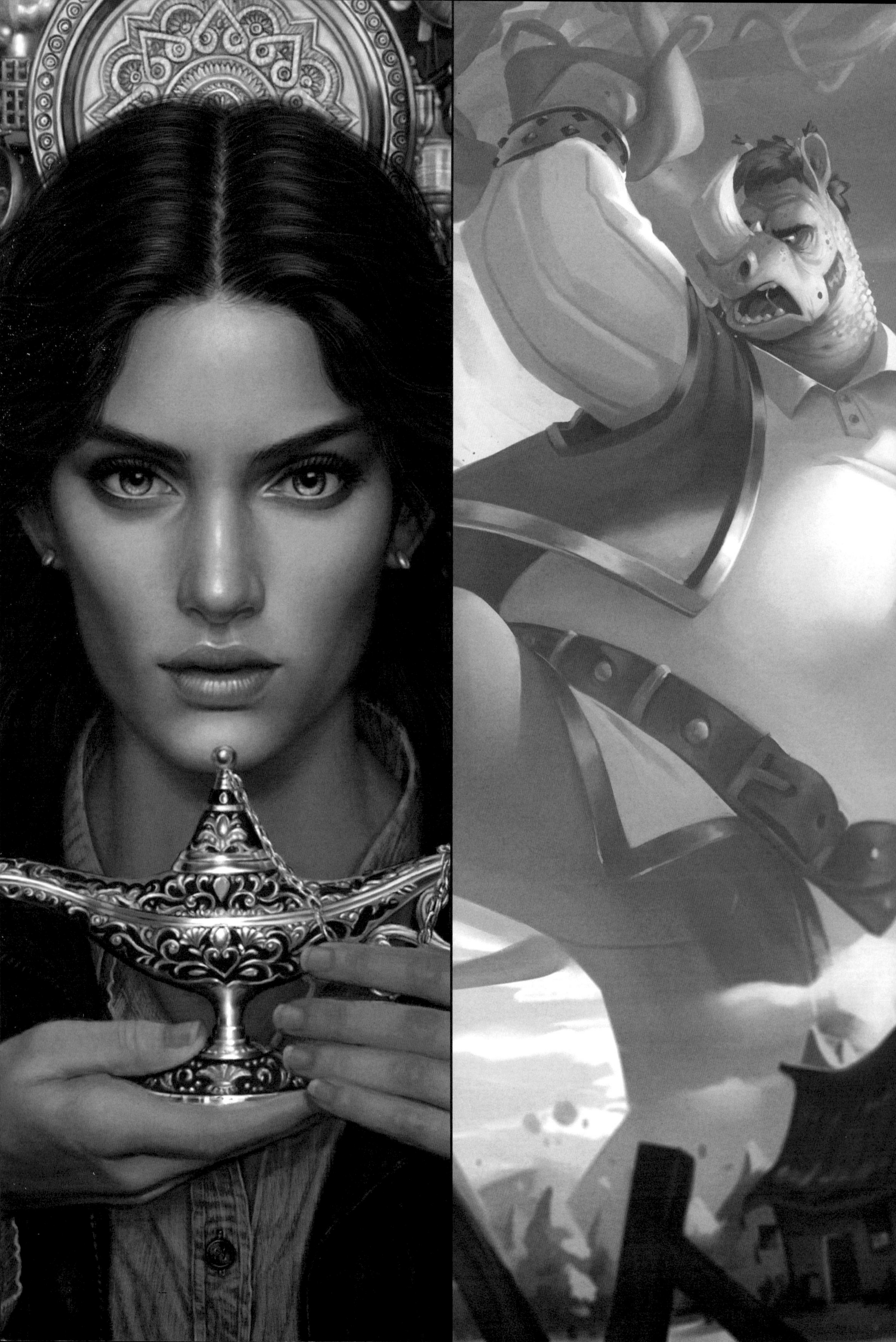

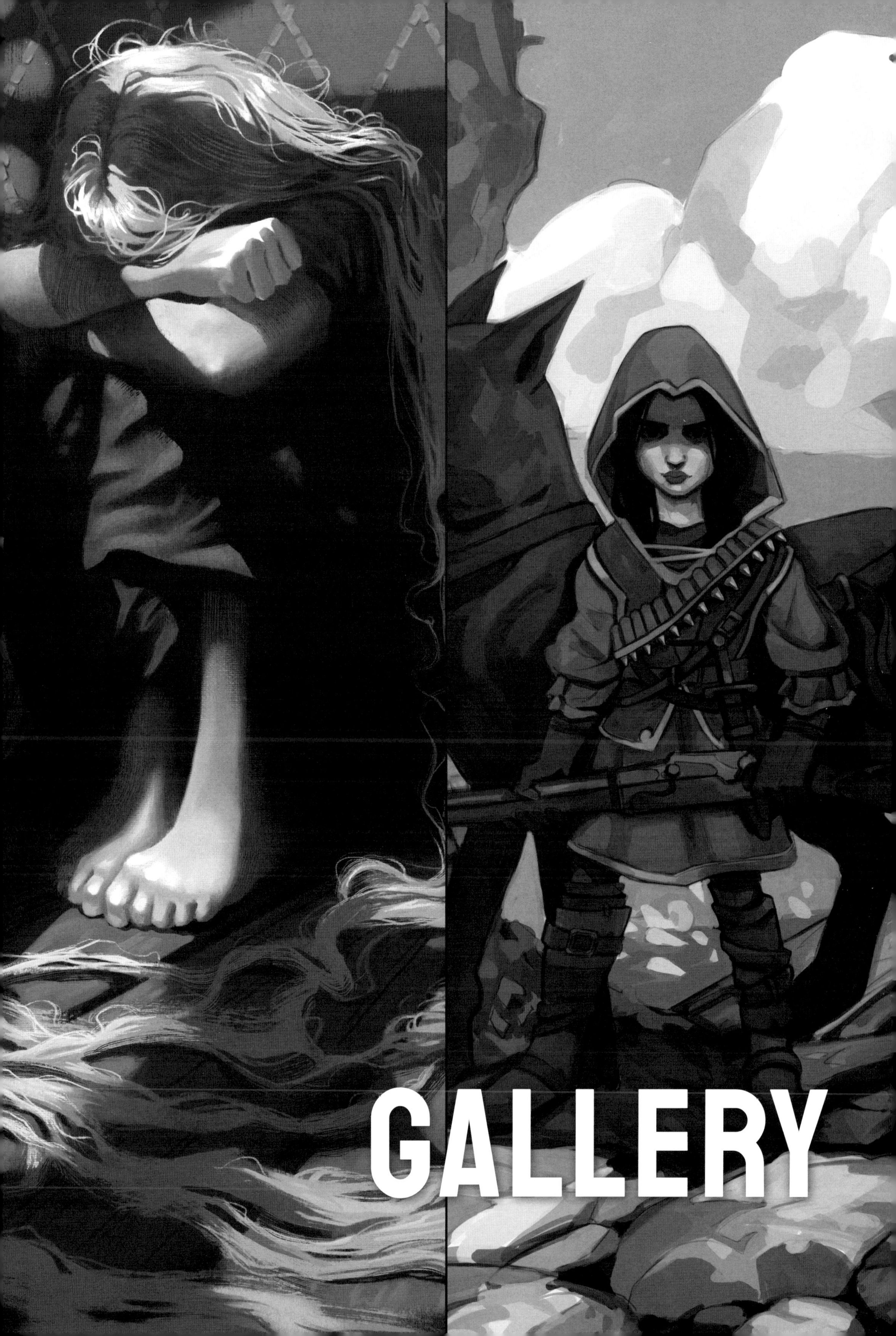

GALLERY

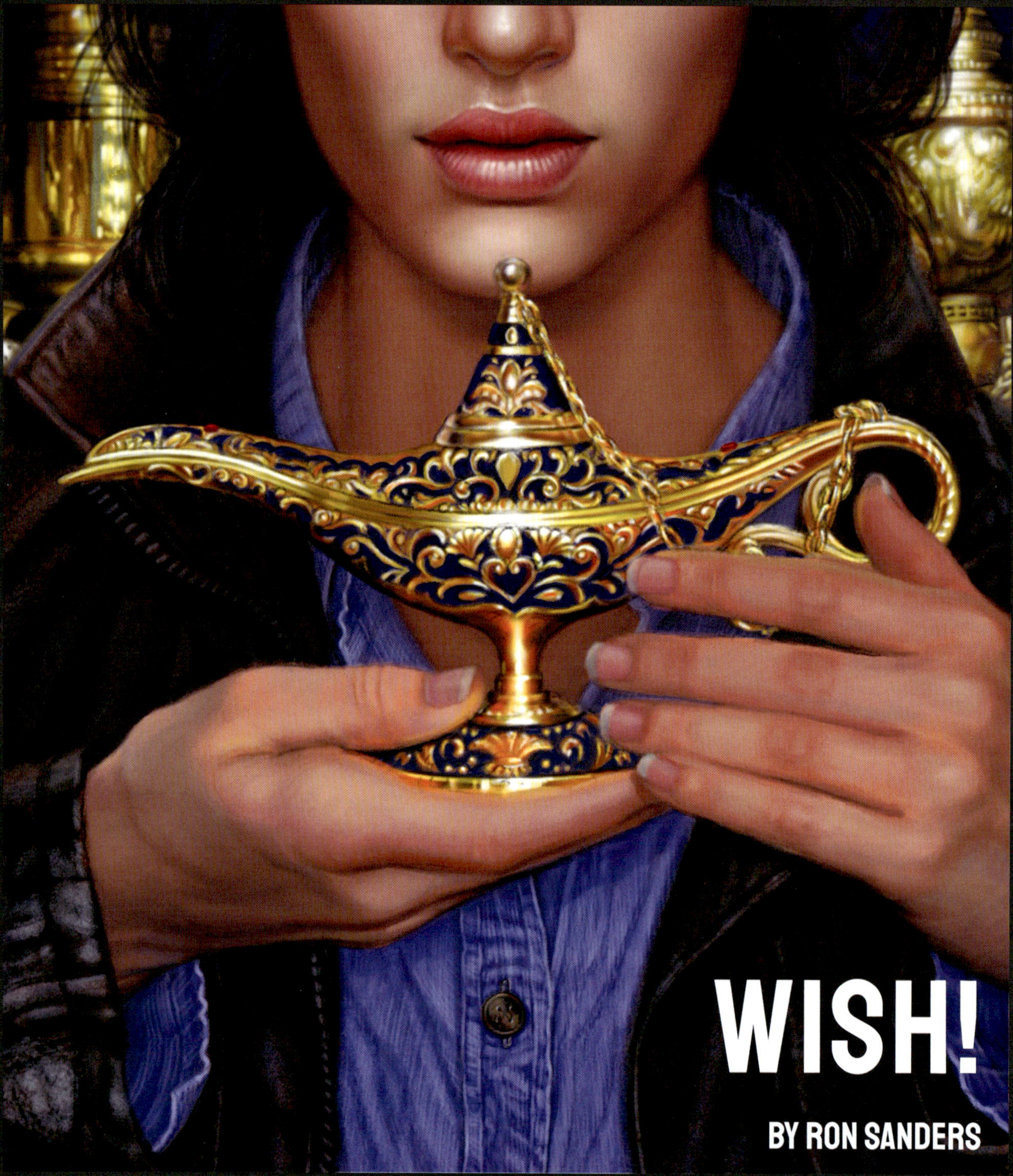

WISH!

BY RON SANDERS

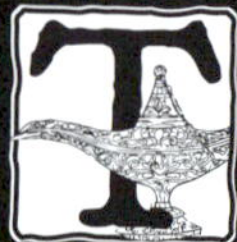

This was the fourth and final painting in a series of fairy-tale portraits, after Snow White, Cinderella, and Rapunzel, that I created to promote my work to the publishing industry. I wrote a contemporary synopsis for each tale, then framed each character in a similar way: holding a significant story element and surrounded by supporting objects or environments. In *WISH!*, my adaptation of the Aladdin story, Ameerah Hameed is an archeologist and adventurer with a background in ancient history and religions. She is approached by a mysterious and wealthy patron interested in a particular item of legend: an antique lamp.

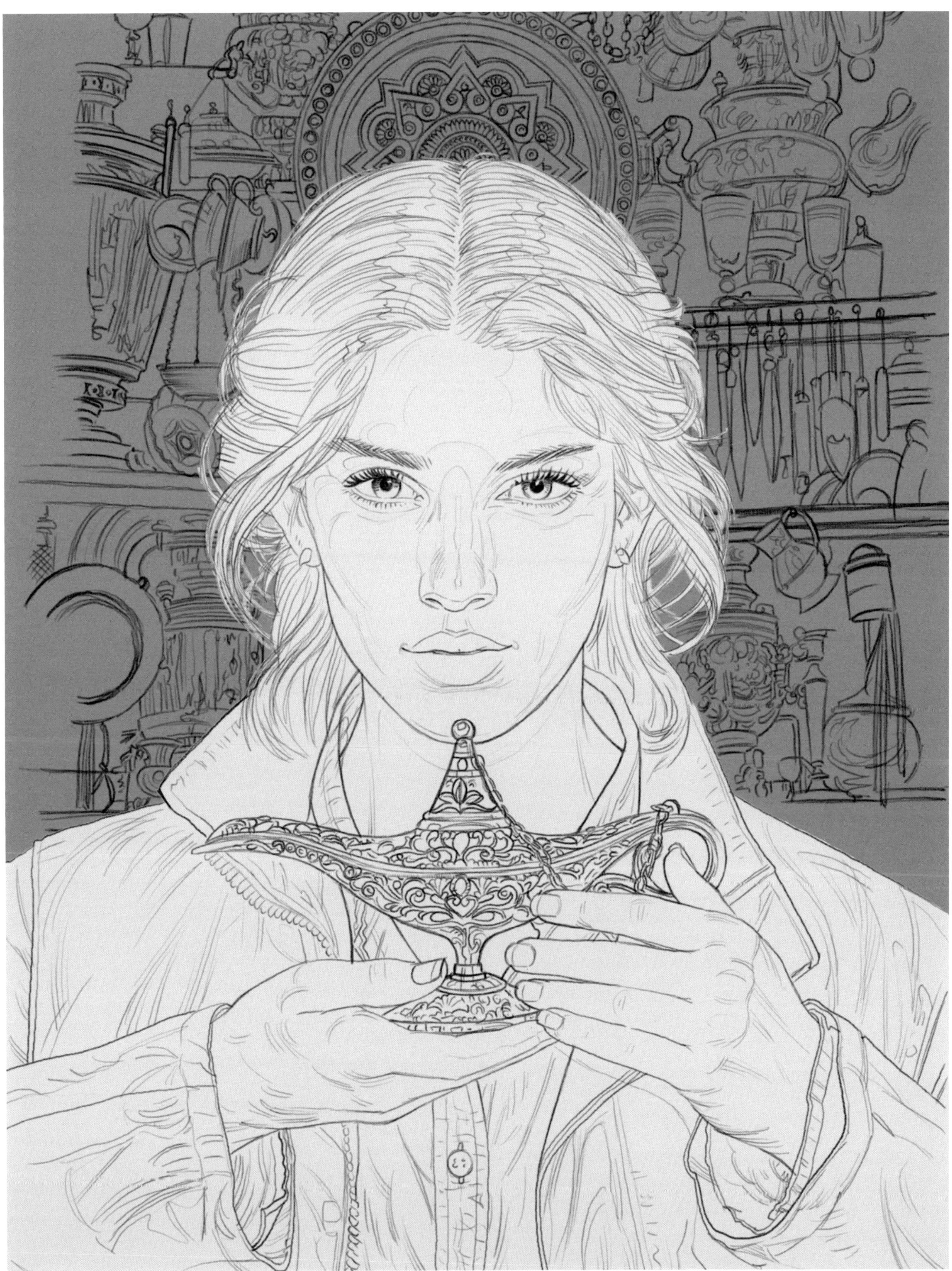

▲ My initial concepts start with a thumbnail sketch, followed by photo reference, hiring models, and using costume and props as needed. I often make a photobashed reference image using those resources, which leads to a final drawing such as this one.

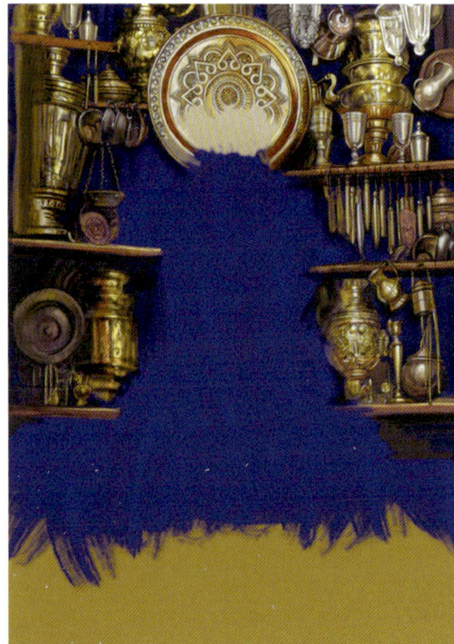

▲ Having the background and foreground separated into their own folders in Adobe Photoshop, I can more quickly work on each section. Here I began roughly blocking in the background, keeping the dominant color scheme of gold and blue in mind.

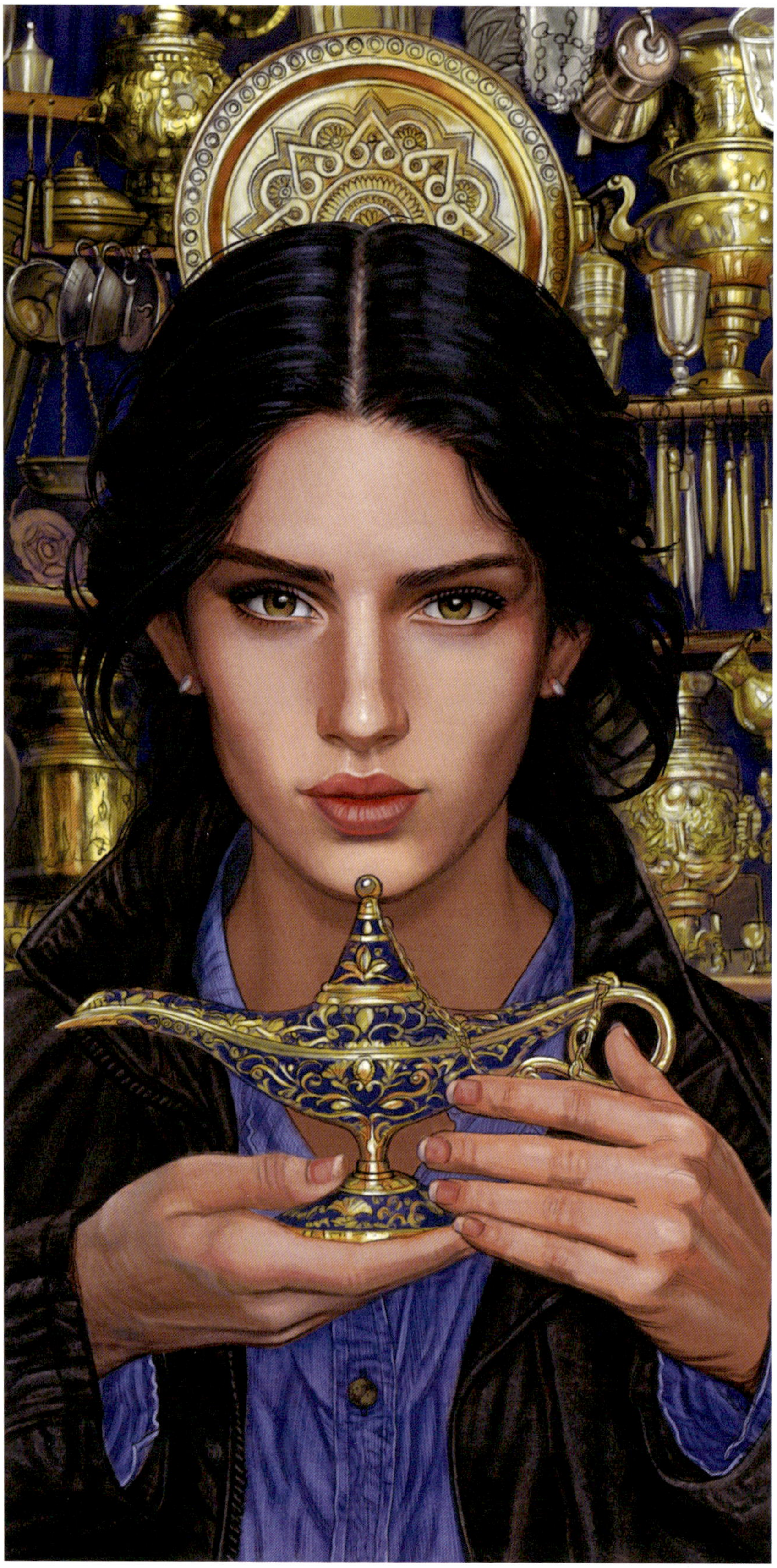

▲ With the background roughed in, I blocked in the main colors of the figure, keeping those separate from the line drawing. I chose to give her honey-colored eyes in keeping with the blue/gold palette.

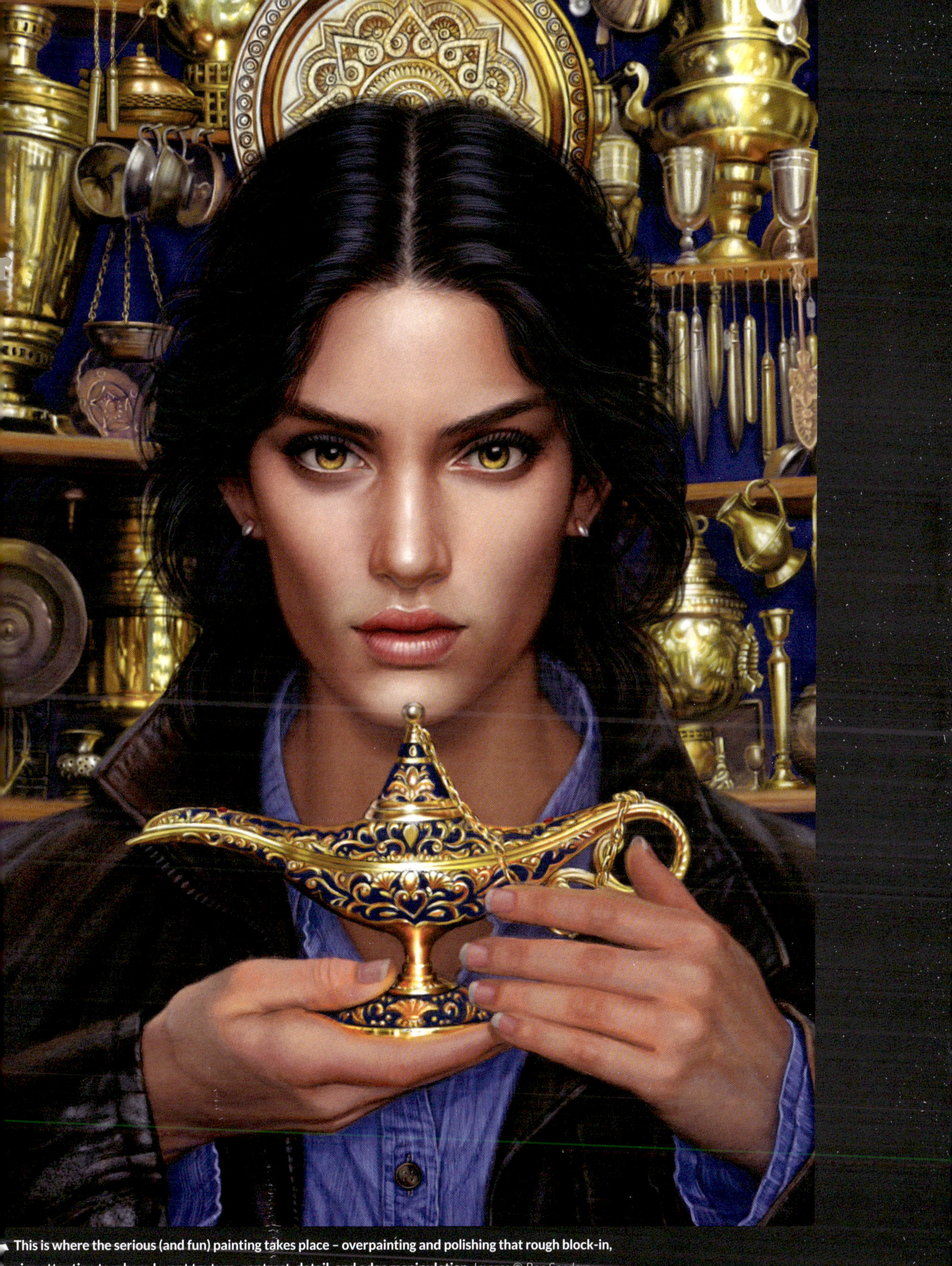

▲ This is where the serious (and fun) painting takes place – overpainting and polishing that rough block-in, paying attention to where I want texture, contrast, detail, and edge manipulation. *Images © Ron Sanders*

JACK AND THE BEANSTALK

BY RYAN HARRELL

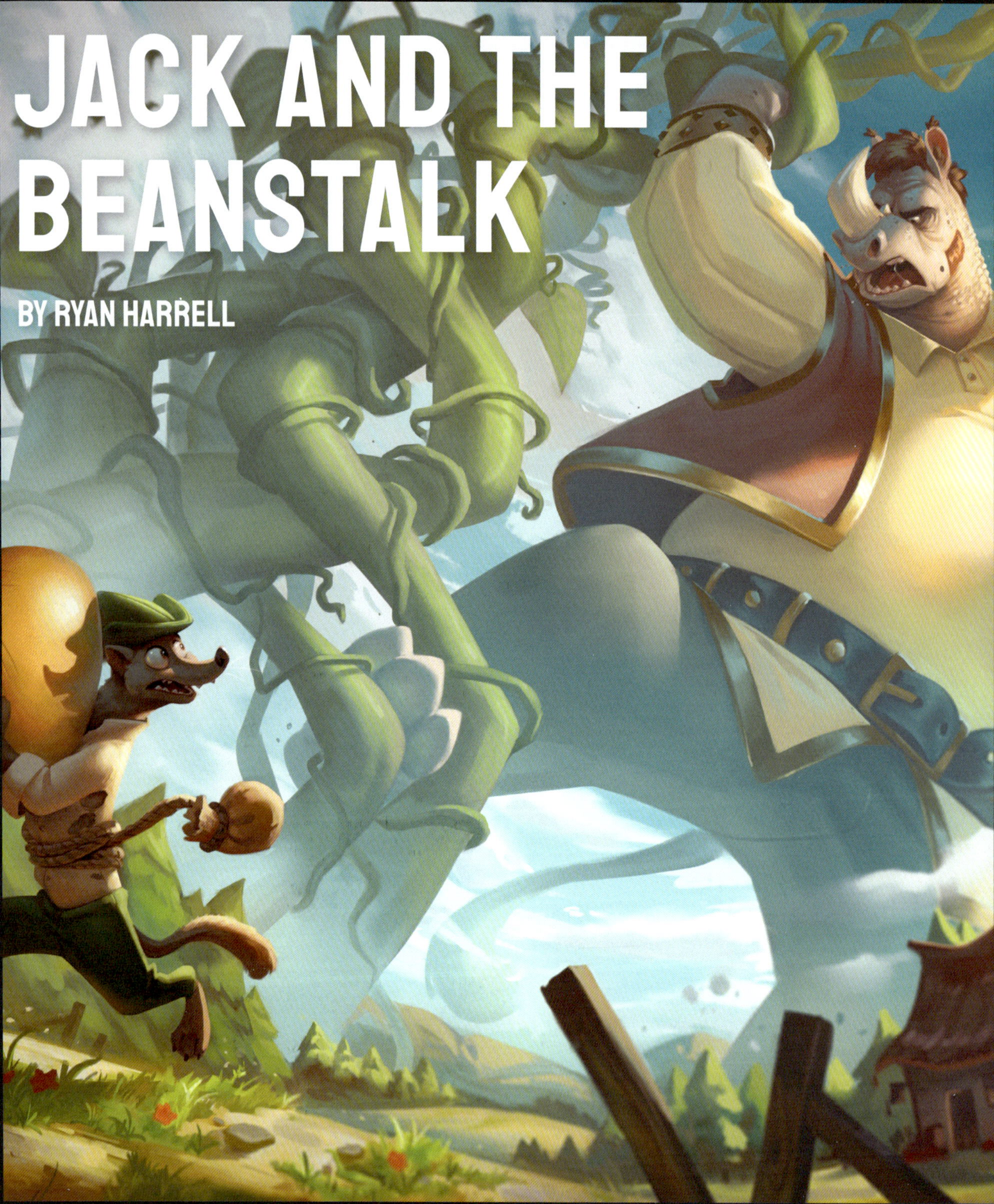

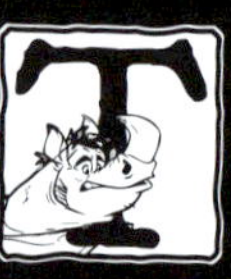

The *Jack and the Beanstalk* fairy tale has caught my attention ever since I was little. Wanting to put my spin on the classic story, I decided to highlight the giant over Jack. To showcase the characters' personalities, I turned them into animals that matched their stereotypes: a giant bulky rhino and a slippery weasel thief. Knowing the giant was the main character, I went into the design process with the goal of making him the focal point.

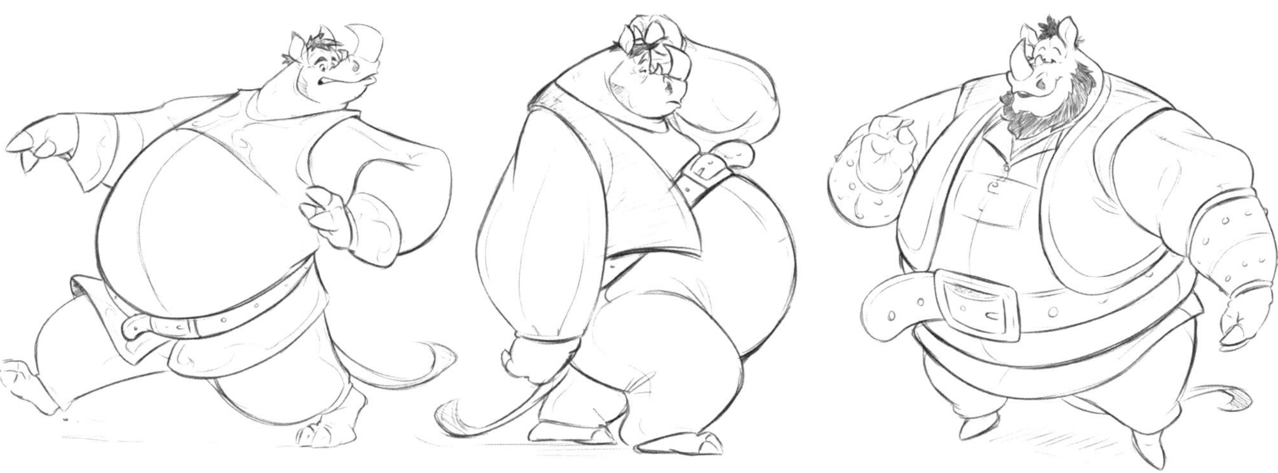

▲ Due to the giant's importance, I focused this early stage on exploring different concepts and shapes for his design. My goal was to find the perfect balance between him being imposing and clumsy.

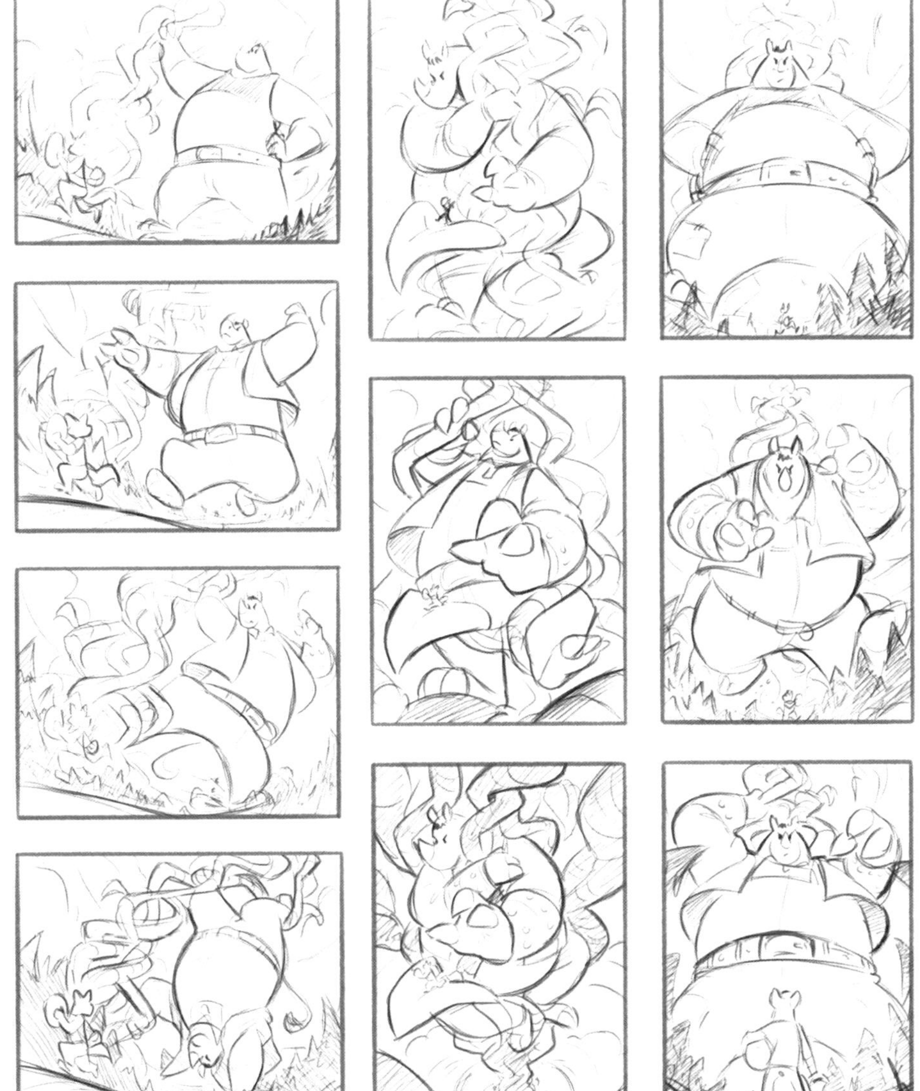

◀ Once I had the giant designed, I explored different composition options using thumbnails. These quick little doodles allowed me to figure out the positioning of the characters and other elements on the page without getting attached to one design.

▼ The last step before painting was exploring values. I played with three lighting scenarios to see which one evoked the right mood for my illustration. I also paid attention to how the lighting drew the eyes of the audience, keeping in mind that the giant is the main character.

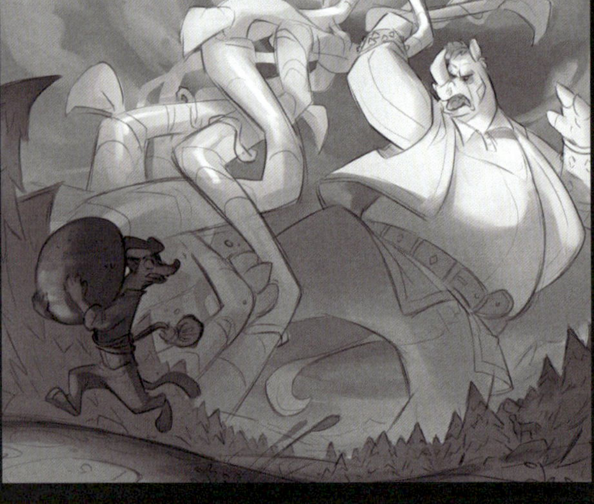

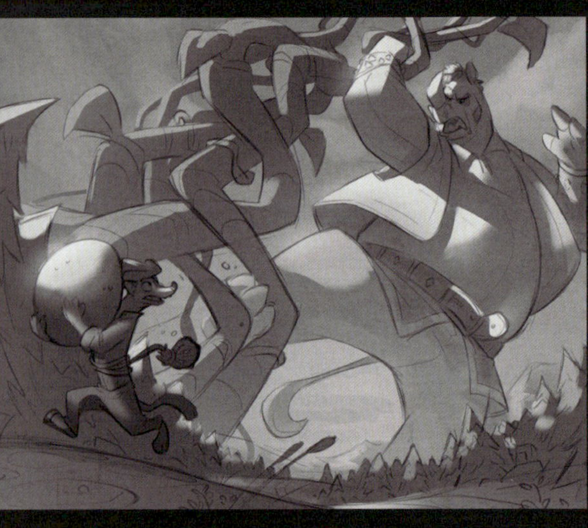

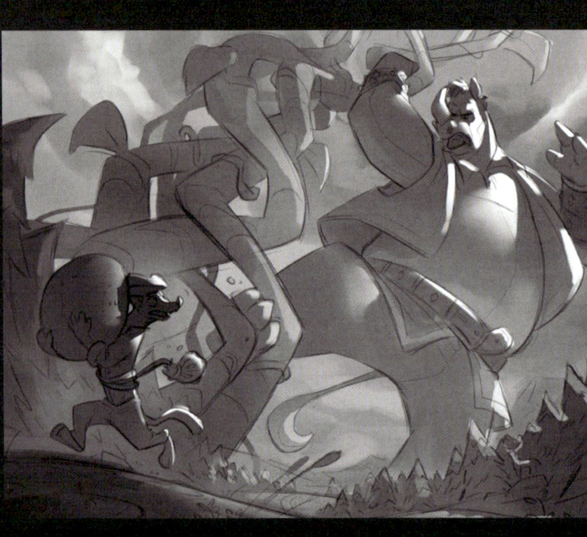

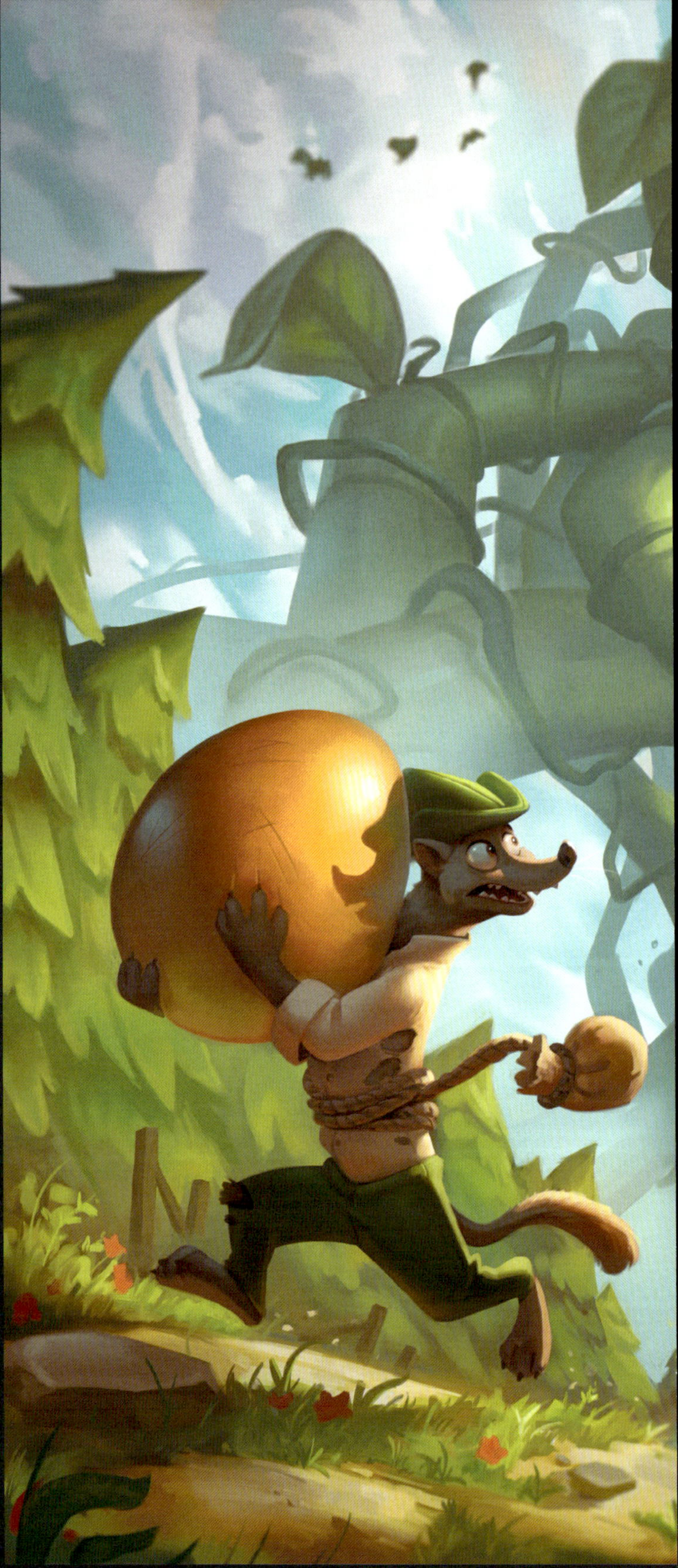

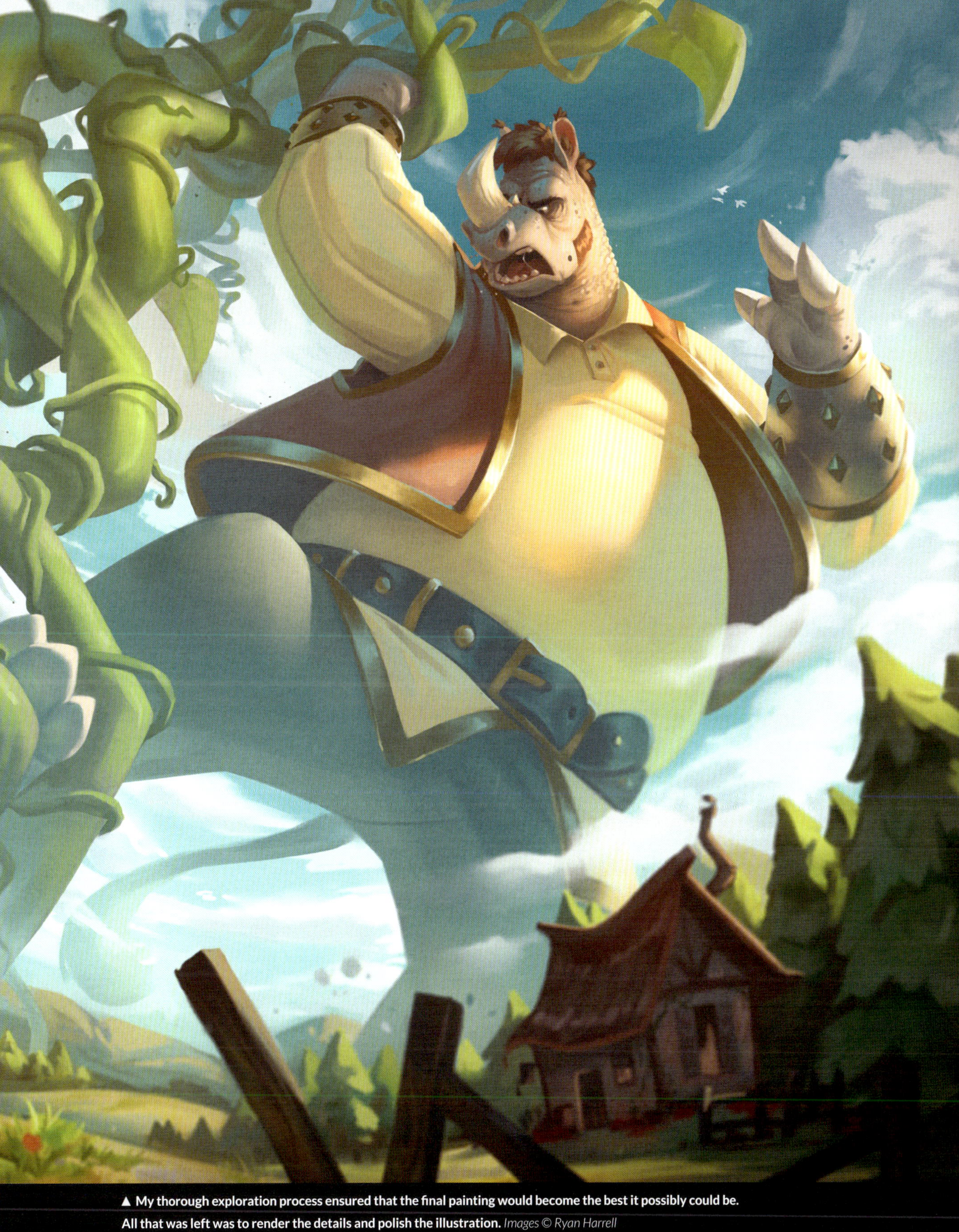

▲ **My thorough exploration process ensured that the final painting would become the best it possibly could be. All that was left was to render the details and polish the illustration.** *Images © Ryan Harrell*

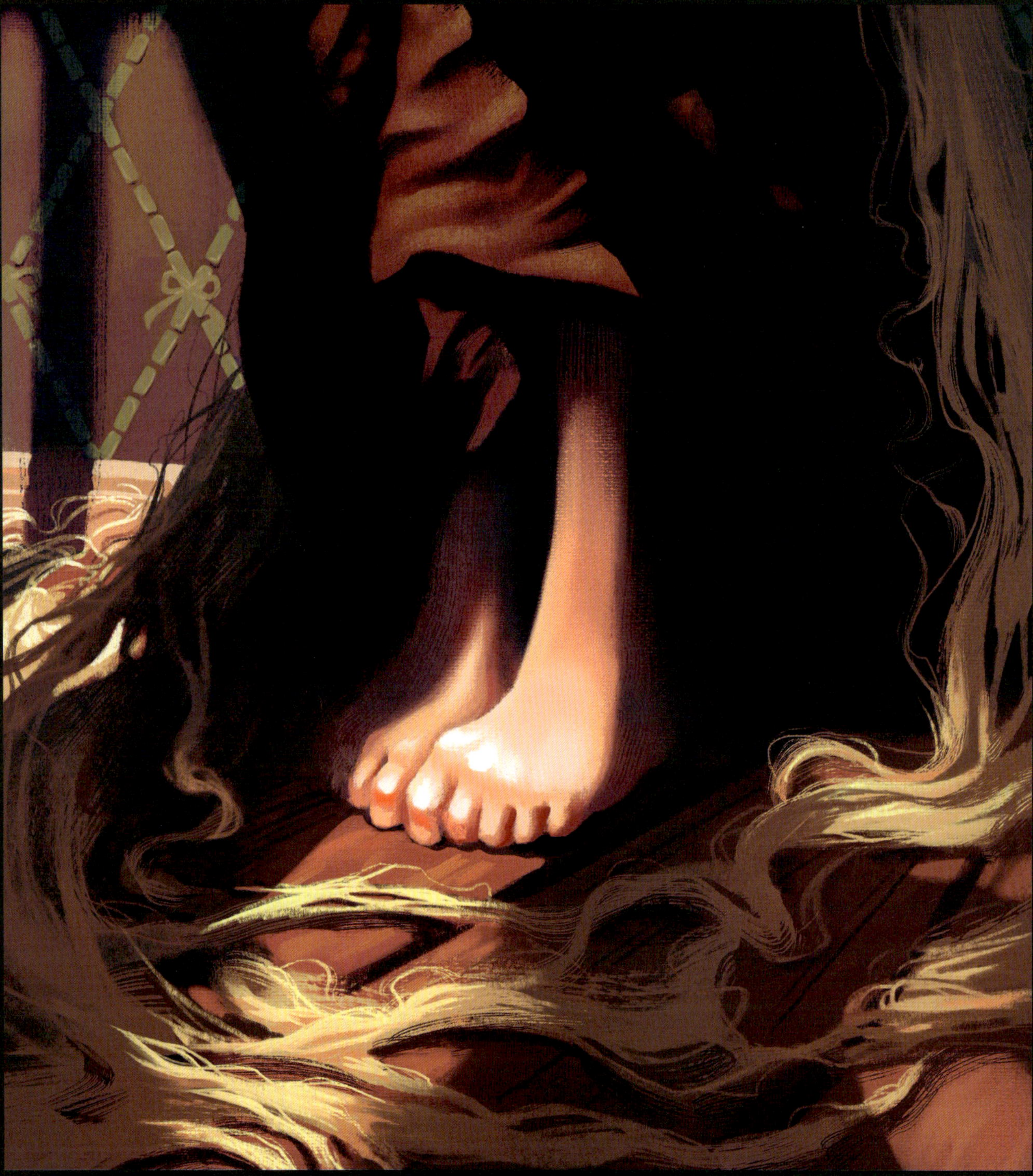

RAPUNZEL

BY KATIE GOLDBERG

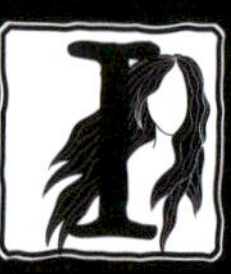

I have always loved Rapunzel and her impossibly long hair. During the Covid pandemic, I felt like I could truly relate to her predicament of being locked up for a long time. However, most movies and storybooks I have seen depict her as patient and perfectly put together. For this piece, I wanted to show a more realistic version of Rapunzel, frustrated and unkempt, with messy hair and wrinkled clothes.

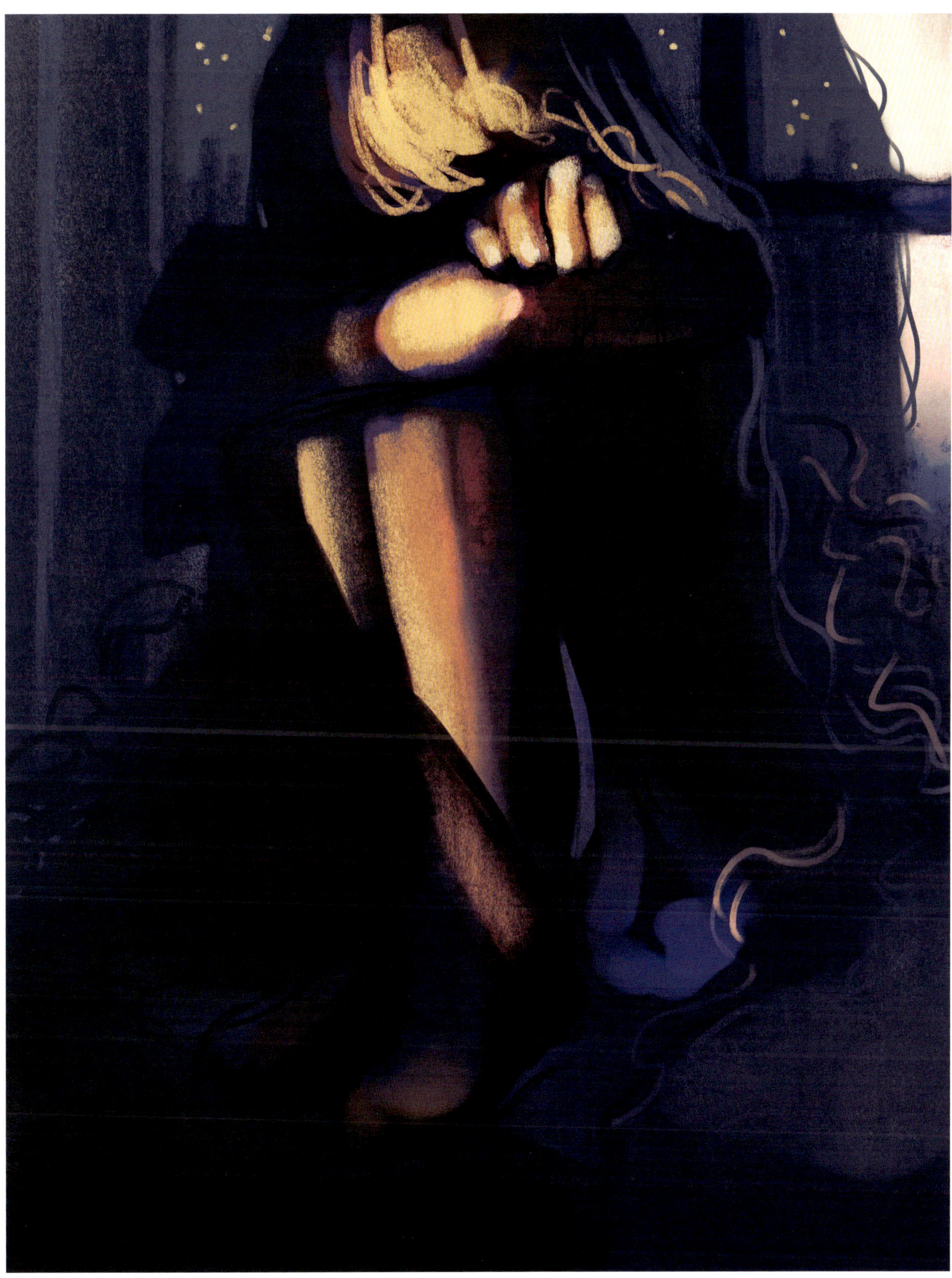

▲ First I drew a quick sketch and blocked in light and shadow to draw attention to the areas that were the most important. I decided on a tight, curled-up position to show how helpless and small Rapunzel felt.

▼ After blocking in the colors, I made the canvas taller to showcase more of Rapunzel's messy hair. I changed the light source to a Gothic rose window to add more drama and interest to the piece.

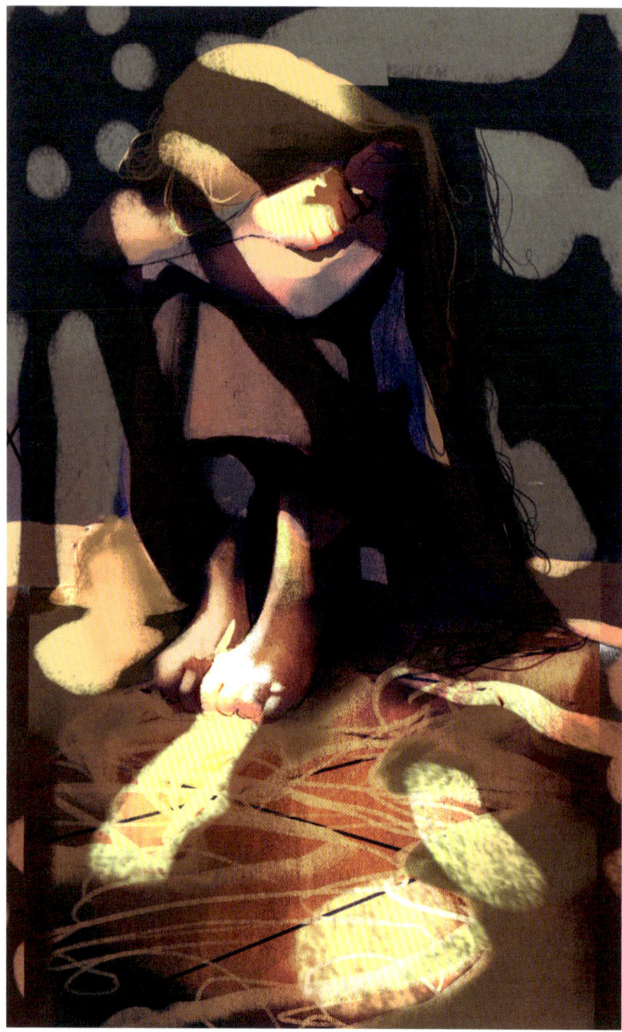

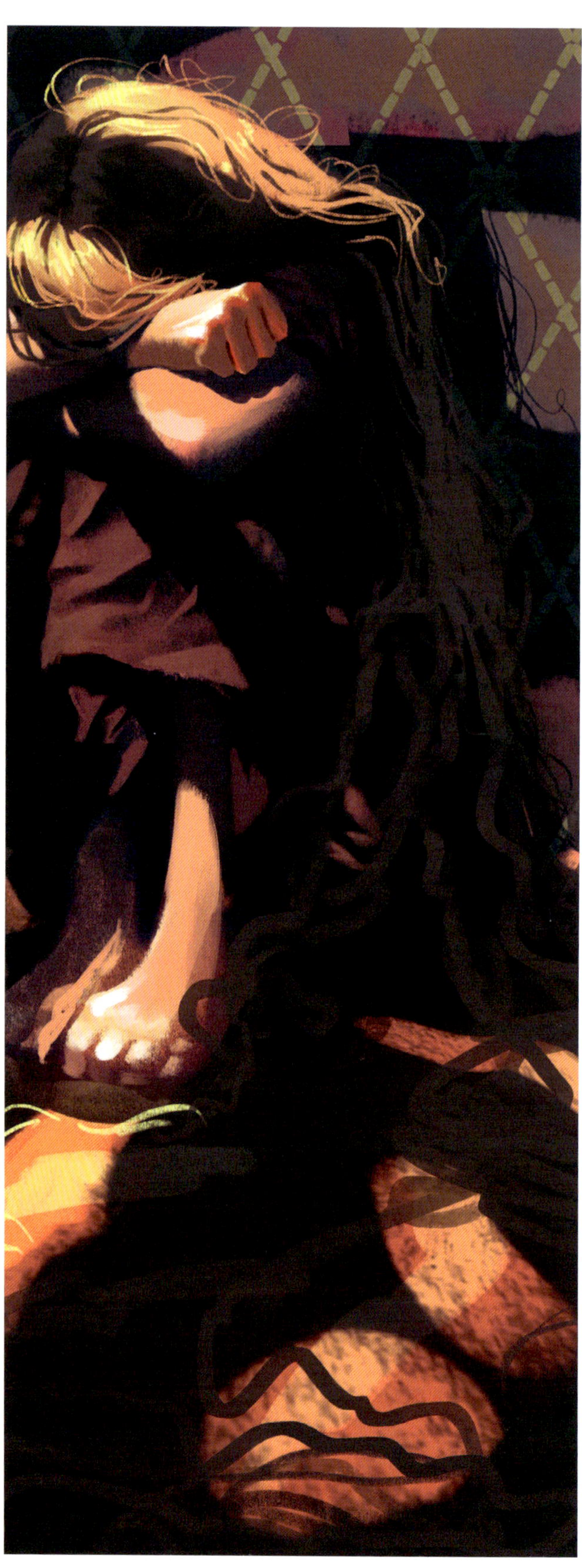

▲ At this stage, I was mostly adding detail to the areas in the light, while keeping the shadows simpler. For the wallpaper, I drew a pattern of criss-crossed ribbons to mimic the walls of a cage.

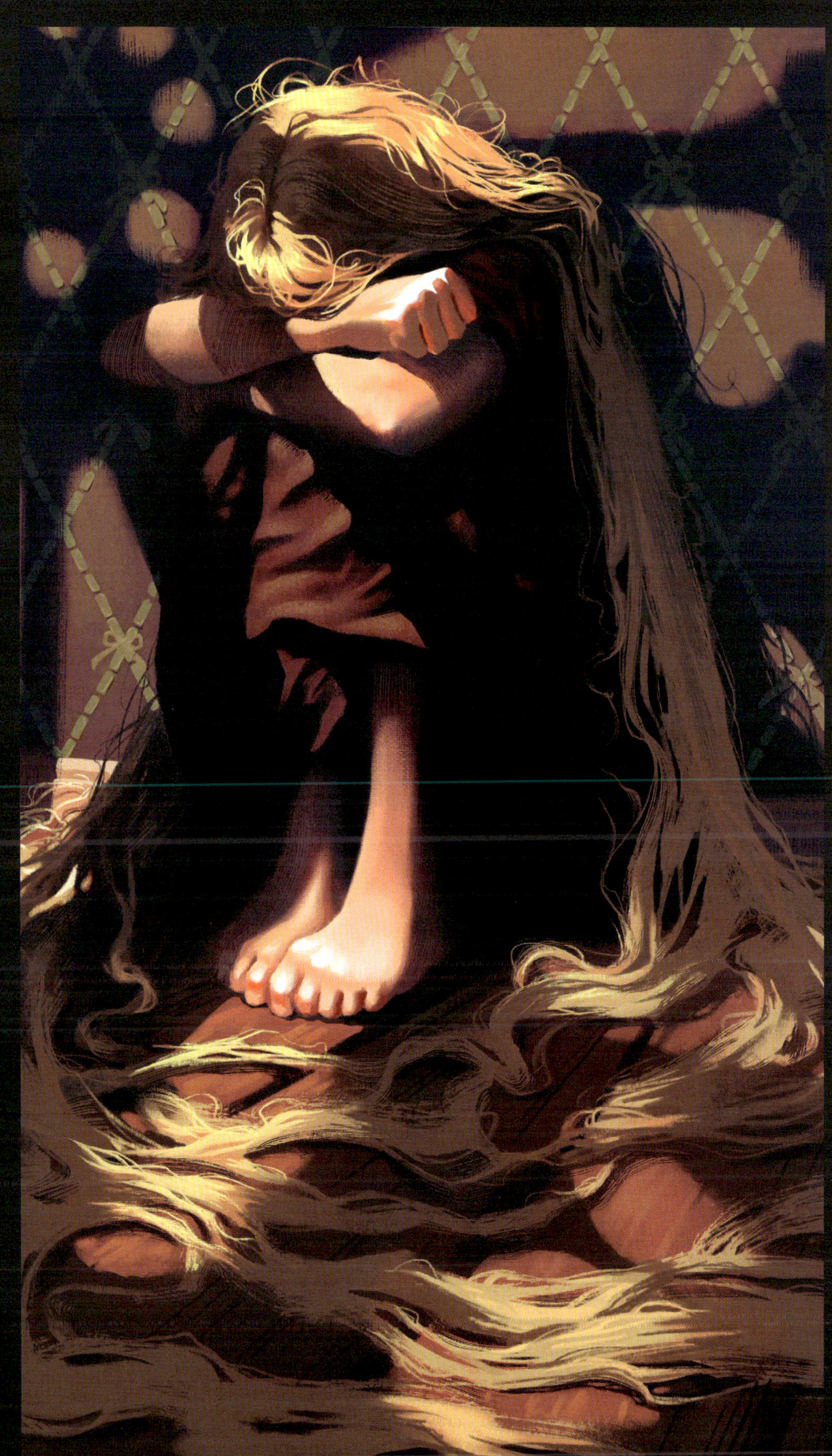

▶ For the finishing touches, I added detail to the shadows by drawing lines following the shapes of the forms. I also added brighter highlights, more color variations, and detail to the hair and floor in the foreground.

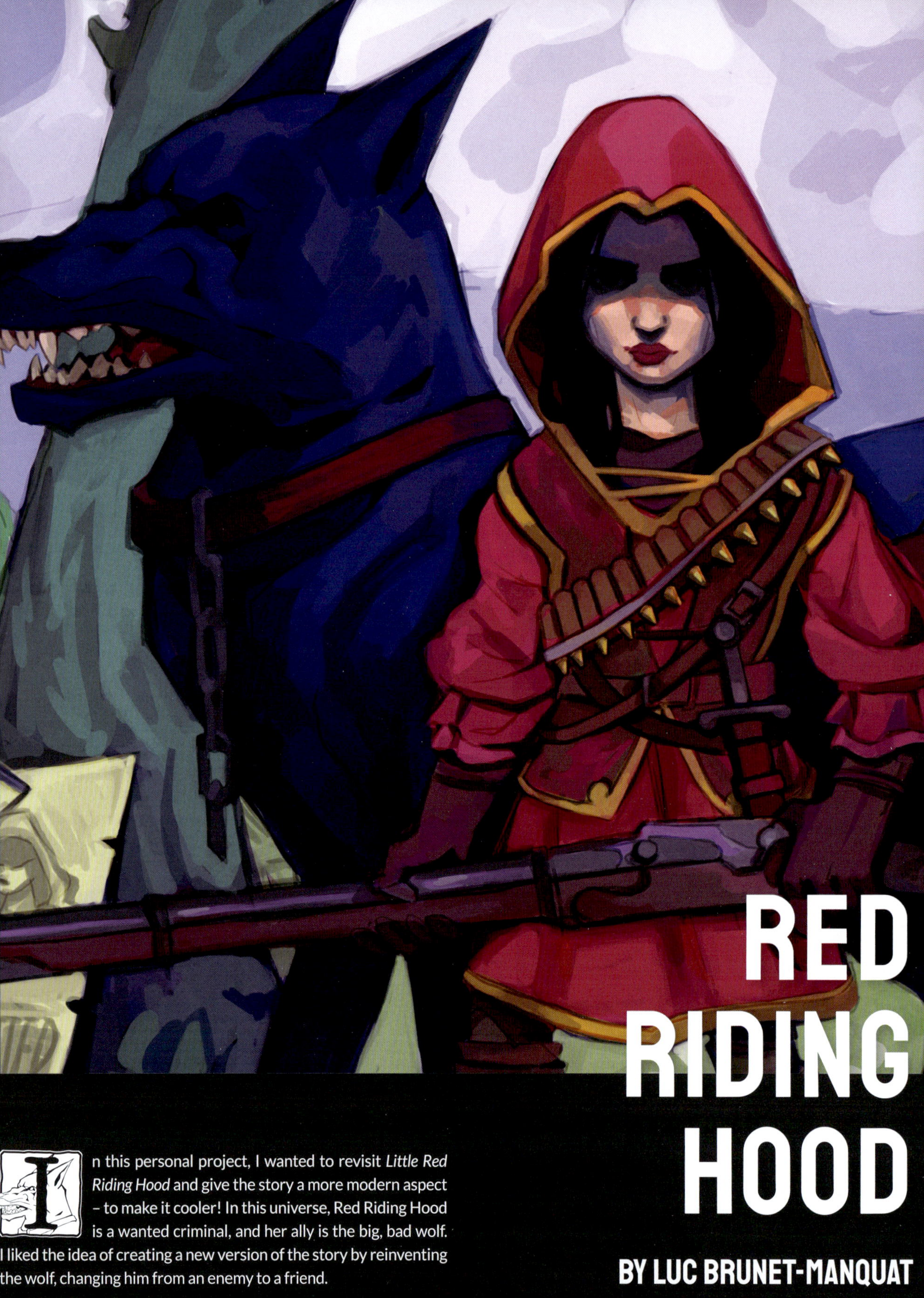

RED RIDING HOOD

BY LUC BRUNET-MANQUAT

In this personal project, I wanted to revisit *Little Red Riding Hood* and give the story a more modern aspect – to make it cooler! In this universe, Red Riding Hood is a wanted criminal, and her ally is the big, bad wolf. I liked the idea of creating a new version of the story by reinventing the wolf, changing him from an enemy to a friend.

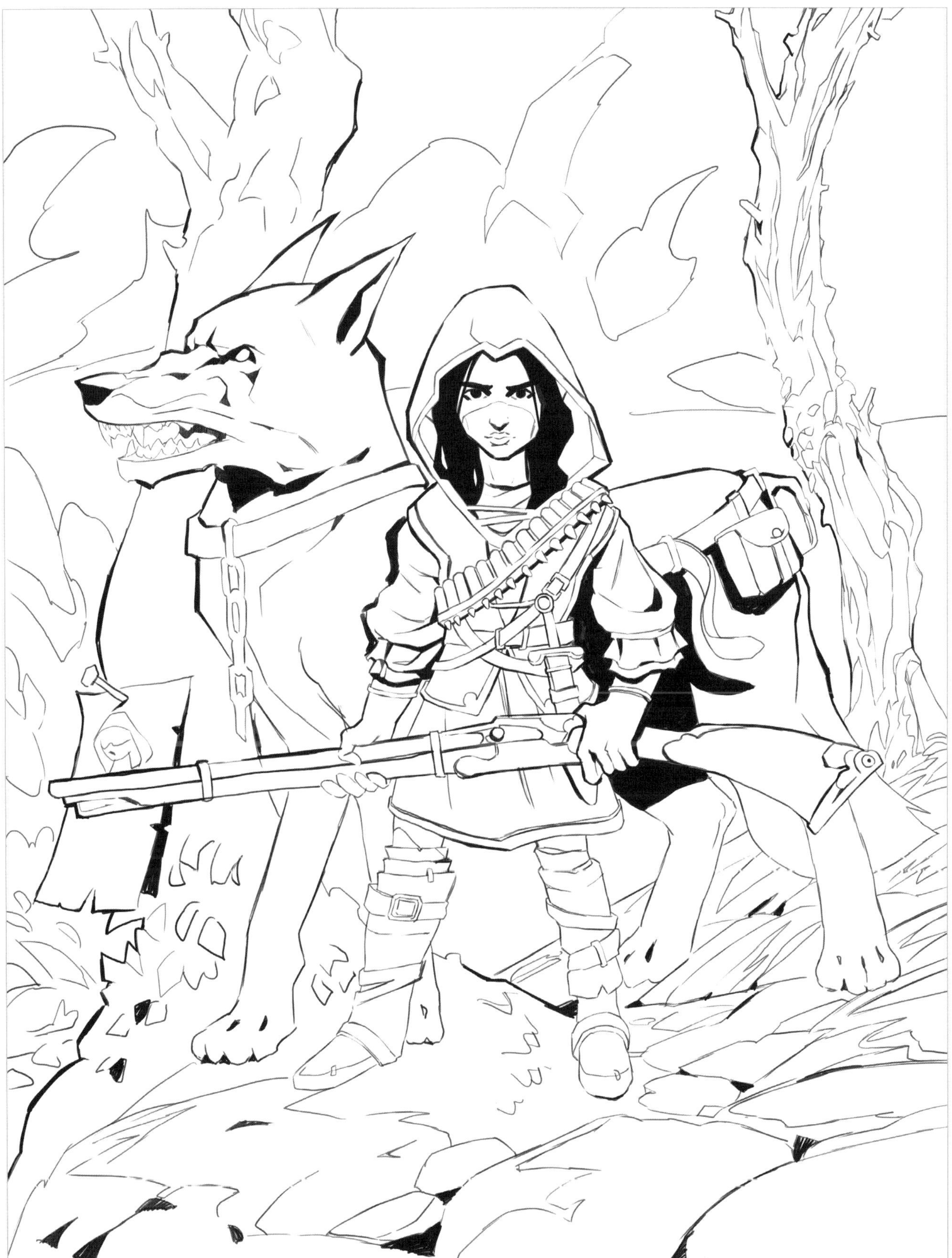

▲ I started with the line art, first making a rough sketch and then drawing this cleaner version over it. For my painting process, I need clean line art and a strong drawing with clear volume.

▼ Next I applied my color, aiming to create a strong base that sets clear intentions for my painting. I tried to create atmosphere just with flat color, using purples, pinks, and blue-greens to create an unusual, magical feel.

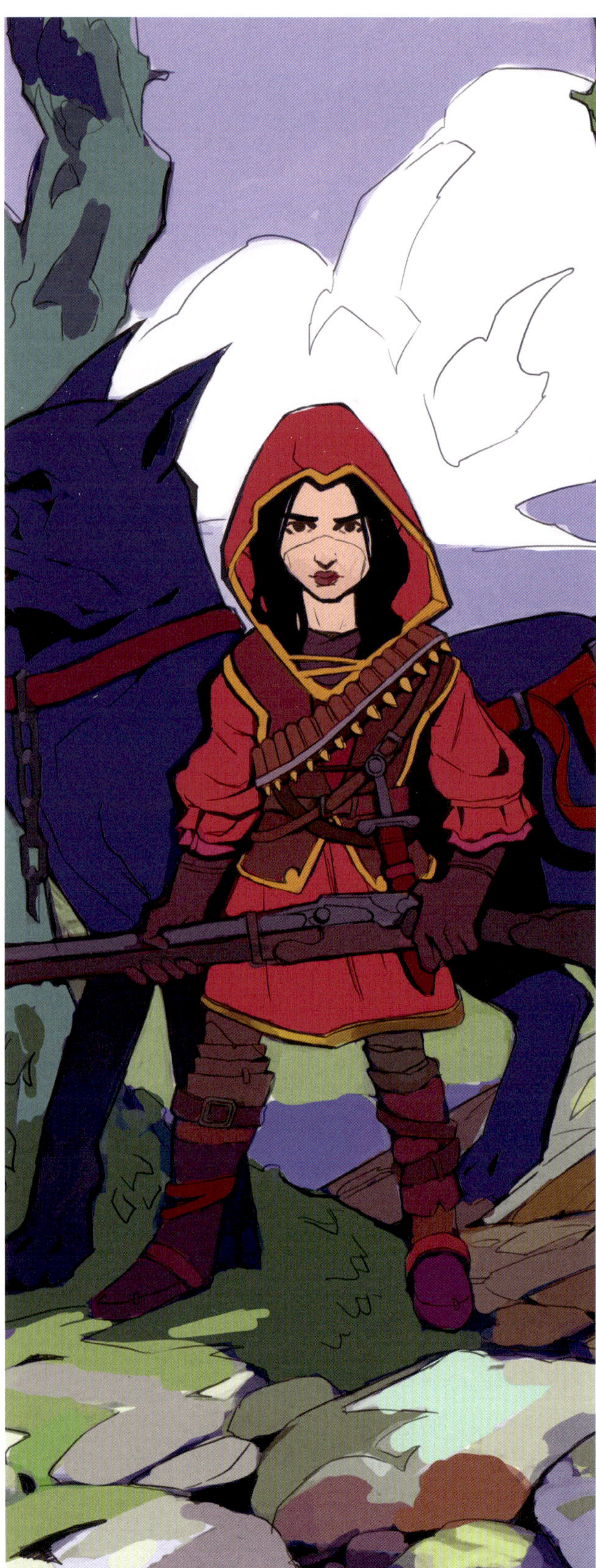

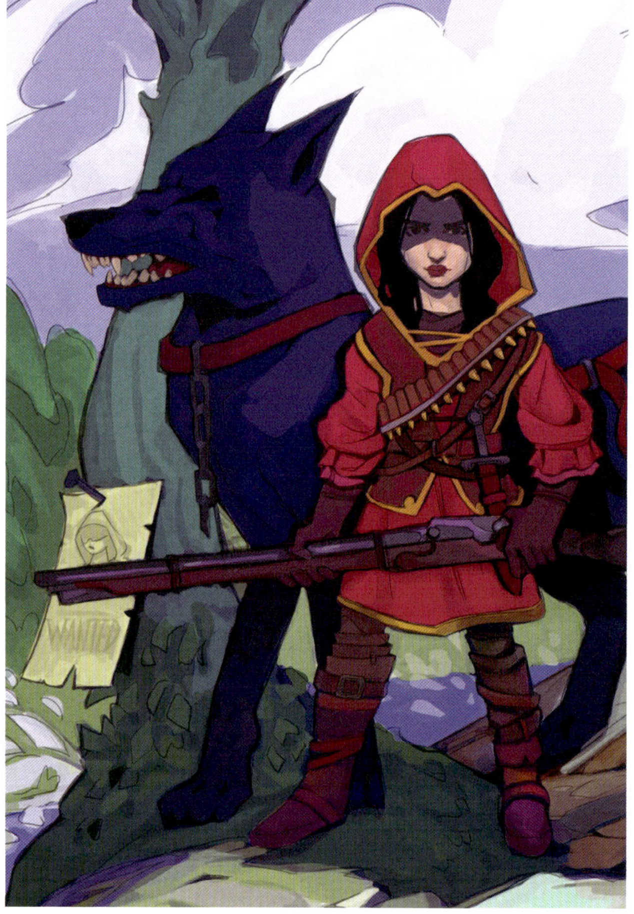

▲ I started to add shadows and variations to my flat colors. The "Wanted" poster is a background detail that shows my Red Riding Hood is a criminal. Even the deep shadow under her hood gives her a shady look, like a bandit's mask.

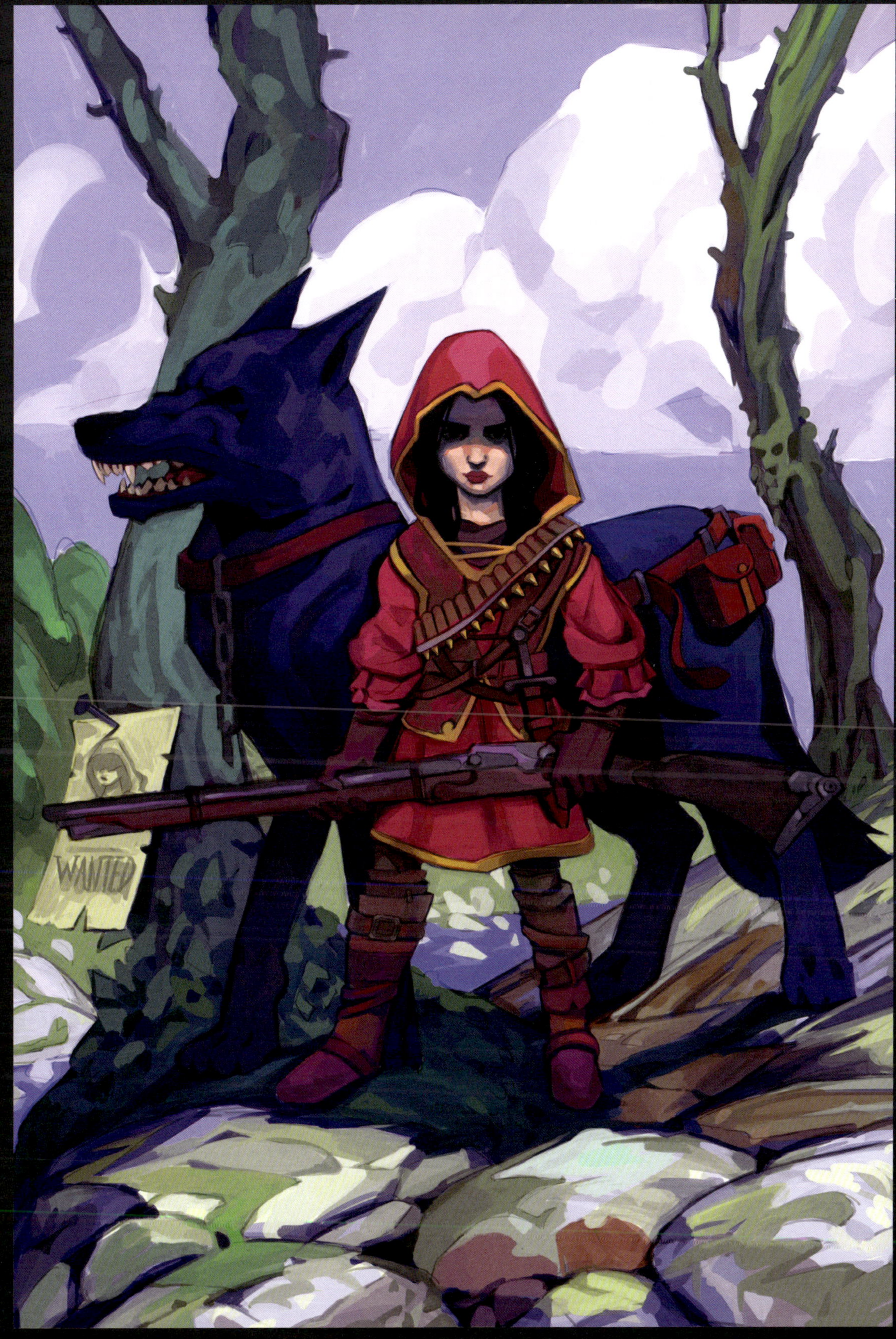

▲ **Finally, I painted over the line art, amplifying the image's contrast and refining the shapes. I aimed for a bold, painterly finish that was not too refined, to allow some sketch lines to still show through.** *Images © Luc Brunet-Manquat*

CONTRIBUTORS

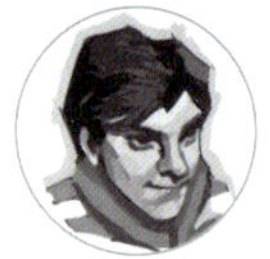

LUC BRUNET-MANQUAT

Luc Brunet-Manquat has been passionate about drawing since he was little. Currently, he is happy to be starting his career as a 2D artist/concept artist junior at Lizardcube.

instagram.com/bm_luc

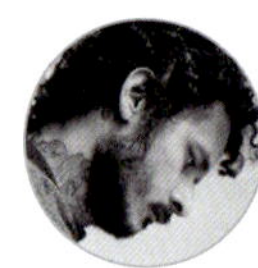

LEO GÓMEZ

Leo Gómez is an illustrator from Colombia, currently based in France. He is a writer of small stories and a passionate filmmaker.

instagram.com/heyleogomez

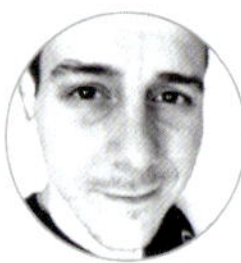

TONY "EIGHT" CAMEHL

Tony "Eight" Camehl is currently a 3D junior artist at Rise FX Munich, and has previously worked for Ubisoft, Framestore, and Spin Master. He loves being creative, exploring ideas in 2D and 3D, and getting lost in fantastical new worlds.

tonyeight.myportfolio.com

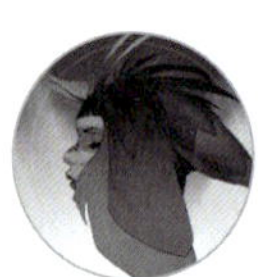

GABRIEL GÓMEZ ALMENZAR

Gabriel Gómez Almenzar is a freelance concept artist and illustrator based in Granada, Spain. He has created concept art for companies such as 31st Union and Luno Pictures, comic covers at Ablaze Publishing, and character designs for Neko Galaxy.

artstation.com/zar

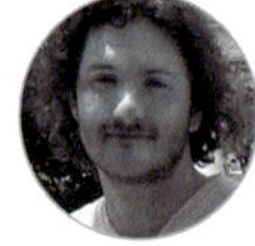

JOSHUA CARSON

Joshua Carson got his foot in the door by illustrating for card games, and now works as an environment concept artist for a video game currently in progress. When not drawing, he enjoys finding inspiration in comics, films, and other visual media.

joshuacarson.artstation.com

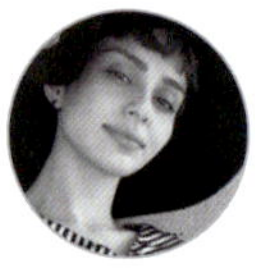

FATEMEH "BLUE BIRDY" HAGHNEJAD

Fatemeh Haghnejad, AKA Blue Birdy, is an illustrator based in Oslo, Norway.

bluebirdy.net

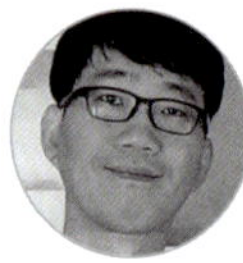

YONGJAE CHOI

Yongjae Choi is a freelance concept artist and illustrator who has worked with Marvel, Xbox Games Studios, Warner Bros. Games, Wizards of the Coast, and Valve.

indusconcept.com

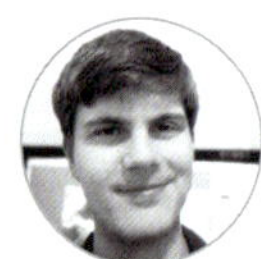

RYAN HARRELL

Ryan Harrell is a visual storyteller who takes stories or everyday moments and puts his own spin on them. They have humorous undertones and feature characters who are heightened by anthropomorphic designs.

kygerstudios.com

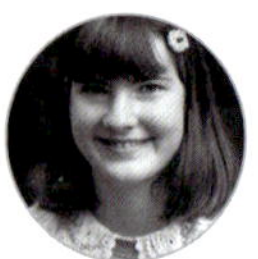

KATIE GOLDBERG

Katie Goldberg is an illustrator studying at Kendall College of Art and Design. She is always looking to find new ways to recreate the whimsy and dreaminess found in fairy tales.

katiegoldberg.art

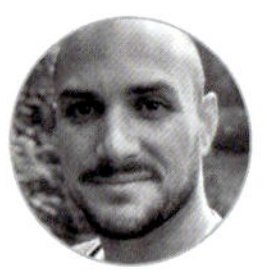

KORY LYNN HUBBELL

Kory Lynn Hubbell is a concept artist located in the Seattle area. He has worked on properties including *Halo*, *Borderlands*, and *Wildstar*. He currently works at Firewalk Studios as a senior concept artist and he has adventures with his family in his spare time.

artstation.com/koryface

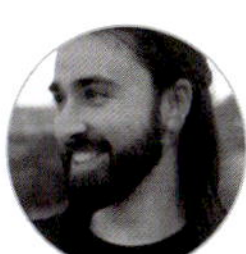

INKOGNIT

João Fiuza, AKA Inkognit, is an illustrator and concept artist specializing in creature and character design. He is also the creator of *Silver Giant*, a world of monsters, spirits, soldiers, and even gods, where imagination runs loose.

inkognit.com

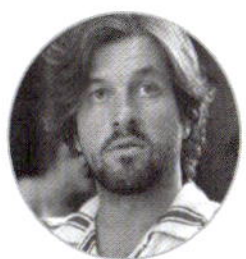

JOÃO MOURA

João Moura is a visual development artist for animated films. Despite a background in architecture, his heart was always set on drawing his favorite characters and places. He loves to spend time with friends and family, hike in nature, or go out for a slice of cake with a sketchbook in hand.

joaomouraart.com

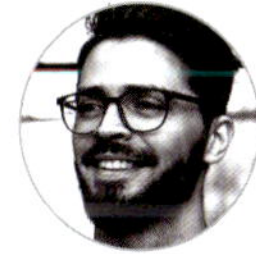

OLIVER ÖDMARK

Oliver Ödmark has been working as a concept artist in the games industry for over 12 years and has worked mostly on AAA games.

artstation.com/oliverodmark

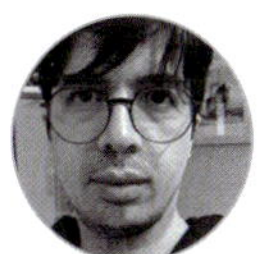

FERNANDO PEQUE

Fernando Peque is a freelance visual development artist from São Paulo, Brazil. His clients include House of Cool, Passion Pictures, Hornet Inc, Shed, Rovio Animation, Headless, Aardman, King, and currently Netflix Animation.

artstation.com/fernando_peque

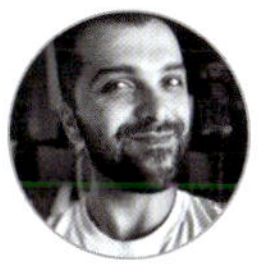

AHMED RAWI

Ahmed Rawi is a concept artist, illustrator, and visual developer working in the video-game and film industries.

artstation.com/rawi

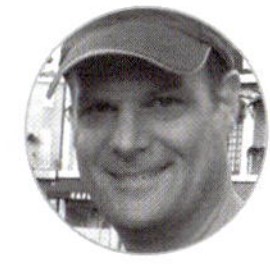

RON SANDERS

Ron Sanders' varied art career has led to work in advertising, editorial, publishing, television, medallic arts, education, limited edition prints, museums, and two dozen fine art galleries.

ronsandersart.com

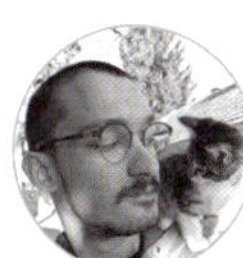

OGNJEN SPORIN

Ognjen Sporin is a fantasy illustrator and concept artist from Serbia. He has been in the art industry for around three years, working for such clients as Netflix Animation, Wizards of the Coast, and Marvel.

artstation.com/ognyendyolic

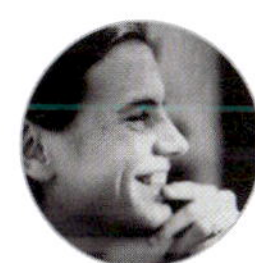

LEROY STEINMANN

Leroy Steinmann is a freelance artist currently based in Switzerland.

instagram.com/leroy_steinmann

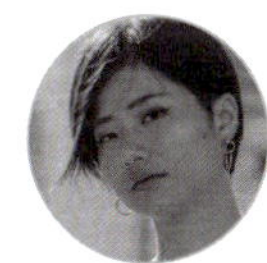

KAINING WANG

Kaining Wang is a concept artist based in Los Angeles, California.

kningart.com

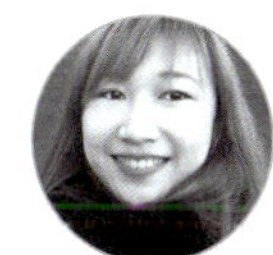

EILENE CHERIE WITARSAH

Eilene Cherie Witarsah is an illustrator and concept artist from Indonesia, creating illustrations, characters, and environments for games and animation. She loves travel videos and documentaries, finding inspiration in cultures all around the world.

artstation.com/eilenecherie

GLOSSARY

AMBIENT LIGHT/SHADOW
The soft, general light and shadow usually created by natural, overcast light. Compared to the hard-edged shadows cast by an object blocking a specific light source, ambient shadows are soft-edged and non-directional.

CHROMATIC ABERRATION
A visual effect originally found as an error in photography, where blurry fringes of color appear around the edges of a subject.

COLOR PALETTE
The selection of colors used in an image, often chosen with the intention of creating a specific mood or emotion in the viewer.

COMPOSITION
The process of placing elements of an image with the intention of creating a specific effect, or the result of this process.

CONTRAST
The level of difference between elements of an image – for example, between lightness and darkness or soft and hard shapes.

FOCAL POINT
The most important area or subject in a composition, emphasized to draw the viewer's attention.

GESTURE
The quality of flow or movement present in an image, design, or figure. A subject with a strong gesture has a strong flow that the viewer's eye will naturally follow.

GRAYSCALE
A color palette that is comprised purely of black, white, and gray values.

HIGHLIGHT
The brightest value area of an image, or the brightest point on an object where it is hit by a light source.

LINE ART
An image comprised of drawn outlines, such as made with a pen or pencil. It can be a preliminary stage before painting or a finished image in its own right.

MIDTONE
A medium value that is neither a shadow nor a highlight. For example, gray is a midtone between black and white.

OPACITY
The level of transparency of a color, layer, or other element. The higher the opacity, the more opaque the result; the lower the opacity, the more translucent.

PERSPECTIVE
In art, the effect of a three-dimensional form on a two-dimensional canvas. Perspective can be achieved by following visual guides such as a horizon line and vanishing points.

RENDERING
In art, the process of developing, refining, and detailing an image until it reaches the desired level of finish.

RULE OF THIRDS
A composition guide in which the canvas is split into thirds horizontally and vertically, creating a grid of nine segments. Focal points can be placed on the intersections of this grid for better balance or impact.

SATURATION
In color theory, the level of vividness and "colorfulness" of a color. A color with high saturation is bolder, richer, or more intense; a desaturated color is lighter, paler, or grayer.

SHADOW
The darkest areas of a scene or subject, caused by a lack or obstruction of the light. The shadows will have the darkest values.

THUMBNAIL
A small, rough sketch, made to quickly explore a design or composition idea.

VALUE
The quality of a color's lightness or darkness. A color with low value is dark, while a color with high or bright value is lighter.

WORKFLOW
The overall process or series of stages followed to achieve a particular result.

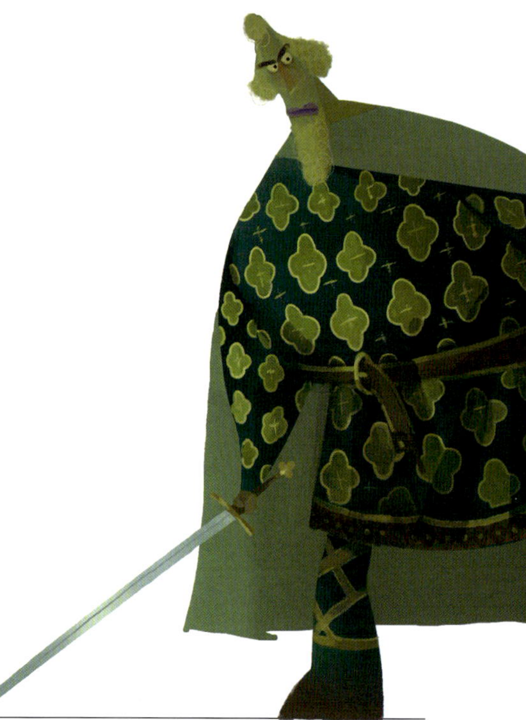

Image © Fernando Peque

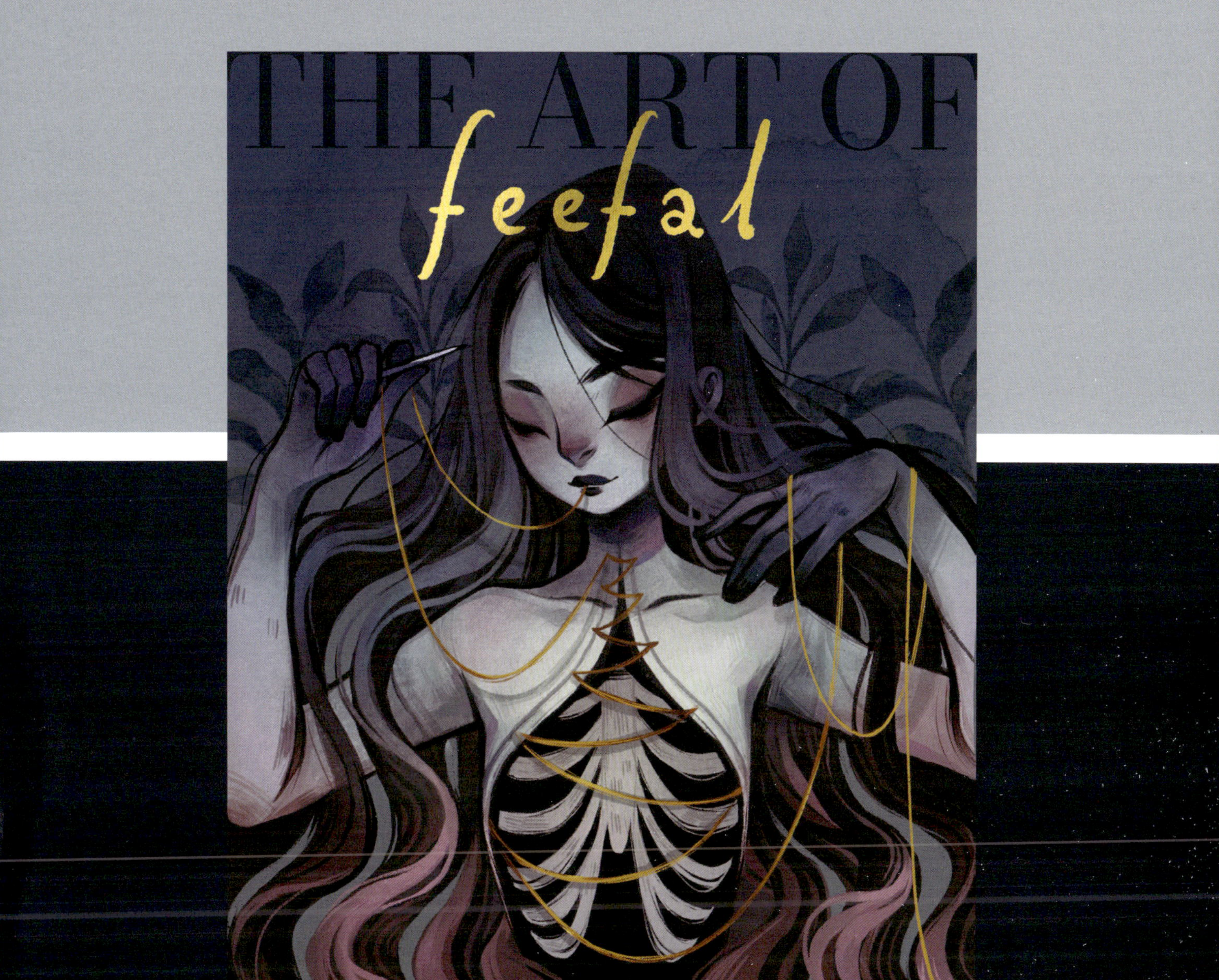
THE ART OF
feefal

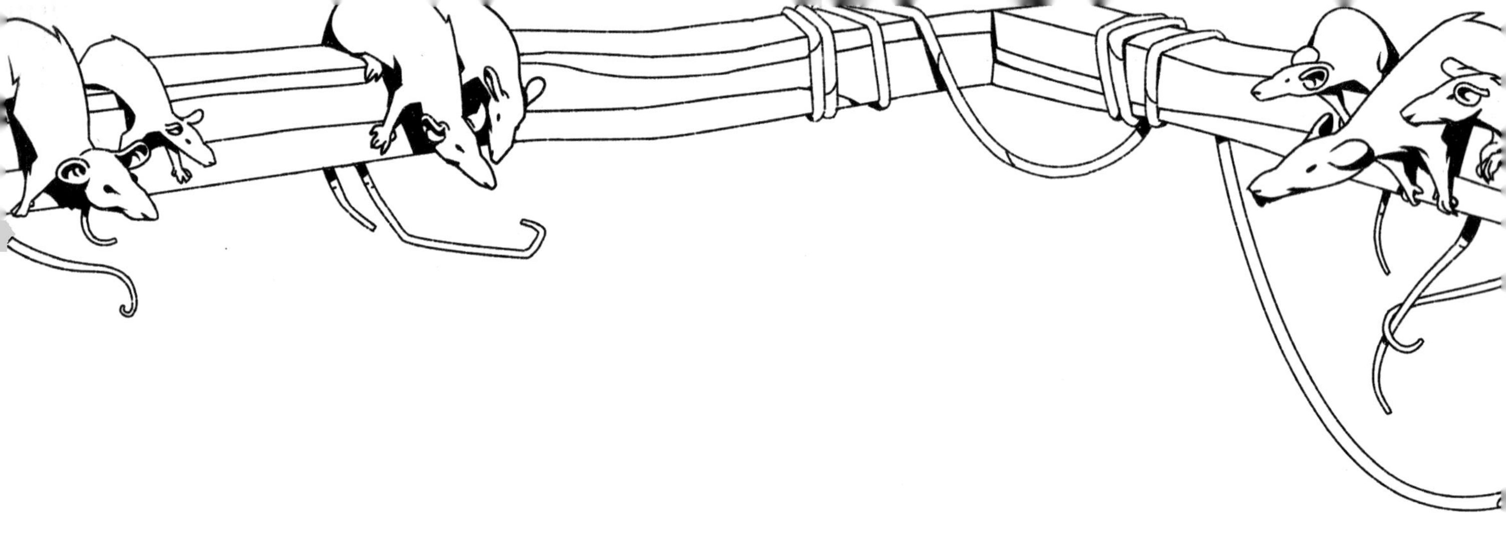

3dtotal Publishing

3dtotal Publishing is a trailblazing, creative publisher specializing in inspirational and educational resources for artists.

Our titles feature top industry professionals from around the globe who share their experience in skillfully written step-by-step tutorials and fascinating, detailed guides. Illustrated throughout with stunning artwork, these best-selling publications offer creative insight, expert advice, and essential motivation. Fans of digital art will enjoy our comprehensive volumes covering Adobe Photoshop, Procreate, and Blender, as well as our superb titles based around character design, including *Fundamentals of Character Design* and *Creating Characters for the Entertainment Industry*. The dedicated, high-quality blend of instruction and inspiration also extends to traditional art. Titles covering a range of techniques, genres, and abilities allow your creativity to flourish while building essential skills.

Well-established within the industry, we now offer over 100 titles and counting, many of which have been translated into multiple languages around the world. With something for every artist, we are proud to say that our books offer the 3dtotal package:

LEARN · CREATE · SHARE

VISIT US AT 3DTOTALPUBLISHING.COM

3dtotal Publishing is part of 3dtotal.com, a leading website for CG artists founded by Tom Greenway in 1999.

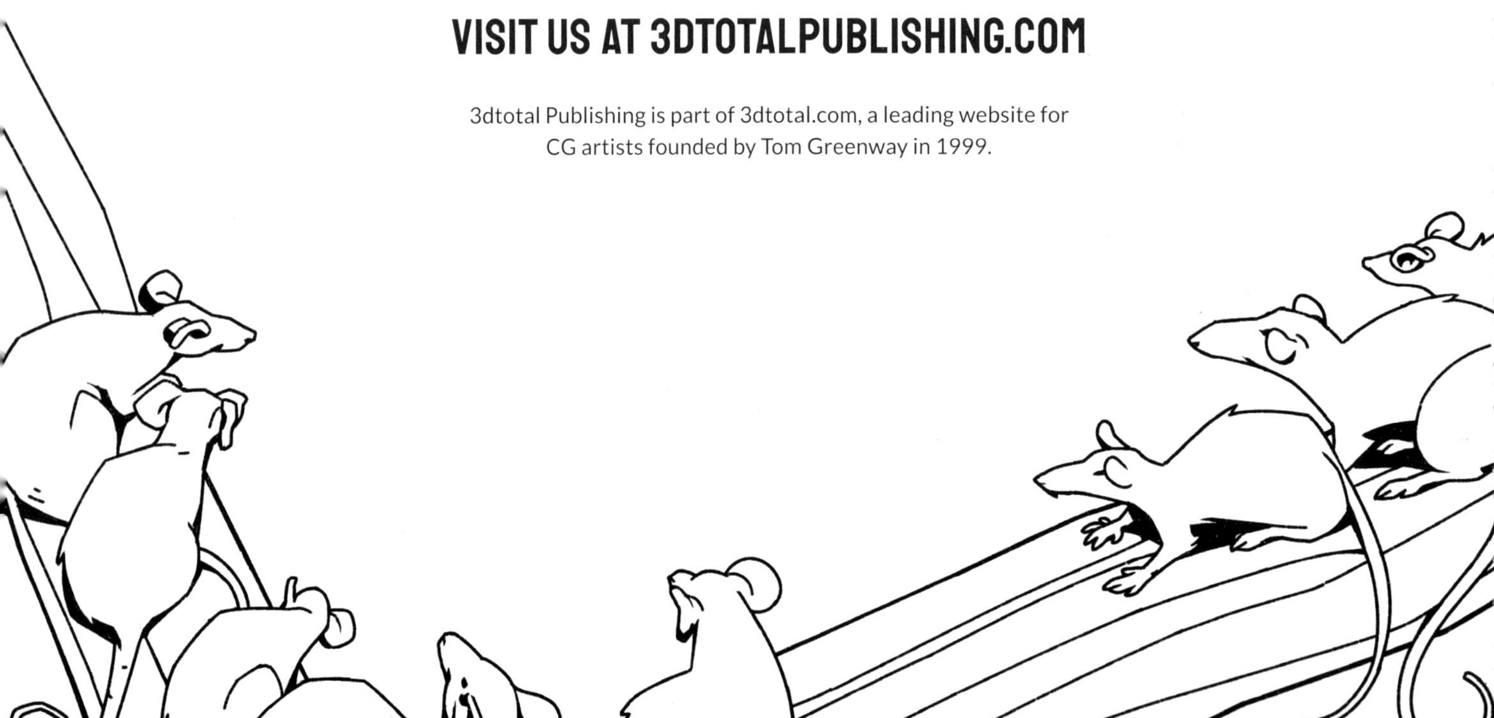